CRIMINOLOGY

CRIMINOLOGY

Chris Hale
Professor of Criminology
at the University of Kent

Keith Hayward
Lecturer in Criminology
at the University of Kent

Azrini Wahidin
Lecturer in Criminology
at the University of Kent

Emma Wincup
Senior Lecturer in Criminology and Criminal Justice
at the University of Leeds

OXFORD
UNIVERSITY PRESS

OXFORD

UNIVERSITY PRESS

Great Clarendon Street, Oxford OX2 6DP

Oxford University Press is a department of the University of Oxford.
It furthers the University's objective of excellence in research, scholarship,
and education by publishing worldwide in

Oxford New York

Auckland Cape Town Dar es Salaam Hong Kong Karachi
Kuala Lumpur Madrid Melbourne Mexico City Nairobi
New Delhi Shanghai Taipei Toronto

With offices in

Argentina Austria Brazil Chile Czech Republic France Greece
Guatemala Hungary Italy Poland Portugal Japan Singapore
South Korea Switzerland Thailand Turkey Ukraine Vietnam

Oxford is a registered trade mark of Oxford University Press
in the UK and in certain other countries

Published in the United States
by Oxford University Press Inc., New York

British Library Cataloguing in Publication Data

Data available

Library of Congress Cataloging in Publication Data

Data available

ISBN 0–19–927036–8   978–0–19–927036–1

10 9 8 7 6 5 4 3

Typeset by RefineCatch Limited, Bungay, Suffolk
Printed in Great Britain
on acid-free paper by
Ashford Colour Press, Gosport, Hampshire

Eight miles from Manhattan is the largest penal colony in the world, a place most New Yorkers could not point to on the map and many do not know exists. Home to 15,000 inmates, Riker's Island is just over the waterway 100 yards from La Guardia International airport. It is a place of invisibility from where, paradoxically, the inmates have an extraordinary view of one of the most famous skylines in the world: a tantalizing sight which no doubt only serves to increase their misery. Such a world of secret punishment sets us a whole series of puzzles for the criminologist—for the sociologist as sleuth! Why, first of all, is punishment hidden when in the past, as the French philosopher Michael Foucault pointed out in *Discipline and Punish*, it was out front and ostentatious: witness the public gallows, the whipping post, the village stocks. And why do so many people need to be punished in a rich, developed country that, supposedly, is the homeland of liberal democracy? In the United States there are 2.1 million people behind bars at any one time, and prison building, management, and maintenance has become a giant industry, vigorously competed for by state and local authorities because of its promise of employment and a pollution-free environment.

But let us look a little closer at Riker's Island: it is the size of a small town of 20,000 inhabitants (including staff) with its own schools, bakers, tailor shop, recreation, medical centre, nursery, and religious facilities. Yet it is scarcely economically sufficient: Riker's costs the US taxpayer over $800 million a year to run. Indeed the average cost of keeping an inmate is $60,000 a year—compare that to the average US wage of $37,000. And as for efficiency, about 75% of inmates will return to Riker's within a year of release. Let us say at this stage that such a paradox is repeated across the developed world—it is not an idiosyncrasy of the United States, however much the scale of imprisonment is exceptional. So a further and seemingly perennial problem occurs for the criminologist: how is such an irrational process possible and why does it persist? But the puzzles do not end here. Let us look at the inmates themselves: what strikes one immediately is that the demographic profile of Riker's is scarcely representative of the wider society. First of all they are over 90% Black and Latino, secondly they are nearly all men, thirdly one quarter have been treated for mental illness and 80% have a history of substance abuse. Lastly and perhaps most definitively, they are poor: 30% are homeless and 90% lack a high school diploma. And such a profile of race, gender, mental instability, and desperate poverty could be repeated in prisons around the globe. Why, then, is the criminal justice system skewed in such a way? Is this the shape of criminality? Each of these dimensions of the inmate population throws up its own series of questions. Is the racial disproportionality of the prison due to racism inherent in the criminal justice system or does it truly reflect the differences in levels of crime between ethnic groups? Is there some genetic characteristic of men compared to women that makes them more aggressive and liable to crime? To what extent can the mentally disturbed be held responsible for their crimes? And are the poor incarcerated the world over because it is the deviance of the poor that we call crimes? Or is all this just another example of the golden rule: it is the people with gold who make the rules?

The study of criminology begs all these questions. It encompasses questions of sociology and psychology, of legal theory and social philosophy, of biology and the social sciences. It is at the crossroads of all these disciplines and more—it is never a marginal concern but one that takes us immediately into the relations of normality and deviance, of order and disorder, of crime and punishment, and indeed of good and evil. Because of this, crime has always been a major staple of the mass media: it is on the news every night. It is the core theme of detective fiction and of 'cops and robbers' drama on television. It alarms us and makes us fearful, but it also entertains and thrills us. We are attracted and beguiled by these images yet so many of them are patently false. The serial killer is an extreme rarity, yet it becomes a major genre of thriller fiction, its depiction a caricature of reality, a 'pornocopia' of sex and violence. Crime in the real world is frequently not detected—the criminal usually gets away. In fiction the intuitive skills and resourcefulness of the detective inevitably lead to the apprehension of the crook yet reality has no such denouement. The depiction of the violent attack from Hollywood blockbusters to video games revolves around 'stranger danger'—the threat of the unknown, of the malicious 'Other'. In most parts of the world this is the very inverse of truth. If you want to know your most likely murderer, look in the mirror. You are most likely to kill yourself, to commit suicide, than be killed by others; of those around you, your best friends and your nearest and dearest, then casual acquaintances are more likely to be your killer than those unknown to you. The stranger will only rarely look back at you, and when it does, the face looking out will be the same age, the same class, the same colour of skin as you. The only exception to this is if you are a woman: a man's face will look back at you (you are most likely to be killed by your husband or boyfriend) and, tragically, if you are a child, it is your mum or dad who will look back at you—only rarely will it be a stranger.

Criminology is intrigued by crime and the images of crime: each 'fact' which seems obvious becomes problematic on examination; each stereotype that we take for granted appears dubious or even prejudiced when we inspect it at close quarters. Our task, then, must be to untangle stereotype from reality, fact from fiction. And the search for the answers to all these questions that we have posed—and many more besides—is an endeavour of great practical importance, for it is only by their solution that we can help ameliorate both the impact of crime and the pains of imprisonment.

It is with such thoughts in mind that I recommend this book to students, practitioners and interested members of the public alike. The editors are to be congratulated for having brought together a group of contributors that pose these and many other related questions surrounding criminology and its uses in an accessible and thought-provoking way. I am certain that this book will become a cornerstone of criminology and criminal justice programs for many years to come.

Jock Young
New York City, NY
January 2005

OUTLINE CONTENTS

DETAILED CONTENTS

PART I Introducing crime and criminology   1

LIST OF FIGURES

LIST OF TABLES

LIST OF CONTRIBUTORS

Deborah Cheney *Lecturer in Law, University of Kent*

Jeff Ferrell *Associate Professor, Texas Christian University, USA*

Frank Furedi *Professor of Sociology, University of Kent*

Chris Greer *Senior Lecturer in Criminology, Northumbria University*

Chris Hale *Professor of Criminology, University of Kent*

Keith Hayward *Lecturer in Criminology, University of Kent*

Olga Heaven *Director of Female Prisoners Welfare Project Hibiscus*

Tim Hope *Professor of Criminology, University of Keele*

Barbara Hudson *Professor in Law, University of Central Lancashire*

Richard Jones *Lecturer in Criminology, Edinburgh University*

Trevor Jones *Senior Lecturer in Criminology, Cardiff University*

Derek Kirton *Lecturer in Social Policy and Social Work, University of Kent*

Wayne Morrison *Reader in Law, Queen Mary College, University of London*

Mike Presdee *Lecturer in Criminology, University of Kent*

Paddy Rawlinson *Lecturer in Criminology, University of Leicester*

Larry Ray *Professor of Sociology, University of Kent*

Heather Shore *Lecturer in Criminology, University of Portsmouth*

Catrin Smith *Lecturer in Criminology, University College Chester*

Terry Thomas *Lecturer in Social Work, Leeds Metropolitan University*

Steve Tombs *Professor of Sociology, Liverpool John Moores University*

Steve Uglow *Professor of Criminal Justice, University of Kent*

Claire Valier *Lecturer in Law, Birkbeck College, University of London*

Azrini Wahidin *Lecturer in Criminology, University of Kent*

Brian Williams *Professor of Community Justice and Victimology, De Montfort University*

Emma Wincup *Senior Lecturer in Criminal Justice, University of Leeds*

Anne Worrall *Professor of Criminology, Keele University*

Guide to the book

Chris Hale, Keith Hayward, Azrini Wahidin
and Emma Wincup

In recent years the expansion of criminology as an academic discipline has been little short of remarkable. Once taught exclusively as a postgraduate subject, criminology is now offered in an ever-expanding range of undergraduate courses at all levels across the university system. To put this into perspective, according to recent figures provided by the UK University and College Admission Service, in Great Britain alone, there are now 792 courses related to criminology offered by fifty institutions. In terms of student numbers, data provided by the same organization confirmed that some 932 students were accepted to single honours Criminology degrees in 2003, while in the same year, 4,050 students accepted a place on a Criminology degree in combination with another subject. One could also point to a large increase in the number of 'applied criminology' courses, such as community justice and policing studies aimed at professionals already working within the criminal justice system or those who hope to pursue a career in criminal justice.

Inevitably such rapid expansion has precipitated the arrival of a whole host of textbooks, course books and handbooks that have sought to introduce developments in criminology and criminal justice to this new generation of students. For all their various merits, none of these works have been able to provide undergraduate criminologists with a single comprehensive and authoritative source that serves as an accessible overview of the most pertinent issues currently facing the discipline. *Criminology* is specifically intended to meet this requirement. It has been produced as a complete package both for students new to criminology and their course lecturers. We also hope that *Criminology* will serve as a useful resource for criminal justice practitioners and interested members of the general public.

For students, *Criminology* offers twenty-seven chapters on core criminological issues that can be used to help them prepare for a seminar discussion, or as the foundation stone for a presentation or essay. Each chapter is self-contained although links are made to relevant discussions in other chapters. Students are also encouraged to use the index to research the topic further. In addition to the substantive discussion, a number of pedagogical features are included. Chapters are accompanied by review questions, suggestions for further reading and relevant websites. Where appropriate, students are guided to additional resources such as sources of data. Key concepts are collated in a glossary at the end of the text. All of this, we hope, adds up to a book that is pitched at an appropriate level for students with no prior knowledge of criminology, yet at the same time is challenging enough to equip them with the skills and knowledge needed for future study.

For lecturers, *Criminology* proffers sufficient material for a course spanning the whole academic year, and allows lecturers responsible for one term/semester courses to dip into the book and select an appropriate mix of topics or restrict their choice to particular sections. Each chapter is complemented by questions that can be used to structure discussions within seminars.

Accompanying *Criminology* is an extensive website carefully designed both to assist students with no prior knowledge of criminology, and to provide course leaders with a range of pedagogic tools aimed at enhancing the student learning experience. The most important resources are links to relevant websites, which allow students to access additional information at the click of a button in order to update and augment the chapter discussions. This is particularly vital given the ever-changing nature of criminal justice policy and shifting patterns of offending and victimization. For lecturers, the website offers brief lecture notes and Powerpoint ® slides for each topic included in the book. The website also contains a 'Testbank' of approximately 300 multiple-choice questions. These can be used by students to test their understanding of the material covered in each chapter and employed by lectures to assess students on a formal and informal basis. Each question is accompanied by feedback to enable students to further their understanding of criminological issues.

This book is arranged around four themes. As its name suggests Part One, 'Introducing Crime and Criminology', introduces students to the core concepts and issues needed for the study of criminology today. To begin with, Wayne Morrison tackles what is perhaps the discipline's most fundamental question: what is crime? Whilst for the uninitiated this may appear a straightforward topic, he moves quickly beyond simple definitions to consider questions of power and legitimacy, each reviewed within a historically and culturally informed discussion of how criminologists define their object of study. This line of enquiry is developed and given further historical colour by Heather Shore in her chapter 'The History of Crime'. Drawing on a plethora of examples, Shore presents a narrative of crime and punishment in England since the seventeenth Century. In doing so she challenges simple understandings of crime and the sources from which they spring.

Bringing the story up to date Tim Hope problematizes the questions surrounding the measurement of crime. How do we know the level of crime? What information is available and how reliable is it? Going far beyond the standard discussions, he presents a provocative and informed account of the problems of measuring crime either from police figures or by using surveys.

Shifting gear the next two chapters provide the student with a comprehensive introduction to how criminological theory has developed and is used. While all the chapters in this book are theoretically informed Keith Hayward and Wayne Morrison offer the reader a series of theoretical vignettes each one of which provides both an accessible introduction to a particular theory and informed signposts to more detailed readings. Although we take the importance of theory as self-evident, not everyone shares this view. Hence, in Chapter 5, Claire Valier presents a strong justification for 'doing theory' and some insightful thoughts on how it should be approached. Valier urges us not to think of theory as an esoteric or abstract exercise but something that exists at the very heart of the criminological enterprise.

Whilst the main thrust of this text is sociological we freely acknowledge the substantial influence psychology has exerted on criminology. In Chapter 6 Keith Hayward casts a sympathetic but critical eye on the interface between these two disciplines, presenting and assessing some of the major psychological theories of crime and their impact on the study of crime and criminal justice. This interdisciplinary approach is further evidenced in Jeff Ferrell's chapter on the cultural significance of crime. His central aim is to examine the way in which crime and culture intertwine within the lived experiences of everyday life. He asserts that a whole host of urban crimes are perpetuated by actors for whom transgression is everything. Ferrell charts a world of underground graffiti artists, BASE jumpers, gang members, street hustlers, pimps, and other 'outlaws', whose distinctive subcultures are increasingly the subject of media, corporate and political interest. Continuing this cultural theme, Chris Greer sharpens the focus specifically to look at the interconnections between crime and the media. In a world in which crime is often packaged as entertainment, Greer asks us to reflect on and unpick these relationships. After critically discussing the dominant theoretical and conceptual approaches, he considers the evidence for the effects of media representations, both on criminal behaviour and on fear of crime.

Part Two, 'Forms of Crime' moves beyond introduction to look at some of the various types of crimes prevalent in late-modern society. Starting with our daily round Mike Presdee examines the way crime is woven into the fabric of everyday life. He looks at the day-to-day offences that constitute the major part of the recorded crime figures arguing that while, historically, volume crime has meant property crime (burglary, theft and criminal damage), now low-level activities labelled 'anti-social' are increasingly coming to dominate the volume crime discourse. Picking up on these themes Emma Wincup's chapter also focuses on crimes which are a feature of many people's daily lives. Problematic use of drugs and alcohol are often linked with property and violent crime although the relationship between drug and alcohol use and crime is more complex than is typically portrayed in media and political discussions.

While violence inevitably features in the previous two chapters, Larry Ray takes discussion to another level providing a systematic overview of some of the main sociological and criminological debates in the area. But more than this he explores changing socio-cultural responses to crimes involving high levels of aggression and violence. Using data from the British Crime Survey, he provides figures on the prevalence of different types of violence within England and Wales and discusses the impact of hate, homophobic and racist crimes. Sharpening the focus still further, in Chapter 12, Terry Thomas tackles a subject typically excluded from criminological textbooks; sexual offending. He argues that these crimes have long been seen as somehow 'different' to other offences, being particularly invasive, exploitative and accompanied by latent or manifest violence. Moreover, he explores the root causes of this type of behaviour and the treatment modalities that are made available to the sexually motivated offender.

A very different type of crime, but one that again is often ignored in student texts is the vitally important area of corporate crime. Steve Tombs examines the emergence of this concept, discussing its meaning and reviewing the extent to which it represents a crime problem. He then considers various dimensions of corporate crime, its visibility, causation and control, questioning society's will to censure and punish company directors and other 'rogue' capitalists. While criminology has tended to concentrate on more 'traditional' forms of criminality, the burgeoning of organized crime on a global scale has provoked increasing academic interest. Paddy Rawlinson looks at a number of its current and previous manifestations, from US street gangs of the 1920s, to the Italian-based family 'mafia' groups, and on to the newer organized crime groups that have emerged from places as geographically and culturally distinct as the former Soviet Union and Colombia. Similarly marginalized from the criminological gaze is terrorism. While other disciplines have begun to engage with this subject in the wake of 9/11, criminology has been slow to regard the dynamics of international terrorism as one of its primary concerns. Addressing this lacuna Frank Furedi provides a general introduction to the subject and poses a series of important questions about how one actually defines terrorism against a backdrop of contemporary fears in a risk averse society.

In Part Three, 'Social Dimensions of Crime' the authors examine how offending, victimization and experiences of the criminal justice system (CJS) may be affected by people's class, gender and ethnicity. Beginning with the complex relationships between crime, economic marginalization and social exclusion, Chris Hale provides a clear introduction to the key issues and debates. Again moving beyond the standard textbook approach of focusing on crime and unemployment, he provides a more rounded critical analysis of the impact of economic factors on offending and victimization. Next, Catrin Smith explores the connections between gender and crime. She examines the different kinds of crimes in which men and women are involved, and considers the complex and changing relationship between masculinity(ies), femininity(ies) and crime. By deconstructing how these relations have been typically understood in criminological theory, she looks at how men and women are dealt with by the CJS.

The treatment ethnic minority groups receive, both as victims and suspects, has rightly had an increasingly high profile in recent years. Following the Steven Lawrence Inquiry (1999) the police have had to face up to accusations of being institutionally racist and of using their powers to stop and search suspected offenders in a discriminatory manner. Approaching this subject in a novel but effective way Olga Heaven and Barbara Hudson use Hibiscus (an organization concerned with the needs of female foreign nationals) as a case study to explore the relationships between 'race', 'ethnicity' and 'crime' and to illuminate these broader issues.

Anti-social behaviour, binge drinking, and street gangs are the latest manifestations of society's perennial concerns about young people and their problem behaviour. Dealing with such matters is the focus of Derek Kirton's chapter. He outlines the key principles around which youth justice has evolved and how the balance between welfare and punishment has shifted over time in line with broader social and political changes. Young people are not the only age group to experience special problems within the CJS. In the final chapter in this section, Azrini Wahidin identifies the key issues and charts current debates in criminology surrounding older offenders, crime, and the CJS.

In Part Four, 'Responses to Crime', the focus shifts to consider how society responds to crime through its treatment of both offenders and victims. If defining crime is a political issue, then how we deal with its consequences certainly is. The process and delivery of criminal justice, the practices of the agencies involved in 'crime control' and the treatment of victimized communities and individuals are all framed by public and political debate. In the second of Chris Hale's chapters he examines the rise in punitive and retributive discourses against broader economic and social changes and documents how these have led to an unseemly competition between the political parties to be the 'toughest team in town'. Picking up this theme Steve Uglow outlines and critiques the role of the CJS in England and Wales. He provides a comprehensive and accessible account of the different parts of the criminal justice system and highlights the linkages and tensions between them.

Picking up on the themes of intensified social control discussed by Hale, Richard Jones looks at how social control now operates in a different register. Over the last two decades, a range of new electronic and digital technologies have come to be employed as tools of formal control, security, exclusion and punishment, bringing with them 'new' social practices which many commentators, rightly or wrongly, have argued are likely to have profound consequences for established civil liberties. Jones's chapter offers the reader a general introduction to theoretical debates surrounding surveillance. It then proceeds with an overview of these new technologies of social control, including the forms they currently take, how they function, and their usage. These uses include both the private sector as a form of surveillance and physical exclusion, and in the public domain as an instrument of criminal justice—for example, the electronic tagging and monitoring of offenders.

From its early stereotyping of victims as blameworthy (contributing in some way to their own problems), victimology, the study of victims, has developed a more critical and reflexive edge. With the growth of a vocal and organized victim movement in the last twenty years or so, encompassing everything from Mothers Against Guns to Victim Support, victimology has been increasingly foregrounded within criminology. Brian Williams narrates the story of its development as a discipline, traces the general increase in interest in issues of criminal victimization and addresses how the criminal justice system should respond to victims.

Trevor Jones's discussion of policing draws out the important distinction between 'policing' and the public organizational structure 'the police'. He achieves this task by exploring the workings of a number of agencies, in both the public and private sector, engaged in governance and regulation. After outlining the historical development of the police in Britain and exploring the multitude of roles performed by the police, he considers the different models of policing in operation today and their perceived effectiveness. The key role of discretion, and how this can lead to the exercise of police powers in a discriminatory manner, is also critically assessed. This opens up an analysis of 'cop culture' and attempts by the police to overcome allegations of racial discrimination and poor relations with minority ethnic and other 'hard to reach' communities.

The next pair of chapters look at the treatment of convicted offenders. Anne Worrall begins by exploring the development of punishment in the community from the nineteenth century onwards. Focusing mainly, but not exclusively, on England and Wales, it deals largely with the punishment of adult offenders. She highlights the range of community penalties available to sentencers, and notes how these have expanded rapidly throughout the twentieth century. She then considers the use of these penalties for different groups of offenders (for example, by analysing any gender differences) and different groups of offences. Worrall then reviews the controversial issue of the introduction of private sector bodies to manage some forms of community penalties, such as curfew orders with electronic monitoring. Finally she summarizes the debates about the effectiveness of community penalties as a means of reducing re-offending and diverting offenders from custody.

The use of imprisonment and the reasons for its popularity, despite little evidence of its effectiveness, is at the centre of Deborah Cheney's chapter. She demonstrates how prison regimes have evolved and couches the debate within the theoretical discourses of punishment, rehabilitation, deterrence, incapacitation and retribution. The chapter then explores the rise of the prison population in England and Wales over the past decade. In particular she asks how this has affected the ability of HM Prison Service to reduce re-offending by offering constructive and rehabilitative regimes, and to assist prisoners to lead a law abiding life both during and after sentence. The chapter goes one step further and questions whether prison itself can actually achieve all, or indeed any, of its aims.

The production of this book has been a mammoth undertaking involving twenty-six contributors from seventeen different institutions. Whilst this has inevitably thrown up a number of editorial headaches, we think the end result has been worth the struggle. The editors truly believe that we have produced the most accessible and comprehensive undergraduate text for criminology students and anyone else interested in the study of crime, deviance and criminal justice. Thus, we would like to take a moment here to thank all the contributors for their patience and good grace in the face of our editorial diktats!

Likewise we must also thank our editor Sarah Hyland who has been a model of forbearance and much needed calmness during the book's long gestation. We should also acknowledge her predecessor, Patrick Brindle, who originally commissioned the book before departing for other editorial pastures—not we hope as a result of this project!

Above all we would like to dedicate this book to the interested criminological reader. We hope you find it a useful resource and aid to study. Welcome to the wonderful and exciting world of criminological research.

Chris Hale, Keith Hayward, Azrini Wahidin and Emma Wincup
Canterbury, October 2004

Guide to the companion web site

Criminology is accompanied by an interactive website which you can find and access at www.oup.com/uk/booksites/criminology. The website has been written in such a way as to be closely integrated with the book, and to provide students and lecturers with ready-to-use teaching and learning resources. They are available free-of-charge, designed to complement the textbook and offer additional materials which are suited to electronic delivery. All these resources can be downloaded and are fully customizable allowing them to be incorporated into an institution's existing virtual learning environment ('VLE').

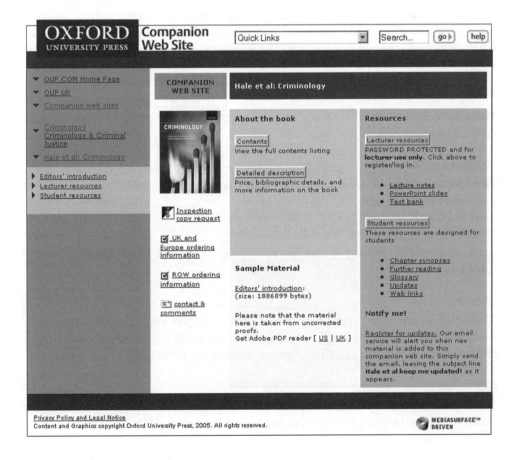

Lecturer resources

These resources are password-protected to ensure that only lecturers can gain access. Lecturers may use these free resources to complement their own teaching notes or as a platform to update and restructure their courses. Registering is easy: click on 'Lecturer Resources' on the companion website, complete a simple registration form which allows you to chose you own user name and password, and access will usually be granted within 48 hours.

Test Bank

The Test Bank is a fully customizable resource containing ready-made assessments with which to test students. Offering versatile testing tailored to the content of this book, each answer is accompanied by feedback to explain to the student why their answer is correct or incorrect and where in this book they can find further information. The test bank is downloadable into Questionmark Perception, Blackboard, WebCT, and most other virtual learning environments (VLEs) capable of importing QTI XML. The test bank questions are also downloadable in formats suitable for printing directly by the lecturer.

Lecture notes and PowerPoint slides

These complement each chapter of the book and are a useful resource for preparing lectures and handouts. They allow lecturers to guide their students through the key concepts, ideas and theories and can be fully customized to meet the needs of the course, enabling lecturers to focus on the areas most relevant to their students.

Student resources

These are accessible to all students, with no registration or password access required, enabling students to get the most out the textbook.

Chapter synopses

These provide a succinct overview of the topics covered in each chapter, allowing you to locate relevant material.

Glossary

A useful one-stop reference point for all the keywords and terms used within the textbook.

Web links

A selection of annotated web links, chosen by the chapter author, allows students to easily research those topics that are of particular interest to them. These links are checked and updated regularly to ensure they remain relevant and up to date.

Further reading

Sources recommended by the chapter author for additional reading to assist in understanding important issues and developing a broader knowledge of the subject.

Updates

This is an indispensable resource that allows students to access changes and developments in a particular area that have occurred since publication of the book. These are added to the website as and when they occur and with page references to enable students to easily identify which material has been superseded and allowing them to keep up to date with new developments without buying a new book. Pages are available for download in various formats and can be printed for easy reference.

Part One

INTRODUCING CRIME AND CRIMINOLOGY

1

What is crime?
Contrasting definitions
and perspectives

Wayne Morrison

INTRODUCTION

Crime, we are told, is today a salient fact, an integral part of the risks we face in everyday life. In both scholarly and public opinion crime is associated with harm and violence; harm to individuals, destruction of property and the denial of respect to people and institutions. It is clear that we face pressing problems of a practical and scholarly nature in understanding crime. But we lack agreement on the most basic question, namely *what is crime*? This battle over definitions, of categorizing events as crimes or other things, is no tame affair. In a bid to make sense of the diversity of opinions, definitions and perspectives surrounding this question, this chapter will introduce students to the complex inter-relationships surrounding the various ways that crime is constructed and objectified, before setting out some of the different perspectives that people actually take towards defining crime in practice. Many of the issues outlined in this chapter will be picked up in the substantive chapters that follow in this text.

BACKGROUND

Crime operates as a core concept in modern society. It seems like a common sense category but this is only a superficial appearance. Its widespread use, moreover, makes it necessary to ask what boundaries can be placed around the use of the term 'crime'. What does its use mean for us, individually, as speakers of the word, and collectively, as social groups that use the concept? The first part of that question raises issues of objectivity and relativism; in other words is there a settled or 'objective' way of calling things crime or must our use of the term crime be subjective and lead to relativism? The second part leads us on to reflexivity, in other words what is the role, function and consequences of our reliance upon 'crime' (and its related concepts, such as 'punishment') as an organizing concept in social life? These are difficult issues and lead analysis onto the acts of power of the agencies responsible for acts of public speech. For example, the legislature and the courts—and the bodies responsible for enforcing the terms of that speech, notably the police and the agencies of punishment, the prisons and other instruments of coercive social control (see Chapters 21, 22, 26 and 27). This section will concentrate upon the first part of the question while the frameworks within which different approaches make sense will be discussed in the following sections.

It is clear that there has been a great deal of variation in history and across different jurisdictions as to what has been defined as a crime. Some of the major figures in history have been termed criminals by a state process that was considered legally valid at the time. In ancient Greece, Socrates (d. 399 BC)—who we remember through Plato's dialogues as one the greatest philosophers of all time—was condemned by a court for the crime of corrupting the youth of Athens with his teachings. He died by taking hemlock after refusing the aid of his supporters to free him. In Roman occupied Palestine, Jesus Christ was condemned and crucified along with 'two common thieves'; Martin Luther King was imprisoned for his role in the 1960s US civil rights movement. While in prison he wrote his *Letter From Birmingham Jail*, an essay that stands as one of the classic writings on civil disobedience (in which he argues that one has a duty to disobey unjust laws, but also to abide by the lawful processes of the State including any punishment so ordered). Likewise, Nelson Mandela was convicted for activities against the apartheid state of South Africa and served twenty-six years in prison before his release. He subsequently became the first democratically elected President of South Africa. Are we to call individuals like these 'criminals'? Or do we say that it was a mistake to have ever called them that?

Writing in the late nineteenth century, the French sociologist Emile Durkheim—often referred to as the 'father figure of sociology'—pointed out that a great deal of social change has occurred as the result of people going against the settled rules and opposing the interests of those in power (see Chapter 4 below). According to Durkheim, a society that had no crime would be 'pathologically over-controlled':

> According to Athenian law, Socrates was a criminal, and his condemnation was no more than just. However, his crime, namely, the independence of his thought, rendered a service not only to humanity but to his country. It served to prepare a new morality and faith which the Athenians needed, since the traditions by which they had lived until then were no longer in harmony with the current conditions of life. (Durkheim, 1966: 71)

Following Durkheim we do not look at 'crime' as something that exists in abstraction, or define it as reflecting some form of simple, plain factual situation. Instead 'crime' is a complex interaction of many processes: from the society having created a concept of 'crime', to people identifying some event as a crime; from the responses to the event so called, to the behaviour and formal activities of state agencies that may or may not process the persons responsible as 'criminals' and punish them. These interactions all take place against the backdrop of the cultural world inhabited at that time. In understanding these interactions it is also important to notice what was not done, what was avoided, as much as cataloguing what was done. This is the subject of the next section.

Defining crime: confronting events and understanding processes

Reflecting upon the processes involved in claiming certain actions or events as crimes serves as a route into analysing differences and similarities in actual events and their role within the sets of beliefs, understandings and reactions to others that enables our societies to cohere. Consider the following examples of social events. Are they crimes?

- In 1781 The *Zong* was a slave ship owned by a large Liverpool slaving company employed on the well-tried route from Liverpool to West Africa and thence with a cargo of slaves to the Caribbean. On 6 September it sailed from West Africa with a cargo of 470 slaves bound for Jamaica. Twelve weeks later, closing on its destination, the *Zong* had already lost more than sixty Africans and seven of the seventeen-man crew because of dysentery brought on by severe overcrowding. The *Zong's* captain ordered that sick slaves should be thrown overboard both to preserve dwindling supplies of water and to allow the shipping company to claim their loss against insurance. One hundred and thirty-one slaves were thrown overboard and drowned, even though it had rained and there was plenty of water. None of the sick sailors were thrown overboard.

- On 5 July, 1884, the yacht the *Mignonette*, crewed by four men and a cabin boy, sank in a storm 1,600 miles off the Cape of Good Hope. The crew put to sea in a small open boat with no supply of food or water except a can of turnips. By 24 July, the men were in a terrible condition and agreed to kill the cabin boy who was virtually dying. One of the men, Dudley, killed him with a knife and all four drank his blood and fed on his body. Four days later a passing boat picked them up. It is accepted that the boy would not have lived and the men probably would have died if they had not eaten him.

- On 6 August 1945, US forces dropped an atomic bomb called 'Little Boy' on the Japanese city of Hiroshima. Three days later they dropped another called 'Fat Man' on Nagasaki. By the end of 1945, less than six months later, the Hiroshima bomb had caused 140,000 deaths, and the Nagaski bomb 70,000. Five years later the totals were 200,000 and 140,000. At the time the reason was put forward that the use of atomic devices was necessary to shorten the war and save allied lives. Was this a crime? Does it matter to your opinion that at the Tokyo International Military Tribunal set up to judge Japanese war criminals, the only judge with any previous experience of 'international law', the Indian judge Pal, issued a full dissenting judgement. He refused to accept the prosecution of the Japanese defendants as he considered that the Allies too should be tried and punished for crimes committed during the war, in particular for the dropping of the Atomic bomb.

- In 1994, after the plane carrying the President of Rwanda was shot down, government military forces along with perhaps as many as 50,000 civilians armed with knives and machetes systematically killed more than 800,000 out of the 1,000,000 minority Tutsi population and at least 20,000 moderate Hutu in a three-month killing spree. This received very little international attention and the United Nations withdrew its small peacekeeping force due to an absence of Security Council pressure to protect anyone. Most commentators believe that if international action had been taken the majority of the 820,000-plus people killed would have been saved.

- In 1999, the government of a major European country facing legitimacy problems have their secret service agents stage a 'terrorist attack' on their own citizens killing 200. They then blame the attack upon separatist 'terrorist' movements in one of the other provinces of the country. As a result they engage in a military crack down in which 100,000 civilians lose their lives. Four years later militant separatists, several of whom have lost their families in the military action seize a school and take hostages. Government forces try to free the children, but in the following action 400 hostage children lose their lives.

- Inmates in a government prison learn that another inmate sentenced for a relatively minor crime has admitted to a cellmate that he has sexually abused children in the past. The inmates convene their own court, try the inmate and find him guilty. As a sentence they beat him up breaking both his legs and kneecaps and leave him permanently crippled. Are their actions a crime, or are they justly punishing him?

- The owner of a factory operates in breach of health and safety regulations and keeps the fire escape exits locked. As a result of a fire on the premises many of the factory staff burn to death. Is this a crime, or an industrial accident?

- In 2003 many thousands of abortions were carried out in the US in accordance with the valid law. Members of the pro-life movement claim that the doctors carrying out the operations are guilt of murder—are they? One pro-life member shoots and kills a well-known abortion performing doctor, because he says the doctor was breaking God's will and he needed to be punished.

The examples could be multiplied. Certainly all 'crimes' are unique events, however, are there common characteristics to some of these events that mark them off for special recognition and thus mean they are crimes? Is there a coherent way of distinguishing key factors and ensuring that 'we', that is the representatives of a community, come to an agreement as to what makes up a crime, or, indeed, what should then follow from agreeing that a crime has taken place? Or does the issue of agreeing on what is crime actually show how divided 'we' are? If we answer each event with a yes, that those events should be accepted as a crime, are we merely being emotive? (Emotivism is defined as a use of language that asserts something which cannot logically be backed up in such a way that it convinces the majority of others to agree.) Can we separate what *is* legally a crime (that is, it is contrary to the valid law) from what we feel ought to be a crime? Or is this way of distinguishing things a mistake? Is it a lazy way out of the dilemma of our responsibility towards the world? What then can we learn from following through the above examples?

- The *Zong* actually went to trial as an insurance case. The boat owners had claimed insurance on the dead slaves as they said they were simply 'property' that had been thrown overboard out of necessity. The original jury agreed and ordered the underwriters to pay insurance on them, but the underwriters appealed and we do not know if any insurance money was ever paid out. Meanwhile, a group of people around a prominent individual called Glanvill Sharp, tried to get the authorities to prosecute the crew for murder, but they were unsuccessful. The system did not want this to be called a crime. As Walvin (1992) argues, if this event had been called 'murder', it would have unpicked the legality of the whole slave system and the international trade in it. As a result people around Glanvill Sharp got together and formed an anti-slavery and abolitionist movement that ultimately changed the system.

- In the case of the cabin boy who was killed and eaten, the men were prosecuted and the case of Dudley and Stephens (1884) became a leading case for the proposition that necessity cannot be a defence against the charge of murder in English law. The judge who heard the case made a wonderful statement that it was always the duty of the captain of a ship to look after his passengers and crew before himself. Of course the *Zong* was not mentioned in argument! The men were sentenced to death, but this was reduced to six months' imprisonment. In fact it was a custom of the sea for men in similar conditions to cast lots and the person with the shortest lot to be killed and eaten (Simpson, 1984). In this example the men had agreed to do this, but the cabin boy was so weak that they decided to kill him without casting lots. The Admiralty opposed the trial as they did not want the customs of the sea upset, but another government department insisted on charges.

- No one has ever faced charges in respect of the atomic bomb, although Sellars (2001: 66), relying upon a biography of the US President Harry Truman (written by his daughter, Margaret) relates a stag dinner hosted by Truman in early 1953. At this dinner, the famous wartime British leader, Winston Churchill, had the bad manners to ask Truman if he had his response ready for when they both were to stand before St Peter and told to justify using the atomic bombs. This caused considerable shock, which was alleviated when the party organized a mock trial of Churchill with Truman as judge and a jury consisting of the US Secretary of State and other close US colleagues and Generals. Acquittal resulted, though Sellars could not find in Margaret Truman's account the reason; perhaps, Sellars surmised, 'they sensed that their own hands were dipped in blood. Or perhaps, they reasoned that it did not matter anyway. After all, even in real life tribunals, no one ever punishes a victor.'

Time for reflection: what are the consequences if we accept the definition of crime that is presented in most criminal law textbooks: namely a crime is some conduct (an act or omission) which, when it leads to a certain state of affairs, is treated in that jurisdiction as being capable of leading to prosecution and punishment? Glanville Williams (1955: 107), for example, defined crime as 'an act that is capable of being followed by criminal proceedings, having one of the types of outcome (punishment etc) known to follow these proceedings'. This in practice is the definition of crime most commonly accepted, as was brought out by Tappan's famous injunction that criminology accepts as its object of study crime, defined as 'an intentional act or omission in violation of criminal law (statutory and case law), committed without defence or justification, and sanctioned by the State as a felony or misdemeanor' (1947: 100). But this means that there is no common element to a crime other than the fact of the prior legal procedure defining such and such act or omission as a crime. It also means that so far in the events considered only the act of killing the cabin boy was a crime, and that was a near thing. In the great age of sail it is probable that many cases occurred where crews ended up in open boats or stranded on desolate shores and one of their company was killed and eaten. But they drew lots, thus when they were picked up everyone could be satisfied that the custom of the sea had been followed and no crime occurred and the authorities were never involved.

- In the case of Rwanda we face a situation, which most commentators now say, was the most easily preventable mass crime of the twentieth century. The attention of the world's media was on events in South Africa where Nelson Mandela was elected President and apartheid ended peacefully. When the first killings began ten Belgian UN soldiers were killed with the result that the UN withdrew the mission and all attempts to get intervention failed in particular because of US reluctance caused in part by the previous killing of eighteen US servicemen in Somalia. The subsequent official US line was that they did not have proper information; they did not appreciate the full picture. We now know that they knew fully what was going on and that President Clinton had ordered that the term 'genocide' not be used as that might trigger calls for the US to intervene, not to mention the quasi-legal obligation to take action as a country that had ratified the Genocide Convention (see, for example, 'US chose to ignore Rwandan genocide', *The Guardian*, 31 March, 2004). Thus, deliberate US inactivity was one of the crucial factors that condemned to death the equivalent of the US domestic homicide total for 1950–2000. It would be literally unthinkable for President Clinton to face penal sanctions in connection with these deaths; for his deliberate inactivity to be called a 'crime'. He was, however, pursued by extremely expensive legal proceedings (costing more than a UN force that would have deterred or at least stopped the main killings of the genocide) for most of his second term in office. The question to be ascertained in those particular proceedings, which included impeachment hearings, was did he commit a crime or misdemeanour when he stated that an activity with a certain female intern at the White House, later found to be an oral sexual act, did not constitute 'sexual relations'. He was acquitted.

• The situation with the 'major European country' and terrorism equates to what many have claimed the situation is between Russia and Chechnya. In the context of the current 'war on terror', most governments say that Chechnya is an internal matter for Russia, in effect closing their eyes to massive human rights violations, death and destruction.

• The action of the prison inmates constitutes 'self-help'. It is deemed a crime and not justified 'punishment' in part because one of the principles that modern society is founded on is that the State claims a monopoly upon legitimate violence. There are many examples of groups that organize themselves in such a way that they almost constitute a state within a state—such as the Mafia or transnational drug dealing organizations—taking on state-like roles and procedures. In doing so they pose a threat to the State's existence and since the sixteenth century the dominant mode of large-scale social organization has been the 'nation-state'. It is the nation-state that has the authority to define what sort of activities can be deemed crimes within its boundaries and only officials of the nation-state are authorized to carry out punishments. (As this chapter is written, October 2004, American and Iraqi forces are waiting until after the US election to attack the Iraqi city of Falluja to establish government control. A key point has been that 'in Falluja, the insurgents are free to carry out their own brand of justice, like the public lashings of people suspected of theft and rape, and the videotaped beheading of . . . one of the city's National Guard commanders' (Filkins, 2004).) The English for capital punishment comes in part from the Latin word *capitalis* which means 'of the head', and was originally by decapitation, literally 'a capital offence'. The symbolism of the beheading is the denial of the legitimacy and the ability of the State to function and its replacement by a counter-state group.

• The final three examples are simplified examples based on real cases. They allow us in the words of the Norwegian criminologist, Nils Christie, to hold up the processes in which crime is identified and reacted to as a mirror revealing a picture of social relations not otherwise seen. Take the example of the factory owners. In the early 1990s similar fires caused the deaths of hundreds of workers in the US, Thailand and China.

In the North Carolina Chicken Processing Plant fire of 1991, twenty-five workers died and forty-nine were injured when a fire broke out and all but one of the nine fire escapes was locked. The owners had locked the doors and boarded up the windows to prevent the staff stealing food; however, no security fence had been constructed or any security guard hired. Nineteen of the twenty-five dead were single mothers, predominantly black— blacks had only been allowed to work in the factories of the south since the 1970s and even then they were unionized and unable to bargain for reasonable conditions. Blame for the fire was attributed to various local, federal and state agencies. It had not been visited by health and safety officers for over eleven years and had already experienced several minor fires that year. There was no trial, the owner pleaded guilty to twenty-five counts of manslaughter, while his son and another manager went free as part of the plea bargain arrangement. To the extent that it was reported and picked up in the media, the fire revealed the conditions of work for many in the semi-rural areas of the US and demonstrated the divided nature of social life in the US. But if one thought that defining something as a crime invokes sympathy for the victims and that political measures would be likely to be taken to reduce victimhood or harm, this case is sobering; for less than two years later insurance companies and the business lobby in North Carolina got together and introduced legislation to reduce compensation for injured workers. Moreover, crime in Anglo-American jurisprudence is an individualist responsibility; in other words crime usually can only be proven when specific individuals are implicated and responsibility can be fixed upon them Thus, it is individuals who are blamed and not the system. This can be seen even more clearly from another case where on 10 May, 1993, fire broke out at the Kader toy factory outside Bangkok, Thailand. Managers had locked exit doors to make sure the workers could not steal the toys. Hundreds of workers, mostly young women were trapped inside. Officially 188 were killed, with 469 injured, many seriously, after they were forced to leap from second, third and forth floors of the buildings to avoid being burnt to death. Blame was fixed on the managers. But did the fault lie only with the managers? The fire occurred at the height of the Simpsons craze and the factory was producing Simpson toys: a melted Bart became the symbol of the tragedy and the consequences of the new global capitalist/consumer economy. The following quote is from a Malaysian labour activist, Tian Chua, who writes from prison where he had been detained from April 2001, without being charged, for attempting to organize Malaysian workers without government permission (you may note the politics here, for if she was actually charged with a 'crime' most jurisdictions require a court appearance where at least a minimal level of proof is brought forward in order that the person remains in custody!).

> The bodies of Bart Simpson scattered all over the ground—some half burned, some without heads or limbs, some half completed . . . Kader was one of the largest toy manufactures in Asia. It was also a typical multinational company which moved around for cheap labour. Kader was jointly owned by Thai and Hong Kong capitalists. It mainly produced toys for European & American markets . . . The toy industry is a sector which produces fun and joy. Toys bring laughter to children and parents. However, the tragedy of Kader fire revealed the sorrows and suffering behind toy manufacturing. Kader made us aware that workers use their sweat, tears and blood to exchange happiness for children around the world. (quoted, 2Bangkok.com, accessed 19/10/04)

In 1993, another fire broke out in the Zhili Toy factory in Shenzhen, China, with eighty-seven deaths. Here we come to the difference between a sociological/critical criminological reading of these events as crimes and a more legalist or narrowly focused criminological interpretation of the event. From the sociological or critical criminological perspective, the international connections between market driven consumption, demands for cheap but well-produced products, and the avoidance of operating according to full health and safety measures are apparent and have considerable bearing on the fire. From a more narrowly focused understanding of crime, those factors are all 'externalities'; what is of concern in ascertaining whether the events were a crime is then only the immediate actions and mental states of those who locked the doors and those who should have ordered them to be open. Moreover, what of the issue of responding to the victims and preventing future similar incidents? Whereas earlier, well published industrial fires, such as the Triangle Shirtwaist Factory fire of 1911 in New York (where nearly 150 people died because of locked fire exits), led to labour agitation and improved regulations of working conditions, the conditions for workers in the so-called developing world are at the mercy of multinational corporations that can quickly relocate to cheaper, less regulated locations. The international press gave Kader some attention, but today writers say very little has improved:

> Thailand's limited building and safety codes, minimal wage levels and factory regulations are not enforced. Indeed, the government in Thailand attracts foreign capital to its shores by openly advertising the lack of restrictions on the exploitation of workers. The Kader factory was no aberration. All the horrors of nineteenth century European capitalism—child labor, dirty and unsafe working conditions, shanty housing—are on display everywhere in Bangkok. (Symonds, 1997: 58–9)

So, even if we were to agree to call this a crime, the consequence may be that a small group of individuals are blamed and punished, but the wider social conditions that caused social harm are pushed to one side and overlooked. This leads several criminologists to say we should not concentrate upon 'crime' as an organizing concept, but replace it instead with 'social harm' or protection of 'human rights' (see, for example, Hillyard *et al.*, 2004).

To summarize this section: we are therefore talking about complicated and changing interactions of governmental and discursive power, public concerns and the different roles of officials who control key decision-making processes (see Chapter 21) as well as the media that highlights certain issues and downplays others (see Chapters 7 and 8). There are complex factors at work that influence how the edifice of public administration—including what the literature refers to as 'the criminal justice system'—relates to and processes events that may or may not be termed crimes.

REVIEW QUESTIONS

1 Under the law of society X, it is lawful to keep slaves and any slave that escapes or attempts to escape commits a serious offence; it is also a crime for any person to consciously assist in the escape of a slave or not to report a slave to the authorities if they come across an escaped slave [assume that there are no international conventions concerning slavery]. While on holiday in X you meet a person you realize is an escaped slave but do not report them; in fact you allow them to stay in your hotel room. Are you a criminal? Is the slave? Your partner decides that they must obey the law and they report you to the authorities with the result that you and the slave are sent to prison, has your partner done anything wrong?

2 Using internet sources and the library, research the Bhopal disaster in India 1984. Who was at fault and has justice been achieved in response to that event? What role if any does racism or corruption play?

Frameworks of choice and logic: the politics of criminology and the definition of crime

So far we have explored matters with respect to practical examples. We have seen how in practice and in the literature there is much disagreement over defining exactly what a crime is. McCabe (1983: 49) says 'there is no word in the whole lexicon of legal and criminological terms which is so elusive of definition as the word "crime" '! How then can a discipline that has as its common focus the study of crime ever have a settled focus? The history of criminology can be read as revolving around this question. It has been said that most definitions of crime involve a drastic circularity and that criminological explanations relying upon them become tautologies. Perhaps it is the effect of this, but criminology as a scholarly discipline has moved in circles over many of its central issues. One problem is that the definition of crime adopted by an individual reflects the whole world perspective of that individual and the social groups they reside within. We are faced with various distinctions, controversies and frameworks of logic that are related to our view of the world and mankind's place in it. There include choices between the following assertions or claims:

- Crime is some action or omission that causes harm in a situation that the person or group responsible 'ought' to be held accountable and punished, irrespective of what the law books of a state say.

- Crime is an action against the law of God, whether as revealed in the holy books, such as The Bible, Koran or Torah or that we instinctively recognize as against God's will, irrespective of what the law books of a state say. If the State law books allow something that we know to be against God's will this does not change its status—it is still a crime.

- Crime is an act or omission that is defined by the validly passed laws of the nation-state in which it occurred so that punishment should follow from the behaviour. Only such acts or omissions are crimes.

- If there is no public authority capable or ready to police social activity and punish offenders, then there is no crime. Crimes and criminals only exist when a public body has judged them such according to accepted procedures. Without the State and the criminal law there is no crime. Without criminal justice systems there are no criminals.

- Crime is an irrelevant concept as it is tied to the formal social control mechanism of the State; deviance is a concept that is owned by sociology, thus our study should be the sociology of deviance, rather than criminology.

We can identify at least four frameworks in which to make sense of how crime is defined:

- (a) crime as a *social construction*;
- (b) crime as a product of religious authority/doctrine;
- (c) crime as a reflection of nation-state legality;
- (d) more recent concepts beyond the nation-state derived from social and political theory.

Criminology, and indeed, our present position more generally contain the legacy of the earlier positions. Let us look briefly at each in turn.

Social construction

Social construction is a highly influential and controversial current perspective. In summary it argues that our concepts and the practical consequences that flow from using them are the products (constructions) of social interaction and only make sense within the communities in which that interaction takes place. In other words, 'crime' is a label created in social interaction, but once created it has both a symbolic and practical reality. We endow the world with symbols and respond to the meanings contained in them. Language and other symbolic systems codify these meanings and by using language we impose a grid on reality; the law is a particularly strong grid system. In this case we create terms of crime and punishment that enable us to identify and distinguish different events. But these terms also impose certain consequences, as in the following statement from a very influential book on criminal justice: 'When a crime is committed, justice must be done . . . a failure to punish crime is wrong and a community that does not punish its criminals is derelict in its moral duty' (Gross, 1979: xv and 18). In many accounts crime and punishment are linked as if they were unproblematic concepts reflecting a reality in which crimes are committed as a matter of identifiable facts and once the person responsible is identified certain processes must logically follow. However, those who accept social construction argue that since language and other symbolic systems are social products, this is a socially constructed grid. It is a social choice to recognize such and such an event as a crime, or such and such a person as a 'criminal'. Some other term and therefore some other course of action could be used. Two consequences follow. In one we have a research project of following through the creation of the use of the concept 'crime and its actual allocation to particular events or situations (the process of criminalization). A second consequence is that we can argue that there is no particular natural level of use of the concept crime, that it can imprison us in particular techniques of social ordering and it may be better to abolish its use. This was stated clearly by the Dutch abolitionist lawyer, Louk Hulsman:

> categories of 'crime' are given by the criminal justice system rather than by victims of society in general. This makes it necessary to abandon the notion of 'crime' as a tool in the conceptual framework of criminology. Crime has no ontological reality. Crime is not the object but the product of criminal policy. Criminalization is one of the many ways of constructing social reality. (Hulsman, 1986: 34–5)

Drawing upon anthropological evidence of how different social groups identified troublesome situations and individuals, the American criminologist Howard Becker (1963) and others developed an influential school of thought in sociology known as labelling theory (see Chapter 4). This holds that the terms crime, deviance or punishment are labels, variously applied by acts of power and not some natural reflection of events. The full potential of labelling theory was not realized. When Becker wrote, for example, he only mentioned in passing the gender divide in which men made the rules in society for other men and women. Today, in the hands not only of feminists but deconstructionists, labelling theory leads in a more radical social constructionist theory in which a multi-sided account of criminalization is given (see Chapter 4). In its abolitionist forms, such as with the Norwegian criminologist Nils Christie (2004), the major challenge for criminology is to understand the social processes of the application of these basic labels and, by implication, if we follow through the process we might come to an understanding that may lead to a lowering of the rate of 'crime' by abandoning the entire processes of criminalization. His central assertion undercuts the common-sense views of crime and disorder:

> Crime does not exist. Only acts exist, acts often given different meanings within various social frameworks. Acts and the meanings given to them are our data. Our challenge is to follow the destiny of acts through the universe of meanings. Particularly, what are the social conditions that encourage or prevent giving the acts the meaning of being crime? (Christie, 2004: 3)

Crime does not exist. Only acts exist, acts often given different meanings within various social frameworks. Acts, and the meanings attached to them . . . but is this actually so and even if this was the case, could humans really accept such a radical view?

Crime in 'the city of God'

The phrase 'city of God' comes from the Christian writer St Augustine (354–410), but could with only slight modification be used to describe Islamic or Judaic systems; it refers to the world view where we humans live in a universe created by God and his commands. Social construction theory is denied by many people who see in it the consequences of human ambition to position ourselves as the masters of the world and our destiny. Instead, very significant numbers of people believe that God created the universe and allocated a place for humans within his creation. To enable us to know something of his intentions God also sent messages to humanity through prophets and other forms of revelation; these messages were collected in books of authority of which the Koran, the Bible and the Torah are best known. Each lays out various rules in terms of imperatives and warnings of the consequences if these are not followed. Let us fear God, says the Koran, 'verily, God is witness over all'. God will prepare shameful woe for those who disobey his rules. To the followers, the laws of God lay out the path to heaven and redemption. There is no problem of the legitimacy of these rules and the definition of what should be crime since God's will is the ultimate driving force of creation—even if humans have been endowed with free will and the capacity not to see the truth. There are numerous problems for social order in a complex grouping: a crucial one is who can agree on the exact message from God, what happens to constrain conflicting interpretations? As Blaise Pascal put it: 'men never do evil so openly and contentedly as when they do it from religious conviction'. Take as examples two crime-related words that have found their way into our English dictionary: thuggery and assassination. The derivation of thuggery is from the Sanskrit *sthag*, to conceal. For centuries a religious sect existed in India to rob and murder. A conservative estimate is that they killed well over a million people between 1740 and 1840 until suppressed by British colonial authorities. Thugs were devotees of the goddess Bhowani or Kali, the 'Black Mother', the Hindu goddess of death and destruction. Gangs of men operated to murder and rob, strangling their victims as sacrifices to Kali. When caught Thugs looked forward to their execution as a quick route to paradise. The English word assassination comes from the Muslim world, where after the death of the prophet Muhammad, three of his early successors were killed with daggers. A group, 'assassins', was founded by Hasan Ibn al-Sabbsh, whose followers killed rival Sunni Muslims, and many Muslim caliphs (ultimate leaders) have been killed over the subsequent centuries. The Assassins killed as acts of piety and sought to replace an allegedly corrupt Sunni regime with a supposedly ideal Shiite one; when caught they accepted their death.

Throughout the western world the horrors of the massive religious conflicts of the late middle ages resulted in the separation of Church and State. The city of God became replaced by the city of man and religious belief was deemed in practice to be a personal matter. For much of its history criminology has been a secular discipline, an applied science of the nation-state; but there are now serious arguments that it has been badly compromised by neglecting to engage with the religious belief systems that many people live by (Knepper, 2001).

Nation-state legality

From the seventeenth century, slowly and with many oppositions, a secular view of crime arose where crime is understood as an act or omission as defined by the sovereign authority in factual charge of a specific territory—the nation-state. It is important to note the full implications of this view. First: the substance of what is made criminal is a matter of the 'will' of the sovereign body, the Parliament, the courts, and the Senate. Second: as liberal jurisprudential writers, such as H.L.A Hart (1961) emphasize, the fact that something is made a crime does not necessarily mean it is immoral. While in practice many crimes will be based on the shared perceptions of the people, arising from customs, religious beliefs and common-sense conceptions of what is acceptable and unacceptable; crimes are simply posited by the rule-making power centres of the State. Third: it follows that to be called a criminal is a status conferred by the legal and political process of the State, there is no such thing as a natural criminal or a born criminal (cf. Chapter 4). As Korn and McCorkle express it, this was forgotten by much individualist focused criminology, which took a naturalist view of the terms 'crime' and 'criminality'.

> The use of the term criminal to identify persons occupying a potential and removable status is in sharp contrast to the view that criminality is a sickness, a biological condition, or a type. The failure to distinguish between the ideas of status and type has led to costly errors and lost directions in criminology. It has led many to mistake the fact of a fairly clear legal category for the existence of an equally identifiable category of persons with similar characteristics. It has led brilliant investigators into life-long searches for common biological, social, or psychological traits. Despite the failure of these investigations to isolate within the offender a single characteristic not found in the law-abiding, the search for common factors continues to preoccupy those who are still unaware that the object of their quest is the product of a semantic confusion. (Korn and McCorkle, 1959: 48)

Those authors were also 'realists', saying that 'irrespective of laws, an act is not a crime until the offender is caught, tried and punished'. The consequences for criminology were clear since the knowledge base requires first the achievement of political control by a state over territory, secondly institutional processes of recognition and interpretation of activity as criminal, and lastly the scholarly reflection upon that ascription and processes of dealing with those defined. By implication where the State has not instituted a situation of 'continuous political control' there can be no criminological reflection; criminology (at least in its conventional or mainstream forms) was the applied science of the nation-state and where the nation-state did not define crime, there was no criminological knowledge (see Hogg, 2002, and Morrison, 2005, for arguments for a contemporary criminology beyond the nation-state).

Beyond nation-state definitions of crime

Modern western societies have largely defined crime in the terms laid down by the nation-state. A crime is an act or omission that leads to penal sanction in accordance with the constitutionally valid procedures of that nation-state. Thus nation-state *A* will prohibit the smoking of cannabis, while nation state *B* may say that within specified areas (for example, the coffee shops of Amsterdam) it is allowed. The examples can be multiplied; thus relativism—and, say some, the holocaust. It does not take a great leap of the imagination to see the policy of the extermination of European Jews (and all others if the State could have power over them) written into the manifesto of Hitler and adopted when the legitimate sovereign of the German people. Hitler's aggressive expansionist policies brought about World War II and after it several of the surviving Nazis were tried for the crime of waging aggressive war and associated crimes against humanity. While we now see the Holocaust as the icon of crime in the twentieth century, at the time and today many commentators say that logically it would not have been a crime if the extermination of the Jews had remained an internal state policy. Perhaps no writer has expressed this better than George Steiner:

> I wonder what would have happened if Hitler had played the game after Munich, if he had simply said, 'I will make no move outside the Reich so long as I am allowed a free hand inside my borders'. [The death camps of] Dachau, Buchenwald, and Therasienstadt would have operated in the middle of twentieth-century civilisation until the last Jew had been made soap. There would have been brave words on Trafalgar Square and in Carnegie Hall, to audiences diminishing and bored. Society might, on occasion, have boycotted German wines. But no foreign power would have taken action. Tourists would have crowded the Autobahn and spars of the Reich, passing near but not too near to the death-camps (Steiner, 1967: 150).

Even if we were to agree with Steiner as a tragic matter of fact, this would clearly be an affront to notions of our common humanity. Hence it is essential that we engage in a movement to construct a framework for defining crime that is neither tied to any one particular view of religion, nor to the confines of the nation-state.

Within criminology a well-known attempt was made by the Schwendigers who asked if criminologists were 'defenders of order or guardians of human rights'? They suggested that our individualist focused conceptions of crime needed to be broadened so that we could define whole 'social systems as criminal'. They argued that an expanded definition of 'crime as a label for social systems' become a 'warrant not for controlling atomistic individuals, or preventing an atomistic act, but rather for the regulation or elimination of social relationships, properties of social systems, or social systems as a whole' (Schwendiger and Schwendiger 1975: 136). Post World War II, a number of international conventions have tried to create a system for the recognition and processing of international crime under such titles as 'crimes against humanity' or 'genocide'. This is an expanding framework, though at present it is characterized more by words than actual deeds, and instances of international intervention are controversial (see Morrison 2004).

One other attempt may be noted, perhaps the most common within the sociological imagination, namely to replace crime by the concept of 'deviance'. Many of the work published within the criminological enterprise from the 1960s focused on the 'sociology of deviance' in order that criminality might escape from legality and create its own frame of reference. The problem was that deviance was, and remained, a sociological construct. In the public consciousness crime was the dominant and seemingly the most useful category.

This failure of sociological criminology to create a discourse that could engage successfully with the public and the political power centres is reflected in the recent book *The Culture of Control* by David Garland (2001), one of the most respected writers in criminology and the sociology of punishment. Garland highlighted the current dilemma surrounding the question of 'what is crime?' by pointing out the practical ways in which crime is approached and perceived in contemporary society. Garland did not refer to crime merely as an increasing factual reality (which is in itself a contestable proposition), nor indeed did he refer to the more complex category of the social fear of crime and ask how we can distinguish the reality of crime from the public and media image of crime; his theme was that *crime was now a core category of governing*. In his narrative, the perception that crime had increased had given rise to a new culture particularly in the US and UK, which he termed the 'culture of control'. His text was published shortly before the terrorist attacks of 11 September 2001, but those events—and the huge changes to notions of security throughout the western and Muslim worlds—have demonstrated the interdependence of the actions of defining events as crimes and modes of social governance. Some called the events of 11 September a great crime. Others called it an act of war, while still others, alternatively, said that the terms used were unimportant, for the real task was to inquire as to why certain people were motivated to carry them out? How one reacted to those events, however, was in considerable part a result of controlling how one defined their nature. Or put it another way: the consequences that the acts invoked were not predetermined, there was a range of possible reactions; once those events were defined in such or such a way, then the range of social reactions was constrained. Thus we end where we began, by re-emphasizing the diversity of opinions, definitions, perspectives and complex interrelationships that surround what at first sight may seem a simple question: what is crime?

1 'The criminal law is the source of crime; without the law we would not have crime'. Discuss.

2 What value is there in advocating an 'abolitionist' approach, such as that espoused by Nils Christie or Louk Hulsman?

CONCLUSION

Defining crime is not a matter of common sense or simply following an accepted procedure. In the examples given in this chapter we can see some of the complex political and economic forces that shape how we define crime in practice—such as US domestic political pressure to downplay knowledge of the events in Rwanda, and to ensure that the specific term that would have described them as a great crime—genocide—was not used, while other domestic political pressures where behind the desperate attempts to define Clinton's explanation of his 'personal' life as a crime. What can we learn? The case of the *Zong*, for example, may seem a long time ago, but:

> On Boxing Day 1996, the crew of an old rusting freighter the *Yiohan* forced over 300 passengers off the ship and on to a small craft designed for a third of that number. Over 280 were drowned when the boat went down. Four years later, fishermen in Sicily were still hauling in corpses and body parts with their catches (*Observer*, 10 June 2001). The tragedy received very little press coverage: only the *Observer* ran the story, as an expose of the ship's captain. (Webber, 2004: 133)

Webber's point is that of course this was not seen as a modern crime of the system, rather the problem was that of the illegal immigrants and those individuals that preyed upon them (who were not apprehended or punished). In the case of the *Zong*, the demand for cheap labour fed the 18th Century slave system of enforced migration. Today we enforce barriers and impose the label criminal on those who seek to voluntarily migrate outside the strict 'legal' conditions governing official migration.

We have a lot to learn from history in this area. Even if we can only conclude that in defining crime there is no easy answer, only controversy and struggle.

QUESTIONS FOR DISCUSSION

1 Why is it so difficult to agree upon a definition of crime?

2 'The crimes that the public are most concerned about are not the real risks that we face.' Discuss.

3 'The solution to the problems of defining crime will be found only by escaping from the confines of the nation-state. We need some universal standards to use as our reference to define crime.' Discuss.

4 Take an area, such as drug prohibition, and follow through how and when this was prohibited. Ask whose interests are served by this criminalization policy? Is criminalization a cause of social harm?

GUIDE TO FURTHER READING

Most textbooks have either a chapter or a section on defining crime. These vary drastically in quality and can be repetitive.

The classic discussion is Keith Bottomley, 'What is Crime?', Chapter 1 of *Criminology in Focus* (1979, Oxford: Martin Robertson).

One of the better recent discussions is John Tierney, *Criminology: Theory and Context* (1996, London: Prentice Hall), Chapter 1 'Criminology, Crime and Deviance: some Preliminaries', and Chapter 2 'Measuring Crime and Criminality'.

Perhaps the best recent single chapter is Stuart Henry and Dragan Milovanovic, *Constitutive Criminology: Beyond Postmodernism* (1996, London: Sage), Chapter 5, 'Definitions of Crime and Constructions of the Victim'.

See also Chapter 2 'A Crime by Any Other Name . . .' in Jeffrey Reiman's . . . *And the Poor Get Prison: Economic Bias in American Criminal Justice* (1996, Needham Heights: Allyn & Bacon) for examples of industrial accidents and other events that cause great harm not being called crimes.

On the rise and fall of the sociology of deviance Colin Sumner's 'The Sociology of Deviance: an Obituary' (1994, Buckingham: Open University Press), is wonderful reading.

For an instructive and relevant essay on the contrast between mainstream criminology and more realist conceptions of harm see Phil Scraton's 'Defining "power" and challenging "knowledge": critical analysis as resistance in the UK' in *Critical Criminology: Issues, Debates, Challenges*, Kerry Carrington and Russell Hogg (eds) (2002, Devon: Willan).

Nils Christie's *A Suitable Amount of Crime* (2004, London: Routledge) is an excellent consistent analysis of the proposition that 'crimes are in endless supply. Acts with the potentiality of being seen as crimes are like an unlimited natural resource. We can take out a little in the form of crime—or a lot' (p. 10).

The best argument that crime needs to be replaced by concepts of social harm is *Beyond Criminology: Taking Harm Seriously*, Paddy Hillyard, Christina Pantazis, Steve Tombs and Dave Gordon (eds) (2004, London: Pluto).

For the need for criminology to move beyond the nation-state see Morrison, *Criminology, Civilisation and the New World Order* (2005, London: Glasshouse).

WEB LINKS

Lexis ONE
http://ww.lexisone.com
A free legal research site providing searchable case law and a whole host of other useful research aids.

The Emile Durkheim Archive
http://durkheim.itgo.com/anomie.html
A detailed website dedicated to the French sociologist.

Amnesty International
http://www.amnesty.org
Find out more about the campaign for international human rights legislation and human rights abuses.

REFERENCES

Becker, H. (1964) *Outsiders*. New York: Free Press.

Brown, D. and Hogg, R. (1992) 'Law and order politics—left realism and radical criminology: a view from "down under", in R. Mathews and J. Young (eds), *Issues in Realist Criminology*. London: Sage.

Christie, N. (2004) *A Suitable Amount of Crime*. London: Routledge.

Durkhein, E. (1966) *The Rules of Sociological Method* (trans S.A. Solovay and J.H. Mueller, (ed) G.E.G. Catlin). New York: Free Press.

Filkins, D. (2004) 'List of Iraqi cities where US troops won't go is growing longer'. *International Herald Tribune*, 6 September.

Garland, D. (2001) *The Culture of Control*. Oxford: Oxford University Press.

Gross, H. (1979) *A Theory of Criminal Justice*. New York: Oxford University Press.

Hart, H.L.A. (1961) *A Concept of Law*. Oxford: Clarendon Press.

Hogg, R. (2002) 'Criminology beyond the nation state: global conflicts, human rights and the "new world disorder" ', in Kerry Carrington and Russell Hogg, *Critical Criminology*. Cullompton: Willan.

Knepper, P. (2001) *Explaining Criminal Conduct*. Durham, North Carolina: Carolina Academic Press.

Korn, R. and McCorkle, L. (1959) *Criminology and Penology*. New York: Henry Holt & Co.

McCabe, S. (1983) 'Crime', in D. Walsh and A. Poole (eds) *A Dictionary of Criminology*. London: Routledge and Kegan Paul, pp. 49–52.

Morrison, W. (2004) 'Criminology, genocide, and modernity: remarks on the companion that criminology ignored', in Sumner C. (ed) *The Blackwell Companion to Criminology*. Oxford: Blackwell.

Morrison, W. (2005) *Criminology, Civilisation and the New World Order*. London: GlassHouse.

Schwendiger, H. and Schwendiger, J. (1975) 'Defenders of Order or Guardians of Human Rights?' in Ian Taylor *et al.* (eds) *Critical Criminology*. London: Routledge & Kegan Paul.

Sellars, K. (2002) *The Rise and Rise of Human Rights*. Phoenix Mill: Sutton.

Symonds, P. (1997) *Industrial Inferno: The Story of the Thai Toy Factory Fire*. London: Labour Press Books.

Tappan, P. (1947) 'Who is the Criminal?', *American Sociological Review* 12: 96–102

Walvin, J. (1992) *Black Ivory: A History of British Slavery*. London: HarperCollins.

Webber, F. (2004) 'The war on migration', in *Beyond Criminology: Taking Harm Seriously*, Paddy Hillyard *et al.* (eds), London: Pluto Press.

Williams, G. (1955) 'The Definition of Crime', 8, *Current Legal Problems*.

Website accessed: www.2bangkok.com/2bangkok/Simpsons

2

History of crime

Heather Shore

INTRODUCTION

The aim of this chapter is to provide readers with an overview of the history of crime in Britain. But why does a student of criminology need to know about history? Or more specifically, why do criminologists need a history of crime? Modern day penological theory and penal practices, criminal law, policing, juvenile justice, and public order, all have a historical context. It is important for students to understand the evolution of the practices, institutions, theories, and systems with which they are concerned. The purpose of this chapter, then, is to explore these developments and their broader historical contexts, and in doing so to clarify the various issues and paradigms which have come to characterize the history of crime. This chapter is divided into four sections. The first will consider the nature and definition of criminality over time, looking particularly at youth crime and the idea of the 'criminal class'. The following three sections will explore the different stages of criminal justice, focusing on the process of prosecution, the role of policing, and the theory and practice of punishment over time.

BACKGROUND

Arguably, the earliest influential theoretician of law was Sir William Blackstone who published his, *Commentaries on the Laws of England* between 1765 and 1769. The *Commentaries* were the first document to fully elucidate the form and function of the English criminal law, which had undergone considerable change since the constitutional changes and crisis of the seventeenth century.[1] Indeed, the eighteenth century was something of a watershed in terms of theories of criminality and penality. From the mid-eighteenth century a number of commentators published on the problems of policing and prostitution, the care of disorderly youth, the state of the prisons, and the nature of punishment. Thus, Henry and John Fielding (1707–54 and 1721–80), Jonas Hanway (1712–86), John Howard (1726–90), Patrick Colquhoun (1745–1820), and Jeremy Bentham (1748–1832) were the most important voices in the shaping of eighteenth and early nineteenth century criminal justice.[2] Whilst their reputation and contribution has been recognized historically, we should also remember that most of these figures had what we might call a practitioner role in the criminal justice system. For example, the Fielding's were magistrates, Hanway founded the Marine Society, an institution for delinquent boys, Howard was a county sheriff, and Colquhoun was a magistrate (Emsley, 1996a). The connection between practice and theory continued in the nineteenth century, but broader social and political contexts shifted the focus. Increasingly, theories of criminality were to be shaped by scientific and medical discourses, and in the later nineteenth century the work of the anthropologist Cesare Lombroso (1876) has been seen as highly significant (Pick, 1989). However, the earlier history of such pseudo-sciences as *physiognomy* and *phrenology* which had been discredited by the 1850s, were also influential in the shaping of European criminal justice responses.

It has become one of the paradigms of the history of crime that both traditional and *revisionist* approaches have tended to focus on the eighteenth and nineteenth centuries. Whilst, as this chapter will show, earlier histories of crime had their place, it was the periods of more dramatic shifts in society and the social order which have caught historians attention. Moreover, as we can see from the development of theory, it was in these periods that contemporaries started making the clearest connections between social action, domestic policy and the control of crime. In the early eighteenth century, criminal justice was overwhelmingly local, the community and the parish controlled law enforcement, punishment was a matter of discretion and negotiation, and where it did take place, served to some extent as a public mechanism for order and stability. By the late nineteenth century, the State had taken over much of the running of the justice system, and it was state agencies and institutions that played out criminal justice at both a local and national level. Moreover, whilst public and private conceptions of justice were not mutually exclusive, the establishment of a professional police force, the formalization of summary juris-diction and rationalization of criminal trial, the development of the *total institution* and the professional-ization of the criminal justice sector were significant watersheds.

However, the history of crime that is available to us as researchers, teachers and students is also shaped by access to, and survival of, sources. Historians' methodologies have often been shaped by parallel developments in other disciplines and by broader political developments. Until the 1960s much of the history of crime that existed was uncritically based on a narrative reading of mainly elite sources. Thus, the parliamentary blue books, covering Select Committees, Inquiries and Royal Commissions were the key sources that defined the '*Whiggish*' histories of the earlier twentieth century. Most of these traditional approaches focused on the idea of progress, on the achievements of the 'great' men and women, the Fieldings, Howards, Peels and Frys, and on the triumph of a humanitarianism which was implicitly shaped by Victorian liberal ideas of modernity.[3] This was gradually to change in the post-World War II period when a combination of factors saw a new generation of historians entering into the profes-sion. The product of an expanded higher education system in the 1960s and 1970s was a body of vigorous young researchers who had been politicized by an era characterized by the anti-war movement, by sexual politics, by civil rights, and to some extent by theoretical Marxism. Moreover, the emergence of the social sciences encouraged a more interdisciplinary approach to history, and those historians who were constructing, '*history from below*'.

Critical *positivist* approaches were particularly influential to historians of crime, who started to appreci-ate the value of *quantitative* methods in understanding crime over time. This focus on the counting of crime, complemented by the focus on non-elite readings of criminality, put the archive and particularly the county-archive at the centre of historical research into crime. However, by the later 1980s the limita-tions of *quantitative* methods were the subject of considerable debate. Survival of records was inconsis-tent across time and place; moreover, the statistics constructed by historians, as well as those left by our forebears, were not always reliable (Emsley, 1996a: 21–55; Sharpe, 1999: 59–63). Methodologies were questioned, and the realization that interpretation was based on the limitations of 'known' crimes resulted in the emergence of new wave of approaches and perspectives. Nowadays, empiricism and *quantitative* methods tend to be incorporated within a more holistic approach. The impact of post-modernist theory and more cultural readings of sources have made historians of crime think twice about their own interpretation of primary material. Currently, a stronger engagement has been sought between historians of crime and criminologists, and to some extent with practitioners in the criminal justice system. Arguably, a more nuanced approach to understanding our criminal past will emerge out of these relationships and collaborations. I hope that the student reading this chapter will gain an understanding of the importance of such an interdisciplinary approach.

Defining crime

The problem of the 'hardened' offender, and as an extension, of the 'criminal classes', was one that was continually to exercise the minds of the Victorians. Yet, as historians of crime have recognized, these typologies can be found in descriptions of London's social life at least from the Elizabethan period (McMullan, 1984). By the eighteenth century the impact of population growth, immigration and manufacture helped increase public as well as State anxiety about crime. The metropolis was perceived as the nerve centre for crime, and increasingly contemporaries were thinking in terms of some sort of economic organization (Howson, 1970). The criminal gang, the highwayman, the street-robber and the thief-whore, were key figures in the criminal typologies that can be found in the biographies and literatures of crime that proliferated in this period. Despite the State's anxieties about crime, and the prevalence of the picturesque, reading the eighteenth century texts the abiding concern seems to have been about the juxtaposition of wealth and poverty, the closeness of the city streets crowding all classes, not only the criminal, into the urban melting-pot. Criminality was seen much as more as part of a life-style risk, to which we could all succumb. This view of crime was to stay substantially the same until the early decades of the nineteenth century. In this period the changes in criminal justice paralleled by a sense of deepening social crisis, resulted in a reformulation of ideas about criminality. At the start of the century, these reformulations focused upon the most vulnerable members of society: the young.

Juvenile offenders

From the early nineteenth century, juvenile delinquency was increasingly being singled out as a social problem. In 1815 the Committee for Investigating the Causes of the Alarming Increase of Juvenile Delinquency in the Metropolis was formed, and the report that they published the following year opened the floodgates to a rush of parliamentary Select Committees, investigations and pamphlets concerned with juvenile crime. Recent work has suggested that the main motivations behind this groundswell was a mixture of generational fears, coincident with the end of the French wars, a re-focusing of attention on the outdated prison system, and the growing influence of reform (King, 1998; Shore, 1996). Increasingly, the need to separate children from adults throughout the whole of the criminal justice system became paramount. In the 1820s a number of acts were passed which were partially designed with the juvenile in mind. The Malicious Trespass Act of 1820, the Vagrancy Act of 1824, and the Larceny Act of 1827 allowed for varying forms of summary processing to be resorted to in the case of petty crimes and minor theft. Overwhelmingly, these acts singled out the trivial and mundane crimes which juvenile offenders were most likely to commit. Moreover, as Susan Magarey argued in her important article, the passage of the 1829 Metropolitan Police Act reinforced this process by focusing the early energies of the new police on petty offences and more vulnerable offenders (1978). As discussed above, the development of summary jurisdiction and juvenile justice in Britain went hand-in-hand, a relationship that was formalized with the passage of the Juvenile Offenders Act of 1847, which allowed children under the age of fourteen to be tried in petty sessions summarily, and a further Act of 1850 which allowed the age limit to be raised to sixteen. From this point on criminal children were increasingly diverted to summary jurisdiction, although the Juvenile Court was not established until the early twentieth century, under the 1908 Children's Act. The legislative journey of the later nineteenth century was to focus almost wholly on the institutional care of the juvenile.

Strategies to deal with juveniles in institutions developed in two ways. On the one hand, the State felt that the new prisons and penitentiary, the apparatus of reform, were adequate to house and to reform juvenile offenders. Peel's Gaol Act of 1824 allowed for greater classification and separation of juveniles. Institutions would be rebuilt or refurbished with separate juvenile specific accommodation. On the other hand, the philanthropic sector established a number of refuges and schools where juvenile offenders could be given useful training. Ultimately the passage of the Industrial and Reformatory Schools Acts between 1854 and 1857 incorporated elements of both the State and voluntary systems. The principle of separate confinement of juvenile offenders was to be finalized in 1876 under the Education Act, which established day industrial schools and truant schools. As a result of the reformatory movement of the later century, there was a significant decline of children in prison, and most children placed in prison were there on remand, or in lieu of paying a fine. This was addressed by the Industrial Schools Act of 1866, which detained such children in the workhouse, and more successfully in the Youthful Offenders Act of 1901, which empowered the courts to remand a child 'into the custody of any "fit person" . . . who is willing to receive him' (Radzinowicz and Hood, 1986: 627–8).

The drive to separate the child from the adult prisoner was underpinned by the desire to nip crime in the bud. Increasingly, commentators saw the control of and intervention in juvenile offenders' lives as the key to preventing future generations of 'hardened' recidivist criminals. Partly this seems to have been a reflection of real concern about marginalized children, and the need to provide viable solutions. However, it was also a reflection of the shifting attitudes to criminality in this period. Contemporaries were increasingly seeking to categorize juvenile offenders by the nature and level of their offending (Carpenter, 1851; Shore, 1999: 95). The classification and categorization of criminals, both juvenile and adults, was largely engendered by the new forms of disciplinary institutions which were being built and developed in this period. Thus, in theory at least, the new penality allowed for the matching of sanction to prisoner. However, arguably, the classification of the criminal was also a reflection of broader attempts to discipline the poor, and the new industrial classes (Ignatieff, 1978). From the mid-nineteenth century the idea of the working class was to be paralleled by the emergence of a much more threatening criminal class.

The criminal class

Allusions to the criminal class became common from the mid-century. Whilst fears about criminal subcultures have most frequently, and understandably, been based on the metropolis, Glasgow, Cardiff, Liverpool, Birmingham, and most of the ports and other growing urban and industrial conurbations, had areas identified as belonging to the criminal class (Jones, 1982: 85–116). In reality, the identification of certain areas as 'crim-inal districts' owed much to concerns about public health and sanitation issues, and to increased police surveillance. Whilst such areas had always been present, the portrayal of criminality became more intense in the later nineteenth century. The combination of more effective policing, the rise of social evangelicalism, the impact of imperial racist discourses, and the emergence of a threatening casual labour class, all helped bring atten-tion to the 'criminal classes'. Gareth Stedman-Jones' groundbreaking study of the eco-nomic and political disenfranchisement of the London poor in Victorian society has shown how changes to the labour market resulted in the emergence of a threatening casual labouring class, located overwhelmingly in the east of the city (1971). The prob-lematization of the casual poor was further underlined by political reform. The reform acts of 1832 and 1867 which resulted in the enfranchisement of a significant proportion of the working class arguably contributed to the further disenfranchisement of the remaining poor. Whilst, charitable schemes provided morally cleansed housing and rec-reation for the respectable working-man and his family, the residuum were physically ghettoized, and perceived in opposition to the respectable working class. For many Victorian commentators the poor were synonymous with the criminal class.

The 'mission' to rescue the urban poor was legitimized by the 'othering' of the poor. In the context of Victorian imperialism, where missionaries and politicians were evangeli-calizing to the native 'other' in Africa and India, the comparisons with outcast London were, for too many contemporaries, startling (Marriott, 1999: xi–l). From the mid-nineteenth century, the influence of the natural sciences, of physiological approaches to criminality like *phrenology*, and the impact of organic and hereditary explanations for crime, typified by the work of Cesare Lombroso (1835–1909) and Havelock Ellis (1859–1939) in the later nineteenth century, saw the criminal and the 'criminal class' biologic-ally identified as 'other'. Moreover, the fact of massive Irish and Jewish immigration from the 1840s, and 1890s respectively, and particularly the presence of the politically danger-ous refugee, emphasized the notion of the underworld as the 'otherworld'. The casual residuum then was increasingly constructed through a new set of agendas based on the impact of mass immigration, the revelations of slum clearance (particularly anxieties about public health and disease) and the re-formulation of imperial and racial discourses.

Finally, changes in law enforcement, increasingly centered on the identification, sur-veillance and supervision of criminal districts in London. After 1829, the increase in police activity clearly aided in the redefinition of criminal and poor space in towns and cities, and surveillance and supervision was now seen as a key role of the new police. With the establishment of a Detective Branch in 1842, and its reformation as the CID in 1877 (Petrow, 1994), criminals and criminal networks were much more effectively mapped and identified. The police identification and consequently, stigmatization of certain areas as 'dangerous', added to the creation of the underworld, and the criminal class who were its inhabitants. The perception of a threatening 'criminal class' enabled a system which labelled and categorized convicts, culminating in the passage of the Habitual Criminals Act of 1869.

REVIEW QUESTIONS

1 Historians have argued that the Victorian period was one in which there was an 'invention' of the juvenile delinquent. Do you agree with this assessment? In which ways was the juvenile 'invented'?

2 How far did the fundamental changes to late eighteenth and nineteenth century society and culture affect understandings of and attitudes to crime and criminality? What was the impact of industrialization, urbanization, immigration and the increasing secularization of society, on public and private responses to crime?

3 Why did the Victorians believe in the existence of the 'criminal class'? Is it fair to argue that the 'criminal 'class' was predominately an urban problem?

The criminal justice system

The way in which criminal justice systems evolve over time is undoubtedly central to the student of crime. However, for the historian of crime the mechanics of that change is less significant than the political and social shifts which structured and propelled it. Moreover, for most historians it is the impact of developments in criminal justice upon its subjects that most concern them. Thus, the processes and institutions of criminal justice take precedence over the technicalities of legislation. These latter are left more properly to historians of legal process (Radzinowicz, 1948–86; Baker, 2002).

Prosecution

The major difference between the system of prosecution in the eighteenth century and the one which was to evolve by the end of the nineteenth century, was that the former was essentially victim-led. Thus, historically the English legal system provided for any private citizen to initiate a prosecution. Justice was essentially a face-to-face matter between victim and offender. However, if you were a victim of crime it was not always necessary or desirable to prosecute the offender. The costs of prosecution were prohibitive, particularly for those who could neither afford legal advice, nor to lose valuable wages. Moreover, alternative sanctions were available. Communities were not averse to dispensing forms of rough justice as a way of disciplining petty offenders, and maintaining social stability (Sharpe, 1999: 123–5). If the offender was known to you, a servant say, or relative, you might agree to enter into private negotiations and settlement rather than take the person to court. Other victims would use newspapers or handbills as a way of advertising for the return of their stolen goods, offering a reward in return for no questions asked (Emsley, 1996a: 182–3). As a result of these informal responses to crime, entrepreneurial systems of law enforcement flourished, with rewards and gratuities for informers often providing the incentive to deal with crimes through extra-legal means. This system was countered by legislation passed during the later eighteenth and early nineteenth centuries that allowed expenses towards the cost of prosecution. By the time of Peel's Criminal Justice Act of 1826, expenses were paid to all prosecutors where there was a conviction, to witnesses, and in the case of some misdemeanors as well as felonies.

However, financial considerations were not the only factor to encourage prosecution. The increasing abolition of the capital sentence during the early nineteenth century, for example for picking pockets in 1808, and in 1820 for shoplifting, meant that people were more willing to consider prosecution.

Police prosecution

The most significant shift in the prosecution process was to come with the formalization and professionalization of law enforcement from the mid-nineteenth century. With the establishment of the metropolitan police in 1829, the police were to take a much more significant role in the prosecution process. Petty street crime and public order offences were increasingly seen as the remit of the police. With the extension of professional policing to the counties and boroughs during the 1830s, the police role in prosecution was strengthened, and by the late nineteenth century the police had come to dominate the prosecution process (Emsley and Storch, 1993).

Institutions

The nature of the court setting was also to change over the course of the eighteenth and nineteenth centuries. The extension of summary jurisdiction (the transfer of offences from quarter session to petty session) during the early nineteenth century was to have its greatest impact on the trial of young offenders (Shore, 1999: 29–34). Traditionally, the prosecution of crime had to go through a series of stages before it reached court, depending on the nature of the crime. Petty crimes such as gambling, assault, trespass, regulatory offences, certain poaching offences, and other misdemeanours were tried summarily in front of a magistrate or two, sitting informally in his front parlour or in a room in a local tavern (Shoemaker, 1991: 6; Emsley, 1996a: 183). However, if a case brought before the magistrate was judged a felony, the offender would then be committed to trial at a higher court. An indictment would be prepared, which would then be submitted to the Grand Jury, who would then decide whether the case should proceed. If your case was sent to a higher court, it would be heard either at the Quarter Sessions or at the Assize court. The former met four times a year in counties and towns, the latter met twice a year in most major county towns. Assizes were generally reserved for the more heinous of crimes, and special assizes could be called if a local example needed to be made. For metropolitan London, the equivalent of the Assizes was the Old Bailey, which was to be re-housed and renamed the Central Criminal Court in 1834. In practice, at all these stages there was a level of discretion and negotiation (King, 2000). As a consequence, the course of eighteenth century prosecution has been controversially debated by a number of historians in the 1970s and 1980s, most importantly through the work of Douglas Hay who contended that the English criminal law was one of the instruments of ideological control and terror available to the ruling class at this time (Hay, 1975).

The greatest shift in this process during the nineteenth century was, as has already been suggested, the extension of summary jurisdiction, and the wider role of the police as prosecutors. After the mid-nineteenth century these functions increasingly combined with the advent of the police court, which dispensed justice in the case of misdemeanors and some petty crime. The concept of the petty session, the magistrate hearing, was also expanded. In political terms this restructuring of summary jurisdiction was most vociferously shaped by the proponents of juvenile justice. A series of acts were passed during the nineteenth century which led to the increase in the numbers of offenders tried in front of magistrates in a petty session (without a jury present), and a decrease in those tried at the higher courts. This was a rationalization of criminal justice that by the late nineteenth century would bear much more relation to modern court systems.

REVIEW QUESTIONS

1 Explain the changes in the way justice was dispensed between the early modern and modern period? What were the implications of this change for the victim of crime?

2 What was meant by 'discretionary justice'? Who had the power to exercise discretion in the criminal justice system?

3 Why did the police become so involved in the prosecution process? What does this tell us about the changing relationship between the police and the magistracy?

Policing

Traditionally, historians have focused on the 1829 Metropolitan Police Act as the great watershed of British law enforcement history. Before this time, it is argued, progress in policing could mainly be pinpointed to a few far-sighted individuals. However, it took the emergence of a new humanitarianism, along with the social anxieties engendered by urbanization, population rise, and industrialization, to really fuel change. This is a largely benign view of police history, focused narrowly on the interplay between administrative and legislative shift on the one hand, and the biography of police reformers on the other. Not surprisingly, with the advent of social history in the 1970s, and the influence of Marxism, a much more conflictual version of police history has now been established alongside these more traditional accounts. However, both approaches tend to see the early nineteenth century as the key period for the making of the English police. More recently though, historians of the early modern period have done much to enlarge and extend our understanding of law enforcement over time.

Policing before the police

The common stereotype of pre-modern forms of policing is one of ineptitude, followed closely by corruption. Yet, many early modern communities had systems of law enforcement that worked, and once we take a closer look at the early nineteenth century, we see that there are more continuities with the earlier period than was previously acknowledged. Whilst there was no formal police force prior to the nineteenth century, there were lots of different forms of policing. The major difference with the earlier period was that policing was effected on a local, parochial basis, and as a result of this, the local community, usually in the form of the parish vestry, had a greater involvement in the policing of their village, or parish. The other difference was that policing was effectively unpaid. Stipendiary magistrates did not appear until the eighteenth century, and until this time, magistrates, constables, and the watch were largely dependant on a variety of rewards and handouts to make their position worthwhile (parishes did hire full-time watchmen, but the extent to which this was an organized system varied from parish to parish).[4] James Sharpe makes the point that police in the early modern period, need to be understood in a much broader sense, to encompass forms of urban and parochial government, not just uniformed and professional law-enforcement officers (1999: 261–2).

Eighteenth century law enforcement has suffered something of a bad press from historians. The passage of various royal proclamations in London and its suburbs from the late seventeenth century, as a response to worries about what we might effectively call street crime, created a situation which encouraged entrepreneurial forms of policing to flourish. Hence, the system of rewards that came into prominence in the early eighteenth century, seemed, at least in the metropolis, to engender high levels of corruption amongst its law enforcement officials. However, by concentrating on corrupt thief-takers like the notorious, and often ubiquitous Jonathan Wild (Howson, 1970), historians have sometimes undermined more serious analysis of eighteenth century policing.[5] The intricacies of the reward system have been expertly handled by Leon Radzinowicz (1948–86, vol. 3); however, more recently historians like Elaine Reynolds (1998) and John Beattie (1986, 2001), have readdressed this situation with much fuller examinations of policing on the ground. Their work has shown how local policing was often very effective and suited the needs of early eighteenth century communities. Community involvement in street policing, particularly in a period where the victim was more centrally involved in the prosecution process, was considerable. Self-interested parish vestries were keen to control the behaviour of the 'idle and disorderly' in their neighbourhoods. From the late seventeenth century, in urban centres, a combination of local parishioners, reforming magistrates, and constables came together to form the Societies for the Reformation of Manners, whose implicit concern was to clean the streets of prostitutes, vagrants and others whose behaviour was defined as disorderly (Shoemaker, 1992). These societies colluded with criminal justice in the early eighteenth century, in the face of heightened concern about street crime, often relying on the activities of informers and the more surreptitious elements of law enforcement. As a result, by the 1730s, a popular backlash against the reforming societies saw them driven underground, though they were briefly resurrected towards the end of the century. The eighteenth century was punctuated by calls for reform: of the police, of the prisons, of the criminal justice system. However, it was a combination of factors such as urbanization, population growth and migration, but also changing attitudes to street life, and public space, which prompted both reformers and parishioners to push for change.

Evolution and watersheds

The role of the police evolved rapidly over the course of the nineteenth century. By the latter part of the century the police were still subject to a considerable amount of public criticism. Much has been written, in recent years, to undermine the traditional Whig narrative of police reform in the nineteenth century. The watersheds of police reform were, in essence, the 1790s, and the 1820s–30s. In 1795 Patrick Colquhoun published *A Treatise on the Police of the Metropolis* (1795). In 1792 the Middlesex Justices Act was passed, establishing seven police offices for London, manned by stipendiary magistrates. In 1798, generally attributed to the influence of Colquhoun, a private police force was set up to guard the commerce of the river Thames; in 1800 this organization was taken over by the government and remodeled as the Thames River Police (Emsley, 1996b). The later period was marked by the passage of the Metropolitan Police Act of 1829, the Rural Constabulary Act of 1839, and the County and Borough Police Act of 1856. Recent research has concentrated on two areas. First, as discussed above, it has focused on the continuities between the old police and the new. Second, it has considered the evolution of law enforcement outside London.

Because it was the seat of government and because of its size and concerns about metropolitan crime, London tended to host most new initiatives in policing. However, the concentration on London belies the extent of policing experiments in other parts of the country. The Cheshire Police Act had also been passed in 1829, and many provincial towns had efficient police by the 1830s. More generally, the combination of the Lighting and Watching Act (1833) and the Municipal Corporations Act (1835) gave local authorities in Britain a considerable amount of power and leeway to reorganize their systems of police. The shift to considering provincial police reform has necessarily broadened research on issues connected with rural policing. Recent work has shown how crucial the permissive 1839 Constabulary Act was in rural areas. The country gentry put their resolve firmly behind Peel's message of prevention, and whilst the installation of a police force was piecemeal and more gradual in the countryside, by the mid-nineteenth century it was clear that both urban and rural England had seen the transition to a 'policed' society (Phillips and Storch, 1999). However, the police were not greeted universally with open arms, and resistance has been well documented. Robert Storch's classic articles on police resistance in class-conscious working-class communities, particularly those of the northern textile towns, show how they opposed the presence of the police through extra-parliamentary means, such as anti-police disturbances (1975; 1976). However, working-class victims of crime could also see the advantages of the 'new police'. As we have already seen, one of the major effects of the establishment of the police was the transference of the prosecution process from the victim to the police. As a result working-class people were more willing to report petty crime, and even to involve the police in domestic altercations (Jones, 1992: 214). By the end of the nineteenth century, the police were a central institution in British society. Moreover, it was not only in preventative policing that developments had occurred. The emergence of more specialized branches of police work was to be a major feature of the later nineteenth and early twentieth centuries (Emsley, 1996b).

Punishment

For governments, practitioners, and academics, punishment—its level, economic viability, application, and appropriateness has dominated much of the discussion about crime and its control (Morgan, 1994: 891). Moreover, the nature of imprisonment is at the centre of that debate. The soaring prison population, combined with much higher numbers of long-term sentences, problems of disorder, and unpalatable conditions have meant that penality is a constant challenge for home secretaries. Historically, at least superficially, these concerns seem very familiar. Certainly, if we consider the middle decades of the nineteenth century, when debates about the specific nature of penal servitude were played out alongside a widespread programme of penitentiary building, it is often tempting to draw parallels. However, if we take a broader view of punishment over time, we can trace both continuities and some very marked changes in such responses to crime.

Gallows to penitentiary

Perhaps the most distinct shift in the punishment of offenders historically has been the move from public, physical sanctions, such as whipping, but more notoriously, forms of torture, and execution, to the more 'private' punishment of penal servitude. This dichotomy is one that has been argued persuasively and famously by the late French philosopher, Michel Foucault, in his groundbreaking study of English and French criminal justice, *Discipline and Punish: The Origins of the Prison* (1977). Foucault's analysis of the prison is shaped by a broader understanding of the shifts and strains of eighteenth and nineteenth century society. Thus, the growth of the State, and of a surveillance society, paralleled by the professionalization of medicine, and the development of psychiatry are key determinants in Foucault's version of penality. Other historians have seen the rise of the penitentiary as more closely related to the impact of the industrial revolution, and the predominance of new forms of work and workplace, which called for a more disciplined and controllable workforce (Ignatieff, 1978). Nevertheless, there are a number of difficulties with the way in which historians have considered this undoubted watershed. One of these is the assumption that early modern forms of penality and punishment were necessarily problematic. Until the nineteenth century, punishment took the form of a variety of physical and fiscal sanctions. Besides execution, whipping, and branding had also been used, alongside the extensive use of fines. The house of corrections and bride-wells already combined the idea of discipline, work and punishment, in a way which has become more readily identified with nineteenth century reforms. The existing gaols and prisons were designed as remand institutions for prisoners awaiting trial. However, the dominant image of early modern punishment is the public execution. Perhaps unsurprisingly, much of historians' debate about continuity and change in punishment has focused on the capital sentence (Innes and Styles, 1993).

In the swath of penal debates which were to appear in Britain from the later eighteenth century, the dominant model was improvement and reformation (through physical conditions and education and religious strategies). The enlightenment penal reformers such as Cesare Beccaria (1738–94) on the continent and John Howard (1726–90) in England, posited a more rational prison system which, they argued, would move away from the barbaric system of the past. Writing at a time when their contemporaries were very receptive to new ideas about penality, these authors had a significant impact on the development of political debates. Yet, the linear progressive model of prison reform has been undermined by historians. Clearly, this was a system in need of some overhaul. Conditions in many of the old penal institutions were undoubtedly poor, and it was not uncommon for early modern gaols to be managed as a commercial venture (Forsythe, 1983). Moreover, as Joanna Innes (1987) has pointed out, reformatory institutions such as the houses of correction and bridewells were considered a largely appropriate way of dealing with petty offenders, including vagrants and prostitutes. Reform in the eighteenth century then was not a sudden break with the past, but more a combination of enlightenment ideas, a new sensibility about institutions and institutional life that could also be seen reflected in attitudes to the lunatic asylum or the workhouse, broader social, ideological and economic factors, such as the emergence of an increasingly industrialized workforce and workplace, and only in part a response to what were seen as the excesses of the 'bloody code'.

This was a legislative trend that extended the death penalty by statute after 1688. During the course of the eighteenth century, the number of crimes for which you could be executed dramatically increased (from around fifty in 1660 to 160 by 1750 and 288 by 1815). Historians such as Douglas Hay (1975) and Edward Thompson (1975) argued that the ruling classes' of the eighteenth century used the criminal law as an ideological tool, exploring the role of justice, mercy, terror, and discretion in the criminal justice system. However, closer examination of the Bloody Code, has revealed that it frequently remade the definition of crime, rather than created 'new' offences. Often the legislation was incredibly specific, thus 'Destroying Westminster Bridge' was a single offence; 'Destroying Fulham Bridge' was another (Emsley, 1996a: 251). Indeed the majority of people who were executed in the eighteenth century were done so under legislation which had much older roots (Innes and Styles, 1993: 243–5). Finally, it should be noted that there was a considerable gap between the number of capital sentences and actual executions during the eighteenth century (Emsley: 253–2). Douglas Hay has seen the threat of the capital statute, and the use of exemplary executions, as a way in which the ruling class maintained its power (1975: 17–63).

Punishment or reformation?

By the late eighteenth century, the various strands of debate about criminal justice had crystallized into a penal strategy that focused centrally on the reformation of the offender. However, the nature of this reformation was not so straightforward, and for much of the nineteenth century the tension between the more punitive and reformatory elements of punishment were to dominate both discourse and actual practice. Much of this debate was focused upon the prison, in particular newly built penitentiaries which were to be the site of many of the penal experiments of the nineteenth century. However, other, older forms of punishment persisted. Transportation to Australia replaced transportation to the American colonies, as a major penalty for those found guilty of serious crime from the late eighteenth century.

During the early nineteenth century Britain embraced what has been described as the age of the 'great confinement'. The old system was replaced with one that was to become dominated by penal servitude. For much of the nineteenth century, penality was under review, with contemporaries seeking a balance between punishment and reformation. Perhaps the most startling element of the new penality was the emergence of the penitentiaries, realized in the building of Millbank penitentiary in 1816. The idea of the penitentiary was to combine the disciplinary regimes of silence and separation with educational and religious instruction. The 1778 penitentiary act created two national penitentiaries (male and female) which were to be centrally administered. For a variety of reasons, but not least due to the disruption of the French wars, the scheme took several decades to materialize. The war itself was to contribute to the shifting opinions of the government regarding penality. The administration of substantial numbers of prisoners of war for a relatively long period undoubtedly influenced plans for the national penitentiaries (Emsley, 1996a: 266–7). Moreover, the ideals of Jeremy Bentham's Panopticon, were also incorporated in the recommendations of the Holford Committee (1810), which met to look into the question of the prisons (McConville, 1981: 111–12). Bentham's architectural realization of the prison was closely bound with adherence to three principles. First, there was the rule of lenity, which signalled the move from bodily suffering associated with the old penal system. Second, there was the rule of severity, which posited the principle of less eligibility. Third, there was the rule of economy, that the system should essentially be cost effective. The Holford Committee generally shared these views, and to a greater or lesser degree, they underpinned the regimes established in Britain's institutions over the next few decades.

The system that was to evolve by the end of the nineteenth century had learnt from the lessons of the past. Whilst elements of the silent and separate system (also known as the Auburn and Philadelphia system which had been established in North America) could still be found, the worst excesses of the penal experiments of the early nineteenth century were removed. That system had not lived up to its reformatory promise, solitary confinement had a counter-productive effect on the morale of prisoners, and a number of highly publicized cases of suicide and insanity brought it into discredit. The separation of prisoners had more success. This was to be engendered by the classification of different categories of prisoner, particularly through the Gaol Acts of the 1820s, though this theory was not always put into practice. Despite this, the principles of Benthamite penality were to be echoed in the Penal Servitude Acts of 1853, 1857 and 1864. Penal servitude differed from a sentence of imprisonment in a number of ways, and was envisaged as a direct replacement for transportation, seven years transportation equalling seven years' penal servitude. Essentially penal servitude consisted of a mixture of separate confinement and hard labour, followed by probation in the form of a ticket-of-leave. It was kept for those convicted of more serious crimes (those who would previously have been transported) and thus went hand-in-hand with the Habitual Criminals Act, and the Prevention of Crimes Act which was passed in 1871, and tightened supervision of convicted criminals (Petrow, 1994: 75–82).

REVIEW QUESTIONS

1 To what extent was the 'Bloody Code' a real reflection of punishment in the eighteenth century?

2 How 'reformatory' was the penal system of the nineteenth century? What methods were used to effect reform?

3 Why was the death penalty increasingly replaced by penal servitude in the nineteenth century? To what extent can it be argued that this was the product of a more humanitarian society?

CONCLUSION

This chapter has sought to explain some of the continuities and changes which have characterized the attitudes to crime and management of criminal justice in the past. Historians interested in society and in the lives of the poor have frequently turned to the criminal justice system. Such studies have illuminated many areas which are central to the work of historians, sociologists and criminologists alike. Historians of course, have to work within the limitations of their sources, and for the most part this means that we are largely looking at elite perceptions of crime. Nevertheless, an understanding of historical sources such as quarter sessions and assize records, police reports, legal documents, newspapers, parliamentary papers, as well as the vast literature that reformers and social commentators produced, is crucial if we are going to understand the complexities of modern day criminal justice.

In this chapter I have shown that the later eighteenth and the nineteenth centuries have been a key reference point for historians of crime. Whilst recognizing strong continuities with the early modern period, the broader developments in state and society that occur from the later eighteenth century have left us a legacy that modern practitioners still at times grapple with. In penality, in particular, we see the legacy of the past in the Victorian prisons that are still in use. The prison system is faced with problems of overcrowding, rather than as in the past when inmates were denied a nutritional diet and basic education.

In this volume Deborah Cheney has discussed the role of modern prisons. Anne Worrall has considered the current vogue to return to community punishment, echoing the traditions of pre-modern society, where community justice was a key form of control in both village and urban parishes. The juvenile justice system also owes much to its earlier manifestations. The public and the penal definition of what a juvenile delinquent is and the appropriate treatment for them, as Derek Kirton shows in this volume, is still in conflict. Modern policing is still characterized by tensions. Corruption charges, public inquiries and internal reorganization continue much as they did in the nineteenth century. Nevertheless, historical systems of criminal justice do need to be considered in the contexts of the societies in which they developed. Elsewhere in this volume, Chris Greer, Jeff Ferrell and Mike Presdee, have considered the relationship between crime and broader social and cultural forms.

Indeed, it is important for the student of criminology to have some basic understanding of the economic upheaval, social conflict, cultures, and political development of the eighteenth and nineteenth centuries, to understand the changes I have discussed. The impact of industrialization, of the market economy, the demographic changes that led to a shift to an urban – based population, the reorganization of local government, new forms of state management, all combine in this period to produce new reformulations of crime and responses to it. What we also have to remember, is that these were changes in society that did not only affect the criminal justice system, but reached in many ways into the lives of the working class people who formed the vast majority of those who moved through the criminal justice system. In 1834 the reorganization of the poor relief system led to a re-evaluation and revamping of the workhouse system. Indoor relief in the workhouse paralleled the prison, as did a series of institutions for the poor. The workplace also changed dramatically in this period, urban manufactories and later factories, fundamentally changed traditional patterns of work and workplace practices. Developments in public health, education, and housing should also be taken into account. The student of criminology, I would argue, needs some sense of the historical framework. This now provides the benchmark to understanding the developments and background to the institutions that both serve to protect and punish us both in terms of policy and practice.

QUESTIONS FOR DISCUSSION

1   What are the potential problems with using historical criminal statistics?
2   How far do you agree with Douglas Hay's assessment that eighteenth century society 'was a society with a bloody penal code, an astute ruling class who manipulated it to their advantage, and a people schooled in the lessons of Justice, Terror and Mercy' (1975)?
3   Why did the criminal justice system undergo so much change during the nineteenth century? How much was this a break with the past?
4   How far is it possible to argue that the nineteenth century was subject to periodic 'moral panics' about violent crime?
5   The Old Bailey Sessions Papers were journalists' accounts of the crimes tried at the Old Bailey from the late seventeenth century. They are available at the Old Bailey Online (website address provided below). What sort of crimes did people commit in the eighteenth century? How were offenders sentenced? What age/gender patterns can be traced?

GUIDE TO FURTHER READING

Beattie, J.M. (1986) *Crime and the Courts in England, 1660–1800*, Oxford: Clarendon Press.
A classic and exhaustive account of the mechanisms of criminal justice in late seventeenth century and eighteenth century Surrey. Despite its local focus, this book has become a handbook for students seeking to understand how courts actually worked in the past.

Emsley, C. (1996a) *Crime and Society in England, 1750–1900* (2nd edn), London: Longman.

This is the most useful and authoritative overview of the history of crime from the later eighteenth century and in the nineteenth century. An invaluable introductory text book.

Hay, D., Linebaugh, P. and Thompson, E. P. *et al.* (1975) *Albion's Fatal Tree: Crime and Society in Eighteenth Century England*, London: Allen Lane.

Since its publication in 1975 this collection of essays by many of the luminaries of the crime history field, has provoked much debate and some controversy. In particular Douglas Hay's groundbreaking chapter has become a classic contribution to our understanding of the eighteenth century criminal justice system.

King, P. (1998) 'The Rise of Juvenile Delinquency in England, 1780–1840', *Past and Present*, 160: 116–66.

A useful overview of the perceived rise of juvenile crime from the late eighteenth century, this provides an empirical and *quantitative* analysis of the subject, with a survey of the reform texts of the time.

Zedner, L. (1991) *Women, Crime, and Custody*. Oxford: Clarendon Press.

A gendered reading of the nineteenth century criminal justice system. This book adds much to our understanding of penality in the Victorian period, and the relationship between broader cultural and social attitudes and criminal justice.

WEB LINKS

http://www.met.police.uk/history/index.htm

The History of the Metropolitan Police Service, including a timeline of police history.

http://www.oldbaileyonline.org/

The Proceedings of the Old Bailey Online, records of the trials that have taken place at the Old Bailey from 1674 to 1834.

http://www.rossbret.org.uk/

Rossbret UK Institutions, includes information and links on British institutions including prisons, reformatories, workhouses, asylums and industrial schools.

http://www.evergreen.loyola.edu/%7Ecmitchell/

The Tyburn Tree: Public Execution in Early Modern England, history of execution in England, includes contemporary images and last dying speeches.

REFERENCES

Baker, J.H. (2002) *An Introduction to Legal History* (4th edn). London: Butterworths.

Beattie, J.M. (1986) *Crime and the Courts in England, 1660–1800*. Oxford: Clarendon Press.

Beattie, J.M. (2001) *Policing and Punishment in London, 1660–1750: Urban Crime and the Limits of Terror*. Oxford: Oxford University Press.

Beccaria, C. (1767) *Dei Delitti e Delle Pene*. London.

Carpenter, M. (1851) *Reformatory Schools for the Children of the Perishing and Dangerous Classes and for Juvenile Offenders*. London: C. Gilpin.

Emsley, C. (1996a) *Crime and Society in England, 1750–1900* (2nd edn). London: Longman.

Emsley, C. (1996b) (2nd edn). *The English Police*. London: Longman.

Emsley, C. and Storch, R. (1993) 'Prosecution and the Police in England Since 1700', *Bulletin of the International Association for the History of Crime and Criminal Justice*. 18: 45–57.

Forsythe, W.J. (1983) *A System of Discipline. Exeter Borough Prison, 1819–1863*. Exeter: University of Exeter.

Foucault, M. (1977) *Discipline and Punish: The Origins of the Prison*. London: Allen Lane.

Hay, D. (1975) 'Property, authority and the criminal law', in D. Hay, P. Linebaugh, E.P. Thompson (*et al.*), in *Albion's Fatal Tree: Crime and Society in Eighteenth Century England*. London: Allen Lane, 17–63.

Howard, J. (1777) *The State of the Prisons in England and Wales*. Warrington.

Howson, G. (1970) *Thief-Taker General: The Rise and Fall of Jonathan Wild*. London: Hutchinson.

Ignatieff, M. (1978) *A Just Measure of Pain: The Penitiary in the Industrial Revolution, 1750–1850*. London: Macmillan.

Innes, J. (1987) 'Prisons for the poor: English Bridewells, 1550–1800', in F. Snyder, D. Hay (eds), *Labour, Law and Crime: An Historical Perspective*. London: Tavistock Press.

Innes, J. and Styles, J. (1993) 'The crime wave: recent writing on crime and criminal justice in eighteenth-century England', in A. Wilson (ed), *Rethinking Social History*.

Jones, D. (1982) *Crime, Protest, Community and Police in Nineteenth-Century Britain*. London: Routledge & Kegan Paul.

Jones, D. (1992) *Crime in Nineteenth Century Wales*. Cardiff: University of Wales Press.

King, P. (1998) 'The Rise of Juvenile Delinquency in England, 1780–1840', *Past and Present*, 160: 116–66.

King, P. (2000) *Crime, Justice and Discretion in England, 1740–1820*. Oxford: Oxford University Press.

Magarey, S. (1978) 'The Invention of Juvenile Delinquency in Early Nineteenth-Century England', *Labour History* [Canberra], 34: 11–27. (Reprinted in Muncie, J., McLaughlin, E. and Hughes, G. (2002), *Youth Justice: Critical Readings in History, Theory and Policy*. London: Sage, pp. 159–72).

Marriott, J. (1999) 'Introduction', in J. Marriott and M. Matsumura (eds), *The Metropolitan Poor: Semi-Factual Accounts, 1795–1910*, 5 vols. London: Pickering and Chatto, vol. 1, xi–l.

McConville, S. (1981) *A History of English Prison Administration, volume 1: 1750–1877*. London: Routledge & Kegan Paul.

McMullan, J. (1984) *The Canting Crew: London's Criminal Underworld, 1550–1700*. New Brunswick, New Jersey: Rutgers University Press.

Morgan, R. (1994) 'Imprisonment', in M. Maguire, R. Morgan and R. Reiner (eds), *The Oxford Handbook of Criminology*. Oxford: Clarendon Press, 889–948.

Petrow, S. (1994) *Policing Morals: The Metropolitan Police and the Home Office, 1870–1914*. Oxford: Clarendon Press.

Phillips, D. and Storch, R. (1999) *Policing Provincial England, 1829–1856: The Politics of Reform*. Leicester: Leicester University Press.

Pick, D. (1989) *Faces of Degeneration: A European Disorder, c. 1848–1918*. Cambridge: Cambridge University Press.

Radzinowicz, L. (1948–86, 5 volumes). *A History of the English Criminal Law*. London: Stevens & Son.

Radzinowicz, L. and Hood, R. (1986): *A History of the English Criminal Law: Volume 5, The emergence of penal policy in Victorian and Edwardian England*. Oxford: Clarendon Press.

Reynolds, E. (1998) *Before the Bobbies: the Night Watch and Police Reform in Metropolitan London, 1720–1830*. Basingstoke: Macmillan.

Sharpe, J.A. (1999) *Crime in Early Modern England, 1550–1750* (2nd edn). London: Longman.

Shoemaker, R. (1991) *Prosecution and Punishment: Petty Crime and the Law in London and Rural Middlesex, c. 1660–1725*. Cambridge: Cambridge University Press.

Shoemaker, R. (1992) 'Reforming the city: the reformation of manners campaign in London, 1690–1738', in L. Davison, *et al.* (eds), *Stilling the Grumbling Hive: the Response to Social and Economic Problems in England, 1689–1750*. Stroud: Alan Sutton, 99–120.

Shore, H. (1999) *Artful Dodgers: Youth and Crime in Early Nineteenth Century London*. London: Royal Historical Society.

Stedman-Jones, G. (1971) *Outcast London: A Study in the Relationship Between Classes in Victorian Society*. Oxford: Clarendon Press.

Storch, R.D. (1975) 'The Plague of Blue Locusts: Police Reform and Popular Resistance in Northern England, 1840–57', *International Review of Social History*, 20: 61–90.

Storch, R.D. (1976) 'The policeman as domestic missionary: urban discipline and popular culture in northern england, 1850–80', *Journal of Social History*, Summer: 481–509.

Thompson, E.P. (1975) *Whigs and Hunters: The Origins of the Black Act*. London: Allen Lane.

NOTES

1. The crisis of the English Civil War (1642–8), and the subsequent *restoration* of the monarchy in 1660, wrought significant developments in the law, the operation of the State, and the role of parliament and other government institutions.

2. Henry and John Fielding were police magistrates and social reformers (Henry was also the author of the influential pamphlet, *An Inquiry into the Causes of the late Increase of Robbers, etc*, (1751) and novels including *Tom Jones* (1749)). Jonas Hanway was also a social reformer, and the founder of the Marine Society (1756) in London, which trained delinquent boys for service in the navy. John Howard was a penal reformer, and the author of *The State of Prisons in England and Wales* (1777). Patrick Colquhoun was a magistrate and police reformer. Jeremy Bentham was a philosopher and jurist. In the 1780s he devised a plan for the 'Panopticon'—a model prison where all prisoners would be observable by (unseen) guards at all times.

3. Robert Peel was home secretary from 1822, and is credited as the main architect of the 1829 Metropolitan Police Act (he was later Prime Minister between 1834–5 and 1841–6). Elizabeth Fry (1780–1845) was a Quaker and prison reformer, noted for her work with female prisoners.

4. The watch were paid civilians who guarded and patrolled the streets at night. They were eventually superseded by the passage of the various metropolitan and county police acts of the nineteenth century.

5. Jonathan Wild (c. 1682–1725) was a receiver of stolen goods, informer, and prototype organized crime chief who operated in London in the early eighteenth century. He was executed at Tyburn in 1725.

3

What do crime statistics tell us?

Tim Hope

INTRODUCTION

Other chapters in this book explore the meaning of the concept 'crime' (Morrison, Chapter 1). In this chapter, the definition of 'crime' refers to a category of human acts that are proscribed by law and for which those responsible, if found guilty, are liable to some form of judicial punishment. The custodian of these kinds of acts is, of course, the State. In this sense, then, crime is a 'property' of the State (Christie, 2004). So, too, are 'statistics'. Dictionary definitions point to the origins of the term, even before the adoption of numerical systems of accounting, as arising out of the act of administration and government itself—of state affairs, or statecraft. This is true still: even though other, non-government bodies can collect statistics, and alternative analyses and interpretations of statistics are possible, there is a real sense that 'statistics' are the 'arithmetic of politics' (Dorling and Simpson, 1999). In contemporary society, statistics have become an important medium of governance—simultaneously informing and obscuring the various risks, including crime, around which we increasingly orient our daily lives and from which we expect our governments to protect us (Rose, 1999). Thus, both 'crime' and 'statistics', as they will be discussed in this chapter, are bound-up fundamentally with the operation and function of the State itself. Crime Statistics, then, are *the accounts* that the State compiles of the actions of its agencies concerning those acts which the law proscribes.

BACKGROUND

There are broadly two polar views held about crime statistics: on the one hand, there is what we might call the *realist* view. This sees the official record as an indicator of the state of crime in society. Thus, even though there may be a 'dark figure' of crime out there—which ultimately may be unfathomable—in this view, it remains possible to refine and develop our statistics so that they aspire to, if not actually ever perfectly achieve, an accurate reflection of the underlying extent, pattern and trend of crime in society. Clearly, experience may suggest that some indicators—for example, statistics of crime recorded by the police—can be inaccurate and subject to biases of various kinds, some of which will be discussed below. Other measurement and estimation techniques have emerged, for example, *crime victimization surveys*, which promise improvements in accuracy and corrections of bias. Nevertheless, the intention is to use these statistics as indices of the amount of crime in society. There are two broad traditions of use here: first, *administration*, where crime statistics provide government (and the electorate) with intelligence about society that assists in the deployment and management of the State's criminal justice resources. As the recent *Review of Crime Statistics for England and Wales* puts it: 'there is general agreement that the overarching purpose for collecting information on crime should be to reduce the impact of crime on society' (Home Office, 2000; 9). A second use is *research*, which sees social statistics as 'social facts'—that is, indicators of the condition of society as a whole—the analysis of which reveals something about how society operates. The progenitor of this tradition is Emile Durkheim's classic nineteenth century study of suicide (Durkheim, 1979).

Against the realist position, there is the *constructivist* perspective. In contemporary criminology this view stems largely from Aaron Cicourel's study of *The Social Organisation of Juvenile Justice* (1968). Based on research into the organization of juvenile justice in an American city, and how the various officials and others saw the process, Cicourel concluded that official statistics could be understood only with reference to the way in which the agencies responsible for them carried out their work. In this view, official statistics tell us as much, if not more, about the organization that produces them than about the phenomenon—that is crime—that they are suppose to measure. Because they are *social constructs*, statistics do not give a clear or objective view of the phenomena they purport to measure because they confuse details about crime with they way it is reacted to and dealt with by the relevant authorities.

Should the student of criminology bother with crime statistics at all? At one extreme, there may be those—at one time disparagingly referred to as 'positivists'—who still believe that crime statistics can be used (more or less) as an objective measure of the state of crime in society. Sections of the public, media and politicians may still think this. They will want to use crime statistics as true measures of the level of crime, or worse, the moral health of society. Nowadays, no criminologist would take such a naive and uncritical view of official statistics. Nevertheless, official crime statistics continue to be used in many studies. Largely, this is for *pragmatic* reasons: the questions asked of them are interesting and important. For example, how much crime is there, has it increased or declined? But there are no more reliable alternative ways available to measure them. For all their faults, official statistics of crime are public records, whose cost of collection is borne by the State. They have a comprehensive, standard coverage of all of the jurisdictions for which the State is custodian, and can be related to other state statistics, particularly those taken from the national Census of Population to provide profiles of levels of crime in different types of community. Criminologists will continue to use official statistics in their work, not least because governments themselves also use them as tools for measuring the performance of criminal justice agencies, particularly the police, and for accounting to the public.

At the other extreme, are those who might be thought of as 'impossibilists', who see official crime statistics as fatally flawed not just because they cannot measure crime separately from the actions of the agencies that produce them, but because the important social and cultural processes that go to make up the process of defining and reacting to crime and deviance are themselves not amenable to statistical measurement and analysis. In this view, quantitative measurement of cultural definitions—meanings and linguistic tropes about crime—is impossible. On the contrary, the analysis of such phenomena has its own logic and canon of procedures that are inimical to the mathematically-based logic of statistics and risk analysis.

Students of criminology will need to make up their own minds as to where they stand on these issues—of course, after a careful reading of this and the other chapters in this book! The stance taken here is pragmatic. It will be realistic enough to say that there are phenomena 'out there' that are capable of being measured in principle and that the careful use of statistics can illuminate many issues that may not be grasped properly by more subjectively oriented approaches to understanding. However, it also recognizes the constructivist argument that the various phenomena of crime in society cannot be divorced from the practices of the agencies that define, report and record them. This is an important area of social enquiry itself. If, philosophically, crime cannot be divorced from its control, statistics neverthe-less can be used to illuminate the interplay between the two or, at the very least, the operation of control itself. Nor is this merely an academic exercize. The more politicians, government, and the media use and cite statistics in justification of their actions, or lack thereof, the more that citizens—including students of criminology—will need to know about how those statistics are produced and how reliable they are as a basis for political decisions; especially if democracy is to work properly. Thus, this chapter will offer a brief 'consumers' guide' to some of the key issues concerning the construction of crime statistics.

What is a crime statistic?

The chapter will focus on arguably one of the most popular of the crime statistics—the *crime rate*—that is, the measure that gives an index of crime occurring in a particular jurisdiction for a specific time period. Police records have been the main source for constructing crime rates. In recent years, however, governments have begun to look for other ways to collect crime statistics—usually commissioning large-scale population (that is, crime victimization) surveys for the purpose. There are broadly two reasons for this. First, a realisation that the various potential biases in official records (discussed below) result in an inaccurate measure of the extent, scale and pattern of crime in society, which causes particular problems in trying to compare jurisdictions, to estimate trends over time, or to explain patterns and trends. Second, reliable statistics have become even more important as governments concern themselves with assessing the performance of criminal justices agencies, particularly the police, whose purpose is seen increasingly as a 'service' to the community, especially to reduce crime and provide security and protection for citizens (see, for example, Home Office, 2003).

As with all 'statistics' there are three different components or uses. These are:

- *Counts*—that is, the actual number of offences occurring within a given referent of time and space—for example, the number of burglary offences in England and Wales per year.

- *Frequencies*—that is, how the counts of criminal offences are distributed amongst a population—for example, how many people are victims, and how frequently are they victimized?

- *Rates*—that is, expressing the count of criminal incidents as an indicator or characteristic of the population or jurisdiction that produced it, typically as a ratio of another characteristic of the population; for example, the rate of burglary per 10,000 residents of the County of Staffordshire.

The following sections of this chapter will look at these three component statistics of 'the crime rate', in turn. Particular attention is paid to how the statistics are defined and how their measurement is constructed.

REVIEW QUESTIONS

1 What is the difference between a 'realist' and a 'constructivist' view of crime statistics? What is the approach adopted here?

2 What are the three different components of a crime statistic?

Counting crime

Who counts?

Crimes are counted by those agencies that have official (legislated) responsibility for receiving complaints about, or otherwise uncovering, incidents of crime on behalf of the State. In the UK, and other countries such as the USA, Canada, Australia and New Zealand that share a common legal tradition (the 'common law'), these agencies are usually designated law enforcement agencies. Most commonly in the UK this is the public police service, which has jurisdiction over specific territorial areas, though there are other agencies that also collect crime records for specific jurisdictions such as the British Transport Police (for railways, airports, docks, etc) and Customs and Excise (regarding the importation of goods). The situation differs however with other countries, for example in Europe, that have different legal traditions, and where the police have different relations with the criminal justice system—for example, working as prosecutors' or courts' agents—or where other regulatory and law enforcement bodies can receive complaints and initiate enquiries into matters that result in criminal proceedings. Even so, as modern states have evolved, it is the statutory, professional police agencies that became the chief custodians of the crime statistics with primary responsibility for counting crime on behalf of the State.

What is counted?

Many things that people experience, witness or perpetrate could be classifiable as crime. Sometimes, for instance, people do not know that these incidents are crimes. The retort 'I'll get you!' during a heated exchange between, say, two irate neighbours could end up as an offence of 'threatening behaviour'. Or people do not want incidents to be considered as crimes, or more particularly do not want the police to intervene in what they see as their 'private' disputes, even if there is good reason that they should. For instance, the abused woman in domestic violence may be too afraid to report her abusive partner to the police while the abuser will not want his abusive behaviour to be known about or punished. Sometimes, people are not even aware they have been victims of crime—after all, the most successful confidence tricks or internet scams are those where the victim remains completely oblivious, even while their pockets and bank accounts are being pillaged.

The police have little knowledge about most crime at the time it occurs and without victims or witnesses telling them about it they will remain ignorant. Thus, the British Crime Survey (BCS), a crime victimization survey (see below), found that the police were present at the scene in only about 3 per cent of incidents experienced by respondents. Generally, there are more incidents and events in people's everyday lives that might warrant a police response than are ever brought to their attention.

Not only is there a 'dark figure' of unreported crime, but there is also a 'grey figure' (Bottomley and Pease, 1986)—the disparity between estimates of what members of the public say they report to the police and the number of crimes actually recorded. The difference is considerable. For instance, from estimates from the 1999 BCS, of the two-fifths of incidents experienced by victims that they said they had reported to the police, only slightly over half appear to have been recorded in the returns made by police to government (Kershaw, *et al.*, 2000). Thus, there are two sources of 'bias' in police-recorded counts of crime—*the propensity of the public to report crime* and *the practice of the police in recording it.*

How is crime counted?

The official count of crime is published by the State. In England and Wales, historically, this has taken the form of the published series of *Criminal Statistics*. Reports of both official statistics and BCS findings are now published together in the *Home Office Statistical Bulletin* series, and are also available via the internet (www.crimestatistics.org.uk). While research studies of police work and recording practices (discussed below) shed some light on how the official statistics are constructed, their accuracy and biases can only be estimated in comparison with alternative ways of counting crime. There are two additional sources of information that can shed some light on how the crime experiences of the public make their way into the official criminal statistics—*police incident logs* and crime victimization *surveys*. These can be compared with the official statistics to reveal some of the processes of (and potential biases due to) reporting and recording. In turn, each also has their limitations as a source of information on crime.

REVIEW QUESTIONS

1 Who has responsibility for counting crime, and for what purposes are crime statistics collected?

2 What are the two general sources of bias in official crime statistics?

Recording incidents as criminal offences

The decision by the police to record an incident reported to them as an offence is a *negotiated outcome*, with the police balancing a number of considerations, usually with some permitted (and some acquired) discretion. There is only one reason for the police to record a complaint or reported incident as a crime—*prima facie* evidence that an offence might have been committed—but there are a variety of reasons why the police do *not* record incidents.

Variation in discretionary police recording practice is likely to be the main influence on disparities in the recording (as distinct from the reporting) of crime. Some of this lies in the way different police forces have interpreted the often complex *Home Office Counting Rules*.[1] As their name implies, these set out how, and in what ways, incidents are to be recorded and counted as offences. The most recent overhaul of the Counting Rules occurred in 1998, largely as an effort to improve the correspondence between numbers and types of incidents and recorded offences. Some of the disparity in recording is also due to different approaches taken when incidents are reported. The *Review of Crime*

Statistics for England and Wales (Home Office, 2000) discovered the existence of two recognizable models of police recording practice: a *prima facie* model which faithfully records as crime the details of allegations made by the public; and an *evidential* model which subjects complaints to some investigative selection prior to recording (Burrows *et al.*, 2000); the former tending to produce a greater number of recorded crimes than the latter. As an illustration of how these approaches might affect the counting of crime, some years ago, a study estimated that the much greater crime rate of Nottinghamshire, compared to its surrounding counties, was due largely to zealous, *prima facie* recording of incidents, including the counting of series of milk-bottle thefts as separate incidents! (Farrington and Dowds, 1985). Efforts to standardize recording practices amongst police forces have resulted in the implementation of the *National Crime Recording Standard* (NCRS), including further amendment of the Counting Rules, with effect from April 2002.

There are a number of reasons why a reported incident may not be recorded:

- The police decide there is *insufficient evidence* that a crime has occurred. For example, a mobile phone reported stolen may have been found and returned.

- There is little chance of an offender being *detected* and prosecuted successfully.

- The victim (complainant) *withdraws* the complaint and thus will not be willing to give evidence in court.

- The police exercize *discretion* in the recording of incidents, for example, as a result of police cultural prejudices and biases against certain types of complainant or complaint (Reiner, 1992). For example, until relatively recently, the police tended not to record officially incidents of 'domestic violence' reported to them.

- The police feel an *obligation* to record crime because other parties may require an official recognition of an incident. For instance, insurance companies usually require victims to report incidents to the police as a condition of meeting their claims regarding loss of property. In part, this helps protect insurers against the possibility of victims fraudulently claiming compensation for losses from burglaries that have not taken place, since this would entail lying to the police as well. Thus, 78 per cent of BCS burglaries with loss are reported to the police, with 98 per cent of these recorded by the police. In contrast, 49 per cent of attempts and no loss burglaries are reported to the police, with only 44 per cent of these recorded.

- The police are under pressure to record, or not, as part of accounting for their individual or organizational *performance* (Bottomley and Pease, 1986). The government nowadays sets the police targets for reductions in crime, leading to the use of crime statistics as a measure of police 'performance'. The 'clear-up rate'—the proportion of recorded crimes detected or otherwise dealt-with—also constitutes a measure of police performance, and has been open to much criticism because it can be manipulated through various recording practices (McCabe and Sutcliffe, 1978).

- The police may employ a range of 'covert' practices to massage the figures (for many reasons, including those noted above), generally known as *cuffing* (Bottomley and Coleman, 1981), where complaints are deliberately not recorded.

- Offenders frequently want their admissions to be *'taken into consideration'*—that is, as TICs—in the hope of more lenient treatment in sentencing. Sometimes these admissions just affect the rate of detection. Sometimes, though, when offenders admit to committing offences that have not been recorded hitherto (known as *secondary detections*), they result in increasing the number of recorded offences as well.

Comparing counts of incidents and offences

For many years in Britain, the police have kept a record—or log—of incidents attended by officers. With the advent of computer systems, and the widespread use of telephones to report incidents, manual recording of incidents has given way to computerized systems. Typically, calls for police service, either through the emergency '999' system or to a local police station, are received at a call centre; details are then taken by a despatcher who assigns available police officers to investigate. Having conducted their enquiries and taken necessary action, the officers will confirm the nature of the incident and an outcome code will then be assigned to the incident log. If officers have evidence that a crime has been committed, they will complete a crime report which will be entered onto the police crime recording information system. For future reference, there is usually a link between the incident log and the crime recording system. Numbers or details of incidents attended by the police are not usually published. Counts of *notifiable offences* (defined according to the *Home Office Counting Rules*) are extracted from the police forces' crime recording systems and returned to the Home Office for processing, eventually finding their way in aggregate form into the published *Criminal Statistics*.

In recent years, the computerization of police records and information systems has helped to provide a picture of how the profile of 'incidents' reported to and/or attended by the police matches the profile of 'crime' recorded by them. As might be expected, there is nothing like a perfect match. Yet what a comparison of the profiles of incidents and crimes reveals is not so much whether the police are providing a good or bad service as the contrast between police work as a service to the public, and police work in the control of crime.

Most research-based answers to the enquiry 'what do the police do?' point to the plethora of different kinds of calls-for-service from the public and the range of responses by the police—from emergency assistance, informal handling, referral, counselling, note-taking, as well as crime-recording. The same raw material provides information on two separate but related activities—police work, and crime. However, both rest fundamentally upon the same basis—the relationship between the public and the police. For each incident, the public take decisions to invoke (call-up) police authority with regard to their 'troubles' and concerns—these include, but are not necessarily restricted to, matters that are criminal as defined by statute. The police make decisions about treating those troubles as a public concern. Different kinds of incident reported to them evoke different kinds of responses. The part played by the police can vary, as can their role as law officers or as a public 'emergency' service. In some incidents where the evidence and attitude of the complainant point clearly towards a crime having been committed, the police responsibility is to record it as a notifiable offence. Other incidents, such as traffic accidents (or the proverbial 'cats-up-trees') are usually not crimes at all; and in between, there is a grey area where police officers can, and are usually entitled to, exercise substantial discretion as to whether or not to record an incident as an offence.

Basic differences between incident-based and crime-based profiles of police work are illustrated in a study undertaken with my colleagues Professor Susanne Karstedt and Dr Stephen Farrall. The research was carried out in an English county, comprising some 1.4 million residents, covering (for England) a large geographic area, with a representative spread of communities—from affluent to poor, including ethnic minorities—and land uses—from the densely urban to the sparsely rural. As part of a research project, access was given to data from both the incident and crime information systems for the entire calendar year of 2000. The incident data contained records of incidents attended by police officers, mostly in response to calls from members of the public. The crime information system contained records of 'crime reports', initiated by attending or investigating police officers. In the research, we sought to count the number of reported incidents and the number of recorded crimes. In order to make some comparison, we needed to group incidents and crimes into broadly similar categories. The classification was not always easy, nor exactly equivalent, other than within broad classes of incidents and crimes. Nevertheless, the results are illustrated in Table 3.1.

Table 3.1 shows that there were over six times more incidents than there were recorded crimes (the third column of Table 3.1). Second, just over a half of all reported incidents did not have criminal equivalents, comprising a wide and diverse range of incidents, accidents, other emergencies, and duties where a police presence was needed, including road traffic matters. Yet, even when comparing recorded crimes with incidents that could be construed as criminal, the respective profiles of incidents and recorded crimes differed quite considerably. It is possible that some of this disparity could have been due to multiple calls from the public about the same offence. Nevertheless, different types of criminal incident had different levels of 'excess' reporting, relative to the number of crimes recorded. Thus, anti-social and violent criminal incidents involving people,

Table 3.1 Incidents reported ('calls') and notifiable offences ('crimes') recorded by an English County Constabulary for the year 2000 (percentages)

	Incidents	Crimes	Ratio of incidents to crimes
Nuisances and conflicts	24	30	4.9
Violence	9	9	6.0
Burglaries and thefts	14	58	1.5
Other incidents	41	–	
Other crimes	–	3	109.0
Roads and related incidents	11	–	
Total Number	733,695	118,503	6.2

Note: These records were compiled for a period before the changes brought in by the National Crime Recording Standard, implemented in April 2002.   *Sources:* Hope *et al.* (2001).

including incidents of nuisance, conflict and violence, comprised the majority of calls from the public to the police about incidents where an offence might have been committed (that is, 69 per cent of all possibly criminal incidents), while acquisitive property crime (largely burglaries and thefts of various kinds) comprised the majority of recorded crimes (58 per cent). Anti-social and violent incidents exceeded recorded crimes by a ratio of five reported incidents to one recorded crime, while acquisitive incidents exceeded crimes by only one-and-a-half to one. Thus, the profiles of public reporting and police recording differed both in volume and type of incident.[2]

As already noted, the police may be responding to the nature of the incident in question but they may also be responding to the different needs of the community. For example, concern about 'anti-social behaviour'—including noisy neighbours or young people scuffling in public—may be made by residents whose primary concern is for the police to control the situation or to move-on the troublemakers. In these situations, an arrest (and resulting crime report) may be the last resort when other means have failed. In sum, comparing the different profiles of incident and recorded crime statistics can tell us something about the extent of crime, the public's demands on the police service, and the way in which the police respond to such demands.

REVIEW QUESTIONS

1 What are the different reasons for the police under-recording crime?

2 What is meant by the 'prima facie' and 'evidential' approaches to recording crime?

3 What is the purpose of the Home Office Counting Rules, and of the National Crime Recording Standard?

4 To what kinds of incident are the police called most frequently? How does the profile of incidents differ from the profile of recorded crime?

Reporting crime to the police

We have already seen how the official statistics of crime might be affected by the recording of crime by the police. Yet, because of the fact that people do not necessarily report all the crime victimization they experience (for reasons described below), it is possible that differences in official crime rates between communities, or trends in crime rates over time, also may reflect the public's propensity to report crime to the police. As noted, crime victimization surveys—such as the BCS or the US National Crime Victimization Survey (NCVS)—have evolved as an alternative measure of crime in the community. Typically, these are (large-scale) sample surveys of general populations. Their method is usually described as *self-report* since it asks respondents to tell the survey's interviewers about incidents in which they have been a victim, usually over the past six to twelve months. Yet, if crime victimization surveys aim to give a more accurate estimate than official statistics, how accurate are they in turn? Broadly, their accuracy depends upon two things: the *coverage* of the survey; and its accuracy of *measurement*.

Coverage of household crime victimization surveys

Crime victimization surveys may not measure all crime for the following reasons:

- They are surveys of *private individuals*, who are asked to report on both their personal crime victimization experiences (for example, violence, robbery and theft) and on property crime victimization suffered by their household (for example, burglary, car crime, vandalism). Crimes against *corporate organizations*—including, firms, retailers, local authorities, hospitals and educational establishments—are not included, amounting to a sizeable number of offences.

- They are samples of the population and may have particular *sample-selection biases*. The BCS does not capture the experiences of young people (below sixteen years) because it does not sample this age group. It also only samples people in their homes, thus failing to reach both the homeless, and those living in institutions. Generally, certain population groups are harder for interviewers to find at home than others, especially young people and inner-city dwellers, whose lifestyles lead them to be out and about a lot. Telephone surveys, though cheaper than face-to-face interviews, obviously rely on widespread telephone ownership.[3] Nowadays, the BCS uses a postal address system for sampling. Previously, surveys used the Register of Electors; however, non-registration for the 'Poll Tax' during the 1980s lead to large numbers of people disappearing from the Electoral Register; likewise, increasing non-voting generally (and non-registration to vote) has lead to the Electoral Register ceasing to be a reliable sampling frame. And some people, for a variety of reasons, simply refuse to take part. Unfortunately, research suggest that all these population groups tend to have substantial experience of crime victimization and/or abuse, thus leading to an under-estimation of the count in victimization surveys, and a biased profile of victimization risk for the population as a whole.

- *Measurement of offences*—because surveys rely upon the self-report method, they may not include offences where: victims are *unaware* they have been victimized (as in the case of successful frauds, or crimes committed against them by corporate bodies, because they are not usually asked such questions); and so-called *victimless crimes*, such as prostitution or drug misuse.

- *Rarity of crime*—statistically speaking, crime victimization is a relatively rare event, experienced by few people in the population at any one time (see the section on frequency below). Thus, in order to gain sufficient counts of victims and offences for reliable statistical analysis, it is necessary to have large samples, and long(ish) recall periods. In practice, only central governments (and occasionally local or regional governments) can afford to sponsor crime victimization surveys on a regular basis. In 2000, the Home Office increased the sample size of the BCS to around 40,000 partly in order to obtain reliable estimates of crime for the 43 police force areas of England and Wales.

- *Geographic clustering*—crime is not distributed equally amongst communities; the majority of victims, and of offences, occur in relatively few areas (see section on rates below). Alongside their large scale, surveys also have to selectively sample particular

Table 3.2 Table of frequencies of victims of household property crime over the previous twelve months in four areas of social housing, 1990

Number of crimes	Frequency of households	Percentage of households	Cumulative percentage of households
0	1423	82.0	82.0
1	212	12.2	94.2
2	49	2.8	97.1
3	27	1.6	98.6
4	12	.7	99.3
5	2	.1	99.4
6	4	.2	99.7
7	3	.2	99.8
9	2	.1	99.9
13	1	.1	100.0
Total	1735	100.0	

Note: Household property crime includes incidents of: burglary, theft from a dwelling, and criminal damage. For details of the survey see Foster and Hope (1993).   *Source:* Foster and Hope (1993).

areas—usually 'inner city' residential areas—in order to obtain reliable samples of victims. Unfortunately, this means that the sample can become less representative of the population as a whole, who are mostly non-victims, living in lower crime areas (see Table 3.2). Surveys such as the BCS that employ face-to-face interviewing also select their samples in geographically-clustered areas, so as to reduce survey costs, such as the travelling time for interviewers. Generally, although the clustering of respondents can produce biased estimates—because 'birds of a feather flock together' (people living near each other are often similar socially)—these biases can be handled mostly by statistical correction. However, there remains the potential for bias if the survey's cluster selection method 'misses' to some extent the geographical clustering of groups at-risk of crime victimization.

Accuracy of measurement in crime surveys

This set of issues and biases arise from the process of interviewing.[4]

- *Knowledge of incidents*—the BCS interviews one respondent per household to answer questions both about personal experiences of victimization and those of the household collectively (usually property crimes). However, respondents may not know about, and will not report, the crime experiences of other household members.

- *Not telling*—there are various reasons for respondents not telling survey interviewers about crime victimization, including: *load and fatigue*—too many crime experiences or too many questions may make the respondent unwilling to divulge all their experiences; *concealing*, for instance, if there is a personal relationship between the victim and the offender (as in domestic violence) because of feelings of shame, or fear of reprisal, or if the victim feels culpable or responsible for the incident in some way (for example, an assailant receiving an unlucky blow in a fight may end-up the 'victim'). Means of ensuring greater anonymity, sympathy and/or confidentiality during the interview process may help to reduce concealment (for instance, a change to the use of Computer Assisted Personal Interviewing by laptop, with an element of anonymous self-completion, may have increased the count of domestic violence in the British Crime Survey).

- *Memory-decay*—or less politely, forgetting. The more distant the event, the less likely respondents are to remember it.

- *Telescoping*—conversely, especially serious or worrying events which occurred some time ago (that is, outside the survey's recall period) may be brought-forward in time—as in, 'it only seemed like yesterday'—because they remain a worrying memory from which victims may not have recovered fully.

- *Education*—surveys ask questions, and rely on people's understanding and memory. Education trains people in understanding and remembering (all those exams!); so, the more educated you are, the more likely you are to recall incidents, and also to cooperate fully with the interviewer (for which, read examiner!).

- *Multiple and series incidents*—in order to make their counts comparable to official crime counts, surveys try to measure crime as discrete, unrelated, incidents, but for some people—again, 'domestic violence' is an illustrative example—their experience of crime is so frequent, and the 'crime' itself is so much a condition of their everyday lives that it is nearly impossible to count or separate instances of these crimes into separate incidents.

- *Interview conditions*—who the interviewer is, where the interview takes place, whether others are present, what procedures of recording (for example, the CAPI example above), ensuring confidentiality and so on, are all likely to produce different responses, greater or less recall, different admission rates, etc. Matching interviewers with interviewees may also affect response rates if it creates greater understanding or trust between interviewer and respondent—for example, appropriate matching according to ethnicity, gender, age, culture and linguistic background can all increase trust and response.

What do crime surveys tell us about the reporting of crime?

The main reason given in official reports of the results of crime victimization surveys for the differential reporting of incidents to the police is the intrinsic characteristics of *incidents*. Comparison between reporting rates for different types of offence (for example, Kershaw *et al.*, 2001), alongside questions directly asked of victims about their decisions to report incidents (Mayhew *et al.*, 1993), point to assessments of the seriousness or triviality of the offence, as well as to the more ambiguous responses of perceived police ineffectiveness[5] and being able to deal with matters privately (Coleman and Moynihan, 1996). Where applicable, considerations of loss and the validation of insurance claims are also likely to affect victims' assessments. These are especially likely to result in high reporting and recording rates where insurance is widespread, as in household contents insurance, or compulsory as in theft of cars, where insurance claims are likely to be made. Thus, according to the 1996 British Crime Survey, victims of motor vehicle theft reported 97 per cent of incidents to the police, while only 36 per cent of attempted vehicle thefts were reported.

Against this view is another which points to the 'discriminatory' nature of reporting decisions applied by, and recording practices applied to, particular *types of complainant* which biases official statistics. Observational research on police-public encounters has generally found person-based selectivity on the part of the police in their decisions to record complaints and allegations from and against particular types of people, including selective treatment of particular social groups such as young people, members of ethnic minorities, the unemployed and economically disadvantaged (Reiner, 1992; Black, 1980; Reiss, 1971). Yet it is difficult to distinguish between what Reiner terms 'discrimination'— 'a pattern of exercise of police powers which results in some social categories being over-represented as targets for police action' (1992: 157)—and 'differentiation'—a disproportionate exercize of police powers against some social categories relative to their presence in the population. A general difficulty is that 'social' selectivity in the types of incident, and person, coming to police attention, is confounded with the potential for 'institutional bias' in police culture and practice in the way they respond to persons coming to their attention.

A difficulty for research is separating out the *general propensity* of different population groups to report crime to the police, even if they are witnesses rather than victims (which may be due to differences in their confidence in the police, or their sense of public duty, or community spirit), from the specific *need* to report crime because they have been a victim (where victims are seeking some kind of service, or are obliged to report by their insurers). The BCS only asks victims about their actual reporting of their current incidents reported in the survey and not the general population about its general propensities in reporting incidents to the police. Likewise, 'incident-tracking' studies pre-select from amongst incidents reported to the police 'those which either definitely, *or might have*, incorporated allegations of crime' (Burrows *et al.*, 2000, original emphasis; see also Farrington and Dowds, 1985).

The greater disparity between calls and crimes for incidents of nuisance and disorder, than for incidents of acquisitive crime (Table 3.1), may reflect differences between the reporting of incidents witnessed by members of the public and the reporting of crime experienced by victims. A study of victims of property crime, identified in the BCS, used statistical techniques to estimate general propensities to report crime by taking into account differences in risk of victimization as well as incident-specific characteristics (MacDonald, 2001). Having done this, the research still found that younger, male or unemployed victims were less likely, while people of Indian Subcontinental ethnic origin were more likely, to report their victimization to the police. Further, victims who had a low opinion of police efficacy were less likely, while those who were worried about burglary were more likely, to report incidents. It would seem, at least with regard to their own personally-experienced victimization, that members of the public exercise a degree of choice—albeit constrained—over their decision to call the police and that this may reflect their perceptions of the likely response of the police to them as well as their own need to call.

Counting crime

Much of the attention paid to the reporting and recording of incidents to the police has been concerned with matters of bias of the resulting indicators extracted from them. Much of this preoccupation reflects a particular, instrumental way of viewing these figures; that is, as an index of a *real* phenomenon (crime) calling for a specific control response—criminal justice—by the State. Yet, since most of the incidents that find their way into the official accounts would not come to the attention of the State without being initiated by private citizens, these figures also represent a *social construction*, the 'policing of communications about risk in late modern society' (Ericson and Haggerty, 1997; 70). Here, the public are communicating their needs to the police as much as the police are collating evidence on behalf of the State of the need for crime control. Thus a *crime rate*, rather than being simply a record of police activity, or an indicator of the demand for crime control, may actually represent the aggregated outcome of the interaction of two processes—the *invocation of police authority* by the public in respect of difficult and troubling incidents—and the *criminalization of incidents* through the application of the criminal law by the police in respect of those incidents. In their own ways, both recorded criminal statistics and the crime victimization surveys that seek to supplement them, are each the outcome of *dialogues* between the citizen and the State; as with all dialogues, they reflect both what is being said, and how it is being received.

REVIEW QUESTIONS

1 What are the factors that lead to unrepresentative (biased) results from sample surveys of crime victimization?

2 What are the factors that affect the accuracy of measurement in crime victimization surveys?

3 What are the kinds of reasons victims have for reporting crime to the police?

The frequency of crime victimization

The count of crime can be arranged in various ways. In this section, we look briefly at the count as an attribute of individual *households* (the next section looks at it as an attribute of *groups*). As described above, a crime victimization survey asks respondents to report the number of crime victimization incidents they have experienced over a particular recall period. These can be arranged as a table of the crime frequency for the particular sample. An example of a frequency distribution is given in Table 3.2.[6] This lists the number (frequency) of households reporting particular levels of the count of crime throughout its range, in this case from zero to thirteen times. We can see at a glance that the distribution is quite distinctive—the large majority of households (82 per cent) did not suffer any household property crime in the previous twelve months, while only 5.8 per cent of

Table 3.3 Table of frequencies of incidents reported by victims of household property crime victimization over the previous twelve months in four areas of social housing, 1990

	Frequency of households	Frequency of incidents	Percentage of incidents	Cumulative percentage of incidents
0	1423	0	0	0
1	212	212	40.4	40.4
2	49	98	18.7	59.1
3	27	81	15.4	74.5
4	12	48	9.1	83.6
5	2	10	1.9	85.5
6	4	24	4.6	90.1
7	3	21	4.0	94.1
9	2	18	3.4	97.5
13	1	13	2.5	100.0
Total	1735	525	100.0	

Note: Household property crime includes incidents of: burglary, theft from a dwelling, and criminal damage. For details of the survey see Foster and Hope (1993).   *Source:* Foster and Hope (1993).

households experienced more than one crime.[7] And although the average for the sample as a whole was only 0.3 incidents per household per annum, the range of incidents, and hence the variability of frequencies of victimization in the sample, was much greater.

The consequences of this peculiarity can be seen in Table 3.3. Relatively few households appear, at any one time, to 'produce' most areas' crime rates—the 5.8 per cent of households experiencing more than one crime incident account for 59.6 per cent of all the household property crime in their areas. In recent years, such findings (replicated in other research) have excited much interest from policy makers. If we could predict which households are likely to be *repeat victims*, and could do something to prevent the repeat victimization occurring, then we might be able to reduce a great deal of crime, relatively inexpensively (see Pease, 1998). On this example (Table 3.3), by targeting the 18 per cent of households who were victims, we would encounter the 6 per cent of residents (but 33 per cent of victims) who are the repeat victims (that is, experiencing two or more victim incidents) producing 60 per cent of crime (Table 3.2). Such, anyway, is the promise, and policy research and development continues to explore and test whether such inferences can be drawn from the frequency distribution, and whether the ambition can be realized in practical crime prevention projects, and at what cost. That task cannot concern us here; but it does give an illustration of how crime statistics can stimulate crime prevention policy making.

The rate of crime victimization

The sample frequency distribution discussed in the previous section was drawn from areas that had crime victimization rates greater than the national average. A *crime rate* is an attribute of a population *group* (in the above case, the 'groups' were households from each of four areas of social housing). Even so, the conventional idea of a crime rate—usually expressed as the number of crimes divided by the size of the population in the area in which the crimes were counted (Bottomley and Pease, 1986)—may be misleading. While a population denominator may serve the useful purpose of comparing rates across jurisdictions of different population sizes (on the natural assumption that, other things being equal, the bigger the population the greater the number of crimes committed), this particular way of conceptualizing a crime rate may also mask other characteristics of the distribution of crime amongst groups. For instance, a programme of research work during the 1990s sought to 'unpack' other features of the crime victimization rate (Trickett *et al.*, 1995; Trickett *et al.*, 1992) by employing the heuristic idea of crime-flux (Hope, 1995). The simple idea behind the notion of crime-flux is that the commonplace crime rate—called the crime incidence rate—can be decomposed into two distinct statistics that combine together. Thus:

(1) The crime *prevalence* rate = no. of victims (V) ÷ no. in population (P) = V ÷ P.

(2) The crime *concentration* rate = no. of victimization counts (C) ÷ no. of victims (V) = C ÷ V.[8]

Therefore, the crime incidence rate = prevalence × concentration = (V ÷ P) × (C ÷ V).

The sample structure of the BCS during the 1980s and 1990s made it possible to compute 'pseudo-crime rates' for small areas.[9] The three rates could then be computed for the clusters of respondents in each pseudo-area, and then ranked from lowest to highest. In turn, average crime rates could be calculated for each decile of the area-ranking—that is, from the 10 per cent of areas with the lowest crime rates, through to the 10 per cent of areas with the highest crime rates. Figure 3.1 illustrates the results of this computation on data drawn from the 1992 BCS.

Figure 3.1 shows the relationship between area incidence and prevalence rates. For low crime areas there is little difference. However, as the rates increase, the incidence rate diverges markedly from the prevalence rate, which seems to grow in a more linear fashion. As defined above, the gap between incidence and prevalence rates—which is by far greater in the highest crime rate areas—can be accounted for, computationally, by the crime concentration rate—that is, the (frequency) rate at which victims are victimized—which is essentially the group-level equivalent of the individual victimization

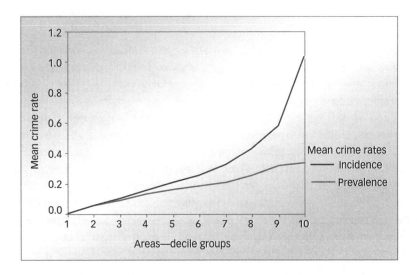

(frequency) distribution illustrated in Table 3.3. A paper by Trickett *et al.* (1992) confirmed, statistically, that 'what is different about high crime areas' is their greater rate of concentration of victimization. In other words, in high crime areas, victims are on average victimized more frequently (than would be expected by chance) than in low crime areas; or alternatively, high crime areas have more repeat victims than low crime areas. Yet, as with all statistical findings, these results raise more questions than they give answers—none of which, unfortunately, can be pursued here.

REVIEW QUESTIONS

1 What is 'crime-flux'?

2 What are the two statistical components of the crime incidence rate?

3 What is different about high crime areas?

CONCLUSION

Statistical description versus statistical analysis

A final point can be made about crime statistics from the data presented in the two previous sections. That is, the statistical analyses presented here are still essentially *descriptive*. Although they suggest intriguing areas of research enquiry, and practical investigation, they do not in themselves prove any thing much about the various social processes that might be producing these observed statistical distributions. To undertake that task requires, initially, the formulation of hypotheses, drawn from theory, from which can be constructed *hypothetical models* that can then be tested against empirical data, and the results used subsequently to revise our theoretical, explanatory models. In other words, the production of reliable counts, frequencies and rates of crime is the start, rather than the end point, of statistical analysis.

There are obvious dangers in leaving matters at the descriptive level without enquiring further as to what social-statistical processes might be producing the observed distributions—not least in drawing the wrong conclusions. Thus, the data on the two distributions of crime victimization—of households and areas—presented in the previous two sections merely suggest that there might be a relationship—or *correlation*—between the two. But it is a common saying in statistical analysis that 'correlation is not causation'. In this case, then, it would be as wrong to conclude (without further analysis) that 'high crime areas' are the consequence of a residential concentration of 'repeat victims'—what is sometimes called a *compositional* explanation—as it would be to conclude that the distribution of repeat victimization is a consequence of the social characteristics and relations that are peculiar to high crime areas—what is called a *contextual* explanation. Further analysis and investigation would be needed to sort out, in effect, which of the distributions of crime victimization—households or areas—was 'causing' the other; or indeed whether there was any genuine relationship between the two that could not be accounted for by some other factor that resulted in the merely coincidental, or spurious, correlation between the prevalence of victims, and the incidence of victimization. Finding that such correlations exist—or even that it has the particular form illustrated in Figure 3.1, invites speculation and further enquiry but does nothing to confirm or validate those speculations, at least until plausible hypotheses have been tested.

Crime statistics as a social construction

To see crime statistics as a social construction in no way invalidates statistical research effort to investigate and explain them. The contemporary approach to the use of crime statistics differs from earlier uses. Rather than treat the statistics literally as an objective measure of a quantity called crime that exists as a social fact 'out there'—what was once called in textbooks the *positivist* approach—the role of statistical analysis is to develop and test explanations (models) that best represent the observed (or sampled) data and which take into account, or treat as an object of statistical study in its own right, the various social processes that lie behind them. Crime statistics are the product of a dialogue between reporter and recorder, between citizen and state. Thus, rather than being an unfortunate set of biases that need to be circumvented, analysis of the various social processes leading to those biases tells us about the dialectic at the heart of criminology—the relationship between deviance and its regulation.

QUESTIONS FOR DISCUSSION

Should a criminologist bother with criminal statistics at all?

1 What does a comparison with either; (a) police incident logs; or (b) crime victimization surveys tell us about the reliability of official recorded crime statistics?

2 How representative and accurate are crime victimization surveys as a measure of crime, what are the principle sources of bias and inaccuracy in such surveys?

3 What does analysis of the frequency, and the rate, of crime victimization tell us about the distribution of crime?

GUIDE TO FURTHER READING

The following provide overviews of criminal statistics and their relationship to criminology in Britain. They also contain information on other types of criminal statistic not considered in this chapter:

Bottomley, K. and Pease, K. (1986) *Crime and Punishment: Interpreting the Data*, Milton Keynes: Open University Press.

Coleman, C. and Moynihan, J. (1996) *Understanding Crime Data; Haunted by the Dark Figure*, Buckingham: O.U. Press.

Maguire, M. (2002) 'Crime statistics: the "Data Explosion" and its implications', in M. Maguire, R. Morgan and R. Reiner (eds) *The Oxford Handbook of Criminology* (3rd Edn), Oxford: Oxford University Press.

WEB LINKS

www.crimestatistics.org.uk

Up-to-date information on crime statistics in England and Wales.

Home Office Statistical Bulletins

Recent reports on criminal statistics and findings from the British Crime Survey. There are published periodically. (Previous reports on the BCS were published in the *Home Office Research Studies* series. Information on these sources can be obtained from the Home Office Research, Development and Statistics (RDS) Directorate at www.homeoffice.gov.uk/rds. Previously, crime statistics were published in the annual statistical series *Criminal Statistics*.)

www.ojp.usdoj.gov/bjs

Information on crime statistics for the USA from the Bureau of Justice Statistics, US Department of Justice.

www.europeansourcebook.org

Information on crime statistics for European countries from the Council of Europe *European Sourcebook of Crime and Criminal Justice Statistics*.

REFERENCES

Durkheim, E. (1979) *Suicide: a study in Sociology*. London: Routledge and Kegan Paul.

Black, D. (1970) 'Production of Crime Rates'. *American Sociological Review*, 35: 733–48.

Black, D. (1980) *The Manners and Customs of the Police*. New York: Academic Press.

Bottomley, K. and Pease, K. (1986) *Crime and Punishment: Interpreting the data*. Milton Keynes: Open University Press.

Bottomley, K. and Coleman, C. (1981) *Understanding Crime Rates*. Farnborough: Gower.

Burrows, J., Tarling, R., Mackie, A., Lewis, R. and Taylor, G. (2000) *Review of Police Forces' Crime Recording Practices*. Home Office Research Study 204. London: Home Office.

Christie, N. (2004) *A Suitable Amount of Crime*. London and New York: Routledge.

Cicourel, A. (1968) *The Social Organisation of Juvenile Justice*. New York: Wiley.

Coleman, C. and Moynihan, J. (1996) *Understanding Crime Data: Haunted by the Dark Figure*. Buckingham: Open University Press.

Dorling, D. and Simpson, S. (1999) *Statistics in Society: the arithmetic of politics*. London: Arnold.

Ericson, R.V. and Haggerty, K.D. (1997) *Policing the Risk Society*. Oxford: Clarendon Press.

Farrington, D. and Dowds, E. (1985) 'Disentangling criminal behaviour and police reaction' In D. Farrington and J. Gunn (eds.) *Reactions to Crime*. Chichester: John Wiley.

Foster, J. and Hope T. (1993) *Housing, Community and Crime: the impact of the Priority Estates Project*. Home Office Research Study No. 131. London: HMSO.

Home Office (2000) *Review of Crime Statistics: a discussion document*. London: Home Office.

Home Office (2003) *The National Policing Plan, 2004–2007*, November 2003. London: Home Office.

Hope, T. (1995) 'The Flux of Victimisation', *British Journal of Criminology*, 35 (3): 327–42.

Hope, T., Karstedt, S. and Farrall, S. (2001) *The Relationship between Calls and Crimes*. Innovative Research Challenge Fund. Report to the Home Office.

Kershaw, C., Budd, T., Kinshott, G., Mattinson, J., Mayhew, P. and Myhill, A. (2000) *The 2000 British Crime Survey: England and Wales*. Home Office Statistical Bulletin 18/00. London: Home Office.

Kershaw, C., Chivite-Matthews, N., Thomas, C. and Aust, R. (2001) *The 2001 British Crime Survey: first results, England and Wales*. Home Office Statistical Bulletin 18/01. London: Home Office.

McCabe, S. and Sutcliffe, F. (1978) *Defining Crime: a Study of Police decisions*. Oxford: Blackwell.

MacDonald, Z. (2001) 'Revisiting the Dark Figure: a Microeconometric Analysis of the Under-reporting of Property Crime and its Implications', *British Journal of Criminology*, 41: 127–49.

Mayhew, P., Aye Maung N., and Mirrlees-Black, C. (1993) *The 1992 British Crime Survey*. Home Office Research Study No. 132. London: HMSO.

Pease, K. (1998) Repeat Victimisation: taking stock. Crime Detection and Prevention Series Paper 90. London: Home Office Police Research Group.

Reiner, R. (1992) 'Police research in the United Kingdom: a Critical Review', in M. Tonry and N. Morris (eds) *Modern Policing*. Crime and Justice: a review of research, Volume 15. Chicago: University of Chicago Press.

Reiss, A.J. (1971) *The Police and the Public*. New Haven, Conn.: Yale University Press.

Rose, N. (1999) *Powers of Freedom: Reframing Political Thought*. Cambridge: Cambridge University Press.

Skogan, W.G. (1986) 'Methodological issues in the study of victimisation', in E. Fattah (ed) *From Crime Policy to Victim Policy*.

Trickett, A., Ellingworth, D., Hope T. and Pease K. (1995) 'Crime Victimisation in the Eighties: Changes in Area and Regional Inequality', *British Journal of Criminology*, 35 (3): 343–59.

Trickett, A., Osborn D.R., Seymour, J. and Pease, K. (1992) 'What is Different About High Crime Areas?' *British Journal of Criminology*, 32: 81–9.

NOTES

1. The Home Office Counting Rules are not publicly available.

2. The precise nature and scale of these disparities may have been peculiar to the police force in question, or have now changed as a result of Home Office effort to bring about consistent recording practice amongst police forces via the implementation (in April 2002) of the National Crime Recording Standard.

3. Although telephone ownership has greatly increased in Britain, poorer and more mobile households have tended not to have access to land-line telephones, at least until relatively recently; for this reason, the BCS has kept to face-to-face interviewing.

4. A good if somewhat dated guide to these methodological issues is Skogan (1986).

5. It is not clear from the wording of the question asked in the BCS whether this is a perception of police ineffectiveness *per se* or whether it is a perception restricted to the specific incident in question.

6. The data in Table 3.2 (and Table 3.3) are taken from a crime victimization survey carried out in four areas of social housing, with high crime rates, in 1990. The tables record frequencies of household property crime, that includes: burglary, theft from a dwelling, and criminal damage to the dwelling and its attached property. For further details of the survey, and the study from which it derives, see Foster and Hope (1993).

7. We can also run a statistical test on this sample frequency distribution which confirms what we might

have suspected visually, that it is highly unlikely that these frequencies could have arisen by chance and therefore the sample distribution truly represents the population from which the sample is drawn.

8. This also provides an index of the degree of repeat victimization.

9. Specifically, sampled respondents were 'clustered' within each of the survey's small area 'primary sampling units'.

4

Theoretical criminology: a starting point

Keith Hayward and Wayne Morrison[1]

INTRODUCTION

Theoretical criminology is a vast, sprawling subject that straddles more than two centuries of intellectual thought and a range of academic disciplines. It is not therefore something that readily lends itself to summary in a short stand-alone chapter. Instead, our aim here is to offer those new to the subject a 'starting point', a very general (and hopefully gentle) introduction to some of the main criminological theories that have sought to explain and account for crime and criminality in the modern age. If this chapter is a starting point, then our first task must be to point out where next for those interested in theorizing crime in more detail? The following textbooks each provide excellent introductions to the rudiments of criminological theory:

Theoretical Criminology by George Vold, Thomas Bernard and Jeffrey Snipes (2002, Oxford: Oxford University Press).

Criminological Theory: Context and Consequences by Robert Lilly, Francis Cullen and Richard Ball (2002, London: Sage).

Understanding Deviance by David Downes and Paul Rock (2003, Oxford: Oxford University Press).

Criminology: Theory and Context by John Tierney (1996, Hemel Hempstead: Prentice Hall).

Essential Criminology by Mark Lanier and Stuart Henry (1998, Boulder, CO: Westview Press).

An Introduction to Criminological Theory by Roger Hopkins-Burke (2001, Cullompton: Willan).

Criminology: A Textbook by Katherine S. Williams (2004, Oxford: Oxford University Press).

Criminological Theories: Traditional and Non-traditional Voices and Themes by Imogene Moyer (2001: Thousand Oaks, CA: Sage).

Theoretical Criminology: From Modernity to Postmodernism by Wayne Morrison (1995, London: Cavendish).

Theories of Crime and Punishment by Claire Valier (2001, London: Longman).

BACKGROUND

Perhaps the first thing worth pointing out to those new to the subject is the overlapping nature of much criminological theorizing. Although our approach in this chapter is to break down theories into short, independent sections, it is important to recognize that criminological theory is not something that is easily compartmentalized. It is essential, therefore, to think critically about both the origins and the contemporary roles of criminological theories, rather than just repeating some learning of their basic outline/structure. One must also bear in mind that, whilst criminological theory is often viewed by many as an abstract, even esoteric enterprise (on this particular point see the following chapter by Claire Valier), in reality its impact over the last century in areas such as crime control (see Chapters 21 and 22), juvenile justice (see Chapter 19), and public and penal policy (see Chapters 10, 26 and 27) has been profound and far-reaching. One need only think of the role played by criminological theory in such diverse policy initiatives as the 1970s 'welfarist' movement within youth justice, and the 'zero tolerance' policing phenomenon of the 1990s to recognize the influential, indeed potent, force of theory. In this sense, theoretical criminology should be seen as a vital, living subject, and not some historical or intellectual fancy. Finally, one should recognize that the collection of theoretical vignettes gathered together here is anything but exhaustive. A great number of other criminological theories abound from 'peacemaking' criminology (Quinney, 1991) to control-balance theory (Tittle, 1995), all of which compete for attention against/with each other in the vibrant—if, at times, exasperating—world of criminological theory.

The theories—a beginners guide

The founding doctrines

For much of modernity (roughly the last 200 years) social scientists believed that the problems of modern society would be overcome or at least managed by the careful, scientific pursuit of relevant knowledge and the application of this knowledge to a specific set of problems (for a good general introduction to the debates around modernity see Bocock and Thompson, 1992; Hall and Gieben, 1992). The basket of differing approaches that we may say collectively constitutes academic criminology should thus be seen as part of this enterprise (see Bierne, 1993; Garland, 1994; Morrison, 2004). Certainly the discipline's two (highly contrasting) founding doctrines, the 'classical' and 'positivist' approaches to the study of crime, were fundamentally concerned with using the techniques and methods of enlightened science and philosophy to make good on their shared goal: the reduction and control of crime within modern, industrialized societies.

Classicism

The first sets of writings typically considered as criminology are labelled *classical criminology* and date from the late eighteenth century. It was a movement born of a combination of fear and optimism: fear of the breakdown of society, fear that there was no longer a God around which to centre things, and fear of the mob, the ragged, poverty-stricken masses that were increasingly drawn to the burgeoning cities of Western Europe; optimism in the sense of the steadfast belief that, as modernity unfolded, it would bestow social science with enlightened knowledge about the human condition. Classical scholars thus put their faith in these new 'sciences of man' in the belief that they would help create greater social stability.

Importantly, with classicism, the new intellectual instruments of modernity were employed not in a bid to understand the ultimate causes of human behaviour; rather the task was to find ways of controlling and directing behaviour by affecting *rational motivation*. In other words, the underlying social conditions of crime were unimportant. Instead the emphasis was on administration, ordered systems that would free society from arbitrary authority and open it up so that the basic true forms of the human condition would become visible. To this end, classical scholars set about reforming the system of investigation and punishing offences. A reasonably coherent, rational intellectual structure was developed which legitimated the creation of a system of criminal justice based on equality and proportionality.

The central figure in classicism's development was the Italian, Cesare Beccaria (1738–94). In *On Crimes and Punishment* ([1764] 1963) Beccaria considered crime 'injurious to society'. It was this injury to society, rather than to the immediate individual(s) who experienced it (or for that matter the abstract sovereign), that was to direct and determine the degree of punishment. Beccaria claimed that criminal law should bind and guide society by laying out clear, rational rules. The rules are laid down by a legitimate body guided by a new science of decision making, namely *utilitarianism* (or the assumption that all social action should be guided by the goal of achieving the greatest happiness for the greatest number: see relatedly Hume [1739] 1978). From this viewpoint, the punishment of an individual for a crime was justified, and justifiable only, for its contribution to the prevention of future infringements on the happiness of others. Accordingly, Beccaria reasoned that, certain and quick, rather than severe, punishments would best accomplish these goals. Torture, execution, and other 'irrational' activities must be abolished. In their place there were to be quick and certain trials and, in the case of convictions, carefully calculated punishments determined strictly in accordance with the damage to society caused by the crime. Beccaria proposed that accused persons be treated humanely before trial, with every right and facility extended to enable them to bring evidence on their own behalf. (In Beccaria's time accused and convicted persons were detained in the same institutions, and subjected to the same punishments and conditions.)

Classicism was given further impetus by the British philosopher, Jeremy Bentham (1748–1832). Like Beccaria, Bentham insisted that prevention was the only justifiable purpose of punishment, and, furthermore, that punishment was too 'expensive' when it produced more evil than good, or when the same good could be obtained at the 'price' of less suffering. He recommended penalties be fixed so as to *impose an amount of pain in excess of pleasure that might be derived from the criminal act*. It was this calculation of pain compared to pleasure that Bentham believed would deter crime, it was his key for unlocking the functionality of human nature: 'Nature has placed mankind under the governance of two sovereign masters, pain and pleasure. It is for them alone to point out what we ought to do, as well as to determine what we shall do' (Bentham, [1789] 1982).

Famously, Bentham also attempted to radicalize imprisonment, an institution then used merely to hold persons awaiting trial or debtors. He spent much of his life trying to convince authorities that an institution of his design, called a 'Panopticon', would solve the problems of correction, of poverty, of idleness and mental instability. There were three features to the panopticon. First, the architectural dimension; the panopticon was to be a circular building arranged so that every cell could be visible from a central point providing a hierarchy of continuous surveillance. The omniscient prison inspector would be kept from the sight of the prisoners by a system of 'blinds unless . . . he thinks fit to show himself'. Second, management by contract; the manager would employ the inmates in contract labour and he was to receive a share of the money earned by the inmates, but he was to be financially liable if inmates who were later released re-offended, or if an excess number of inmates died during imprisonment. Third, the panopticon was to be open to the inspection of the world. Bentham's panopticon idea was never fully implemented (although two prisons were built along his design in France and one in the US). The panopticon keeps its importance not for the institutions actually constructed, rather for the type of disciplinary rationality the scheme displays (on this point see Chapter 23). Indeed, in many ways, the panopticon remains the very embodiment of classicism.

In a bid to illustrate our earlier point that theoretical criminology is a vibrant, living subject, and not some historical fancy it is worth pointing out that many of the central ideas of classicism continue to endure within criminology today, not least the notion of rationality, which has been resuscitated in recent years by proponents of rational choice theory (see Clarke and Cornish, 1985; Roshier, 1989).

REVIEW QUESTIONS

1 What were the primary concerns of classical criminologists?

2 From where did classicism draw its ideas? In which areas of criminal justice did they hope to implement these ideas?

3 What has been the legacy of classicism within mainstream criminology?

Key readings

Beccaria, C. ([1764] 1963) *On Crimes and Punishments*. Indianapolis: Bobbs-Merrill.

Bentham, J. (1791) *Collected Works of Jeremy Bentham*. London: J. Bowring

Clarke, R. V. G. and Cornish, D. B. (1986) The Reasoning Criminal: Rational Choice Perspectives on Offending. New York: Springer Verlag.

Textbook reading/secondary review

Lanier, M. and Henry, S., Chapter 4 ('Classical, Neoclassical and Rational Choice Theories') in *Essential Criminology* (1998). Boulder, CO: Westview Press.

Criminological positivism

While positivism is a broad term which includes a number of differing applications (see Morrison, 1995: chapters 6–9; Giddens, 1974), for the purposes of introducing criminological theory, we can say that it represents a field of criminological inquiry that emerged in the early nineteenth century which argued that criminality could be studied scientifically using methods derived from the natural sciences. Most famously, criminological positivism is associated with the Italian medical doctor, Cesare Lombroso (1835–1909). Lombroso laid claim to founding a new science—the 'science of criminology' that took as its focus not the criminal law or its related rational administrative practices (as with classicism), but the 'criminal (person)'. Thus, in sharp contrast to classicism, Lombroso's answer to the problems of criminal behaviour lay in *biology*, specifically a complex set of externally visible physiological variations that, he claimed, marked out certain individuals as predestined to commit crime. By observation and careful measurement of the bodily features of the criminal, Lombroso attempted to prove scientifically that those who broke the law were physically distinct from those who did not—this is the centrepiece of nineteenth century criminological positivism.

Lombroso conducted thousands of post-mortem examinations and physiological studies of prison inmates and non-criminals. He concluded that the criminal existed, in the natural order of things, as a lower form of human evolution than the average man, with very distinct physical and mental characteristics (see editions of *L'Uomo delinquente*, first published in 1876). Lombroso proffered a four-fold classification:

(a) born criminal, those with true atavistic features;

(b) insane criminals, including idiots, imbeciles, and paranoiacs as well as epileptics and alcoholics;

(c) occasional criminals or criminaloids, whose crimes were explained largely by opportunity; and

(d) criminals of passion who commit crime because of honour, love or anger. They are propelled by a (temporary) irresistible force.

Later, additional categories gave some allowance for the influence of social factors (on this particular point see the work of another Italian positivist, Enrico Ferri (1856–1929)) and he speculated somewhat as to the interaction of genetic and environmental influences (thus providing, to some extent, a precursor to socio-biological theories, see below). However, although Lombroso went some way to developing a multiple factor approach, he never really moved beyond the principle that the true 'born criminal' was responsible for a large amount of criminal behaviour.

Importantly, Lombroso was not alone in his search for the 'criminal type' (see also the work of the aforementioned Ferri and Raffaele Garofalo (1852–1934)—there has been, and indeed still is (see below), a number of scholars and research projects dedicated to reducing the problem of crime to the problem of the criminal. For this reason, one should be aware that positivist criminology does not begin and end with the Italian deterministic tradition (*scuola positiva*). It also extends to include various other early schools of criminological thought. For example, the work of early nineteenth century 'social ecology' scholars such as the Frenchmen André-Michel Guerry and the Belgian Adolphe de Quételet is also typically described as positivist in the sense that it sought to unearth objective, 'law-like' scientific knowledge about crime (in their particular case, via the moral analysis of early crime statistics and how they might help us better understand what they described as 'the social mechanics of crime', see Beirne 1993 chapters 3 and 4).

REVIEW QUESTIONS

1 What were the main methods employed by the nineteenth century positivists?

2 What value can we place on this form of criminology?

3 Is the positivists' ultimate aim of a purely 'scientific' form of criminology a valid one?

Key readings

Lombroso, C. (1911) *Crime: Its Causes and Remedies*. Boston: Little Brown.

Ferri, E. (2003) 'Causes of Criminal Behaviour' in Muncie, J., McLaughlin, E., and Hughes, G. (eds) *Criminological Perspectives: A Reader*. London: Sage.

Beirne, P. (1993) *Inventing Criminology: Essays on the Rise of 'Homo Criminalis'*, Albany, New York: State University of New York Press. Chapter 6.

Textbook reading/secondary source

Morrison, W., Chapter 6 ('Criminological Positivism 1: The Search for the Criminal Man, or the Problem of the Duck') in *Theoretical Criminology: From Modernity to Postmodernism* (1995) London: Cavendish.

Individual perspectives

Biological and genetic explanations of crime

Biological explanations of crime appear to offer the promise that, if humans were examined like other animals, the 'laws of nature' that govern 'human behaviour' could be established and accounted for. Under this perspective, human behaviour is determined by factors that, while universal to the species, reside to a greater or lesser extent in the constitution of the individual—individuals are therefore, to an extent, predetermined into a life of crime. In this sense, this line of work can be seen as extending from the Italian positivist school inspired by Lombroso. The following are a small selection of some of the better-known examples of the biological approach to the study of crime:

William Sheldon's 'body type' theory—Sheldon's famous (1942) study attempted to link body-build and personality. He famously divided humans into three body types, or 'somatotypes' (see relatedly, the slightly earlier work of the English criminologist, Charles Goring (1913) and the Harvard anthropologist, A.E. Hooton (1939)):

(a) endomorphs: a heavy, soft or round build; relaxed, sociable, extrovert personality;

(b) mesomorphs: well-developed, muscular, athletic build; active, dynamic, aggressive (sometimes violent) personality;

(c) ectomorph: small, lean, delicate/weak build; hypersensitive, intellectual, sensitive, introverted personality.

Some individuals are 'pure types', while others are 'hybrids' incorporating elements from two, or even three of the builds in their physique. Sheldon argued that delinquents were characterized by a preponderance of mesomorphs, some indication of endomorphy, and a marked lack of ectomorphs. Sheldon concluded this pattern differed from that found in non-criminal populations, demonstrating that there were differences in the physiques of delinquent and non-delinquent males. More recent studies, of course, have concluded that no such link between body type and crime actually exists. But, even today, this does not deter those who are desperate to reinstate constitutional factors (for example, Cortes and Gatti's 1972 study that argued that crime was caused by an interaction between biological and social factors, hence the term 'biosocial perspective').

Genetic transmission theory—Throughout the twentieth century a series of studies have tried to ascertain the *hereditary* nature of crime. Simply stated, this is the idea that certain criminal tendencies are inherited—a criminal is born not made. For example:

- In the 1920s, the German physician Johannes Lange began the tradition of 'twin studies', where the criminal records of identical and fraternal twins were contrasted. Work continues in this area today.
- Raymond Crowe (1974) and Barry Hutchings and Sarnoff Mednick's (1975) work in the area of 'adoption studies'. Here the aim is to compare the criminal behaviour of adopted children with that of their biological parents. If the behaviour of the children more closely resembles the biological parents rather than the adoptive parents, then there is a strong case for genetic transmission theory.

There have been numerous other specific biological theories, such as:

- the attention given to the 'XYY Syndrome' in the 1960s (a chromosomal abnormality that was controversially linked to violent crime) (for example, Sandberg *et al.*, 1961)
- research into biochemical and hormonal imbalances and criminality in the 1920s and 1930s (for example, Berman 1921).
- the link between testosterone and aggression (for example, Moyer 1971)
- Kathy Dalton's (1961) work on the relationship between PMT and female criminality.

Today there are still those who continue to try and reinstate constitutional factors into the study of crime. In their controversial recent work *Crime and Human Nature* (1985) Wilson and Hernstein devote several pages to reproducing diagrams and photography used by Sheldon, and conclude that 'wherever it has been examined, criminals on the average differ in physique from the population at large' (see 'Right Realism' below).

In conclusion, this body of work is inevitably plagued by the same problems encountered by the Italian positivists; specifically, it is constantly hampered by its inability to control for complex and interacting environmental and social influences. Thus, all informed scholars who claim that biology plays a strong role in criminality now no longer talk in terms of a dominating role; rather a picture is drawn of behaviour resulting from the interaction of the biological make-up of the organism with the physical and social environment.

REVIEW QUESTIONS

1 Can criminality be inherited?

2 If we accept that crime is not a natural phenomenon but is socially constructed, is it possible to explain crime in terms of individual pathology?

3 How much emphasis can criminology afford to place on questions of biology?

Key readings

Sheldon, W. H. (1942) *The Varieties of Temperament*. New York: Harper.
Ciba Foundation Symposium 194 (1996) *Genetics of Criminal and Antisocial Behaviour*. Chichester: Wiley.
Wilson, J. Q. and Herrnstein, R. (1985) *Crime and Human Nature*. New York: Simon and Schuster.

Textbook reading/secondary source

Williams, K. S., Chapter 6 ('Influences of Physical Factors and Genetics on Criminality') in (2001) *Criminology: A Textbook* (Oxford: Oxford University Press).

Psychological explanations of crime

The key psychological theories of crime and the relationship between psychology and criminology more generally are discussed in detail in Chapter 6 below ('Psychology and crime: understanding the interface' by Keith Hayward).

Early sociological perspectives

The term 'sociological perspective' is used here to refer to a specific segment of criminological approaches that deal with crime from a distinctly social perspective. Namely, those theories rooted in functionalism that find their origins with Emile Durkheim (although he never referred to his own theories in these terms) but have undergone many transformations (particularly in the hands of Robert Merton) and were dominant from the 1920s to the 1950s.

Functionalist theories see society as an integrated whole, where ultimately all parts or subsystems operate in an integrated ('organic') and coordinated way. A healthy society is one where balance is achieved—which (according to this theory) is the natural tendency of social functioning. Individuals are perceived to undergo a process of 'socialization', where they are taught appropriate role behaviours and values that contribute to the overall functioning of the system as a whole. It is conventional today, of course, to attack functionalism for its inherent conservatism and assumption of consensus.

The influence of Emile Durkheim (1858–1917)

Durkheim's original thesis still appears quite shocking: namely, that a certain level of crime is not only inevitable but also functional to society. He argues that because crime produces a social reaction (that is, rituals of sanction and punishment, whether repressive or restitutive)—it serves to rebind the various parts of society and its members into a strengthened whole. Further, in a social order predicated on stabilizing mechanisms and conformity, sources of innovation and change are rare, so deviance is also valuable in challenging established moral values.

Durkheim argued that crime is normal in society because there is actually no extra social, or natural, dividing line between criminal activity and other more acceptable activities. The dividing line is an ongoing process of demarcation and labelling, which serves to differentiate between acceptable and unacceptable behaviour. The use of the concept of crime is merely the strongest labelling procedure which works to maintain social solidarity. Its effectiveness actually comes from the process of punishment and social emotions which are engendered within society. For by observing the punishment of people, and engaging in the feeling of moral and social outrage at the offence, individuals become bound to the common perception of the justified and unjustified, *the right and wrong*. Punishment becomes inevitable. Durkheim's thinking in this area is illustrated in the following much-quoted passage: 'Imagine a society of saints, a perfect cloister of exemplary individuals. Crimes, properly so-called, will there be unknown; but faults which appear venial to the layman will create there the same scandal that the ordinary offence does in ordinary consciousness. If, then, this society has the power to judge and punish, it will define these acts as criminal and will treat them as such' (Durkheim, 1965: 68).

He therefore calls upon us to consider that crime is actually a factor in public health, an integral part of social organization. That does not mean to say that there are not (socially) abnormal or pathological levels of crime, but that both the absence of crime and a surplus of crime are socially pathological. A society in which there is no crime would be a rigidly over-policed oppressive society. But a society which is experiencing too high a crime rate is a society in which the balance between regulation and individuality has broken down. Hence his conception of *anomie* (literally, the condition of normlessness), a condition in which individuals feel no identification with any system of values and thus have no reluctance to commit crime.

Durkheim argued that the economic structure of capitalism, with its strong emphasis on self-interested behaviour was itself a major cause of *anomie*. Likewise the forced division of labour associated with industrialized societies locates individuals in a structure of specialization and economic hierarchy where their position is not freely chosen but thrust upon each person by the accident of birth. As a result, many individuals find themselves estranged, resentful and aspiring to social positions that are in fact arbitrarily closed off to them. Robert Merton was to call the reaction to this situation 'an anomie of injustice'.

REVIEW QUESTIONS

1 What does Durkheim mean when he says that crime serves an important social function?

2 What assumptions about human nature are contained in Durkheim's theories?

3 What social factors might underpin anomie today?

Key readings

Durkheim, E., Chapter 3 ('Rules for the distinction of the normal from the pathological') in *The Rules of Sociological Method* ([1895] 1982). New York: Free Press.

Taylor, I., Walton, P. and Young, J., Chapter 3 ('Durkheim and the break with analytical individualism') in *New Criminology: For a Social Theory of Deviance* (1973). London: Routledge and Kegan Paul.

Textbook reading/secondary source

Downes, D. and Rock, P., Chapter 4 ('Functionalism, deviance and control') in *Understanding Deviance* (2003) Oxford: Oxford University Press.

Vold, G., Bernard, T. and Snipes J., Chapter 6 ('Durkheim, anomie, and modernization') in *Theoretical Criminology* (2002) Oxford: Oxford University Press.

Strain theory—the work of Robert Merton (1910–2003)

In the hands of Robert K. Merton, functionalism was radically amended (along with the meaning of *anomie*). Under the Mertonian rubric, it was not that individual criminals did not have the same goals and aspirations as non-criminals, but rather that they lacked legitimate means to achieve them. Thus, the typical problem in modern societies is the *gap* between the ideal of a truly meritocratic society and the arbitrary realities of one's determining birth position (class, gender, ethnicity and so on) within the social structure. Ironically, the rise of literacy and the onset of institutions of universal education serves to make this situation worse, making promises about opportunities that the society is not able to deliver. Merton famously articulated this situation in terms of a *strain theory* of deviance (1938), that is, the variable response of individuals' adaptations (including criminal ones) to tensions between a highly stratified social structure and the mass of cultural messages present in contemporary life (for example, advertisements for products that purport to instil identity etc).

Merton's theorizing was a challenging moment because it considerably blurred the positivist boundary between 'them' (the criminal) and 'us' (the non-criminal). Following Merton, no longer was the criminal essentially different from the good citizen.

In turn, strain theory was taken a step further by Albert Cohen whose classic (1955) study, *Delinquent Boys*, included not only material goals but also social status, drawing on the idea of 'culture' as the realm of meaning as distinct from social structure. Culture, under this rubric, enables people to 'solve' problems created for them by the social structure by investing their lives—including their criminal activity—with an 'acceptable' meaning. For Cohen, for example, it allowed boys to lay claims to the great American value of achievement—if not at school, then in other (deviant) activities. Today the relevant value might be consumer culture, 'the fostering of the propensity to *consume* irrespective of the material possibilities of such a course' (Downes and Rock, 1988: 94; see also Hayward, 2004).

The final step in this journey was the idea of subcultures (see Chapter 7). For is there not a problem in the assumption that everyone is part of the one overarching system of norms and values (white, middle class, imbued with the Protestant ethic)? Rather—and still maintaining the key theme that deviant actors *share the values* of the dominant culture—was it not more appropriate for theory to explore the diversity of cultures within any one set of national boundaries? Throughout this body of work (see also Cloward and Ohlin (1960)), the issue of conflict was less at the individual level and more portrayed as a clash of cultures. Occasionally teetering on the brink of racism (it took an incredible interest in immigrant groups in the US), subcultural theory became a huge industry in the 1960s, applied primarily to areas such as youth culture and sexuality.

Key readings

Merton, R. K. (1938) 'Social structure and anomie' *American Sociological Review* 3: 672–82.
Cohen, A. (1955) *Delinquent Boys: the Culture of the Gang*. New York: Free Press.
Agnew, R. (1992) 'Foundation for a general strain theory of crime and delinquency', *Criminology*, 30: 47–87.

Textbook reading/secondary source

Downes, D. and Rock, P., Chapter 5 ('Anomie') in *Understanding Deviance* (2003) Oxford: Oxford University Press.

The Chicago School of Sociology

To understand the Chicago school it helps to know something of Chicago itself. By the 1930s, Chicago had expanded to a population of more than three million. One of the striking features of this phenomenal expansion was the extent to which the city had become home to a panoply of ethnic groups, both African Americans escaping the rural poverty of the South and European immigrants.

The Chicago school's version of milieu—ecology—drew upon bio-ecological notions of plant adaptation and association that emphasized orderly spatial distribution as both enabling adaptation to the environment and maximizing the use of resources. Park (1925) postulated that human communities were closely akin to any natural environment in that their spatial organization and expansion was not the product of chance, but instead was patterned and could be understood in terms analogous to the basic natural processes that occur within any biotic organism. Thus, Park maintained that the city could be thought of as a *super-organism*; an amalgamation of a series of sub-populations, each unified at one level by race or income or business interests. Accordingly, each of these groups acted 'naturally' in that they were underpinned by a collective or organic unity. Furthermore, not only did each of these 'natural areas' have an integral role to play in the city as a whole, but each community or business area was interrelated in a series of 'symbiotic relationships'. Close observation of these relationships enabled Park to conclude that, just as is in any natural ecology, the sequence of 'invasion-dominance-succession' was also in operation within the modern city.

Such thinking was developed by Park's colleague Ernst Burgess (1925) in his concentric zone theory which contended that modern cities expanded radially from an inner-city core. Burgess identified five main concentric zones in Chicago—which in turn came to stand for all cities. At the centre was the business district (1), an area of low population and high property values. This, in turn, was encircled by the 'zone in transition'

(2)—crucial from the crime point of view—characterized by run-down housing, high-speed immigration, and high rates of poverty and disease. Then followed the belts of: (3) working-class housing; (4) middle-class housing; and, ultimately, (5) the affluent suburbs.

The (unfortunately named) 'invasion' aspect arises because, once immigrants establish themselves, they seek to leave the zone in transition and live in a more prosperous zone (typically zone 3). This makes the zone in transition itself a great place of flux and restlessness, not exhibiting a proper 'biotic balance' with its (always temporary) inhabitants. Also, it is itself always subject to invasion from the expansion of the core, business, district (and, in anticipation, property speculators hence keep the rents low, and the buildings unrepaired). The Chicagoans used the term 'social disorganization' to characterize the unstructured and fluid ethos of this social space with its disturbed social equilibrium, and to account for its higher rate of crime.

One influential study by Shaw and McKay (1931, 1942) mapped out juvenile court referral rates and found that these correlated closely to the zones, with the highest level in socially disorganized areas and progressively diminishing in the other zones (irrespective of demographic/ethnic composition). This was a momentous breakthrough that did much to dispel earlier criminological theories that located the root cause of crime in the individual (or populist racist theories of criminal ethnic minorities). Instead it was now the neighbourhood, the area and the immediate environment that was the key factor in promoting delinquent values, largely through youth culture (rather than parent–child relations). Having established this important position, Shaw and McKay went on to claim that socially disorganized neighbourhoods perpetuate a situation in which delinquent behaviour patterns are *culturally transmitted* 'down through successive generations of boys, in much the same way that language and other social forms are transmitted (1942: 166). This observation, along with Edwin Sutherland's (1939) theory of *differential association*, was an important strand in subsequent criminological theories that attempted to account for crime by reference to deviant subcultures.

Strongly related to their substantive arguments, the other important feature of the Chicago School was their *method*. Unlike Shaw and McKay who relied (perhaps naively) on official statistics, the majority of the Chicago school took their lead from Robert Park, a former newspaper journalist, who proceeded from the premise that the best way to study crime was through the close observation of the social processes distinctive to the city. In this they were positivists to the extent that they sought first-level facts or data through which to get to some underlying level of social reality (which would provide the explanatory connections). But their key contribution was in the area of *qualitative* methods—*participant-observation* and the *focused interview*. Such techniques enabled the Chicagoans to 'enter the world of the deviant' and compile ethnographic data on hobos and 'taxi-dancers', racketeers and street-gang members (see, for example, Thrasher, 1927; Cressey, 1932; Anderson, 1975). The influence of this method can clearly be seen in subsequent writers of the labelling perspective, such as Howard Becker (see below).

The work of the Chicago School was criticized primarily at the explanatory level—whether its theories about social organization and disorganization did not rely on unexplored assumptions about consensual values, and whether the claim about the effect of environment was too strong (the so-called 'ecological fallacy'). What has survived most strongly (apart from their contribution, already noted, to qualitative methods and the study of social actions from the deviant's perspective) has been the observational tradition of collecting data about the spatial organization of crime. In Britain a number of area studies combined (uneasily) 'mini-ethnographies' of primarily working-class areas with a positivist search for definitive factors in the turn to crime. More recently, under the banner of administrative and environmental criminology (see Bottoms, 1994), the interest in area studies of the offender's *residence* has shifted to a concern with the location of criminal *offences*, and the notion of crime 'hot spots' (see Sherman *et al.*, 1989).

REVIEW QUESTIONS

1 Can locality itself be considered a causal factor in explaining crime and other social problems?

2 Was the ecological analogy useful or did it ignore some of key forces that are present within city life?

3 What has been the legacy of the Chicago School within contemporary criminology?

Key readings

Park, R.E. (1925) 'The city: suggestions for the investigation of human behaviour in the urban environment' in Park, R.E., Burgess, E.W. and McKenzie, R.D. (eds), *The City*. Chicago: Chicago University Press.

Shaw, C.R. and McKay, H.D. (1942) *Juvenile Delinquency and Urban Areas*. Chicago: University of Chicago Press.

Anderson, N. (1975) *The Hobo: The Sociology of the Homeless Man*. Chicago: University of Chicago Press.

Textbook reading/secondary source

Vold, G., Bernard, T. and Snipes, J., Chapter 7 ('Neighbourhoods and crime') in *Theoretical Criminology* (2002) Oxford: Oxford University Press.

The 'labelling' perspective (including social interactionism)

'Labelling' is the term that the American sociologist Howard Becker, writing in the 1960s, used to describe the profound effect on a person of naming them as deviant. Such social 'proclamations' transform the doing of a deviant act into a core part of a person's identity—a symbolic reorganization of self—that, in a theatrical metaphor, 'pre-scripts' their future performances according to their new, conferred, role as deviant. Becker, and also Erving Goffman (1968), studied many examples of such roles, from 'becoming a marijuana user' to the 'sick role' involved in becoming a patient.

As a theoretical development, the labelling perspective proved devastating both to the whole positivist tradition of investigating the 'criminal', and to the established way in which criminology analysed the criminal justice system. These paradigms are challenged if we can no longer use words such as 'offender' or 'criminal or 'deviant'—all 'naming words'—simply as given, 'natural' categories describing the world as it just exists. What happens to these obvious vocabularies when we become aware of the social processing— the *work*, as Becker puts it—that has gone into creating the characterization of the person before us?

For Becker and fellow *symbolic/social interactionists*, the primary moments in this process was what was at stake in the labelling and the individual's way of dealing with this. Such analysis drew upon a mix of theoretical frameworks, including the philosophical pragmatism of George Herbert Mead ([1934]1962), and his distinction between the 'I' and the 'me' (I as observer/me as object of observation). For Mead, no (wo)man is an island; the self does not pre-exist interaction with others. Labelling as social or symbolic interactionism thus takes as its starting point the notion that people *lack* a strong sense of self—of who they are and what they can do—and rely on constant processes of social exchange.

Equally important was the role of linguistic and visual components in the construction—*and* interactive negotiation—of meaning. Deviance, like any action or mode of being, only becomes deviance when it enters social life by receiving a linguistic response. Social control is thus not so much an external force but embedded in the very meanings we confer on acting and being. By the same token, the use of language also provides individuals with resources for 'negating' blame—what David Matza called 'neutralisation techniques' by which we tell ourselves, for example, that 'everybody does it' or 'she was asking for it' (Sykes and Matza, 1957). Labelling theory can thus lead to strong associations with subculture theory when attention is paid to the elaboration of deviant 'worlds' with a sympathetic 'audience'.

For mainstream criminologists, more directly interested in formal social control and the criminalization process, labelling theory could also be absorbed in a straightforward causal way as part of the aetiology of 'the criminal' (and the formation of a criminal 'career'). This meant turning sociological theories on their head: it was not that deviance produced social control as a reaction but, rather, that social control produced deviance. Lemert (1951), for example, distinguished between 'primary deviance' (the original act—whose causes remained—were heuristically assumed to be unknown) and 'secondary deviance (that is, deviance resulting from the labelling attached to the original act). Such re-incorporation of labelling theory reputedly caused Becker much distress, leading him to say that he wished that he had never invented the term. It must also be remembered that crime as such had not been the core focus of the theorizing but, rather, any mode that came to be seen as deviant. From this perspective, labelling theory leads away from the effects of criminalization on the individual and wonders instead what rules and labels tell us about society. Why do societies *react* the way they do, penalizing different particular acts and in different particular ways at different historical moments and parts of the world? (see Sumner, 1990; Cohen, 1972).

REVIEW QUESTIONS

1 How does the labelling perspective differ from both classicism and positivism?

2 Identify a significant 'label' by which you define yourself. How does that label condition how you act?

3 What is important about the distinction between deviant *acts* and deviant *people*?

Key readings

Becker, H. S. (1963) *Outsiders*. Free Press of Glencoe: Collier-Macmillan
Goffman, E. (1968) *Stigma: Notes on the Management of a Spoiled Identity*. London: Penguin.

Textbook reading/secondary source

Lilly, R., Cullen, F. and Ball, R., Chapter 5 ('The irony of state intervention: labelling theory') in *Criminological Theory: Context and Consequences* (2002) London: Sage.

Downes, D. and Rock, P., Chapter 6 ('Symbolic interactionism') in *Understanding Deviance* (2003) Oxford: Oxford University Press.

Marxist/radical criminology

The late 1960s and 1970s saw dramatic changes in the study of crime. Moving on from the soft libertarianism of theories of deviancy and labelling theory, the emphasis was now to be the *political economy* of crime. Political economy implied a basic commitment to the idea that capitalism was criminogenic. Broadly, this meant a recognition that society was fundamentally organized around class-based structural antagonisms. Where more traditional criminology operated around naive consensual assumptions about shared values and socially functional processes, Marxism saw conflict not as social or individual pathology but as the social norm. In Britain, this turn to a Marxist inspiration was announced in Taylor, Walton and Young's groundbreaking work *The New Criminology* (1973).

At the explanatory level, focusing on the 'political economy' of capitalism as criminogenic meant potentially two different aspects of causation. The first (more classically Marxist) was that the causes of criminal activity were to be found in the structure and operation of market relations, including the commodification of human labour—and to be studied at the direct level of the economy. Typical concerns would be the relation between unemployment and crime (Box, 1987) or the claim that crime reduces surplus labour by providing a black economy (Chambliss, 1975). Such issues have been developed (particularly in the USA) to encompass the interplay of different power economies (not only class, but also race and gender) notably in the work of James Messerschmidt (1993), who offers a version of the 'kick the dog' syndrome as a basis of crime (loosely, you pick on the person who is lower than you in the hierarchies).

Second—and far more prominent in British theorizing (in turn reflecting the origins of this movement in deviancy and labelling theory) is the question of criminalization— what is criminalized and what forms does that criminalization take? This is where we find out what a society values as its core concerns and, more subtly (and this has to be acknowledged as a Durkheimian insight), what is also revealed by forms of social processing of infractions. Much of the most productive work on this theme looked at the past, partly inspired by the work of social historians such as E.P. Thompson (1975), Eric Hobsbawm (1972) and Marx's own great text on the criminalization of the theft of wood. The transition from feudalism to capitalism showed very dramatically how new social arrangements produced new criminalizations geared to the motor of a new economic system driven by the capitalist institution of private property as an alienable commodity (that is, that could—and must—only be bought and sold on the marketplace). As illustrated by the eighteenth century introduction of legislation imposing capital punishment for poaching game, installing the new system and driving out the old one was simultaneously, (a) dramatically coercive on the part of the rising bourgeoisie; (b) complex in the mobilization of class resistance (with feudal aristocrats and 'their' peasants acting together in defence of the old way of life); and (3) subtle in its associated ways of disciplining the new factory workforce into an appreciation of the basic capitalist equation: time = money (see Thompson 1968).

This kind of work in turn led in different directions. On the one hand, the conjunction of 'macro-power' (criminal law/coercion/death penalties) with 'micro-powers' was echoed in the work of Michel Foucault (1977) and Dario Melossi (1990) and to emphasize the continuities in disciplinary/policing mechanisms between prisons, factories and schools (see Chapter 23). On the other hand, *The New Criminology*, reinforced by the tone of social historians' texts (such as Hobsbawm's *Bandits*) had an undeniable tendency to romanticize 'the criminal' as proto-revolutionary or at least social critic—in Marxist terms, implying a degree of class-conscious warfare.

Finally, at the political and professional level, what was involved was a fundamental self-examination in which criminologists were urged to become aware of and, ideally, disengage from, their professional collusion with the State. Criminologists must stop being useful 'problem solvers' and become '*problem-raisers*' (Nils Christie). An important background paper of this period was Stan Cohen's (1981) 'Footprints in the Sand', which linked state-recognition (and funding!) with professional criminologists' positivist tendencies towards measurable indices, in turn necessarily oriented to potential points of individual intervention. The target was identified as 'correctionalism'—the ideology and very real practices of dealing with crime as a problem of the individual law-breaker seen as in need of alteration. Adapting Marx's *Theses on Feuerbach*, the slogan was: 'the point is not to change the individual—the "criminal"—but to change society.'

REVIEW QUESTIONS

1 Should certain types of law-breakers be seen as class warriors?

2 In what different ways can crime and criminalization be explained by reference to political economy?

3 Why were historical studies so important to Marxist-inspired criminology?

Key readings

Taylor, I., Walton, P., and Young, J. (1973) *New Criminology: For a Social Theory of Deviance*. London: Routledge and Kegan Paul.

Quinney, R. (1974) *Critique of the Legal Order: Crime Control in Capitalist Society*. Boston: Little Brown.

Box, S. (1983) *Crime, Power and Mystification*. London: Tavistock.

Textbook reading/secondary source

Jones, S., Chapter 10 ('Conflict, Marxist and Radical theories of crime') in *Criminology* (2001) London: Butterworths.

Gender and crime: the feminist perspective

Feminist-influenced writing started in criminology in earnest in the 1970s and has provided a fertile source of challenges and critiques to the mainstream criminological enterprise. Traditional and radical criminology stood accused not only of neglecting the study of women but falsely implying that the theories produced were theories of crime, rather than being what they actually were—theories of males committing crime. As a result, it was not surprising that women 'did not fit' the standard explanations. Even on the rare occasions when they have been considered, typically they been portrayed in very stereotypical ways (for example, Lombroso, see below).

As a preliminary exercise, let us begin with 'the facts' as given by crime statistics. The most striking fact is that women have always featured to a much lesser extent than men. In the latest crime statistics for England and Wales 80 per cent of crime is committed by men. Moreover, crimes committed by females tend to be less serious (for more on this point see Chapter 17 below). What implications, then, could be drawn from such analysis of statistics?

Traditional criminology dealt with these statistical facts in two different ways. On the one hand, it regarded them as fictional—a type of scepticism about statistics that identifies a huge reluctance on the part of men (whether as victims or criminal justice agents) to label women as criminals. While commentators such as Otto Pollak (1950) saw this as part of a system of oppression of women (an idealization that functions to keep them in their place, that is, the home), his deeply problematic depiction of women is itself 'backed up' with stereotypes about women as cunning deceivers excellent at concealing their true crime rate, especially in the home whose privacy provides many opportunities for abusing their families. On the other hand, the fact of women's non-delinquency was taken as correct, the key question about women being, why were they so conformist? (Lombroso). Here a further repertoire of stereotypes provided 'answers', concerning women's less individualized, non-achievement oriented natures. Consequently, those women who *did* commit crimes appeared as 'doubly deviant', departing from social and feminine norms—and often receiving explanations in terms of medical or psychological pathology.

This line of critique continued through the history of criminology up to the present day, documenting criminology's deficiencies writer by writer (for example, Heidensohn, 1968, 1996; Klein, 1973; Smart, 1976).

The question then was, how should feminist criminology develop after critique? The dilemma posed was incorporation/assimilation or existing as a 'special topic'. On the one hand, should women be treated 'equally' and be subject to the same sorts of explanations as men? On the other hand, should there be special explanations relating to women's differences? Hence one dominant strand in feminist criminology unwittingly reproduced Lombroso's question (why are women so conformist?) while rejecting his (biologistic pseudo-evolutionary) answer. Posed in the language of social control theory, women's non-deviance was to be understood in terms of the internalization of social norms *and* the nature of external informal controls, largely through family responsibilities, applied throughout women's lives (see Heidensohn 1985; Cain 1989).

Other approaches tended to step sideways, sometimes querying why feminism, in an era of radical critique, was so anxious to 'sign up' to categories such as 'criminality': why reproduce the most criticized categories of criminological theory? Alternatively, much attention was focused on women as *victims* of crime, especially rape, including their 'second victimization' in the courtroom. Attention thus became more socio-legally oriented and also connected with campaigns to change criminal law or the law of (sexual character) evidence. Conventional victimology was also shown to be symptomatically deficient, especially, again in the area of rape.

One of the most vivid responses to the dilemma has been to argue that criminology was, in fact, correct all along to be studying men because men *are* the problem. But while past theories have been implicitly written from a male standpoint, they have not really confronted the issue of masculinity as such (see Messerschmidt 1993; Jefferson 1996; Collier 1998 for recent attempts to correct this lacunae; for more on this particular point see also Chapter 11 below). The subject of gender and crime is discussed in more detail in Chapter 17 of this volume ('Gender and crime' by Catrin Smith).

REVIEW QUESTIONS

1 Draw up a list of diverse crimes and account for how gender differences might account for different levels of involvement.

2 What have been the main achievements of feminist perspectives in criminology?

3 How has feminism transformed the discipline of criminology?

Key readings

Heidensohn, F. (1994) 'Gender and crime' in Maguire, M., Morgan, R. and Reiner, R. (eds) (1st edn), *The Oxford Handbook of Criminology*. Oxford: Oxford University Press.

Gelsthorpe, L., 'Feminist methodologies in criminology: old wine in new bottles' in Gelsthorpe, L., and Morris, A., *Feminist Perspectives in Criminology*. Milton Keynes: Open University Press.

Jefferson, T. (1997) 'Masculinities and crime' in Maguire, R., Morgan, M. and Reiner, R. (eds) (2nd edn), *The Oxford Handbook of Criminology*. Oxford: Oxford University Press (Second edition).

Textbook reading/secondary source

Hopkins-Burke, R., Chapter 10 ('Feminist perspectives') in *An Introduction to Criminological Theory*. (2001) Willan: Cullompton.

Criminological realism

After the intellectual energy brought into the area by the labelling perspective, Marxism, and a host of other influences in the 1960s and 1970s, the mid–1980s saw a return to basics. Crime rates seemed to move upwards in the face of increasing poverty and the attempts of criminology to come up with workable theories designed to control/reduce crime. Writers from the political right, such as James Q. Wilson, asserted that the time had come to stop attempting to explain crime and simply concentrate instead on controlling it (a position that became known as right realism). At the same time, a 'nothing works' message came from several commentators who investigated the supposed success rates of penal measures and a general public perception surfaced in the US and UK that the criminal justice system had gone soft on the criminal. Meanwhile, on the political left, many critical criminologists had become deeply disillusioned with the 'outdated' Marxism associated with radical criminology, not least its 'utopian' dreams of a revolutionary politics. In the face of an increasingly complex world, the desire for simplistic solutions reasserted itself—enter criminological 'realism'.

Right realism

Based largely around the work of James Q. Wilson (Wilson, 1985), right realism emerged in the United States during the 1970s, as a direct response to the aetiological crisis in criminology. Unlike left realists (see below), right realists accept prima facie that crime has risen dramatically in the post-war era and that, furthermore, if left unchecked will continue to rise, irrespective of improved social conditions, unless governments change their overall approach to the problem of crime. Consequently, right realists are interventionists primarily interested in the issue of societal order. As a consequence, they rarely flinch from deploying those two old stalwarts of the right—incapacitation and criminal law—as a general deterrence and as a means of protecting the propertied.

The central plank of Wilson's thesis is that, at a community level, crime begets crime. Or to use his favourite analogy, if a window is smashed in a building and not replaced, it indicates to the immediate community that no one cares about the property; consequently it will only be a matter of time before other windows are smashed and the building falls prey to criminals (Wilson and Kelling, 1982). Wilson describes this as the 'developmental sequence' of crime and disorder. This being the case, it is essential that governments acknowledge this pattern and implement specific policy initiatives to address it. Wilson further argues that governments should finally wake up to the fact that they can do little to attack the root cause of crime, and should strive instead for more 'realistic goals' and instigate a series of measures that will have a real and quantifiable affect on both recorded crime and importantly, the *fear of crime*—the measures to which he refers, primarily centre around a new and somewhat controversial role for the police.

Wilson asserts that if inroads are to be made in areas of high crime and urban decay, then police work needs to be based around 'order maintenance' and 'crime prevention'. In other words a shift in police practices from 'incident orientated policing' to 'community-orientated policing'. Briefly, this means expanding the practice of everyday police work to include certain social problems that he believes greatly affect levels of crime. In his own words: 'It means defining as a problem whatever a significant body of public opinion regards as a threat to community order. It means working with the good guys, and not just against the bad guys' (Wilson and Kelling, 1989). Effectively, then, the primary task for the police should be to establish order in problem areas by undertaking a systematic, hands-on, street level assault on anti-social behaviour—a policy referred to by some as 'zero tolerance policing'. Police officers are encouraged to 'sweep the streets of undesirables', and clamp down on behaviour like drunkenness, rowdiness, prostitution, begging and vandalism. The theory behind this approach is that if significant inroads can be made in the level of lesser crimes in an area, then eventually more serious crimes will also 'cave-in' and neighbourhoods can begin to shed the skin of endemic criminality.

More controversial are views held by certain right realists concerning causality. While, originally, it was enough for right realists simply to refute the liberal orthodoxy that crime is a by-product of poor social conditions, more recently they have accounted for this by suggesting that criminality is in fact a complex composite of socio-environmental (especially familial), psychological and contentiously biological factors. Drawing on the behaviourist psychology of Hans Eysenck (1970), Wilson and Hernstein argue in *Crime and Human Nature* (1985) that certain personality traits—whether levels of intelligence or indeed levels of psychopathy—are the outcome of *genetic inheritance*. However, they are keen to point out that these traits do not in themselves result in criminal or deviant behaviour. What is of equal if not greater importance is the early 'social conditioning' and positive reinforcement that an individual experiences within key social environments (in this sense their ideas correspond with contemporary control theories, see below). The stress placed by Wilson on hereditary factors has resulted in this aspect of his work being decried as 'neo-positivism', and Wilson himself dismissed as an old-fashioned moral conservative. More controversial still was Hernstein and Murray's 1994 book *The Bell Curve*, in which it was suggested that black people and Latinos are over-represented within the US 'underclass' because of lower IQ and a resulting lack of 'self-control'. Other features, such as the experience of unemployment or location in the social hierarchy, are regarded as spurious and seen simply as a direct consequence of individual-level differences which are either inherited or caused by family-school processes at an early age. Needless to say, such assertions were met with a considerable challenge by commentators from the political left.

REVIEW QUESTIONS

1 What mutual ground exists between right and left realists?

2 Why are right realists typically described as 'interventionists'?

3 What policing practices are associated with 'zero tolerance policing'? What is this approach to street crime hoping to achieve?

Key readings

Wilson, J. Q. (1985) *Thinking About Crime*. New York: Vintage Books.

Wilson, J. Q. and Kelling, G. (1982) 'Broken Windows' *Atlantic Monthly*, pp. 29–38.

Wilson, J. Q. and Herrnstein, R. (1985) *Crime and Human Nature*. New York: Simon and Schuster.

Textbook reading/secondary source

Lilly, R. Cullen, F. and Ball, R., Chapter 8 ('Conservative criminology: revitalizing individualistic theory') in *Criminological Theory: Context and Consequences* (1995) London: Sage.

Left realism

In the UK a movement called new left realism (owing its roots to the radical energies of the 1970s and a decline of utopian thinking), loosely grouped around members of Middlesex University, originated as a political platform with a message to the left to take crime seriously as a pressing practical problem. In many ways, the emergence of left realism can be seen as a response to both the rise of the 'neo-positivism' of right realism and the significant political and cultural transformations that took place in the 1980s and 1990s—not least, the continued hegemony of capitalism and the subsequent fall of communist Eastern Europe. Although it would be doing a disservice to imply that new left realism might simply be viewed as a way in which radical criminology sought to free itself from its limiting ideological roots, it is fair to state that left realism provided a more pragmatic, policy-oriented approach to the problem of crime than much previous critical criminology. Rather than the focus placed by radical criminology on macro political theory and in particular the crimes of the powerful, left realism views crime from both ends of the social structure.

The disenchantment with radical criminology (or left idealism as left realists now prefer to call it) came about for several reasons. First, as mentioned above, several of the leading lights of radical criminology had grown tired of the inherent Marxist 'utopianism' that underpinned 1970s British radical/critical criminology. Second (and by the same token), the move to left realism was mediated by several positions adopted within radical criminology that were perceived by realists as being either morally ambiguous or just plainly too liberal, in particular, radical penology's attempts to abolish the prison system and certain liberal positions adopted concerning drug use. Third, left realists took issue with the view asserted by many radical criminologists that there had been no real increase in levels of crime in the post-war era. (Radical criminology had always dismissed the 'aetiological crisis', claiming that the continued rise in recorded crime was a fallacy and that statistical evidence to that effect could be explained by police preference and anomalies in the recording processes.) Fourth, and most fundamentally, many former radicals upheld the belief that left idealism was 'failing to take crime seriously'. Left realists argued that because of its lopsided concern with the crimes of the powerful, radical criminology had lost touch with the reality of 'normal crimes'. Traditionally, left idealism upheld the view that offenders themselves were victims of social inequality and racial and class biases. Consequently, many radicals dismissed (and often celebrated!) lower-class crime as political (or indeed quasi-revolutionary) action. Left realists however, have tended to shy away from this position. While the realist approach does not lose sight of the fact that the working-classes are often the victims of the crimes of the powerful ('the working-class is a victim of crime from all directions . . . one sort of crime tends to compound another' Lea and Young 1984: 264), they now place a greater emphasis on those members of society who are the *victims* of (normal) crime. Thus we see a significant shift in criminological attention away from the *working-class law-breaker to the working-class victim*.

Following this line of thought, left realists look at the social and symbiotic relationship between the victim, the offender, and both formal and informal controls in a bid to better understand both the anxieties of victims (and 'the fear of crime' generally) and offender motivations. This more comprehensive approach has a twofold purpose:

(a) it enables left realists to wrest the 'law and order' initiative out of the hands of the conservative right; and

(b) it produces a less ideologically tainted picture of contemporary crime.

A picture made considerably clearer by undertaking widescale empirical enquiry into levels of crime within society. For left realists the official crime statistics collated by the government are inaccurate indices that are not only highly subjective, but also corrupted by political and state agency bias. Instead, they favour (and indeed pioneered) the use of victim surveys and other types of localized crime surveys as a means of extracting more accurate data on the incidence of crime in a given locality (for example, Jones *et al.*, 1986).

As the name implies, left realism maintains that the best way to accomplish a reduction in crime is by developing common-sense policies that will have a quantifiable impact on crime and the fear of crime across all societal levels; but particularly among those most often victimized—the poor and the socially deprived. What is more, for maximum effectiveness, these 'realistic' initiatives should be implemented at local or 'community' level rather than nationally or regionally. As Lea and Young (1984: 267) explain: '[t]he organisation of communities in an attempt to pre-empt crime is of the utmost importance'. In their emphasis on pragmatic community reform and crime prevention practices, left realists are very much reappropriating policies traditionally favoured by conservatives and right realists. Indeed, as noted earlier, many of the initiatives they advocate are strikingly similar to those championed by right realists and administrative criminologists. However, left realists are keen to stress that these localized policies are infused by an underlying socialist ethos. This emphasis on community and the inclusion of marginalized and disenfranchised segments of society within localized crime-control initiatives is a central component of contemporary left realism (see Taylor *et al.*, 1996).

Needless to say, the main criticism of the left realist approach stems from the established radical and critical criminological tradition. For critical criminologists, the development of the left realist approach has been a major ideological step backwards.

REVIEW QUESTIONS

1 How does left realism differ from more traditional forms of Marxist criminology?

2 What are the key ideological differences between left realism and right realism?

3 What practical solutions might left realists employ in an effort to reduce crime on a troubled inner-city housing estate?

Key readings

Lea, J. and Young, J. (1984) *What is to be done about Law and Order?* Harmondsworth: Penguin.

Kinsey, R., Lea, J. and Young, J. (1986) *Losing the Fight Against Crime*. Oxford: Blackwell.

Matthews, R. and Young, J. (1992) *Issues in Realist Criminology*. London: Sage.

Textbook reading/secondary source

Hopkins-Burke, R., Chapter 15 ('Left realism') in *An Introduction to Criminological Theory* (2001) Willan: Cullompton).

Control theory

American criminology, largely through the work of Travis Hirschi (1969), took up a reading of Durkheim's ideas and combined this with the assumption of classical criminology (that a tendency to crime is normal in any human being) to argue that criminal behaviour results from a failure of conventional social groups (family, school, social peers) to bind or bond with the individual. In other words, to maintain social order, society must teach the individual *not to offend*. Control theorists argue that we are all born with a natural proclivity to violate the rules of society; thus, delinquency is a logical consequence of one's failure to develop internalized prohibitions (controls) against lawbreaking behaviour.

In his early 'social bond theory', Hirschi focused on *how* conformity is achieved—this was a theory not of motivation, but of *constraint*. Put simply, what is it that stops individuals from offending? Hirschi outlined four major elements of the social bond:

(a) *Attachment*: the ties that exist between the individual and primary agents of socialization (parents, teachers, community leaders etc.). It is a measure of the degree to which law-abiding persons serve as a source of positive reinforcement for the individual.

(b) *Commitment*: investment in conformity or conventional behaviour and a consideration of future goals which are incompatible with a delinquent lifestyle.

(c) *Involvement*: a measure of one's propensity to participate in conventional activities (sports, pastimes, work etc).

(d) *Belief*: acceptance of the moral validity of societal norms.

Delinquency was thus associated with weak attachments/bonds to conventional institutions and modes of conduct.

In 1990 social bond theory was considerably updated/augmented with the publication of Gottfredson and Hirschi's *A General Theory of Crime*. In this work, the emphasis shifts from external to *internal* controls. In other words, in proposing a theory of low *self*-control, Hirschi moved away from his classic *social* bonding formulation to present differential rates of self-control as a set of individual propensities that give differing propensities to refrain from, or to commit crime, at all ages, and under all circumstances. Gottfredson and Hirschi's theory states that individuals with high self-control will be 'substantially less likely at all periods of life to engage in criminal acts' (1990: 89), while those with low self-control are highly likely to commit crime.

The source of low self-control is seen as ineffective or incomplete socialization, especially ineffective childrearing. Parents who are attached to their children, supervise their children closely, recognize the lack of self-control in their children, and punish deviant acts will help to socialize children into social control. Such children will generally not become delinquent as teenagers or engage in criminal acts as adults. The explicit disapproval of parents or others about whom one cares is the most important negative sanction. School and other social institutions contribute to socialization, but it is the family in which the most important socialization takes place. Consequently, unlike with social-bond theory, peer groups are relatively unimportant in the development of self-control and in the commission of delinquency or crime (the four key elements of social bonding theory—belief, attachment, commitment and involvement—are virtually absent from Gottfredson and Hirschi's theory). Once formed in childhood, the amount of self-control that a person has acquired remains relatively stable throughout life.

The authors also spell out the policy implications of self-control. According to self-control theory, official actions taken to deter crime in adulthood are not likely to have much effect. Self-control, they contend, is already fixed, and therefore only preventative policies that take effect early in life and have a positive impact on families have much chance of reducing crime and delinquency.

These variants of control theory, however, have not gone uncriticized (see Morrison 1995 for an extended critique of control theory). For example, commentators have pointed out the tautology in the self-control hypothesis; specifically, that propensity towards crime and low self-control appears to be one and the same. More accurately, Gottfredson and Hirschi do not identify operational measures of low self-control as separate from the very tendency to commit crimes that low self-control is supposed to explain. To avoid this tautological problem, conceptual definitions or operational measures of self-control must be developed that are separate from measures of crime or propensity towards crime. Unless that step is taken, this theory will remain untestable; much of the empirical work that picks up on the theory strives to develop indices of what self-control can be taken as.

REVIEW QUESTIONS

1 Describe what you consider is meant by the term 'self-control'. What are its constitutive elements?

2 Outline how control theories differ from other criminological theories you have studied.

3 Control theory is predicated on a set of values—but whose values?

Key readings

Hirschi, T. (1969) *Causes of Delinquency*. Berkeley CA: University of California Press.

Gottfredson, M. and Hirschi, T. (1990) *A General Theory of Crime*. Stanford CA: Stanford University Press.

Reis, A. J., (1951) *Delinquency as a failure of personal and social controls, American Sociological Review*, 16: 196–207.

Textbook reading/secondary source

Vold, G., Bernard, T., and Snipes, J., Chapter 10 ('Control theories') in *Theoretical Criminology* (2002) Oxford: Oxford University Press.

Cultural criminology

In recent years there has been something of a revival of interest in the aetiological question. Some of the most thought provoking work in this area can be found in a particular variant of contemporary critical criminology known as cultural criminology (see Hayward and Young, 2004; Ferrell, 1999; Ferrell and Sanders, 1995, Ferrell *et al.*, 2004). Simply stated, cultural criminology emphasizes the role of image, style, representation and meaning both within criminal subcultures, and in the mediated construction of crime and crime control. Utilizing an eclectic mix of intellectual influences, this new body of work explicitly sets out to develop a 'postmodern' theory of crime (see Katz, 1988; Lyng, 1990; Henry and Milovanovic, 1996), wherein criminal behaviour is reinterpreted as a technique for resolving certain psychic conflicts that are in turn viewed as being indelibly linked to various features of contemporary life (Presdee, 2000; Hayward, 2004). One of the great strengths of the 'cultural approach' is that it tackles the subject of crime and criminalization from a variety of new perspectives and academic disciplines—from subcultural analyses to critiques of oppressive structures, from social theory to phenomenology. In effect, its remit is to keep 'turning the kaleidoscope' on the way that we think about crime, and importantly, the legal and societal responses to it. Whilst it is undoubtedly the case that many of the key themes of cultural criminology have been 'voiced' elsewhere in the criminological tradition (most notably in the writings of Robert Merton and David Matza, see above), it is clear that this dynamic body of work offers something new—not least because of the way it seeks to reflect the peculiarities and particularities of the late modern socio-cultural milieu. Cultural criminology and the relationship between culture and crime more generally are discussed in more detail in Chapter 7, 'Crime and Culture' by Jeff Ferrell.

Key readings

Ferrell, J., Hayward, K., Morrison, W., and Presdee, M. (2004) *Cultural Criminology Unleashed*. London: GlassHouse Press.

Ferrell, J. and Sanders, C.S. (1995) *Cultural Criminology*. Boston: Northeastern University Press.

Presdee, M. (2000) *Cultural Criminology and the Carnival of Crime*. London: Routledge.

Textbook reading/secondary source

Morrison, W., Chapter 13 ('Culture and crime in the postmodern condition') in *Theoretical Criminology: From Modernity to Postmodernism* (1995) London: Cavendish.

CONCLUSION

Trying to summarize 200 years of criminological thought in one short chapter was a difficult, daunting and some might say rather foolhardy task. It was certainly very difficult deciding on what to include and what to leave out. The trained criminological eye will inevitably point to certain gaps in the 'story', but we hope they will forgive us the broad sweep of our narrative. After all, the chapter is meant purely as a 'starting point'. Moreover, much effort has been made to point the interested student to classic studies and further secondary readings for each of the chapter's ten theoretical themes. We hope, indeed urge, you to follow these signposts. We should also point out that this chapter is not intended to be read in isolation—rather it should be studied in tandem with Claire Valier's following chapter, *Theoretical Criminology 2*: 'Just theory': theory, crime and criminal justice. All theories need to be unpicked and deconstructed if we are to understand what lies behind them and thus fully comprehend the political and social forces that brought them into existence. We feel that, read together, these two chapters represent an excellent 'starting point' from which to begin your own personal theoretical journey.

WEB LINKS

www.theorynetwork.net

Check out all the latest news about the British Society of Criminology's *Theory Network Group* This site includes some excellent links to various theorists and philosophers.

www.asc41.com

The website of The American Society of Criminology. The ASC is the pre-eminent organization of academic, theoretical and applied criminology in the United States.

www.crimetheory.com

'An educational resource for the learning, researching and teaching of theoretical criminology' maintained by Bruce Hoffman, Department of Sociology, Ohio University.

www.sagepub.com/journal.aspx?pid=173

Theoretical criminology: An international journal for the advancement of the theoretical aspects of criminology.

REFERENCES

Anderson, N. (1975) *The Hobo: The Sociology of the Homeless Man*. Chicago: University of Chicago Press.

Beccaria, C. ([1764] 1963) *On Crimes and Punishments*. Indianapolis: Bobbs-Merrill.

Beirne, P. (1993) *Inventing Criminology: Essays on the Rise of 'Homo Criminalis'*. Albany, New York: State University of New York Press.

Bentham, J. ([1789] 1982) *A Fragment of Government and an Introduction to the Principles of Morals and Legislation*. London.

Berman, L. (1921) *The Glands Regulating Personality*. New York: Macmillan.

Bocock, R. and Thompson, K. (eds), (1992) *Social and Cultural Forms of Modernity*. Buckingham: Open University Press.

Bottoms, A.E. (1994) 'Environmental criminology' in M. Maguire, R. Morgan, and R. Reiner (eds), *The Oxford Handbook of Criminology*. Oxford: Oxford University Press.

Box, S. (1983) *Crime, Power and Mystification*. London: Tavistock.

Box, S. (1987) *Recession, Crime and Punishment*. London: Macmillan.

Burgess, E.W. (1925) 'The growth of the city' in R.E. Park, E.W. Burgess, and R.D. McKenzie (eds), *The City*, Chicago: University of Chicago Press.

Cain, M. (1989) *Growing Up Good*. London: Sage.

Chambliss, W.J. (1975) 'Towards a Political Economy of Crime', *Theory and Society* 2, pp. 149–70.

Clarke, R.V.G. and Cornish, D.B. (1985) 'Modelling offenders' decisions: a framework for policy and research' in Tonry, M. and Morris, N. (eds) *Crime and Justice: An Annual Review of Research*, 6.

Cloward, R. and Ohlin, L. (1960) *Delinquency and Opportunity: A Theory of Delinquent Gangs*, New York: The Free Press.

Cohen, A. (1955) *Delinquent Boys: the Culture of the Gang*. New York: Free Press.

Cohen, S. (1972) *Folk Devils and Moral Panics*. London: MacGibbon and Kee.

Cohen, S. (1981) 'Footprints in the sand: a further report on criminology and the sociology of deviance in Britain' in *Crime and Society: Readings in History and Theory* by M. Fitzgerald, G. McLennan and J. Pawson (eds). London: Open University Press.

Collier, R. (1998) Masculinities, Crime and Criminology. Buckingham: Open University Press.

Cornish, D.G. and Clarke, R.V.G. (1986) *The Reasoning Criminal: Rational Choice Perspectives on Offending*. New York: Springer-Verlag.

Cortes, J.B., and Gatti, F.M. (1972) *Delinquency and Crime: A Bio-psychological Approach*. New York: Seminar Press.

Cressey, P. (1932) *The Taxi-Dance Hall*. Chicago: University of Chicago Press.

Crowe, R.A. (1974) 'An adoption study of anti-social personality', *Archives of General Psychiatry*, 31: 785–91.

Dalton, K. (1961) 'Menstruation and crime', *British Medical Journal*, 2 1752–53.

Downes, D. and Rock, P. (1988) *Understanding Deviance*, Oxford: Oxford University Press.

Durkheim, E. (1965) *The Rules of Sociological Method*, trans. Solovay and Mueller. New York: Free Press.

Eysenck, H. (1970) *Crime and Personality*. London: Paladin.

Ferrell, J. (1999) 'Cultural Criminology', *Annual Review of Sociology* 25: 395–418.

Ferrell, J. and Sanders, C.R. (eds), (1995) *Cultural Criminology*. Boston: Northeastern University Press.

Ferrell, J., Hayward, K.J., Morrison, W., and Presdee, M. (2004) *Cultural Criminology Unleashed*. London: GlassHouse.

Ferri, E. (2003) 'Causes of Criminal Behaviour' in Muncie, J., McLaughlin, E., and Hughes, G. *Criminological Perspectives: A Reader*. London: Sage.

Foucault, M. (1977) *Discipline and Punish: The Birth of the Prison*. London: Penguin Books.

Garland, D. (1994) 'Of crime and criminals: the development of criminology in Britain' in M. Maguire, R. Morgan and R. Reiner (eds), *The Oxford Handbook of Criminology* Oxford: Oxford University Press.

Giddens, A. (1974) *Positivism and Sociology*. London: Heinemann.

Goffman, E. (1968) *Stigma: Notes on the Management of a Spoiled Identity*. London: Penguin.

Goring, G. (1913) *The English Convict*. London: Darling & Son.

Gottfredson, M. and Hirschi, T. (1990) *A General Theory of Crime*. Stanford CA: Stanford University Press.

Hall, S. and Gieben, B. (1992) *The Formations of Modernity*. Cambridge: Polity.

Hayward, K.J. (2004) *City Limits: Crime, Consumer Culture and the Urban Experience*. London: GlassHouse Press.

Hayward, K.J. and Young, J. (2004) 'Cultural criminology: some notes on the script' Theoretical Criminology, 8 (3): 259–73.

Heidensohn, F. (1968) 'The Deviance of Women: a Critique', *British Journal of Sociology*, 19.

Heidensohn, F. (1996) *Women and Crime*. London: Macmillan.

Henry, S. and Milovanovic, D. (1996) *Constitutive Criminology: Beyond Postmodernism*. London: Sage.

Herrnstein, R.J. and Murray, C. (1994) *The Bell Curve: Intelligence and Class Structure in American Life*. New York: The Free Press.

Hirschi, T. (1969) *Causes of Delinquency*. Berkeley CA: University of California Press.

Hobsbawm, E. (1972) *Bandits*. Harmondsworth: Penguin.

Hooton, E.A. (1939) *The American Criminal: An Anthropological Study*. Cambridge MA: Harvard University Press.

Hume, D. ([1739] 1978) *A Treatise on Human Nature*. Oxford: Oxford University Press.

Hutchings, B. and Mednick, S.A. (1975) 'Registered criminality in the adopted and biological parents of registered male criminal adoptees', in R.R. Fieve, D. Rosenthal and H. Brill (eds) *Genetic research in Psychiatry*, Baltimore: Johns Hopkins University Press.

Jefferson, T. (1996) 'Introduction to the masculinities', Special edition of the *British Journal of Criminology*, 36.

Jones, T. MacLean, B. and Young, J. (1986) *The Islington Crime Survey*. Aldershot: Gower.

Katz, J. (1988) *The Seductions of Crime: Moral and Sensual Attractions in Doing Evil*. New York: Basic Book.

Kinsey, R., Lea, J. and Young, J. (1986) *Losing the Fight Against Crime*. Oxford: Blackwell.

Klein, D. (1973) 'The Etiology of Female Crime: a Review of the Literature', *Issues in Criminology*, 8.

Lea, J. and Young, J. (1984) *What is to be done about Law and Order?* Harmondsworth: Penguin.

Lemert, E.M. (1951) *Social Pathology*. New York: McGraw Hill.

Lombroso, C. (1876) *L'Uomo Delinquente*. Milan: Hoepli.

Lyng, S. (1990) 'Edgework: a Social Psychological Analysis of Voluntary Risk-Taking', *American Journal of Sociology* 95: 876–921.

McLaughlin, E. (2001) 'Functionalism' in E. McLaughlin and J. Muncie (eds), *The Sage Dictionary of Criminology*. London: Sage.

Matthews, R. and Young, J. (1992) *Issues in Realist Criminology*. London: Sage.

Mead, G.H. ([1934]1962) *Mind, Self, and Society: From the Standpoint of a Social Behaviorist*. Chicago, IL: University of Chicago Press.

Melossi, D. (1990) *The State of Social Control*. Cambridge: Polity.

Merton, R.K. (1938) 'Social Structure and Anomie', *American Sociological Review* 3: 672–82.

Messerschmidt, J. (1993) *Masculinities and Crime*. Lanham MD: Rowman and Litchfield.

Morrison, W. (1995) *Theoretical Criminology: From Modernity to Post Modernism*. London: Cavendish.

Morrison, W. (2004) 'Lombroso and the Birth of Criminological Positivism: Scientific Mastery or Cultural Artifice?' in J. Ferrell (*et al.*) *Cultural Criminology Unleashed*. London: GlassHouse.

Moyer, K.E. (1971) 'The physiology of aggression and the implication for agression control' in R.G. Green and E.I. Donnerstein (eds) *The Control of Aggression and Violence*. New York: Academic Press.

Park, R.E. (1925) 'The city: suggestions for the investigation of human behaviour in the urban environment' in R.E. Park, E.W. Burgess and R.D. McKenzie (eds), *The City*. Chicago: Chicago University Press.

Pollak, O. (1950) *The Criminality of Women*. New York: A.S. Barnes.

Presdee, M. (2000) *Cultural Criminology and the Carnival of Crime*. London: Routledge.

Quinney, R. (1991) *Criminology as Peacemaking*. Bloomington IN: Indiana University Press.

Roshier, B. (1989) *Controlling Crime*. Milton Keynes: Open University Press.

Sandberg, A.A., Koepf, G.F., Ishiara, T., and Hauschka, T.S. (1961) 'An XYY human male', *Lancet* 262: 488–9.

Shaw, C.R. and McKay, H.D. (1931) *Social Factors in Juvenile Delinquency*. Washington DC: Government Printing Office.

Shaw, C.R. and McKay, H.D. (1942) *Juvenile Delinquency and Urban Areas*, Chicago: University of Chicago Press.

Sheldon, W.H. (1942) *The Varieties of Temperament*. New York: Harper.

Sherman, L.W., Gartin, P.R. and Buerger, M.E. (1989) 'Hot spots of predatory crime: routine activities and the criminology of place'. *Criminology* 27: 27–55.

Smart, C. (1976) *Women, Crime and Criminology: A Feminist Critique*. London: Routledege

Sumner, C. (1990) *Censure, Politics and Criminal Justice*. Milton Keynes: Open University Press.

Sutherland, E. (1942) *Principles of Criminology*. Philadelphia: J B Lippincott.

Sykes, G.M. and Matza, D. (1957) 'Techniques of neutralization'. *American Sociological Review* 22.

Taylor, I. Walton, P. and Young, J. (1973) *New Criminology: For a Social Theory of Deviance*. London: Routledge and Kegan Paul.

Taylor, I., Evans, K. and Fraser, P. (1996) *A Tale of Two Cities: Global Change, Local Feeling and Everyday Life in the North of England: A Study in Manchester and Sheffield*. London: Routledge.

Thompson, E.P. (1968) *The Making of the English Working Class*. Harmondsworth: Penguin.

Thompson, E.P. (1975) *Whigs and Hunters*. London: Allen Lane.

Thrasher, F.M. (1927) *The Gang: A Study of 1,313 Gangs in Chicago*. Chicago: Chicago University Press.

Tittle, C. (1995) *Control Balance: Toward a General Theory of Deviance*. Boulder CO: Westview Press.

Wilson, J.Q. (1985) *Thinking About Crime*. New York: Vintage Books.

Wilson, J.Q. and Kelling, G. (1982) 'Broken windows', *Atlantic Monthly*, pp. 29–38.

Wilson, J.Q. and Herrnstein, R. (1985) *Crime and Human Nature*. New York: Simon and Schuster.

NOTE

1. This chapter has been adapted from *Theoretical Criminology* (Morrison and Hayward 2001), a subject guide used in connection with the University of London's External Laws Programme. Our thanks go to the External Programme for kindly allowing us to reproduce sections of that text here.

5

Just theory: theory, crime and criminal justice

Claire Valier

Whatever else we do as criminologists, we are engaged in a moral enterprise . . . The criminologist, although not likely educated as a moral philosopher, operates with an implicit moral philosophy, and is engaged in the construction of moral philosophy.

(Quinney, 2000: 194)

INTRODUCTION

At a criminology conference not so very long ago, two delegates could be heard discussing which talks they should attend. Looking down the programme one of them, pointing out a session and then turning over the page, said to the other, 'Oh that one's theory, just theory'. The other fellow nodded in agreement and the two then moved on. 'Just theory': this rather peremptory comment suggests that the kind of session one need not attend is 'only theory'. On this view, one's time is better devoted to something else of greater merit or importance. The dismissive words imply that theory can be avoided, as nothing substantive or substantial, nothing concrete, little of substance. Theory is not driven by numbers. Quite often it has no graphs, no charts and tables, no survey and questionnaire results. Often there are no classifications, models, formulae and predictions. There are no statistics, no correlations, and most often no numbers at all. For those who only see worth in certain quantitative styles of study there is nothing real, nothing persuasive. There is nothing that will change anything. There is just theory, only theory. There is no counting, so theory does not count. The words of the delegate are more than merely coincidental. They indicate a certain uncertain status of theory in criminology as, at best, inconsequential. Nevertheless, if others had spoken they doubtless would have said that criminology cannot do without theory. Some may have said that theory has ever been central to the imagination that vivifies the discipline and moves it on. Our errant delegate was, of course, thinking of theory in negative terms, imagining theory on the basis of what it is not. Fortunately, the phrase 'just theory' suggests another approach from which theory can be considered. This, doing justice to theory, apprehends it in terms of what it can and does offer, instead of what it has no aspiration to do. Theory profoundly questions common-sense notions of crime and punishment. Moreover, a 'just theory' goes beyond critique to develop an ethics of criminal *justice*. This is a matter of envisaging just responses to crime. Making theory work in this way is to make theory count, far beyond the horizons of the customary notions of counting.

This chapter takes up the notion of 'just theory' as a means of introducing readers to some questions about the connections between theory, ethics and criminal justice. First of all, the character and the merits of doing theory work in criminology are discussed. Given the regularity with which theory is said to be 'difficult', some useful strategies for improving learning and teaching in this area are presented. Note the use of the phrase 'doing theory'. The chapter will offer some suggestions to enable reflection upon and discussion of the 'doing' of 'doing theory'. Clearly theorists may subscribe to various understandings of just what they are doing when they are 'doing theory'. This author has no pretensions whatsoever to the authoritative and the prescriptive. The chapter hence does not make claims about what all theorists do, or what all theorists ought to do. Rather than saying what theory definitively is, some insights are offered into what theory can do. The point is to provide an opportunity for readers to think about what theory is good for, and what might constitute a good theory. A key phrase to be borne in mind throughout reading the chapter is 'just theory'. This little phrase encapsulates the argument that an effective theory must also be an ethical theory, that is, a theory that aspires to the ethical. For this reason, in thinking about what 'doing theory' might mean, the chapter will consider the notions of criminology as a moral enterprize and of the criminologist as a moral witness. All in all, the chapter gives a sense of the pleasures, the pitfalls and the rewards, of doing theory. We can now wave goodbye to the two conference delegates. Despite their dismissive attitude, this chapter affirms that theory is not only alive and well, but undergoing something of a renaissance at present. Moreover, theory is an activity that is very much 'where the action is' in contemporary criminology.

Theory matters

Now that an indication has been given of the kinds of questions that this chapter will be looking into, we can move on to begin to talk about theory matters. Far from being immaterial, theory matters a great deal. What's more, there are certain matters with which theory is particularly well-equipped to deal. These are moral questions, which are central to criminological inquiry. A similar argument can be made about the centrality of ethical questioning to the study of law or of society (Douzinas and Warrington, 1994; Bauman, 1993, 1995). When the field of enquiry is crime and criminal justice, questions about morality and ethics are inescapable. As Anthony Bottoms (2002: 24) says, 'if they are to be true to their calling, all criminologists have to be interested in morality'. This kind of study is especially timely at present. The study of criminal justice ethics is particularly warranted, given the punitive measures, and the heated justifications of them, that have come to the fore. Because criminal justice matters are now highly emotive, it is necessary to ask to what extent these are just feelings. It must be asked whether in the strong emotions that infuse the practices of criminal justice today, moral values and convictions are being brought to bear. As Mona Lynch (2002) has shown in an excellent analysis of internet communications around the American death penalty, punishment is now popularly spoken of in terms of the moral imperative of harsh, severe penalties. It is less that people argue for 'tough' measures as effective deterrents, than that they feel severe punishments ought to be inflicted, as what the offender deserves. The acute moral dilemmas at the heart of criminal justice hence return strikingly to the fore, although they are seldom debated with subtlety in everyday discourse. Theory, as I have said, is well suited to the kind of moral questioning that is needed today. In this way, theory has a particularly timely role to play.

What would a just theory, that is, a theory that aspires to justice, entail? Thinking of just responses to crime is not to approach criminal justice as a self-evident, obvious entity, a set of discrete institutions and their practices. The analysis would not begin with the criminal justice *system*, that is, with how the police, the courts, and the prisons work. Instead, a starting point would be to take criminal *justice* as a problem for consideration. In fact one would even begin from the idea of 'criminal justice' as a contradiction in terms. An initial premise would be that justice after crime poses a grave problem. However enticing the promise of justice may sound, it remains just that, a promise. With this proviso in mind, there is neither the expectation of, nor the seeking for easy answers, for the questions are difficult ones. The theorist reflects upon the hazards and costs of securing order through criminal justice systems. He or she keeps in mind the words of the philosopher and theologian Martin Buber (1947–70: 7), when he said 'injustice as a means to justice renders justice unjust'.

How is theory itself to be judged? This is a hotly contested question, for there has been quite some acrimony between theorists and those who pursue 'scientific', quantitative methodologies. Sometimes this dispute has dominated discussion of the purposes and value of theory. It is appropriate for the author of this chapter to declare her position on this matter. This is that the contributions of theory are invaluable, and are not reducible to judgement by the scientific, 'positivist' criminologies, according to their criteria. Nevertheless, it is possible to find statements from scientific criminologists to that very effect. For instance, Ronald Akers (2000: 12) states baldly that 'the primary criterion for judging a theory is its verification or refutation by empirical research'. It is clear that such a statement relies upon a limited idea of what theory is and what it is for. Theory work offers a vision of intellectual rigour quite different from the tenets and practices favoured by scientific styles of criminology. Indeed some have taken the time to compose trenchant critiques of the scientific criminologies, which favour quantitative methods and tend to be focused on official policy and practice (Taylor, Walton and Young, 1973; DiCristina, 1995; Walters, 2003). These critiques have considered quantitative criminologies to be unjustifiably narrow in scope, and beholden to the policy maker's agenda. Worse still, the critique of scientific criminology has held it to be equivocal if not overtly conservative. Nevertheless, it should be remarked that there is nothing inherently progressive about theory. Theory too can be conservative; can be a way of re-enforcing the status quo. There can be conservative moments within any text. A schematic contrast of quantitative criminology versus theory would probably be expressed as one of predictive science versus utopian critical reflection. Both of these modes of research look to a future, and both make change a matter for discussion. Yet they do this in very different ways. Instead of the acrimonious battling of theory and quantitative criminology, a more fruitful approach recognizes that criminology is a broad church. This means both that no way of 'doing criminology' needs to be written off, and no methodology should be privileged over others. Anyway, as Bottoms (2002) has noted, while some criminologists prioritize empirical work and others theoretical work, good empirical research has to be theoretically informed, and some theoretical work does draw insights from empirical studies. It seems that the greatest amount of dialogue goes on between theory and qualitative empirical research, with positivist empirical criminologies often appearing inattentive to theory. Nevertheless, too bold a contrast need not be made across the board, as some critical and reflexive variants of quantitative research are practised. In this connection, theory can work to expand the notion of what counts as data, for instance seeing the reading of images as significant.

That divisive and rather unproductive dispute having been dealt with, albeit in brief, we can proceed to think about theory itself. Theory is aimed at critique and the formation of alternative vistas of criminal justice, and not at evaluation. This means that its practices depart considerably from those of the quantitative criminologies. For those who prefer such styles, theory can seem esoteric, vague, or ill-disciplined, because it goes about its business in different ways. Nevertheless, it is not the case that in theory 'anything goes.' Clearly some theories are deemed better than others, for theory has its own forms of granting legitimacy and relevance. Instead of asking how theories should be judged, one can ask what matters in theory. What matters to, and among, theorists? Consider the statement that 'Bertie is a talented theorist'. What would you understand if you heard those words being said? What does it mean to be good at theory, or to have a talent for theory? Relatedly, what would it mean for a theory to be spoken of as 'a good theory'? At this point it should be made clear that there is no protocol of criteria for identifying a good theory. Nevertheless, some reflections upon what counts in theory can be offered, in the spirit of stimulating discussion. The purpose of this discussion would be to consider the kind of approaches and skills to be fostered if the aim is to produce good theory and good theorists.

In thinking of the 'good theory' and the 'good at theory', we can consider several matters. These include complexity, erudition, elegance, profundity, reflexivity, originality, resonance, and ethical stance. Each of these is material to the success of a theory and will be considered in turn. The word 'complexity' refers to the difficulty level of something. Theory is studious. It is not dogma, polemic, reporting, commentary, or simple opinion. It is a carefully considered, scholarly discourse in which one thinks, reads and writes. Moreover, criminal justice is the site of ethical dilemmas, for which there are no ready answers. Theory is just the thing for this, for it is eminently able to engage sensitively with the grey areas that inevitably pertain when the questions are those concerning crime and criminal justice. This feature of complexity is indicated when a text is described as 'subtle', 'sophisticated', or 'nuanced.'

A theorist is sometimes described as erudite, or a theory as elegant. These words suggest that the work shows the scholar to be well-read and knowledgeable, and his or her work to be written well. Good writing is sometimes called 'polished'. This word suggests matters like succinctness, clarity, the ability to present a striking turn of phrase, and the organization of the article into an apposite structure. Similar words that are sometimes seen are 'panache' and 'finesse', which suggest that the charms of a theory, and the pleasures of the text, are being considered. Evaluative terms like these indicate that the beauty of the text is worth considering and is a component if its efficacy. Of course, to say 'pleasure' or 'beauty' is not to say that the text speaks of pleasant things, or seeks to make that of which it speaks sound pleasing. Pleasure and beauty can also reside in the hauntingly poignant, and are part of the evocation of the tragic. This matter of the elegant is a tricky one, and is of course highly subjective. There is an art to writing well, which cannot be learned in a formulaic way. Perhaps to some extent good writing skills can be built up through reading things that are eloquent, and reflecting upon why they come across so well. Now we come to the description of a text as 'profound'. Profundity is an aspect of theory denoting the extent to which it goes beyond the superficial. Profundity is sometimes related to scope. Theory work shows that the deep analysis of a single event, text, or instance can be as important for criminology as the evaluation of large data sets or the production of broadbrush historical or comparative analyses. These analyses of telling instances are often written as critical interventions at a particular moment. They are sometimes spoken of as 'cutting edge', and can suggest concepts and arguments that others go on to apply in other areas.

The significance of originality perhaps sounds fairly obvious, yet still merits further consideration. As Edward Said (1983: 127) has pointed out, there is a lengthy tradition in the western world of connecting the notion of theory with that of originality. Theory is often linked with imagination, with daring and even dangerous thoughts. Why might this be the case? Theorists take seriously areas of inquiry that might otherwise be disregarded, and can hence produce novel analyses of contemporary developments. For instance, there is considerable activity in the cultural analysis of crime and criminal justice (see Lovell, 2001; Nickoli *et al.*, 2003; Ferrell *et al.*, 2004). This cultural analysis tends to envisage not data, but artefacts. The difference is that to think of 'things' as artefacts is to take an interest in the conditions of their emergence, and the ways in which they attain significance. This approach has been productive of a splendid array of perspectives, which are brought to bear in looking into and writing about crime and punishment. One notable aspect of theory's originality is its eclecticism. Theory is a rich site of interdisciplinarity. Distinctive and theoretically informed styles of research have addressed a wide range of areas. A substantial series of sets of literature could be mentioned here. The length of this chapter only permits me to mention a few recent contributions. For instance, theorists have engaged with literary studies and the history of art (Valier, 2000; Ruggiero, 2003), the history of crime and criminal justice (Brown, Pratt, 2002), film and television studies (Rafter, 2000; Sarat, 2001; Wilson, 2003), and social theory (Young, 1999; Garland, 2001).

Theory is sometimes called 'moving' and 'touching'. Words like these indicate the 'resonance' of theory, the way in which it strikes deep chords with readers. One aspect of resonance is the frequency with which theorists tackle questions of power and difference that really matter to students. Theory's resonance is also related to its foregrounding of *reflexive* modes of scholarship and study. Reflexivity is a term that refers to the ability to address the conditions and the limitations of one's own work, as part of the very process of producing that work. Theory work requires a good deal of self-questioning. Instead of beginning with a hypothesis, to be proved or disproved, theory work is open-ended. This feature of theory is particularly evident in the influential French philosopher Michel Foucault's (1926–84) descriptions of his scholarly work as an 'experience'. The latter is a word that in the French used by Foucault means both something one goes through, or that happens to one, and an experiment:

> If I had to write a book to communicate what I have already thought, I'd never have the courage to begin it. I write precisely because I don't know yet what to think about a subject . . . In so doing, the book transforms me, changes what I think . . . I don't develop deductive systems to apply uniformly in different fields of research. When I write, I do it above all to change myself and not to think the same thing as before (Foucault, 1981/1991: 27).

Instead of the objectivity that is often claimed by those who work in scientific styles of criminology, theorists usually acknowledge and reflect upon their subjective investments in what they write. Instead of the assumption that evidence is available wholly aside from any particular beliefs brought into the activity of researching, theory is overtly reflexive. Theory hence features as that activity in which there is the realization that one's work is that in which one is implicated. This is not a matter of recognizing and avoiding 'bias', a term that implies that there is a neutral, value-free, stance from which one could write. Theory is instead a scholarly practice dedicated to the taking of a critical stance towards itself, to the questioning of both presuppositions and implications. Some would make the claim that reflexive study generates more honest, and to that extent more accurate, versions of what crime and criminal justice are. Others would envisage reflexive study as part of the transformative project of education (see for instance Freire, 1972).

Then there is the matter of ethical stance. Morality is a word that refers to our relations with others, our duties to them, and the standards of right conduct that should be followed. Ethics is a discourse, a critical reflection upon moral values and convictions, about good and bad, justice and injustice, rights and responsibilities. Ethical stance refers to the way in which a theorist takes up a position on these matters. It also concerns the extent to which he or she considers the ethical implications and consequences of what is being written. A related matter might be called ethical depth, by which one might designate the subtlety with which the theorist considers the 'justice' of criminal justice. Theory is good for this kind of study. As Anthony Bottoms (2002) has pointed out, there has been a tendency in which scientific criminologies have engaged in the derogation of moral discourse. Such a denigration of moral questioning reduces crime and criminal justice to mere technical matters. For some, this really does not get to the heart of the matter. Bottoms makes a convincing case that moral arguments can be used effectively to criticize or defend criminal justice institutions and their practices. All this perhaps sounds very serious. But if theory is sometimes thought to be 'heavy' that is because it does not speak of matters that can or ought to be taken lightly. Nevertheless, just because what is at stake are deep and oftentimes grave matters, it does not mean that theory is doomed to be deadly. Luckily, theory is readily engaging, and students are more likely bedazzled than bored rigid.

You will notice that there are no formal definitions in, or attached to, this chapter. Theory is not about definitions. Just as theory is not about enumeration, it is also not about striving to define and categorize. Theory is not about definition, a term that should be understood as de-finition, a matter of setting limits, of delimiting, separating and containing. Instead, theory is about opening up, about opening up thought, questioning, critique and discussion. Being good at theory requires the development of sophisticated critical and analytical skills, through which one's questioning powers are enhanced. It is to elucidating these skills and prompting reflection upon how they may be enhanced that the chapter now turns.

Doing justice to the text

It is sometimes said that theory is hard work; that it is difficult to read, to write, to teach, and to learn. Phrases like 'not for the fainthearted' are heard. Fortunately, it is also said that theory courses can turn out to be really rewarding. Moreover, it is not too unusual to hear students speak of 'loving theory', speaking of theory with evident enthusiasm and enjoyment. What is to be made of this divergent response? To my mind, a productive way of approaching this question is to reflect upon and discuss what might be called 'the challenges of theory'. Theory is indeed challenging, and theory courses can be experienced as a rollercoaster of highs and lows. This is not because theory is overly complicated or obtuse. What however is the case is that theory makes a specific set of demands upon the reader. These may differ somewhat from those previously encountered. First of all, theory is sometimes accused of being 'full of jargon'. Like any advanced scholarly discourse, theory has a specialist vocabulary with which the reader must become acquainted. This is not a matter of being obscurantist or arcane, but simply reflects the fact that the author speaks of complex matters and requires a conceptual vocabulary adequate to the task. A second point to be borne in mind is that theory challenges self-evidences and the commonsensical. This means that readers are required to think unfamiliar thoughts. Sometimes readers must think about and discuss troubling things, that they find personally challenging. For instance, most students are ready to express sympathy for the victims of crime, but offer considerable resistance to extending any consideration to the plight of offenders. This makes for a simplistic 'us and them' approach to the ethical dilemmas of criminal justice (see Mentor, 2000). Some texts make considerable demands upon the reader, in terms of demands upon the imaginative powers, and the ability to suspend judgement, or at least not to rush to hasty judgements. Theory, above all, is not about stating the obvious! For this very reason, theory offers to the reader the opportunity to think anew, to see things in a different light. This is not an easy task. One must not favour or reject theories according to how well they conform to initial opinions and beliefs. A third aspect of the 'difficulty' of theory is its abstraction. To be good at theory is to develop an enthusiasm and a knack for holding abstract arguments and concepts in the mind's eye. Not all theories can be, or even should be, related to situations, events, and actions from your own knowledge and experience. It will be necessary, at least now and then, to make an 'imaginative leap.'

A fourth and final point related to the so-called difficulty of theory concerns the subtle reading skills that students need to develop while engaged upon theory courses. Unfortunately the activity of reading theory is seldom considered during a course of study. When reflection upon reading has not taken place, students can fail to see reading skills as inherent to the task of learning theory. Enhancing your reading skills is important because one thing that theorists do is to engage in the close and considered reading of a range of texts. Most works in theory are not transparent to readers throughout the entire body of the text. However, this does not mean that they are inaccessible. When reading theory, it is necessary to take one's time. This requires commitment and patience. To get to grips with it, it will be necessary to read a text more than once, and to devote a keen attention to key passages. Given that the study of theory requires students to hone their reading skills, some useful reading strategies are presented below. While looking through these, and thinking about how you might use them, you should bear in mind that reading is an active experience, in which the reader creatively interacts with the text. It is hence a mistake to approach the text with the attitude that it will 'tell you everything that you need to know' on a particular subject. In addition, remember the words above about the transformative effect of studying theory. This means that as you work on and with the text, it works on you. This dual effect has been described by the French critic Roland Barthes (1915–80), who once wrote: 'And no doubt that is what reading is: rewriting the text of the work within the text of our lives' (1970/1995).

Keeping these words in mind, read the following list of reading strategies, which are intended to make the experience of reading more effective and more enjoyable. The list should encourage reflection upon what you are doing when you are reading a text:

- While nothing prescriptive can be said about getting in the mood for reading, and about how best to maintain focus during reading, some reflections on this might prove useful. One possible approach is to imagine that the author is there beside you, whispering the words into your ear. Listen carefully, or you will miss hearing what is being said to you. Others might imagine the author watching them while they read, as the French philosopher Sartre (1964/1967: 42) did. Different readers will prefer different reading modes. The practice of imagining oneself listening to the voice of the author has the advantage of emphasizing the language used, in its tone and tenor as well as its specific vocabulary and grammar.

- There may be unfamiliar language here and there, with which you have no prior acquaintance. This may consist of unusual vocabulary, or specialist terminology. Be prepared to find out about, and reflect upon, new words and phrases. There are a number of criminology glossaries, dictionaries and encyclopedias available (for instance, see Munice and McLaughlin, 2001). These books work on the basis that all definitions are at best provisional, are often contested, and are only offered as useful steps within a broader learning process.

- After reading the text, consider what struck you in it. What came across to you as particularly thought provoking?

- Gloss, or make a précis of, the kernel of the main argument. Journal articles usually commence with an abstract that presents this kind of summary, so one way of developing this skill is to read some good abstracts.

- Keep in the mind's eye a picture of how the principle argument was constructed. How was it built up?

- Identify and interpret key passages. How do your interpretations differ from those of others?

- Draw out important quotations and paraphrase them. One useful activity is to imagine that you have been asked to find an epigraph, akin to that with which this chapter commences. This should be highly suggestive of the questions considered in the text.

- Look at the language used by the theorist. For instance, look for telling metaphors, analogies and vignettes. The theorist uses these to substantiate the argument. How do these devices work to persuade the reader? The theorist may use the *double entendre*, a phrase that has a double meaning, as in the main title to this chapter. Often the title for the piece is a telling one, and thinking about the title chosen can prompt effective learning. How does the title work both to promote interest and to indicate content? What alternative titles could have been presented?

- Sometimes the theorist engages in a little etymology, the analysis of word derivations. Looking back to the origins and heritage of a word can be revealing, and assists us in gaining a more subtle sense of its meaning.

- Classic texts have an enduring appeal. Sometimes the author will engage with one of these as an important part of their work. There is no substitute for close reading of the classic texts in the discipline. Just reading a commentary on them will not suffice. They are classics for a reason. Apart from their intellectual contributions to the discipline, they are usually particularly well written, and much can be learned from their style of asking questions and of persuading the reader.

- The notion of classic texts calls up the idea of a canon of works that have become seen as 'greats.' The canon is the dominant imagined memory of the landmark texts in the history of a discipline. English Literature cherishes certain texts, penned by individuals like Chaucer, Shakespeare, Donne, Byron and Keats. Criminology too has its canon of texts that are deemed particularly worthy and important. It is necessary therefore to consider why some texts are included and others are not. It is also possible to keep in mind that a text is not wholly conservative or progressive simply by dint of its inclusion in or exclusion from the canon.

- Look for the main concepts that the text employs. How do these depart from the use of the same concepts by other theorists? If new concepts are presented, in what ways do they both build upon, and differ from, older concepts?

- Who do you think the book or article is addressed to? Do you feel that it really speaks to you? In what respects does it speak to your concerns? How does it sustain your attention? At what points did you feel yourself moving away from what was being said? Were there moments when you would have liked to interrupt the author? What would you have said to him or her?

- Journals often include reviews of new books. One fruitful exercise is to imagine you are writing a book review of a certain text, and then to read some published reviews. How does your review differ from the others?

- Once you are well into your course of study, look back and think about which texts have made an impression on you. Have any of them made you rethink your assumptions about crime and criminal justice?

Clearly this is not an exhaustive list. Neither is it prescriptive. It simply constitutes some useful suggestions. With luck it may build some confidence, and some enthusiasm, for the task of reading. Remember that this list of strategies is not a checklist, but rather a number of points furnishing a basis for discussion.

While engaged upon these reading strategies, it is important to keep an open mind, and to keep in mind the requirement to do justice to the text. Whether one agrees with the author or not, it is important to remember that any text is the result of a great deal of time and effort on the part of its author. Furthermore, in publishing the fruits of his or her labour, the author is seeking discussion with readers. It is necessary therefore to strive to hear what he or she has to say. In keeping an open mind, one proceeds along the lines that critique is not a matter of a choice between celebration or denunciation of a text. Critique is considerably more sophisticated than mere praise or condemnation, and is not just about what one likes. That is something that needs to be constantly reaffirmed when what is being read is texts about crime and criminal justice. When what is being read is about emotive matters, seeming gut-responses can come to the fore. While it is right and appropriate to acknowledge that reading is a subjective experience, it should also be a reflexive one. Doing justice to the text involves thinking about what criticisms need to be made, thinking of what seem the most important and worthwhile criticisms. It also involves a notion of being fair to the author, of looking to what he or she is trying to achieve with the text. This might be called 'appreciative inquiry'. Part of this inquiry would be to think of the moment within which the text was written, for no text appears from nowhere. This is to see an article as a situated intervention, engaged in and with its times. Then, and only then, can a just critique be mounted, in which one challenges what the author has argued. Pointedly, a fair reading does not 'trash' the text or its author. There is a great difference between critiquing a text and rubbishing it. A fair reading also does not make a straw man of the text or its author, which is then knocked down. Reading, above all, is not, as David Wood (1992: 2) puts it 'the use of a sacrificial victim to exhibit one's own position'. The imperative of doing justice to the text, and the problems encountered when working with this requirement in mind, have been discussed by the French philosopher Jacques Derrida (2003). Derrida (1915–2004) speaks of a relation of both fidelity and betrayal, in which the author is followed up to a certain point, but also departed from. He emphasizes that to follow the thought of the author, is also inherently to depart from it. This is the case because all reading is an interpretation. One does not simply repeat what the author has said, for invention is part of all reading. There are subtle movements between the hearing of the author's voice and the making of a response to the text. Perhaps something of this might be summed up by the question 'what do you make of this text?' The question does not only ask what you understand by the text. It also asks what you are making with your reading of it. This might be called 'constructive criticism'. Again the words of Roland Barthes are suggestive. In a little piece called 'Research: The Young' (1972/1986), he emphasized the unique contribution of reading and writing as modes of scholarship in the arts and humanities. In doing so, Barthes (1972/1986: 70) drew a picture of students and authors over the years as 'a living collection of readers'. In this utopian vision readers engage passionately with texts, work on detailed interpretations of them, working reflexively, thoughtfully, and with generosity to one another. He emphasized the process of reading and writing inherent to theory studies as communicative, a process in which one 'de-scribes' the writing in an old text, making it anew. In this way he was able to evoke what he called the drama of writing, within which studying and researching is conceived as 'an interlocution—a task on behalf of others, a social phenomenon' (Barthes 1972/1986: 75). Being good in theory then requires the development of reading and writing skills through which close attention is paid to texts.

The criminologist as a moral witness

Interestingly enough, the term 'theory' is derived from the Greek *theoros*, a representative sent to observe formal events in cities other than his own. The earliest 'theorists' were hence onlookers at public performances. The theoros was summoned on special occasions to attest to the occurrence of some event. He, and male he would certainly have been, was required to witness the event's happening and to report upon its having taken place. Only the report of the theoria, as all the theoros were collectively known, could officially certify what had been seen. This involved an active kind of observation, including asking questions and listening to stories. So the theoros was one who went on a journey, who travelled elsewhere than home, to witness events and make an official record of them. The theorist is thus eminently a witness. If the aspiration is to produce just theory, the theorist tries to be a moral witness. Under the notion of journey, one imagines the theorist seeking to move away from and beyond his or her own immediate concerns and initial assumptions. He or she tries to move towards the side of the other person, if you like. Also thinking of this notion of journey, of travelling and of moving, one thinks of the moral witness as moved by the plight of the other. Moved by the other, this theorist is called to bear witness, an act that requires an ethical engagement and not distanced spectatorship. This is a difficult and active engagement fraught with ambiguities. In addition, the theorist takes the reader on a certain journey, moving the reader, challenging and on occasion changing what is thought.

At first glance, the notion of the moral witness might seem unproblematic. However, the idea of moral enterprise comes with quite some baggage. Four decades ago, in his book Outsiders, Howard Becker (1963) introduced the notion of the moral entrepreneur while writing of the labelling process through which dominant groups succeeded in having vast areas of difference censured and even criminalized (see Chapter 4, section 3.5). Becker depicted the moral entrepreneur as one who engaged in concerted and organized activity to alter the moral constitution of society: 'Rules are the products of someone's initiative and we can think of the people who exhibit such enterprise as moral entrepreneurs' (Becker 1963: 146). He explained that moral entrepreneurs were rule creators and rule enforcers. The prototype of the rule creator was, he suggested, the crusading reformer. This was a role that Becker criticized as follows:

> He operates with an absolute ethic; what he sees is truly and totally evil with no qualification. Any means is justified to do away with it. The crusader is fervent and righteous, often self-righteous (ibid: 148).

The moral entrepreneur is characterized here as rigidly moralistic. 'He' also is depicted as dogmatic, as forthright, as overly assured in his convictions. The moral entrepreneur is probably the one who shouts the loudest and the longest. Note also that moral enterprise means the elaboration of rules, of rigid distinctions between the good and the 'evil'. This person does not sound very subtle in their approach to others, seeing things in black and white. This person also does not seem very reflexive. He is judgemental rather than questioning.

In contrast to the moral entrepreneur, the efforts of whom he clearly disapproved, Becker (1963: 176) emphasized a relativistic view, advising that deviance be viewed as 'simply a kind of behaviour some disapprove of and others value'. For Becker, deviant behaviour was ultimately behaviour so-labelled by those with the power to define (see Valier 2001, Chapter 5). His work criticized the exaggerated and unnecessarily censorious reactions of moral entrepreneurs, the press and the legal system, to what he considered to be innocuous forms of difference. Crucially, the negative conception of moral enterprise came with a refusal to make judgements about forms of crime and violence themselves. The role of social reaction theories in questioning accepted and apparently self-evident definitions and categories of crime was exceptional. Nevertheless, in emphasizing the act of labelling, difficult questions about the inherent badness of some acts are ignored. Among critical criminologists (see Chapter 4) then, for some time the very notion of the moral entrepreneur was dubious if not anathematic. Moral debate and argument remained more visibly the domain of the right. For instance Nils Christie, in *Limits to Pain* (1981) wrote that: 'Moralism within our areas has for some years been an attitude or even a term associated with protagonists for law and order and severe penal sanctions, while their opponents were seen as floating in a sort of value-free vacuum'. However, a number of genres did emerge that insisted on reintegrating a moral and ethical dimension into critical criminology, and furnish intellectual resources for the discussion of moral witnessing. We will now proceed to consider some of these.

Characterizing criminology as a kind of moral philosophy, Richard Quinney (1998/ 2000) described the criminologist as he or she that bears witness. His starting proposition was that the central object of inquiry in criminology, crime, is by definition a matter of suffering. This, he told the reader, means that criminology as a discipline is about suffering. Criminologists, for Quinney, are not only students of suffering, but those who bear witness to suffering. This onus on bearing witness places an emphasis on the responsibility of the criminologist to pay true witness. For Quinney this is not only a matter of producing accurate knowledge about crime. Correctness is also a matter of rightness, or 'right understanding', which requires the adoption of a specific moral stance, from which one bears witness. This moral stance leads Quinney (1998/2000: 180) to write of criminology as a kind of peacemaking, 'the non-violent criminology of compassion and service'. As far as Quinney is concerned criminologists are, whether they know it or not, and whether they like it or not, moral entrepreneurs. In this way, criminology becomes reconsidered as a kind of vocation, or difficult calling.

Look at the epigraph to this chapter again, and a little more closely. Quinney uses the phrase 'engaged in'. He emphasized in his book that witnessing is an active practice. It is moot at this point to dispel the mythological status of theory as mere speculation, in the common sense of being divorced from all reality and all effectivity. Phrases like 'armchair theory' and 'ivory tower' are sometimes used to censure theory as impractical and founded on nothing of any substance. They are quite wide of the mark. As Quinney made clear in his book, the practice of criminology as moral questioning and critique is not disengaged from action and change, and is not based on a lack of experience. More broadly, there is no need to separate theory from practice and from the 'real world'. Theory is not only a reflection upon things but also an engagement with them, an engagement that creates change. The term 'engagement' also suggests the personal. Clearly crime and punishment are matters upon which people have strong feelings of one kind or another. They involve questions that are taken personally by many. Furthermore, note that the term 'engaged' suggests involvement. The criminologist is not construed as somebody who is sheltered from the harsh realities of life. He or she is not a neutral observer. On the contrary, Quinney's moral entrepreneur is affected by the suffering in the world and wants to do something about it. He addresses the reader through the term 'we'. His approach is to evoke a collective movement, within which 'we as criminologists' all have responsibilities as witnesses to crime. Quinney's words evoke a collectivity of criminologists as moral witnesses through a dual, or doubled, mode of addressing the reader. Rather than being just a descriptive term describing what criminologists do, Quinney's writings appeal to criminologists to turn reflexively to moral witnessing. His words have a mobilizing effect of calling upon criminologists to reconsider, and in some respects reorientate, their view of the discipline and their own activities within it. Happily there is now a space for moral argument within the critical criminologies. This of course assumes diverse forms. Some write of the apprehension of injury and suffering, of how they can be made visible, or are rendered invisible. For instance Stan Cohen, in *States of Denial* (2001), has written of the manifold strategies through which a blind eye is turned to violence and suffering. Shoshana Felman (1997), on her part, has evoked one striking aspect of the legendary blindness of justice. She wrote of the extent to which the heated O.J. Simpson murder trial set two traumas, of race and of gender, in competition with each other, each battling for exclusive visibility. Witnessing must be inherently reflexive. It must question its own modes of seeing and of making visible.

Just responses to crime?

Writing 'just theory' is about envisaging just responses to crime. To think further about what might count as just, a useful distinction can be drawn between reaction and response. The moral entrepreneurship criticized by Becker in *Outsiders* was depicted by him as reactionary and negative. A reaction occurs as an opposition to something else. It is provoked by that something, and has connotations of being involuntary and violent. The term has strong associations with the retrogressive and the conservative. The word 'response', however, carries a different weight. It has the dual sense of reply and of responsibility. The notion of a response produces the image of an attentive respondent. This ideal respondent has listened to what has been said before making an answer, and enquired into what is going on before making an intervention. Response itself seeks a reply, and hence envisages ongoing connection. Response looks to the future, seeking to move on through questioning and negotiation, rather than stopping things dead and looking back if not in anger in antipathy. Response then is of the order of openness rather than of negativity, curtailment, containment and elimination. Of course this is to draw two ideal types, of reaction and response. Really things are somewhat more complex than this, and the notion of a 'just response' is an aspiration, just as justice remains, however tantalizingly, a promise. Nevertheless, the notion of 'response' seems a fruitful and appropriate one in terms of understanding what is going on in the moral witnessing to which the criminologist aspires. It is hence possible to cautiously take up the notion of moral witness. This is not as an entrepreneurship of rule-making that looks towards firm precepts, an activity of dogmatic assertion.

The criminologist not only bears moral witness to the sufferings associated with crime, but also to those associated with criminal justice systems. We will now proceed to consider something of both of these, addressing them according to the following two statements:

(a) The criminologist is a witness to crime.

(b) The criminologist witnesses, and makes, responses to crime.

These two aspects of witnessing are not unrelated, but we will think about them separately, the one after the other, for the time being. We shall begin by thinking about the notion of the criminologist as a witness to crime. This is by no means a self-evident matter. As mentioned above, Quinney points out that crime is suffering, calls the criminologist a witness to suffering, and evokes a 'we' that might collectively bear witness. Nevertheless, as Susan Sontag (2003: 16) has written, 'No "we" should be taken for granted when the subject is looking at other people's pain'. It is necessary to reflexively cast a critical eye upon the assumption that 'we' all see, feel and respond to the sufferings of crime in the same way. The notion of witnessing crime calls for both sensitivity and subtlety. It is something about which theory has had plenty to say. In particular, black and feminist criminologies, and scholars in the fields of holocaust and genocide studies, have engaged with these difficult questions. The moral witnessing of crime is to take a careful and considered approach to the position and the demands of the victim of crime. In the last few decades of the twentieth century there began a striking revival of interest in the victim of crime, as the basis for a new and emotive morality of criminal justice. Regrettably, this was all too often an integral part of the movement towards severe punitive sanctions, as though paying due attention to the plight of the victim necessarily entailed 'being tough on' the offender. Victims' right advocates frequently called for harsher penalties to be inflicted upon criminals. While this demand for strong punishment is not univocal among victims, it attracts vastly more attention than the voices of those victims who call for restraint. Two decades ago warnings were already being issued about the dangers of crime victim movements. Ezzat Fattah (1986: 12) stated firmly that inhumane treatment of the offender should not be a corollary of humanitarian consideration for the victim. He went on to proscribe the bifurcation that was already apparent to him, through which one not only limits the direction of compassion, sympathy, pity to the victim, but is actually aggressive and cruel to the offender, writing:

> Humaneness is indivisible. We cannot be humane to one party and inhumane to the other, be kind to the victim and cruel to the offender. We cannot preach justice for the aggressed and at the same time tolerate injustice toward the aggressor (Fattah, 1986: 13).

These words of warning were not heeded by policy makers, who have tended to use the vengeful voice of the crime victim to legitimate harsh measures. 'Justice for victims' became the clarion call of the day, as though there was nothing problematic in that statement at all. What has all too often resulted is what David Garland (2001) has aptly called the 'zero-sum game' of victims' rights. This is a situation in which 'rights for victims' is taken to mean 'offenders have no rights'.

This problem leads us to look at the second statement, and to think about the criminologist as witnessing, and making, responses to crime. First of all, there is the idea that the criminologist is a witness to punishment. The idea of witnessing punishment is both literal and metaphorical. As concerns the former, there are a number of thoughtful accounts published by individuals who have attended executions. Robert Johnson (1989/ 1992) wrote of his experience in attending an electric chair execution in America. He emphasized the cold, unemotional, bureaucratic mechanisms through which the death penalty is administered. Johnson wrote of the emotional distance carefully maintained by the death team of prison officers. He told of instances in which the meticulous procedures threatened to break down, as when the condemned man stumbled moment-arily on the way to the chair. Johnson, watching this man being killed, gave witness to his inability, in the face of the death of this other person, to ignore his humanity: 'The strapped and masked figure sat before us, utterly alone, waiting to be killed . . . A faceless man breathed before us in a tragicomic trance, waiting for a blast of electricity that would extinguish his life. Endless seconds passed. His last act was to swallow, nervously, pathetically, with his Adam's apple bobbing. I was struck by that simple movement then, and can't forget it even now. It told me, as nothing else did, that in the prisoner's restrained body, behind that mask, lurked a fellow human being' (Johnson 1989/1992: 280).

Johnson's paper is called 'This Man Has Expired', which are the official words pro-nounced to verify the death of the condemned. In their coldly factual tone, and their procedural correctness, they epitomize the bureaucratic, emotionless efficiency that dehumanizes the inmate. It is also possible to read and write about prisoner's accounts of their experiences awaiting capital punishment, of which there is a lengthy heritage, including classic works by Fyodor Dostoevsky (1955: 47–8) and Maurice Blanchot (1994/ 2000), as well as those currently on death row.

In addition to analysing accounts of witnessing executions, the criminologist as a moral witness considers the ethics of imprisonment. Prisons, which are discussed in Chapter 27 of this book, are special moral places, and an important locus for the activity of moral witnessing. This is the case because in the prison, ordinary and taken for granted rights are suspended. Prisons are, as Nils Christie (2000) argued in *Crime Control As Indus-try*, institutions for pain infliction. Against the drive in prison numbers, he posited what he called the counterforces of morality. Furthermore, the dominant rationale of imprisonment today does not aim at restoring offenders into social interaction. Prisons are instead places of spatial confinement. This has led Zygmunt Bauman (1998), noting both the trend of mass imprisonment and the regimes of the maximum security prison, to write of the prison as premised on estrangement from others. We can listen here to a voice from one such place, to some lines from a poem written by an inmate of a maximum security prison:

'In the tombs,
I once asked the living dead,
Why have you forsaken humankind?
He answered, "It's only a job."
In the tombs . . .'
(Abdullah, 1995/1996: 27)

These few lines, penned in an infamous American 'supermax prison', are a condensed testimony to the human cost of the bureaucratic style of today's prisons, and their estranging, dehumanizing tendencies. Albert Camus once wrote, 'It is no man's right to despair of another, to consider he has no chance of making amends' (Camus 1957/ 1961). Seen in this light, and whether it is capital punishment at stake or long-term imprisonment with little eye to reintegration into society, imprisonment today is, as Bauman (1998: 114) put it 'ethically worrying'. There is a lengthy and richly diverse body of literature drawing upon a range of theoretical resources within which criminologists have given witness to the pains of the 'criminal justice' system (see, for instance Wincup, 1999; Liebling, 2000).

If the criminologist is a moral witness to punishment, he or she is duty bound to think of alternative, more just, responses to crime. One such response is restorative justice, which is discussed in Chapter 24 of this book. This is a set of criminal justice practices, and a movement of penal reform, commonly described as a contrast to the 'punitive justice' of contemporary times. As its primary exponents freely admit, restorative justice is about values, and about the restoration of the moral order. It is about the restoration of 'community', a cherished socio-ethical ideal that is at the heart of thinking around the potential and pitfalls of restorative justice. Nevertheless, there is a need for caution when criminologies evoke the 'we'. The manner in which 'community' has been invoked within restorative justice discourses has been the subject of some critical scrutiny. This is the case because, as several authors have noted, there is a threat of violence inherent in the constitution of the 'we' within communitarian thinking on crime. As Nicola Lacey warned, 'amid all the welter of cosy appeals to what "we" think, do, understand or feel, there appears to be no critical space in which to reflect upon the processes of inclusion and exclusion which characterize "us" '(Lacey 1998: 138–9). Stuart Scheingold (2000) and Richard Delgado (2000) similarly criticized the implicit uniformity, coerciveness and authoritarianism of restorative justice. In fact, Delgado went so far as to allude to the 'atavistic appeal' of restorative justice. An individual who has done much to question the claims and the promises of restorative justice through theoretical critique is George Pavlich. In 'The Force of Community' Pavlich (2001) wrote of the potent and persuasive, yet ominous, unifying strategy within restorative justice discourses. This, he explained, tends to assume a homogeneous, harmonious community based on consensus and devoid of fundamental disagreements. This, as Pavlich points out, is not only hard to believe in, but deeply problematic.

So we have been thinking about two statements, as follows:

(a) The criminologist is a witness to crime.

(b) The criminologist witnesses and makes responses to crime.

I mentioned above that these two aspects of witnessing are not unrelated. Clearly the possibility of making just responses to crime requires careful reflection on the activity of witnessing crime. Witnessing becomes an eminently reflexive enterprise, within which the criminologist thinks critically about 'seeing' events, 'hearing' testimonies, and 'bearing' witness.

CONCLUSION

The study of criminal justice requires authors and students alike to consider difficult moral questions. Therein arises the necessity for theory, and specifically the necessity of something that has been imagined in this chapter as 'just theory.' Theory is eminently suited to this task of critical engagement. In answer to the dismissive approach to theory, as that which doesn't achieve much, and changes little, one can reply that it is actually vital. However, the purpose of this chapter has not been to make exclusive claims for theory. The point has not been to suggest something along the lines of 'only theory can do this.'

The chapter has instead offered some insights into what theory is good for and what theory is good at. The chapter has employed the notion of 'just theory' as a device to stimulate debate and discussion around the question of what makes a good theory. In this connection, the ideas of criminology as a moral enterprise and of the criminologist as a moral witness have been considered. It has been emphasized that in thinking about criminal justice ethics, there is no moral high ground to be taken. Above all, a just theory is not a matter of firm rules, easy answers, and axiomatic statements.

QUESTIONS FOR DISCUSSION

1 Why is theory important in the study of crime and criminal justice?

2 Anthony Bottoms has argued for 'the inescapability for criminologists of an engagement with critical morality' (Bottoms, 2002: 27). Unpack this quotation, discussing its constituent words and the ideas that they represent.

3 What do you understand by the phrase 'just theory'?

4 How can the criminologist be thought of as a moral witness to punishment?

5 To what extent can restorative justice be thought of as a just response to crime?

GUIDE TO FURTHER READING

A: Introductory texts

No canon of authoritative texts can be recommended as a definitive source for effective learning about theory in criminology. Nevertheless, there are a number of textbooks and other introductory publications that are of assistance to the aspiring theorist:

(1) Valier, C. (2001) *Theories of Crime and Punishment*. London: Longman.

This textbook provides an overview of the principal theories of crime and punishment from the late eighteenth century to the present day. The political and cultural context for each theory, as well as its intellectual antecedents, are drawn out.

(2) Hudson, B. (2003) *Understanding Justice: An Introduction to Ideas, Prespectives and Controversies in Modern Penal Theory (2nd edn)*. Milton Keynes: Open University Press.

This text supplies an introduction to the ideas and controversies that have arisen within law, philosophy, sociology and criminology about the punishment of criminals.

(3) Sumner, C. (1994) *The Sociology of Deviance: An Obituary*. Milton Keynes: Open University Press.

This engaging text documents the formation of the field of sociology of deviance from its conception in the work of Durkheim to the work of the critical criminologists. The book explores the theoretical matrix that held the sociology of deviance together and sets it in the context of culture, politics and social change.

(4) Lacey, N. (ed.) (1994) *Criminal Justice*. Oxford: Oxford University Press.

This book is a Reader, and provides a broad selection of previously published articles and book extracts.

(5) Sparks, R. and Loader, I. (2002) 'Contemporary landscapes of crime, order and control' in Maguire, M., Morgan, R., and Reiner, R., (eds), *Oxford Handbook of Criminology (3rd edn)*. Oxford: Oxford University Press.

This chapter provides an introduction to some ways in which crime and crime control are currently being theorized.

B: Advanced texts

The following texts are recommended as interesting and inspiring examples of theory work:

(1) Lynch, M. (2000) 'The Disposal of Inmate #85271' in Sarat, A. and Ewick, P. (eds), *Studies in Law, Politics and Society*. Stamford, CN: Jai Press.

This essay is a sensitive and subtle account of the experience of being witness to an execution. It shows to full force the ethical problems raised by the sanitized, bureaucratic administration of the death penalty.

(2) Sarat, S. (1997) 'Vengeance, Victims and the Identities of Law' *Social and Legal Studies* 6(2): 163–89.

This article casts a critical eye upon the manner in which victim impact statements have furthered the renewed legitimacy of vengeance in criminal justice.

(3) Lippens, R. (2003) 'The Imaginary of Zapatista Revolutionary Punishment and Justice. Speculations on "the First Postmodern Revolution" ' *Punishment & Society* 2: 179–95.

This thoughtful article looks into the alternative visions of justice and punishment arising within the communications of the Zapatista rebels of Mexico. It is an excellent instance of the theorist's keen interpretative power as shown through a reading of a single image.

(4) Duff, R.A. (2000) *Punishment, Communication and Community. Oxford: Oxford University Press.*

This is an excellent book about the justification of punishment, encompassing retributivism and abolitionism.

(5) Valier, C. (2003) *Crime and Punishment in Contemporary Culture*. London: Routledge.

This book addresses the matter of why questions about crime and punishment are so deeply emotive today.

WEB LINKS

www.theorynetwork.net
British Society of Criminology Theory Network. This site aims to be both informative and inspiring. It includes a comprehensive series of links on theory and a bibliography for teaching and learning theory.

REFERENCES

Abdullah, L. (1995/1996) 'The Tombs' in Rich, A. (ed), *The Best American Poetry 1996*. New York: Scribner.
Akers, R. (2000) *Criminological Theories. Introduction, Evaluation and Application* (3rd edn). Los Angeles, CA: Roxbury Publishing.
Barthes, R. (1970/1995) *S/Z: An Essay*. New York: Hill and Wang.
Barthes, R. (1972/1986) 'Research: The Young' in *The Rustle of Language*. Oxford: Blackwell.
Bauman, Z. (1993) *Postmodern Ethics*. Oxford: Blackwell.
Bauman, Z. (1995) *Life in Fragments*. Oxford: Blackwell.

Bauman, Z. (1998) *Globalization: The Human Consequences*. Cambridge: Polity.

Becker, H. (1963) *Outsiders. Studies in the Sociology of Deviance*. New York: Macmillan.

Blanchot, M. (1994/2000) 'The Instant of My Death' in *The Instant of My Death and Demeure*. Stanford, CA: Stanford University Press.

Bosworth, M. (2001) 'The past as a foreign country: some methodological implications of doing historical criminology', *British Journal of Criminology* 41: 431–42.

Bottoms, A. 2002 'The relationship between theory and research' in R. King and E. Wincup (eds), *Doing Research on Crime and Criminal Justice*. Oxford: Oxford University Press.

Bottoms, A. (2002) 'Morality, crime, compliance and public policy' in A. Bottoms, and M. Tonry (eds), *Ideology, Crime and Criminal Justice. A Symposium in Honour of Sir Leon Radzinowicz*. Cullompton: Willan.

Brown, M. (2001) 'Race, science and the construction of native criminality in colonial India', *Theoretical Criminology* 5: 345–68.

Buber, M. (1947/1970) *Ten Rungs. Hasidic Sayings*. New York: Schocken.

Butler, J. (1993) 'Endangered/endangering: Schematic racism and white paranoia' in R. Gooding-Williams (ed), *Reading Rodney King. Reading Urban Uprising*. New York: Routledge.

Camus, A. (1957/1961) 'Reflections on the Guillotine' in *Resistance, Rebellion and Death*. London: Hamish Hamilton.

Christie, N. (1981) *Limits to Pain*. Oxford: Martin Robertson.

Christie, N. (2000) *Crime Control as Industry. Towards Gulags, Western Style*. London: Routledge.

Cohen, S. (2001) *States of Denial: Knowing About Atrocities and Suffering*. Cambridge: Polity.

Delgado, R. (2000) 'Goodbye to Hammurabi: Analyzing the Atavistic Appeal of Restorative Justice'. *Stanford Law Review* 52: 751–75.

Derrida, J. (2003) 'Following Theory' in M. Payne and J. Schad (eds), *Life. After. Theory*. London: Continuum.

DiCristina, B. (1995) *Method in Criminology: A Philosophical Primer*. New York: Harrow and Heston.

Dostoyevsky, F. (1955) *The Idiot*. Harmondsworth: Penguin.

Douzinas, C. and Warrington, R. (1994) *Justice Miscarried: Ethics, Aesthetics and the Law*. Hemel Hempstead: Harvester Wheatsheaf.

Fattah, E. (1986) 'On some visible and hidden dangers of victim movements' in *From Crime Policy to Victim Policy. Reorienting the Justice System* Basingstoke: Macmillan.

Felman, S. (1997) 'Forms of Judicial Blindness, or the Evidence of What Cannot Be Seen'. *Critical Inquiry* 23: 738–87.

Ferrell, J., Hayward, K., Morrison, W., and Presdee, M. (eds) (2004) *Cultural Criminology Unleashed*. London: GlassHouse.

Foucault, M. (1981/1991) 'How an "Experience-Book" is Born', *Remarks on Marx*. New York: Semiotexte.

Freire, P. (1972) *Pedagogy of the Oppressed*. London: Sheed and Ward.

Garland, D. (2001) *The Culture of Control: Crime and Social Order in Contemporary Society*. Oxford: Oxford University Press.

Johnson, R. (1989/1992) 'This Man Has Expired: Witness to an Execution' in S. Gould (ed), *Moral Controversies. Race, Class and Gender in Applied Ethics*. Belmont, CA: Wadsworth.

Lacey, N. (1998) *Unspeakable Subjects: Feminist Essays in Legal and Social Theory*. Oxford: Hart.

Liebling, A. (2000) 'Prison suicide and prisoner coping', *Crime and Justice* 26: 283–360.

Lovell, J. (2001) 'Crime and Popular Culture in the Classroom: Approaches and Resources for Interrogating the Obvious', *Journal of Criminal Justice Education* 12(1).

Lynch, M. (2002) 'Capital Punishment as Moral Imperative: Pro-death-penalty Discourse on the Internet', *Punishment & Society* 4(2).

Mentor, K. (2000) 'Humanizing criminal justice education: Alternatives to "us" versus "them" ' in G. Goodwin and M. Schwartz (eds), *Professing Humanist Sociology*. Washington DC: American Sociological Association.

Muncie, J. and McLaughlin, E. (eds), (2001) *Sage Dictionary of Criminology*. London: Sage.

Nelken, D. (1994) *The Futures of Criminology*. London: Sage.

Nickoli, A., Hendricks, J. and Osgood, E. (2003) 'Pop Culture, Crime and Pedagogy', *Journal of Criminal Justice Education* 14(1).

Pavlich, G. (2001) 'The Force of Community' in H. Strang and J. Braithwaite (eds), *Restorative Justice and Civil Society*. Cambridge: Cambridge University Press.

Pratt, J. (2002) *Punishment & Civilization*. London: Sage.

Quinney, R. (1998/2000) *Bearing Witness to Crime and Social Justice*. State University of New York Press.

Rafter, N. (2000) *Shots in the Mirror*. Oxford: Oxford University Press.

Ruggiero, V. (2003) *Crime in Literature. Sociology of Deviance and Fiction*. London: Verso.

Said, E. (1983) *The World, the Text and the Critic*. Cambridge: Harvard University Press.

Sarat, A. (1997) 'Vengeance, Victims and the Identities of Law', *Social and Legal Studies* 6(2): 163–89.

Sarat, A. (2001) *When the State Kills: Capital Punishment and the American Condition*. Princeton NJ: Princeton University Press.

Sartre, J.-P. (1964/1967) *Words*. Harmondsworth: Penguin.

Scheingold, S.A. (2000) 'Constructing the New Political Criminology: Power, Authority and the Post-Liberal State', *Law & Social Inquiry* 23(4): 857–95.

Sontag, S. (2003) *Regarding the Pain of Others*. London: Penguin.

Taylor, I., Walton, P., and Young, J. (1973) *The New Criminology: For a Social Theory of Deviance*. London: Routledge and Kegan Paul.

Valier, C. (2000) 'Looking daggers: reading the scene of punishment' *Punishment & Society* 2(4): 379–94.

Valier, C. (2001) *Theories of Crime and Punishment*. London: Longman.

Walters, R. (2003) *Deviant Knowledge: Criminology, Politics and Policy*. Cullompton: Willan.

Wilson, E. (2003) *Cinema's Missing Children*. London: Wallflower Press.

Wincup, E. (1999) 'Researching women awaiting trial: dilemmas of feminist ethnography' in F., Brookman, L., Noaks and E. Wincup (eds), *Qualitative Research in Criminology*. Aldershot: Ashgate.

Wood, D. (1992) 'Reading Derrida' in *Derrida: A Critical Reader*. Oxford: Blackwell.

Young, J. (1999) *The Exclusive Society: Social Exclusion, Crime and Difference in Late Modernity*. London: Sage.

6

Psychology and crime: understanding the interface

Keith Hayward

INTRODUCTION

Many students new to academic criminology are often confused by exactly what role psychology plays in the contemporary criminological enterprise. Very often they have visions of a discipline preoccupied with offender profiling, forensic crime analysis, and the study of psychopathic or mentally impaired serial killers. This chapter aims to set the record straight by providing students with a brief introduction to some of the main points of interface between criminology and psychology. It combines a general review of some of the more prominent psychological explanations of criminal behaviour with some brief examples of how this work has come to be employed in criminological theory and practice. At various intervals, the chapter also adopts a more reflexive stance in a bid to develop some critical insights into the way that 'criminological psychology' is portrayed and perceived within the popular imagination. In this sense, the viewpoint taken here is very much that of a criminologist's perspective of psychology (for an opposite perspective see Hollin, 2002).

BACKGROUND

It has become a cliché to say that recent years have been marked by an increasing popular fascination with the subject of crime and criminality. Yet, in terms of understanding the ever-growing 'psychologistic preoccupation' among criminology students, it is worth pausing to consider some of the reasons behind this current 'fascination'. As Ian Taylor (1999: 2) pointed out, much of this interest is attributable to powerful cinematic and televisual representations of forensic or criminological psychology that serve both to popularize and legitimize various forms of 'analytically individualist criminology'. In Taylor's words, this 'is a form of common-sense criminology organized around 'the criminal', and particularly 'the criminal mind' as an 'object of analysis', and also complicit in the task of identification, prevention and containment of the individual [psychologically distinct] criminal' (ibid.).

In these representations, criminal psychology is frequently portrayed in a very favourable light, almost as if it were a sort of 'secret science', its practitioners capable of feats of identification and detection that far exceed the laboured efforts of the police and other state agencies (Ainsworth 2000: 1–3). Moreover, in these accounts, the mundane, prosaic aspects of crime rarely feature. Instead we are offered up a steady diet of crimes that contain a highly charged emotional (typically pathological) dimension—rape, child abduction, stalking, hate crimes, sexual homicides and other forms of expressive violence.

The attraction of this type of fiction (and increasingly non-fiction; see the recent Channel Four documentary series, *The Real Cracker*) is that it suggests criminological psychology is capable of identifying and understanding 'uniqueness', of identifying whom we should trust and whom we should fear. Whether it is Robbie Coltrane's compelling portrayal of the forensic psychologist Fitz in the Granada Television series *Cracker*, or the mass of popular crime-psychology titles that occupy the shelves of the 'Real Crime' section in high street bookshops, the message is always the same: that crime is about *individual difference* and that psychology holds the key to understanding that difference. I would argue that the impact of such representations of crime has been far-reaching, not least in the way it has contributed to how crime and criminality are currently perceived and understood within the contemporary socio-cultural imagination (Furedi 2004: 30). Today, the popular image of the criminal is no longer that of an 'economically marginalized' or 'socially under privileged' offender, but of an 'emotionally disturbed' or 'psychologically distinct' individual.

In stark contrast, criminology as an academic discipline has tended, in the main, to focus on wider questions concerning the complex relationship(s) that exist between crime, criminal justice and society—something that should immediately be apparent from the diverse range of chapters that comprise this volume. This is not to suggest that sociological criminologists discount the many important gains made by psychologists in understanding a whole range of abnormal and extreme criminal behaviour, both in terms of individual and collective action. Rather, simply to point out that, in the majority of cases, most academic criminologists approach the subject of crime and criminality from a much broader perspective that includes not just the 'causes of crime', but also questions about how crime is itself constructed (see Chapter 1), and how society and the State seek to both control and to respond to crime (see Chapters 21 and 22).

It should be obvious, then, even from this most schematic of introductions that, despite a shared interest in criminal behaviour, criminology and psychology have often made rather uneasy bedfellows. In the next section, as attention turns to the main psychological explanations of criminal behaviour, I will make some intermittent comments about how this relationship has ebbed and flowed over the last 100 years or so. In the meantime, however, in a bid to keep to my introductory remit and (more importantly perhaps in terms of disciplinary politics!) to illustrate a sense of even-handedness, I will conclude this section with the following passage from Putwain and Sammons' introduction to criminological psychology:

> The contribution that psychology can make to criminological issues tends to reflect the strengths and weaknesses of psychology as a discipline. On the positive side, psychologists undergo rigorous training in research methodology, and are therefore well placed to carry out their own investigations and experiments and to comment on and evaluate the work of others. On the negative side, psychology tends to emphasize *individual* factors at the expense of *social* factors. For example, psychological explanations of criminal behaviour tend to concentrate on why *individuals* become offenders by considering factors such as personality and brain function. In contrast sociological approaches tend to emphasize social factors such as poverty and social class . . . Neither approach is foolproof and each complements the other. When taken in isolation, each approach can only provide part of the whole picture, but when taken together they provide a more comprehensive understanding of crime (Putwain and Sammons 2002: 2–3).

Key psychological explanations of criminal behaviour

Introduction

Some brief historical context

Generally speaking, psychology and criminology emerged as distinct disciplines at a very similar historical moment—the latter half of the nineteenth century. Typically, one associates the birth of modern criminology with the work of Cesare Lombroso (1835–1909) and his fellow members of the Italian positivist school (*scuola positiva*; see Chapter 4, for a general introduction to positivism and other key moments in the historical development of criminology). At this point, of course, the nascent 'science of criminology' was still fundamentally preoccupied with matters relating to the individual actor, the so-called 'criminal person or type' (see Beirne 1993: Chapters 2 and 3; Morrison 2004 for recent commentaries). Only later would it broaden its horizons to include wider social and economic factors in accounts of crime. Psychology, meanwhile, had begun to coalesce around the early experimental research of the German, Wilhelm Wundt (1832–1920)—the first person to call himself a psychologist—and the American, William James (1842–1940). (Sigmund Freud, of course, began his career as a neurologist and thus his early work was very much rooted in biology. It was not until slightly later that criminal psychologists took up his psychodynamic theory of personality; see below.)

Such contemporaneous development is not surprising, for both disciplines should be seen as clear products of modernity's faith in enlightened science and philosophy. If modernity was about anything it was about the belief that society's failings would be overcome or at least managed (controlled) by the careful, scientific pursuit of relevant knowledge and the application of this knowledge to a specific set of problems. The then fledgling disciplines of criminology and psychology exemplified such ideals; protagonists of both 'sciences' steadfastly believing that rational scientific analysis could 'make sense' of human behaviour by identifying flaws and categorizing traits and types. No longer would there be talk of humans possessing a 'soul' or a 'spirit'—or indeed of 'good' and 'evil'. Instead, the psychologist and the criminologist would be the objective recorder of 'personality' and 'criminality' respectively—only later would these two sub-fields collide.

Some basic psychological 'distinctions' explained

Perhaps the most enduring (and over-simplified) controversy within psychology is the 'nature versus nurture debate'. In simple terms, the controversy revolves around the *origins* of individual human behaviour/personality. Carlson and Buskist neatly summarize the debate, whilst also pointing out that, as with various other aspects of psychology, what initially appear to be clear-cut distinctions are in fact rather blurred:

'Is it [personality] caused by biological or social factors?' 'Is it innate or learned?' 'Is it a result of hereditary or cultural influences?' 'Should we look for an explanation in the brain or in the environment?' Almost always, biology, innateness, heredity, and the brain are placed on the 'nature' side of the equation. Society, learning, culture, and the environment are placed on the 'nurture' side. Rarely, does anyone question whether these groups of items really form a true dichotomy . . . most modern psychologists consider the nature-nurture issue to be a relic of the past. That is, they believe that *all* behaviours, talents, and personality traits are the products of both types of factors: biological and social, hereditary and cultural, physiological and environmental. The task of the modern psychologist is not to find out which one of these factors is more important but to discover the particular roles played by each of them and to determine the ways in which they interact. (1997: 99–100)

Such is also the case with psychological understandings of criminality. While, countless criminological psychologists have, over the years, sought to identify a single biological (that is, 'nature') explanation of crime, such attempts have born little fruit (for a brief introduction to the some of the major biological and genetic explanations of crime— William Sheldon's 'body type' theory; genetic transmission theory; twin and adoptee studies etc.—see Chapter 4; see also Hollin, 1989: 23–34; Lanier and Henry, 1998: Chapter 5; Bartol 2002: Chapter 3; and in more detail Jeffrey 1994; Ciba Foundation 1996). Indeed, the idea that human behaviour is determined by factors that, while universal to the species, reside to a greater or lesser extent in the *constitution of the individual*, is now distinctly unfashionable (cf. Mednick *et al.* 1987; Raine 1993 for more recent attempts to reassert the role of genetics in criminal behaviour). To put it more bluntly, few psychologists still cling to the idea that certain individuals are somehow predetermined into a life of crime. Instead, the 'nature-nurture' dichotomy is seen to be less an absolute distinction and more an interacting framework for thinking about causal factors in the commission of crime.

Another key definitional distinction, and one that often trips up students new to the subject, is the one that outlines the two major schools of thought within criminological psychology: cognitive psychology and behavioural psychology. Once again, as the following quote makes clear, the two approaches are anything but mutually exclusive:

> Cognitive theories place the study of psychology in the *mind*; they see human action as the result of driving or compelling mental forces or to be the result of mental reasoning and beliefs. These theories take account of *internal feelings* such as anger, frustration, desire and despair. In fact, all activity is seen as the result of *internal mental processes*. In contrast, the behavioural theorists, whilst taking account of internal factors, place them in a *social context*. They see that internal mental processes can be affected and even altered by *certain factors in the environment which either reinforce or discourage the behaviour*. Clearly there is no strong dividing line between these two. *A degree of overlap is likely, whilst some psychological theories may not fit neatly into either school*. (Williams 2004: 170 [emphases added])

I will return to these two schools of thought at various intervals in the chapter. In the meantime, suffice it to say that criminological psychology is a multi-faceted discipline which, despite its overall goal of striving to understand, explain and predict criminal behaviour, typically tends to shy away from making any major pronouncements about there being a single or universal cause/explanation for deviant action. That said, criminological psychology has made significant strides in applying 'psychological theory and investigation to understanding (and attempting to change) criminal behaviour' (Hollin 2002: 144). Moreover, since its emergence as a significant sub-discipline in the early 1960s, criminological psychology (along with its 'sister' discipline, legal psychology (see Müller *et al.*, 1984; Bartol and Bartol, 1994; Kapardis, 1997; Gudjonsson and Hayward, 1998; Adler, 2004) has proven to be of considerable practical use, both in terms of police work and to those working within the legal profession (see below). Indeed, such has been the rise of criminological psychology as a disciplinary variant in its own right, that recent years have seen the publication of a whole host of excellent textbooks aimed at introducing the reader to the subject (for example, Hollin, 1989, 1992; Blackburn, 1993; Feldman, 1993; Ainsworth, 2000; Bartol, 2002; Putwain and Sammons, 2002; McGuire, 2004). Readers new to this area would do well to access one of these texts for a good general synopsis of the interface between psychology and criminology. Now, however, I wish to proceed by focusing on some of the main psychological theories of criminal behaviour. Again, I should point out that what follows is only the briefest of snapshots of some of the more prominent psychological explanations of crime.

Psychoanalytical theories of crime

Most readers will have some understanding of the term psychoanalysis and the work of the Austrian psychiatrist, Sigmund Freud (1856–1939). However, few will be aware of the considerable impact his thinking had on criminological psychology. Despite the fact that, in reality, Freud himself had very little to say about crime, his ideas served as the cornerstone for a whole host of theories that sought to understand crime and deviance by recourse to psychoanalytic techniques—even though many of these subsequent so-called 'psychoanalytical theories' of crime very often represented something of an adulteration (or more charitably, an augmentation) of classic Freudian psychoanalytic theory (see Freud, 1935; Kline, 1984). Let us start at the beginning, by introducing some of the central tenets of Freud's thinking.

Freud's great achievement was to highlight the way that innate desires and repressed emotions shape individual human behaviour. For example, according to Freudian thinking, violent, aggressive or sexually deviant acts should be seen as expressions of buried internal (psychic) conflicts that are the result of traumas or deprivations experienced during childhood (see below). To fully appreciate this perspective one must first understand how Freud perceived the human mind. In simple terms, Freud argued that the mind was comprised of three provinces: the *ego*, the *id* and the *super-ego* (Figure 6.1).

First, the *id* represents the primitive, instinctive, animalistic portion of the 'unconscious mind'. It is here that the primeval human desires reside: that is, fundamental biological and physiological concerns such as innate sexual urges (*libido*); the 'life instinct' (*Eros*) or drive for life; the destructive 'death instinct' (*Thanatos*); and the desire to eat, sleep and be comfortable and so on. The goal of the *id* is simple: to gratify instincts at all costs. According to Freud, the unconscious desires and urges that well up in the id are wholly unresponsive to the demands of reality and are instead governed by what he

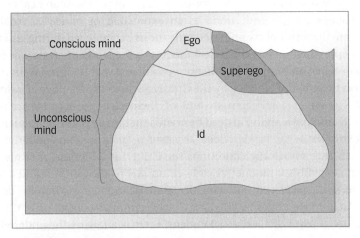

Figure 6.1 The 'pyramid' diagram of Freud's notion of the psyche

Source: Carlson & Buskist Psychology: *The Science of Behaviour* (Allyn & Bacon 1997).

termed 'the pleasure principle'. Needless to say, over the years, such drives have been of considerable interest to criminal psychologists (see, for example, the work of Lorenz 1966; Storr 1970). Second, the ego relates (primarily) to the 'conscious mind', and acts as a sort of 'mediating device' between the two opposing mental forces of the id and the super-ego. Because of the conscious recognition within the individual that 'every act has a consequence', Freud claimed that the ego was driven by the 'reality principle'. Finally, the (largely conscious) super-ego is the 'repository of moral values' and the seat of guilt within the individual. Perhaps the best way to perceive the super-ego is as a sort of internal 'nagging parent' or moral or ethical guardian. Importantly, especially for psychoanalytical theories of crime, the super-ego develops as a result of a series of early social experience(s) (and, for Freud at least, admonishments) that serve to engender in the individual an internal 'source of self-criticism based on the production of guilt'.

In crude terms, Freud maintained that human behaviour should be thought of as a 'struggle between the internalized psychic forces of the id and the super-ego'—with the ego constantly striving to maintain a suitable balance. It is this checking and controlling process that is of vital importance to Freudian psychoanalysis. Over time, and largely formed through learned behaviour, the ego strives to undertake a complex mental balancing act between the primeval desires of the id and the internalized conscience of the super-ego, whilst all the time seeking to work out the best way in which to actually 'serve' the id by meeting some of its requirements: 'A baby learns that it is fed only after crying, and a child learns to say "please" in order to obtain things. It learns that in some circumstances, giving into the id leads to punishment and unpleasantness, and so it may not follow its desires in order to avoid these consequences . . . Slowly, the ego develops and controls or tempers the id' (Williams 2004: 172).

But what does all this mean in terms of understanding criminal behaviour? The key thing here is this process by which the super-ego is formed. As mentioned above, a well-developed super-ego is the result of early social interactions with parents (or with those acting in loco parentis). Consequently, for proponents of psychoanalytical criminology, criminal behaviour can be understood as an expression of buried internal (mental) conflicts that are the result of traumas or deprivations experienced during childhood.

The first to apply such psychoanalytical models to the study of crime was the former schoolteacher August Aichorn (1925). Aichorn postulated that traditional environmental factors (such as those being outlined by the Chicago School of Sociology at a similar time; see Chapter 4) were not sufficient in and of themselves to account for individual involvement in criminal activity. Instead he argued that many of the delinquent children he studied exhibited what he described as *latent delinquency*—an 'underlying predisposition' which psychologically conditions the child 'for a lifetime of crime'. In other words, a failure to establish productive early emotional relationships resulted in a breakdown in the *socialization process*, 'allowing the latent delinquency to become dominant: a state which Aichorn describes as "dissocial". The criminal behaviour is therefore the result of a failure of psychological development, thereby allowing the underlying, latent delinquency to govern the behaviour' (Hollin, 1989: 35). In even plainer terms, for Aichorn childhood delinquency is the product of a badly structured/supervized early childhood (whether as a result of parental neglect or over-indulgence). This being the case, his remedy was straightforward, delinquent children must be provided with a well-supervized, pleasant social environment that will encourage the type of emotional relationships which, in turn, will help develop a well-established *super-ego*.

Following Aichorn, the importance of early childhood development on behaviour was further emphasized by a whole host of psychoanalysts—including most famously, the work of Abramson (1944) and Alexander (Alexander and Staub, 1931; Alexander and Healy, 1935) on failure to control drives associated with the 'pleasure principle'; and Healey and Bronner's (1936) research into the Freudian concept of 'sublimation', or the way that 'unsatisfied instinctual desires' are often channelled into other forms of behaviour, including deviance. However, perhaps the most influential figure in this field was the British developmental psychologist, John Bowlby (1907–90). Bowlby's achievement was to solidify the link between *maternal deprivation* and antisocial behaviour (Bowlby, 1944; 1951). This commitment to understanding behaviour by recourse to early familial circumstances is made abundantly clear in the following quote:

> No variables have more far-reaching effects on personality development than a child's experiences within the family. Starting during his first months in his relation to both parents, he builds up working models of how attachment figures are likely to behave towards him in any of a variety of situations, and on all those models are based all his expectations, and therefore all his plans, for the rest of his life. (Bowlby, 1973: 369)

More specifically, what was important for Bowlby was the close, loving relationship between mother and child. Consequently, any rejection or separation between mother and child during early child development is likely to prove highly problematic. Indeed, according to Bowlby's sample groups, such ruptures in familial relations will be disproportionately represented in serious cases of delinquency in later life.

Bowlby's writings, along with other related research (for example, Little, 1965; Rutter, 1972), proved extremely effective in terms of influencing governments and generating policy initiatives. Not least, ideas about maternal deprivation and other later so-called 'broken home theories' were a central element in the rehabilitative 'welfarist' movement in youth justice of the 1960s and 1970s (see Chapter 19). However, these early forays into the psychology of the offender did not sit well with everyone. Many commentators objected strongly to the lack of scientific rigour associated with this early psychoanalytical criminology (specifically the '*tautological*' and 'untestable' nature of the intra-psychic Freudian approach). Others meanwhile questioned the extent to which the psychoanalytical approach relied upon the interpretative expertise of the analyst in teasing out the particular link between the criminal act and the hidden unconscious drive—a link that, for many, was simply too convoluted and contingent. That said, the psychoanalytical approach to deviance, and other subsequent theories derived from psychoanalysis (see below), went on to exert considerable influence within both psychology and criminology for many decades to come (see Garland, 1994: 42–60; Valier, 2001). Not least, its enduring legacy is the concrete link it cemented in the minds of many practitioners and caregivers between chaotic early child development and behavioural problems in later life.

Behavioural and social learning theories of crime

In contrast to theories of crime that suggest the root cause of deviance lies with primitive instinctive drives and internal psychodynamic struggles, behavioural and social learning theories—as the name clearly implies—assert instead that crime and deviance are *learned responses*. The starting point for this expansive body of work was Edwin Sutherland's (1883–1950) renowned sociological theory of 'differential association' (1947). For Sutherland, behaviour—including crime—is a social product, a result of different interactions and patterns of learning that occur in the intimate personal groups and surrounding social circumstances that encapsulate the individual. According to Sutherland, such groups teach 'definitions'—including special skills, motivations, norms and beliefs—either 'unfavourable' or 'favourable' to the violation of the law (that is, in the latter case, the *association* of an individual with a group, or indeed a community, that is both ingrained with criminal traits and norms, and also isolated from more positive anti-criminal traits and attitudes). Despite criticisms of differential association (not least questions about why, under shared conditions, individuals still tend to behave very differently from each other) Sutherland's work was extremely influential, ushering in a whole host of subsequent theories that sought to prove that the determinants of behaviour reside *outside the individual*.

This line of thinking inevitably chimed loudly with the shift already underway within American psychology towards 'behaviourism' (see, for example, Watson 1913 for an early example). But as Clive Hollin makes clear, rather than making for harmonious relations between psychology and criminology, this apparent convergence in thinking surrounding the role of *external stimulants* in the development of behaviour, instead heralded a parting of the ways for the disciplines, as behavioural psychologists continued to focus their attention exclusivly on the *individual behaviour* rather than the wider external circumstances in which that behaviour was forged. Consequently, 'psychology failed to connect with criminology and the opportunity for a genuine academic alliance slipped away' (Hollin, 2002: 150). The uneven and, at times, strained relationship between psychology and criminology now underway.

Psychological developments in learning theory meanwhile drew further strength from the behavioural research of B.F. Skinner (1904–90), and especially his principles of 'operant learning' (1938,1953). Crudely stated, operant learning suggests that 'behaviour is determined by the environmental consequences it produces for the individual concerned'. Put another way, behaviour that leads to 'awards' will increase (that is, is 'positively reinforced'); behaviour that produces an unpleasant stimulus (that is, is 'punished') is avoided: 'Any such behaviour, driving a car, writing a letter, talking to a friend, setting fire to a house, is *operant* behaviour. Behaviour does not occur at random; environmental cues signal when certain behaviours are liable to be reinforced or punished . . . the Antecedent conditions prompt the Behaviour which in turn produces the Consequences—the ABC of behavioural theory' (Hollin, 1989: 40).

Among the first to suggest that criminal behaviour could be understood in terms of operant learning was C.R. Jeffrey (1965) and his *theory of differential reinforcement* (see also more recently Akers, 1985). By combining the principles of Skinner's operant learning with Sutherland's differential association, Jeffrey maintained that, although criminal behaviour might well be the result of pervasive socio-cultural norms and attitudes within a given locality (*à la* Sutherland), it is also greatly affected by the particular consequences (or 'reinforcements' in Skinnerian terms) that deviance produces for the individual. For example, 'The majority of crimes are concerned with stealing where the consequences are clearly material and financial gain: the gains may therefore be seen as positively reinforcing the stealing' (Hollin 1989: 41). Such an approach has the advantage of overcoming the main problem associated with differential association. By focusing on *individual learning histories* (that is, unique reward and punishment experiences), differential reinforcement theory explains how, despite shared environmental conditions, individual actors ultimately behave very differently.

While Skinner and Jeffrey did not wholly discount the role of internal mental processes in their particular brand of behaviourism, neither did they feature prominently in their analyses. The first to actively integrate 'internal processes' into learning theory was the psychologist Albert Bandura (1973, 1977; also Rotter, 1954). Bandura's 'social learning theory' hypothesis was an uncomplicated one: individual behaviour is something learnt at the *cognitive level* by observing and then imitating the actions of others. Most famously, Bandura conducted an experiment in which a group of infants watched a film depicting an adult violently attacking an inflatable rubber 'Bobo' doll (see Figure 8.2). In subsequent tests, this group were significantly more likely to repeat the aggressive behaviour toward the doll than were the members of a control group who had not been exposed to the film—indeed, this second group behaved more passively throughout the whole experiment. Because of the emphasis Bandura placed on 'learnt aggression', his findings quickly found support within criminological psychology (for example, Nietzel 1979).

Such experiments suggested that, not only does social learning take place at the familial and sub-cultural level, but also via the observation of cultural symbols and media 'role models' (see Chapter 8). 'For example, a child may learn to shoot a gun by imitating television characters. He or she then rehearses and fine tunes this behavioural pattern by practising with toy guns' (Bartol, 2002: 128). Naturally, just like other operant behaviour, cognitively learned behaviour is further 'reinforced' or 'punished' via the process of socialization ('The behaviour is likely to be maintained if peers also play with guns and reinforce one another for doing so', ibid.).

This interest in the relationship between wider social and cultural determinants and individual criminal behaviour could have heralded the onset of a productive, collaborative relationship between criminology and psychology. Not for the last time, however, this opportunity for disciplinary accord would be largely squandered. While behavioural and social learning theories continued to develop, by the end of the 1970s most criminal psychologists had turned their back on this approach, choosing instead to pursue a very different course based around theories of criminal behaviour concerned with the identification of individual *personality traits*.

Trait-based personality theories

The study of individual personality traits is nothing new in psychology (see, for example, Allport, 1937; Cattell, 1965). As we saw earlier, one could even view Freud's work as the study of personality development. Yet, while Freud saw abnormal behaviour as the product of unconscious desires and motivations, the new 'Trait-based personality theories' set out to identify and classify particular personality characteristics, and to empirically measure how these traits become assembled differently in different people. The central figure in this shift towards understanding human behaviour via 'psychometric' statistical testing was Hans Eysenck (1916–97). Eysenck's work is especially pertinent to the current discussion as his goal was the creation of a general psychological theory of crime (1977; Eysenck and Gudjonsson, 1989).

Eysenck had little time for the 'sociological turn' in the study of crime and deviance, something made abundantly clear in the following quote: 'In many ways we disagree with various sociological theories that have become so popular since World War II but which, we believe, are fundamentally erroneous and counter to the fact' (Eysenck and Gudjonsson, 1989: 1 cited in Bartol, 2002: 70). Instead Eysenck stressed the fundamental role of inherited genetic predispositions (especially in relation to the cortical and auto-nomic central nervous systems) in determining the way each individual responds to environmental conditioning. In other words, Eysenck subscribed to the view that an individual's personality—including those personality traits that he considered constitu-tive of the criminal personality—was largely the product of their genetic make-up. Yet, this was no simple return to biological determinism (see Chapter 4), rather Eysenck's theory was a fusion of biological, socio-environmental and individual factors.

Because Eysenck spent much of his life's work constantly retesting and augmenting his theory of crime, his key assertions are not easily summarized, however, the following passages by Lanier and Henry provide a succinct general synopsis (for more detailed summaries see Eysenck, 1984; Bartol, 2002: 70–85; Hollin, 1989: 53–9):

> Eysenck claimed to show that human personalities are made up of clusters of traits. One cluster produces a sensitive, inhibited temperament that he called *introversion*. A second cluster pro-duces an outward-focused, cheerful, expressive temperament that he called *extroversion*. A third dimension of personality, which forms emotional stability or instability, he labelled *neuroticism*; to this schema he subsequently added *psychoticism*, which is a predisposition to a psychotic breakdown. (Lanier and Henry 1998: 119).

Eysenck plotted the personality traits of the individuals he studied on a very rudimentary graph that has since become one of the most famous diagrams in all psychology (Figure 6.2). Although something of an oversimplification, Eysenck concluded that most people in society would reside somewhere near the middle of the axis (that is, within the inner 'square'), but that what was important in terms of explaining criminal behaviour were those individuals who featured at the extremes of the diagram.

> Normal human personalities are emotionally stable, neither highly introvert or extrovert. In contrast, those who are highly neurotic, highly extroverted, and score high on a psychoticism scale have a greater predisposition toward crime, forming in the extreme the psychopathic personality. Eysenck explained that such personalities (sensation seekers) are less sensitive to excitation by stimuli, requiring more stimulation than normal, which they can achieve through crime, violence and drug taking. These people are impulsive, being emotionally unstable. They are also less easy to condition and have a higher threshold or tolerance to pain. Low IQ can [also] affect the ability of such personalities to learn rules, perceive punishment, or experience pain, as in biological theory. (ibid.)

Taken at face value, Eysenck's theories seem convincing. Yet, a trawl through the mass of empirical research undertaken in an attempt to test his propositions reveals a more ambiguous picture—not least many of these studies point to a number of significant methodological and theoretical flaws. Crucially, whilst there is general support for his

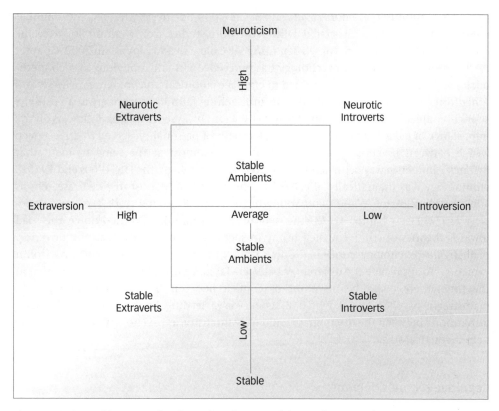

Figure 6.2 Eysenck's personality dimensions for neuroticism and extraversion

contention that offenders will score highly on both the psychoticism and neuroticism dimensions, there is little evidence to support the crime-extroversion connection. Furthermore, a common charge often labelled at the trait-based approach is that it is inherently tautological: 'Stealing may be taken as an indicator of impulsiveness and impulsiveness given as the reason for stealing. Thus a recurrent criticism of trait-based theories is that they represent correlational rather then causal connections' (ibid: 121).

These and various other criticisms aside, the wider influence of the trait-based approach to deviance can be seen in the continued growth of psychometric questionnaires and other related diagnostic devices that have emerged out of this field of research. These include early examples of so-called 'personality inventories' such as the Minnesota Multiphasic Personality Inventory (MMPI) (first proposed in 1939) to British equivalents like the British Maudsley Personality Index (MPI) and Eysenck-inspired self-report questionnaires such as the Eysenck Personality Inventory (EPI) and its subsequent iterations. Basically, the idea here is that specific personality traits can be measured and assessed by asking the individual a battery of specially designed questions (or more recently by testing responses to a series of images). Such assessments are then used to predict, prevent and treat future deviant behaviour.

Inevitably, many commentators have pointed out the intrinsic problems associated with statistical attempts to measure anything as complex and multifaceted as personality (see most famously, Taylor *et al.* 1973: 44–61)—not least the all too familiar methodological pitfalls associated with self-report studies (for a criminology-specific introduction to the problems of self-reporting see Coleman and Moynihan 2002: Chapter 3). Yet, most of this type of psychology has proceeded virtually oblivious to such methodological criticism and has continued to embrace empirical psychometric methods and other forms of quantitative analysis. This unflinching faith in psychology as a positivist science, coupled with the continued emphasis placed by Eysenck and his followers on the importance of *biological factors* in the development of personality, served to drive a deep wedge between psychology and criminology. For almost at the same moment that Eysenck's influence was being felt most acutely in psychology (the late 1960s and 1970s), criminology was dramatically affected by a new wave of Marxist-inspired research, as announced by Taylor, Walton and Young in the groundbreaking work *The New Criminology* (1973) (see Chapter 4). As (the majority of) criminology turned down the road towards theories of crime couched firmly in sociological and political economic terms, mainstream psychology continued down the experimental, empirical path. As Hollin explains: 'To appreciate the differences between Taylor *et al.* and Eysenck, is to see that at the time, there could be no point of contact between the new criminology and mainstream psychology (of which Eysenck was a leading figure)' (2002: 155). Such disharmony between the disciplines would only intensify, as psychology embarked on its next theoretical stage.

Cognitive theories of crime

Such was the speed at which cognitive theory impacted on psychology its emergence on the scene is often described in terms of a 'cognitive revolution' (Baar, 1986). Drawing on the early work of the Swiss child psychologist, Jean Piaget (for example, 1954), and Lawrence Kohlberg's (1969) notion of 'progressive moral development', cognitive theory 'has as its major theme how mental thought processes are used to solve problems—to interpret, evaluate, and decide on the best of actions. These thought processes occur through mental pictures and conversations with ourselves' (Lanier and Henry, 1998: 126). More simply, it is an attempt to understand the way people think via investigations of such concepts as intelligence, memory structure, visual perception and logical ability (see also M.W. Eysenck and Keane, 1997 for a comprehensive overview of mainstream cognitive psychology).

The first major cognitive study to make an impression on criminology was Yochelson and Samenow's infamous *The Criminal Personality* (1976; see Glueck and Glueck, 1950 for a precursor study). In an expansive three-volume work, Yocheslon and Samenow set themselves the ambitious task of 'mapping the criminal mind'. The positivist zeal with which they undertook this task is made clear in the following quote by Samenow:

> I shall expose the myths about why criminals commit crimes, and I shall draw a picture for you of the personality of the criminal just as the police artist draws a picture of his face from the description. I shall describe how criminals think, how they defend their crimes to others, and how they exploit programs that are developed to help them. (Samenow 1984: 5)

All this from a sample group of only 240 offenders, each one of whom had been adjudged 'not guilty by reason of insanity' and who, at the time of study, were institutionalized in a psychiatric hospital in Washington DC. After several thousands of hours of qualitative interviewing Yocheslon and Samenow identified '52 errors of criminal thinking' or 'problematic thinking styles' that, they claimed, taken together constituted 'the criminal personality'. These included inter alia 'chronic lying', irresponsible decision making, 'super optimism', 'distorted self-image', and a lack of empathy for others' (a trait that has since been made much of in contemporary cognitive-behavioural programmes for sex offenders; see below). According to Yochelson and Samenow, such 'cognitive distortions' ensure that '[C]riminals *think differently* from responsible people' and, moreover, that 'Crime resides *within the person* and is "caused" *by the way he thinks, not by his environment*' (Samenow 1984: xiv, cited in Lanier and Henry, 1998: 127, emphases added). Naturally, such assertions have implications in terms of how one treats the offender. Indeed it is within the sphere of contemporary treatment programmes that the influence of cognitive theory has been greatest—I will thus return to this subject in more detail below. In the meantime, it is worth pausing to reflect on some of the much-voiced criticisms of Yochelson and Samenow's *The Criminal Personality*, as these critiques also serve to illustrate many of the problems associated with various other types of empirical psychology concerned with statistically measuring or 'mapping' the complexities of the human criminal personality.

To start with, little distinction is made between the various types of criminal studied. Thus, their assertion that all criminals share the same thought patterns/processes is highly problematic—does a violent offender, for example, share the same cognitive distortions as an embezzler? Second, by focusing so intently on internal thought process and dysfunctional cognitions, Yochelson and Samenow downplay the importance of both psychobiological *and* socio-environmental influences. Third, theories of crime that stress cognitive irregularities are seen as tautological in that certain behaviours are said to be indicative of cognitive processes, while these same cognitive processes are then used to explain away the behaviour. Fourth, and perhaps most obviously, Yocheslson and Samenow's sample was comprized only of *incarcerated* offenders. Yet, while one cannot deny the existence of these and several other theoretical and methodological flaws, it is hard not to be drawn to some of their ideas about cognitive reasoning, especially in relation to interpersonal relationships. Unsurprising, then, that many other psychologists have chosen to pursue this line of inquiry and in so doing have developed a body of work that, not only greatly augments Yocheslson and Samenow's research, but which has since gone on to be enthusiastically received by practitioners working in the treatment arena.

A central assumption of *The Criminal Personality* is that a criminal's erroneous thinking can be corrected if they are first taught to construct a 'moral inventory' of their everyday thoughts, and then, by working with a practitioner, to identify and ultimately eradicate any dysfunctional cognitions (Samenow 1984: 6–7). Although something of an over-simplification, this is the rationale behind the majority of cognitive therapeutic interventions that seek to correct problems experienced by offenders in their everyday lives. For example, such programmes typically concentrate on cognitive considerations such as:

- insufficient levels of *self-control* (that is, impulsivity or the failure to delay gratification) (for more on the role of self-control more generally within criminological theory, see Chapter 4);
- an inability *to feel empathy for others*—especially victims;
- deficits in basic *social problem-solving skills*—the type of skills we all employ to negotiate interpersonal relationships and everyday struggles;
- problems in the interpretation of *visual and situational cues* (e.g. a great deal of research suggests that violent individuals not only perceive fewer social cues than non-violent people, but that they are also much more prone to interpret social cues in a hostile fashion) (see Crick and Dodge's 1994, 1996 work on social information processing);
- an inability to distinguish between which facets of personal life are subject to *internal control* (i.e. are governed by one's own actions) and those which are subject to *external control* (i.e. are governed by the actions of others).

Cognitively inspired treatment programmes are currently very popular within the UK criminal justice system, being employed in increasing numbers both within the prison setting and as an alternative to custody. However, while these correctional programmes have often proved successful at reducing certain forms of persistent offending, ultimately they remain fundamentally limited in scope—primarily in the sense that they never really offer a full and inclusive explanation of why someone becomes involved in criminality (or, for that matter, decides to stop). That said, perhaps this is not really the point. These cognitively inspired programmes make little attempt to consider traditional criminological concerns such as the inequalities associated with class, race, gender and socio-economic deprivation. Instead, the goal is the distillation of crime and criminality to rigid 'narratives of feeling' and formalized, reductionist understandings of the social world. Only when this process is complete will the individual offender then be in a position to assume responsibility for his or her actions. As Wayne Morrison points out, such psychotherapeutic practices represent the new wave of governmental and institutional weapons in the fight against crime, a discourse preoccupied solely with strategies of pacification and control (see Garland 1997, 2001 for a more general introduction to criminological thinking in this area)—with the psychologist as independent arbiter of acceptable behaviour and intention:

> Psychology presents a variety of tools and knowledges: methods of awareness (which strive to make a self visible to the person) . . . The aim of these knowledges and methodologies is to visualize the healthy, and get rid of pathological aspects. The task is to change anxiety into excitement through techniques of self-reflection and self-examination, and thereby to ensure that we become a reflexive self, more able to redirect our [internal] forces. Thus we can learn processes of control over ourselves which the behavioural manipulators claim they can exercise from without . . . We learn a language and a technique, a process which makes us governable, and yet offers us the possibilities of governing ourselves. This reflects the dialectics of modernity: control and autonomy, responsibility and inclusivity, civilization and citizenship. (Morrison 1995 163–4)

Theory into practice: some examples of the way psychology is employed within criminal justice

This final section will focus on some of the more prominent practical applications of psychology within the sphere off criminal justice (see Adler, 2004 for a general introduction). Students should recognize that, once again, what follows here is only an introduction and that, needless to say, countless other practical interfaces abound (see, for example, HM Prison Service and the National Probation Service, 2003; Towl, 2004).

Recent psychological developments in rehabilitation and treatment

The most obvious place to start is with psychological attempts at rehabilitation, as the various treatment programmes put forward by psychologists naturally draw heavily on many of the psychological theories and principles outlined in the previous section. The key point here is that psychologically based rehabilitation models operate on very different principles to traditional judicial sanctions such as imprisonment or fines. To start with they are less concerned with *punishing the offender* than with reducing the 'risk' of re-offending. Consequently, 'they are based on psychological theories of offending, rather then the (sometimes rather vague) notions of "human nature" on which judicial sanctions often seem to be based' (Putwain and Sammons, 2002: 147).

Since the 1980s numerous psychologically based treatment programmes have been pioneered, both within and outside the custodial setting. However, I have chosen here to concentrate on what are perhaps the two most common initiatives—*cognitive behavioural treatments for offending* based on cognitive and social learning theories of crime, and *token economies* based more specifically on operant conditioning theories.

As Anne Worrall makes clear in her chapter on punishment in the community in this volume, the nature of probation intervention has changed radically in the past two decades. The disillusionment and pessimism encapsulated in Robert Martinson's infamous 1974 remark that 'nothing works' in penal interventions (see Chapter 26, this volume) epitomized the lack of confidence in the efficacy of established offender treatment/ supervision modalities, heralding a 'crisis in confidence' both in the National Probation Service specifically and the 'welfarist' treatment paradigm more generally (see, for example, Bean, 1976; Hudson, 1987). This loss of confidence lasted until the early 1990s and the emergence (initially in North America) of cognitive behavioural programmes based in large part on a new wave of psychological research—or more accurately, a new spirit of collective endeavour and reciprocity between learning, behaviour and cognition theorists (see McGuire, 1995 on the subsequent initiatives associated with the 'What

Works?' conferences; and Raynor, 2002; Lipsey *et al.*, 2004 for recent commentaries on developments in this area).

As mentioned above, rather than attempting to change the whole personality or circumstances of an offender, cognitive behavioural programmes focus on specific unacceptable behaviours and seek to modify these by correcting distortions in the way offenders think about their crimes. The practitioner's primary goal therefore is to get the offender to 'face up' to their crimes and accept responsibility for their actions (instead of blaming the victim or their social circumstances). Likewise, treatment programmes also concentrate both on correcting problem behaviours (such as anger management, drunk driving or deviant forms of sexual arousal), and the acquisition of new social and inter-personal skills that will help the offender better deal with certain situations that, previously, had triggered anti-social or criminal behaviour. Typically, these strategies are bundled together in the form of a treatment/correction 'programme', which in turn draws 'together a series of planned and sequential learning opportunities into a cumulative sequence, covering an appropriate curriculum of skills and allowing plenty of opportunity to reinforce learning through structured practice' (Raynor, 2002: 1185).

Since their emergence in the UK in the early 1990s, the use of such programmes has grown exponentially. Jill Peay, for example, estimates that, by 2001, 'over 100 prisons were running such programmes, with five specific programmes in prisons and nine in the probation service having been accredited' (2002: 775). The interesting thing to note here about such growth is the way that cognitive behavioural programmes are now employed as a 'mainstream application' within the contemporary probation system. No longer are they employed simply as a means of treatment for chronic offenders with various personality disorders, or as a way of assessing, managing and ultimately *reducing the risk of re-offending* among sexual and violent offenders (see Kemshall, 2001; Jones, 2000: 151–6; and Kemshall, 2003 more generally). Increasingly, these programmes are offered to offenders involved in a much more general—dare I say it, even commonplace—range of so-called 'anti-social behaviours' (see McGuire, 2004: Chapter 6). Clearly, this is more evidence of the widening of what Wayne Morrison described above as the net of governmental structures of self-reflection and self-examination.

Leaving this more critical point aside, the incredible growth of cognitive behavioural treatment programmes have resulted in them being a somewhat difficult phenomenon to define accurately (see McGuire, 2000). Consequently, as Hollin explains, the relationship between theory and effective practice in this area has, on occasion, been a somewhat disjointed one:

> . . . rather then the purist sequence of a theory leading to the design of an intervention, so producing outcome evidence by which to amend theory and practice, 'What Works' has started from a quite different position. The meta-analyses have brought together a disparate batch of treatment outcome studies and distilled their effective components. In an about turn, the position has been arrived at whereby positive treatment outcome data have outstripped theory. (2002: 167)

Inevitably, this situation throws up certain problems in terms of moving the field forward, yet it should not blind us to the fact that a significant number of these therapies have proven highly successful in the treatment of both adult and juvenile offenders (see

Andrews *et al.*, 1990; Lipsey and Wilson, 1998; Redondo *et al.*, 1999). It is for this reason that many psychologists and practitioners are highly optimistic about the future potential of cognitive-behavioural rehabilitative strategies (Vennard and Hedderman, 1998). Some even suggesting that work in this area offers the potential for establishing 'genuine cross-disciplinary collaboration' between psychological and criminological research (Hollin, 2002: 168). However, before we get carried away, we need also to consider the concerns of many criminological researchers that the current enthusiasm for cognitive behavioural practices could result in the further marginalization of 'traditional' programmes such as basic literacy and social skills. Moreover, commentators such as Pat Carlen have pointed to the problematic way in which many of the programmes that constitute the 'What works' movement are assessed and evaluated:

> The verity of the 'programmer's' claims to 'success' are often 'proven' by dubious self-report questionnaire evidence from prisoners that a programme 'works'—usually in terms of changing prisoners' understanding of their offending behaviour (Indeed, in view of all these 'program-mers' and 'counsellors' claiming to have found the philosopher's stone in relation to changing offenders' behaviour, it is truly amazing that the prisons have not been emptied by now!). (Carlen, 2002: 120)

Another psychologically based treatment modality to have gathered momentum since the 1980s (although less so in the UK) is the idea of the *token economy*. Only feasible within the prison/institutional setting, the token economy is a system whereby, having complied with an agreed list of 'desirable behaviours' (for example, establishing courteous or positive relations with a member of staff, or completing a set of pre-arranged chores), offenders receive 'tokens' which they can then exchange for *reinforcers* such as confectionary, soft drinks or visits home. The programmes are based on the basic principles of operant conditioning theory: that is, if all behaviour is learnt through 'reinforcement and punishment', then 'bad behaviour' can be 'unlearned' through 'lack of reinforcement', and good behaviour 'learned' via the process of 'positive reinforcement'. While early research into these schemes threw up some interesting findings (for example, Ayllon and Milan, 1979), subsequent research into the longer-tem rehabilitative value of token economies has cast considerable doubt on the lasting benefits of this approach. Indeed, most studies concluded that token economies were only of real benefit when employed as a means of managing offenders within the institutional setting.

Psychology and police work

In the modern police force, psychology seems to play an ever-expanding role (see Reiser, 1973; Bull *et al.*, 1983; Ainsworth and Pease, 1987; Hollin, 1989: Chapter 5). For example, it is employed *inter alia* as a major tool in the following areas:

- the selection and training of police recruits;
- analysing the values, norms and perceptive skills of police officers as they proceed through their careers;
- training and ultimately improving the way officers conduct interviews with

witnesses (see for example, Geiselmen *et al.*, 1985 on the idea of the 'cognitive interview'; McGurk, 1993);

- understanding the way police officers deal with work-related stressors such as complaints made against them by the public or being faced with a violent or dangerous confrontation (see, for example, Terry 1981)

- improving the ability of police officers to retrieve, recall and interpret events that may have a bearing on a criminal investigation (see Clifford and Bull, 1978)

- improving interrogation techniques (Gudjonsson, 1992)

- understanding and improving officer decision making in riot and firearm situations

- and, of course, most famously (and perhaps most contentiously) as a key component in the construction of offender profiles.

Let us look briefly at some of these areas.

The complex and multifaceted nature of contemporary police work has ensured that many forces around the world increasingly rely upon the use of psychological testing in their selection processes. The goal behind using tests like the Minnesota Multiphasic Personality Inventory (MMPI) (see above) or other similar psychometric questionnaires is straightforward: either to 'screen out' candidates who exhibit unwanted characteristics such as deceitfulness or racism, or who by their responses to situational tests illustrate that they may be prone to high levels of stress or anxiety; or to 'screen in' candidates who exhibit desirable personality traits such as honesty or the ability to think calmly when confronted with potentially volatile situations (see Burbeck and Furnham, 1985; Yuille, 1986).

This type of psychological analysis of the personalities of police officers and their decision-making strategies does not stop at recruitment stage. The psychological scrutiny of police work has extended to virtually all aspects of policing—from the way officers negotiate their daily administrative duties, to how they cope with more challenging situations such as a hostage scenario or the violent death of a fellow officer (see for example, Fridell and Binder, 1992). Central to this field of study is the notion of the distinct 'police personality' (Evans *et al.* 1992). This argument follows that, whether by 'predisposition' (that is, characteristics already present in the individual prior to joining the police), or via the process of 'socialization' (that is the compliance with and ultimate acceptance of the dominant norms and values already embedded within police culture), police officers hold a very different set of attitudes and values than the rest of the population. The psychological findings in this area are decidedly mixed. While there is some evidence to suggest that police officers in various countries do share higher than average instances of certain personality characteristics such as 'authoritarianism' (Colman and Gorman, 1982), 'conservatism' (Cook, 1977) and 'extraversion' (Gudjonsson and Adlam, 1983), there is no conclusive evidence to indicate whether or not these tendencies existed prior to joining the police or were subsequently learnt on the job. Consequently, psychologists conclude that there is thus much need for more detailed longitudinal studies to be carried out in this area.

Perhaps the most celebrated application of psychology within police work is the notion of the psychological *offender profile* (see Jackson and Bekerian, 1997; Ainsworth, 2001;

Holmes and Holmes, 2002 for general introductions). Certainly the role of the 'offender profiler' has, over the last decade or so, become a major theme within the mass entertainment industry, featuring in a slurry of TV shows and hit movies such as *Manhunter* and *Red Dragon*. Consequently, the idea of the so-called 'mind hunter' now holds something of a fascination with both the general public, and a great many students new to academic criminology—a number of whom often labour under the misapprehension that an undergraduate degree in criminology could lead to a formal 'job' as an offender profiler (see Gudjonsson and Copson (1997) for a guide to what profilers actually do):

> 'The best way to become a profiler is to become a chartered forensic psychologist or a chartered forensic psychiatrist, and then, after you've done that, wait ten years and then wait to be asked.' Dr Julian Boon, the British psychologist and offender profiler (*The Real Cracker*, Channel 4 TV, 2001)

While definitions of profiling abound—each new book offering its own iteration—the following statement by Swanson *et al.* still stands as one of the clearest expositions:

> The purpose of the psychological assessment of a crime scene is to produce a profile, that is, to identify and interpret certain items of evidence at the crime scene which would be indicative of the personality type of the individual or individuals committing the crime. The goal of the profiler is to provide enough information to investigators to enable them to limit or better direct their investigations. (1984: 700–1)

One of the key questions surrounding profiling concerns which crimes are suitable to be profiled (Pinizzotto, 1984; Stevens, 1995). While some maintain that profiling is only applicable in crimes that indicate a high degree of psychological abnormality (such as violent, sexual assaults, 'motiveless' murders or paedophilia), others claim that the practice could be extended to include a range of other crimes that do not necessarily involve personal contact or clinical disorders. Rider (1980), for example, has produced psychological profiles of the economic arsonist; Boon has applied profiling to various cases of extortion; while others have attempted to develop a profile of the political terrorist (see Strentz, 1988). This debate is interesting in the way that, to a certain degree, it mirrors the divide that exists between the two major approaches to profiling: the crime scene analysis approach favoured by the FBI Investigative Support Unit (formerly the Behavioural Science Unit), and the 'investigative psychology' approach as favoured by the British psychologist David Canter and his various proponents (see Ainsworth, 2001; Chapters 6 and 7 for introductions to these different approaches).

Essentially, the FBI's approach is to cross reference crime scene evidence (such as levels of violence or mutilation, timing of the offence, body disposal/position, or levels of premeditation and so on.) with established 'offender typologies' to determine a working personality profile of the perpetrator(s), thus enabling the authorities to better focus their investigations. However, whilst these typologies have considerable 'discriminatory power', they inevitably rely upon the 'subjective judgements' of the individual profiler (see Ressler and Shachtman, 1992). Such reliance upon individual intuition has led many to question the empirical value of this approach, with critics such as David Canter (1994) and Philip Jenkins (1994) asserting that individual hunches and rigid typologies based primarily on interviews with notoriously distrustful (often psychopathic) offenders are no basis for a systematic science.

The second approach is different in that it eschews the so-called informed speculation—or what David Canter has described as the 'flash of insight'—that is a key feature of the FBI approach. Instead it seeks to construct a situational/geographic profile of the offender(s) based on the assumption that the offender, like most people, acts consistently over time (the criminal consistency hypothesis). It is for this reason that the investigative psychology approach is not limited solely to crimes such as murder and rape, and that it can also be used to profile a whole range of more prosaic crimes. The goal of investigative psychology profiling, then, is to identify intelligible patterns between things like time and location of offence (Canter and Larkin, 1993; Canter and Gregory, 1994), factors surrounding victim selection and, if the victim survived (for example, non homicidal rape cases) a close analysis of the offender's behaviour (Canter and Heritage, 1990) and speech patterns. Canter's goal, then, is the rigorous application of applied psychological principles to the study of offender profiling.

Canter's work was originally based on five aspects of the interaction between the victim and the offender—the five-factor model:

(1) *Interpersonal coherence* assumes that offenders will deal with their victims in a manner similar to the way they treat people in their day-to-day lives.

(2) *The significance of time and place* may provide analysts with clues about the offender's mobility and even his residence.

(3) *Criminal characteristics* are used by researchers and analysts to place offenders into broad categories, from which subcategories can be selected or developed.

(4) *Criminal career* is an assessment as to whether the offender may have engaged in criminal activity before and what type of activity it most likely was.

(5) *Forensic awareness* draws in part from Step 4 above, criminal career. It is an assessment of the scene and evidence to determine if the offender has any special knowledge of evidence gathering procedures used by the police.

Source: *Criminal Investigation* (Chapter 8) by Swanson, C.R., Chamelin, N.C. and Territo, I. (2002) New York: McGrawHill.

Despite optimistic noises about the growing 'scientific' rigour of offender profiling, significant doubts still remain about its empirical legitimacy—not least the problem of how one measures the accuracy and thus the ultimate value of profiles. Certainly it has proven difficult to establish reliable data on the overall effectiveness of personality profiles, something due in no small part to the fact that there is considerable 'variability' in the way that profilers go about 'compiling' their profiles (Bekerian and Jackson, 1997: 212). Likewise, when a profile does appear to have been useful in facilitating an arrest, it can often prove difficult to ascertain exactly whether the success was due to the profile or was in fact simply the result of traditional police inquiries. Such scepticism, however, has done little to dampen down the popular appeal of offender profiling within the public's imagination. As Ainsworth suggests: the 'exclusive focus upon the type of profiling most often portrayed in the media is misleading and often unhelpful. The portrayal of "experts" with their intuitive minds and amazing powers of deduction may do little to educate the public as to the real role which profilers, or more correctly forensic psychologists, might play in crime investigation' (2001: 181).

Psychology and the courtroom

The last two decades have witnessed a growing mass of psychological research produced on various aspects of the legal process. A detailed account of what is often referred to as legal psychology is beyond the compass of this chapter. Instead I have chosen here to introduce three key areas of overlap between psychologists and those working in the legal profession: the pre-trial role of psychologists and psychiatrists in the assessment of mentally disordered offenders; the psychological research into eyewitness testimony; and the decision-making strategies and psycho-social dynamics of jurors/juries.

For more detailed summaries of the practical and theoretical work that constitutes the field of psycho-legal studies see Farrington *et al.* (1979); Lloyd-Bostock (1981); Müller *et al.* (1984); Losel *et al.* (1992); Bartol and Bartol (1994); Maguire *et al.* (2000); Kapardis (1997). For interesting commentaries on both the common ground and the various mutual problems that exist between psychology and law, see the review articles by Tapp (1976) and Monahan and Loftus (1982).

Mental disorder and criminal responsibility

The question of whether mentally abnormal—or, more accurately, 'mentally disordered'—offenders should be incarcerated in prisons and institutional facilities or cared for within the community is an incredibly complex and contentious one (see Peay, 2001 for an excellent summary). Such an extensively documented subject is not easily summarized, yet it would be remiss of me not to point out briefly the important, if at times indefinite (see Roberts, 1996), role played by psychiatric and psychological evidence in the legal processes surrounding mentally disordered offenders.

The key problem in this area is one of definition: mentally disordered offenders simply do not constitute a distinct group. As Jill Peay makes patently clear: 'Mental disorder' . . . is a term of acute terminological inexactitude. Definitions of mental disorder act like a concertina, expanding and contracting in order to accommodate different client groups with little or no coherence. Their mismatch frequently results in uncertainties and anomalies' (2001: 753). Inevitably, these definitional problems ensure that there is a ready need for the assessment expertise of the psychiatrist, not least in relation to *mens rea* (the notion of criminal intent) and the thorny question of whether or not the offender was in a sound psychological state of mind when committing the criminal act (Prins, 1986).

Such clinical testimony, along with various other courtroom roles played by the psychologist—such as the expert witness (see MacKay *et al.*, 1999) and the role of advisor to counsel—ensure 'that psychiatric and psychological evidence is increasingly prevalent and influential in criminal proceedings' (Peay, 2001: 766). Indeed, the wealth of empirical studies undertaken within psychology into abnormal behaviour (some of which have been discussed above), in tandem with the long history of predominantly medical diagnoses proffered by psychiatrists, have served as the catalyst for the modification of the law's approach to a number of issues concerning criminality and mental health—even to the point where forensic psychologists are occasionally asked to assist in making recommendations to Parliament.

The psychology of eyewitness memory

Many of us have witnessed an accident or a crime in the course of our daily round. Depending on its seriousness, we are often asked to recall the details of the event, whether by witness statement or police interview, or perhaps even via an artist's impression, photo-fit or identity parade (Putwain and Sammons, 2002: 111–19). In every case, it is essential that the police and other authorities be provided with accurate and reliable information. To assist in this process, a body of work has emerged in recent years based on the psychology of eyewitness memory (and testimony) (see Clifford and Bull, 1978; Loftus, 1979; Gudjonsson, 1992; Ainsworth, 1998; Heaton-Armstrong *et al.*, 1999 for comprehensive overviews). The goal of these studies is to better understand the processes and problems associated with memory:

> Most people seem to think that our memory works passively like a video recorder. We can 'play back' information in exactly the same form that it was recorded, providing an accurate and objective record of the world. If our memory worked like this then eyewitness memory would not raise any issues. Witnesses would be able to provide accurate accounts of events with no loss of detail and identify suspects without any chance of error. Unfortunately, memory does not work like this. Witnesses can sometimes provide only hazy recollections of events, sometimes contradicting themselves and mistakenly identifying suspects. (Putwain and Sammons, 2002: 97)

By way of summary, one can state that the psychology of eyewitness memory focuses on three stages of the memory process: *acquisition*, *retention* and *retrieval* (see Cohen, 1999):

(a) *Acquisition (or encoding) stage—the witnessing of the incident*: This stage can be affected by time factors like the length of time spent witnessing the event; the time of day when the event took place (studies show that witnesses recall more details about crimes that took place in daylight than at night); the nature of the incident witnessed (for example, the so-called 'weapon focus effect', where victims of gun-related crime often recall intimate details about the firearm, but very little about other aspects of the crime).

(b) *Retention (or storage) stage*: Research in this area has shown that this stage of the memory process can be affected by the duration of time that passes between witnessing a crime and the request to retrieve the details; and whether the witness discusses the events with others prior to giving evidence—the so-called contamination effect.

(c) *Retrieval stage—the process of giving evidence*: Studies around the retrieval of information have highlighted that memory can be affected by subtle changes in the way the questions are worded/inferred; or by the process of *expectation*, where witnesses often tend to report what they expected to see (on such points, see the large body of work by the psychologist, Elizabeth Loftus).

Psychology of the jury

As with other areas of the legal process, criminological psychology has had much to say about courtroom dynamics and, in particular, the way that juries arrive at their decisions (see Ainsworth, 2002: chapter 7 and Hollin, 1989: 161–71 for student-friendly introductions). Importantly, one should point out that because of the obvious inherent practical and ethical difficulties of studying actual jury decision-making strategies, much of the psychological research in this area is the product of experiments conducted on mock juries/trials. Summarized below are a few of the main research areas:

(a) *Eyewitness testimony*: research suggests that juries place considerable emphasis on eyewitness testimony when weighing their decisions—even when counsel has cast doubt on the veracity of the eyewitness (see Loftus, 1974).

(b) *The effects of pre-trial publicity on the jury*: experimental studies in this area have found clear evidence to suggest that juries are prejudicially affected by exposure to pre-trial publicity, a process that does not appear (in mock trials at least) to be offset by judicial instruction.

(c) *Levels of confidence displayed by witnesses*: perhaps unsurprisingly, research indicates that jurors tend to place most faith in witnesses who display a confident manner when testifying.

(d) *The extent to which jurors perceptions about defendant characteristics such as attractiveness, gender, race, age, status/qualifications and demeanour affect their decision-making* (see Fife-Schaw 1999).

(e) *Jury selection procedure*: In the United States the 'screening out' of jurors who counsel believe may have the 'wrong type of personality' to try a particular case has become a major area of psychological research (see Kassin and Wrightsman, 1983). Indeed, this practice of *voir dire* has become a specialism of certain trial lawyers—as illustrated most publicly in the trial of O.J. Simpson.

(f) *The social dynamics of how a group of twelve jurors arrive at their verdict.*

(g) *The problems associated with children's testimony.*

REVIEW QUESTIONS:

1 What are the limitations of psychologically—based rehabilitation programmes?
2 Is offender profiling a systematic science or just intuitive guesswork?

CONCLUSION

It is hoped that this chapter has provided the reader with a solid introduction to the various ways in which psychological research has contributed to our understanding of crime and the criminal justice system. On the way, I hope it has also helped to shatter some of the popular myths and 'media-created' assumptions about criminological psychology. In particular, my goal has been to dispel the erroneous conception of criminal psychology as a sort of 'secret science' (wherein its practitioners are capable of identifying and detecting something as specific and observable as a psychologically distinct criminal mind or personality).

We have also seen that, despite the fact psychological research has frequently served as an important driver of change in society's attitudes and responses to crime, there still exists a slightly uneasy relationship between criminology and psychology. Certainly, we still find ourselves in a situation where advocates of one discipline are often working independently of those in the other. In part this is due to the disciplinary schisms that are an intrinsic part of the history of Western social sciences. That said, I have endeavoured to highlight some of the more productive interactions between these areas of ongoing research. It remains to be seen if a more conciliatory approach may lead to a greater consensus or convergence in 'scientific knowledge'.

QUESTIONS FOR DISCUSSION

1 What early behavioural characteristics/traits might be listed as predicators of violent crime? Do you agree with the statement that 'most psychological problems have their roots in some sort of trauma yet to be resolved'?

2 Think about some of your own characteristics, traits and behaviours. To what extent have these behaviours been learned, either via 'positive reinforcement', 'differential association' or via the observation of cultural symbols and media 'role models'?

3 Is it really possible to empirically map something as complex as the human personality? Moreover, could you make the argument that psychology is not really a science?

4 What are the social and cultural factors behind the public's fascination with criminal psychology?

GUIDE TO FURTHER READING

Ainsworth, P. (2002) *Psychology and Policing*, Cullompton: Willan.

A good general introductory account of the way in which psychological principles and practices are applied to policing.

Bartol, C.R. (2002) *Criminal Behaviour: A Psychosocial Approach*, Upper Saddle River, NJ: Prentice Hall.

An engaging and helpfully frequently updated introduction to the role of psychology in understanding criminal behaviour.

Blackburn, R. (1993) *The Psychology of Criminal Conduct: Theory, research and Practice*, Chichester: Wiley.

A detailed and comprehensive account of many of the themes discussed in this chapter.

Hollin, C. R. (1989) *Psychology and Crime: An Introduction to Criminological Psychology*, London: Routledge.

Despite being over fifteen years old, this book continues to provide the most comprehensive and accessible review of the literature on criminological psychology.

Kapardis, A. (1997) *Psychology and Law: A Critical Introduction*, Cambridge: Cambridge University Press.

A general introduction to psychology's various contributions to criminal justice and socio-legal studies.

WEB LINKS

http://www.clas.ufl.edu/users/gthursby/psi/

Link to the *Psychology World Wide Web Virtual Library*, a site that keeps track of psychology related websites.

http://www.psychology.org/

The Encyclopaedia of Psychology website.

http://www.psychologyinfo.com

A private US internet resource run by Donald J. Franklin, Phd, that provides general and accessible information about the practice of psychology, see more specifically http://www.psychologyinfo.com/forensic/

http://faculty.washington.edu/eloftus/

The homepage of Elizabeth Loftus, one of the leading researchers in eyewitness testimony and other aspects of legal psychology. The site has various links to her books and articles.

http://www.freudfile.org/

A website dedicated to the life and work of the psychoanalyst Sigmund Freud.

http://www.bps.org.uk/index.cfm

Website of the British Psychological Society.

REFERENCES

Abrahamson, D. (1944) *Crime and the Human Mind*. New York: Columbia University Press.

Adler, J.R. (2004) *Forensic Psychology: Concepts, Debates and Practice*, Cullompton: Willan.

Aichorn, A. (1925) *The Wayward Youth*. New York: Meridian Books.

Ainsworth, P.B. (1998) *Psychology, Law and Eyewitness Testimony*, Chichester: Wiley.

Ainsworth, P.B. (2000) *Psychology and Crime: Myths and Realities*. London: Longman.

Ainsworth, P.B. (2001) *Offender Profiling and Crime Analysis*. Cullompton: Willan.

Ainsworth, P.B., and Pease, K. (1987) *Police Work*. London: Methuen.

Akers, R. (1985) *Deviant Behaviour: A Social Learning Approach*. Belmont, CA: Wadsworth.

Alexander, F., and Healy, W. (1935) *Roots of Crime*. New York: Knopf.

Alexander, F., and Staub, H. (1931) *The Criminal, The Judge and the Public*. New York: Macmillan.

Allport, G.W. (1937) *Personality: A Psychological Explanation*. New York: Holt.

Andrews, D., Zinger, I., Hoge, R.D., Bonta, J., Gendreau, P., and Cullen, F. T. (1990) 'Does correctional treatment work?: a clinically-relevant and psychologically informed meta-analysis', *Criminology* 28, 369–404.

Ayllon, T., and Milan, M. (1979) *Correctional Rehabilitation and Management: A Psychological Approach*. New York: Wiley.

Baars, B.J. (1986) *The Cognitive Revolution in Psychology*. New York: Guildford Press.

Bandura, A. (1973) *Aggression: A Social Learning Analysis*. Englewood Cliffs, NJ: Prentice Hall.

Bandura, A. (1977) *Social Learning Theory*. New York: Prentice Hall.

Bartol, C.R. (2002) *Criminal Behaviour: A Psychosocial Approach*. Upper Saddle River, NJ: Prentice Hall.

Bartol, C.R. and Bartol, A.M. (1994) *Psychology and Law*. Pacific Grove, CA: Brooks/Cole.

Bean, P. (1976) *Rehabilitation and Deviance*. London: Routledge.

Beirne, P. (1993) *Inventing Criminology*. Albany, NY: State University of New York Press.

Bekerain, D.A., and Jackson, J.L. (1997) 'Critical issues in offender profiling' in J.L. Jackson and D.A. Bekerian (eds) *Offender Profiling: Theory, Research and Practice*. Chichester: Wiley.

Blackburn, R. (1993) *The Psychology of Criminal Conduct: Theory, Research and Practice*. Chichester: Wiley.

Boon, J.C.W. (1997) 'The contribution of Personality Theories to psychological profiling' in J.L. Jackson and D.A. Bekerian (eds) *Offender Profiling: Theory, Research and Practice*. Chichester: Wiley.

Bowlby, J. (1944) Forty-four juvenile thieves: their characters and home life. *International Journal of Psycho-Analysis*, 25: 19–52 and 107–27.

Bowlby, J. (1951) *Maternal Care and Mental Health*. World Health Organization: London: Her Majesty's Stationery Office.

Bowlby, J. (1973) *Separation: Anxiety and Anger. Volume 2 of Attachment and Loss*. London: Hogarth Press.

Bull, R.H.C., Bustin, B., Evans, P., and Gahagan, D. (1983) *Psychology for Police Officers*. Chichester: Wiley.

Burbeck, E., and Furnham, A. (1985) 'Police Officer Selection: a Critical Review of the Literature', *Journal of Police Science and Administration* 13: 58–69

Canter, D. (1994) *Criminal Shadows*. London: Harper Collins.

Canter, D., and Gregory, A. (1994) 'Identifying the Residential Location of Rapists' *Journal of the Forensic Science Society*, 34: 169–75.

Canter, D., and Heritage, R. (1990) 'A Multivariate Model of Sexual Offence Behaviour: Developments in Offender Profiling', *Journal of Forensic Psychiatry*, 1: 185–212.

Canter, D. and Larkin, P. (1993) 'The environmental range of serial rapists' *Journal of Environmental Psychology*, 13: 63–69.

Carlson, N.R. and Buskist, W. (1997) *Psychology: The Science of Behaviour*. Boston, Mass: Allyn and Bacon.

Cattell, R.B. (1965) *The Scientific Analysis of Personality*. Harmondsworth: Penguin.

Ciba Foundation (1996) *Ciba Foundation Symposium 194: Genetics of Criminal and Antisocial Behaviour*. Chichester: Wiley.

Clifford, B.R. and Bull, R. (1978) *The Psychology of Person Identification*. London: Routledge.

Cohen, G. (1999) 'Human memory in the real world' in A. Heaton-Armstrong, E. Shepherd and D. Wolchover (eds) *Analysing Witness Testimony*, London: Blackstone.

Coleman, C. and Moynihan, J. (2002) *Understanding Crime Data*. Buckingham: Open University Press.

Colman, A.M., and Gorman, L.P. (1982) 'Conservatism, dogmatism, and authoritarianism in British police officers', *Sociology* 16: 1–11.

Cook, P.M. (1977) 'Empirical survey of police attitudes', *Police Review* 85: 0142, 1078; 1114; 1140.

Copson, G. (1995) *Coals to Newcastle? Part 1: A Study of Offender Profiling*, London: Police Research Group Special Interest Series/Home Office.

Crick N.R., and Dodge, K.A. (1994) 'A review and reformulation of social information processing mechanisms in children's social adjustment', *Psychological Bulletin*, 115: 74–101.

Crick N.R. and Dodge, K.A. (1996) 'Social information processing in reactive and proactive aggression', *Child Development*, 67: 993–1002.

Evans, B.J., Coma, G.J. and Stanley, R.O. (1992) 'The police personality: Type A behaviour and trait anxiety', *Journal of Criminal Justice*, 20: 429–41.

Eysenck, H. (1977) *Crime and Personality*. London: Routledge.

Eysenck, H. (1984) 'Crime and Personality' in Müller, D.J. *et al.* (eds) *Psychology and Law*, Chichester: Wiley.

Eysenck, H. and Gudjonsson, G. (1989) *The Causes and Cures of Criminality* New York: Plenum Press.

Eysenck, M., and Keane, M. (1997) *Cognitive Psychology: A Student's Handbook*. Hove: Psychology Press.

Farrington, D.P., Hawkins, K., and Lyod-Bostock, S. (1979) *Psychology, Law and Legal Process*, London: Macmillan.

Feldman, P. (1993) *The Psychology of Crime*. Cambridge: Cambridge University Press.

Fife-Schaw, C. (1999) 'The influence of witness appearance and demeanour on witness credibility' in A. Heaton-Armstrong, E. Shepherd, and D. Wolchover, (eds) *Analysing Witness Testimony*. London: Blackstone.

Freud, S. (1935) *A General Introduction to Psychoanalysis*. New York: Liveright.

Fridel, L.A. and Binder, A. (1992) 'Police Officer Decision Making in Potentially Violent Confrontations', *Journal of Criminal Justice* 20: 385–99.

Furedi, F. (2004) *Therapy Culture*. London: Routledge.

Garland, D. (1994) 'Of Crimes and criminals: the development of criminology in Britain' in Maguire, M. R. Morgan and R. Reiner (eds), *The Oxford Handbook of Criminology*. Oxford: Oxford University Press.

Garland, D. (1997) ' "Governmentality" and the Problem of Crime: Foucault, Criminology and Sociology' *Theoretical Criminology* 1(2): 173–214.

Garland, D. (2001) *The Culture of Control*. Oxford: Oxford University Press.

Geiselman, R.E., Fisher, R.P., MacKinnon, D.F., Holland, H.L. (1985) 'Eyewitness Memory Enhancement in Police Interview: Cognitive Retrieval Mnemonics Versus Hypnosis', *Journal of Applied Psychology* 70: 401–12.

Glueck, S., and Glueck, E. (1950) *Unravelling Juvenile Delinquency*, New York: Harper and Row.

Gudjonsson, G.H. (1992) *The Psychology of Interrogations, Confessions and Testimony*. Chichester: Wiley

Gudjonsson, G.H., and Adlam, K.R.C. (1983) 'Personality Patterns of British Police Officers' *Personality and Individual Differences* 4: 507–12.

Gudjonsson, G.H., and Copson, G. (1997) 'The role of the expert in criminal investigation' in J.L. Jackson and D.A. Bekerian (eds) *Offender Profiling: Theory, Research and Practice*. Chichester: Wiley.

Gudjonsson, G.H. and Hayward, L.R.C. (1998) *Forensic Psychology: A Guide to Practice*. London: Routledge.

Healy, W., and Bronner, A.F. (1936) *New Light on Delinquency and its Treatment*. New Haven, Conn: Yale University Press.

Heaton-Armstrong, A., Shepherd, E. and Wolchover, D. (eds) (1999) *Analysing Witness Testimony*. London: Blackstone.

HM Prison Service and the National Probation Service (2003) 'Driving Delivery: A strategic framework for psychological services in prisons and probation' HM Prison Service, NPS, London: Applied Psychology Group.

Hollin, C.R. (1989) *Psychology and Crime: An Introduction to Criminological Psychology*. London: Routledge.

Hollin, C.R. (1992) *Criminal Behaviour: A Psychological Approach to Explanation and Prevention*. London: Falmer Press.

Hollin, C.R. (2002) 'Criminological psychology' in M. Maguire *et al.* (eds) *The Oxford Handbook of Criminology* (3rd edn). Oxford: Oxford University Press.

Holmes, R.M. and Holmes, S.T. (2002) *Profiling Violent Crimes: An Investigative Tool*. London: Sage.

Hudson, B. (1987) *Justice Through Punishment*. London: Macmillan.

Jackson, J.L. and Bekerian, D.A. (eds) (1997) *Offender Profiling: Theory, Research and Practice*. Chichester: Wiley.

Jeffrey, C.R. (1965) 'Criminal Behaviour and Learning Theory' *Journal of Criminal Law, Criminology, and Police Science*, 56: 294–300.

Jeffrey, C.R. (1994) 'Biological and Neuropsychiatric Approaches to Criminal Behaviour' in G. Barak (ed) *Varieties of Criminology: Readings from a Dynamic Discipline*. Westport, Connecticut: Praeger.

Jenkins, P. (1994) *Using Murder: The Social Construction of Serial Homicide*. New York: Aldine de Gruyter.

Jones, S. (2000) *Understanding Violent Crime*. Maidenhead: Open University Press.

Kapardis, A. (1997) *Psychology and Law: A Critical Introduction*. Cambridge: Cambridge University Press.

Kassin, S.M. and Wrightsman, L.S. (1983) 'The construction and validation of a juror bias scale', *Journal of Research in Personality*, 17, pp. 423–442.

Kemshall, H. (2001) *Risk Assessment and Management of Known Sexual and Violent Offenders: A Review of Current Issues*. Police Research Series Paper 140. HMSO.

Kemshall, H. (2003) *Understanding Risk in Criminal Justice*. Open University Press: Maidenhead.

Kline, P. (1984) *Psychology and Freudian Theory*. London: Methuen.

Kohlberg, L. (1969) 'Stage and sequence: the cognitive-developmental approach to socialization' in D.A. Gosling (ed) *Handbook of Socialization Theory and Research*. Chicago: Rand McNally.

Lanier, M., and Henry, S. (1998) *Essential Criminology*. Boulder, CO: Westview Press.

Lipsey, M.W., and Wilson, D.B. (1998) 'Effective intervention for serious youth offenders: a synthesis of research' in R. Loeber and D.P. Farrington (eds) *Serious and Violent Juvenile Offenders: Risk Factors and Successful Interventions*. Thousand Oaks, CA: Sage.

Lipsey, M.W., Landenberger, N.A. and Chapman, G.L. (2004) 'Rehabilitation: an assessment of theory and research' in C. Sumner, (ed) *The Blackwell Companion to Criminology*, Oxford: Blackwell.

Little, A. (1965) 'Parental deprivation, separation and crime: a test on adolescent recidivists', *British Journal of Criminology* 5: 419–30.

Lloyd-Bostock, S. (1981) *Psychology in Legal Contexts: Applications and Limitations*. London: Macmillan.

Loftus, E.F. (1974) 'The Incredible Eyewitness', *Psychology Today*, December 117–19.

Loftus, E.F. (1979) *Eyewitness Testimony*. Cambridge: Harvard University Press.

Lorenz, K. (1966) *On Aggression*. New York: Harcourt Brace World.

Losel, F., Bender, D., and Bliesener, T. (eds) (1992) *Psychology and Law: International Perspectives*. Berlin: Walter de Gruyter.

McGuire, J. (ed) (1995) *What Works: Reducing Reoffending*. Chichester, John Wiley.

McGuire, J. (2000) *Cognitive Behavioural Approaches: An Introduction to Theory and Research*. London: HMSO.

McGuire, J. (2004) *Understanding Psychology and Crime*. Maidenhead: Open University Press.

McGuire, J., Mason, T., and O'Kane, A. (eds) (2000) *Behaviour, Crime and Legal Process: A Guide for Practitioners*, Chichester: John Wiley.

McGurk, B.J., Carr, M., and McGurk, D. (1993) *Investigative Interviewing Courses for Police Officers*, London: Home Office.

Mackay, R.D., Colman, A.M., and Thornton, P. (1999) 'The admissibility of expert psychological and psychiatric testimony' in A. Heaton-Armstrong, E. Shepherd, and D. Wolchover (eds) *Analysing Witness Testimony*, London: Blackstone.

Mednick, S.A., Moffitt, T.E., and Stack, S.A. (1987) *The Causes of Crime: New Biological Approaches*. Cambridge: Cambridge University Press.

Monahan, J., Loftus, E.R. (1982) 'The Psychology of Law', *Annual review of Psychology*, 33: 441–75.

Morrison, W. (1995) *Theoretical Criminology: from Modernity to Post-modernism*. London: Cavendish.

Morrison, W., (2004) 'Lombroso and the Birth of Criminological Positivism: Scientific Mastery or Cultural Artifice?' in J. Ferrell (*et al.*) *Cultural Criminology Unleashed*, London: Glass House.

Müller, D.J., Blackman, D.E., and Chapman, A.J. (eds) (1984) *Psychology and Law*. Chichester: John Wiley and Sons.

Nietzel, M.T. (1979) *Crime and its Modification: A Social Learning Perspective*. New York: Pergamon.

Peay, J. (2002) 'Mentally disordered offenders, mental health and crime' in M. Maguire *et al.* (eds) *The Oxford Handbook of Criminology* (3 edn). Oxford: Oxford University Press.

Piaget, J. (1954) *The Construction of Reality in the Child*. New York: Basic Books.

Pinizzotto, A.J. (1984) 'Forensic psychology: criminal personality profiling' *Journal of Police Science and Administration*, 12: 32–40.

Prins, H. (1986) *Dangerous Behaviour, the Law and Mental Disorder*, London: Tavistock.

Putwain, D. and Sammons, A. (2002) *Psychology and Crime*. London: Routledge.

Raine, A. (1993) *The Psychopathology of Crime: Criminal Behaviour as a Clinical Disorder*. San Diego, CA: Academic Press.

Raynor, P. (2002) 'Community penalties: probation, punishment and "What Works" ' in M. Maguire *et al.* (eds) *The Oxford Handbook of Criminology* (3rd edn). Oxford: Oxford University Press.

Redondo, S., Sanchez-Meca, J., and Garrido, V. (1999) 'The influence of treatment programmes on the recidivism of juvenile and adult offenders: a European meta-analytic review, *Psychology, Crime and Law*, 5: 251–78.

Reiser, M. (1973) *Practical Psychology for Police Officers*. Springfield, ILL: C.C. Thomas.

Ressler, R. and Shachtman, T. (1992) *Whoever Fights Monsters*. New York: St Martins.

Rider, A.O. (1980) 'The firesetter: a psychological profile', *FBI Law Enforcement Bulletin*, 49 (6): 6–13.

Roberts, P. (1996) 'Will you stand up in court? On the admissibility of psychiatric and psychological evidence', *Journal of Forensic Psychiatry* 7: 63–78.

Rotter, J.B., (1954) *Social Learning and Clinical Psychology*. Englewood Cliffs, NJ: Prentice Hall.

Rutter, M. (1972) *Maternal deprivation Reassessed*. Harmondsworth: Penguin.

Samenow, S.E. (1984) *Inside the Criminal Mind*. New York: Times Books.

Skinner, B.F. (1938) *The Behaviour of Organisms*. New York: Appleton.

Skinner, B.F. (1953) *Science and Human Behaviour*. New York: Macmillan.

Stevens, J.A. (1995) 'Offenders in profile' *Policing Today*, August.

Storr, A. (1970) *Human Aggression*, Harmondsworth: Penguin.

Strentz, T. (1988) 'A terrorist psychological profile', *Law Enforcement Bulletin*, 57: 11–18.

Sutherland, E. (1947) *Principles of Criminology*. Philadelphia: Lippincott.

Swanson, C.R., Chamelin, N.C., and Territo, L. (1984) *Criminal Investigation*. New York: McGraw-Hill.

Tapp, J.L. (1976) 'Psychology and law: an overture', *Annual review of Psychology*, 27: 359–404.

Taylor, I., Walton, P. and Young, J. (1973) *The New Criminology*. London: Routledge.

Terry, W.C. (1981) 'Police Stress: the Empirical Evidence', *Journal of Police Science and Administration*, 9: 61–75.

Towl, G.J. (2004) 'Applied psychological services in Prisons and Probation' in J.R. Adler (ed) *Forensic Psychology*. Cullompton: Willan.

Valier, C. (2001) 'Psychoanalytic Criminology' in McLaughlin, E., and Muncie, J. (eds) *The Sage Dictionary of Criminology*. London: Sage.

Vennard, J., and Hedderman, C. (1998) 'Effective Interventions with offenders' in P. Goldblatt and C. Lewis (eds) *Reducing Offending: An Assessment of Research Evidence on Ways of Dealing with Offending Behaviour*. Hove Office Research Study No. 187, London: Hove Office.

Watson, J.B. (1913) 'Psychology as the behaviorist views it', *Psychological Review*.

Yochelson, S. and Samenow, S. (1976) *The Criminal Personality*. New York: Jason Aronson.

Yuille, J.C. (1986) 'Police Selection and Training: The Role of Psychology'. Dordrecht: Martinus Nijhoff.

7 Crime and culture

Jeff Ferrell

INTRODUCTION

In contemporary society, criminal practices and cultural dynamics intertwine within the experiences of everyday life. Many common forms of criminality emerge out of criminal and deviant subcultures that are themselves shaped by shared conventions of meaning, symbolism, and style. These subcultures in turn produce intensely collective experiences and emotions that define their members' identities and reinforce their members' marginal social status. At the same time those who undertake enterprises conventionally defined as 'cultural'—popular music, art photography, film and television programmes—regularly confront public accusations of promoting criminal and delinquent behaviour, and at times face criminal justice actions ranging from police raids to obscenity trials. In today's society, all of these phenomena—criminal identities, popular controversies, crime control campaigns, experiences of crime victimization—are increasingly offered and displayed for public consumption. Moreover, all of these phenomena take shape within a larger mediated universe—a universe in which criminal subcultures appropriate popular images and create their own forms of mediated communication; political leaders launch public campaigns of criminalization and panic over crime and criminals; and everyday citizens go about consuming crime as news and entertainment. Because of this, criminologists today realize that a critical awareness of cultural dynamics is necessary if we are to understand even the most basic dimensions of crime and crime control.

BACKGROUND

Over the past few decades a number of criminologists have attempted to locate issues of crime and crime control within broader cultural dynamics. Generally speaking, culture refers to the shared symbolic environment in which the members of social groups operate—that is, their shared way of life within which everyday objects, practices, and interactions come to have meaning. In examining cultural dynamics, then, criminologists have investigated those features of everyday life that embody issues of symbolism and representation, and that therefore define the meaning of crime and crime control. During the 1970s, for example, the British 'Birmingham School' of cultural studies, and the radical theorists associated with the 'new criminology' (for example, Taylor et al., 1973, see Chapter 4 above), began to examine the mass media's role in constructing understandings of criminal subcultures and in contributing to crime control. Stanley Cohen (2002 [1972/1980/1987]) documented the media's role in casting members of youth subcultures as folk devils who symbolize danger and threat, and allegedly embody larger social problems. Through this process, Cohen argued, the media and public officials are also able to construct moral panic around otherwise inconsequential criminal events and identities, a sense among the public that a particular crime or criminal is in fact symptomatic of far greater social harms. Similarly, Jock Young (1971) showed how the police, public officials, and the media operate in such a way as to 'amplify' the reality of a criminal problem, rather than to solve it;

and others (Hall *et al.*, 1978) revealed that public officials and the mass media at times generate public concern over crimes and alleged crime patterns as a way of furthering their own political agendas.

During this same period, criminologists and sociologists in the US began to investigate the dynamics of illicit subcultures, and to develop a criminological perspective that came to be known as labelling theory (see Chapter 4 above, for more). In a groundbreaking book, Howard Becker (1963) demonstrated that the meaning of human activity is in large part defined by others' responses to it—in the case of crime and deviance, by the labelling of certain activities as criminal or deviant. Moreover, Becker showed, some groups and institutions hold far greater power than others to assign such labels; in many cases, it is the work of moral entrepreneurs—powerful individuals or groups pushing their own moral agenda—that results in activities being labelled criminal or deviant. Given this, Becker and others (Polsky, 1998 [1967]) argued, criminologists cannot simply rely on conventional understandings of groups labelled criminal or deviant; instead they must go inside the subcultures of such groups to explore the distinctive rituals, symbols, and practices that emerge there.

From the first, then, criminologists' attempts to account for the cultural context of crime and crime control have relied on a variety of disciplines. As the field of cultural studies emerged over the past few decades, so did criminologists' willingness to investigate often ignored dimensions of social life (popular culture, style and fashion, entertainment), and their understanding that these dimensions were essential to the practice of crime and crime control. As criminologists developed labelling theory and similar perspectives on crime's contested meaning, they relied on the insights offered by sociology, and specifically on the sociological approach known as symbolic interactionism—an approach that understands social reality to be constructed out of ongoing, meaningful social interaction. In addition, criminologists interested in cultural dynamics came to see the essential role of the mass media in constructing everyday understandings of crime and crime control, and so borrowed perspectives from fields like media studies and film studies. In this sense, the study of crime and culture intertwines with subjects explored elsewhere in this volume—among them 'media images of crime', 'crime and everyday life', 'young people and crime', 'criminological theory', and 'surveillance'.

Today, criminological interest in the cultural dynamics surrounding crime and crime control is flourishing. In many criminological works, an inquiry into the traditional subject matter of criminology—crime, criminals, policing, courts—has now been recast as an inquiry into 'media images of' or 'representations of' these phenomena. Moreover, many criminologists have now moved beyond simply studying the mass media's role in creating images or accounts of crime, and to an understanding that crime, crime control, and the media are endlessly entangled in a series of media loops (Manning, 1998) whereby each phenomenon reflects and embodies images of the other. Criminological understandings of criminal subcultures are also developing. Following the lead of early researchers (Hebdige, 1979), criminologists continue to explore style as the symbolic medium through which illicit subcultures define and display their identities, crime control agents respond to the subculture's public presence, and mass media institutions appropriate and portray subcultural images. Continuing to investigate also the internal meanings of these subcultures, criminologists embrace their own first-hand, appreciative understanding of criminality, their own sense of criminological verstehen (see below, and Ferrell, 1997), as they attempt to penetrate the situated logic and emotion of these worlds. In this way, for example, they are able to make sense of moments of illicit edgework (Lyng, 1990) in which subcultural skills and values become manifest in the experience of extreme risk. In fact, current criminological interest in the cultural and subcultural dynamics of crime and crime control is such that a new form of criminological research and theory has recently evolved: cultural criminology (Ferrell and Sanders, 1995; Presdee, 2000; Ferrell *et al.*, 2004; also Chapter 4).

Crime and culture

Among the many intersections of culture and crime, five in particular offer significant insights into the complex cultural dynamics within which the practice of crime and crime control takes shape.

Subculture and style

Much of the illicit behavior that criminologists study is organized and defined by criminal subcultures. Criminal subcultures provide repositories of skill from which subcultural members learn the techniques essential to successful criminal conduct, whether they be the skills needed for efficient automobile theft, surreptitious embezzlement, or effective violence. Perhaps more importantly, these subcultures create a collective ethos, a fluid set of values and orientations that define their members' criminal behaviour as appropriate, even honourable; in this way criminal subcultures also function as counter-cultures, ways of life that oppose and defy conventional understandings of legality, morality, and achievement. In most cases, these subcultural orientations come to be embodied in the subculture's distinctive style—subtle conventions of dress and comportment, distinctive linguistic codes often incomprehensible to the outsider, and everyday rituals designed to mark the boundaries of subcultural membership. Given this constellation of skills, attitudes, and styles, criminal subcultures operate as much more than proximities of personal association among their members. They become symbolic communities, communities of shared meaning that define for their members the nature of criminality perhaps more than does the criminal act itself.

Understood in this way, the powerful pull of criminal subcultures operates in ways that are as much cultural as interpersonal. Dressed in clothes that embody a host of illicit sartorial codes, fluent in the nuances of subcultural argot, wrapped in the defiant assurance of an 'outlaw' identity, a street gang member or race track hustler maintains subcultural membership even when no others are around; the subculture continues to surround its members even when they wander from it. At the extreme, this cultural dynamic suggests to criminologists that criminal subcultures can operate effectively even when their members have never come face-to-face; this dynamic in turn suggests to those concerned with controlling criminal subcultures and their dissemination that the task will not be as simple as arresting one member or another.

In the US, for example, hip hop graffiti writers have for many decades operated within conventions of style so carefully constructed that writers could effectively communicate status and meaning by way of 'tags' and murals even when they had never met, and could therefore know and understand one another as members of a shared urban subculture even without direct association. More recently, transcontinental freight trains have emerged as the preferred medium for hip hop tags and murals, and with them an illicit subculture that now stretches from New York City to Los Angeles, communicating, solidi-fying—even recruiting—by means of dislocated subcultural symbolism (Ferrell, 1998). At the other end of the technological spectrum from rusty freight trains and spray paint cans, illicit cyber-communities now operate within a welter of fabricated identities and stylized language practices that form powerful, encompassing associations among strangers around the world. In fact, it is just this symbolic construction of the subculture itself, this profound lack of face-to-face interaction, that keeps on-line communities of child pornographers or prostitutes so impenetrable to outside authorities (Jewkes, 2003; Jenkins, 2001).

And yet of course legal authorities themselves increasingly understand this cultural dynamic as well, and so turn to these very subcultural symbols and styles in their attempts to prevent or control criminal activity. Watching for the emergence of new linguistic or sartorial styles among marginal groups, instituting surveillance programmes based on subtleties of appearance or comportment, constructing official 'gang lists' on the basis of young people's sport shoes and tattoos, reading gang graffiti for signs of impending trouble, legal and political authorities contribute their own complex of meanings to these subculture styles and symbols, and so themselves come to participate in this ongoing cultural interplay (Ferrell, 2004). In doing so, they raise a host of troubling questions regarding definitions of crime and legitimate measures of crime control—questions that are essentially cultural in nature. Is it appropriate for probation officers to violate the probation of juvenile offenders on the basis of a juvenile's new 'gang' tattoo or choice of 'gang-related' attire (Miller, 1995)? Is 'racial profiling' or 'terrorist profiling' in the US and Great Britain an appropriate response to subtle displays of criminal affiliation, or in fact a form of institutionalized racism based on unfair stereotypes? Most broadly, in their attempts to respond to the symbolism and style of marginal subcultures, do legal authorities in effect criminalize the lives and activities of those on the margins by defining their styles as de facto indicators of criminality?

However powerful—or appropriate—is the response of legal authorities to the styles of illicit subcultures, there is another external response that likely has a more powerful effect—and along the way forges yet another link between crime and culture. Increasingly, clothing manufacturers, advertisers, and other member of the corporate economy recognize that the illicit styles of gang members, graffiti writers, street hustlers, pimps, and other 'outlaws' lend a degree of street legitimacy to fashion, music, and other commodities, especially when these commodities are designed for sale to young people (see Hayward, 2004: 166–73 for a series of examples of what he describes as 'the commodification of transgression'). Because of this, corporations carefully appropriate the symbolism and style of illegal subcultures, blending these styles into new product lines, and incorporating these styles in sophisticated marketing campaigns designed to promote new products. Losing ground to Japanese motorcycles and on the brink of bankruptcy, Harley-Davidson Motorcycles reinvented its product line, building the previously illicit, after-market styles of the outlaw biker subculture into the motorcycles produced in the Harley-Davidson factory, and promoting these newly stylized motorcycles through corporate advertizing campaigns; as a result, the company was reborn as a viable, profitable, and high-profile icon of leisure consumption (Lyng and Bracey, 1995). Similarly, as Heitor Alvelos (2004) has recently shown, corporate marketers in the UK and elsewhere have begun to copy the symbolism, style, even the placement of street graffiti—to the point that the legal, street-level graffiti of corporate advertising campaigns is at times indistinguishable from the illegal graffiti of hip hop graffiti writers and other illicit artists. In this way, corporate marketers, like legal authorities, add yet another layer of cultural meaning to the illicit codes of criminal subcultures—and in doing so, often do more to undermine the subcultural integrity of these codes, to sanitize their illicit purpose, than the legal authorities themselves.

REVIEW QUESTIONS

1 By displaying illicit styles, do members of criminal subcultures 'invite' legal surveillance and control? Are legal authorities justified in using these styles as indicators of criminality? If so, in what circumstances, and with what limitations?

2 Is it appropriate for major corporations to market the styles of illicit subcultures to young people and others? Should parents or school authorities be concerned if young people begin wearing clothes, or using language, associated with criminal subcultures?

Edgework, adrenalin, and criminological verstehen

While the lives of those engaged in criminal activity are sometimes shaped by their stylized subcultural identities, and by the response of others to these identities, a recent body of cultural criminological research has shown that they are often shaped by something else as well: a variety of intensely emotional and intensely meaningful collective experiences (Katz, 1988; Lyng, 1990; Ferrell, 1996; Hayward, 2004 Chapter 5; Jackson-Jacobs, 2004). In investigating a wide range of criminal activities, from street fighting to firesetting, criminologists have found that criminals often embrace the extreme risk and danger that accompanies their criminal activity; rather than shying away from such risk, or seeing it only as an unfortunate consequence of their illicit occupations, they come to enjoy it—to the point that they regularly report being 'addicted' to the dangerous experiences, to the 'adrenalin rushes', of criminality.

Often outsiders misunderstand this enjoyment of extreme risk as embodying out-of-control, haphazard orientations on the part of wildly violent criminals; others assume that this enjoyment of danger constitutes some sort of nihilistic death wish on the part of those disconnected from conventional morality. In fact, criminological research shows, it is neither. Instead of seeking death in these moments of extreme risk, criminals seem to be seeking a more vivid version of life itself, an experience that transcends the conventions of everyday living. And rather than being simply the product of out-of-control individuals, these 'edgework' experiences seem clearly to embody the work of criminal subcultures, integrating as they do illicit subcultural skills with moments of profound danger. Moreover, it is precisely these subcultural skills and attitudes that define the allure of edgework experiences; in such moments the counter-cultural values of the subcultural are confirmed at the level of existential experience, the value of the subculture's illicit skills now measured, and proven, against the risk of violent failure. After all, a burglar's skills matter most when silently jemmying open a window, a graffiti writer's most when spray painting a midnight alley wall. In the words of a member of the BASE jumping subculture, a woman who utilizes carefully honed subcultural skills to execute illegal, low-level parachute jumps from bridges and buildings, 'It isn't a death wish like everybody thinks it is. You know you're alive when you do this, every sense is working. . . . You want to live so you can do it again' (in Ferrell, 2002: 85).

The regularity with which members of illicit subcultures talk of 'adrenalin rushes' and 'addiction' to them, with which they dismiss the notion of a 'death wish', suggests yet another cultural dimension of these experiences: their meaning is constructed not only out of shared subcultural skills, but out of shared subcultural language. As criminological researchers have found time and again, subcultural members define the nature and importance of these experiences by talking about them—and by talking and thinking about them within a shared subcultural argot, or slang, that both defines particular experiences as unique to the subculture, and closes the meaning of these experiences to outsiders. In the seconds surrounding a moment of edgework, later in the evening over a pint, or years later as part of subcultural lore, the powerful meanings of edgework are constructed and reconstructed as they are negotiated within the linguistic structure of the subculture. As the criminologist Donald Cressey (1954) once argued in regard to 'compulsive' crimes, what appear to be ephemeral, individual experiences in this sense remain soundly collective and thoroughly cultural, defined as they are within shared 'vocabularies of motive'. And as with subcultural style, the collective conceptualization of edgework experiences ensures that an individual caught up in a moment of illicit excitement operates within the boundaries of the subculture, even when no one is there to notice.

At the same time existentially invigorating and subculturally meaningful, these edgework experiences provide further evidence for the powerful 'seductions' of crime (Katz, 1988); in them criminologists begin to glimpse a dynamic so powerful that criminals consistently characterize it as 'addictive'. The prevalence of these edgework experiences also suggests a significant critique of certain criminological theories. They cast doubt on 'rational choice' and 'routine activity' theories of criminality, theories that presume a sort of mechanistic, calculative rationality underlying criminal acts and situations; on the contrary, these edgework experiences reveal criminal acts animated by risk and excitement, and criminal situations sought after for their seductions (Young, 2003). More broadly, as Katz (1988) has argued, the vivid, seductive experiences of crime's 'foreground' call into question the usual assumption that criminological theories can account for crime by focusing primarily on 'background' or structural factors such as social class or ethnic inequality. While these background factors certainly remain interwoven with criminal acts, as do the existing codes and conventions of various criminal subcultures, they seem clearly to take on meaning inside the act itself, rather than simply 'causing' it in some exterior, deterministic fashion. Finally, the specific dynamics of these edgework experiences undermine—both conceptually and practically—crime control or crime deterrence models based on aggressive policing strategies. As the catalyst that brings these edgework experiences to life, risk is essential to their subcultural meaning and vitality— and so, as illicit edgeworkers regularly report, increased risk of legal apprehension generally amplifies, rather than diminishes, the adrenalin-fuelled seductions of the experience.

To the extent that moments of edgework and subcultural excitement shape the reality of criminality, conventional criminological methods of research must be reconsidered as well. Methods that simply accumulate crime statistics or tabulate survey responses cannot penetrate the negotiated meanings of these vivid foreground experiences; instead, methods are needed that can situate criminologists as close as possible to the immediacy of criminal situations and events. Because of this criminologists concerned with the dynamics of crime and culture, and especially those interested in investigating subcultural dynamics, often utilize field research or ethnographic methods that place criminologists, again as best as possible, inside the actual lives and experiences of criminals (see for example Ferrell and Hamm 1998). Pushing this methodology further still, these criminologists often pursue the goal of achieving criminological verstehen— a deep, even emotional understanding of the dangerous experiences that define criminality—as a way of gaining criminological insight unavailable to others. Such a methodology of course challenges conventional notions of research 'objectivity', and of criminology as a 'social science' of crime and crime control; it also raises for criminologists difficult issues of morality and legality. Still, if the meaning of crime is largely constructed in the immediacy its experience, how else are criminologists to investigate and understand it?

REVIEW QUESTIONS

1 Are there types of crime that are not shaped by edgework and excitement? If so, how is this category of criminality different from that defined by edgework?

2 Should there be moral or legal limits placed on verstehen-oriented criminological research with criminals? Are there types of crime for which we should not seek emotional understanding? Why not?

Culture as crime

If by 'culture' we mean the world of images and symbols, the complex symbolic environment of everyday life, then in contemporary society we can identify certain individuals and groups especially involved in constructing this cultural environment: artists, musicians, photographers, film makers, and television directors, for example. Some of these individuals and groups create forms of culture traditionally thought of as 'high culture', forms such as gallery and museum art, and fine art photography. Others produce television programmes, commercial films, popular music, and other cultural forms more commonly thought of as 'popular culture'. No matter what the cultural realm in which they operate, though, these individuals and groups remain vulnerable to having their cultural enterprises, and their cultural products, redefined as criminal. Time and again, fine art photographers whose work focuses on nude figures or sexually explicit subjects face accusations of producing not art, but obscenity and pornography. Musicians, producers, distributors, and retailers involved with musical forms as different as punk, heavy metal, and rap are regularly accused of disseminating obscene lyrics, and of influencing young listeners to commit assault, murder, or suicide. In the same way, television programmes, popular films, even animated cartoons are often blamed for inciting crime and delinquency, and for spinning off 'copy-cat crimes' in imitation of their content. In some cases these accusations of criminality simply circulate in the public realm; in other cases legal charges are brought, arrests made, and convictions gained. In either case, moral entrepreneurs and others regularly work to reconstruct cultural enterprises as criminal endeavours, to reconceptualize culture as crime.

Significantly, two often hidden threads run through the majority of theses cases, linking the criminalization of cultural forms as different as museum photography and rap music. First, those attempting to connect cultural products to crime often operate from a remarkably simplistic assumption: that cultural products directly induce imitative behaviour in those exposed to them, causing a 'copy-cat' reflex among listeners or viewers. In fact, cultural criminologists argue, this reductionist assumption fails on two fronts: it mistakenly reduces the complex workings of the cultural milieu to some sort of simple triggering mechanism, and it likewise reduces the complexities of human perception to a model of robotic reaction. Certainly the swarm of mediated images that saturates everyday life shapes to some degree the frameworks of perception and understanding within which individuals operate; in contemporary society, the sheer breadth of the mediated environment all but ensures that it will play a part in individuals' efforts to make sense of the world around them. This very breadth, though, also ensures that individuals will sort and assemble a remarkable range of cultural influences in constructing their values and behaviours, rather than responding unthinkingly to a single image or lyric. In this sense, the meanings and effects of cultural products reside less in the products themselves than in the interactions that surround them; their potential links to crime and delinquency are less predetermined than they are negotiated. And, to the extent that these negotiations take place within various criminal and non-criminal subcultures, yet another layer of ambiguous cultural meaning is added to the world of mediated information.

That complexities of cultural meaning and perception would be ignored in debates over culture's criminal or criminogenic (that is, crime-causing) properties is not surprising in light of a second thread running through these debates: their essential role within heated 'culture wars' over morality, sexuality, and ethnicity. In the great majority of cases, accusations linking cultural products to crime have emerged within larger political battles, and specifically as part of reactionary campaigns against cultural outsiders of one sort or another. This pattern becomes evident when one notices the identities of the accusers and of those accused. Cultural reactionaries, religious fundamentalists, and other conservative moral entrepreneurs regularly identify as obscene the works of gay photographers and of feminist, lesbian, and gay performance artists, and especially those works which allegedly embody anti-Christian images. In both Great Britain and the US, producers and performers of politically progressive punk music face police raids, confiscation of records and promotional materials, and charges of obscenity and distribution of harmful materials to minors. Rap musicians and producers, even record store owners stocking rap records, confront arrests, obscenity convictions, and carefully organized police boycotts that in many ways reproduce earlier, racialized condemnations of 'race music' styles like jazz and rock 'n' roll. In each of these cases, accusations of criminality emerge not from individual outrage, but as part of well-funded and highly publicized campaigns. And while some of these campaigns have in fact resulted in criminal charges and convictions, they in many ways succeed even when they do not. Publicizing allegations of criminality, publicly accusing artists and musicians of criminal conduct, these campaigns seem designed primarily to criminalize marginal groups at the level of image and perception, and thus to contribute to their ongoing stigmatization.

Operating in this way, these campaigns of pointed criticism against particular cultural producers, these organized moral panics over the criminogenic effects of everyday culture, embody a revealing irony: they don't stand apart from everyday culture so much as they participate in it. Such campaigns are themselves cultural enterprises, occupying the same mediated terrain as those they critique. Artists, photographers, and musicians work to create one set of cultural meanings around their work, defining it in terms of aesthetics, enjoyment, or social progress; those who accuse them of criminal behaviour work to create an alternative set of understandings shaped by orientations toward obscenity, crime, and delinquency. In this sense both groups contribute to the always-contested debate over crime and culture, and both groups do so through the same channels: press conferences and press releases, the distribution of evocative images, the organization of marketing campaigns and media coverage. Caught up in a series of self-reinforcing media loops, both groups construct their own images, and offer for public display images of the other's images, continually blurring as they do the boundaries separating culture from crime.

REVIEW QUESTIONS

1 If, in a court trial, the claim was made that the crimes of the accused had been caused by exposure to violent media images—that is, that the accused had simply committed a 'copy-cat' crime, and was therefore not personally culpable—what evidence could be presented to support this claim? What evidence could be presented to rebut this claim?

2 What guidelines might be developed to balance the potential harm of violent media imagery against humanistic values regarding freedom of speech and expression? Should mediated free expression be limited by concerns over its potential harm?

Crime, culture, and public display

Producing and disseminating countless images of crime, criminal justice, and victimization, the mass media put crime issues on display for everyday public consumption. But this is not the only way in which crime issues are displayed in contemporary society; they are also displayed as part of everyday social activities and interactions, and as part of the built environment within which social life goes on.

While crime is conventionally thought of as a secretive activity conducted away from public view, residual indicators of criminality often remain available for public scrutiny. Abandoned automobiles stripped of their parts, broken locks and unhinged gates, gang or hip hop graffiti on city walls, tyre tracks across a village green—all suggest something of criminal activity, and so become symbols that various groups and individuals 'read' for signs of safety or threat. In fact, one of the most prominent and politically influential criminological perspectives to develop in recent decades is based on an alleged understanding of this interplay between crime and public display. According to the model of 'broken windows' (Wilson and Kelling, 2003 [1982]), broken windows and other public displays of petty criminality signal a lack of surveillance or concern, in this way offering a symbolic invitation to more serious forms of criminality, and ultimately setting in motion a downward spiral of criminal disorder. Utilized as the scholarly justification for aggressive street policing strategies against beggars, homeless populations, graffiti writers, and others who commit visible 'quality of life' crimes in urban areas, this 'broken windows' thesis has significantly altered the politics and policing of the contemporary city.

From the perspective of cultural criminologists, however, the political utility of the 'broken windows' thesis has far exceeded its usefulness as an accurate, scholarly understanding of crime and public display. Certainly conservative politicians have found it a convenient foundation for their focus on the alleged criminality of marginal urban populations—but in this same context, cultural criminologists have found 'broken windows' to be an inadequate and politically distorted analysis of crime and culture. Arbitrarily assigning a series of abstract meanings to images and to imagined audiences, the 'broken windows' thesis in fact misses, rather than unmasks, the complex nuances of meaning and perception that link culture and crime. Depending on situational context, for example, a building's broken windows can offer, instead of an invitation to criminality, any number of alternative meanings to any number of audiences: a personal grudge, problems of absentee ownership, anticipated urban development, even informal community accommodation of the homeless. Likewise, urban graffiti can suggest to various groups a remarkable range of meanings, among them pride in ethnic heritage, an

Figure 7.1 Early hip hop graffiti: New York City subway train, c. 1970. The crown above the COCO 144 tag signifies Coco's claim to be a king in the emerging hip hop graffiti subculture.

Source: © Hulton Archive.

informal demarcation of drug sale territories, even the substitution of a symbolic status system for interpersonal violence. None of these symbolic meanings is self-evident or assured; each is negotiated day-to-day amidst the swirl of urban populations. Because of this, accurately understanding public display as a key nexus between crime and culture requires attentiveness and long-term emersion in everyday situations—not abstract political posturing.

Similarly complex issues emerge in considering public displays of crime control and crime prevention. Motivated by fear of crime, desperate to guard themselves against it, individuals at times display their fear for all to see, buffering their homes with 'No Trespassing' signs and their front gardens with displays of surveillance that coalesce into what Mike Davis (1992) has described, in a study of Southern California suburbia, as 'angry lawns'. Similarly, the sorts of 'target hardening' strategies often recommended as effective crime prevention sometimes operate as contradictory symbolic practices, with newly spiked fences, well-trained guard dogs, and expensive CCTV cameras suggesting that in this location there is indeed something worth protecting—and worth stealing. At a larger level, criminal justice agencies increasingly embrace the policing of public space through environmental design—that is, through the integration of symbolic control structures into public settings. Arguing that such structures can signal surveillance and control while at the same calming fear of crime, environmental designers utilize thorny bushes, CCTV cameras (whether activated or not), specially designed fences and park benches, and permanently elevated compartments (in which a police officer may or may not be hiding) to quite literally build displays of social control into the public environment. In doing so, of course, they at times transform policing from a process of human interaction into a display of symbolic control, and reconstruct open public space as significantly less open and public (Ferrell, 2002).

Perhaps the most evocative of contemporary public displays are those symbolizing the collective sorrow surrounding crime victimization and violence. The death of a celebrity often generates a broad and largely spontaneous public display of collective grief, with cascades of flowers, condolence notes, and photographs affixed to fences or piled in doorways; the massive accumulation of flowers in front of Kensington Palace following the death of Princess Diana stands as a particularly striking example. High-profile crime events and public tragedies likewise elicit countless public commemorations of loss and sorrow, as with the thousands of informal public shrines that emerged in Manhattan (and elsewhere) following the bombings of the World Trade Center. At other times, public memorials emerge in response to acts of victimization seen by the public as particularly egregious, or in the midst of moral panic over a perceived pattern of victimization; shrines and memorials dedicated to abducted or murdered children often develop in this context. Throughout the US, Mexico, Greece, Italy and other countries, friends and family members likewise build shrines to those lost to automotive violence; such shrines are often constructed at the location of a deadly automotive wreck, at times even incorporating pieces of the wreckage along with flowers, photographs, and personal memorabilia (Ferrell, 2003). In all of these cases, such public memorials forge yet another link between crime and culture as they help construct the collective meaning of crime victimization, begin to create a new symbolic identities for the victims of crime, and organize opportunities for ongoing, shared public commemoration.

Faced with the proliferation of these public memorials, criminal justice agencies have developed a variety of responses. Some have moved to prohibit such memorials on the grounds that they encourage illegal public gatherings and pose a distracting danger to motorists and other members of the public. Other agencies have attempted to regulate and standardize the memorials, setting limits on their size, location, and temporal duration, and working to bring their construction and maintenance under the jurisdiction of the agencies themselves. Still other criminal justice and governmental agencies have enacted procedures to protect these informal public memorials on the grounds that they often embody significant cultural traditions, and offer important opportunities for the expression of collective grief. Yet as different as they are, all of these official responses affirm the importance of these memorials, and of other public displays, as components of the symbolic environment within which we makes sense of crime and justice.

REVIEW QUESTIONS

1 As you move about your everyday environment, what symbols of crime, crime control, or crime victimization do you see? How do you interpret these in terms of your own sense of safety or vulnerability?

2 How might a person's interpretations of public displays associated with crime or crime control vary based on that person's gender, sexual orientation, social class, age, or ethnic origin?

Media, crime, and crime control

In contemporary society the mass media provide the preponderance of the public's information on crime and crime control (see also Chapter 8). In order to understand public support for particular crime control policies, then, or public concerns over everyday criminality, the various media of mass communication must be examined. When they are examined, a significant pattern emerges: the mass media transmit not only information, but emotion. In both news and entertainment programming, the mass media regularly overemphasize the threat posed by street-level crime in comparison to the harms of corporate criminality; focus on the criminal victimization of strangers rather than the dangerous intimacies of domestic or family conflict; and overplay violent criminality in comparison to more pervasive, non-violent property crime. While these particular patterns of sensationalism result in some part from political manipulation of the media, and from the media's reliance on official sources, they seem to be driven in large part by the media's ongoing desire to build television ratings, sell newspapers and magazines, and increase profits. Yet whatever their source, the cumulative effect of these distortions remains soundly political; they regularly amplify and misdirect public fears over crime, set inappropriately punitive public agendas regarding crime control, and ready the public for the next moral panic over crime and criminality.

In this sense contemporary media do not simply report, with greater or lesser accuracy, on existing crime and crime control issues; instead, the media actively participate in constructing the social reality of these very issues. Politicians and moral entrepreneurs utilize the media to deploy evocative crime imagery as they work to consolidate political power or criminalize marginal groups. Policing agencies increasingly coordinate their operations with those of existing media institutions, and develop their own channels of mediated communication and surveillance, in the interest of gaining public support, recruiting new members, and apprehending criminals. At the same time, everyday policing operations themselves become fodder for 'reality' television programming, with televised police chases and high-profile sting operations presented in the form of morally-charged entertainment. All the while, commercial films, popular music, and nightly television programming offer a swarm of crime and crime control characterizations, by turns celebrating and condemning the activities of outlaws, police officers, and judges. In the end, this ongoing stream of dramatic imagery accumulates into a vast cultural stockpile, a complex of images, symbols, and meanings by which individuals and groups come to make sense of crime, violence, and crime control. In doing so, they participate in a looping, self-fulfilling process by which symbols of criminality or images of violence refer not so much to external experience as to other images and symbols, as each new mediated moment references earlier mediated meanings and understandings.

Not surprisingly, those occupying criminal or criminalized worlds also participate in this endless process of mediated negotiation. Street gangs, skinheads, hip hop graffiti writers and other groups maintain websites designed to present their own understandings of crime and society. Urban skateboarders shoot illicit videos as they defiantly trespass on private property or skate across the very physical barriers designed to control them. Outlaw BASE jumpers wear helmet-mounted video cameras to record their own illegal parachuting from bridges and buildings, circulating these videos within the BASE jumping underground, and often selling them to mass media outlets as a way of raising funds for the next illegal jump (Ferrell, Milovanovic, and Lyng, 2001). Within progressive political groups, videographers and 'camcordistas' play an increasingly important role, as they employ video cameras to document police misconduct during street protests and to create their own alternative news footage. In this sense, as McRobbie and Thornton (1995) have noted, marginal groups are not always passive victims of the moral panic constructed around them; with the emergence of new media technologies, they are at times able to create their own images of crime and crime control, to counter the construction of moral panic, and to turn mediated moral panic to their own ends. In this way both the mass media and the micromedia of marginal or criminal groups engage in an endless appropriation and reinvention of each other's images and understandings.

These contemporary perspectives on mediated meaning as an essential component of crime and crime control continue the refinement of key concepts such as 'moral panic' and 'moral entrepreneurship'; these perspectives also expand the conceptual range of labelling theory. In the contemporary world, the labelling process—that is, the labelling of certain individuals, groups, and activities as criminal—can be seen operating not only among individuals and within institutions, but amidst an emergent mediated environment. As political leaders, policing agencies, mass media organizations, and illicit subcultures produce images of crime and crime control—and contested images of each other, and of each others' images—they engaged the public in negotiating the meaning of crime itself.

In this sense, these public, mediated negotiations of crime's meaning offer us also an image of the labelling process writ large. Yet despite these important conceptual advances, much scholarly work on media, crime, and crime control remains to be done.

In particular, the many and varied audiences for these public negotiations require closer attention; the actual meanings of mediated crime imagery in the daily lives of various groups and populations, its lived effects inside their everyday experiences, often remain more imagined than investigated.

REVIEW QUESTIONS

1 What can be done to correct the mass media's distortion and over-dramatization of crime issues?

2 Is it appropriate for criminal or criminalized groups to produce their own websites and videos? Should there be limits on these sorts of illicit media?

CONCLUSION

In the many confluences of crime and culture, certain patterns can be seen time and again. Subcultures organized around criminal or marginal behaviour emerge also as communities of shared symbolism and meaning, encoding common experience in counter-cultural values and expectations, inventing rituals that confirm and celebrate legal marginality, and indulging in nuances of alternative language, demeanour, and style. For their part, legal authorities attend to these symbolic displays in their efforts at surveillance and control, often policing the culture of crime as much as crime itself; corporate marketers work to appropriate such displays, hoping to capture something of their edgy currency; and the mass media utilize such symbolic displays as dramatic markers of criminality, drafting from them gross caricatures of criminality in the interest of constructing folk devils and moral panic. In this way, all the parties to crime and crime control operate within a common if contested cultural milieu, shaping the reality of crime through the medium of symbolism and style. In turn, these negotiations of meaning develop within larger cultural frames: a mediated environment already saturated by crime as news and entertainment, a political culture cut through by controversies linking art and music to crime and criminality, and a human landscape dotted with public displays of criminality, crime control, and crime victimization. And yet, within this contested cultural vortex, members of criminal subcultures continue to find experiences of edgework and adrenalin—experiences of intense, situated affirmation—if only for a moment.

This ongoing cultural construction of crime and crime control intertwines with other areas of criminological concern as well, many of them considered in this volume. It is of course within this larger context of culture and crime that the importance of critically analyzing 'media images of crime' (see Chapter 8) begins to make sense. In addition, the links between 'crime and everyday life' (see Chapter 9 below) can be seen to be as much cultural as experiential, constructed as they are out of culturally manufactured perceptions of crime's consequences, and experiences given meaning within broader cultural frames of reference and interpretation. 'Young people and crime' (see Chapter 19) seem especially to be connected by way of illegal or marginal subcultures, stylized representations of illicit identity, and mediated images of criminality—and for young people and others, the experience of edgework and adrenalin offers one of many powerful links between 'psychology and crime' (see Chapter 6 above). As already seen, such stylized identities in turn provide opportunities for 'surveillance' on the part of legal authorities (see Chapter 23 below). In these ways the study of crime and culture has become an essential component in the larger practice of criminological inquiry—and yet it has also begun to take shape as a distinctly cultural criminology that today contributes to the pantheon of 'criminological theory' (see Chapter 4).

Perhaps most importantly, the connections between crime and culture continue always to evolve; crime and crime control can best be understood not as accomplished cultural facts, but as ongoing cultural processes. For this reason any attempt to document the subtleties of subcultural style or to catalogue the range of mediated crime representations becomes, at the moment of its writing, a cultural history—important in its own right, but already a step behind the emerging trajectory of crime and culture. And for this reason it is essential that students—those who are already becoming the next generation of criminological scholars—become involved in researching and analyzing the connections between crime and culture. Existing scholarship, no matter what its merits, can never be enough; it can only offer a foundation from which to build new understandings of crime and culture.

This task takes on particular significance when the contemporary politics of crime and culture are considered. The intersection of culture and crime is today emerging as an essential domain of political and moral conflict; it is here that fundamental issues of human identity and social justice are being contested. The scope and effects of everyday surveillance and criminal profiling; the balancing of free expression versus the potential for social harm; the negotiation of boundaries separating art from obscenity, or popular culture from pornography; the legitimacy and popularity of competing crime control agendas; the proper role of various media forms in the policing of contemporary society—all of these issues take shape in the interplay of crime and culture. Because of this, the critical analysis of crime and culture is no abstract intellectual exercise; it is, at its best, an exercise in engaged citizenship and informed activism.

QUESTIONS FOR DISCUSSION

1 Select a controversial issue having to do with crime or crime control—the legal rights of immigrants, for example, or the prevalence of domestic violence. Using only images culled from the mass media and popular culture, create a visual essay that presents your critical understanding of this issue.

2 Construct a set of guidelines for mass media coverage of everyday crime. Consider not only the fairness and accuracy of particular news reports, but ways to ensure that the cumulative effect of ongoing crime reporting is helpful to the public's understanding of larger crime issues.

3 If the possession and consumption of coffee were to be made illegal, what sort of illicit subculture might evolve among users of coffee? What sorts of subcultural values, styles, rituals, and experiences might emerge? Why?

4 If, upon the event of your death, your family and friends built a public memorial to you, what sorts of images and cultural references would you want included in it?

5 This chapter has discussed the styles, rituals, and practices of criminal subcultures. But what is the subculture of policing in Great Britain? In what ways is this police subculture similar to, or different from, the subcultures formed by criminal or marginalized groups?

GUIDE TO FURTHER READING

Ferrell, J., Hayward, K., Morrison, W. and Presdee, M. (eds) (2004) *Cultural Criminology Unleashed*. London: GlassHouse Press.

This book expands the theoretical and substantive range of cultural criminology, and includes research into culture and crime across a variety of local, regional, and national settings.

Ferrell, J. and Sanders, C.R. (eds) (1995) *Cultural Criminology*. Boston: Northeastern University Press.

The first book to define the new criminological approach known as 'cultural criminology', this work builds from earlier British and American studies of crime and culture, and includes chapters on mass media, music, subcultures, and style.

Cohen, S. (2002 [1972, 1980, 1987]) *Folk Devils and Moral Panics* (3rd edn). London: Routledge.

Now in its third edition, this book remains a classic study in the intersections of culture and crime. The ongoing vitality and importance of Cohen's 'folk devil' and 'moral panic' concepts are highlighted in a new introduction to this third edition.

Presdee, M. (2000) *Cultural Criminology and the Carnival of Crime*. London: Routledge.

This book utilizes the lens of cultural criminology to examine a wide range of everyday practices—raving, joyriding, and sadomasochism, for example—and finds among them the shattered remains of human carnival.

Hayward, K. (2004) *City Limits: Crime, Consumer Culture and the Urban Experience*. London: GlassHouse Press.

This book offers the reader a series of unique cultural insights into the way that urban space is changing. Expanding the vision of criminology by drawing on cultural studies, social theory, urban studies, architectural theory and research into urban consumerism practices, Hayward argues that consumption is now central to understanding the crime-city relationship.

Crime, Media, Culture: An International Journal. London: Sage.

This new criminological journal provides a forum for international research into crime and culture. The journal includes works on crime and media, and on the cultural dynamics of crime and criminal justice; it also includes photographs and photographic essays relating to crime and culture.

Silver, Tony, director (1983) *Style Wars*. New York: Plexifilm.

Produced by Henry Chalfant, this historic documentary traces the evolution of hip hop graffiti within the larger hip hop culture of music and dance.

Valdez, Luis, director (1982). *Zoot Suit*. Los Angeles: Universal Studios.

Based on the highly regarded stage play, this film examines the historical emergence of the stylized Latino Zoot Suiter in the United States (particularly Los Angeles), and explores the cultural politics of the 1940s 'zoot suit riots' in Los Angeles.

WEB LINKS

Art Crimes http://www.graffiti.org/

An extensive, updated archive of hip hop graffiti images, this site also includes a variety of resources and links regarding hip hop graffiti.

CultureX http://www.indiana.edu/~culturex/

Maintained by Professor Stephanie Kane, this site offers a guide to issues in culture, law, and crime.

StopViolence.Com http://stopviolence.com/ and
Paul's Justice Page http://www.paulsjusticepage.com/

Maintained by Professor Paul Leighton, these two sites offer a variety of resources, essays, images, and links relating to contemporary crime and crime control issues.

REFERENCES

Alvelos, H. (2004) 'The Desert of Imagination in the City of Signs: Cultural Implications of Sponsored Transgression and Branded Graffiti' in J. Ferrell, K.J. Hayward, W. Morrison and M. Presdee (eds), *Cultural Criminology Unleashed*. London: GlassHouse Press.

Becker, Howard S. (1963) *Outsiders: Studies in the Sociology of Deviance*. New York: Free Press.

Cohen, Stanley (2002 [1972, 1980, 1987]) *Folk Devils and Moral Panics* (3rd edn). London: Routledge.

Cressey, Donald (1954) 'The Differential Association Theory and Compulsive Crime', *Journal of Criminal Law and Criminology* 45: 49–64.

Davis, M. (1992) *City of Quartz*. New York: Vintage.

Ferrell, J. (1996) *Crimes of Style: Urban Graffiti and the Politics of Criminality*. Boston: Northeastern University Press.

Ferrell, J. (1997) 'Criminological Verstehen: Inside the Immediacy of Crime', *Justice Quarterly* 14(1): 3–23.

Ferrell, J. (1998) 'Freight Train Graffiti: Subculture, Crime, Dislocation', *Justice Quarterly* 15(4): 587–608.

Ferrell, J. (2002) *Tearing Down the Streets: Adventures in Urban Anarchy*. New York: Palgrave/Macmillan.

Ferrell, J. (2003) 'Speed Kills' *Critical Criminology* 11(3): 185–98.

Ferrell, J. (2004) [1995]. 'Style Matters', reprinted in J. Ferrell, K. Hayward, W. Morrison, and M. Presdee (eds) (2004) *Cultural Criminology Unleashed*: 61–63. London: GlassHouse Press, forthcoming.

Ferrell, J., Hayward, K.J., Morrison, W., and Presdee, M. (eds) (2004) *Cultural Criminology Unleashed*. London: GlassHouse Press.

Ferrell, J., Milovanovic, D., and Lyng, S. (2001) 'Edgework, Media Practices, and the Elongation of Meaning', *Theoretical Criminology* 5(2): 177–202.

Ferrell, J., and Hamm, M. (eds) (1998) *Ethnography at the Edge: Crime, Deviance and Field Research*, Boston: Northeastern University Press.

Ferrell, J. and Sanders, C.R. (eds) (1995) *Cultural Criminology*. Boston: Northeastern University Press.

Hall, S., Critcher, C., Jefferson, A., Clarke, J. and Roberts, B. (1978) *Policing the Crisis: Mugging, the State, and Law and Order*. London: Macmillan.

Hayward, K.J. (2004) *City Limits: Crime, Consumer Culture and the Urban Expression*. London: GlassHouse.

Hebdige, D. (1979) *Subculture: The Meaning of Style*. London: Methuen.

Jackson-Jacobs, C. (2004) 'Taking a Beating: Narrative Gratifications of Fighting as an Underdog' in J. Ferrell, K.J. Hayward, W. Morrison and M. Presdee (eds), *Cultural Criminology Unleashed*: 231–244. London: GlassHouse Press.

Jenkins, P. (2001) *Beyond Tolerance: Child Pornography on the Internet*. New York: New York University Press.

Jewkes, Y. (ed) (2003) *Dot.cons: Crime, Deviance and Identity on the Internet*. Devon, UK: Willan.

Katz, J. (1988) *Seductions of Crime: Moral and Sensual Attractions in Doing Evil*. New York: Basic Books.

Lyng, S. (1990) 'Edgework: A Social Psychological Analysis of Voluntary Risk Taking' *American Journal of Sociology* 95: 851–86.

Lyng, S. and Bracey, Jr., M.L. (1995) 'Squaring the One Percent: Biker Style and the Selling of Cultural Resistance' in J. Ferrell and C.R. Sanders (eds), *Cultural Criminology*: 235–76. Boston: Northeastern University Press.

Manning, P. (1998) 'Media Loops' in F. Bailey and D. Hale (eds) *Popular Culture, Crime, and Justice*: 25–39. Belmont CA: West/Wadsworth.

McRobbie, A. and Thornton, S.L. (1995) 'Rethinking "Moral Panic" for Multi-Mediated Social Worlds', *British Journal of Sociology* 46: 559–74.

Miller, J. (1995) 'Struggles Over the Symbolic: Gang Style and the Meanings of Social Control' in J. Ferrell and C.R. Sanders (eds), *Cultural Criminology*: 213–34. Boston: Northeastern University Press.

Polsky, N. (1998 [1967]) *Hustlers, Beats, and Others*. New York: Lyons Press.

Presdee, M. (2000) *Cultural Criminology and the Carnival of Crime*. London: Routledge.

Taylor, I., Walton, P. and Young, J. (1973) *The New Criminology*. New York: Harper & Row.

Wilson, J.Q. and Kelling, G.L. (2003 [1982]). 'Broken Windows: The Police and Neighborhood Safety' reprinted in E. McLaughlin, J. Muncie, and G. Hughes (eds.), *Criminological Perspectives: Essential Readings* (2nd edn): 400–441. London: Sage.

Young, J. (2003) 'Merton with Energy, Katz with Structure: The Sociology of Vindictiveness and the Criminology of Transgression', *Theoretical Criminology* 7(3): 389–414.

Young, J. (1971) 'The Role of the Police as Amplifiers of Deviancy, Negotiators of Reality and Translators of Fantasy' in Stanley Cohen (ed), *Images of Deviance*, 27–61. Harmondsworth, UK: Penguin.

8

Crime and media: understanding the connections

Chris Greer

We live in an age of 'media saturation', an age in which media play an increasingly central role in everyday life. It is also an age in which high crime rates and high levels of concern about the crime have become accepted as 'normal'. The rapid and relentless development of information technologies over the past one hundred years has shaped the modern era, transforming the relations between space, time and identity (see Giddens, 1991; Castells, 1996; Jewkes, 2002; Greer, 2004). Where once 'news' used to travel by ship, it now hurtles across the globe at light speed and is available 24 hours-a-day at the push of a button. Where once cultures used to be more or less distinguishable in national or geographical terms, they now mix, intermingle and converge in a constant global exchange of information. Where once a sense of community and belonging was derived primarily from established identities and local traditions, it may now also be found, and lost, in a virtual world of shared values, meanings and interpretations. In short, media are not only inseparable from contemporary social life; they are, for many, its defining characteristic. Understanding the connections between crime and the media is central to understanding the cultural place that crime and media occupy in our social world.

This chapter is an introduction to the investigation of crime and media. My main aim is to present a summary of some of the major themes and debates which have shaped the research agenda. But I also want to sharpen the focus of investigation on some less well rehearsed issues. The chapter is divided into four principal sections. The first offers some background information and addresses the crucial question of why exploring media images of crime and control is important. The second section considers how scholars have gone about researching crime and the media, and presents an overview of the main findings. The third section critically discusses the dominant theoretical and conceptual tools which have been used to understand and explain media representations of crime? And the fourth section considers the evidence for the effects of media representations, both on criminal behaviour and on fear of crime. Finally, I will offer some tentative suggestions about useful areas for future research and investigation.

BACKGROUND

Fortunately, though sections of the popular press may suggest otherwise, most of us have little first-hand experience of serious criminal victimization. Our understanding of the crime problem—how much crime is out there, what types of crime are most prevalent, who is most at risk, what are the best responses—mostly derives from sources other than personal experience. Paramount among these are the media. The media, then, are key producers and purveyors of 'knowledge' about crime, disorder and control. For this reason alone, media representations are worthy of in-depth investigation.

But precisely what kinds of knowledge do these representations generate, and to what effect? Below are some of the key questions which have perplexed students of crime and the media:

- Is it possible to discern a coherent picture of 'the crime problem' from the media and, if so, does this picture bear any resemblance to what we may claim, however tentatively, to know of the 'reality' of crime and disorder?

- Do the media merely reflect, objectively and impartially, what happens in the world, or are they active agents in socially constructing 'mediated realities' in which certain values, interests and beliefs are promoted, while others are downplayed, or even actively suppressed?

- Do the media reproduce and reinforce prejudice and the stereotyping of marginalized groups, or actively challenge it?

- Do the media undermine or fortify the existing structures of power and authority?

- Does violence in the media make us more aggressive, more fearful, or both?

Concern about the pernicious influence of the media is perennial, and academic research exploring media representations of crime dates back to the early 1900s (Pearson, 1983; Bailey and Hale, 1996). Yet despite literally thousands of studies, these key questions have generated few straight answers. It is important to be clear that the media cannot (if they ever could) be usefully thought of in the singular, like some monolithic, unified institution to be understood through generalized statements and assumptions. The media *are* a multiplicity of institutions, organisations, processes and practices which are hugely diverse in composition, scope and purpose (Fiske, 1990; Briggs and Cobley, 1998). Today there are more media forms (television, newspapers, magazines, radio, the Internet, mobile phone Wireless Application Protocol (WAP) technology) and greater levels of diversity within each individual form (satellite, cable and digital television), than ever before. Understanding media, therefore, requires a critical and reflexive appreciation both of the diversity of forms and formats involved and of the complexity with which images, texts, messages, signs are produced, transmitted and received.

One of the key points to grasp—and one of the issues I want to communicate most forcefully—is that we do not all use, interpret, and respond to media representations in the same way. Images of violent crime, for example, may repel some and attract others, disturb some and excite others, frighten some and anger others. I, along with the other contributors in this collection, am keen to encourage you to look beyond the instinctive desire to tackle complex dilemmas with simplified accounts and generalizations. The relationship between media images and the world around us is so fascinating precisely because it is complex and hard to pin down.

Researching crime and media

Research on crime and the media can be broadly split between studies which are primarily either quantitative or qualitative. Quantitative analyses are concerned first and foremost with measuring the *amount* of crime, violence or control in the media—for example, the number of crime stories reported in a newspaper, or the number of violent incidents appearing in a television programme. The 'media picture' of crime is then compared and contrasted with the 'real world' picture, normally derived from official criminal statistics. Quantitative approaches have traditionally predominated in research on media content. Qualitative analyses, by contrast, are concerned primarily with investigating the *nature* of media representations of crime, violence and control. Though they often incorporate some quantitative component, qualitative research is more interested in untangling the complex processes through which media images are produced, exchanged and interpreted—for example, by exploring the use of language, the forces and constraints that shape media production, or the wider influence of the economic, political and cultural environment. Both quantitative and qualitative analyses may be equally concerned with media effects.

Each approach has its strengths and weaknesses, but some of the limitations of purely quantitative research are particularly noteworthy. Official statistics are a very poor indicator of crime rates and, in fact, may arguably reveal more about the reporting and recording practices of the police and the public than they do about actual levels of offending (Maguire, 2002). Quantitative claims about the relationship between media images and the statistical 'reality' of crime, therefore, need to be treated with caution. More fundamentally, because quantitative analyses cannot tackle the crucial issue of meaning, for many they can only ever provide a superficial description of media representations of crime rather than a deeper understanding, which would generally be the favoured research outcome. Nevertheless, quantitative research can offer important insights into patterns and trends in the representation of crime, as well as generating useful data on which more substantive qualitative investigations can be based.

The nature and extent of crime in the media

A virtually universal finding in the literature is that media representations exaggerate both the levels of serious interpersonal crime in society and the risk of becoming a crime victim. This is the case for studies of newspapers (Marsh, 1991), television (Gunter *et al.*, 2003) and radio content (Cumberbatch *et al.*, 1995), across both news and entertainment media (Reiner *et al.*, 2000a), and literary crime fiction (Knight, 2004). The representation of crime, most significantly in the news media, is largely event-oriented in that it focuses on specific criminal cases and incidents rather than wider debates around causes, prevention, or policy (Rock, 1973; Greer, 2003a). All media forms focus overwhelmingly on violent or sexual offences.

Calculations of the proportion of news space devoted to crime may vary considerably depending on the definition of 'crime' adopted, and the types of material included and excluded on that basis. Some studies, for example, may only include news reports of particular criminal events or court cases (Ditton and Duffy, 1983; Smith, 1984). Others, in addition to considering news reports, may also include feature items, editorial pieces and letters to the editor (Ericson *et al.*, 1987). Studies may also expand the definition of 'crime' to explore a wider range of deviant acts, such as corporate offending (Cavender and Mulcahy, 1998; Tombs and White, 2001), environmental crime (Lynch *et al.*, 2000), and state violence (Herman and Chomsky, 1994). 'Popular' (normally tabloid) news outlets are generally found to include a greater proportion of crime stories reported in a more sensationalistic style than 'quality' (broadsheet) ones (Graber, 1980; Schlesinger and Tumber, 1994). Estimates of the amount of crime in the UK news media range from an overall average proportion of 4 per cent in one study (Roshier, 1973) to 13 per cent in another (Williams and Dickinson, 1993). A summary of content analyses in the US found the proportion of crime news to range from just over one per cent, to more than 30 per cent (Marsh, 1991). In the entertainment media, an average of around 25 per cent of US

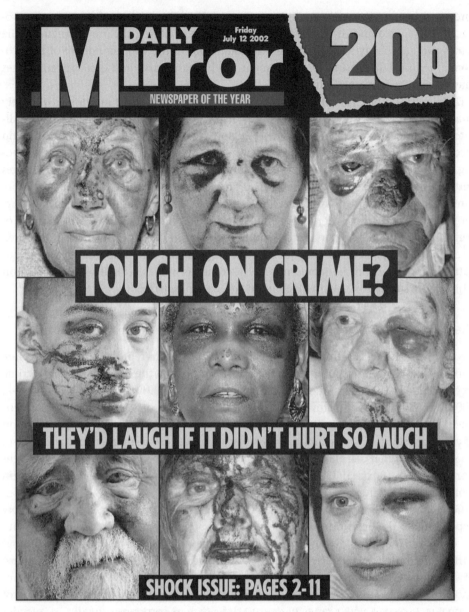

Figure 8.1 Tough on crime? They'd laugh if it didn't hurt so much.

Source: © Mirrorpix.

and UK primetime television programming, and around 20 per cent of film releases are crime stories (Dominick, 1978; Allen *et al.*, 1997; Reiner *et al.*, 2000a).

Given the limitations of purely quantitative analyses, many of these studies have also attempted to develop a qualitative appreciation of media representations by investigating their structure, meaning and origins, or by scrutinizing language, style, presentation and context. A number of studies have adopted this kind of approach. My own research provides one useful illustration. In *Sex Crime and the Media: Sex Offending and the Press in a Divided Society* (2003a), I investigated changes in reporting throughout the 1980s and 1990s within a context of ongoing political conflict (Greer, 2001a, b; 2003b). Quantitatively, the amount of press attention to sex crime increased massively over the period, more than trebling between 1985 and 1997. Qualitatively, reports became increasingly case-based and featured ever-diminishing levels of discussion around wider issues like crime prevention and personal safety. Significantly, on the few occasions on which advice was forthcoming, it was nearly always in relation to cases involving a predatory sex attacker on the loose. Compounded by the use of emotive and sometimes highly inflammatory language, and the selective reporting of only certain types of sexual offence, the prevalent but deeply misleading notion that strangers pose the greatest threat was consistently reinforced.

In order to explain these and other findings, the representation of sex crime was located within the wider contexts of social, political, economic and cultural change in late modernity. A range of factors were found to be of particular significance. These included: growing competition in the newspaper market; the power relations between journalists, editors and news sources; the impact on social awareness of particular high profile cases; the relentless campaigning activities of victim groups; changes in the political climate in Northern Ireland; and wider cultural shifts in thinking about sex and crime, and law and order more generally. Collectively, these factors have contributed to increasing the newsworthiness of sex crime and altering, sometimes radically, popular consciousness about the full range of sexual offences. The resulting intensification of public interest is not necessarily a bad thing; the problem of sexual violence is now a public issue, no longer 'hidden' behind social awkwardness and cultural taboos. But a parallel consequence has been the generation of a media space in which the reporting of sex crime is increasingly event-oriented, progressive discussion and debate are increasingly rare, and press representations become ever-more starved of useful information.

Qualitative studies employ a range of research methodologies, including interviews—with journalists, editors and producers, police and probation officers, and victims and offenders—audience research—focus groups to explore what media representations 'mean' to media consumers—and ethnography—immersing oneself in the natural environment of the research subjects (for example, exploring crime journalism through working in a newsroom). The significant contribution of this type of research is to offer the potential for explanation and understanding over description (see Soothill and Walby, 1991; Jenkins, 1992, 1994; Sparks, 1992; Kitzinger and Skidmore, 1995; Allen *et al.*, 1997; Reiner *et al.*, 2000a, b; Reiner, 2001; Leishman and Mason, 2003).

REVIEW QUESTIONS

1 Why is it both important and useful to study crime and the media?

2 What are the main differences between quantitative and qualitative methods of content analysis and what are their respective strengths and weaknesses?

3 Can a coherent picture of the crime problem be discerned from media representations? If so, what is it, and is it accurate?

This section has provided a brief review of the research literature on the content of media representations of crime and control and drawn attention to some of the factors that may influence that content. The aim in the next section is to establish a clearer picture of the forces and influences that shape media representations of crime.

Theorizing crime and media

Crime news is not simply plucked out of thin air. Nor does it exist in a vacuum. It is the end result of a complex process of selection, processing and prioritization, and is shaped by interactions between journalists, editors, their working conditions, the wider environment and, crucially, news sources. News sources are those individuals, organizations and institutions which provide the information to journalists on which news stories are often based. In relation to crime news, key sources include the police, probation, prison and court services, politicians, penal reform groups, victim organisations, and a host of other interested parties.

Reporting crime takes time, money and effort. Editors and producers seek to maximize the efficiency and cost effectiveness of this process by concentrating limited resources around sources which can offer consistently reliable and reportable crime material within the rhythms of the news production process. Powerful criminal justice institutions like the police and the judiciary routinely produce a significant volume of reportable information, and are therefore extremely useful to crime journalists. For this reason, they enjoy what Hall *et al.* (1978) refer to as 'privileged access' in the media: that is, they find it easier than less powerful, or less useful (in news terms), organizations to have their views or version of events publicized. This 'privileged access' is further enhanced by the credibility and cultural authority—the 'expert status'—associated with official agencies on matters of crime and control (Ericson *et al.*, 1989, 1991). That journalists are to an extent reliant on powerful institutional sources is undeniable. The consequences of this reliance, however, and the wider implications for the democratic flow of information and the objectivity and impartiality of the news product, may be interpreted very differently depending on the theoretical approach adopted.

Media theory and crime news production

Analyses of media production can be broadly distinguished according to two opposing media theories: radical and liberal pluralist. Radical approaches are influenced by the theories of Karl Marx and Antonio Gramsci, among others, and stress the unequal distribution of economic and cultural power throughout society, and its impact on media production. Liberal pluralist interpretations are underpinned by the ideals of classical liberal theory, and emphasize the principles of freedom, choice and democracy, and their impact on media production. There are numerous variations on each perspective, but in their simplest terms, radical readings see the mass media as controlling people, while liberal pluralist readings see the mass media as serving them. The liberal pluralist approach is capable of capturing both political left and right positions. The radical view is more explicitly associated with the political left. Since the vast majority of criminological debate in this area has concentrated on news production, this will provide the focus for the discussion that follows.

At the radical extreme, the 'propaganda model' views the media as an extension of the State's apparatus of ideological control. Over three decades, Ed Herman and Noam Chomsky have argued that economic, political, military and cultural elites conspire to control the content and flow of media information, filtering out or delegitimizing dissenting views to protect ruling class interests (Chomsky, 1989; Herman and Chomsky, 1994). Through analysing media coverage of 'terrorism' and the media's alleged collusion in the 'criminalization' of non-friendly regimes, the authors argue that the key actors in the news production process are not journalists, who are seen as largely powerless, but media owners, who share interests in common with other elite groups. In this critical materialist interpretation of news production—underpinned by Marxist theory—the function of the news media is to 'manufacture consent' around elite ideas in the name of the 'national interest' and, in so doing, to engender political compliance and acceptance of the established order.

A less conspiratorial approach is the 'hegemonic model', based on the neo-Marxist writings of Antonio Gramsci (1971). Here the media are viewed not as the direct mouthpieces of the powerful, but as sites of contestation on which alternative viewpoints actively compete for ideological dominance, or hegemony. Due to their privileged access, however, criminal justice institutions are able advance a 'primary definition' of crime-related issues, which frames the terms for any ensuing debate and subverts competing viewpoints, though these may still be heard, to marginal status (Hall *et al.*, 1978). Though journalists may think they are autonomous, in practice they are constrained to reproduce the elite 'ideas' of the dominant sources on which they rely, in turn, helping to make these the 'ideas' of everyone. This is why, it is suggested, crime reporting tends to favour an elite (conservative) portrayal of the crime problem—an issue of working-class minority youth offending (not white collar corruption or state violence), requiring greater punishment and control of particular groups (not government accountability and corporate regulation) (Fishman, 1978; Barlow *et al.*, 1995).

The radical perspective, in its various guises, contrasts with liberal pluralist media theory (Gans, 1980; Koss, 1984; Hetherington, 1985). Liberal pluralists concede that certain official interests are advantaged in the media. But they insist that any significant source bias or pressure from media owners is offset by journalistic professionalism (in particular the requirements of objectivity and balance), the ideological and stylistic diversity of the media, and what is viewed as open and equal competition between a wide range of groups for media access and influence. Journalists insist upon, indeed pride themselves upon maintaining high levels of professional autonomy and are actively encouraged in this pursuit by colleagues who share the same system of values (Gans, 1980). Any pressure to follow a particular line, apply a particular 'spin', suppress a particular piece of information, or in some other way distort the 'truth status' of the news will be forcefully resisted.

Nor does the 'privileged access' of powerful institutions guarantee definitional control. Journalists, and other social actors, both can and do challenge the established order. This is clear, for example, when the high-profile exposure of scandal (political, sexual, economic) forces senior politicians to resign from office (Thompson, 2000), or the credibility of criminal justice agencies is undermined by media exposés evidencing corruption, incompetence, or institutional racism. In the liberal pluralist view, then, the media act as 'fourth estate'—exposing injustice and holding the powerful to account. They provide a voice for marginalized groups and, in so doing, defend the integrity of the democratic process (Blumler and Gurevitch, 1995).

In practice, the power relations between journalists and sources are more fluid than radical scholars have tended to argue, but more constraining than liberal pluralists suggest (Greer, 2003a). The radical position tends to overstate the dominance of official agencies and rather understates the ability both of journalists to challenge the status quo, and of other competing groups to enter and, sometimes with alarming effectiveness, reframe the terms of a given debate (Miller, 1993). Marginal groups prepared to proactively deliver news 'fit to print' are attractive to journalists with tight deadlines and, in that way, may have their views circulated over and above more powerful institutions which sit back until approached. The victim-centred nature of contemporary crime narratives places victim groups (like Victim Support and Rape Crisis) in a strong position to advance their values, interests and beliefs in media discourse, whether these beliefs coincide with 'official' viewpoints or not (Greer, forthcoming). The radical view also assumes, on some level, the existence of an 'elite consensus' which is then promoted by some unified constellation of ruling class interests (McNair, 1998, 1999). This interpretation overlooks the considerable levels of conflict and competition both between and within political and economic elites (the ongoing debates around a European Constitution, the legality of the 2003 war in Iraq, the privatization of public services), and fails to recognize that access to the media changes over time.

On the other hand, liberal pluralists understate the various influences within news agencies which severely limit journalists' freedom to report 'objectively and impartially', and the fact that competition for media access and influence is clearly not equal. Journalists are required to produce news which is not only pitched at the right market (for example, broadsheet or tabloid), but which also reflects the appropriate editorial position, regardless of their beliefs as individuals. If a newspaper takes a hard line on youth offending, for example, journalists at that newspaper are professionally obliged to reflect that position in their reports. Failure to do so may result in stories being 'spiked' (that is, not run), individuals being passed over for promotion or, in extreme cases, dismissal. And it is beyond doubt that criminal justice agencies maintain a clear definitional advantage, if not guaranteed definitional control, on issues of crime and justice. Less powerful or marginalized groups can gain access, sometimes to great effect, but they generally need to work harder and more creatively to have their views heard. These constraints have real consequences for the production and dissemination of crime and justice knowledge, and cannot be simply disregarded on the basis of claims to professional autonomy, ideological diversity and equal competition.

Postmodernist thinking maintains that there is no general explanation, still less some grand theory, capable of accounting for news production in all its diversity and complexity (Brown, 2003). Many postmodernists argue that in societies where images, signs and codes are constantly recycled through the media, it is no longer possible to distinguish with any certainty between 'image' and 'reality', the 'represented' and the 'real' (Baudrillard, 1983; Poster, 1990); *how* crime policy is presented becomes more important than *what* the policy actually is. In an age of media proliferation, political spin, ubiquitous public relations operatives, and ever-more sophisticated media audiences, perceptions of credibility and the balance of definitional power may shift from story to story. Different media in different markets uphold different agendas, manufacture different products, cater to different audiences and are constrained by different pressures and demands. Relationships of power and authority, dominance and subservience, exist at all levels of the news production process—between more and less senior journalists, between journalists and sources, between journalists, sources and the law, and between journalists, sources, the law and the public. The nature, content and ideological substance of 'crime news' is the outcome of a complex dialectical interplay between a diversity of dynamics, interests and influences.

News values and newsworthiness

On 26 December 2003, Iran was struck by an earthquake which killed more than twenty-five thousand Iranian citizens. This was a natural disaster on a massive scale, and the second story reported on the UK evening News at Ten. The headlining item disclosed that an English police officer had been shot.

It would be neither possible nor desirable to report everything that happens in the world. Only a tiny fraction of events, criminal or otherwise, are deemed sufficiently 'newsworthy' to merit media attention. News values are the criteria that determine 'newsworthiness'. They enable journalists and editors to decide which stories to run and which to drop, which are headliners and which are fillers, which are the most important details and which are the least. Having 'a good nose for a story', then, may equally be interpreted as having a well-honed appreciation of news values.

Table 8.1 outlines three different, but overlapping, interpretations of what it is that make events in general, and criminal events in particular, worthy of media attention.

News values help to explain the broad profile of media representations of crime and control. Interpersonal crimes of sex and violence can be more easily presented as dramatic and titillating than non-violent crimes—for example, most property and white collar offences. By focusing on people (as victims and offenders) and events rather than abstract issues and debates, crime reporting is individualized and simplified, which also contributes to the common association of crime with individual pathology rather than wider social, structural and political influences. Crimes are more newsworthy if they involve famous or notable people. Indeed, in an increasingly secular society, some suggest that the culture of celebrity is for many a more powerful source of social cohesion than religion (Rojek, 2001). Although names will generally be included where possible, one of the most compelling images in crime narratives is that of the 'unknown' predatory stranger. As the producers of reality crime shows like *Crimewatch UK* or *America's Most Wanted* and countless newspaper editors know only too well, few stories capture the public imagination as forcefully as the killer on the loose, especially when the (potential) victims are children. In addition to their inherent drama, individualization and violence, such narratives possess a unnerving sense of immediacy and a palpable risk of further attacks. They have a clear capacity to fulfil that increasingly important, commercially driven journalistic imperative; the requirement to shock (Greer, 2003b).

Table 8.1 Criteria of newsworthiness

Galtung and Ruge (1965)	Chibnall (1977)	Jewkes (2004a)
Threshold (importance)		Threshold (importance)
Unexpectedness (novelty)	Novelty (unexpectedness)	
Negativity (violent, harmful, deviant, sad)		Violence
Unambiguity (clear and definite)	Simplification (removing shades of grey)	Simplification (removing shades of grey)
	Dramatisation (action)	
Frequency (timescale, fit within news cycle)	Immediacy (the present, fit within news cycle)	
Elite-centricity (powerful or famous nations or people)	Personalization (notable individuals, celebrities)	Celebrity or high-status (notable individuals)
	Structured Access (experts, officials, authority)	
Composition (balance, fit with other news)		
Personification (individual focus or causality)	Individual pathology (individual causality)	Individualism (individual focus or causality) Children (young people)
Continuity (sustainability)		
	Graphic presentation	Spectacle or graphic imagery
	Visible/spectacular acts	
Meaningfulness (spatial and cultural relevance)		Proximity (spatial and cultural relevance)
Consonance (fit with existing knowledge and expectations)	Conventionalism (hegemonic ideology)	Predictability (expectedness)
	Titillation (exposes, scandal)	
		Risk (lasting danger)
	Sexual/political connotations	Sex
	Deterrence and repression	Conservative ideology or political diversion (deterrence, distraction from wider problems)

Sources: Galtung and Ruge (1965); Chibnall (1977); Jewkes (2004).

I have suggested elsewhere that all of these news values are mediated by the overarching notion of proximity; that is, spatial nearness and cultural meaningfulness of an event (Greer, 2003a). How dramatic or shocking a particular crime story is will depend on the extent to which it resonates with the consumer. Crimes, and indeed any events, happening close to home are perceived as both spatially and culturally 'close', and will generally be considered more newsworthy than the same crimes, or events, happening far away. This is particularly the case if the latter occur in non-western countries, which are widely perceived as more spatially and culturally distant. The news value of proximity helps to explain why the story of one police officer being shot at home was considered more newsworthy than twenty-five thousand citizens being killed by an earthquake in Iran.

REVIEW QUESTIONS

1 What are the principal characteristics of the radical and liberal pluralist readings of news production? How does each reading view journalistic freedom and source power?

2 What are the main strengths and weaknesses of the radical and liberal pluralist readings, and what contributions has postmodernist thinking offered?

3 What is it that makes some crimes so eminently reportable, whilst others are scarcely mentioned?

The previous sections have reviewed the literature on the nature and extent of representations of crime and control in the media, and offered an overview of some of the main theoretical and conceptual tools used to understand why media representations take on the form that they do. The next section considers the evidence for media effects.

Problematizing crime and media

When toddler James Bulger was murdered by two ten-year-olds in 1993, enormous attention was directed at the film *Child's Play III*, and other 'video nasties', as a likely cause (Muncie, 1999; Barker, 2001). Director Oliver Stone was prosecuted (unsuccessfully) amidst claims that his graphically violent film *Natural Born Killers* (1994) incited a number of copycat murders (Carter and Weaver, 2003). And when two teenagers shot twelve classmates and one teacher in Columbine in 1999, before killing themselves, the music of Marilyn Manson, the Hollywood film *The Basketball Diaries*, and violent computer games were all cited as possible causes (Muzzatti, 2003).

Few today would suggest that media representations have no influence on their audiences. Rather, the debate has been around the nature, extent and significance of that influence. Two schools of thought have dominated. On the political right, the concern has been that media images glamorize crime and violence, undermining respect for authority and the rule of law and encouraging criminality. On the political left, it has been that media images of crime and deviance increase public fears and anxieties, helping to win support for authoritarian measures of control and containment. Both of these viewpoints have their supporters and detractors. The evidence for the criminogenic effects of the media will be considered first.

Media violence and the problem of 'effects'

Research on media effects has for decades sought to demonstrate a causal relationship between media violence and violent thoughts and behaviours in the real world. Typically, subjects (most often children) are exposed to some aggressive stimulus (say, a short violent film) within a controlled setting (frequently a laboratory or office), and then observed to see if they think or behave more aggressively than a control group not exposed to the aggressive stimulus. Myriad variations have been conducted on this 'stimulus-response' (SR) format, variously controlling for participant characteristics, type of violence shown, duration of exposure, and so on.

In a frequently quoted statistic, more than 70 per cent of studies claim to demonstrate that media violence does cause real life violence (Andison, 1977; Howitt, 1998). In the classic example, children exposed to a short film in which aggressive interaction with an inflatable 'Bobo doll' was rewarded performed more imitative aggression (for example, striking the Bobo doll with a mallet after having observed it in the film) than those who had viewed non-aggressive interactions, or interactions in which aggression was punished (Bandura *et al.*, 1961, 1963). The authors concluded that aggressive behaviour may result, to a significant extent, from 'social learning'. Furthermore, the effects of media violence, though typically small, appear to diminish over time, but not disappear entirely (Livingstone, 1996). Huesmann (1995) concluded after a twenty year follow-up study that children who watched more violent television at age eight had secured significantly

Figure 8.2 Bandura's Bobo doll experiment.

Source: © Albert Bandura.

more violent criminal convictions in adulthood, even after controlling for social class and intelligence levels. The relationship between childhood exposure to television violence and later criminality has been supported in a host of other studies (see Paik and Comstock, 1994; Wilson *et al.*, 1998).

Such 'evidence' of criminogenic media effects is regularly cited by right-wing moral campaigners as justification for greater controls and censorship (Barker and Petley, 2001). But these claims should be treated with caution. Effects research has been heavily criticized on methodological, theoretical and conceptual grounds. Gauntlett (2001), and others (Howitt, 1998; Murdock, 2001; Reiner, 2002; Carter and Weaver, 2003), have identified a number of problems with the 'effects model'. Some of the most pertinent are summarized below.

- Counting 'units' of violence in accordance with the pre-established definitions of the researcher ('this is violence, this is not'), ignores the different meanings that people attach to acts and behaviours and implicitly assumes not just that we all think the same way, but that we all think the same way as the researcher.

- It is dubious to suppose that how subjects behave in controlled laboratory or field experimental situations (where they know they are being observed), sometimes toward inanimate objects (for example, an inflatable doll), reflects how they will behave in the real world toward real people.

- There is an assumption that only certain types of person are susceptible to the influences of media violence—mostly children, who are considered helpless victims, but sometimes also 'uneducated' or 'working class' populations, who apparently lack the maturity and sense most people take for granted.

- Different forms of violence—for example, in cartoons, soap operas, and horror movies—are often conflated, treated as equal in weight, and reduced to statistical data lacking any sense of plot or context. Whether violence is rewarded or punished, realistic or humorous, perpetrated by a 'hero' or a 'villain', may influence its impact profoundly.

- A correlation—violent people enjoy violent media—is not the same as a causal relationship—people are violent *because* of violent media. Media representations may provide technical knowledge about committing violent crimes, but that does not mean they also provide the motivation to use it.

- Whether intended or not, effects studies play into the hands of conservatives and right-wing moral campaigners who wish simplistically to blame the media for society's ills, rather than addressing more intractable sources of crime like social inequality, prejudice and stereotyping.

- Media influence, short term or cumulative, can never be disaggregated entirely from other social, psychological and cultural influences, yet studies routinely search for a 'pure' (negative) media effect. Prosocial images, though rarely considered, may be every bit as powerful as anti-social ones, and perhaps even more so.

While some critics have challenged the validity of the entire effects enterprise (Barker and Petley, 2001), others are less damning. Carter and Weaver (2003: 8), for example, recognize the limitations, but maintain that the effects tradition 'needs to be engaged with intelligently, rather than rejected out of hand as ill informed'. A growing body of work is using sophisticated methods of audience research to investigate the reception and interpretation of media images, not in isolation, but as part of an ongoing process of interaction, both with other media images and with the 'material and social realities of people's lives' (Kitzinger, 1999: 11; see also Buckingham, 1993, 2000; Philo, 1999). Gauntlett (1997), for example, has explored the influence of mass media on children by inviting young participants to make their own videos, and Hunt (1997) has studied the complex ways in which 'raced subjectivity'—racial sense of identity and community—influences the viewing and interpretation of images of racial violence.

Despite growing appreciation of the complexity of media influence, claims of a straightforward cause-and-effect relationship persist. A seemingly direct recreation of Bandura's Bobo doll experiment was offered up by Labour peer Professor Robert Winston as conclusive 'once and for all' evidence of the link between media violence and real violence in an article appearing in *The Guardian* newspaper supplement in January 2004. Though the second half of the article did include some qualification, the relationship between media violence and real world violence was presented as clear and unambiguous. The availability of more sophisticated approaches, therefore, is no guarantee that those approaches will be used. As with the media-violence debate, the connections between media and fear of crime are also highly contestable. It is these connections that are considered next.

Seeing is believing

The question of whether children mimic violent images they watch on television has been debated for decades. But now, says Robert Winston, he has witnessed an experiment that finally proves they do.

Robert Winston
Wednesday 7 January, 2004
The Guardian

One of the most revealing pieces of television I have watched recently concerned an experiment in which I was loosely involved. Four three-year-olds sit in a room where they view events in an adjoining playroom on a TV screen. An actor enters the playroom and the three-year-olds see the man gently cuddling a life-size rubber doll. Then the children are led individually into the same room and each is filmed. Without prompting, all stroke or kiss the doll, mimicking what they have just seen.

A little later, the children are back in the viewing room. This time the TV shows a man coming into the playroom with a large wooden hammer. The toddlers see him beating the doll vigorously. When these normally well-behaved children are led back into the playroom, each attacks the doll viciously. One toddler, normally shy and retiring, is completely carried away—his violence continuing even when his mother comes in and tells him to stop. It is some time before he can be dragged off and calmed down.

continued

---

continued

It is worth remembering that, in contemporary Britain, the average three- or four-year-old now watches a screen for around five hours each day, and more than 50 per cent of three-years-olds have a TV set in their bedroom. . . .

. . . Is there really hard scientific evidence that watching television affects how children communicate?

Well, yes—and the evidence grows steadily. Studies of boys, initiated in the 60s, showed that children aged six to 10 exposed to violent behaviour on TV were far more likely to demonstrate aggressive behaviour than adults in follow-up studies 15 or more years later. In separate projects, Dr Huesmann of Ann Arbor University in Michigan, and Dr Jeffrey Johnson in New York State, have shown that such aggressive traits are increased even when other factors such as social deprivation, intelligence and parenting skills are taken into account.

By the time they are 18, American children will have seen around 16,000 simulated murders and 200,000 acts of violence on TV. Hardly surprising, then, that much of this research come from the US. But research is beginning to show that violence on television may not always cause children to be aggressive—the evidence suggests that this is true around 10 per cent of the time. The kind of violence viewed may be important; children seeing 'unbelievable' violence for example, may gain over-optimistic impressions about the body's ability to withstand attack.

As parents, can we counter the effect of television violence? One worrying feature in Britain is that so many TV sets are in a child's bedroom; this means that the mediating effect of watching with a parent, the ability to discuss and interpret what has been seen, is lost. So perhaps we should reconsider placing this particular one-eyed monster in the bedroom, so often used by parents as a distracting, calming influence. But a sense of proportion is needed. We must not fail to recognize that television can be a hugely positive influence in children's lives, [and] one of the greatest educators in contemporary society . . .

Source: © Guardian Newspapers Limited 2004.

Media and fear of crime

Fear of crime first registered on the policy agenda in the early 1980s, when the British Crime Survey suggested it was becoming as big a problem as crime itself (Hough and Mayhew, 1983). Its consequences may range from not walking home alone at night to withdrawing from society altogether and living in isolation (Ferraro, 1995). Given the centrality of fear of crime in the public and political imagination, understanding its origins is an important criminological undertaking. Fear of crime is influenced by a range of social and demographic variables—perceptions of risk and vulnerability, age, social class, geographical location, ethnicity, and experience of criminal victimization (Box *et al.*, 1988; Davis, 1994; Hale, 1996). Media representations, though enormously diverse, are only one possible influence among many. As such, their significance remains a matter for debate.

Probably the best known research in this area is the 'cultivation analysis' of Gerbner *et al.*, which over several decades has employed content analyses and survey questionnaires to assess quantitatively the influence of violence on prime-time US television (Gerbner and Gross, 1976; Gerbner *et al.*, 1994). The central finding is that 'heavy' television viewers (those who watch most TV—more than four hours per day in Gerbner's studies) cultivate a world-view which more closely resembles the 'television message' than 'light' television viewers (those who watch less than two hours per day). Because television overstates both the seriousness and risk of criminal victimization, portraying the world as 'mean and scary', heavy viewing is said to cultivate higher fear of crime.

While supported in some studies (Hawkins and Pingree, 1980; Morgan, 1983), others have failed to replicate the cultivation effect (Gunter, 1987; Cumberbatch, 1989), and a number of empirical and theoretical weaknesses have been identified. It does not necessarily follow, for example, that people who watch the most television watch the most crime. An exaggerated sense of the risk of crime is not the same as fear of crime, yet these distinct concepts are easily confused. And many of the limitations of quantitative content analyses more generally—the distinction between forms of violence, the subjective definition of what violence is, the direction of influence, the relative importance of non-media factors—apply equally to cultivation studies of fear of crime.

In an attempt to address these weaknesses, more recent studies, including revised work by Gerbner and colleagues, have paid greater attention to the nature, form and context of crime and violence in the media. While earlier studies considered violent incidents as decontextualized units, recent work considers the complete scene, in which the consequences of violence are also shown, or the entire programme, in which the *overall* message may be one of restored order and reassurance, rather than dread and fear (Potter *et al.*, 1995, 1997). The extent to which images of crime and violence resonate with consumers' lives may be crucial to their impact. Schlesinger *et al.* (1992), for example, found that women may be particularly sensitive to images of interpersonal attacks. Partly on this basis, concerns have been expressed that the highly unrepresentative focus on 'real' violent and sexual interpersonal crimes in the BBC's long running reality show *Crimewatch UK* may increase levels of fear in sections of the viewing audience (Schlesinger and Tumber, 1993; Kidd-Hewitt, 1995; Jewkes, 2004a).

The proximity (spatial and cultural nearness) of crime may also be significant. Recent research on US television news concluded that local crime coverage generates more fear than national coverage, particularly within individuals who have experienced victimization and perceive television accounts to be realistic (Chiricos *et al.*, 2000; see also Eschholz *et al.*, 2003). The purely quantitative approach limits any explanation of these findings, though they are supported in studies on US newspaper readership (Heath, 1984). A recent UK study, however, suggests that local newspaper reporting has no bearing at all on fear of crime. Using a combination of quantitative and qualitative methods, participants kept diaries charting their daily fears and anxieties about crime, and related these directly to press coverage. Local crime reporting was perceived as 'background noise' which had little impact on participants' lives (Roberts, 2001: 12). National crime coverage, by contrast, was actually found to reduce fear of crime by reassuring news consumers that their communities are comparatively safe (see also Heath and Petraitis, 1987).

Aside from illustrating the contradictory nature of the research findings, these examples further demonstrate the usefulness of developing qualitative research approaches which consider the everyday contexts within which media images are consumed, and help not only to describe the relationships between media and fear of crime, but also to explain and understand them. While the relationship between media images and fear of crime has proved difficult to demonstrate conclusively, it is beyond doubt that media can have a profound influence on sections of the population at certain times. It is with this in mind that the next section considers the sociological theory of moral panic.

Moral panics and multi-mediated societies

The term 'moral panic' refers to the disproportionate and hostile social reaction to a group or condition perceived as a threat to societal values. It involves sensational and stereotypical media coverage, public outcry and demands for tougher controls. As the name suggests, the panic may subside as rapidly as it erupted (Goode and Ben-Yehuda, 1994; Murji, 2001). Moral panics have most often emerged around youth-related issues, particularly subcultural forms of youth expression and identity—for example, punk, acid house, rave and the wider drugs culture—but football hooliganism, satanic child abuse, and the re-housing of child sex offenders in the community have also been the source of recent panic (Best, 1990; Jenkins, 1992; Silverman and Wilson, 2002).

In the original analysis, Cohen (1972) queried the social reaction to the Mods and Rockers disturbances in 1964, when boredom and bad weather one Bank Holiday resulted in a few fights, lots of noise and some windows being smashed. Though the damage was minor, the national press exaggerated and sensationalized the disturbances using phrases like 'day of terror' and 'hell-bent on destruction'. News reports predicted further violence, demanded tighter controls, and portrayed Mods and Rockers as 'folk devils'—a symbol not just of youth delinquency, but of wider permissiveness and social decline. Cohen (1972) demonstrates how the labelling and marginalization of Mods and Rockers, and the emphasis on mutual antagonism, created a 'deviancy amplification spiral' in which future disturbances were virtually guaranteed. These disturbances seemed to justify initial fears, resulting in more media coverage, more public outcry, more policing, and thus the spiral of reaction continued. The moral panic occurred at a time of rapid social change. In particular, the increase in youth spending power and sexual freedom—defiantly flaunted and revelled in by so many young people—blurred moral and class boundaries and challenged the traditional ethics of hard work and sobriety, generating uncertainty and hostility among 'respectable society'. The 'creation' of Mods and Rockers, then, provided scapegoats or 'folk devils'—a deviant minority against whom the conforming (nostalgically reactionary adult) majority could unite at a time of conflict and change.

In a radical, Gramscian analysis of 'hegemonic crisis' at a time of economic recession, political decline and class unrest in the 1970s, Hall *et al.* (1978) argue that the State orchestrated a moral panic around 'mugging', casting in the central role the image of the black street criminal. The creation of this 'folk devil', again against which all 'respectable citizens' could unite, tapped into escalating fears around crime, race and social decline, and allowed the State to reassert and relegitimate itself—'policing the crisis', crucially with the consent of the people, by stamping down hard on the problem from above.

Critics of moral panic theory have questioned the attribution of 'disproportionality' to social reaction because this assumes some superior knowledge of the objective reality of the issue, against which the reaction can be measured, and a tacit assumption about what a 'proportionate' reaction would look like (Waddington, 1986). Left realists, in particular, have committed to 'take crime seriously' and insist that crime and fear of crime cannot simply be dismissed as groundless media-induced hysteria (Matthews and Young, 1992). Others have gone further, suggesting that in multi-mediated societies the concept of moral panic needs to be reformulated (McRobbie and Thornton, 1995; Ungar, 2001). While folk devils were once helpless against their demonization, they may now find themselves being vociferously supported in the same mass media that castigate them. They may also provide counter-definitions and explanations in any number of alternative media outlets. While moral panics were once rare, they are now commonplace, and even commercially desirable. One of the best ways of promoting (and selling) records, clothes, books, films—most popular cultural commodities, in fact—is actively to court controversy and generate a little 'panic'. Few things get in the way of commercial success, particularly of youth-oriented products, more than 'conventional approval'.

REVIEW QUESTIONS

1 What does the 'effects' model propose, and how has effects research been criticized?

2 Compile a list of factors, other than media representations, which might influence fear of crime. Which of these do you think are most/least important?

3 Can you think of any recent moral panics? On what basis would you say that the term 'moral panic' is justified?

CONCLUSION

This chapter has provided an overview of some of the main issues and debates which continue to inform the scholarly investigation of crime and the media. You should now have a sense of the nature and extent of crime, violence and control in media content, an understanding of some of the dominant theoretical and conceptual tools used to explain and understand media representations, and a working knowledge of the evidence for, and against, media effects. Equipped with this knowledge and insight, you can now explore in greater detail any issues which have challenged your assumptions, tested your critical faculties, or stimulated your imagination.

The themes developed in this chapter should not be considered in isolation, but as part of a much wider criminological enterprise which seeks to 'make sense' of our social world and to understand matters of crime, deviance and control from a diversity of perspectives. Some of the chapters in this volume deal with the related matters of, for example, theory, youth, policing and social control. Others describe new movements and orientations within criminology, borne out of the increasing popular, political and intellectual fascination with deviance and disorder. Cultural criminology, in particular, is highly sensitized to the significance of media, image, style and representation to the processes of criminalization, control, resistance and identity (see Chapter 7; see also *Theoretical Criminology*, special issue on Cultural Criminology, 2004).

Today, image and representation penetrate all areas of social existence. Political and media processes have become inseparable (Manning, 2001). To stand any chance of winning public hearts and minds,

Figure 8.3 The September 11, 2001 attacks on New York's twin towers.

Source: © Reuters/CORBIS.

political parties and other interest groups must at least appear capable of addressing the problem of crime. One of the most effective ways of achieving this is by advancing claims in the media, and rebutting the claims of others (Beckett, 1997). The media thus constitute a fiercely contested terrain on which a diversity of groups, interests and ideologies compete to appear the most knowledgeable, credible, legitimate—the experts in the field; for with 'expert status' comes media access, definitional influence and, ultimately, political power.

Crime and justice events are reported as they happen, high-profile 'celebrity' trials are broadcast live, and the growth in 'reality' programming continues to erode the boundaries between news and entertainment, fact and fiction (Fishman and Cavender, 1998). Initiatives of crime prevention and social control increasingly rely on surveillance technologies like CCTV to monitor and regulate public space (McCahill, 2002). Media are also increasingly used by offenders, as recent scares about 'cyberstalking' and paedophiles' use of the Internet to 'groom' children clearly illustrate (Jewkes, 2003). Global acts of terrorism are designed with maximum media visibility in mind. The destruction of New York's twin towers on 11 September, 2001 was also an exercise in media politics (Castells, 2004). Global live coverage of the horror served both as the ultimate humiliation of the imperial power of the US and a calling to like-minded fundamentalists to share in the struggle. These are just some of the issues underpinning current and future interest in crime and the media research.

Media representations tap into and reinforce social and political concerns. They help shape public sensibilities, fears, anxieties and appetites. They provoke public outcry and, at times, generate moral panics. They serve as ideological weapons in the ongoing struggle for hegemony. They impart important, but often mixed, messages about the nature and extent of 'the crime problem', how we should think and feel about it, who is most at risk, and what is to be done. They indicate, however inaccurately, the State of the nation. But they also entertain. 'Crime talk' (Sasson, 1995), in whatever form, simultaneously elicits fear and fascination; it is a major source of concern, but also of distraction, escapism, and moral reassurance (Sparks, 1992; Greer and Jewkes, forthcoming). Crime sells. It always has.

Whether as news, fiction, or that expanding cultural form that lies somewhere in between, the sheer quantity of crime in the media illustrates that we have an insatiable appetite for narratives of deviance and control. And there is evidence to suggest we are growing hungrier (Reiner *et al.*, 2000a). Given the close interrelationship between the political, commercial and cultural significance of crime and disorder, it is small wonder it features so prominently across all media and markets. As the boundaries between fact and fiction (the represented and the real) become increasingly diffuse and uncertain, so the importance of understanding the connections between crime and the media becomes more concrete.

QUESTIONS FOR DISCUSSION

1 Design and conduct your own content analysis of newspaper crime reporting. Make sure you include both quantitative and qualitative considerations.

2 Compare coverage of the same crime or justice event in at least three different media forms (newspaper, Internet, television, radio). How and why does representation differ between media forms and organizations?

3 Watch an episode of your favourite crime drama or a recent film and note the portrayal of policing and criminal justice. Are the representations favourable or critical?

4 Re-read the article 'Seeing is believing' by Professor Robert Winston, boxed text, pp 170–1. What are Professor Winston's main claims and, based on your understanding of effects research, how might they be challenged or supported?

5 Keep a 'crime diary' for a week and record your thoughts and feelings about crime and personal safety. Do media representations have any impact on your fear of crime?

GUIDE TO FURTHER READING

For a book-length exposition of many of the issues and debates discussed here, students are enthusiastically directed towards Yvonne Jewkes's *Media and Crime* (London: Sage, 2004). Written at a slightly more challenging level, this textbook develops the complex relationships between crime and media forms and effects in late modernity.

For a more condensed review, Robert Reiner's 'Media Made Criminality: The Representation of Crime in the Mass Media', in Mike Maguire, Rod Morgan and Robert Reiner's (eds) *The Oxford Handbook of Criminology* (Oxford: Oxford University Press, 2002) is also excellent.

The most useful edited collections include Stanley Cohen and Jock Young's (eds) *The Manufacture of News: The Social Construction of Crime and Deviance* (revised edition, London: Constable, 1981) and, more recently, David Kidd-Hewitt and Richard Osborne's (eds) *Crime and the Media: The Post-Modern Spectacle* (London: Pluto Press, 1995), Richard Ericson's (ed) *Crime and the Media* (Aldershot: Dartmouth, 1995) and Paul Mason's (ed) *Criminal Visions: Representations of Crime and Justice* (Cullompton: Willan, 2003). These books present accessible explorations of a comprehensive range of media-crime issues, written by key scholars in the field.

Students should also look out for the new journal *Crime, Media, Culture: An International Journal* (London: Sage Publications), edited by myself, Yvonne Jewkes and Jeff Ferrell. *Crime, Media, Culture* (CMC) provides a forum for debate for the increasing number of researchers working at the interface between criminology, media studies and cultural studies and, in addition to more conventional scholarly articles, includes photographic essays, international research think-pieces, and reviews of relevant crime-media material.

Also, keep an eye on *Criminal Justice Matters* (London: CCJS), an extremely useful journal which should be compulsory reading on all introductory criminology courses. *Criminal Justice Matters* (CJM) regularly features short articles on media-related issues written by key figures, and has a number of special editions specifically on crime and the media.

WEB LINKS

http://www.lexisnexis.com
Lexis Nexis is probably the best resource for conducting online searches of news and other print media from around the world. Access requires a password, which most universities should be able to supply.

www.jc2m.co.uk
The *Journal of Crime, Conflict and Media Culture* is a recently launched e-journal, edited by Paul Mason, which contains high quality contributions from leading scholars in the areas of media culture, criminal justice and conflict.

www.spiked-online.com
Spiked is an independent online publication which offers an alternative and always critical take on the news stories of the day. Its self-stated priorities are liberty, enlightenment, experimentation and excellence.

http://www.theory.org.uk

Theory.org.uk is a fun and accessible website maintained by David Gauntlett, which includes information on media effects, key social and cultural theorists, and plenty of links to other useful media-oriented sites.

http://www.ccms-infobase.com

The Communication, Cultural and Media Studies Infobase contains a wide range of salient links, definitions, and issues for debate—pitched at an introductory undergraduate level—which are easy to navigate.

REFERENCES

Allen, J., Livingstone, S. and Reiner, R. (1997) 'The Changing Generic Location of Crime in Film: A Content Analysis of Film Synopses', in *Journal of Communication*, 47: 89–101.

Andison, E. (1977) 'TV Violence and Viewer Aggression: A Cumulation of Study Results, 1956–1979', in *Public Opinion Quarterly*, 41, 3: 314–31.

Bailey, F. and Hale, D. (1998) *Popular Culture, Crime and Justice*. Belmont, CA: West/Wadsworth.

Bandura, A., Ross, D. and Ross, S. (1961) 'Transmission of Aggression Through Imitation of Aggressive Models', *Journal of Abnormal and Social Psychology*, 63: 575–82.

Bandura, A., Ross, D. and Ross, S. (1963) 'Imitation of Film-Mediated Aggressive Models', *Journal of Abnormal and Social Psychology*, 66: 3–11.

Barker, M. (2001) 'The Newson Report: A Case Study in Common Sense', in M. Barker and J. Petley (eds) (2001) *Ill Effects: The Media/Violence Debate* (2nd edn). London: Routledge.

Barlow, M., Barlow, D. and Chiricos, T. (1995) 'Economic Conditions and Ideologies of Crime in the Media: A Content Analysis of Crime News', in *Crime and Delinquency*, 41, 1: 3–19.

Baudrillard, J. (1983) 'The Precession of the Simulacra', in T. Doherty (ed) *The Postmodern Reader*. Hemel Hempstead: Harvester Press.

Beckett, K. (1997) *Making Crime Pay: Law and Order in Contemporary American Politics*. Oxford: Oxford University Press.

Best, J. (1990) *Threatened Children*. Chicago: University of Chicago Press.

Blumler, J. and Gurevitch, L. (1995) *The Crisis of Public Communication*. London: Routledge.

Box, S., Hale, C. and Andrews, G. (1988) 'Explaining Fear of Crime', in *British Journal of Criminology*, 28: 340–56.

Briggs, A. and Cobley, P. (eds) (1998) *The Media: An Introduction*, London: Longman.

Brown, S. (2003) *Crime and Law in Media Culture*. Buckingham: Open University Press.

Buckingham, D. (1993) *Children Talking Television: The Making of Television Literacy*. London: Falmer Press.

Buckingham, D. (2000) *The Making of Citizens: Young People, News and Politics*. London: Routledge.

Carter, C. and Weaver, C.K. (2003) *Violence and the Media*. Buckingham: Open University Press.

Castells, M. (2004) *The Power of Identity* (2nd edn). Oxford: Blackwell.

Castells, M. (1996) *The Rise of the Network Society*. Oxford: Blackwell.

Cavender, G. and Mulcahy, A. (1998) 'Trial by Fire: Media Constructions of Corporate Deviance', in *Justice Quarterly*, 15, 4. 697–719.

Chermak, S. (1995) *Victims in the News: Crime and the American News Media*. Boulder, CO: Westview Press.

Chibnall, S. (1977) *Law and Order News: An Analysis of Crime Reporting in the British Press*. London: Tavistock.

Chiricos, T., Padgett, K. and Gertz, M. (2000) 'Fear, TV News, and the Reality of Crime', in *Criminology*, 38, 3: 755–85.

Chomsky, N. (1989) *Necessary Illusions*. London: Pluto Press.

Cohen, S. (1972) *Folk Devils and Moral Panics: The Creation of the Mods and Rockers*. London: MacGibbon and Kee.

Cohen, S. and Young, J. (eds) (1981) *The Manufacture of News: Social Problems, Deviance and Mass Media*, revised edition. London: Constable.

Cumberbatch, G. (1989) 'Violence in the Media: The Research Evidence', in G. Cumberbatch and D. Howitt (eds) *A Measure of Uncertainty: the Effects of the Mass Media*. London: John Libbey.

Cumberbatch, G. and Howitt, D (eds.) (1989) *A Measure of Uncertainty: the Effects of the Mass Media*. London: John Libbey.

Cumberbatch, G., Woods, S. and Maguire, A. (1995) *Crime in the News: Television, Radio and Newspapers: A Report for BBC Broadcasting Research*. Birmingham: Aston University, Communications Research Group.

Curran, J. and Gurevitch, M. (eds) (1996) *Media, Culture and Society* (2nd edn). London: Arnold.

Davies, P., Francis, P. and Greer, C. (eds) (forthcoming) *Victims, Crime and Society*. London: Sage.

Davis, M. (1994) 'Beyond Blade Runner: Urban Control. The Ecology of Fear', in E. McLaughlin, J. Muncie and G. Hughes (eds) (2003) *Criminological Perspectives: Essential Readings* (2nd edn). London: Sage.

Ditton, J. and Duffy, J. (1983) 'Bias in the Newspaper Reporting of Crime', in *British Journal of Criminology*, 23, 2: 159–65.

Doherty, T. (1083) (ed) *The Postmodern Reader*. Hemel Hempstead: Harvester Press.

Dominick, J. (1978) 'Crime and law enforcement in the mass media', in C. Winick (ed) *Deviance and Mass Media*. London: Sage.

Ericson, R., Baranek, P. and Chan, J. (1987) *Visualising Deviance: A Study of News Organisation*. Milton Keynes: Open University Press.

Ericson, R., Baranek, P. and Chan, J. (1989) *Negotiating Control: A Study of News Sources*. Milton Keynes: Open University Press.

Ericson, R., Baranek, P. and Chan, J. (1991) *Representing Order: Crime, Law and Justice in the News Media*. Milton Keynes: Open University Press.

Eschholz, S., Chiricos, T. and Gertz, M. (2003) 'Television and Fear of Crime: Programme Types, Audience Traits and the Mediating Effect of Perceived Neighbourhood Racial Composition', in *Social Problems*, 50, 3: 395–415.

Ferraro, K. (1995) *Fear of Crime: Interpreting Victimisation Risk*. New York: State University of New York, Albany.

Fishman, M. (1978) 'Crime Waves as Ideology', in *Social Problems*, 25: 531–43.

Fishman, M. and Cavender, G. (eds) (1998) *Entertaining Crime: Television Reality Programmes* New York: Aldine de Gruyter.

Fiske, J. (1990) *An Introduction to Communication Studies* (2nd edn). London: Routledge.

Franklin, B. (ed) (1999) *Social Policy, the Media and Misrepresentation*. London: Routledge.

Galtung, J. and Ruge, M. (1965) 'Structuring and selecting news', in S. Cohen and J. Young (eds) (1981), *The Manufacture of News: Deviance, Social Problems and the Mass Media*, revised edition. London: Constable.

Gans, H. (1980) *Deciding What's News*. London: Constable.

Gauntlett, D. (1997) *Video Critical: Children, the Environment and Media Power*. London: John Libbey.

Gauntlett, D. (2001) 'The Worrying Influence of "Media Effects" Studies', in M. Barker and J. Petley (eds) (2001) *Ill Effects: The Media/Violence Debate* (2nd edn). London: Routledge.

Gerbner, G. and Gross, L. (1976) 'Living with Television: the Violence Profile', in *Journal of Communication*, 26, 1: 173–99.

Gerbner, G., Gross, L., Morgan, M. and Signorielli, N. (1994) 'Growing up with Television; The Cultivation Perspective', in J. Bryant and D. Zillman. (eds) *Media Effects*. Hillsdale, NJ: Lawrence Erlbaum.

Giddens, A. (1991) *Modernity and Self-Identity: Self and Society in the Late Modern Age*. Cambridge: Polity.

Goode, E. and Ben-Yehuda, N. (1994) *Moral Panics: The Social Construction of Deviance*. Oxford: Blackwell.

Graber, D. (1980) *Crime, News and the Public*. New York: Prager.

Gramsci, A. (1971) *Selections from the Prison Notebooks*. London: Lawrence and Wishart.

Greer, C. (2001a) *Crime in the Press: A Case Study of Sex Offending in Northern Ireland*, Unpublished PhD Thesis, The Queen's University of Belfast.

Greer, C. (2001b) 'Risky Business', in *Criminal Justice Matters*, 43: 28–29.

Greer, C. (2003a) *Sex Crime and the Media: Sex Offending and the Press in a Divided Society*. Cullumpton: Willan.

Greer, C. (2003b) 'Sex Crime and the Media: Press Representations in Northern Ireland' in P. Mason (ed) *Criminal Visions: Representations of Crime and Justice*. Cullompton: Willan.

Greer, C. (forthcoming) 'Constructing victimhood: media representations of crime and suffering', in P. Davies, P. Francis and C. Greer (eds) *Victims, Crime and Society*. London: Sage.

Greer, C. (2004) 'Crime, media and community: grief and virtual engagement in late modernity', in J. Ferrell, K. Hayward, W. Morrison and M. Presdee (eds) *Cultural Criminology Unleashed*. London: Cavendish.

Greer, C. and Jewkes, Y. (2005) 'Extremes of Otherness: Media Images of Social Exclusion', in *Social Justice (special edition on Emerging Imaginaries of Regulation, Control and Oppression)*, 32, 1.

Gunter, B. (1987) *Television and the Fear of Crime*. London: John Libbey.

Gunter, B., Harrison, J. and Wykes, M. (2003) *Violence on Television: Distribution, Form, Context and Themes*. London: Lawrence Erlbaum.

Hale, C. (1996) 'Fear of Crime: A Review of the Literature', in *International Review of Victimology*, 4: 79–150.

Hall, S. Critcher, C. Jefferson, T. Clarke, J. and Roberts, B. (1978) *Policing the Crisis: Mugging, the State and Law and Order*. London: Macmillan.

Hawkins, R. and Pingree, S. (1980) 'Some Processes in the Cultivation Effect', in *Communication Research*, 7: 193–226.

Heath, L. (1984) 'Impact of Newspaper Crime Reports on Fear of Crime: Multi-Methodological Investigation', in *Journal of Personality and Social Psychology*, 47, 2: 263–76.

Heath, L. and Petraitis, J. (1987) 'Television Viewing and Fear of Crime: Where is the Mean World?', in *Basic and Applied Social Psychology*, 8, 1/2: 97–123.

Herman, E. and Chomsky, N. (1994) *Manufacturing Consent: The Political Economy of the Mass Media*. New York: Pantheon.

Hetherington, A. (1985) *News, Newspapers and Television*. London: Macmillan.

Hough, M. and Mayhew, P. (1983) *The British Crime Survey*, Home Office Research Study 76. London: HMSO.

Howitt, D. (1998) *Crime, the Media and the Law*. London: Wiley.

Huesmann, A. (1995) *Screen Violence and Real Violence: Understanding the Link*, Media Aware, PO Box 1354, Auckland: New Zealand.

Hunt, D. (1997) *Screening the Los Angeles 'Riots'*, New York: Cambridge University Press.

Jenkins, P. (1992) *Intimate Enemies: Moral Panics in Contemporary Great Britain*. Hawthorne, NY: Aldine de Gruyter.

Jenkins, P. (1994) *Using Murder: The Social Construction of Serial Homicide*. Hawthorne, NY: Aldine de Gruyter.

Jewkes, Y. (2002) *Captive Audience: Media, Masculinity and Power in Prisons*. Cullompton: Willan.

Jewkes, Y. (ed) (2003) *Dot. Cons: Crime, Deviance and Identity on the Internet*. Cullompton: Willan.

Jewkes, Y. (2004a) *Media and Crime*. London: Sage.

Jewkes, Y. (2004b) 'Media representations of criminal justice', in J. Muncie and D. Wilson (eds) *Student Handbook of Criminal Justice and Criminology*. London: Cavendish.

Kidd-Hewitt, D. (1995) 'Crime and the media: a criminological perspective', in D. Kidd-Hewitt and R. Osborne (1995), *Crime and the Media: The Post-Modern Spectacle*. London: Pluto Press.

Kidd-Hewitt, D. and Osborne, R. (eds) (1995) *Crime and the Media: The Post-Modern Spectacle*. London: Pluto Press.

Kitzinger, J. (1999a) 'A sociology of media power: key issues in audience reception research', in G. Philo (ed) *Message Received*. London: Longman.

Kitzinger, J. and Skidmore, P. (1995) 'Child Sexual Abuse and the Media', Summary Report to ESRC. Award no. R000233675. Report available from Glasgow Media Group.

Knight, S. (2004) *Crime Fiction 1800–2000*. Basingstoke: Palgrave Macmillan.

Koss, S. (1984) *The Rise and Fall of the Political Press in Britain*. London: Hamish Hamilton.

Leishman, F. and Mason, P. (2003) *Policing and the Media: Facts, Fictions and Factions*. Cullompton: Willan.

Livingstone, S. (1996) 'On the Continuing Problem of Media Effects', in J. Curran and M. Gurevitch (eds) *Mass Media and Society*. London: Arnold.

Lynch, M., Stretesky, P. and Hammond, P. (2000) 'Media Coverage of Chemical Crimes, Hillsborough County, Florida, 1987–1997', in *British Journal of Criminology*, 40, 1: 112–26.

Maguire, M. (2002) 'Crime statistics: the "data explosion" and its implications', in M. Maguire, R. Morgan and R. Reiner (eds) *The Oxford Handbook of Criminology* (2nd edn). Oxford: Oxford University Press.

Maguire, M., Morgan, R. and Reiner, R. (eds) (2002) *The Oxford Handbook of Criminology* (3rd edn). Oxford: Oxford University Press.

Manning, P. (2001) *News and News Sources: A Critical Introduction*. London: Sage.

Marsh, H.L. (1991) 'A Comparative Analysis of Crime Coverage in Newspapers in the United States and Other Countries From 1960–1989: A Review of the Literature', in *Journal of Criminal Justice*, 19, 1: 67–80.

Mason, P. (ed) (2003) *Criminal Visions: Representations of Crime and Justice*. Cullompton: Willan.

Matthews, R. and Young, J. (1992) (eds) *Rethinking Criminology: the Realist Debate*. London: Sage.

Mawby, R. (2002) *Policing Images: Policing, Communication and Legitimacy*. Cullompton: Willan.

McCahill, M. (2002) *The Surveillance Web: The Rise of Visual Surveillance in an English City*. Cullompton: Willan.

McLaughlin, E. and Muncie, J. (eds) (2001) *The Sage Dictionary of Criminology*. London: Sage.

McLaughlin, E., Muncie, M. and Hughes, G. (eds) (2003) *Criminological Perspectives: Essential Readings* (2nd edn). London: Sage.

McNair, B. (1998) *The Sociology of Journalism*. London: Arnold.

McNair, B. (1999) *News and Journalism in the UK: A Text Book* (3rd edn). London: Routledge.

McRobbie, A. and Thornton, S. (1995) 'Rethinking "Moral Panic" for Multi-Mediated Social Worlds', in *British Journal of Sociology*. 46, 4: 559–74.

Miller, D. (1993) 'Official Sources and "Primary Definition": The Case of Northern Ireland', *Media, Culture and Society*, 15: 385–406.

Morgan, M. (1983) 'Symbolic Victimisation and Real World Fear', in *Human Communication Research*, 9, 2: 146–57.

Muncie, J. (1999) 'Exorcising demons: media, politics and criminal justice', in B. Franklin (ed) *Social Policy, the Media and Misrepresentation*. London: Routledge.

Muncie, J. and Wilson, D. (2004) (eds) *Student Handbook of Criminal Justice and Criminology*. London: Cavendish.

Murdock, G. (2001) 'Reservoirs of dogma: an archaeology of popular anxieties' in M. Barker and J. Petley (eds) (2001) *Ill Effects: The Media/Violence Debate*, (2nd edn). London: Routledge.

Murji, K. (2001) 'Moral panics', in E. McLaughlin and J. Muncie (eds) *The Sage Dictionary of Criminology*. London: Sage.

Muzzatti, S. (2003) 'Criminalizing Marginality and Resistance: Marilyn Manson, Columbine and Cultural Criminology', paper presented at the American Society of Criminology Conference, Denver, Colorado, November 2003.

Newburn, T. (ed) (2003) *Handbook of Policing*. Cullumpton: Willan.

O'Connell, M. and Whelan, J. (1996) 'The Public Perceptions of Crime Prevalence, Newspaper Readership and "Mean World" Attitudes' in *Legal and Criminal Psychology*. 1: 179–95.

Osborne, R. (1995) 'Crime and the media: from media studies to post-modernism', in D. Kidd-Hewitt and R. Osborne (eds) *Crime and the Media: The Post-Modern Spectacle*. London: Pluto Press.

Paik, H. and Comstock, G. (1994) 'The Effects of Television Violence on Anti-Social Behaviour: A Meta-Analysis', in *Communication Research*, 21, 4: 516–46.

Pearson, G. (1983) *Hooligan: A History of Respectable Fears*. London: Macmillan.

Philo, G. (ed) (1999) *Message Received*. London: Longman.

Poster, M. (1990) *The Mode of Information: Poststructuralism and Social Context*. Cambridge: Polity Press.

Potter, W., Vaughan, M., Warren, R., Howley, K., Land. A. and Hagemeyer, J. (1997) 'Aggression in Television Entertainment: Profiles and Trends', in *Communication Research Reports*, 14: 116–24.

Potter, W., Vaughan, M., Warren, R., Howley, K., Land. A. and Hagemeyer, J. (1995) 'How Real is the Portrayal of Television Aggression in Television Programming?', in *Journal of Broadcasting and Electronic Media*, 39: 496–516.

Reiner, R. (2001) 'The Rise of Virtual Vigilantism: Crime Reporting Since World War II', in *Criminal Justice Matters*, 43: 4–5.

Reiner, R. (2002) 'Media Made Criminality: The representation of crime in the mass media', in M. Maguire, R. Morgan and R. Reiner (eds) *The Oxford Handbook of Criminology* (3rd edn). Oxford: Oxford University Press.

Reiner, R. (2003) 'Policing and the media', in T. Newburn (ed) *Handbook of Policing*. Cullumpton: Willan.

Reiner, R., Livingstone, S. and Allen, J. (2000a) 'Casino culture: media and crime in a winner-loser society' in K. Stenson and D. Cowell (eds) *Crime, Risk and Justice*. Cullumpton: Willan.

Reiner, R., Livingstone, S. and Allen, J. (2000b) 'No more happy endings? The media and popular concern about crime since the Second World War', in T. Hope and R. Sparks (eds) *Crime, Risk and Insecurity*. London: Routledge.

Roberts, M. (2001) 'Just Noise? Newspaper Crime Reporting and the Fear of Crime', in *Criminal Justice Matters*, 43, Spring 2001: 12–13.

Rock, P. (1973) 'News as eternal recurrence' in S. Cohen and J. Young (eds) (1981) *The Manufacture of News: Social Problems, Deviance and the Mass Media*, revised edition. London: Constable.

Rojek, C. (2001) *Celebrity (FOCI)* London: Reaktion Books.

Roshier, R. (1973) 'The Selection of Crime News by the Press', in S. Cohen and J. Young (eds) (1981) *The Manufacture of News: Deviance, Social Problems and the Mass Media*, revised edition. London: Constable.

Sasson, T. (1995) *Crime Talk: How Citizens Construct Social Problems*. Howthorne, NY: Aldine de Gruyter.

Schlesinger, P., Dobash, R.E., Dobash, R. and Weaver, C.K. (1992) *Women Viewing Violence*. London: British Film Institute.

Schlesinger, P. and Tumber, H. (1993) 'Don't have Nightmares: Do Sleep Well', in *Criminal Justice Matters*, 11: 4.

Schlesinger, P. and Tumber, H. (1994) *Reporting Crime: The Media Politics of Criminal Justice*. Oxford: Clarendon Press.

Silverman, J. and Wilson, D. (2002) *Innocence Betrayed: Paedophilia, the Media and Society*. Cambridge: Polity Press.

Smith, S. (1984) 'Crime in the News', in *British Journal of Criminology*, 24, 3: 289–95.

Soothill, K. and Walby, S. (1991) *Sex Crime in the News*. London: Routledge.

Sparks, R. (1992) *Television and the Drama of Crime: Moral Tales and the Place of Crime in Public Life*. Buckingham: Open University Press.

Stenson, K. and Cowell, D. (eds) (2000) *Crime, Risk and Justice*. Devon: Willan.

Surette, R. (1998) *Media, Crime and Criminal Justice: Images and Realities* (2nd edn). Belmont, CA: West/Wadsworth.

Thompson, J.B. (2000) *Political Scandal: Power and Visibility in the Media Age*. Cambridge: Polity.

Tombs, S. and White, D. (2001) 'Reporting Corporate Crime out of Existence', in *Criminal Justice Matters*, 43: 22–24.

Ungar, S. (2001) 'Moral Panics versus the Risk Society: The Implications of the Changing Sites of Social Anxiety', in *British Journal of Sociology*, 52, 2: 271–91.

Waddington (1986) 'Mugging as a Moral Panic: A Question of Proportion', in *British Journal of Sociology*, 37, 2: 245–59.

Williams, P. and Dickinson, J. (1993) 'Fear of Crime; Read All About It; The Relationship Between Newspaper Crime Reporting and Fear of Crime', in *British Journal of Criminology*, 33, 1: 33–56.

Wilson, B.J., Donnerstein, E., Linz, D. *et al*. (1998) 'Content analysis of entertainment television: the importance of context', in J. Hamilton (ed) *Television Violence and Public Policy*, Ann Arbor, Michigan: University of Michigan Press.

Winston, R. (2004) 'Seeing is Believing', in *The Guardian, G2*, 7 January, 2004.

Wykes, M. (2001) *News, Crime and Culture*. London: Pluto Press.

Zedner, L. (2002) 'Victims', in M. Maguire, R. Morgan and R. Reiner (eds) *The Oxford Handbook of Criminology* (3rd edn). Oxford: Oxford University Press.

Part Two
FORMS OF CRIME

9 'Volume crime' and everyday life

Mike Presdee

INTRODUCTION

We all carry within us a view of crime that is partly created by personal experience and partly by what we read, view and hear. Film, literature and the media all tell a story of crime that we store away in our consciousness to be used when we make decisions in our everyday lives such as where we might walk at night, who we might fear or be wary of, who we might trust or not. In other words we all think we 'know' something about crime. What we think it is, where we think it takes place and who the supposed criminals are—the what, where and whom of crime. We read about 'true' crime that typically tends to be spectacular crime—great robberies, serial killers, gang leaders or sexual predators (see Howitt, 1998; Reiner, 2002 for general introductions). The names come and go, entering the realm of popular culture, all the time adding to our collective understandings of crime (see Chapter 8 above). These acts need to be 'wicked', 'evil', or simply 'spectacular' before we categorize them within the collective conscience as crime, yet such crimes make up only a very small part of 'recorded' or 'reported' crimes in any given year. It remains the case that the vast majority of crime, is 'petty' by nature and often considered by us all to be unimportant, or not really 'proper' crime at all. We might buy something cheap at a garage sale which we consider to be 'a good buy', or just remove something lying around that we assume is no longer wanted (Ferrell, 2005). We might 'fiddle' expenses; do some 'cash work' that we fail to declare to the Inland Revenue; 'spin' our CVs; pull a 'sicky' when we want a day off work; or take 'things' home from our place of business as a 'perk' of the job. In other words, we simply do not consider these acts to be crimes and ourselves criminals. They are simply a part of everyday life (Gabor, 1994). Yet it is here, located in the hustle and bustle of everyday life that the vast majority of reported crime—what increasingly is referred to as 'volume crime'—occurs, whether 'property' or 'behaviour' based.

BACKGROUND

The use of the term 'volume crime' is a fairly new concept in criminological writing and arises out of what was previously described as the 'crimes of everyday life' (Felson, 1998; Carrabine et al., 2002; see relatedly Baldwin and Bottoms, 1976; Cohen and Felson, 1979; Figlio et al., 1986; Brantingham and Brantingham 1991, 1993). The aim of this body of work was to explore the ways in which the experiences of modern life make us all vulnerable to crime and criminality. In particular, it creatively examined the ways in which the minutiae of our lives lead us to be either offenders or victims of crime. The way we travel to work, to shop, to our leisure. Where we live, how we live, and with whom we live. Our age, our gender, our ethnicity, whether we work, study or are unemployed. When we work and what we work at. All were seen, and are still seen, as a constitutive part of the dynamics of everyday crime.

As an obvious example of this thesis, consider the everyday life of the average university student. The annual British Crime Survey clearly shows that being both young and a student makes you more susceptible to being a victim of crime. You spend your days on a busy campus surrounded by lightly engaged strangers; your car is often left for long periods in an unattended car park; you live in mass accommodation blocks; you often party long and late; and very often have limited financial resources. All these factors make for what David Garland has described as a micro 'crime-prone society' (2001: 91); a set of spatial and temporal circumstances that frequently culminate in students becoming the victims of both property crimes and acts of so-called 'anti-social behaviour'. In such circumstances, students and occasionally staff are themselves often tempted to become involved in the criminal marketplace (Dodd *et al.*, 2004: 54; see also Fisher and Sloan, 1997 for a policy summary). Marcus Felson in *Crime and Everyday Life* (1998), talks of a university campus in this way:

> A college campus is a giant delivery system. It funnels students, faculty, staff, and various products into one general location and moves them from building to building to deliver education. It also delivers crime opportunities. Students and their property may play several roles in crime. University employees fit the same bill. The university itself owns many items worth stealing and provides many corners where illegal action can occur . . . All crime is local—every offender goes from some local area to another. The minimal elements of crime converge locally. The physical and social processes generating crime therefore are intricately related. (Felson, 1998:75; see relatedly Rengert *et al.*, 2001)

One should also be aware that the contemporary term 'volume crime' also evokes a much more managerial dimension than previous concepts which have sought to explain/define crime. By this I mean that it extrapolates from the crimes of everyday life those particular offences that are seen by the government, the police, and other criminal justice agencies as the most socially pressing and in need of attention. This redefinition should be seen as part of a wider ideology of late modern social control (a series of instrumental administrative and bureaucratic strategies solely concerned with the 'management of crime'; see Garland, 2001 for an overview, and Chapter 23 below). Inevitably this process has political as well as criminological connotations, with politicians now scrambling to define which offences are, or are not, on the political agenda. The result is the inclusion of a new discourse of 'anti-social behaviour' within the context of 'volume crime'. This now allows a much wider spectrum of behaviours to be defined as anti-social. For example, where drunkenness, substance abuse, begging and other strictly illegal activities used to be the focus of state agency concern, now their remit has extended to behaviours that are more generally perceived as 'disorderly', such as 'fly-tipping, pestering people, bullying, games in inappropriate areas, loud music' and the like (Home Office Report 26, 2004: 4). Activities such as these (typically associated with young people) are all now increasingly classified as anti-social acts and subject to the criminalization process.

What is or is not deemed to be volume crime is, as mentioned above, both defined and determined by politicians and criminal justice agencies alike. It is a fluid concept forever being redefined in line with political considerations, crime trends and, importantly, changes in social and cultural aspects of everyday life (see Chapter 1 above). In this sense, then, and given the material and behavioural dimensions associated with volume crime, we must pay particular attention to changes in relation to both: (a) what we own, and how we protect it—as this inevitably impacts on levels and modalities of property crime; and (b) how we behave and interact with each other within social contexts. Consider, for example, the impact that late modern consumer culture has had both on the physical and structural nature of urban space and also at the level of individual subjective emotions—what Keith Hayward has described as 'the hidden patterns of behaviour and the new and distinct forms of subjectivity precipitated and engendered by a fast-paced consumer society' (2004: 1, for more on this point see below). Not only will changes in these areas affect what we buy, how we buy it, and how we protect what we buy, but it also brings about changes in our cultural lives. Ten years ago alcohol-related violence and general drunkenness were problems contained within the end of the working week. In contemporary society, changing social and leisure patterns mean that people can now 'party' seven days a week, irrespective of the time of day (Measham *et al.*, 1998; Hobbs *et al.*, 2000, 2003). As a consequence, noise and drunken behaviour become ever more visible social problems. From the State's perspective such behaviour also threatens to disrupt working life and thus is something that increasingly falls under the rubric of anti-social behaviour. In what follows, I will explore both property crime and anti-social behaviour in more detail and in direct relationship to our experiences of everyday life.

REVIEW QUESTIONS

1 In what ways do the patterns of your everyday life make you susceptible to property crime?

2 Examine your own ideas about crime and criminals and how these perceptions affect your everyday behaviour.

Property crime and everyday life

What is property crime?

Property crime is not just the single event of theft or robbery but concerns all the dimensions involved in the taking, distributing and buying of stolen goods. In the latest *Crime in England and Wales 2003/2004* report published by the Home Office (Dodd *et al.*, 2004), Laura Ringham and Martin Wood interpret data from the British Crime Survey (BCS) to draw a statistical sketch that demonstrates the diversity and extent of property crimes in England and Wales. For example, it estimates 2,121,000 vehicle thefts in the year 2003/4 (which included 241,000 stolen vehicles, 1,337,000 thefts from vehicles and 543,000 attempts of theft); 943,000 burglary offences; 622,000 thefts from the person; and 1,321,000 'other thefts of personal property'. Robbery and mugging offences (estimated at 399,000) are classified as crimes of violence rather than property crimes even though both involve the loss of property, including, for example, mobile phone theft (see Figure 9.1). Property crime also includes both the £1.8 billion of retail shop theft (often called shoplifting), as well as the £1.5 billion 'pilfered' from shops by employees (often described by employees as 'perks') (*Retail Express*, 28 September 2004). Whilst such statistical data is useful for criminologists in terms of identifying patterns and trends in particular types of crime (see Chapter 2 above), it tells us very little about the more complex social dimensions involved in the processes of property crime. For example, property crime happens not just in the street, but also at home, at work, even at school. It can happen when we are awake or asleep. How then can we explain the complex processes and dynamics associated with property crime? What are the social dimensions involved and how has it become so much a part of all our everyday lives?

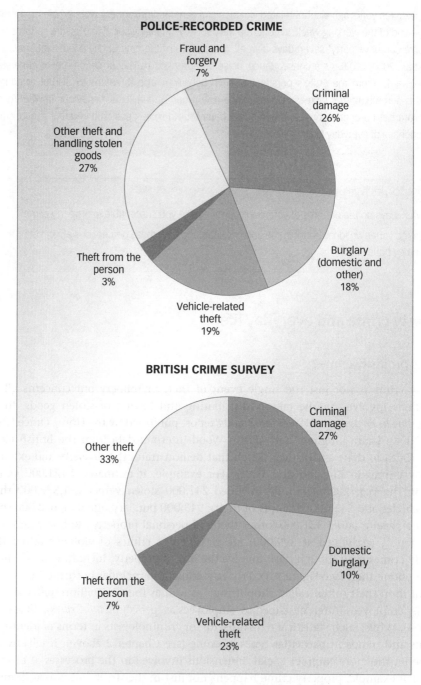

Figure 9.1 Police recorded and BCS property crime broken down by offence, 2003/04

Source: Crime in England and Wales 2003/04. Tricia Dodd, Sian Nicholas, David Povey and Alison Walker (London: HMSO: 2004), p. 45.

Explanations

Markets

Above all else volume property crime is about the identification of markets and the dynamics associated with the production, distribution and consumption of commodities (see Clarke, 1999; and Kock *et al.*, 1996 for an interesting analysis of the market for stolen electrical goods). In this sense, the illegal economy is driven by much the same basic dynamics as the formal legal economy. Producers wish to maximize profits, and need to distribute goods and services to consumers who in turn must be satisfied that they have received value for money. The successful criminal, then, must either identify a market and seek out goods to feed it, or start with a commodity and then find a suitable market for distribution (see the mass of research on 'crime markets' by Mike Sutton, especially his work on the Market Reduction Approach (MRA) to tackling theft and illegal trading, for example, Sutton 1995; Sutton *et al.*, 1998, 2001).

For example, the growing consumer boom in China has recently created a soaring demand for scrap metal, with prices rising from £40 a tonne in 2000 to £120 a tonne in 2004. The result is a lucrative and illegal scrap metal market (*The Times*, 13 March 2004). Here, then, is a market identified by criminal protagonists that has resulted in the increased theft of such bizarre items as 'man hole' covers—eighty being stolen in Gloucester in one year, with 150 disappearing in Cambridgeshire in the space of three weeks. Another example of an emerging criminal market involves the end product of a consumer society—the disposal of waste. Once again, the costs involved in the disposal of unwanted products have risen in the last ten years as a result of more and more controls and regulations over waste disposal practices. The result has been the creation of illegal waste disposal services that dump unwanted goods throughout the countryside in a process known as 'flytipping'. The cost of cleaning up the countryside of such consumer detritus is in the end, of course, borne by local communities.

The products of criminal activities need of course to be acquired in the first place, either from individual people or from legal businesses. Most consumer items have a 'life' of their own which determines their desirability and value. Felson, for example, identifies in grid form these connections between theft and the 'stages of a product's life' (see Table 9.1) that clearly shows the rise and fall of property theft during the life of particular mass commodities. However, there are also 'specialist' markets that do not necessarily follow these rules. The markets in stolen artworks and stamps, for example, are especially lucrative. There even exists a specialist stolen pedigree dog market, with certain breeds attracting up to £3,000 per dog.

Once a market has been established and a 'product' stolen then the next element of the process, that of distribution, comes into play. Without an efficient distribution network, theft remains small scale, for personal use and consumption only. The ability to distribute stolen goods is therefore an essential element of property crime.

Distribution

There is, then, a need for criminal producers to identify and seek out both a population of people that make up a particular market place, and a means of safely distributing and delivering stolen property to those consumers (see Sutton *et al.*, 2001: 15–18). This

Table 9.1 Theft and stages of the product life cycle

	Product Innovation	Product Growth	Product in Mass Market	Product Saturation
Product users	Few and special	Growing and general	Many and universal	Nearly everyone
Ease of product use	Difficult to use	A bit easy to use	Some are easy to use	Wide range of usability
Ease of product transportation	Difficult to carry	A bit difficult to carry	Easy to carry	Easy to carry
Price	Prohibitive price	Price coming down	Wide price range	Low price
Theft risk	Not often stolen	Thefts accelerate	Epidemic of thefts	Declining thefts

Source: Felson, M. (1998) 'Crime & Everyday Life'. Sage: Thousand Oaks, CA, p. 187.

process takes many forms. Professional 'garage' sales, weekly car boot sales and market places, including antique markets and auction houses, provide easy outlets for stolen goods. There are few controls over these activities and goods circulate quickly and are difficult to trace back to the original seller. Likewise, friendship and family groups quickly become distribution 'networks' for stolen goods. Even motorway service areas often emerge as convenient sites for the distribution of stolen goods. These areas are like crowded local market places made up of a transitory population where within hours both seller and buyer are many hundreds of miles away and most likely impossible to trace. Lastly, in impoverished rundown urban areas, second hand shops often provide an outlet for stolen goods. Normally, property sold here is in poor condition and overpriced but still allows a segment of the population to consume like other members of the population and as such become part of the local economy. With few questions asked, and even fewer answers given, everyone appears happy—except of course the original owner or legitimate producer of the property. Marcus Felson once again neatly sums up the living, organic, criminal aspects of everyday crime when he writes:

> Crime feeds off the physical form of local life, whether in a village, town, city, suburb, or university campus. That form is organized by how people and things move about in everyday life. In the ways that they move around, people often prevent crime, whether they are aware of it or not, and both people and things sometimes contribute to crime in their presences or absences. People are sometimes offenders or combatants, sometimes targets or guardians, sometimes buyers or sellers of illegal goods. As they move through time and space, people also come into contact with products, some of which are stolen, some of which are sold as illegal goods or used for illegal acts. Everyday life thus sets the stage for people to break laws, hurt each other, and even hurt themselves. (Felson 1998:75)

Consumers

In the past criminology has too often concentrated on the 'producer' of criminal goods (the thief) or the sales staff (the dealers) and even occasionally the CEOs or top managers (the crime 'Barons'), rather than analysing the role of the consumers of criminal commodities. What is it then that makes us become consumers of other people's stolen property? Why is it that millions of normally law-abiding citizens come to act no differently to common criminals? What dynamics are at work that are so powerful as to lead such large numbers of people into the processes of crime? How many of us have been tempted to buy what we know are stolen goods? A cheap mobile phone, phone cards, clothes, CDs and DVDs, bikes and bits of bikes, tools, TVs, computers and computer games. The bargains are there as long as we can put out of our mind the fact that we are partaking in a criminal activity. But do we only consider price or are there deeper and more personal dynamics that lead us into the cycle of property crime? To fully understand the suspension of reality that takes place when we buy stolen property we must take a moment to understand the motivations behind such purposes.

Property crime offences, both estimated and recorded, make up the majority of criminal acts (notwithstanding the fact that most property crimes have shown a decrease in recent years). This demonstrates that one of the central defining dynamics of personal identity in contemporary society—that is the conspicuous ownership and consumption of commodities—is permanently under threat of violation. If our personal identity becomes reliant on what we consume and own, then property crime often becomes an act of *personal* violence, a violation felt deeply by the individual (rather than society as a whole) and thus closely connected to what we as individuals desire, need or want at any given time. The whole notion of property crime therefore comes to rest on our insatiable need to consume as a central activity within society (see Lury, 1996; Miles, 1998; Edwards, 2000 for general introductions to the subject of consumer culture). We now live in a consumer society where 'to have is to be'. Where 'we are what we consume'. Or as Eric Fromm so brilliantly expressed it:

> In a culture in which the supreme goal is to have . . . and to have more and more . . . and in which one can speak of someone as 'being worth a million dollars', how can there be an alternative between having and being? On the contrary, it would seem that the very essence of being is having; that if one has nothing, one is nothing. (Fromm 1976: 3)

The very act of consuming and 'becoming' involves both deeply desiring a commodity and obtaining access to it through legal or illegal markets. Everyday items that make us what we want to 'be' are imbued with such social status that often many of us will acquire them by whatever means necessary. It is through this dynamic of desire and wanting that we become both victim and offender. Commodities such as mobile phones, jeans, watches, hand bags, music CDs and film DVDs—are all highly desirable items. Indeed this desirability is unlikely to be affected just because these goods are now being sold in illegal markets. Consider, for example, the healthy market in counterfeit—or 'knock off'—products, from unlicensed generic prescription drugs to 'designer label' clothing.

In this way property crime is defined through the very process of the coming together of culture and economics that creates through its social dynamics criminal market places. That is property crime becomes an integral part of the fabric of everyday life. Out of this fabric arise such seemingly bizarre or abstract criminal markets as the illegal wild fish market, and even a large market in stolen caravans (*The Times*, 16 August 2004). Each reflecting the personal identities and everyday lives of particular groups as they go about affirming their identities through the consumption of stolen goods.

We cannot escape the premise that criminal markets and the culture of consumption go together. Illegal crime markets and criminal consumption are thus at the very heart of volume property crime, something which in turn is driven by the overwhelming desire to 'have' in order to 'be'. As I have said elsewhere, these desires:

> [no] longer respect the limits and cultural boundaries produced in the past to protect the institution of ownership. This new and all encompassing consumer culture creates a confused consumer psyche where anxiety and its social antidotes are themselves producing much so called 'social disorder' and 'transgression', as groups and individuals attempt to make sense of a life increasingly mediated through the new and distinct processes associated with late modern consumerism. The search for the thwarted promise of happiness through consumption leads many to hedonism and seemingly irrational acts. (Presdee 2000: 279)

Everyday cultural processes, then, inextricably link culture with crime, investing commodities with cultural meanings and understandings. The mobile phone industry, for example, is a site of production where sheer desirability and technological style are seductively woven together, creating a continuing demand for the 'latest models'. By employing a 'seduction of the new', each new marketing campaign encourages us to be ashamed of our current phone. Indeed a *Carphone Warehouse* advertisement in 2002 played on the theme of personal embarrassment through the use of an outdated handset. In such a highly personalized and therefore pressurized market place both criminal acquisition and criminal consumption are seemingly inevitable. Under these circumstances is it any surprise that mobile phone theft has become one of the UKs fastest growing crimes?

REVIEW QUESTIONS

1 Try and identify the various criminal markets that you might come across in your everyday life.

2 By examining the emotions of consumption, analyse the image and identity you are seeking through your own consumption strategies.

Anti-social behaviour and the politics of control

The emergence of anti-social behaviour

As Prime Minister in the mid 1990s, John Major introduced a high profile 'back to basics' campaign. His goal was to foreground the importance of family values, moral fortitude, and discipline at school and work in an attempt to counteract the ever growing, and increasingly visible 'anti-social' activities of the new so-called 'yob culture'. The campaign made much of the threat posed by anti-social behaviour to the lives and well being of 'ordinary' citizens. According to John Major and his fellow Conservatives, young people were out of control, laziness was rife, and infidelities within families were destroying the British way of life. At the time, the Labour opposition leader, Tony Blair, viewed such an approach to crime and deviance as a cheap electioneering stunt, and gained considerable political capital when eventually the campaign collapsed under the weight of 'Tory Sleaze' including a series of sensational sex scandals involving Conservative MPs. However, once in power, the current Labour government quickly took up the 'battle cry' again, only this time the 'back to basics' rubric was replaced with a war on anti-social behaviour. The mythical 'yob' was once again cast as a threat to 'decent' citizens, a sort of enemy within, eating away at order through disorder, creating a generalized feeling of insecurity throughout the population.

This puritanical approach defines that which interrupts the processes of organized production as 'anti-social', and identifies a perceived general lack of discipline for work and social order as the major ill confronting contemporary societies. Worklessness and 'bad behaviour' become a social and moral weakness to be controlled and criminalized. As a result anti-social citizens must be considered 'disturbed' or 'depraved' or 'dangerous' or all three and in need of precise definition to enable legislation to be enacted that would control such undesirable behaviour.

The defining process

The present Labour Government began the 'defining' process in September 2003 by identifying through its Anti-social Behaviour Unit's 'one day snapshot' of anti-social behaviour, over 60,000 anti-social reports within a twenty-four hour period (Home Office, 2003). They further identified another 250,000 neighbourhood disputes that were reported to local authorities and environmental agencies in one year alone.

Reflecting the present Government's concerns regarding anti-social behaviour the Home Office produced its report *Defining and Measuring Anti-Social Behaviour* (2004) which in turn built on the 2003 White Paper 'Respect and Responsibility: Taking a stand against anti-social behaviour'. These publications served to set out a working definition of what anti-social behaviour is and how community practitioners might apply that definition to particular communities. However, right from the outset there was considerable concern about definitional boundaries. They begin by saying:

> People's understanding of what constitutes anti-social behaviour is determined by a series of factors including context, location, community tolerance and quality of life expectations. As a result, what may be considered anti-social behaviour to one person can be seen as acceptable behaviour to another. The subjective nature of the concept makes it difficult to identify a single definition of anti-social behaviour. (Home Office 2004: 3)

They also recognized the shortcomings of the definition set down by the Crime and Disorder Act (1998) that defined the anti-social as: 'Acting in a manner that caused or was likely to cause harassment, alarm or distress, to one or more persons not of the same household as the defendant'. This definition defines the anti-social not through what it is, but by examining the effect that so-called anti-social behaviour has on people and society. However, in order to bring more precision and focus to the defining process, the Home Office have continued their attempts to proscribe a particular range of social actions as being anti-social. Again they tried to avoid 'demonizing' or 'excluding' specific groups such as young people, or socially excluded sections of the population like the homeless, or those involved in drug rehabilitation programmes. Even so, a number of respondents felt that a specific 'youth nuisance' category should be added to the typology, recognizing that groups of young people are often perceived as a problem. (The BCS 2002/03 showed that 25 per cent of the public perceived 'teenagers hanging around' as the biggest ASB problem in their local area.) Ultimately, however, the decision was taken not to include a youth category in the typology, as it was felt that anti-social behaviour should be defined by the nature of the activity not the age of the perpetrator (Home Office, 2004: 5).

Instead, the Government embarked on a much more subtle strategy. As Table 9.2 makes clear, the Home Office typology of anti-social behaviour includes a whole host of activities primarily associated with young people, such as the playing of loud music, joyriding, graffiti, hooliganism, playing games in inappropriate places, and skateboarding and cycling in pedestrianized areas. This defining process ensures that it is young people rather than adults who become trapped by the rubric of anti-social behaviour, further adding to what has been described as the 'creeping criminalisation and control of youth' (see Jeffs and Smith, 1996; Hayward, 2002).

It is quite clear, then, that the present government, like governments before it, have little understanding about the realities of everyday life for young people in contemporary society. In particular, their search for fun, excitement, and an escape from the boredom of everyday routines. As I have said elsewhere:

> Excitement, even ecstasy (the abandonment of reason and rationale), is the goal . . . the quest for excitement is directly related to the breaking of boundaries, of confronting parameters and playing at the margins of social life in the challenging of controllers and their control mechanisms . . . It is the realm of resentment and irrationality par excellence and also the realm of much crime. It is that part of social life that is unknowable to those in power and which therefore stands outside of their consciousness and their understanding. They cannot understand it or indeed even 'read' it as real life, but only as immoral, uncivilized, obscene and unfathomable social behaviour. (Presdee 2000: 7–8)

Or in the context of the present chapter, 'unfathonable social behaviour' becomes defined as anti-social behaviour and rendered understandable, knowable and therefore preventable through control mechanisms.

The government has further extended the binary social/anti-social categorization of social behaviour by attempting to identify particular behaviours that are most likely to cause 'alarm', 'distress' and 'harassment' within specific communities. Take, for example, the recent furore over binge drinking and the way it has been cast as the number one social problem within certain urban locations (see Measham, 1996, 2005). In Post-industrial cities, urban regeneration has resulted in the rapid development of the night-time economy as cities have re-invented themselves as sites of consumption and leisure (Hobbs et al., 2002, 2003; Measham, 2004). Often the regeneration and re-zoning of these urban spaces is accompanied by the relaxation of local licensing laws enabling people to drink into the early hours of the morning. In turn this is blamed for the rapid growth of anti-social behaviour, creating both a fear of inner city areas and a demand for more

Table 9.2 RDS typology of anti-social behaviour

Misuse of public space	Disregard for community/ personal well-being	Acts directed at people	Environmental damage
Drug/substance misuse & dealing Taking drugs Sniffing volatile substances Discarding needles/drug paraphernalia Crack houses Presence of dealers or users **Street drinking** **Begging** **Prostitution** Soliciting Cards in phone boxes Discarded condoms **Kerb crawling** Loitering Pestering residents **Sexual acts** Inappropriate sexual conduct Indecent exposure **Abandoned cars** **Vehicle-related nuisance & inappropriate vehicle use** Inconvenient/illegal parking Car repairs on the street/in gardens Setting vehicles alight Joyriding Racing cars Off-road motorcycling Cycling/skateboarding in pedestrian areas/ footpaths	**Noise** Noisy neighbours Noisy cars/motorbikes Loud music Alarms (persistent ringing/ malfunction) Noise from pubs/ clubs Noise from business/ industry **Rowdy behaviour** Shouting & swearing Fighting Drunken behaviour Hooliganism/loutish behaviour **Nuisance behaviour** Urinating in public Setting fires (not directed at specific persons or property) Inappropriate use of fireworks Throwing missiles Climbing on buildings Impeding access to communal areas Games in restricted/ inappropriate areas Misuse of air guns Letting down tyres **Hoax calls** False calls to emergency services **Animal-related problems** Uncontrolled animals	**Intimidation/ harassment** Groups or individuals making threats Verbal abuse Bullying Following people Pestering people Voyeurism Sending nasty/ offensive letters Obscene/nuisance phone calls Menacing gestures *Can be on the grounds of:* Race Sexual orientation Gender Religion Disability Age	**Criminal damage/ vandalism** Graffiti Damage to bus shelters Damage to phone kiosks Damage to street furniture Damage to buildings Damage to trees/ plants/hedges **Litter/rubbish** Dropping litter Dumping rubbish Fly-tipping Fly-posting

Source: Research Development and Statistics Directorate.

controls over perceived rises in alcohol related crime (see the following chapter by Emma Wincup). Both the user and the seller of alcohol are seen here as anti-social, with licensees being controlled through legal frameworks, leaving consumers to be controlled by the criminal justice system or by local social control programmes. For example, in Sunderland, the local authority saw fit to employ a 'drink reduction officer' to assist in controlling and changing the perceived anti-social recreational behaviour of local people (*Sunderland Echo*, 16 March 2004; see also Winlow 2001 for a more general discussion of alcohol related crime in a North-East city). This example illustrates the increasing criminalization of everyday leisure activities.

Everyday 'order' and the anti-social

In his book *Understanding Social Control* Martin Innes discusses the notion that in contemporary society there is a growing sense of insecurity that feeds the need for ever more controls over certain sections of the community. He goes on to state that:

> We are living through a period of history where the control apparatus is being reconfigured. It is evident that the conduct of social control in late-modern societies is very complex, involving a range of state and non-state agencies, using an array of layered and interlocking technologies, strategies and ideas ... There is an accompanying sense that the reach of social control is extending and the social control network is expanding ... it seems as if more and more people are subject to some form of control. (Innes 2003: 144)

This reconfiguring involves not just the control of individuals through behaviour orders, but also the control of segments of society such as 'youth' or the 'homeless' or the 'poor'. For example, young people have been barred from particular areas at particular times through the use of generalized curfews enacted for no other reason than they may be at risk of committing anti-social behaviour in the future. Such was the reasoning for the suggested ban on under sixteen-year olds from the 'West End' of London after 9 p.m. in the evening and the barring of young people in Rossendale, Lancashire, from 'playgrounds' after 6 p.m. in winter and 9 p.m. in summer (Presdee, 2000: 111). As Jeffs and Smith remark this approach is problematic because it criminalizes 'perfectly legal and acceptable behaviour on the grounds of age ... to select young people and criminalize them for doing what the rest of the population can freely do is doubly discriminating' (Jeffs & Smith, 1996: 11).

A collection of government acts including the Anti-social Behaviour Act 2003, the Police Reform Act 2002 and the Criminal Justice and Police Act 2001, have combined to create a considerable raft of social control measures to direct social behaviour and punish those who transgress through the issue of on the spot Fixed Penalty Notices (FPNs) (a number of which are now being issued on a trial basis to children as young as ten). These 'on the spot' fines can be issued by the Police, community support officers or any one else accredited by the Chief Constable of a particular region. Such fines serve to bring an immediacy to punishment that is aimed at reinforcing the unacceptable and anti-social nature of a particular range of behaviours. At the present time fines are issued as set out in Table 9.3.

Table 9.3 Current fixed penalty notices for disorder (Criminal Justice and Police Act 2001)	
Wasting police time	£80
Knowingly giving a false alarm to the fire brigade	£80
Knowingly giving a false alarm to a person acting on behalf of the fire brigade	£80
Causing harassment, alarm or distress	£80
Using a public electronic communication system to cause alarm or distress	£80
Drunk and disorderly	£80
Sale of alcohol to a person under 18	£80
Buying alcohol for a person under 18	£80
Delivering, or allowing delivery of, alcohol to under 18	£80
Throwing fireworks in a thoroughfare	£80
Contravention of firework regulations and giving false statements	£80
Theft	£80
Destroying or damaging property	£80
Trespass on a railway	£50
Throwing stones on a railway	£50
Drunk on a highway	£50
Drinking in a designated public area	£50
Consuming, or allowing the consumption of alcohol under 18	£50
Depositing and leaving litter	£50

Source: The Penalties for Disorderly Behaviour (Amount of Penalty) (Amendment No. 2) Order 2004 No. 2468.

This ratcheting up of everyday techniques of social control does not stop with the issuing of FPNs. The range of anti-social behaviours now identified under various statutes is stunning in its comprehensiveness, including everything from:

- controls over gardening (the banning of high hedges over two metres);
- graffiti removal orders against those whose properties have been targeted;
- holding 'raves' and other such unauthorized gatherings in-doors as well as outside;
- cycling on footpaths;
- selling spray paint;
- using airguns under 17;
- two or more young people on the street after 9 p.m. and before 6 a.m;
- selling fireworks to under 18s;
- throwing fireworks;
- begging.

These contemporary forms of social control are mechanisms and responses to what Stan Cohen identified, with typical foresight, as:

[c]rime, delinquency and allied forms of deviant and/or socially problematic behaviour (i.e. *Anti-social behaviours*) which are actually conceived of as such, whether in the reactive sense

(after the putative act has taken place, or the actor has been identified) or in the proactive sense (to prevent the act). (Cohen: 1985: 3)

What Cohen described in the 1980s as 'socially problematic behaviour' is now commonly referred to as anti-social behaviour and is seen by Government as a threat to the flimsy and fragile existence of social order. The idea that social controls should be instituted as a form of situational crime prevention comes alongside the idea of social control as a form of protection against 'yob culture' and other perceived threats to social order, thereby allowing the State to increase its powers to intervene in everyday social life.

In many ways, this approach can be seen as a consequence of a general and identifiable loss of confidence and patience in the ability of family structures to ensure everyday order (see Wilson, 1985; Taylor, 1999: 42–50 for criminological introductions to this point). As Innes remarks:

> Over the past two decades, there has been a particular focus upon the family as an object of control because of the popular concerns relating to physical and sexual abuse . . . but also, due to fears that the family's effectiveness as a mechanism of informal social control is waning. The dramatic rises in recorded crime between the 1960s and mid–1990s were causally attributed to the increase in number of single mothers and families without fathers, by politicians who, for ideological reasons, found this a more palatable explanation, than to look at the structural inequalities caused by their liberalisation of free market mechanisms (Mooney, 1998). (Innes, 2003: 57)

For the State, the identified rise in anti-social behaviour, is a result of bad parenting rather than, for example, in the case of alcohol-related crime and disorder, due to changes in the alcohol industry and the changing social and spatial dynamics associated with the late modern night-time economy. By defining anti-social behaviour so widely both in what it is and who commits it the present government has ensured that it has become the new 'volume crime', thus allowing more political and practical attention to be concentrated on it. This cycle creates a new crime agenda that legitimates Government actions on social control.

REVIEW QUESTIONS

1 Make a list of all the social behaviours you and your friends regard as anti-social. Which do you think are the most important and how might they best be tackled?

2 Who currently has the power to identify particular behaviour as acceptable or not?

CONCLUSION

In this chapter we have identified the major elements of volume crime, both in terms of property crime and anti-social behaviour. We have discussed the underlying dynamics of property crime as being connected to the acquisition, distribution and consumption of stolen goods that make up what we call criminal markets. For each element we have teased out how the internal dynamics of the market are reliant on each other and make up the process of property crime. We have shown the importance of the identification of a market in the setting-up of the process of property crime; that there must also be distribution networks to enable goods to be offered for sale and consumers to ensure the process is successfully completed. We have examined closely the tensions involved in the social act of consumption and the way that the emotions of consumption interplay with the process of the formation of personal identity. We have suggested therefore that it is important to recognize that property crime is not just about the 'thief' but also involves those who handle stolen goods and those who consume them. In this way we expand our criminological concerns to include all those who are involved and play a part (no matter how seemingly insignificant) in the process of crime. In doing so we suggest, they become an inescapable and integral part of the crime process itself.

In the second half of the chapter we positioned the concept of anti-social behaviour as volume crime. We identified how the activities of young people, the poor, and the socially excluded are increasingly being targeted as 'anti-social' and perceived by the State as a product of the breakdown in social order. We showed how at the heart of the anti-social behaviour debate is a desire by the State and Government to increase its controlling mechanisms over the everyday lives of increasing numbers of its citizens. In doing so we suggested that anti-social behaviour legislation and regulation subjects a greater proportion of people to the realms of the criminal justice system.

QUESTIONS FOR DISCUSSION

1 By examining both national and local newspapers, especially court roundups in local presses, examine the approaches they take to everyday crime. What do they include, who do they include and what is absent from these accounts?

2 Discuss the question whether 'bad parenting' is responsible for most crime and the perceived break down in order.

3 Can legislation create 'good' behaviour?

4 Is it ever possible to isolate oneself from the everyday happenings of a consumer society?

GUIDE TO FURTHER READING

Criminal Justice Matters, Issue 57, Autumn 2004, 'Whose Justice'.
A series of accessible articles on anti-social behaviour written by academics and practitioners.

Felson, M., *Crime and Everyday Life*. Thousand Oaks, CA: Sage.
An interesting book concerned with examining how society encourages or inhibits crime in the routine activities of everyday life.

Innes, M., *Understanding Social Control*. Maidenhead: Open University Press.
An interesting theoretical introduction to the way societies respond to a variety of forms of deviant behaviour.

Mike Sutton 'Supply by theft: does the market for second-hand goods play a role in keeping crime figures high?' *The British Journal of Criminology*, 35 No. 3, 400–16.
A useful academic analysis of the way crime markets function.

Chapter 1 ('Youth crime: representations, discourse and data') in John Muncie's *Youth and Crime* (2nd edn). London: Sage.

A clear, concise introduction to some of the key issues surrounding contemporary youth crime.

WEB LINKS

http://www.statistics.gov.uk/CCI/nscl.asp?ID=5004

The 'crime and justice' page of the National Statistics Online web page. These pages provide a whole host of statistical information about such things as Police Cautions and other sentencing data.

http://www.guardian.co.uk/Archive/0,4271,00.html

This is the 'archive' page of the UK daily newspaper *The Guardian*. Search under 'anti-social behaviour' for a plethora of articles, many of which adopt a very similar critical line to the one set down in this chapter.

http://www.homeoffice.gov.uk/crime/antisocialbehaviour/index.html

The 'Anti-social behaviour' page on the Home Office's website.

http://www.homeoffice.gov.uk/crime/alcoholrelatedcrime/index.html

The 'Alcohol related' crime page on the Home Office's website.

http://www.hmso.gov.uk/acts/acts1998/19980037.htm

A full digital version of the 1988 Crime and Disorder Act. Check out the various sections on anti-social behaviour.

http://www.youth-justice-board.gov.uk/YouthJusticeBoard/

The website of the Youth Justice Board, including information on everything from Youth Offending Teams to Pre Court Orders.

REFERENCES

Baldwin, J. and Bottoms, A.E. (1976) *The Urban Criminal*. London: Tavistock.

Brantingham, P.J. and Brantingham, P.L. (1991) *Environmental Criminology*. Prospect Heights, Ill: Waveland.

Brantingham, P.J. and Brantingham, P.L. (1993) 'Environment, routine and situation: toward a pattern theory of crime' in R.V. Clarke and M. Felson (eds). *Routine Activity and Rational Choice: Advances in Criminological Theory 5*, New Brunswick, NJ: Transaction Books.

Carrabine, E., Cox, P., Lee, M. and South, N. (2002) *Crime in Modern Britain*. Oxford: Oxford University Press.

Cohen, L. and Felson, M. (1979) 'Social Change and Crime Rates: a Routine Activity Approach' *American Sociological Review* 44: 588–608.

Clarke, R.V. (1999) *Hot Products: Understanding, Anticipating and Reducing Demand for Stolen Goods*, Police Research Series paper 112. London: HMSO.

Dodd, T., Nicholas, S., Povey, D. and Walker, A. (2004) *Crime in England and Wales 2003/4*. London: Home Office.

Edwards, T. (2000) *Contradictions of Consumption: Concepts, Practices and Politics in Consumer Society*. Buckingham: Open University Press.

Felson, M. (1998) *Crime and Everyday Life* (2nd edn). London: Pine Forge Press.

Ferrell, J. (2005) *Empire of Scrounge*. New York: New York University Press.

Figlio, R.M., Hakim, S. and Rengert, G.F. (1986) *Metropolitan Crime Patterns*, Monsey, New York: Willow Tree Press.

Fisher, B. and Sloan, J.J. (1997) *Campus Crime: Legal, Social and Policy Perspectives*. Springfield, ILL: Charles C Thomas Publishers.

Gabor, T. (1994) *Everybody Does It! Crime by the Public*. Toronto: University of Toronto Press.

Garland, D. (2001) *The Culture of Control*. Oxford: Oxford University Press.

Hayward, K. (2002) 'The vilification and pleasures of youthful transgression' in J. Muncie, E. Hughes and E. McLaughlin, (eds), *Youth Justice: Critical Readings*. London: Sage.

Hayward, K. (2004) *City Limits: Crime, Consumer Culture and the Urban Experience*. London: Cavendish.

Hobbs, D., Lister, S., Hadfield, P., Winlow, S. and Hall, S. (2000) 'Receiving Shadows: Governance and Liminality in the Night-time Economy', *British Journal of Sociology* 51 (4): 701–17.

Hobbs, D., Hadfield, P., Lister, S. and Winlow, S. (2003) *Bouncers: Violence and Governance in the Night-time Economy*. Oxford: Oxford University Press.

Home Office (2003) *Respect and Responsibility: taking a stand against anti-social behaviour*.

Howitt, D. (1998) *Crime, the Media and the Law*. Chichester: Wiley.

Innes, M. (2003) *Understanding social control: Deviance, Crime and Social Order*. Maidenhead: Open University Press.

Jeffs, T. and Smith, M. (1996) 'Getting the dirt bags off the street-curfews and other solutions to juvenile crime', *Youth and Policy*, no. 53: 1–14.

Kock, E., Kemp, T., and Rix, B. (1996) *Disrupting the Distribution of Stolen Electrical Goods*, Crime Detection and Prevention Series, paper 69, London: HMSO.

Lury, C. (1996) *Consumer Culture*. Cambridge: Polity.

Measham, F. (1996), 'The "Big Bang" approach to sessional drinking: Changing patterns of alcohol consumption amongst young people in north west England', *Addiction Research*, Volume 4, No. 3: 283–99.

Measham, F., Parker, H. and Aldridge, J. (1998), 'The Teenage Transition: From adolescent recreational drug use to the young adult dance culture in Britain in the mid-1990', in R. Power (ed), *Journal of Drug Issues*, Special Edition, Contemporary Issues Concerning Illicit Drug Use in the British Isles, Volume 28, No. 1: 9–32.

Measham, F. (2004), 'Play Space: Historical and socio-cultural reflections on drugs, licensed leisure locations, commercialisation and control', *International Journal of Drug Policy*, Special Edition: Social theory in drug research and harm reduction, forthcoming.

Measham, F. (2005), 'The Decline of Ecstasy, the Rise of "Binge Drinking" and the Persistence of Pleasure', *Probation Journal*, Special Edition: Rethinking Drugs and Crime, forthcoming.

Miles, S. (1998) *Consumerism as a Way of Life*. London: Sage.

Mooney, J (1998) 'Moral Panics and the new right: single mothers and feckless fathers—is this really the key to the crime problem?' in P. Walton and J. Young (eds) *The New Criminology Re-visited*. London: Macmillan.

Muncie, J., Hughes, G. and McLaughlin, E. (2002) *Youth Justice: Critical Readings*. London: Sage.

Muncie, J. (2004) *Youth and Crime* (2nd edn). London: Sage.

Presdee, M. (2000) *Cultural Criminology and the Carnival of Crime*. London: Routledge.

Reiner, R. (2002) 'Media made criminality: the representation of crime in the mass media' in M. Maguire, R. Morgan and R. Reiner (eds), *The Oxford Handbook of Criminology* (3rd edn). Oxford: Oxford University Press.

Rengert, G.F., Mattson, M.T., and Henderson, K.D. (2001) *Campus Security: Situational Crime Prevention in High Density Environments*. Monsey, New York: Willow Tree Press.

Sutton, M. (1995) 'Supply by theft: does the market for second-hand goods play a role in keeping crime figures high?' *The British Journal of Criminology*, 35 No. 3: 400–416.

Sutton, M., Johnston, K., and Lockwood, H. (1998) *Handling Stolen Goods and Theft: A Market Reduction Approach*, Home Office research Study 178. London: HMSO.

Sutton, M., Schneider, J., and Hetherington, S. (2001) *Tackling Theft with the Market Reduction Approach*, Crime Reduction Research Series Paper 8. London: HMSO.

Taylor, I. (1999) *Crime in Context: a Critical Criminology of Market Societies*. Cambridge: Polity.

Wilson, J.Q. (1985) *Thinking About Crime*. New York: Vintage Books.

10 Drugs, alcohol and crime

Emma Wincup

INTRODUCTION

Drug and alcohol use are frequently offered as explanations for crime. The use of so-called 'hard' drugs such as heroin and crack cocaine is cited as one of the causes of a range of crimes, particularly acquisitive crimes; excessive alcohol use is perceived as closely connected with violent behaviour. For many members of the general public and the media, the relationship between drug or alcohol use and criminal activity is clear and the solutions straightforward. This contrasts sharply with the findings of research studies which identify the need for a more complex understanding and consequently, a multi-faceted response.

This chapter is divided into two main parts. The first part focuses on drug use and addresses three key issues: (a) the nature and extent of drug use; (b) the relationship between drug use and crime, (c) and strategies for reducing drug-related crime. In the second part, we explore the same issues in relation to alcohol use. Exploring the relationship between drugs, alcohol and crime is a huge task and it is necessary to impose some editorial boundaries. First, I will be concentrating predominantly on England and Wales. Second, space precludes a detailed consideration of organized crime relating to drug and contraband alcohol markets or the policing of these markets. For introductory overviews of these topics, readers are directed to Bean (2002) and Croall (1998).

Part one: Drugs and crime

BACKGROUND

Attempts to control drug use date back to the Pharmacy Act 1868 which confined the sale of opium to pharmacists. Throughout the twentieth century, other statutes were passed in a piecemeal fashion to strengthen the laws regulating drug use, including a succession of Dangerous Drugs Acts. The 1971 Misuse of Drugs Act consolidated earlier statutes and laid the foundations for existing and future controls on the import, export, possession, use, manufacture and distributions of *controlled* drugs (Jason-Lloyd, 2003). We should pause for a moment and reflect upon the language utilized within the legislation because it is revealing about the ideological assumptions underpinning the Acts and offers an insight into shifting conceptions of drug use across time. By 1971, the language of danger, with its moralistic overtones, had been replaced by the language of control which emphasized the need to control drugs by preventing their misuse at the same time as permitting their correct use in medical contexts.

The 1971 Act divided controlled drugs into categories (see Table 10.1) according to official perceptions of their relative harmfulness when misused. The level of control is expected to be proportionate to official definitions of harmfulness.

Table 10.1 The 1971 Misuse of Drugs Act	
Category	**Examples of controlled drugs**
Class A (most harmful)	Cocaine, Ecstasy, Heroin, LSD
Class B	Amphetamines
Class C (least harmful)	Cannabis, Tranquillisers

Although a series of statutes have been passed since, the 1971 Act continues to be 'the major stepping-stone in the modern regulation of controlled drugs' (Jason-Lloyd, 2003, p. 1:4). An independent inquiry into the Act (Police Foundation, 2000) outlined a comprehensive reform programme, advocating a less punitive approach to possession offences and a more punitive approach to supply. Whilst many of its recommendations have not been implemented, Cannabis was downgraded from a Class B to a Class C drug in 2004, and in most instances possession of cannabis is no longer an arrestable offence (see Barton, 2003 for a more detailed discussion). This move was supported by research findings (May *et al.*, 2002) which suggested that reclassification would allow police officers to respond more effectively to other demands on their time and remove a source of friction between the police and young people.

Legislation is based upon official perceptions of the harm caused by drugs, which may not be shared by all members of society. A number of classic criminological studies illustrate this vividly (Becker, 1963; Young, 1971). These qualitative studies were shaped by symbolic interactionism (see Chapter 4) and focused on cannabis use. They emphasized the plurality of societal norms and values and identify the processes by which drug use is socially constructed as a 'deviant' act and drug users portrayed as belonging to a counter-culture.

The drug 'problem' has been officially defined as a law and order, social, medical and public health 'problem'. These different interpretations have, at different times, influenced the development of UK drug policy. During the 1980s and most of the 1990s, the UK adopted a public health approach to drug policy, initially concerned with reducing the risk drug users pose to themselves and later with risks to wider society (Harman and Paylor, 2002). The public health approach was a response to the realization that unsafe injecting practices could transmit HIV. As the new millennium drew close, a criminal justice approach to drug policy was adopted: problem drug use and offending became increasingly interlinked. Critics of the shift in policy emphasis are numerous, and it has been described as a 'war on drug users' (Buchanan and Young, 2000: 409). However, as Sampson (2002) highlights, 'the dominance of the criminal justice perspective in drug policy is still more apparent than real' because 'the vast bulk of drugs money still goes to health authorities and local government' (p. 6).

The nature and extent of drug use

Commonly used terms to describe drug use include experimental, recreational and problematic, and these are based more on individual opinion than accepted definitions (Health Advisory Service, 2001). In one sense, all drug use is problematic due to the health risks involved and because it can lead to contact with criminal justice agencies.

The difficulties of defining categories of use adequately have been commented on elsewhere (Barton, 2003); however, I offer some working definitions here. Recreational drug use is characteristically centred on the use of cannabis and 'dance drugs' (for example, ecstasy) and whilst these drugs may be used frequently on a recreational basis, unlike problem drug use, recreational use does not involve dependency, regular excessive use or use which creates serious health risks (for example, injecting). Problem drug use typically involves consuming Class A drugs and has the strongest links with offending behaviour.

Estimating the extent of illegal drug use is extremely difficult and there is no comprehensive data source. Criminologists seeking to understand the nature and extent of drug use have to piece together data from official statistics, self-report studies and academic studies.

Official statistics

The Home Office publishes data on the number of offenders charged with drug offences that come to the attention of the police or HM Customs and Excise and are subsequently cautioned, convicted or dealt with in some other way. In 2002, 113,500 people were dealt with for drug offences (Ahmad and Mwenda, 2004). Unlawful possession of controlled drugs, particularly cannabis, was the most common offence and the typical offender was young and male. The majority of episodes of drug use form part of the 'dark figure' of undetected crime; hence drug offender statistics provide little insight into the nature and extent of drug use. An alternative data source is national data on the number of drug users seeking medical treatment. The latest data demonstrate that just over 140,000 individuals received drug treatment in England between April 2002 and March 2003 (Department of Health, 2003). This is likely to represent the 'tip of the iceberg'. It excludes drug users who were unable to, did not wish to or did not need to access treatment. Given these limitations, researchers have developed elaborate models to estimate the prevalence of problem drug use using data gathered from various agencies that problem drug users are likely to make contact with; for example, criminal justice agencies, GP surgeries and hospital accident and emergency departments (Frischer *et al.*, 2004; Hickman *et al.*, 2004; Millar *et al.*, 2004).

Self-report studies

Self-report studies have become the most commonly used means of assessing how many people use, or have used, drugs. However, criticisms of this method are numerous (see Coleman and Moynihan, 1996 for an overview). The two main studies which provide data on drug use for England and Wales are the British Crime Survey and the Youth Lifestyles Survey.

The British Crime Survey (BCS) was established in 1982 as a large survey of adults living in a representative cross-section of private households in England and Wales. Whilst the main focus of the survey is on experiences of crime, data have been collected on drug use since 1994. Respondents enter their answers directly into a laptop computer so that sensitive information can be kept confidential and refusal rates kept to a minimum. The

Table 10.2 Prevalence of drug use in the last month by age group

Type of drug	% used (16–24 years olds)	16–59 year olds
Cannabis	16.2	6.7
Ecstasy	2.6	0.9
Cocaine	1.9	0.9
Amphetamines ('speed')	1.7	0.6
Amyl nitrate ('poppers')	1.7	0.6
Any illicit drug	17.6	7.4

Source: British Crime Survey 2002/3 (Condon and Smith, 2003).

2002/3 BCS (Condon and Smith, 2003) estimated that 36 per cent of 16–59 year olds have used one or more illicit drugs in their lifetime, and 13 per cent have used a Class A drug at least once. Levels of drug use within the past year were lower with 12 per cent of all 16–59 year olds admitting to taking an illicit drug and 3 per cent to using a Class A drug. Levels of drug use within the past month are lower still, and this is illustrated in Table 10.2. The data reveal that usage varied tremendously between drug types and provides further evidence of the strong relationship between drug use and age.

The BCS does have its limitations as a survey of drug use. In addition to the limitations described in Chapter 3, it is important to note that the BCS is a household survey, and therefore excludes some of the groups most likely to be involved in drug use such as homeless people (Fountain and Howes, 2002; Wincup *et al.*, 2003).

The Youth Lifestyles Survey is also a survey of individuals living in private households in England and Wales. Its focus is on offending behaviour. Two sweeps have taken place: the first in 1992/3 (Graham and Bowling, 1995) and the second in 1998/9 (Flood-Page *et al.*, 2000). The second YLS estimated that 27 per cent of young people aged 12–30 had used drugs in the last year. The highest rates were for 21 year olds (54 per cent) and for males (32 per cent). Much smaller proportions admitted to using drugs at least once a month or at least once a week.

Academic studies

Academic studies of drug users are plentiful. In contrast to the work of Becker and Young described earlier in this chapter, often these studies focus on drug users' experiences of the criminal justice system and treatment rather than their drug use *per se*. The available studies have captured the diversity of the drug-using population by exploring different populations such as women (Taylor, 1993), homeless people (Wincup *et al.*, 2003), care leavers (Ward *et al.*, 2003), young offenders (Hammersley *et al.*, 2003), clubbers (Measham *et al.*, 2001) and prisoners (Cope, 2000). We will focus here on the work of Parker and his colleagues whose longitudinal study of over 700 young people has fuelled academic debates around the normalization of recreational drug use among young people.

The study began in 1991 when the young people were aged 14 and ran initially for five years. It was later extended to follow up the research participants for a further three years. Based on their initial findings, the authors (Parker *et al.*, 1998) outline a normalization thesis consisting of six key dimensions, listed below.

(a) widespread availability of drugs;

(b) high levels of drug trying;

(c) a significant minority engage in sustained drug use;

(d) extensive knowledge about drugs;

(e) open-mindedness around future drug use;

(f) drug use is accommodated within youth culture.

Parker *et al.*, like South (2002), argue that drug use is no longer confined to atypical subcultural groups. Instead, it forms part and parcel of growing up in contemporary Britain and is one of a number of ordinary, unremarkable activities (see also Coffield and Gofton, 1994). The normalization thesis has been strongly criticized by others (Shiner and Newburn, 1997; 1999) who suggest that it exaggerates the extent of drug use by young people. They emphasize that many young people do not experiment with illegal drugs and experimentation is often shortlived. Moreover, Shiner and Newburn draw attention to young people's perceptions of drug use as a problematic activity, noting their use of 'techniques of neutralisation' (Sykes and Matza, 1957) such as 'everyone does it' to justify their 'deviant' behaviour.

REVIEW QUESTIONS

1 What are the main sources of data on drug use?

2 What are the strengths and weaknesses of the main data sources?

3 Do you believe that drug use among young people is now normalized?

Exploring the links between drug use and crime

There have been multiple attempts to develop frameworks of the links between drug use and crime. This is a complex task because both drug use and crime encompass a wide range of behaviours, thus the best attempts have broken down the task by focusing on one broad category of crime.

Goldstein (1985: 493) developed what he termed a 'tripartite conceptual framework' to explain the 'drugs/violence nexus'. He suggests that drugs and violence are related in three possible ways. First, the psychopharmological model proposes that some individuals after consuming drugs may exhibit violent behaviour. Second, the economic compulsive model propounds that some drug users engage in economically oriented violent crime, for example robbery, in order to support costly drug use. Third, the systemic model suggests that violence is intrinsic to involvement with illegal drug use because violence is normatively embedded in the social and economic networks of drug users and sellers. This framework helpfully draws out the different ways in which drug use and violence are connected but as Goldstein acknowledges in practice there is considerable overlap between the three models (see Neale (2002) for a detailed critique).

More recently, Seddon (2000) reviewed the literature on the linkages between what he termed 'non-recreational' (that is, problem) drug use and acquisitive crime (theft, burglary, robbery, shoplifting, fraud and deception). He suggests that essentially three models of the relationship have been proposed.

(a) Drug use causes crime. This model suggests that the drug users commit crimes out of economic necessity in order to satisfy uncontrollable needs to obtain drugs which cannot be met via a legitimate income source. From this perspective, a straightforward causal relationship is identified.

(b) Crime causes drug use. This model highlights that for many drug users criminality predates drug-taking. Again, a straightforward causal relationship is acknowledged yet operating in the opposite direction to previous model.

(c) Crime and drug use are related to other factors. Seddon notes that this model is the less well developed in the literature and has yet to be refined into a single coherent position. Nonetheless, it remains an important attempt to move away from causal explanations by suggesting that both crime and drug use are related to other factors.

Reviewing the available evidence

Offering a comprehensive review of the available literature, which may or may not offer support for these models, is beyond the scope of this chapter. More comprehensive overviews can be found elsewhere (Hough, 1996; Seddon, 2000). Instead, I will focus on the key studies which have been published in the past decade.

One major piece of research is the New English and Welsh Arrestee Drug Abuse Monitoring Programme (NEW-ADAM). The research study comprised interviews and voluntary urine tests with arrestees across sixteen locations (Bennett and Holloway, 2004). A similar programme exists in Scotland (McKeganey *et al.*, 2000). Data from the first two years of the NEW-ADAM programme reveal high levels of drug use among arrestees. Just over two-thirds tested positive for one or more illegal drugs and almost two-fifths tested positive for heroin and/or (crack) cocaine. Levels of self-reported drug use were also high with 29 per cent admitting to using heroin and/or (crack) cocaine in the three days prior to their arrest and 64 per cent using any drug. Overall, 18 per cent of the sample were defined as drug misusing repeat offenders, using heroin and/or (crack) cocaine at least once a week and reporting two or more income-generating offences per month.

The data discussed above clearly demonstrate that a high proportion of arrestees are recent users of illicit drugs but shed little light on the nature of the relationship between drug use and crime. However, interviewees' perceptions of the relationship were gathered via interviews. Three-fifths of arrestees who reported using one or more illicit drugs and committing one or more acquisitive crimes in the last year thought there was a connection, rising to 89 per cent of those who reported using heroin and/or cocaine. The majority (83 per cent) suggested they offended to obtain money to buy drugs. Other responses given were that drug use affected their judgement making them more likely to offend (27 per cent) and that they used the money from crime to buy drugs (8 per cent). The study did not collect detailed retrospective data on drug use and crime therefore cannot tell us whether drug use predates crime or vice versa.

Pudney (2002) analysed YLS data to explore the timing of young people's initiation into drug use and offending. He found that crime tends to precede drug use. The average age of onset for crime was 14.5 compared to 16.2 for drugs. Interpreting the findings is challenging because the onset of both offending behaviour and drug use are best viewed as processes rather than one-off events. For example, a drug 'career' may commence with experimenting with alcohol, tobacco, glues and solvents around the age of fourteen moving on to take cannabis and 'poppers' aged sixteen and heroin and crack cocaine aged seventeen or eighteen. We cannot conclude from Pudney's research that crime causes drug use. The situation is more complex than this. The relationship between problem drug use and crime can best be viewed as 'dynamic or interactive' (Edmunds *et al.*, 1998: 10) because drug and criminal careers tend to develop in parallel. For instance, acquisitive crime or sex work can provide people with sufficient money to become involved in drug use, and if the drug use becomes problematic they may become locked into involvement in crime. Additionally, as Pudney concludes, social, economic and family circumstances are key influences on young people's risk of becoming involved in both crime and drug use.

Lloyd (1998) reviewed studies which have sought to identify the risk factors associated with problem drug use. Since drug experimentation and recreational drug use are so widespread, it is not possible to identify groups who are at risk of using drugs in this way. Lloyd concluded that risk factors can relate to the family (for example, parental or sibling drug use; family disruption, poor attachment or communication with parents and child abuse); school (for example, poor educational performance, exclusion); involvement in crime and other conduct disorders (for example, truancy); mental disorder; social deprivation and young age of onset for drug use. He suggests that these factors are highly connected and best viewed as a 'web of causation' (p. 217).

REVIEW QUESTIONS

1 Critically evaluate the different models proposed to explain the relationship between drug use and crime.

2 Consider the following policies. Which models described by Goldstein and Seddon are they linked to?

- Drug treatment for offenders
- Tackling social exclusion
- Prevention programmes for young people at risk of offending
- More intensive policing of drug markets

3 Refer to Chapter 19. How similar are the risk factors for problem drug use and crime?

Breaking the links

In 1998, *Tackling Drugs to Build a Better Britain* (President of the Council, 1998) was launched as the government's ten year strategy to tackle drug misuse and was updated in 2002 (Home Office Drugs Strategy Directorate, 2002). Despite its title, its focus was on England: other parts of the UK were asked to reflect on the implications for their existing strategies and all produced new versions. Fraser and Padel (2002) suggest that attempts to tackle drugs have traditionally operated in three spheres: prevention, treatment and enforcement. All strategies across the UK focus on this trio of interventions. The aims of *Tackling Drugs to Build a Better Britain* are listed below:

(a) to help young people resist drug misuse in order to achieve their full potential in society;

(b) to protect our communities from drug-related and anti-social behaviour;

(c) to enable people with drug problems to overcome them and live healthy and crime-free lives;

(d) to stifle the availability of illegal drugs on our streets.

Drug policy is now largely the responsibility of the Home Office rather than the Department of Health. Change regarding the ownership of drug policy is both a cause and effect of the shift towards a criminal justice approach, premised on the view that drug use causes crime and therefore the link needs to be broken. Providing treatment for drug-using offenders has been central to breaking the link. The criminal justice system can be viewed as ideally placed for targeted interventions because of the large number of problem drug users that come into contact with it and because treatment opportunities exist from the point of arrest through to release from prison (Kothari *et al.*, 2002).

Arrest referral schemes aim to identify problem users at the point of entry into the criminal justice system. This involves the presence of a drug worker in a police custody suite who can conduct a brief assessment, if the arrestee wishes, and refer them to a treatment provider if appropriate. The schemes seek to make best use of a moment of vulnerability when the drug user is most receptive to intervention. Between October 2001 and September 2002, just over 41,000 arrestees were screened by arrest referral workers, and approximately half had never previously accessed drug treatment (O'Shea *et al.*, 2003). Research has suggested that well-designed referral schemes can break the cycle of problem drug use and offending (Edmunds *et al.*, 1998). The essential ingredients of success include sufficiently resourced schemes, ability to establish positive relationships with arrestees and access to appropriate and adequate treatment services. Rhetoric does not match reality (see Mair, 2002). Custody suites are rarely staffed on a continual basis and even when a drug worker is present it may be difficult for them to find the time to assess even those detained for long periods. Arrestees typically face a lengthy wait to access treatment and therefore attrition rates are high. However, if arrestees are charged with the offence and required to appear before the criminal courts, further opportunities for intervention exist (see Table 10.3).

Prior to 1998, no specific sentences for drug-using offenders existed although it was

Table 10.3 Overview of new sentences for drug-using offenders

Sentences	Brief description	Relevant legislation
Drug Treatment and Testing Orders (DTTO)	A community penalty requiring offenders to undergo regular drug testing and to attend treatment.	Crime and Disorder Act (1998)
Drug Abstinence Order (DAO)	A community penalty requiring offenders to undergo regular drug testing.	Criminal Justice and Court Services Act (2000)
Drug Abstinence Requirement (DAR)	The DAR places the same obligations on the offender as a DAO but is attached to another community sentence rather than a sentence in its own right.	Criminal Justice and Court Services Act (2000)

possible to attach a condition of drug treatment to a probation order (now known as a community rehabilitation order). In practice, these conditions were rarely used: probation officers were concerned about the effectiveness of coerced treatment and drug agencies were reluctant to operate mandatory programmes (Bean, 2002). The Drug Treatment and Testing Order (DTTO) is distinct from earlier provisions in that it requires regular drug testing and reviews before the courts. DTTOs are described more fully in Chapter 26. The introduction of treatment which has been various described as 'coercive' or 'enforced' (see Bean, 2002 for a discussion) and 'quasi-compulsory' (Stevens *et al.*, forthcoming) has attracted fierce criticism. A frequently espoused concern is that such measures may disadvantage drug users whose offending is confined to illegal drug use.

DTTOs were piloted at three sites from October 1998 to March 2000 and evaluated (Hough *et al.*, 2003; Turnbull *et al.*, 2000). The pilots were not unequivocally successful but provided important lessons regarding implementation. Reconviction rates were calculated for the 210 offenders involved in the pilot two years after the start of their DTTO: 80 per cent of the sample had been reconvicted. Levels of reconviction were highest for those who had not completed their order (91 per cent compared to 53 per cent). This findings suggests that a key challenge for the criminal justice system is to boost retention rates although relying on reconviction rates as a measures of success is in itself problematic (Lloyd *et al.*, 1994).

The criminal courts have other options if they wish to confer a sentence which tackles an offender's drug use. The requirement to attend an offending behaviour programme such as ASRO (Addressing Substance-related Offending) can be attached to a community rehabilitation order (at the time of writing, the evaluation of the ASRO pilots has not been published). Offending behaviour programmes are based on cognitive behavioural approaches (see Chapter 6). Alternatively, sentencers can choose Drug Abstinence Orders

(DAO) and Drug Abstinence Requirements (DAR). These provisions were piloted between July 2001 and October 2003 and evaluated (Matrix Research Consultancy and Nacro, 2004). The findings point towards evidence of reduced levels of drug consumption, higher levels of treatment contact, higher level of abstinence from heroin and (crack) cocaine and lower levels of offending. However, it is important to note that the findings are based on a small number of cases of offenders receiving DAOs (82) and a much larger number receiving DARs (1,462). DTTOs, DAOs and DARs will no longer exist in their current form once the Criminal Justice Act 2003 is implemented. This creates a new generic community order for offenders aged sixteen and over which will comprise of requirements commensurate with the seriousness of the offences. Drug testing and treatment will form part of the 'menu' of requirements available to sentencers (see Gibson, 2004 for a detailed discussion).

Those sentenced to custody are also afforded opportunities to seek treatment for their drug use through Counselling, Assessment, Referral, Advice and Treatment (CARAT) schemes. However, offering treatment alongside measures such as mandatory drug testing and increased security is fraught with contradictions (Duke, 2003). At present, liberal responses (for example, the issuing of sterilizing tablets to prisoners who inject) operate alongside punitive responses. The official discourse remains centred on 'control', 'order' and 'punishment' rather than harm minimization and treatment. For some prisoners, control will extend beyond the prison gate as the Criminal Justice and Court Services Act 2000 permitted a drug testing requirement to form part of a condition of release from prison.

REVIEW QUESTIONS

1 Does it matter which government department has responsibility for drug policy?

2 What assumptions about the relationship between drugs and crime underpin the sentences described in Table 10.3?

3 Are DTTOs and DAOs effective ways to tackle drug-related crime?

Part two: Alcohol and crime

BACKGROUND

Attempts to restrict alcohol use date back to the nineteenth century. Legislation from the 1872 Licensing Act onwards was introduced to prevent or reduce the problems associated with alcohol intoxication. As Deehan (1999) notes, the legislation covers the responsibilities of the licensee, the behaviour of drinkers and the powers of the police to deal with both. Alcohol legislation is typically perceived as a reflection of social and cultural attitudes in British society. Few would argue that the laws governing the availability of alcohol should be significantly tightened, and more flexible licensing laws (for example, by allowing pubs to open later) have been met with a mixed response. Britain is often described as having a 'wet' culture; in other words, drinking alcohol is widespread and socially accepted as a legitimate and pleasurable activity (Newburn and Shiner, 2001). At the same time, concerns have been expressed about the health and public order implications of problem drinking. Alcohol therefore occupies an ambiguous position in contemporary Britain, associated with pleasure, but also individual and social harms (Newburn and Shiner, 2001). Furthermore, alcohol and related industries are important in economic terms providing employment and a source of government income.

We referred above to 'problem drinking'. This term is used to refer to 'alcoholism' (or 'alcohol dependency') and 'binge drinking'. It is important to distinguish between the two although this task is complicated by the absence of universally accepted definitions. Both patterns of drinking can be contrasted with the officially defined 'sensible' drinking (Department of Health, 1995). Alcohol dependency can be characterized as consuming more than the sensible daily limits and drinking every day. Binge drinking can be defined as drinking half the weekly recommended units of alcohol in a single drinking session. The sensible drinking guidance recommends that men drink no more than three to four units per day and women no more than two to three. This supplements the initial guidance that men should not consume more than twenty-one units of alcohol per week and women no more than fourteen. Exceeding these limits on a regular basis increases the risk to health of the individual but also potentially effects their families and society as a whole.

Reviews of the literature from criminological and public health perspectives have explored how problem drinking can lead to accidents, abuse (in all its forms) in the home, drink-driving, lost productivity at work and violence from minor assaults to homicide (Deehan, 1999; Finney, 2004a, 2004b, 2004c; Prime Minister's Strategy Unit, 2003). Most recently, academic, political and media attention has focused on the extent of alcohol-related violence and disorder in urban centres (Finney, 2004a; Hobbs *et al.*, 2003). In post-industrial cities, urban regeneration has resulted in the rapid development of the night-time economy as cities have re-invented themselves as sites of consumption and leisure (Hobbs, 2003). Consequently, problem drinking places heavy demands on the resources of the health service and criminal justice system, although the night-time economy is largely 'policed' by private security companies (Hobbs *et al.*, 2003).

The nature and extent of alcohol use

Over 90 per cent of adults in Britain consume alcohol, and the majority of people drink sensibly the majority of the time (Prime Minister's Strategy Unit, 2003). Whilst the level of alcohol consumption is now lower than a century ago, consumption levels rose steadily in the second half of the twentieth century. This contrasts with the pattern elsewhere in Western Europe, and if current trends continue the UK will rise near the top of the consumption league by 2013 (Prime Minister's Strategy Unit, 2003).

Data on alcohol consumption can be obtained from a variety of sources. The General Household Survey (GHS) provides data on alcohol use for those aged sixteen and over on an annual basis. Questions are asked about average weekly consumption, as well as consumption on the heaviest day during the week prior to interview. The GHS provides a detailed dataset but we should emphasize here two key findings for 2002 (Richards *et al.*, 2004). The first relates to gender differences: men were not only more likely than women to have drunk alcohol in the previous week but to have consumed a greater amount and on a more frequent basis. The second relates to problem drinking: young people (aged 16–24), especially young males, were the most likely to drink above the sensible limits.

Data for young people aged between eleven and fifteen can be obtained from the annual school-based survey for England. The 2002 survey (National Centre for Social Research and the National Foundation for Education Research, 2003) discovered that approximately a quarter of pupils had drunk alcohol in the previous week, a similar proportion to studies from the mid-1990s onwards. Again, levels of alcohol consumption among males were higher than among females. Data on underage drinking can also be obtained from the YLS. This also suggests that underage age drinking is commonplace, and that levels of alcohol use increase as young people make their transitions to adulthood (Harrington, 2000). Drinking alcohol, and specifically getting drunk, were viewed positively by young people because they lead to increased confidence and greater opportunities for socializing (Harrington, 2000; see also Honess *et al.*, 2000). The extensive literature on teenage drinking is summarized by Newburn and Shiner (2001).

Limited data on alcohol use is also available from the Home Office. Official crime statistics provide information on the number of offenders cautioned for, or convicted of, offences which specifically mention alcohol but are not revealing about the extent of alcohol-related crime. The main 'facts' are presented below;

(a) in 2002, just over 43,000 people in England and Wales were cautioned by the police or found guilty by the courts for offences relating to drunkenness; 86 per cent of them were male (Home Office, 2003);

(b) in 2002, just over 100,000 drivers tested positive for alcohol or refused to be tested, comprising 18 per cent of those tested (Ayres *et al.*, 2004).

REVIEW QUESTIONS

1 What are the main strengths and weakness of the different data sources?

2 Does a 'wet' culture exist in Britain?

3 How can we explain higher level of alcohol consumption among males? (You might find it helpful to refer to Chapter 17)

Exploring the links between alcohol use and crime

The link between alcohol use and crime has been explored extensively, and numerous attempts have been made to develop typologies for understanding the relationship between the two behaviours. Whilst typologies vary, all agree that the link between alcohol and crime is multifaceted. A useful starting point is offered by Hayes (1993) who suggests that the relationship can be characterized in three ways. First, the relationship may be causal because an offender has committed an alcohol-defined offence, an alcohol-induced offence (for example, assaulting someone when drunk) or an alcohol-inspired offence (for example, shoplifting to obtain alcohol). Second, the relationship between alcohol and crime may be contributory: alcohol provides 'dutch courage' to commit an offence, acts as a catalyst, or is offered later as an excuse for offending behaviour. Finally, there may be no relationship between alcohol and crime, with the two behaviours simply co-existing as separate activities.

Similarly, Purser (1995) developed a functional model of the alcohol and crime relationship, distinguishing between the different roles alcohol plays in the offence His five categories are listed below:

(a) offences which specifically mention alcohol;

(b) offences against the licensing law;

(c) offences committed while under the disinhibiting effects of alcohol where alcohol has affected the person's self-control or judgement;

(d) offences resulting from an alcohol problem where alcohol need not have consumed immediately prior to the offences being committed;

(e) offences where alcohol is used an excuse.

Both approaches are helpful but tend to oversimplify the relationship between alcohol and crime. Hayes' typology runs the risk of attributing causality more readily than appropriate whilst Purser's model tends to assume that alcohol and crime are always related, even if alcohol is not always a causal factor in crime. Research on the relationship between alcohol and crime is voluminous and difficult to interpret. A number of researchers have reviewed the available literature (Deehan, 1999; Newburn and Shiner, 2001; Ramsay, 1996; Sumner and Parker, 1995). Rather than repeat their efforts, we will focus here on the most recent studies.

Budd (2003) analysed BCS data in order to estimate the extent of alcohol-related violence. Alcohol-related violence was defined as assaults, robbery and snatch thefts in which the victim considered the perpetrator to be under the influence of alcohol. This perception may, of course, differ from the one held by the perpetrator. She estimated that there were at least one million incidents of alcohol-related violence in 1999: just over a third involved violence between strangers, a further third occurred between acquaintances, a quarter were domestic assaults and 5 per cent were muggings. Approximately half of these incidents took place in the context of the night-time economy, occurring in and around pubs, bars and clubs. The highest rates of victimization were among men aged sixteen to twenty-nine.

Data are available from a number of studies on patterns of alcohol use among offenders. The NEW-ADAM study revealed that 24 per cent of male arrestees and 14 per cent of female arrestees tested positive for alcohol (Bennett and Holloway, 2004). The data can be interpreted in different ways and does not demonstrate a causal relationship between alcohol and crime. A clearer picture emerges from studies of young offenders. Hammersely et al. (2003) found high levels of alcohol use among their sample of offenders in contact with Youth Offending Teams in England and Wales. Ninety-one per cent of the sample had tried alcohol, even though most were aged under eighteen, and around one quarter were categorized as very heavy drinkers (defined as drinking on more than 100 days in the previous year). Statistical analysis revealed that substance use predicts offending, and that alcohol, tobacco and cannabis use were more strongly related to offending than other drugs. However, both offending and substance use were related to other key factors: life difficulties and events, disliking and being excluded from school, lack of positive coping mechanisms and expecting to get into trouble again were related to both substance use and offending. This provides further evidence to challenge the view that alcohol and crime are causally related, and suggests the need to go beyond simplistic interpretations of the data.

The YLS (Flood-Page *et al.*, 2000) also sheds light on the complex relationship between alcohol use and offending. It found that men aged under twenty-one who drank regularly were more likely to be offenders than those who drank occasionally or who did not drink. Among young people aged twenty-two to thirty, there was no relationship between regular drinking and self-reported offending except in relation to violent offences. The data also reveal a link between levels of alcohol consumption and involvement in violent crime: 15 per cent of those who drank alcohol at least five days a week had committed violent offences. Drinking at least five times a week was a predictor of serious or persistent offending for eighteen to thirty year old men but not for those aged twelve to seventeen.

Parker (1996) conducted in-depth interviews with sixty-six persistent offenders aged between 18 and 25. All except three were male, and all were in contact with the probation service. The majority (fifty-two) were current drinkers, and just under half of these (twenty-four) defined their use of alcohol as a problem. The entire sample felt alcohol was sometimes part of the explanation for their offending but even the heavy drinkers did not perceive alcohol as central to their explanations of their own offending behaviour. Parker concluded that the search for a simple correlation between alcohol use and offending is not 'good criminology' (Parker, 1996: 291). He found that through analysis of qualitative motivation accounts, other variables emerged relating to illegal drug use and the desire to pursue a preferred lifestyle, thus attempts to isolate alcohol use as a key variable are misguided. Parker concluded that for persistent young adult offenders alcohol is both an accessory to crime and to a lawful good time, and in the latter respect they are no different to law-abiding young adults.

REVIEW QUESTIONS

1 What are the difficulties of relying upon victims' perceptions of whether the offence was alcohol-related?

2 What interpretations can be offered of the finding that almost one quarter of arrestees test positive for alcohol?

3 Parker suggests the political discourse and media discourse is 'alcohol plus young men equals violent crime'. Should criminologists challenge this view? If so, how might they do it?

Breaking the links

In March 2004, an *Alcohol Harm Reduction Strategy for England* was published (Prime Minister's Strategy Unit, 2004). This was preceded by an interim analysis of the evidence base for the strategy (Prime Minister's Strategy Unit, 2003) and an action plan to tackle alcohol-related crime, disorder and nuisance (Home Office, 2000). In Wales, a substance misuse strategy, which included alcohol, was already in place (National Assembly for Wales, 2000). The *Alcohol Harm Reduction Strategy for England* aims to reduce the harm caused by alcohol misuse through an emphasis on education, treatment and law enforcement. The four key ways that government can act to reduce alcohol-related harm are listed below.

(a) improved and better targeted education and communication;

(b) better identification and treatment of alcohol problems;

(c) better coordination and enforcement of existing powers against crime and disorder;

(d) encouraging the industry to continue promoting responsible drinking and to continue to take a role in reducing alcohol-related harm.

The most common criticism relating to the strategy was the amount of time taken for it to be published. The government declared its intention to introduce a national strategic approach to alcohol in the White Paper *Saving Lives: Our Healthier Nation* (Department of Health, 1999). The publication of an alcohol strategy for England six years after the equivalent for illegal drug use was used to support the argument that despite alcohol being 'our favourite drug' (Royal College of Psychiatrists, 1986), the government's commitment to tackling alcohol-related harm is far less than for drug-related harm.

We will focus here on action to tackle alcohol-related crime and disorder. In order to meet this aim, a programme of work is outlined in the strategy covering five main areas, detailed below:

(a) alcohol-related disorder and anti-social behaviour in towns and cities at night;

(b) reducing level of underage drinking;

(c) managing repeat offenders of alcohol-related crime;

(d) alcohol and domestic violence;

(e) drink-driving.

It is beyond the scope of this chapter to explore the myriad of interventions which could be put in place to tackle the five issues detailed above, but it is possible to map out in broad terms the types of measures needed.

A wide range of interventions are described by Alcohol Concern (1999), Deehan (1999) and Felson (2002), with most being attempts to change the environment in which drinking takes places through a variety of situational crime prevention (SCP) measures. These are 'directed at highly specific forms of crime which involve the management, design or implementation of the immediate environment in which these crimes occur . . . so as to reduce the opportunities for these crimes' (Hough *et al.*, 1980: 1). SCP measures include the use of plastic glasses, serving food with alcoholic drinks, reduced prices for low- and non-alcohol drinks and the abolition of happy hours. Whilst SCP approaches offer a potentially effective means of reducing alcohol-related harm, they are only part of the solution. Criminologists have been urged by Hayward (2004) to adopt a cultural perspective and ask why the majority of violent assaults in the UK involve the use of alcohol in one form or another.

Alongside SCP measures, the criminal justice system can offer opportunities to work with offenders, for example offering programmes for drink-impaired drivers (Hollin *et al.*, 2002) and screening and assessing offenders for alcohol problems at the pre-sentence stage (Raynor and Honess, 1998). In addition, some of the interventions described for drug-using offenders also apply. For example, arrest referral schemes and offending behaviour programmes offered by the probation service will work with problem drinkers as well as drug users. However, there is no equivalent of the DTTO, DAO and DAR.

REVIEW QUESTIONS

1 What are the strengths and weaknesses of situational crime prevention measures as a means to tackle alcohol-related crime and disorder?

2 What might a cultural perspective add to our understanding of how best to reduce alcohol-related crime? (You may find it helpful to refer to Chapter 7.)

3 Should quasi-compulsory treatment along the lines of the DTTO be introduced for offenders whose crimes are alcohol-related?

CONCLUSION

In this chapter, we have pieced together the available evidence, and acknowledged its limitations, to present a picture of drug and alcohol use in England and Wales. We have noted that alcohol use and, to a lesser extent, drug use is widespread but problem use is confined to a minority. Males, especially young males, are most likely to be engaged in problem drug or alcohol use and therefore more likely to come into contact with the criminal justice system.

Reviewing the available evidence suggests that our current knowledge about the relationship between drugs, alcohol and crime remains patchy and prone to misinterpretation. We have explored the dangers of relying upon deterministic explanations and suggested that 'chicken and egg' arguments about whether drug (or alcohol) use leads to crime or vice versa are both simplistic and unhelpful. Instead, we have argued for a more complex understanding of the relationship between drugs, alcohol and crime which acknowledges the role of other social, economic and cultural factors. Current policy is based on a partial understanding of the relationship between drugs, alcohol and crime, and thus its impact is likely to be limited.

Finally, it is important to note that the material on drugs and alcohol has been presented separately to aid understanding of a challenging criminological issue. This approach runs the risk of glossing over the fact that both the causes and effects of problem drug and alcohol use may be similar, and that alcohol is often a common element in polydrug use among offenders (Bennett and Holloway, 2004; Parker, 1996).

QUESTIONS FOR DISCUSSION

1 Look at newspaper reporting of crime. To what extent are drug and alcohol use offered as explanations for offending?

2 Is it possible to obtain an accurate figure of the nature and extent of drug and alcohol use?

3 How can we respond to the commonly held view that the relationship between drugs (or alcohol) and crime is straightforward?

4   What are the main differences between policy responses to drugs and alcohol?

5   Is more legislation likely to reduce levels of drug-related and alcohol-related crime?

GUIDE TO FURTHER READING

Barton. A. (2003) *Illicit Drugs: Use and Control* London: Routledge.

This book illuminates the complexity and diversity of illicit drug use through tracing the historical development of the 'drug problem'.

Bennett, T. and Holloway, K. (2005) *Understanding Drugs, Alcohol and Crime*. Buckingham: Open University Press.

This text provides a succinct overview of current theory and research on the links between drugs, alcohol and crime.

Deehan, A. (1999) *Alcohol and Crime: Taking Stock*, Crime Reduction Series Paper 3. London: Home Office (www.homeoffice.gov.uk/rds).

This short report, aimed predominantly at practitioners, draws together information on the link between alcohol and crime and suggests methods which might reduce alcohol-related crime.

Nacro (2003) *Drugs and Crime: From Warfare to Welfare*. London: Nacro.

Produced by an independent voluntary organization working to prevent crime, this report brings together available evidence on the relationship between drug use and crime and provides a critical analysis of contemporary drug policy.

South, N. (2002) 'Drugs, Alcohol and Crime' in M. Maguire, R. Morgan and R. Reiner (eds) *The Oxford Handbook of Criminology*. Oxford: Oxford University Press.

This chapter covers similar ground to the chapter you have just read, but offers a more detailed discussion of trends in drug and alcohol use and strategies to tackle both the demand for, and supply of, drugs.

Finally, students are strongly encouraged to familiarize themselves with the latest policies on drug and alcohol use. These can be found on government websites: www.strategy.gov.uk (England), www.wales.gov.uk (Wales), www.scotland.gov.uk (Scotland) and www.nio.gov.uk (Northern Ireland).

WEB LINKS

www.drugscope.org.uk

DrugScope is an independent centre of expertise on drugs and aims to inform policy development and reduce drug-related risk. Its website provides authoritative and reliable information on all aspects of drug policies and problems.

www.alcoholconcern.org.uk

Alcohol Concern is the national voluntary agency on alcohol misuse, acting as an umbrella body for 500 local agencies working with alcohol misusers and their families. Its website is a vital part of its aim to act as the principal source of information on alcohol to the general public.

www.ukhra.org

The UK Harm Reduction Alliance (UKHRA) is a campaigning coalition of drug users and professionals working in health and social care, criminal justice and education. The website offers opportunities to join discussion lists and read critical evaluations of contemporary drug policy.

www.homeoffice.gov.uk

The Home Office website contains links to further websites maintained by a range of government departments. It also includes links to a wide range of research publications conducted by or commissioned by the Research Development and Statistics Directorate.

www.dh.gov.uk

The Department of Health website includes a wide range of information on alcohol (prevalence, consumption patterns, health-related issues, alcohol-related harm and expenditure), mainly for England.

REFERENCES

Ahmad, M. and Mwenda, L. (2004) *Drug Seizure and Offender Statistics*, United Kingdom, 2001 and 2002, Home Office Statistical Bulletin 08/04. London: Home Office.

Alcohol Concern (1999) *Proposal for a National Alcohol Strategy for England*. London: Alcohol Concern.

Ayres, M., Futi, R., Perry, D. and Murray, L. (2004) *Motoring Offences and Breath Test Statistics, England and Wales 2002*. Home Office Statistical Bulletin 05/04. London: Home Office.

Barton, A. (2003) *Illicit Drugs: Use and Control*. London: Routledge.

Bean, P. (2002) *Drugs and Crime*. Cullompton: Willan Publishing.

Becker, H. (1963) *Outsiders: Studies in the Sociology of Deviance*. New York: Free Press.

Bennett, T. and Holloway, K. (2004) *Drug Use and Offending: Summary Results of the First Two Years of the NEW-ADAM Programme*, Findings 179. London: Home Office.

Buchanan, J. and Young, L. (2000) 'The War on Drugs—A War on Drug Users', *Drugs: Education, Prevention and Policy*, 7 (4): 409–22.

Budd, T. (2003) *Alcohol-related Assault: Findings from the British Crime Survey*, Home Office Online Report 35/03. London: Home Office.

Coffield, F. and Gofton, L. (1994) *Drugs and Young People*. London: Institute for Public Policy Research.

Coleman, C. and Moynihan, J. (1996) *Understanding Crime Data: Haunted by the Dark Figure*. Buckingham: Open University Press.

Condon, J. and Smith, N. (2003) *Prevalence of Drug Use: Key Findings from the 2002/20003 British Crime Survey*, Findings 239. London: Home Office.

Cope, N. (2000) 'Drug Use in Prison: The Experience of Young Offenders', *Drugs: Education, Prevention and Policy*, 7 (4): 355–66.

Croall, H. (1998) *Crime and Society in Britain*. London: Longman.

Deehan, A. (1999) *Alcohol and Crime: Taking Stock*, Crime Reduction Research Series Paper 3. London: Home Office.

Department of Health (1995) *Sensible Drinking: The Report of an Inter-Departmental Working Group*. London: Department of Health.

Department of Health (1999) *Saving Lives: Our Healthier Nation*. London: Department of Health.

Department of Health (2003) *Provisional Statistics for the National Drug Treatment Monitoring System in England, 2001/2 and 2002/3*. London: Department of Health.

Duke, K. (2003) *Drugs, Prisons and Policy-Making*. Basingstoke: Palgrave Macmillan.

Edmunds, M., May, T., Hearnden, I, and Hough, M. (1998) *Arrest Referral: Emerging Lessons form Research*, Drug Prevention Initiative Paper 23. London: Home Office.

Felson, M. (2002) *Crime and Everyday Life*. Thousand Oaks, CA.: Sage.

Finney, A. (2004a) *Violence in the Night-time Economy: Key Findings from the Research*, Findings 214. London: Home Office.

Finney, A. (2004b) *Alcohol and Sexual Violence: Key Findings from the Research*, Findings 215. London: Home Office.

Finney, A. (2004c) *Alcohol and Intimate Partner Violence: Key Findings from the Research*, Findings 216. London: Home Office.

Flood-Page, C., Campbell, S., Harrington, V, and Miller, J. (2000) *Youth Crime: Findings from the 1998/99 Youth Lifestyles Survey*, Home Office Research Study 209. London: Home Office.

Fountain, J. and Howes, S. (2002) *Home and Dry? Homelessness and Substance Use*. London: Crisis.

Fraser, P. and Padel, U. (2002) 'Editorial', *Criminal Justice Matters*, 47: 3.

Frischer, M., Heatlie, H. and Hickman, M. (2004) *Estimating the Prevalence of Problematic and Injecting Drug Use for Drug Action Team Areas in England*, Home Office Online Report 34/04. London: Home Office.

Gibson, B. (2004) *Criminal Justice Act 2003: A Guide to the New Procedures and Sentencing*. Winchester: Waterside Press.

Goldstein, P. (1985) 'The Drugs/Violence Nexus: A Tripartite Conceptual Framework', *Journal of Drug Issues*, Fall 1985, 293–506.

Graham, J. and Bowling, B. (1995) *Young People and Crime*, Home Office Research Study 145. London: Home Office.

Hammersley, R., Marsland, L. and Reid, M. (2003) *Substance Use by Young Offenders: The Impact of the Normalisation in the Early Years of the 21st Century*, Home Office Research Study 261. London: Home Office.

Harman, K. and Paylor, I. (2002) 'A Shift in Strategy', *Criminal Justice Matters*, 47: 8–9.

Harrington, V. (2000) *Underage Drinking: Findings from the 1998–99 Youth Lifestyles Survey*, Home Office Research Findings 125. London: Home Office.

Hayes, P. (1993) 'A View from the Probation Service', in J. Russell (ed) *Alcohol and Crime: Proceedings of a Mental Health Foundation Conference*. London: Mental Health Foundation.

Hayward, K. (2004) *City Limits: Crime, Consumer Culture and the Urban Experience*. London: Glasshouse Press.

Health Advisory Service (2001) *The Substance of Young Need*. London: Health Advisory Service.

Hickman, M., Higgins, V., Hope, V. and Bellis, M. (2004) *Estimating Prevalence of Problem Drug Use: Multiple Methods in Brighton, Liverpool and London*, Home Office Online Report 36/04. London: Home Office.

Hobbs, D. (2003) *The Night-Time Economy*, Alcohol Concern Research Forum Papers. London: Alcohol Concern.

Hobbs, D., Hadfield, P., Lister, S. and Winlow, S. (2003) *Bouncers: Violence and Governance in the Night-time Economy*. Oxford: Oxford University Press.

Hollin, C., McGuire, J., Palmer, E. Bilby, C., Hatcher, R. and Holmes, A. (2002) *Introducing Pathfinder Programmes into the Probation Service: An Interim Report*, Home Office Research Study 247. London: Home Office.

Home Office (2000) *Tackling Alcohol Related Crime, Disorder and Nuisance Action Plan*. London: Home Office.

Home Office (2003) *Criminal Statistics England and Wales 2002*. London: Home Office.

Home Office Drugs Strategy Directorate (2002) *Updated Drug Strategy 2002*. London: Home Office.

Honess, T., Seymour, L. and Webster, R. (2000) *The Social Contexts of Underage Drinking*, Home Office Occasional Paper. London: Home Office.

Hough, M., Clarke, R. and Mayhew, P. (1980) 'Introduction' in R. Clarke and P. Mayhew (eds) *Designing Out Crime*. London: Home Office.

Hough, M. (1996) *Drug Misuse and the Criminal Justice System*, Drugs Prevention Initiative Paper 15. London: Home Office.

Hough, M., Clancy, A., McSweeney, T. and Turnbull, P. (2003) *The Impact of Drug Treatment and Testing Orders on Offending: Two-year Reconviction Results*, Findings 184. London: Home Office.

Jason-Lloyd, L. (2003) *Drugs, Addiction and the Law*. Huntingdon: Elm Publishing.

Kothari, G., Marsden, J., Strang, J. (2002) 'Opportunities and Obstacles for Effective Treatment of Drug Misusers in the Criminal Justice System in England and Wales', *British Journal of Criminology*, 42 (2): 412–32.

Lloyd, C. (1998) 'Risk Factors for Problem Drug Use: Identifying Vulnerable Groups', *Drugs: Education, Prevention and Policy*, 5 (3) 217–32.

Lloyd, C., Mair, G., and Hough, M. (1994) *Explaining Reconviction Rates: A Critical Analysis*, Home Office Research Study 136. London: Home Office.

Mair, G. (2002) 'Arrest Referral Schemes: First Port of Call for Drug Users in the Criminal Justice Process', *Criminal Justice Matters*. 47: 16–17.

Matrix Research Consultancy and Nacro (2004) *Evaluation of Drug Testing in the Criminal Justice System*, Home Office Research Study 286. London: Home Office.

May, T. Warburton, H., Turnbull, P. and Hough, M. (2002) *Times they are A-changing: The Policing of Cannabis*. London: JRF.

McKeganey, N., Connelly, C., Knepil, J., Norrie, J. and Reid, L. (2000) *Interviewing and Drug Testing of Arrestees in Scotland*. Edinburgh: Scottish Executive.

Measham, F., Aldridge, J. and Parker, H. (2001) *Dancing on Drugs: Risk, Health and Hedonism in the British Club Scene*. London: Free Association Press.

Millar, T., Gemmell, I., Hay, G. and Donmall, M. (2004) *The Dynamics of Drug Misuse: Assessing Changes in Prevalence*, Home Office Online Report 35/04. London: Home Office.

National Assembly for Wales (2000) *Tackling Substance Misuse in Wales: A Partnership Approach*. Cardiff: National Assembly for Wales.

National Centre for Social Research/National Foundation for Educational Research (2004) *Drug Use, Smoking and Drinking among Young People in England in 2003*. London: Department of Health.

Neale. J. (2002) *Drug Users in Society*. Basingstoke: Palgrave.

Newburn, T. and Shiner, M. (2001) *Teenage Kicks? Young People and Alcohol: A Review of the Literature*. York: Joseph Rowntree Foundation.

O'Shea, J., Jones, A. and Sondhi, A. (2003) *Statistics from the Arrest Referral Monitoring Programme from October 2000 to September 2002*. London: Home Office.

Parker, H. (1996) 'Young Adult Offenders, Alcohol and Criminological Cul-de-sacs', *British Journal of Criminology*, 36 (2): 282–98.

Parker, H., Aldridge, J. and Measham (1998) *Illegal Leisure: The Normalization of Adolescent Drug Use*. London: Routledge.

Police Foundation (2000) *Drugs and the Law: Report of the Independent Inquiry into the Misuse of Drugs Act 1971*. London: Police Foundation.

President of the Council (1998) *Tackling Drugs to Build a Better Britain: The Government's Ten Year Strategy for Tackling Drug Misuse*. London: The Stationery Office.

Prime Minister's Strategy Unit (2003) *Alcohol Harm Reduction Project: Interim Analytical Report*. London: Cabinet Office.

Prime Minister's Strategy Unit (2004) *Alcohol Harm Reduction Strategy*. London: Cabinet Office.

Pudney, S. (2002) *The Road to Ruin? Sequences of Initiation into Drug Use and Offending by Young People in Britain*, Home Office Research Study 253. London: Home Office.

Purser, R. (1995) *Alcohol and Crime*, Submission to the All Party Group on Alcohol Misuse.

Ramsay, M. (1996) 'The relationship between alcohol and crime' in C. Bryon (ed) *Home Office Research and Statistics Directorate Research Bulletin No. 38*. London: Home Office.

Raynor, P. and Honess, T. (1998) *Drug and Alcohol Related Offenders Project: An Evaluation of the West Glamorgan Partnership*, Drug Prevention Initiative Paper 14, London: Home Office.

Richards, L., Fox, K., Roberts, C., Fletcher, L. and Goddard, E. (2002) *Living in Britain: Results from the 2002 General Household Survey*. London: Office for National Statistics.

Royal College of Psychiatrists (1986) *Alcohol: Our Favourite Drug*. London: Tavistock.

Sampson, A. (2002) 'Framing the Non-offender', *Criminal Justice Matters*, 47: 6–7.

Seddon, T. (2000) 'Explaining the Drug-Crime Link: Theoretical, Policy and Research Issues', *Journal of Social Policy*, 29(1): 95–107.

Shiner, M. and Newburn, T. (1997) 'Definitely, maybe not: The Normalisation of Recreational Drug Use amongst Young People', *Sociology*, 31(3): 1–19.

Shiner, M. and Newburn, T. (1999) 'Taking tea with Noel: the place and meaning of drug use in everyday life', in N. South (ed) *Drugs: Cultures, Controls and Everyday Life*. London: Sage.

South, N. (2002) 'Debating Drugs and Everyday Life: Normalisation, Prohibition and "Otherness" ', in N. South (ed) *Drugs: Cultures, Controls and Everyday Life*. London: Sage.

Stevens, A., Berto, D., Heckmann, W., Kerschi, V., Oeuvray, K., Van Ooyen, M., Steffan, E. and Uchtenhagen (forthcoming) 'Quasi-Compulsory Treatment of Drug Dependent Offenders: An International Literature Review', *Substance Use and Misuse*.

Sumner, M. and Parker, H. (1995) *Low in Alcohol: A Review of the International Research into Alcohol's Role in Crime Causation*. London: The Portman Group.

Sykes, G. and Matza, D. (1957) 'Techniques of Neutralization: A Theory of Delinquency', *American Sociological Review*, 33(10): 46–62.

Taylor, A. (1993) *Women Drug Users: An Ethnography of a Female Injecting Community*. Oxford: Clarendon Press.

Turnbull, P., McSweeney, T., Webster, R., Edmunds, M. and Hough, M. (2000) *Drug Treatment and Testing Orders: Final Evaluation Report*, Home Office Research Study 212. London: Home Office.

Ward, J., Henderson, Z. and Pearson, G. (2003) *One Problem Among Many: Drug Use among Care Leavers in Transition to Independent Living*, Home Office Research Study 260. London: Home Office.

Wincup, E., Buckland, G. and Bayliss, R. (2003) *Youth Homeless and Substance Use: Report to the Drugs and Alcohol Research Unit*, Home Office Research Study 258. London: Home Office.

Young, J. (1971) *The Drugtakers*. London: Paladin.

11 Violent crime

Larry Ray

INTRODUCTION

This chapter is an introduction to criminological and sociological analysis of violence that will provide you with an overview of some of the main debates and issues along with suggestions for further reading. It begins by raising the question 'what is violence?', which is itself subject to debate and uncertainty. It then examines a key theoretical approach to violence developed by the sociologist Norbert Elias that has placed the understanding of violence in historical context as well as provided a theory accounting for the gradual but uneven diminution of interpersonal violence in modern societies. The chapter then presents summary data on the prevalence of violence in the UK based largely on information from the British Crime Survey (BCS). Next it examines specific issues—aggression and masculinity, violence in the private sphere, racist violence, and homicides. For each type of violence a summary of the data, its prevalence, and discussion of some key explanatory frameworks is given. The chapter ends with some general questions for discussion and a guide to further reading and Internet sources.

BACKGROUND

What is violence? There is no simple answer to this question. The sociological analysis of violence has focused on criminal forms—especially homicide, assault, child abuse, sexual violence and intimate violence—with the result that a research literature has developed that is specialized but lacks overall theoretical coherence (Jackman, 2002). Except for specialist studies of war, revolution and social movements, the sociology of violence tends to focus on interpersonal rather than collective or state violence, and works within a criminal justice framework. 'Violence' tends to be separated from 'legitimate force' so that the killing of a police officer by a civilian is considered 'homicide' (that is, violence) whereas the killing of a civilian by a police officer 'in the line of duty' is generally not. Similarly, the exposure of workers to hazardous working conditions that result in death or injury is not considered violence either because the hazard level is within the law or because the motives of the corporation cannot be verified within legal notions of premeditated intent. Indeed, the definition of violence is contested and this dispute itself is part of the process of identifying ways of resisting violence and the structures that give rise to it (Hearn, 1998). We could say that violence is behaviour that intentionally threatens or does physical harm, and more generally 'involves the infliction of emotional, psychological, sexual, physical and material damage' (Stanko, 1994: 38). Kelly's (1987) famous definition, developed in the context of domestic violence, is a continuum of verbal, emotional and sexual abuses of power. This definition extends violence to include abusive behaviour that might not inflict direct physical harm but ties the concept to 'abuse of power', which is a theme that will be developed here. Like any other behaviour violence is embedded in complex ways in social relations and values. It forms a continuum of types of behaviour that people interpret as threatening or harmful, that includes name-calling, stalking, vandalism and intimidation of violence. Above all, it is surrounded in misleading stereotypes. Violence is often described as 'meaningless'. Violent offenders for example are still imagined as 'out-of-control', psychologically disturbed, distant and different from the rest of us. Yet violence is virtually never without purpose and often takes place between people who know each other. Violence or its threat is generally embedded in social relations where its use has meaning to victims and perpetrators. For example one of the common triggers for a violent incident can be a situation where someone responds to taunts and harassment in an unexpected way—by rejecting a subordinate role and resisting. Finally, it is mainly men who perpetrate violence. Most offenders in England and Wales are male (accounting for about 90 per cent of stranger attacks) and in 66 per cent of attacks on women the assailant is male. 'More than anything else', says Oliver James, 'violence is caused by not being female' (James, 1995: 75).

REVIEW QUESTIONS

1 What is violence?

2 Try to list as many forms of harm as you can and decide whether they would be considered to be 'violence' or not? Why?

3 Why is violence enacted by the State likely to be judged differently from violence against the State?

Violence, the body and the civilizing process

Violence is about relationships to and around the body and more particularly about pain, emotions, control and discipline. As such it is an intensely emotional experience, variously invoking inter alia hatred, pleasure, fear and threat. Hence understanding emotions and their social consequences is central to the process of management and control of violence on interpersonal and wider levels. Recently attention has grown concerning the importance of emotion, and in particular shame, in social life, in opposition to the dominant cognitive focus in the human sciences (for example, Barbalet, 1998), and such concern echoes earlier sociological theories such as those of Simmel, Goffman and Elias. It is beyond the scope of this introductory chapter to do this but there is a need for broader conceptualizing of various forms of hurt, injury and threat within a common theoretical framework.

Norbert Elias (1897–1990), whose work is currently receiving increased attention in sociology and criminology, famously proposed the thesis of a 'civilizing process'. This occurred during the transition between European medieval and modern societies during which complex social, cultural and psychological changes occurred that resulted in a reduction in interpersonal violence. This thesis aimed to reverse the view that industrialization and urbanization are inseparable from *rising* violence. Elias claims that the growth of increasingly mannered social interaction was accompanied by increased public intolerance of violence and cruelty. Repugnance towards physical violence increased with advancing thresholds of shame and embarrassment surrounding the body—acts once performed publicly, such as defecation and sexual intercourse, become intensely private. Most people now regard carnivals of violence, such as public executions, or the torture of animals, as deeply repugnant. Underlying this cultural and psychological shift there is a deepening and widening of interdependencies between people which Elias calls 'figurations'.

In medieval society war is the normal state of society and pleasure is derived from cruelty, destruction and torment evidenced for example in the mutilation of prisoners of war, burning heretics, public torture and executions. In modern societies there is a concentration of the means of violence in the State such that 'If in this or that region the power of central authority grows, if over a larger or smaller area people are forced to live at peace with one another, the moulding of affects and the standards of the economy of instincts are gradually changed as well' (Elias, 1994 [1939], 1: 201). Elias argued that with the centralization of state power there was a growth in personal restraint and mannered conduct, initially in court society, gradually spreading more widely along with the expansion of trade, urban life, a more complex division of labour, and the formation of 'civil society'. The longer and denser were networks of interdependence, the more people were obliged to attune their action to those of others and the less their interactions will be marked by overt violence. Stephen Mennell (1995) offers one example of these changes, pointing to the difference between a medieval and modern journey. A medieval journey was a difficult and dangerous undertaking, along muddy roads on which there were few other travellers and risk of collision was low. However, the medieval traveller had to be alert to dangers posed by animals, other travellers and bandits. This state of alertness required a volatile temperament and eager readiness to fight and a personality that would be impulsive and resort quickly to violence. On the other hand on modern roads the danger of physical attack is low but the risk of collision high. In this context (typical of the interconnected and complex nature of modern society) the development of control systems based on self-regulation, constant vigilance, foresight and self-control is crucial. These require personalities that are not impulsive but rational, calculating, technically competent.

However, in modern society people still feel the need for excitement—which is provided by institutionalized and regulated activities such as sport, in which rules reduce the risk of injury but gratify need for excitement. Sport institutionalizes calculated violence (such as the professional foul) without loss of self-control, while spectators have the opportunity to vicariously enjoy the excitement of contest without the actual violence of earlier spectacles such as gladiatorial struggle. This analysis does raise the issue though of how to explain actual violence among rival spectators, which has become a major topic of research pursued particularly by followers of Elias such as Dunning *et al.* (1987). Their work points to factors such as a change in social composition of spectators and decontrolling emotional controls in explaining spectator violence.

Elias argues that over several hundred years there developed increased sensitivity and repugnance towards violence. Is there any evidence for this? There is evidence that earlier societies were more tolerant of violence than is the case today (ESRC 2002: 9). There is some long-term historical evidence for a declining rate of homicide between the thirteenth and twentieth centuries (shown in Figure 11.1).

These data should be interpreted with caution, however, because of the inadequacy of records over much of this period, changes in key juridical concepts such as *mens rea*, changing rules of evidence and so on. There is evidence that although Britain for example became less violent during the first half of the twentieth century than it had been in the

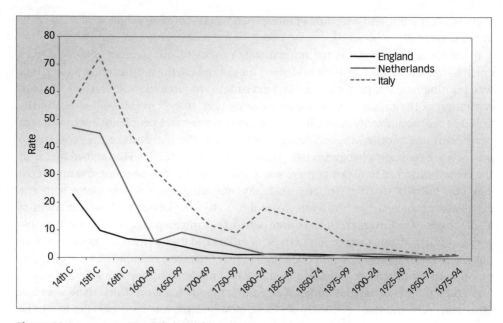

Figure 11.1 Long-term trends in homicide rates for selected countries

Source: Eisner (2001).

nineteenth, levels of interpersonal violence rose again in the latter half and serious violent assaults rose steeply between 1975–96 (see Figure 11.2). Moreover, the pacification of society does not preclude the continued existence of a 'culture of violent solutions' in which its use is commonplace. While Elias acknowledged this, he has been criticized for ignoring the extent to which much violence is hidden, 'private' and endured in silence, and most is kept away from the criminal justice system. This notably applies to domestic violence, which is considered below.

Elias' thesis though has been influential and offers insight into the formation of the modern self through regulation of violence, in ways that for some parallels Michel Foucault's work on similar themes (for example, Smith, 1999). Elias describes the formation of a personality structure governed by self-control and foresight combined with feelings of shame, repugnance and embarrassment towards our own and others' behaviour. The pressures of surviving within highly interdependent social networks lead us to treat others and ourselves as a 'danger zone'—we feel anxiety about our vulnerability to other's behaviour and to our own inner drives (Elias, 1939, 1: 445). The experience of these tensions has two consequences in particular. First, modern human beings draw tight boundaries between themselves and whatever is 'outside', to the point of doubting the 'reality' of our perceptions of the outside world. Second, there is the tendency to see ourselves as free and unique sovereign individuals and deny that we are shaped by the figurations into which we are born. Thus, renunciation of violence forms the modern self as individuated and subject to internal and external techniques of control. This in turn has structured how violence tends to be viewed in sociological and criminological literature as a threat arising in some sense from 'outside'—either from somewhere spatially separate, such as transitory spaces (deserted trains, subways, night

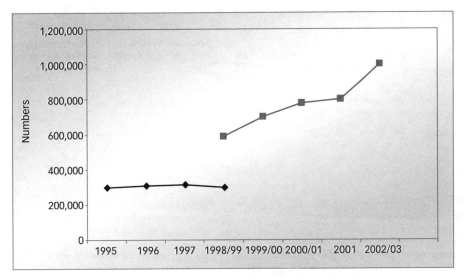

Figure 11.2 Trends in violent crime in England and Wales

Source: Research Development and Statistics (RDS), Home Office. (In 1998/99, the chart shows a break because police were asked to start recording certain new offences—such as 'Common assault', 'Assault on a constable', 'Harassment' and 'Possession of a weapon'.)

metro stations) or from 'below' (the threat to social order from the dispossessed and dark places of our inner psyche). However, one theme in recent studies of violence has been to suggest its routine or habitual nature such that it origins lie within, not outside, and nowhere is safe.

REVIEW QUESTIONS

1 What is the 'civilizing process'?

2 Why is interpersonal violence less in modern than medieval societies?

3 Is it true that the modern person feels repugnance at public displays of violence?

Patterns of violence

Violent crime measured by the British Crime Survey[1] is subdivided into a typology of four groupings based broadly on the relationship between suspect and victim:

- domestic violence—including all violent incidents involving partners, ex-partners, household members or other relatives;

- mugging—comprised robbery, attempted robbery and snatch from the person;

- acquaintance violence—includes wounding and assaults in which the victim new one or more of the offenders, at least by sight;

- stranger violence—includes common assaults and wounding in which the victim did not know the offenders in any way

Table 11.1 Violent incidents by type and gender

	All (000s)	Percentage of all violent incidents	Percentage against men within violence type	Percentage against women within violence type
All violence	2,781	100	62	38
Domestic	501	18	27	73
Mugging	388	14	59	41
Stranger	949	34	83	17
Acquaintance	942	34	60	40

Source: BCS 2002/03.

The figures in Table 11.1 above show the breakdown of types of violence for men and women in England and Wales for 2002/03:

Currently available evidence from the BCS suggests that violent crime in England and Wales is still rare (accounting for about 4 per cent of all crimes), but rose in the 1980s by 40 per cent for male and 90 per cent for female victims. According to the BCS, perpetrators and victims often know each other—either as intimates or acquaintances although the pattern is clearly gendered, with men being represented highly in incidents of stranger violence and women in domestic violence. Victims are most often men aged sixteen to twenty-four (15.1 per cent of that group in the past twelve months), single people living alone (8.9 per cent), single parents (8 per cent), people living in private rented accommodation (7.4 per cent), those living in 'disordered areas' (7.3 per cent) and women between the ages of 16–25 (6.9 per cent). Moreover, ethnic minorities—especially Afro-Caribbean and Pakistani British—have twice the risk of being victims of violent crimes than other Britons.

Fear of violence generally exceeds its statistical risk (Croall, 1998: 93–5) and is likely to give rise to anger about threats of crime (Ditton *et al.*, 1999). Yet young men, who are most at risk from assault, express least worry about it while the elderly (who are least at risk) worry most (Croall, 1998: 93–5). There are problems, however, with these kinds of risk assessments. Questions about fear of crime in the BCS do not relate people's answers to their locality, which for example may have higher than average crime. On the other hand the possibility of risk factors being compounded (for example, if many single parents also live in 'disordered areas' or if many men aged 16–24 are single) is not addressed in these surveys.

Where does violence take place? Violence takes place in all settings although different types are predicted by their settings, often in fairly predictable ways. Masculine confrontation violence is most common in public leisure areas (such as pubs and clubs) and in the workplace. In fact 25 per cent of reported incidents in England and Wales occur at work and of these 75 per cent are perpetrated by members of the public on practitioners and service providers (ESRC, 2002). High-risk professions include the police, public transport, medical, public transport, bouncers, and teachers. Domestic violence takes place largely in the home, where it is probably still under-reported. In 1993, in North

London, one-third of women interviewed reported violence in the home at some time in their lives and one in ten in the past twelve months and the extent of 'women on women' violence may be under-reported too (Hester *et al.*, 1996).

REVIEW QUESTIONS

1 Why might BCS data be a more reliable indication of the prevalence of violence than prosecution rates?

2 What forms of violence are most common?

3 Who is most at risk from violent assault?

Aggression and masculinity

As shown in Table 11.2 below there is a marked gender difference among victims and perpetrators of violence with an excess of prosecutions of men for violent offences in England and Wales:

Table 11.2 Ratio of male and female prosecutions by type of offence	
	Ratio (M:F)
Sexual offences	75:1
Criminal damage	17:1
Common assault	7:1
Violence against the person	5.7:1

Source: Croall (1998: 137).

This gender patterning of crime is not a new trend—males have been over-represented in all major violent crime categories since the collection of crime statistics began and the same pattern is found in all countries. In the USA, for example, men committed 83 per cent of crimes in 1996, and there are similar figures in France and Germany (Croall, 1998: 136). There is a slightly rising trend of convictions for women in the UK—in 1992 only 8.7 per cent of convictions for violence against the person were women while in 2002 this had risen to 10 per cent. In the teenage years the gap between girls and boys in delinquency, broadly defined, is relatively small, although the gap in more serious offending is considerably wider (Smith *et al.*, 2001).

Explaining male violence

While it is often taken for granted that men are more criminogenic than women, recent work has undertaken more complex analysis of the nature of masculinity and its relationship with violent crime. A division has appeared between bio-social, evolutionary approaches on the one hand and sociological explanations on the other.

Evolutionary lag

Evolutionary explanations point out that for 99 per cent of our history humans have lived in small hunting groups in which violence was natural rather than pathological since it aided survival. Masculine violence aided the hunting success and maximized food supply while men competed with one another for reproductive mates. However, this violence would be balanced by a need to preserve the size of the group, thus cultural norms of reciprocity and reconciliation emerged to limit violence (Hatty 2000: 50). However, in modern societies violence has become dysfunctional and is no longer restrained by environmental pressures. Steven Pinker (2002) claims that aggressiveness is largely genetically coded and learned influences such as parental behaviour and role models are largely unimportant.

It is problematic though to suggest that human aggressiveness is a kind of biosocial lag from an earlier developmental state. In a wide-ranging comparative study of violence among humans and other primates, Eric Fromm (1979) argued that human violence has become pathological (detached from self-defence and hunting) and that 'man is the only mass murderer'. Evolutionary theory attempts to explain aggressiveness in terms of a *continuation* of primal tendencies, when in fact humans display *more* destructive violence than other primates do. Evolutionary accounts pay little regard to the symbolic and culturally mediated forms that violence can take (for example in rituals) and cannot easily explain why rates of violence vary between locales and countries. If there is an underlying biological tendency towards masculine violence this should manifest similarly in different cultures and places, which it clearly does not. Further, James (2002) has taken issue with evolutionary theories of human aggression arguing that family influences are critical. He claims that children born to violent parents but raised in peaceable households are no more likely to have violent criminal records than those born to non-violent parents.

Social theories and 'hegemonic masculinities'

There are many social and cultural theories of violent behaviour, stressing social learning, youth sub-cultures, economic inequality (for example, Hearn, 1998; Stanko and Newburn, 1995) and the potential thrill and enjoyment of violence (see Katz, 1988; Ferrell, Chapter 7 and Presdee, 2000). Through the process of gender socialization (how we learn the attributes of 'masculine' and 'feminine' behaviour) violence may acquire different meanings for men and women. Through violence men attempt to affirm a positive self-concept, enhance self-esteem and reclaim personal power, while women on the other hand see violence as a failure of self-control. Further Campbell (1993) suggests that men tend to engage in justifications for violence that minimize their use of violence while women are more likely to express guilt. Justifications for violence are learned speech acts that prepare ground for violence and deploy wider available narratives in society.

In these terms excess male violence reflects patterns of socialization in which the male role involves greater readiness to use violence as a means of control and assertion of power. In Connell's (1995) and Messerschmidt's (1993 and 1997) theory of 'hegemonic masculinities' masculinity is viewed as a crucial point of intersection of different sources and forms of power, stratification, desire and identity.[2] Unlike socialization theories Connell and Messerschmidt emphasize performance and choice rather than passively learnt behaviour. Violent behaviour is *chosen* while calling upon dominant discourses of masculinity for support and legitimation. Connell thus sees crime as a way of 'doing gender'; which manifests differently in social situations structured by the influences of race, class, and age. Violence is a resource that men can call upon based in prevailing idealized cultural conceptions involving the dominance of women, heterosexuality, the pursuit of sexual gratification, independence.

Criminal behaviour is seen here as a resource for 'masculine validation'. For example, white, middle class boys can achieve masculinity through moderate academic success, sports, and preparation for a career. But schools are repressive and authoritarian so these boys will deviate outside of school through for example vandalism, drinking and petty theft. This is 'opposition masculinity' that demonstrates to peers dominance, control, and aggressiveness. White, working class boys on the other hand tend to demonstrate opposition masculinity outside of school, but also in school, through fighting, vandalism and so on. They do still have opportunities in the labour market, however, whereas disadvantaged (racial minority and lower class) boys have even fewer conventional opportunities to accomplish gender (they perceive no future in schooling or good job prospects in the real world), and are more likely to use illegal means like robbery and crimes of violence to demonstrate their masculinity. They are more likely then to engage in serious crime in and out of school.

How useful is the concept of hegemonic masculinity for explaining the predominance of men in violent crime figures? It is limited in that it does not explain the meaning of crime perpetrated by women, while at the same time 'over-predicting' male criminality. There is not a great deal of empirical support for the theory. One exception is Krienert (2003) who undertook a study of 704 offenders in Nebraska and found that masculine traits alone failed to predict violent events. But men with very high 'masculine' traits and few acceptable outlets to assert masculinity (such as education, marital status, children, employment, and income) *were* more likely to have been involved in violent incidents. Even so, the theory lacks a subjective or motivational account of the meanings of violence for perpetrators, and Messerschmidt cannot show why some men are violent and (most) others are not. Like many theories of crime it over-predicts incidence since if the theory were straightforwardly true then the incidence of violent behaviour would be much higher than it is.

'Crisis of masculinity'

Dominant forms of masculinity are at various historical periods thrown into crisis, a process also related to violent behaviour. Suzanne Hatty (2000: 6) comments, 'Violence is the prerogative of the youthful male especially when confronted by the contradictions and paradoxes of thwarted desire and personal and social disempowerment'. This account suggests that unemployment and decline of traditional working class male occupations combined with increasing women's equality provokes a 'crisis of masculinity'. Whereas the fathers and grandfathers of today's young men spent their lives in male spaces of manual work and associated leisure activities, young working class men are often unemployed and spend time at home or on the street. However, home is still a female space whereas the street offers opportunities for alternative experiences of dominance and risk-taking—joyriding, theft, burglary, competition and 'business'—drugs and organized crime. At the same time youth cultures emerge that emphasize and exaggerate features of traditional white working class masculine appearance and behaviour. Nayak (1999) argues that skinhead culture for example represents a consolidation of masculinity, sexuality and white ethnicity in working class culture. Similarly Hebdige (1987) regarded skinheads as expressing a nostalgic exaggeration of white working class characteristics and 'mime of awkward masculinity' that was a macho, working class, white (often racist) 'geometry of menace'. The uniform—boots, braces and cropped hair—represented a caricature of the traditional dress mode of a working man.

Phillipe Bourgeois's (1996) study of Puerto Rican migrants to the US exemplifies this argument. This is an ethnographic study of street-level drug dealers in East Harlem (USA) who had found that the work they had migrated to do was disappearing but they would not take work in service sector, which was regarded as 'women's work'. However, their wives did take this work and gained more financial independence than they had previously had, thereby threatening the basis of male dominance in the household. The men often took refuge in drug economy where there were very violent norms of gang rape, sexual conquest, abandonment of families and 'real manhood' based on devotion to group membership. Thus, the crisis of masculinity is more acute at lower socio-economic locations where violence is way of confirming status in a street culture.

Rich insight into changing cultural representations of masculinity and violence can be found in popular culture and especially the film. Post-World War II masculine heroes showed little emotional sensitivity and were prone to impulsivity and anger. War was 'what good men do' and its portrayal was unproblematic especially since in the war zone sexual differentiation was reaffirmed. In the later genre of 'hard body' films such as *Rambo First Blood Part Two* (1985) and *Die Hard* (1988) violence and single-handed rescue fantasy is unproblematic and unchallenging but also exaggerated, suggesting uncertainty about real life masculine roles. Hard masculine body cinematic representations of combat—robotic masculinity of *Robocop* and *Judge Dread*—concealed a growing crisis in masculinity, in which an alienated individual experiences potency through experiencing and inflicting pain. This idea becomes thematic in recent films and is often related to violence. For example in *Falling Down* (1993) a middle class man (Michael Douglas) divorced and unemployed, unable to visit his children engages in a killing spree against ethnic minorities. David Finder's *Fight Club* (1999) offers a more complex exploration of the crisis of masculinity and violence. Though sometimes pegged as an overtly masculine film, gone is the powerful white masculinity of the 1980s and hard body films of 1990s. It features Jack (the narrator) and Tyler Derby his destructive alter ego whom we find first in a support group for men recovering from testicular cancer ('remaining men together') where following chemotherapy, one character, Bob, has lost his testicles and grown breasts symbolizing masculinity's demise. Jack's addiction to self-help groups has replaced his addiction to consumerism (again 'feminized' activity), which is then replaced by a search for authentic masculinity in the self-inflicted violence of the fight club. But the sole woman character Marla Singer (Helen Bonham-Carter) is dominant in the unfolding plot and enables Jack to renounce violence. However, when the film looks as though it has reverted to a familiar hero-rescue fantasy Jack is unable to prevent the terrorists of Project Mayhem from blowing up large commercial buildings, their falling symbolizing the failure of the masculine corporate world.

REVIEW QUESTIONS

1 Why is violent crime predominantly 'masculine'?

2 What do you understand by 'hegemonic masculinities'?

3 Is there a 'crisis of masculinity'? If so, why should it manifest in violence?

Violence in the private sphere

Closely related to masculinity and violence is the issue of violence against women and children within the family, which can take many different forms, including physical assault, rape and sexual violence, psychological or emotional violence, torture, financial abuse including dowry-related violence, and control of movement and of social contacts. For centuries domestic violence was not considered a serious problem. For example, it is sometimes claimed that in 1782 the English Judge Francis Buller ruled it permissible to beat a wife with a stick no wider than a thumb. There is some doubt as to whether the ruling was ever given, but English Common Law sanctioned violence against women and it is only recently, from the 1980s, that the police have seriously begun to pursue offenders. This change in perceptions of seriousness of domestic violence arose from at least four developments (Pahl *et al.*, 2004):

- feminist activism in the 1970s identified this as an issue that would give practical expression to their more general concern about the position of women;

- the opening of women's refuges made visible what had previously been hidden;

- the growth of Women's Aid, as a coordinating body for the growing number of refuges, brought the activists together to share ideas and experience and to work for increased political visibility for their analysis;

- feminist scholars and activists were energetic in researching the issue and in pressing for more effective and appropriate action by relevant agencies.

How extensive is domestic violence? BCS data records experience of domestic violence both during the past twelve months and during a lifetime. In answer to the question 'have you experienced domestic violence during the past twelve months', 4.2 per cent of women *and* men experienced assault although twice as many women as men had been injured, suffered repeated violence and frightening threats. Although this may create the impression that men and women experience domestic violence roughly equally, victimization takes two distinct patterns. One, accounting for about 10 per cent of cases, which both women and men perpetrate is marked by occasional anger and aggression; the other which is more likely to be 'male' is characterized by severe escalating violence and terrorization (Mirrlees-Black, 1999). This second type is more widespread. When asked about lifetime prevalence, a ratio of 1:4 women report being assaulted by male partner, 1:8 women having been assaulted repeatedly; while 1:6 men reported occasional assault and 1:20 repeated assaults. Further, domestic violence typically escalates so that previous violence is a predictor of further violence—35 per cent of second incidents occur within five weeks of first and domestic violence has the highest rate of repeat victimization of any violent crime (MPS, 2003).

Reported domestic violence varies considerably worldwide (ranging between 10–69 per cent of violent offences in different countries) and definitions vary considerably too, along with levels of culturally accepted violence. Statistics alone offer only limited insight into the issue. Questions such as 'have you ever been abused?' or even behaviourally specific questions might fail to take account of the atmosphere of terror in violent relationships and its effects on children. Some men may enjoy inflicting violence. One of the women interviewed by Hammer (2000: 12) reported that 'the more violence he did to me the happier he would be . . . After he had hit me, he would say "Sit there in front of me, if I see any tears in your eyes then see what happens" '. At the same time men may blame women for provoking violence and adopt the posture of victims (Glasser, 1998), which is a common feature of other violent offenders (Ray *et al.*, 2003). Some estimates suggest that fathers in violent families have abused 70 per cent of children and even those who do not suffer abuse are likely to be aware of what is taking place (WHO, 2002). Such children are likely to suffer from confused and torn loyalties; they may feel ashamed, guilty, isolated and alone; they may respond by trying to protect their mothers, by phoning the police, or most dangerously, by trying to restrain their fathers (WHO, 2002).

The World Health Organization indicates that the triggers for domestic violence are remarkably consistent across all countries and cultures (WHO, 2002). These include:

- 'not obeying the husband'
- 'arguing'
- 'not having food ready'
- 'not caring adequately for children and home'
- 'questioning about money'
- 'going out without permission'
- 'refusing sex'
- pregnancy.[3]

One of the conclusions that can be drawn from this is that domestic violence is primarily about the exercise of power and a response to perceived challenges to male power. Even so, domestic violence occurs more in some settings and places than others and this patterning still requires more specific explanation.

Explanations

Many explanations of domestic violence follow the patterns of explanations of violence in general. There are explanations that focus on individual pathologies (for example, paranoid or narcissistic disorders), socialization (many abusers have come from dysfunctional and violent families) and social structural (for example, poor education, unemployment, low-income and so on). There may be some association between domestic violence and low socio-economic status (as there is for violence in general) but these accounts do not explain middle class domestic violence (for example, Pahl *et al.*, 2004). Feminist researchers suggest that rather than look for specific pathologies amongst perpetrators we should recognize that domestic violence is ubiquitous and a routine means of maintaining patriarchal power and authority. Feminist researchers emphasize factors such as:

- the historically subordinate position of women within marriage;
- women's responsibility for childcare (and consequent exclusion from the labour market and weak economic position in the household);
- patriarchy that reproduces male power/female dependence at all levels—social, cultural and economic;
- machismo cultures and the tacit or explicit approval of male violence.

However, one weakness of these explanations is that, like the theory of hegemonic masculinities, they encounter the problem of over-prediction. If violence were routinely inscribed into intimate heterosexual relations then we would expect to find a higher incidence than we do, even allowing for significant under-reporting. A broader approach that incorporates feminist analysis would be a more multi-factorial one that estimates the risk of domestic violence across a number of dimensions. The model set out in Table 11.3 attempts to combine individual, relationship, community and societal levels of analysis while identifying markers of risk, rather than causes of violence. In this model poverty causes stress, inadequacy, a 'crisis of masculinity' while making it more difficult for women to leave abusive relationships. Social capital refers to social trust that facilitates coordination and cooperation for mutual benefit, so that people believe that a benefit

Table 11.3 Risk factors in domestic violence

LEVEL	Individual	Relationship	Community	Societal
FACTOR	• Young • Alcohol abuse • Depression Personality disorder • Low educational attainment	• Conflict • Marital instability • Economic stress • Dysfunctional families	• Weak community sanctions • Poverty • Low social capital	• Traditional gender norms • Social norms supportive of violence 'macho cultures'

granted now will be repaid indirectly within a community in the future. While this model may explain why some societies and individuals are more violent than others we do not know the specific and relative weights to give the factors nor how they operate on different levels.

Racist violence

Racist violence in the UK came under sharp public scrutiny following the murder of a Black teenager, Stephen Lawrence, by a gang of racist white youths in 1993 and the subsequent public inquiry that reported in 1999 (Macpherson, 1999). Criticism of the police investigation and wider suggestion that the police were 'institutionally racist' resulted in widespread scrutiny of institutional practices in the police and other public organizations of ways in which racism might be inscribed in routine practices and beliefs.[4] Among the UK police it resulted in the creation of many new practices, training, and requirements to report, record and act on allegations of racist harassment and assault. Moreover, the targeting of racist violence, along with domestic and homophobic violence is part of a wider social and legal agenda to tackle 'hate' or bias crimes where the victim is selected on the grounds of their social status. Partly as a result of this, the numbers of recorded racist incidents in England and Wales has risen from 15,000 in 1988 to 25,000 in 1999, and 54,351 in 2003 (see Figure 11.3).

However, the dramatic increase in reporting of racist incidents (within which increasing proportions are serious assaults) was not matched by increases in convictions, representing about 5 per cent of reported incidents. Against this trend, however, it should be noted that the 2000 BCS reports *lower* estimated rates of racially motivated offences (about half of them actual attacks) than in the 1995 survey (280,000 against 390,000). This discrepancy between the BCS and police figures can be explained by greater willingness on the part of victims to report incidents to the police and better recording by the police of incidents reported to them. But the relationship between incidents, reporting and official statistics remains complex.

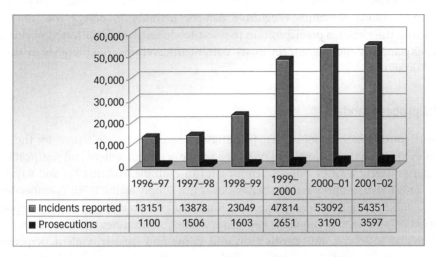

	1996–97	1997–98	1998–99	1999–2000	2000–01	2001–02
Incidents reported	13151	13878	23049	47814	53092	54351
Prosecutions	1100	1506	1603	2651	3190	3597

Figure 11.3 Racist incidents reported to the police in England and Wales

Source: Home Office Racist Incident Reports and CPS Reports 1997–2002.

Explaining racist violence

The existing data provides several causal models of racist violence. These are generally multivariate models although there is again little attempt to weight the various factors cited and they are all usually assumed to be relevant.

Cognitive psychological models

Much of the research in this area follows hypotheses developed in the early 1990s, which in turn drew on classical models of authoritarianism and racism. For example, Heitmeyer (1994) argues that hostility towards foreigners is based on an identifiable process by which feelings of perceived threat develop into racist violence. First, feelings of 'estrangement' appear which are expressed as 'an attitude of distance' and 'contempt'. Second, this fear of foreigners becomes overshadowed by a 'competitive stance fuelled by economic and/or cultural considerations. Third, tolerance disappears and 'complete hatred of foreigners' arises resulting in hostile 'offensive struggle' (Heitmeyer, 1994:17). Bjørgo (1994) focuses on patterns and motives of violence towards immigrants and refugees in Scandinavia where youth gangs often with criminal records perpetrate the majority of racist incidents. Though not necessarily members of extreme right groups, they have been exposed to their propaganda and methods. The majority of cases are planned and/or carried out under the influence of alcohol, although it is generally recognized that this is most likely to be an aggravating rather than causal factor. Beck (2000) claims that pro-violent attitudes towards black and Asian people stem from archaic belief in inferiority of other races and women that are perpetuated by allegiance to wider cultural group experience. These models regard the racist offender as having a distinctive personality that predisposes them to both racism and violence. Violent racism arises from poor and problematic moral reasoning, cognitive defects, inability to accept the impact of violence on the victim, a predisposition to resort to violence and a 'distorted worldview'. These explanatory models inform many current intervention programmes in the UK probation service.

Social process models

There is considerable evidence that perpetrators' racist views are shared by the communities to which they belong and provide a source of reinforcement and justification of their behaviour, at least by not condemning it (for example, Sibbitt 1997 and Ray *et al.*, 2003). This illustrates how human behaviour is not simply 'caused' but is embedded in systems of belief, legitimation and justification within which it appears to be acceptable. Sibbitt (1997) argues that prejudice permeates whole communities that have entrenched problems of socioeconomic deprivation and crime and 'spawn' violent perpetrators through mutually supportive relationships between the perpetrator and the wider community (1997: 101). Hence she speaks of 'perpetrator communities' that scapegoat their problems onto visible minorities who serve to provide an external focus for their dissatisfaction, frustration and alienation. Sibbitt developed a typology of different groups, stratified by generational experiences:

- the pensioners—long-term residents who feel that the area has been 'invaded';
- the 'people next door'—insecure adults who latch onto their parents' racialization of problems;
- the 'problem family'—with poor mental or physical health, who behave abusively towards children who in turn are low achievers and learn racist abusive behaviour;
- racist and antisocial behaviour is then transmitted to younger age groups who although they will have black friends at school learn to participate in racist violence and bullying.

Ray *et al.*, (2002) further found that racist offenders tended to scapegoat South Asians for community problems of unemployment, the decline of local manufacturing, and (somewhat paradoxically) for the rise in local crime. There was evidence here of the kind of 'crisis in masculinity'; noted elsewhere in this chapter. Ray *et al.* (2003) found a contrast between the global city image of central Manchester and the isolated and deprived life on outer-city housing estates from which many racially motivated offenders came. The latter expressed hostility at exclusion that was projected onto South Asians as symbols of an apparently cosmopolitan culture.

A conclusion of these studies is that there are links between deprivation, social and personal disorganization and racist violence. Similar themes arise in the inquiry reports into the disturbances in English towns in 2001, which identify a territorial mentality, residential segregation and the deep fracturing of communities on racial, generational and religious lines. The Home Office reports into the disturbances put considerable weight on residential segregation, which is in turn symptomatic of several underlying structural conditions (Home Office, 2002: 12). These include:

- systematic disadvantage in that many members of ethnic minorities can only afford cheaper housing;

- higher unemployment than in the majority community, especially in Bangladeshi and Pakistani communities;

- cultural cohesion and choice amongst minority communities, which is possibly linked to fear of racist attacks and hostility from the surrounding areas;

- discrimination in council housing allocation that has been a major cause of residential segregation.

Cultural factors

Racism is not confined to areas of deprivation—it also affects rural, suburban and prosperous areas as well as blighted inner city locales (Bowling and Phillips, 2002: 115). It can increase during periods of higher consumption, as it did during the 1990s. In addition to deprivation as a cause of racist violence, there are cultural logics in which deeply rooted fears and beliefs about 'contamination' by other cultures are crucial. One study of racist Internet chat rooms found no reliable connections between unemployment and racist hate but did find a correlation with politicized mobilization, which was associated with fears of threats to integrity and in particular of interracial marriage (Glasser *et al.*, 2002). Again Back (2002) found that white supremacist Internet sites were preoccupied with fears of cultural 'pollution' manifest in 'White Singles' dating pages. These cultural fears are in turn rooted in the colonial past of European nations and a belief in the cultural and 'civilizational' inferiority of ethnic minorities that paradoxically pose a threat because of their supposed global power. Such views are of course part of articulated racist worldviews and other evidence indicates that these are relatively rare even amongst racist offenders (Ray *et al.*, 2003). Nonetheless, these assumptions and fears may be part of the cultural background of racism even when they are not explicitly articulated.

REVIEW QUESTIONS

1 Why did recorded racist incidents in the UK rise during the late 1990s and 2000s?

2 How do you explain racist violence?

3 Are there links between 'hegemonic masculinity' and racism?

Homicides

The most extreme form of violence is homicide. This is rare in the UK and in most other developed countries—generally ranging between ten and twenty per million of the population per annum (slightly less in the UK at nine per million) (United Nations, 1996). There is a strong statistical association between homicide rates and rates of poverty and inequality. Men are more likely to be both victims and offenders than are women and men are more likely to be killed by strangers—the highest risk of victimization in the UK is among Afro-Caribbean men aged between twenty-one to twenty-five. Women are more at risk from spouses or former spouses with twenty per cent of all murders occurring among spouses (Metropolitan Police Service, 2002). Key factors in explaining homicide rates have been shown to include multiple deprivation, low social mobility, income inequality, a high proportion of nineteen to twenty-nine year olds in a locality, and a high correlation between inequality measured by the Gini coefficient and homicide.[5] The relationship between income inequality and homicide rates is remarkably consistent cross-nationally (Daly *et al.*, 2001) although it is unlikely to be sufficient to explain variations in the rate, and other factors will be relevant.

Messner's (1989) now famous study claimed that there was a close relationship between inequality and homicide rates. Savolainen (2000) argues (using anomie theory) that the effect of economic inequality on the level of lethal violence is limited to nations characterized by relatively weak collective institutions of social protection (such as welfare states). He tests this hypothesis with two cross-national data sets drawn from Finland and Mexico. Both settings suggest that the effects of income inequality on homicide can be mitigated by the strength of the welfare state. Nations that protect their citizens from the vicissitudes of market forces appear to be immune to the homicidal effects of economic inequality. This suggests that it is the social disorganization caused by sharp inequality rather than the inequality itself that is the determining factor. Similarly, Kawachi *et al.* (1999) argue that the degree of cohesiveness in social relations among citizens, measured, for instance, by indicators of 'social capital', affect the level of violent crimes, including homicides, that were 'consistently associated with relative deprivation (income inequality) and indicators of low social capital'. Social capital here refers to the extent of voluntary groups, involvement in the community, social networks and levels of social trust. The process that is suggested by studies like these is that relative poverty causes feelings of stress, inadequacy, 'crisis of masculinity' and undermines social capital. This in turn creates a context conducive to risk taking, criminality and increasingly violent competition for resources such as street business and dominance. However, other factors will be relevant too. Messner (1989) pointed out that in addition to inequality, an aggravating factor would be the mechanism by which inequality was reproduced—so that for example inequality based on racist exclusion would result in high levels of diffuse hostility and a high homicide rate. It is worth noting in this context that South Africa, where there is a long and bitter history of apartheid, has one of highest homicide rates in world at 600 per million per annum (United Nations, 1996) These factors may also be compounded by cultural attitudes towards violence. Commenting on higher rates of homicide in southern as opposed to northern states in the US, Cohen and Nisbett (1997) argue that southerners articulate and transmit attitudes that legitimate and encourage violence especially, violence in defence of personal and familial honour.

REVIEW QUESTIONS

1 How is the homicide rate related to inequality?

2 Who is most at risk from homicide?

3 How relevant are cultural factors in explaining the homicide rate?

CONCLUSION

One consequence of the civilizing process is an increased sensitivity to and fear of violence, which constitutes a threat to the integrity of the controlled and individualized self. There is evidence for a gradual diminution of interpersonal violence in modern societies and social and political agendas around the control of violent emotions, such as hate crime legislation, illustrates how the civilizing process has increased repugnance towards violence and its causes. At the same time violence and its threat is a routine part of everyday life for large numbers of people in settings of the street, home, neighbourhood, workplace and leisure activities. A great deal of research focuses on interpersonal violence and is accompanied by theoretical explanations that address the circumstances of individual perpetrators. Clearly, however, violence has multiple manifestations—and most of the theories discussed here point at least implicitly towards wider societal issues. In each type of violent behaviour examined here, explanations raise issues of power and dominance, but also powerlessness and inequality, the effects of which are mediated by broader cultural contexts. In order to develop a more comprehensive theory of violence we need to elaborate the ways in which power and exclusion, and the consequences of increasingly complex patterns of inequality intersect with emotional life and forms of socialization (See Ferrell, Chapter 7). There is clearly an important issue around masculinities and violence that is receiving increasing attention in the literature along with recognition that 'masculinity' cannot (any more than 'femininity') be viewed as a simple construction, but has multiple cultural and psycho-social manifestations. Once we begin to unravel the complex links between social, economic and cultural reproduction, gender socialization and the intersecting dimensions of identity and class—we may begin to understand how violence is embedded in everyday life.

QUESTIONS FOR DISCUSSION

1 What is violence and how are definitions linked to power? Consider different forms of harm to people and whether theses would be considered 'violence' or not. Why?

2 What do you understand by the 'civilizing process'? Is Elias right? How would you decide?

3 How do you explain violence in society? Consider social as opposed to biological explanations.

4 Why do you think violent crime increased in the UK and many other countries in the later twentieth century? Do explanations of violence outlined here account for this?

5 What is the relationship between masculinity and violence? Is there a 'crisis of masculinity' and how might this be connected with violent behaviour?

GUIDE TO FURTHER READING

Bowling, B. (1998) *Violent Racism: Victimisation, Policing and Social Context*. Oxford, Clarendon Press.

This is a detailed analysis of official documents and historical origins of racist violence. Bowling uses a case study to analyse the language of white supremacy and the experience of racist victimization.

Jackman, M.R. (2002) 'Violence in social life' *Annual Review of Sociology* 28: 387–415.

A good overview and critique of current sociological theories of violence and develops a programme for a new approach.

Messerschmidt, J. (1993) *Masculinities and Crime* Rowman & Littlefield.

This has become a key text in theorizing the relationship between masculinities and crime and uses the theory of 'hegemonic masculinities'.

Scheff, T.J. (2000) 'Shame and the social bond: A sociological theory' *Sociological Theory* 18 (1): 84–99.

Develops a theory of the links between social solidarity, emotions, anger and violence. Links with work inspired by John Braithwaite on shame and reintegrative shaming.

Stanko, E.A. (ed) (2003) *The Meanings of Violence* London: Routledge.

A recent collection of chapters based on projects in the ESRC's Violence Research Programme. Offers new insights and data on violent crime.

WEB LINKS

http://www.worldbank.org/poverty/inequal/abstracts/violence.htm

World Bank Poverty Net website. This is a portal into articles, discussions and other material on the relationship between inequality and violence.

http://www.who.int/violence_injury_prevention/violence/world_report/wrvheng/en/ UK

World Health Organization. World report on violence and health.

http://www.homeoffice.gov.uk/rds/bcs1.html

Home Office Research Development Statistics. Provides access to the British Crime Survey.

http://www1.rhbnc.ac.uk/sociopolitical-science/vrp/realhome.htm

ESRC Violence Research Programme website.

http://www.norberteliasfoundation.nl/

The Norbert Elias Foundation. Access to Figurations an on-line journal with discussions and reviews and other Elias related material.

REFERENCES

Barbalet, J.M. (1998) *Emotion, Social Theory, and Social Structure: A Macrosociological Approach*. Cambridge: Cambridge University Press.

Beck, A. (2000) *Prisoners of Hate* New York: Harper Collins.

Bjørgo T. and Witte, R. (eds) (1994) *Racist Violence in Europe*. London: St Martins Press.

Bourgeois P. (1996) *In Search of Respect*. Cambridge: Cambridge University Press.

Bowling, B. and Phillips C. (2002) *Racism, Crime and Justice*. London: Longman.

Campbell B. (1993) *Men, Women, Aggression*. London: Basic Books.

Cohen D. and Nisbett, R. E. (1997) 'Field experiments examining the culture of honor: The role of institutions perpetuating norms about violence', *Personality and Social Psychology Bulletin* 23 (11): 1188–99.

Connell, R. (1995) *Masculinities*. Cambridge: Polity Press.

Croall, H. (1988) *Crime and Society in Britain*. London: Pearson.

Daly, M., Wilson, M. and Vasdev, S. (2001) 'Income Inequality and Homicide rates in Canada', *Canadian Journal of Criminology* 43:219–36.

Ditton, J., Farrall, S., Bannister, J., Gilchrist, E and Pease, K. (1999) 'Reactions to Victimisation: Why Has Anger Been Ignored?' *Crime Prevention and Community Safety: an International Journal*, 1, 3:37–54.

Dunning, E., Murphy, P. and Williams, J. (1987) *The Roots of Football Hooliganism*. London: Routledge.

Eisner M. (2001) 'Modernization, Self-control and Lethal violence. The Long-term Dynamics of European Homicide Rates in Theoretical Perspective', *British Journal of Criminology* 41 (4): 618–38.

Elias, N. (1994) *The Civilizing Process*. Oxford: Blackwells, vol. I.

ESRC (2002) *ESRC Violence Research Programme—Taking Stock*. Royal Holloway: HMSO.

Fromm, E. (1979), *Anatomy of Human Destructiveness*. London: Cape.

Glasser, J., Dixit, J., and Green, D.P. (2002) 'Studying Hate Crime with the Internet: What Makes Racists Advocate Racial Violence?' *Journal of Social Issues* 58(1): 177–93.

Glasser, M. (1998) 'On Violence: a Preliminary Communication', *International Journal of Psycho-Analysis* 79, 5: 887–902.

Hammer, J. (2000) 'Domestic violence and gender relations: contexts and connections' in J. Hammer and C. Itzin (eds) *Home Truths About Domestic Violence*. London: Routledge. pp. 9–23.

Hatty, S. (2000) *Masculinities, Violence and Culture*. London: Sage Publications.

Hearn, J. (1998) *The Violences of Men*. London: Sage.

Hebdige, D. (1987) *Subculture—Meaning of Style*. London: Methuen.

Heitmeyer, W. (1994) 'Hostility and violence towards foreigners in germany' in Børgo and Witte. *Racist Violence in Europe*, pp. 17–28.

Hester, M., Kelly L. and Radford, J. Women (1996) *Violence and male power: feminist activism, research and practice*. Buckingham: Open University Press.

Home Office (2002) *A Report of the Independent Review Team Chaired by Ted Cantle*. London: Home Office.

Jackman, M.R. (2002) 'Violence in Social Life', *Annual Review of Sociology* 28:387–415.

James, O. (1995) *Juvenile Violence in a Winner-Loser Culture*. London, Free Association Books.

James, O. (2002) *They F*** You Up*. London: Bloomsbury.

Katz, J. (1988) *Seductions of Crime—moral and sensual attractions in doing evil*. NY: Basic Books

Kawachi I., Kennedy B.P., Wilkinson R.G. (1999) 'Crime: Social Disorganization and Relative Deprivation', *Social Science and Medicine* 48 (6): 719–7.

Kelly, L. (1987) *Surviving Sexual Violence*. Cambridge: Polity.

Kersten, J (1996) 'Culture, Masculinities and Violence Against Women', *The British Journal of Criminology* 36:381–95.

Krienert, J.L. (2003) 'Masculinity and Crime: A Quantitative Exploration of Messerschmidt's Hypothesis', *Electronic Journal of Sociology* http://www.sociology.org/content/vol7.2/01_krienert.html

Macpherson, W. (1999) *The Stephen Lawrence Inquiry. Report of an Inquiry by Sir William Macpherson of Cluny* (Cm 4262). London: The Stationery Office. http://www.archive.official-documents.co.uk/document/cm42/4262/sli–00.htm

Mennell, S. (1995) 'Civilisation and Decivilisation, Civil society and Violence' *Irish Journal of Sociology*, Vol. 5, pp.1–21.

Messerschmidt, J. (1993) *Masculinities and Crime*. Lanham, Md.: Rowman & Littlefield.

Messerschmidt, J. (1997) *Crime as Structured Action*. London: Sage.

Messner, S. (1989) 'Economic Distribution and Homicide Rates: Further Evidence on the Cost of Inequality', *American Sociological Review*, 54, 4, 597–612.

Mirrlees-Black, C. (1999) *Domestic Violence—Findings from a new BCS self-completion questionnaire*. Home Office: RDS.

Metropolitan Police Service (2003) *Findings from the Multi-Agency Domestic Violence Murder Reviews in London*. London: Metropolitan Police Service.

Nayak, A. (1999) ' "Pale warriors": skinhead culture and the embodiment of white masculinities' in A. Brah, M. Hickman, and M. Mac an Ghaill *Thinking Identities*. London: Macmillan. pp. 71–99.

Newburn, T. and Stanko, E.A. (eds) (1994) *Just Boys Doing Business? Men, Masculinities and Crime*. London. Routledge.

Pahl, J., Hasanbegovic, C. and Yu, M-K. (2004) 'Globalisation and Family Violence', in George, V. and Page, R. (eds), *Global Social Problems and Global Social Policy*. Cambridge: Polity Press.

Pinker, S. (2002) *The Blank Slate—The Denial of Human Nature*. London: Penguin.

Presdee, M. (2000) *Cultural Criminology and the Carnival of Crime*. London: Routledge.

Ray, L., Smith, D., Wastell, L. (2003) 'Understanding racist violence' in E. Stanko (ed) *The Meanings of Violence*. London: Routledge, pp. 112–29.

Savolainen J. (2000) 'Inequality, welfare state, and homicide: Further support for the institutional anomie theory', *Criminology* 38(4): 1021–42.

Sibbitt, R. (1997) *The Perpetrators of Racial Harassment and Racial Violence*. London: Home Office.

Smith, D. (1999) 'The Civilizing Process and the History of Sexuality: Comparing Norbert Elias and Michel Foucault', *Theory and Society* 28,1:79–100.

Smith, D. J., McVie, S., Woodward, R., Shute, J., Flint, J. and McAra, J. (2001) 'The Edinburgh Study of Youth Transitions and Crime' http://www.law.ed.ac.uk/cls/esytc/findreport/wholereport.pdf

Stanko, E. (1994) *Perspectives on Violence*. London: Quartet Books.

United Nations (1996) *Demographic Yearbook*. New York: United Nations.

WHO (2002) *World Report on Violence and Health* (eds) E. Krug, L. Dahlburg, J. Mercy, A. Zwi and R. Lozano Geneva: World Health Organization.

NOTES

1. The British Crime Survey published by the Research Development Statistics branch of the UK Home Office, asks people about crimes they have experienced in the last year and about a range of other crime-related topics. The BCS is a large sample survey, now carried out annually, designed to collect information on the extent and nature of crime and on other crime related issues. See http://www.homeoffice.gov.uk/rds/bcs1.html

2. 'Hegemony' refers to the ways in which the dominance of a group is sustained through culture. Hegemonic masculinity refers to cultural representations of dominant cultural ideals of masculinity that reinforce the subordination of women and marginal masculinities such as gay and racialized minorities (Connell 1995: 77ff).

3. The ESRC's Violence Research Programme found that 2.5 per cent of pregnant women had suffered assault in last twelve months and lifetime prevalence was 13.4 per cent. Women were ten times more likely to be assaulted in pregnancy if they had experienced violence in last twelve months (ESRC 2002).

4. The report defined institutional racism as: 'the collective failure of an organisation to provide an appropriate and professional service to people because of their colour, culture or ethnic origin. It can be seen or detected in processes, attitudes and behaviour which amount to discrimination through unwitting prejudice, ignorance, thoughtlessness, and racist stereotyping which disadvantage minority ethnic people'.

5. The Gini coefficient measures the percentage difference between a hypothetical model of perfect equality (the Lorenz curve) and actual income inequality—so higher Gini coefficients indicate greater income inequality.

12

Sex crime

Terry Thomas

INTRODUCTION

As a category of criminal activity, sexual offending has long been seen as somehow 'different' to other crimes. Crimes of a sexual nature are particularly invasive and exploitative and accompanied by a latent or manifest violence. The victims are usually women or children and the offenders invariably men. Even within the prison community there has been a history of other offenders regarding the sex offender as 'different' and 'by tradition "nonces" are expected to know their place and keep out of the way of "straight cons" ' (Sparks *et al.*, 1996: 179).

In the UK and North America the 'problem' of the sex offender has moved inexorably up the political agenda in the last decade. Sexual offending has become increasingly unacceptable and a range of adjustments have been made within the criminal justice system to improve the investigation of sexual offending, and the prosecution of sex offenders. More punitive sentences have been introduced and new civil measures, such as the sex offender 'register' have been developed to better protect the community.

This chapter examines the nature of sex offending and the forms it takes as well as the enhanced social response made to sex offending over the last ten years.

BACKGROUND

The sexual activities of individuals is usually a matter for them alone, but the very fact that sexual offending has become such a matter of public and political concern demonstrates that not all sexual activities can be just left to the participants.

The reasons for the increased public political attention to sexual offending are many and varied. The feminist movement of the 1970s highlighted the plight of women as victims of male violence and sexual offending. In the 1980s social workers and paediatricians focused on the sexual abuse of children and raised the question of what should happen to the adult perpetrators of these crimes. The 'law and order' lobby of the 1990s generally wanted more punitive punishments for a range of offenders and achieved a degree of success in this direction, encouraged by a rampant tabloid press and—in the case of sex offenders—even street demonstrations that led to vigilantism against identified offenders. In a world beset by changing values, there was some security to be had in knowing that, whatever else may change, the commission of sexual crimes against children was always going to be a constant 'wrong' and action against them would be needed. The 'paedophile' became the 'folk-devil' of our times.

'Folk devils' are those figures in society we are encouraged to dislike and avoid. In the past they have included young offenders, including football hooligans, muggers, punk rockers and those mods and rockers who fought seaside battles in the 1960s. The phenomenon was originally examined by Cohen in his study of mods and rockers and the way in which their activities were exaggerated and distorted by the social reaction in terms of law enforcement, court judgements, and media reaction and then the inter-reaction between those responding agencies. The offenders take on a symbolic significance and the action and re-action that takes place duly spirals into what Cohen called a 'moral panic' (Cohen, 1973).

Sexual activity usually takes place between individuals freely consenting to that activity. Sexual offending only enters the picture when that consent is absent. Consent may also be imagined as a continuum from 'true' consent at one end through to reluctant acquiescence and submission at the other end. It is not an easy stand-alone concept to cover all circumstances. The actual activities engaged in may otherwise be as broadly defined as the parties in which they are involved are willing to agree.

In 2000, the UK Home Office published the final report of its comprehensive review of sexual offences and gave it the title 'Setting the Boundaries'; but even with such a title the Home Office was clear that the review's 'guiding principle was that the criminal law should not intrude unnecessarily into the private life of adults' (Home Office, 2000, para. 0.7).

Consent or free agreement

Consenting, or giving free agreement, to sexual activities is usually premised on the idea that we are talking about mature adults who know the full consequences of what they are doing and are under no duress and subject to no deceptions as to what they are agreeing to; we use the phrase 'consenting adults'. Consent may be impaired when the person giving it lacks the capacity to know the full consequences of what they are doing because they are, for example, an adult with intellectual impairments, or they are too affected by alcohol or drugs to give free agreement. Children are said to lack an adult capacity to consent.

We talk of an 'age of consent' which in the UK is set at sixteen years. Children below the age of sixteen may give a consent but the younger the child the more likely that consent is flawed and ultimately negatived by the child's absence of understanding the full physical and emotional consequences of what they are agreeing to; at such point sexual offending is taking place, and particular laws may be needed to protect children from predatory adults.

The problem of under-age consent is further confused when children under sixteen have engaged in prostitution within the commercial sex industry. The UK still has laws allowing for the prosecution of such children for activities associated with prostitution even though some would say their 'invalid' consent makes them the victims of crime rather than the perpetrators (see below).

The actual 'age of consent' varies over time and from place to place. In England and Wales it was moved up from thirteen to sixteen years in 1885 for heterosexual activities, and remains at sixteen to this day; in Northern Ireland it is seventeen. In Germany it is fixed at fourteen and in Denmark at fifteen. When it comes to homosexual activities the age of consent in England and Wales dropped from twenty-one to eighteen in 1994 and dropped again to sixteen in 2000.

Consent when applied to heterosexual activities is also very much a gender-specific concept. It is the woman who consents and not the man. Such a conceptualization implies that the man 'always' wants sex and the idea of him consenting to sexual activities is almost risible. The term 'free-agreement' in place of 'consent' has been suggested as going some way towards correcting this imbalance (Home Office, 2000: para. 2.10.5), but the current law still uses the word consent.

Even when consent has been present, the UK criminal law may still be invoked with a view to determining the presence of sexual offending. Certain relationships may be declared 'prohibited', such as that between a father and daughter or brother and sister, regardless of whether there was consent. Governments have also seen it as proper to intervene in the interests of protecting public health, as the UK did in prosecuting a group of adult men under the Offences Against the Persons Act 1861 for indulging in sexual activities they had all consented to; the European Court of Human Rights upheld the prosecution (*Laskey, Jaggard and Brown* v UK (1997), 24 EHRR 39).

Teachers are prohibited from having sexual relations with their pupils even if those pupils are over the age of sixteen and have consented. The criminal law considers this to be the offence of 'abuse of trust' which covers anyone working with young people in schools, children's homes or similar settings (Sexual Offences Act 2003, ss. 16–24).

In making a retrospective attempt to unravel whether consent was present or absent at a particular incident, the picture is further confused by the range of complex messages—many of them non-verbal—used by adults to convey agreement or consent. Add to that the fact that sexual activities invariably take place in private and with no evidential witnesses and that external confusion on the truth of the matter is only exacerbated.

Forms of sexual offending

A definitive list of exactly what is and is not a sexual offence is probably impossible to draw up. We might be clear that lack of consent results in rape or indecent assault, and that those entering into a 'prohibited relationship' commit an offence of 'familial sexual abuse', but as we develop the range of possible sexual offences the outer limits are less clear. When the UK sex offender 'register' was first proposed in a 1996 Consultation Paper, a total of thirty-three offences were suggested as possibly leading to registration in England and Wales; the Consultation paper completely overlooked the fact that two different lists would be needed for Scotland and Northern Ireland where the law was different (Home Office 1996: Annex A). When the register was later enacted in law, this figure for England and Wales had dropped to just twelve (Sex Offender Act 1997, Schedule One, para. 1) and more recently there have been proposals to raise the number again (Home Office/Scottish Office 2001: Chapter 4). Scotland and Northern Ireland had lists of twenty and fifteen respectively (Sex Offender Act 1997, Schedule One, paras. 2 and 3).

The categorization of sexual offence can change with a simple change in law. In this way homosexual activities have been decriminalized (Sexual Offences Act 1967), and the rape of a man by another male has been recognized when previously it was not (Criminal Justice and Public Order Act 1994, s. 143). At one time it was presumed a man could not be prosecuted for raping his own wife, but this was changed by court ruling in 1991 and statutory law in 1994 (Criminal Justice and Public Order Act 1994, s. 142). In similar vein boys under fourteen were once assumed incapable of the act of rape, but since 1993 they can be prosecuted over the age of ten (Sexual Offences Act 1993; now in the Sexual Offences Act 2003, s. 1).

In general terms sexual crimes are committed by two groups of people; those who know their victims and those who do not. In the past, rapes, for example, have sometimes been categorized as 'acquaintance rapes' and 'stranger rapes' and the conventional wisdom has long held that children are far more at risk of sexual crime within their families than they are outside of it (although research still suggests we should not underestimate the risk children might be subject to outside of the family (Gallagher *et al.*, 2002)).

Some adults who persistently target children for sexual activities may be described as 'paedophiles'. As such they have entered the lexicon of hatred for our times and been demonized by the press and popular opinion (Silverman and Wilson, 2002). Adult men who have sexually offended against children in schools and children's homes have been the cause of numerous safeguards now put into place to prevent them ever getting such work giving them access to children (Thomas, 2002). At the other extreme a seventeen-year old boy having 'under age' sex with a fifteen year old girl may receive only muted criticism albeit committing the same offences by the letter of the law.

The commercial sexual exploitation of children through under-age prostitution has been tackled by a new focus on the organizers and purchasers of children as the criminals and the introduction of 'exit' strategies for the children now seen as the victims of abuse (Department of Health *et al.*, 2000; Brown and Barrett, 2003).

Some men, including those described as 'paedophiles', have been known to travel across international boundaries specifically for purposes of having sex with children. This travel is premised on the idea that some countries have more relaxed laws and that even when laws are in place they are not enforced with any rigour. This form of abuse is invariably commercial in nature as family poverty in places like Thailand, the Philippines and parts of Eastern Europe, drives children into prostitution. The men travelling to avail themselves of these 'services' have become known as 'sex tourists' (Kane, 1998).

Although 'sex tourism' throws up problems for the destination countries, it has also received attention at home—the sending country—as measures have been put in place to restrict the levels of travel involved. The ultimate answer is to ensure an equivalence of law and law enforcement in all countries to remove any 'havens' that might exist.

The production, dissemination and ownership of pornography, has been considered a sexual offence and especially when that pornography has featured children. The rise of the Internet in the late 1990s meant it became a favoured medium for the dissemination of such material across international borders (Carr, 2004). The UK government responded with its police High Tech Crime Unit to combat Internet crime, and international exercises such as Operation Ore followed. Operation Ore was an FBI led operation from the USA which discovered some 7,000 people in the UK alone—including the rock star Pete Townshend—had subscribed to an illegal child pornography website ('How British police officer set trap for paedophiles', *The Observer*, 19 January 2003).

The point is made that any photographs or film of a child being abused are images of a crime having taken place even though the ultimate viewer may be far removed from that crime; the demand for child pornography has helped 'cause' the crime. In Sweden researchers have tried to track the children so abused in order to help them, and not least to help them with the emotional impact when they know their image has been disseminated (Svedin and Back, 1996).

Criminal processes

The criminal justice system processes sexual offenders just as it processes all offenders. A police investigation is followed by a decision to prosecute, a court hearing and, on a finding of guilt, an appropriate punishment is imposed. The criminal justice system may be conceived of as a series of sub-systems wherein decisions are made concerning the offender; we start by considering the initial police investigation.

Investigating sexual offences

Sexual crimes have not always been readily reported to the police for investigation. As we have noted, sexual activity whether of a consensual or a criminal nature, usually takes place in private. This in itself may lead to a reluctance to report because from the outset it may be just one person's word against another with no corroborating evidence. Add to this the possible shame or stigma experienced by the victim and the phenomena of 'under reporting' begins to take shape.

Further disincentives to report have in the past arisen from police attitudes to receiving reports of sexual crime. Negative attitudes of disbelief and incredulity from police officers and the nature of the investigative questioning have led rape victims in particular, to not bother reporting in the first place. In 1982 the UK's Thames Valley Police featured in a notorious 'fly-on-the-wall' documentary which showed two male officers dismissing a woman's report as nothing less than 'fairy tales' to cover up a consensual sexual experience. In such a climate a crime could often be recorded as 'no-crime' by the police.

Throughout the 1980s and into the 1990s the police—prompted by the Home Office—improved their investigative interviewing and techniques. Realizing that sexual crime takes place in private, they have taken victims' statements more seriously, made efforts to improve the reception of victims and opened special medical suites to ensure that medical evidence can be taken without causing additional distress. Police officer training in this area has been improved and specialist teams of officers created to develop expertise; in Northern Ireland, for example, the Child Abuse and Rape Enquiry Unit—or CARE team—carry out the necessary investigations.

As the police slowly changed their attitudes, women victims became more willing to come forward. What had once been an area of crime 'under reported' now saw the 'reporting figures' start to rise. Research confirmed that the reporting of rape increased threefold between 1985 and 1996 (Harris and Grace, 1999). When the police became custodians of the sex offender 'register' in 1997 and later started partaking in Multi-Agency Public Protection Panels (see below) sexual offending was beginning to move from the margins of police thinking toward the centre. All of this, however, did not stop the Home Office in 2003 still referring to 'sexual offenders (being) significantly under-reported to the authorities' (Home Office, 2003a, p. 82).

Prosecuting sexual offenders

If the problem of sexual crime being 'under-reported' had been partially addressed, there still remained difficulties with the prosecution of alleged sex offenders. At the end of a police investigation, the case information has to be tied up and passed to the Crown Prosecution Service (CPS) for their analysis and decision on whether to take the accused to court. Guided by their own Code of Practice, the CPS needs to decide on the possibilities of winning the case and whether or not prosecution is in the public interest. If the evidence was not sufficient or contained irregularities or the case was, for some reason, not worth bringing to court in the public interest, the CPS would not proceed—or in their language the case would be 'discontinued'.

The Home Office sexual offences review noted a significant fall in the prosecutions for unlawful sexual intercourse with children and confessed 'we do not know why the numbers of prosecutions for USI have fallen so significantly' (Home Office, 2000a: para. 3.2.10). A joint report of the Crown Prosecution Service and HM Inspectorate of Constabulary has further reported a fall in the number of prosecutions and 'a marked decline' in the percentage of successful prosecutions for rape offences.

> . . . the rate of conviction for rape, after trial, has decreased from one in three cases reported (33 per cent) in 1977 to one in 13 (7.5 per cent) in 1999. Furthermore only one in five (20 per cent) reported cases currently reaches the trial stage.
>
> (CPSI/HMIC 2002: para. 1.3)

Evidential difficulties for the CPS with respect to sexual offending include:

- victims who are vulnerable in terms of age or learning disabilities;
- the victim's previous sexual history;
- a prior relationship between victim and offender which can test the victim's willingness to give evidence;
- when the case turns on the issue of 'consent', it is often one person's word against another.

(Harris and Grace, 1999: 26)

A fair hearing in court

A person accused of a sexual crime has the same rights as any other defendant in a criminal court to defend themselves whilst receiving a fair trial. The particular nature of sexual crime, however, has led to the introduction of special measures to help victims give sensitive evidence in what can be the intimidating environment of the court. In the interests of justice these special measures have to be balanced against the defendant's right to a fair trial.

In the late 1980s laws were passed to enable a child victim of sexual crime to give their evidence in court through a live video link to save them having to go into the court itself. These measures were soon followed by laws to allow children to give their evidence by means of a pre-recorded video tape, although they might still have to later make themselves available for cross examination by counsel. These arrangements are still in place and governed by revised Home Office guidelines (Home Office 2002(a)).

Adult women victims of sexual crime have also been given forms of protection in court. In 1976 rape victims were allowed anonymity and this was extended to victims of other sexual offences in 1992. The same 1976 law—the Sexual Offences (Amendment) Act—also gave anonymity to defendants but this was withdrawn by a later law in 1988.

Since 1976, women victims of rape have had the additional protection of limits being placed on the degree to which their past sexual histories could be referred to in court. It was a common form of defence for the defendant to demonstrate, say, a past history of consensual sex between the two parties or a history of promiscuous sexual activity by the woman. Restrictions on these references to past sexual history were at the discretion of the judge and were meant to save the woman from irrelevant 'smearing' and 'innuendo' which made some women feel they were being 'abused' or even 'raped' again by the court process. In practice, however, the restrictions did not work very well and judges were seemingly far too willing to lift them. In 1999 new laws were introduced to strengthen them in the interests of the victim.

The Youth Justice and Criminal Evidence Act 1999, s. 41 strengthened the restrictions on evidence about the sexual behaviour of the victim which could only be given by leave of the court in specified circumstances. This was referred to as 'the rape shield'. Almost the first time the courts came up against the new s. 41, an appeal was made that it prevented the defendant getting a fair trial. The matter was referred to the House of Lords where the appeal was dismissed (*R v A (Respondent) (On Appeal from the Court of Appeal (Criminal Division)* 17 May 2001 [2001] UKHL 25).

The Youth Justice and Criminal Evidence Act also introduced other measures to help sexual offence complainants give evidence if the court believed fear and distress would diminish the quality of that evidence. Screens may be brought in to shield them from the defendant, and the court may even be cleared so the public are not present during the giving of evidence. The arrangements for live video links and pre-recorded video testimony were extended from children to adults who were particularly vulnerable (see Home Office, 2002a for full details).

Punishing the sex offender

Over the last fifteen years the punishments available to courts sentencing sex offenders have been increased in severity. In its 1990 White Paper the government was unequivocal that it wished to give courts the power 'to give custodial sentences longer than would be justified by the seriousness of the offence to persistent violent and sexual offenders, if this is necessary to protect the public from serious harm' (Home Office, 1990: para. 3.13); the new sentences were introduced by the Criminal Justice Act 1991, s. 2(2)(b).

Subsequent laws have gone in the same direction. An automatic life sentence is now mandatory for a person committing a second serious offence; a serious offence includes rape, attempted rape and intercourse with a girl under thirteen (Crime (Sentences) Act 1997). The same Act (s. 52) increased the maximum sentence for gross indecency with a child under fourteen from two years to ten years. Sentences for a sexual offence were lengthened again by the Crime and Disorder Act 1998, ss. 58–9; the lengthening applied to any part of a sentence that involved licence in the community and which followed the custodial element of the sentence. In future that period of supervision in the community under licence could be for as long as ten years.

The Criminal Justice Act 2003 introduced another new punishment that could be used for sex offenders. The worry was that some sex offenders had been imprisoned for a determinate period, had not availed themselves of treatment programmes and were being discharged from custody just as dangerous as when they went in. The idea now was to manage that release and only allow it when the offender was no longer a risk to the public. The Criminal Justice Act 2003, s. 225 provides for 'imprisonment for public protection for serious offences' for offenders who are assessed as 'dangerous' (s. 229) having committed a specified violent or sexual offence. Imprisonment is for a determinate period followed by a 'reviewable' period during which the Parole Board will decided on release.

Measures to help with the rehabilitation of offenders back into the community were denied to people who had committed sex offences. In January 1999, a scheme was started whereby prisoners were released early from prison subject to wearing an electronic tag for the last sixty days of their formal custodial period; this was extended to ninety days in October 2002. This Home Detention Curfew, as it is known, is not available for sex offenders (Criminal Justice and Court Services Act 2000, s. 65).

Offenders who were on the sex offender 'register' and, therefore had obligations to report any change of address to the police as custodians of the 'register' (see below) also found their punishments increased if they failed to comply with their obligations. The Criminal Justice and Court Services Act 2000 increased the possible fine and the maximum term of imprisonment despite the fact that the reported compliance rate was actually running at some 94 per cent (Plotnikoff and Wilson, 2000: 6).

This toughening up of sentences imposed on sex offenders, has not stopped the UK prison service ensuring that comprehensive Sex Offender Treatment Programmes are in place throughout the prison estate. Sex offenders are encouraged to take part in these Programmes, and results have been encouraging (Beech et al., 1998). The problem is that no '100 per cent cure' can be guaranteed and there is always the lurking fear that these offenders will remain a danger.

REVIEW QUESTIONS

1 What are the difficulties in investigating sexual offences?

2 How can we ensure victims get a fair hearing in court?

3 Are longer sentences the best way to protect the public from convicted sex offenders?

Civil measures

At the same time as the UK has brought in new criminal procedures and punishments to deal with the sex offender, there have been parallel moves to introduce a range of civil measures to reduce the risk of re-offending by those sex offenders we know about. The most high profile of these civil measures has been the sex offender register introduced in 1997. The 'register' concept recognizes that many sex offenders have ended their formal period of community or custodial punishment but may continue to pose a risk of re-offending. The idea that these offenders are 'untreatable' and therefore unlikely to change is an idea that dies hard. The conclusion is, therefore, that we need to know just where they are in the community at any one time, and we need to have surveillance and screening measures in place to prevent them engaging in particular work or travel arrangements that might enable them to re-offend.

These civil measures are essentially exercises in risk assessment and risk management. They are dependent on high quality information about the offender and his circumstances being made available to various professionals and practitioners—as well as the courts—charged with this risk reduction task. The decisions they make on receipt of this information should improve aggregate levels of community safety or be more specific decisions leading to individual child protection or the protection of a former victim.

The concept of risk has become all important when considering interventions against people who commit sexual offences, or, indeed, other forms of violent offending. The concept has been with us for a long time and in essence it is about trying to predict a person's future behaviour. Scientists, engineers and insurance officers have refined the idea of risk and its calculation in order to reduce the negative aspects of risk and make the future more manageable.

Practitioners now collate information about sexual and violent offenders, and their social environment to make risk assessments on the likelihood of future offending. Various 'instruments' have been designed to assist the practitioners in this task of collating and then weighing this information in order to improve the accuracy of risk assessment. Just how accurate risk assessment can ever be is a matter of contention.

In general terms risk assessment may be divided into an actuarial and a clinical form. Actuarial risk assessment is a statistical calculation borrowed from the world of insurance, looks at types of offenders and makes a probability estimate of future (re)offending. Clinical risk assessment is more focused on the individual and uses the knowledge and wisdom of practitioners who work with them; clinical assessment can even include the idea of 'gut-feelings'. A lot of practitioners would seek to combine the two forms in their work.

Policy and practice based on risk assessment is inevitably problematic. Predicting the future is always going to be an imprecise science, and the accuracy of risk assessment is always open to doubt. Even robust instruments designed to help may be fallible when implemented quickly by practitioners under pressure. It may even be said to be unethical to take action against people who may offend in the future—but who also may not (see, for example, Feeley and Simon, 1994; Garland, 2001).

Registering the whereabouts of sex offenders

The UK sex offender register is maintained by the police. It is not a discrete 'register' as such but simply a sub-category of the complete national criminal record collection maintained by the police on the Police National Computer. The Republic of Ireland introduced its own register in 2001.

The idea for a register came about in the mid-1990s when various parts of the media picked up on the concept from the USA where federal legislation in 1994 had required all fifty States to have a register in place. More focused research from the University of Manchester supported the register idea (Hughes *et al.*, 1996) and a Home Office Consultation Document formally tabled it in 1996, saying, somewhat tentatively, 'it would help police identify suspects after a crime; it *could* help prevent crimes; and it *might* act as a deterrent' (Home Office, 1996: para. 43, emphasis added). The 1997 Sex Offender Act created the register; today its provisions are in the Sexual Offences Act 2003, ss. 80–96.

The unique feature of the register when it came into operation on 1 September 1997 was that offenders currently in the system or committing designated sexual offences after that date, would be required—in future—to notify the police every time they changed their name or address. In this way the police would have an up to date and more accurate picture of where all these known offenders lived. The exact length of time each offender would have to continue notifying the police was dependent on the severity of the original sentence—the most serious would have to register for life. Failure to register would be an offence in itself and punishable by a fine or imprisonment (for further details see Cobley, 1997).

From the outset the 'register' was criticized for not being retrospective and thereby missing out on an estimated 110,000 sex offenders in the community who had offended *before* the register came into existence (Marshall, 1997). It was also criticized for being too narrowly focused on its designated twelve sex offences (for England and Wales) listed in Schedule One to the 1997 Act. Some people wanted individuals to register even when there had been *no* conviction but, for example, where care proceedings had been taken on a 'substantiated' case of child sexual abuse in a family, but where insufficient evidence existed for a prosecution (see Thomas, 2000, chapter 7). The Government felt unable to act on these criticisms.

In 2000 the Home Office published its first evaluation of the 'register'. Some 94 per cent of those required to register were found to be complying with their obligations and to that extent the 'register' was working well. The police also reported that the 'register' had led to improved working relationships with other agencies like the probation service, who sometimes shared the information on the 'register' (see below). The one thing the evaluation could not say, however, was whether or not the 'register' was making communities any safer and it lamented the fact that 'no single measure of effectiveness emerged from this study as suitable for performance measurement' (Plotnikoff and Woolfson, 2000: 50).

A year later the Home Office published a further consultation paper on the sex offender 'register'. By this time various changes had been made to the 'register' by the Criminal Justice and Court Services Act 2000, including an increase in the punishment for non-compliance, but the consultation paper now proposed yet more changes. New Home Secretary David Blunkett in an introduction to the paper, claimed the 'register' 'had proved a valuable tool in helping protect the public', even though 'experience in implementing it has suggested that aspects could be strengthened' (Home Office/Scottish Office, 2001: 1). The compliance rate was now set at 97 per cent and the numbers on the register totalled 'about 15,000' (ibid.: 11–12).

On the basis of the response to the consultation paper the new changes to the 'register' were announced in 2002. In future, offenders would have to report in person annually to the police to verify their details, changes had to be notified within three days (previously it was fourteen) and changes of addresses of more than seven days had to be notified (previously that was also fourteen). The police got more powers to photograph and fingerprint at each annual visit and more offences were proposed that would lead to registration (for example, serious violent offences where there was evidence that they presented a risk of causing serious sexual harm) (Home Office, 2002b: Chapter 1). All of these changes required new legislation, and the changes were made by the Sexual Offences Act 2003, Part 2 which now replaced the whole of the 1997 Sex Offenders Act.

Multi-agency public protection panels

Once the sex offender 'register' had been implemented, the Home Office was anxious that it should not become a passive list of names that simply gathered dust on the metaphorical shelf. It wanted the list to be interactive and dynamic and something that made an active contribution to community safety. Some voices were heard calling for the register to be open to the public, so the community would know where these offenders lived. Home Secretaries have always resisted that call (see below).

In North Wales a test case on police disclosure of information to the public ruled that such 'controlled disclosures' were in order if they were in the interests of public safety and crime prevention. The disclosures were not to be routine or 'blanket' in nature but should only be where a particularly high risk of re-offending had been noted (*R v Chief Constable of North Wales Police ex p. Thorpe* (1998) *The Times* 23 March). This begged the question of how you decided who, on the register was high-risk, and who would actually make the decision?

The police as custodians of the sex offender 'register' realized that this was going to be their decision to make and to make effective risk assessments they needed the help of others like the probation service. When the register was implemented meetings between the police and probation service started to take place in varying degrees of formality, to consider the risk assessment and risk management of those on the register. Sometimes other agencies such as the local Social Services Department would be co-opted into the discussions.

These initial ad hoc arrangements made in the wake of the register's implementation were knocked into a more formal shape by the Criminal Justice and Court Services Act 2000 (ss. 67–8). In future these meetings would be called Multi-Agency Public Protection Panels or MAPPPs, and although the police and probation services would take the lead, other agencies such as social services, housing or health care professionals could be formally co-opted. MAPPP's would look at three layers of offenders:

(a) those on the register;

(b) violent and other sex offenders imprisoned for more than twelve months;

(c) any other offenders considered to pose a risk to the community.

The local MAPPPs would publish an annual report on their work and the Home Office would produce an annual national review of their work; neither report would name individual offenders. These arrangements were started 1 April 2001 (see Bryan and Doyle, 2003).

First reports suggested that the MAPPP's were not very standardized in their work despite their new statutory status and although the Home Office were pleased with the new structures they did not offer any additional resources to the police or probation to support the MAPPPs.

In 2002 pilot schemes were started to include lay members of the public on to the MAPPPs for them to have a say in the risk assessment work that was being carried out. The plan was to include lay members in all areas of the country during 2004. They were not allowed to divulge confidential information on individuals that they might hear at the meetings.

Managing the 'unregistered' sex offender

The sex offender register was not retrospective. Sex offenders who committed offences before the register's implementation (1 September 1997) were under no obligations to report their whereabouts. An early calculation suggested there were some 110,000 of them in this position (see above). As long as they were not re-offending they were not a problem, but perhaps something was needed if they looked as though they were about to re-offend. The civil measure of the Sex Offender Order was introduced to try and address this problem.

Sex Offender Orders were applied for by the police, on people known to have convictions that would normally have put them on the sex offender register, and who were now believed to be acting in a suspicious way as though they were intent on re-offending and there was, therefore, 'reasonable cause to believe that an order . . . is necessary to protect the public from serious harm' (Crime and Disorder Act 1998, s. 2, as amended by the Police Reform Act 2002).

If magistrates allowed the police application, a Sex Offender Order brought the offender on to the register and also imposed various 'negative' requirements on them to stop the activities that had been interpreted as suspicious by the police. Failure to comply resulted in criminal proceedings. The Order could not impose any 'positive' requirements on the offender to do things (for example, attend a treatment programme). Some ninety-two Orders had been made between 1 December 1998 and 31 March 2001, with magistrates approving 96 per cent of the applications laid before them (Knock, 2002).

Although the Sex Offender Order was a civil measure, a test case in the courts has ruled that the implications of the Order are so serious that criminal procedures have to be adhered to in the courts hearing an application. In other words the civil requirement that the Order be made only on a 'balance of probabilities' was now replaced by the criminal requirement that the Order be made only when its need has been proved 'beyond all reasonable doubt' (*McCann v Manchester Crown Court* [2002] 4 All ER 593). The Sexual Offences Act 2003 later replaced the Sex Offender Order with the Sexual Offences Prevention Order (see below).

Restraining the sex offender

Restraining Orders were introduced by the Criminal Justice and Court Services Act 2000 (s. 66 and Schedule 5) which again amended the Sex Offenders Act 1997. The Restraining Order was made on a sex offender at the point of sentencing at the discretion of the court; no one had to specifically apply for it. The court had to be satisfied that the Order was needed to prevent risk of serious harm to the general public or to an individual; the latter would most likely be the victim of the crime. As with Sex Offender Orders the Restraining Order could only make 'negative' requirements for an offender to desist from certain activities and not 'positive' requirements that they do something. The Order could be for a specific time or for an indefinite period, and breach of the Order would be dealt with as a criminal matter with sanctions of imprisonment or fines. Like the Sex Offender Order the Restraining Order was replaced by the Sexual Offences Prevention Order.

Sexual offences prevention orders

The Sexual Offences Act 2003 (ss. 104–13) replaced both the Sex Offender Order and the Restraining Order by combining them in the Sexual Offences Prevention Order (SOPO). The SOPO contains the two distinct strands of the former Orders with an Order by application or an Order added to a criminal sentence and has similar sanctions for breach of the Order. The SOPO is, however, expanded in scope to cover offences of violence where there is also a sexual component.

Sex offenders who travel abroad

The 'sex tourist' is the person who travels the world intent on having sexual encounters with children. As we have already noted their travel is premised on the notion that some countries have less rigorous laws and less rigorous law enforcement. Mostly these travellers are seeking commercial sex from children acting as prostitutes (Kane, 1998; Barrett, 2000).

In 1997 civil provisions were implemented to allow prosecutions in this country of sexual crimes committed abroad; these measures were contained in the Sex Offenders Act 1997 Part II, and the provisions were first used against a man who had offended in France ('Camp site owner jailed for sex assaults on girls', *Independent* 22 January 2000).

For those on the sex offender register further restrictions were imposed in 2000 with new requirements for registrants to notify the police if they went abroad for more than eight days. The idea was that the police could then notify their counterparts in the destination country who could choose whether they kept an eye on the traveller or not. These provisions were originally in the Criminal Justice and Court Services Act 2000 and are now in the Sexual Offences Act 2003.

Although the registered sex offender now had obligations to notify the police about his proposed foreign travel, the police had no powers to actually stop him going. Proposals to introduce such a power emerged during discussions on the Sexual Offences Bill in March 2003. The Home Office produced a short paper proposing a Foreign Travel Banning Order that the police could apply to the court for. A case would have to be made out to the effect that the person concerned already had offences against children, had subsequently acted in a way indicative of re-offending and there were no realistic alternatives to the Banning Order (Home Office, 2003b). These Orders were renamed as Foreign Travel Orders when introduced by the Sexual Offences Act 2003, ss. 114–22.

The same Home Office paper also proposed adding to the 'register' all those who had offended and been convicted whilst abroad. This requirement was to be for both UK and foreign nationals now resident here (ibid.) and was formalized in the Notification Order that could be applied for when knowledge of such offences was available (Sexual Offences Act 2003 ss. 97–103).

Laws against 'grooming'

One troubling aspect of sexual offending for legislators was the practice of 'grooming' a child for sexual activity by lengthy befriending and often deception. Sex offenders had long been thought to do this, but the use of the internet and 'chat-rooms' whereby adult men could anonymously pretend to be of the same age as their intended victims made the problem more urgent. The proposed answer was the Risk of Sexual Harm Order (RSHO) introduced by the Sexual Offences Act 2003 (ss. 123–29). The police can apply for these Orders if they see a pattern developing and there is an identifiable sexual component to the behaviour. Fines or imprisonment can be imposed for breach of the Order.

REVIEW QUESTIONS

1 Does the registration of sex offenders make communities safer?

2 Are civil measures to 'contain' sex offenders in danger of breaching their human rights?

3 Can we ever fully prevent adults from 'grooming' children for sexual purposes?

Public access to the 'register'?

A disputed aspect of the 'register' has been the debate as to whether the public should have access to it. To put it another way—should residents be told when a convicted sex offender moves into their street so that they can better protect themselves and their families? At present—as we noted above—the UK government has always resisted such demands; in the USA the government has taken an opposite tack and passed federal law (known as Megan's Law) requiring all states to give open access to their registers.

The first attempts to get open access to the UK register were during the 1997 parliamentary debate on the Sex Offenders Bill (Thomas, 2000: 111–2). At one point the Home Secretary at the time looked set to concede open access ('Howard set to name sex offenders', *Guardian* 12 February 1997), but in the end he did not. Later he would say that it had never been his intention to do so 'as it would be tantamount to inviting vigilante activity' (quoted in Silverman and Wilson, 2002: 162). The fear of vigilante activity and of driving offenders 'underground' has remained the primary argument against notifying communities when a sex offender has moved in.

In the summer of 2000, the 'News of the World' newspaper revived the argument for open access following the abduction and murder of eight year old Sarah Payne in Sussex. Calling for a 'Sarah's Law' to reflect the US 'Megan's Law', the newspaper started publishing the names and photographs of the sex offenders it was aware of, and continued to do so for several weeks ('Named, Shamed', *News of the World* 23 July 2000). A frisson of 'paedophile panic' went round the country and not least in Paulsgrove, an estate outside Portsmouth where demonstrations and vigilante activity lasted a week (Silverman and Wilson, 2002, Chapter 8).

When the furore died down, the government still held the line against public access, but it did make amendments to strengthen the 'register' with amendments to the Criminal Justice and Court Services Bill, then going through parliament. The Home Secretary attributed these changes directly to the Sarah Payne murder, saying 'we have I believe, recognized the very strong public concern which her murder has evoked' (Home Office, 2000).

The Home Office will allow, what it calls, 'controlled disclosure' of 'register' information as opposed to public access in accordance with the North Wales Police judgement (see above). The police—as custodians of the register—decide when and where information might be disclosed. Often this is to a school or housing department and occasionally to members of the public with a direct need to know. It was to help the police make these 'controlled disclosure' decisions that meetings began with the probation service and led on to the creation of MAPPPs.

At the time of writing (Spring, 2004) the Home Office still continues to deny public access to the 'register', and indeed what evidence there is on the effectiveness of public access in the USA shows it to be policy that is limited (Lovell, 2001; see also Power, 2003).

REVIEW QUESTIONS

1 Who should know where convicted sex offenders live?

2 Would communities be safer if they knew where sex offenders live?

3 Is vigilantism a justified response to sex offenders?

The 'possibly' dangerous

In the normal course of events any loss of liberty imposed on an individual citizen is carried out by the criminal justice process sentencing that person to a period in custody. Some secondary forms of incarceration take place under the umbrella of mental health legislation taking people compulsorily into hospital. The last and most far-reaching measure proposed to reduce the risk of sex offending, has been the idea of indeterminate sentences.

The idea that the behaviour of certain people can be described as 'dangerous' has—like the concept of risk—been with us for a long time. The Victorians referred to whole

Figure 12.1 A *News of the World* employee, at Times International, following the death of Sarah Payne.

Source: © AFP/Getty Images. Adrian Dennis.

sections of society as the 'dangerous classes', and more recently there has been a 'rediscovery' of the dangerous person (Bottoms, 1977); invariably the dangerous person is the would-be sexual or violent offender. In the past we have incarcerated the dangerous person or transported them to the other side of the world. Today we may still imprison the most dangerous, but we also believe in community sentences and policies of de-carceration and integration back into the community. This presents us with the problem of ensuring a degree of community safety or public protection for the community (see Nash, 1999, chapter 1).

Dangerousness as an adjective describing behaviour has become inextricably linked to 'risk assessment' and 'risk management'. In some senses the word management has moved from being an adjective to being a noun and we now talk of the dangerous person as having dangerous attributes we can identify and isolate as part of a risk assessment. The short comings of risk assessment have already been referred to.

The problem with the sex offender is that (a): he—or more rarely she—may be per-ceived as 'dangerous' before he has actually offended; and (b) he may not necessarily be mentally disordered. In these circumstances neither the criminal justice process or men-tal health provisions can be brought to bear, and the argument has been made that some new system of indeterminate sentence is needed on those few people assessed as 'dangerous', likely to offend, yet not mentally disordered.

In the USA a number of states have introduced such a 'third way' with their laws on civil commitment that permit the civil detention of people categorized as sexually dan-gerous predators. Such people can be removed from the community or—more likely—simply re-categorized as they come near to their release date from prison and further detained under these civil measures when they thought they were going home. A risk assessment has to be made and confirmed by the courts in the form of the civil commit-ment detention (Janus, 2000). Appeals to the Supreme Court that such further detention is 'unconstitutional' have been unsuccessful (*Kansas v Hendricks* (1997) 117 S. Ct. 2072).

In the UK the Home Office has proposed its own form of civil commitment, which it called 'indeterminate sentences' (Home Office, 1999). Since that first proposal there has been much discussion on the topic of 'personality disorders'—which includes sex offenders—and legislative proposals have bounced between the civil and the criminal law. Central to the debate is whether or not the sex offender, now classed as having a 'dangerous severe personality disorder', can ever be treated, and if not—what is the point of detention if not a form of custodial sentence from the criminal courts. As we have seen, the Criminal Justice Act 2003 introduced powers of 'imprisonment for public protection' to keep convicted 'dangerous' people in prison for indeterminate periods beyond their original sentence and until such times as they were no longer a risk to the community.

Attempts to broaden the scope of mental health legislation to include those with dangerous severe personality disorders—even having committed no offence—are still continuing. The conundrum is whether or not they are 'treatable' and just what is 'treat-ment'? The current law (Mental Health Act 1983) requires detention for purposes of treatment. People with severe personality disorders have been turned away by psychi-atrists as 'untreatable'. A Draft Mental Health Bill published in June 2002 tried to widen the definition of treatment to include 'education, training in work, social and independ-ent living skills' (Department of Health, 2002). The Draft Bill was much criticized as being too flexible with this definition and in danger of turning nurses and doctors into prison warders. The Department of Health has said it will revise the proposals (Department of Health, 2003).

REVIEW QUESTIONS

1 How does a person assessed as dangerous prove they are no longer dangerous?

2 Should we be able to detain people who have not offended and are not mentally ill, but still considered 'dangerous'?

3 Should we widen the definitions of 'mental disorder; and 'treatment' to cover people considered dangerous?

CONCLUSION

One of the most marked features of the social response to sexual offending has been the recourse to civil measures to complement the criminal arrangements that have been put in place. The investigation of sexual offending has been improved and the punishments in the criminal courts have been made more severe. The civil measures, however, appear to be of a new character.

The sex offender 'register' and its attendant Multi-Agency Public Protection Panels now form the mainstay of the UK's civil arrangements for greater public protection from sex offenders in the community. The requirements and obligations placed on those who must register have been slowly tightened since the 'register' came on line in September 1997. This tightening and strengthening of the register has caused the Home Office to issue a word of warning and a reminder that a civil measure like the register is *not* a criminal punishment from the courts but is only an administrative measure to improve community safety; the fear is that the two separate entities might get confused:

'It (the register) is a measure aimed at helping to protect the community from sex offenders not an additional penalty for the offender.' (Home Office/Scottish Office 2001: 11)

'Were the registration requirement to become more onerous, there could come a point at which the Act could no longer be seen as an administrative requirement.' (ibid.: 13)

In effect the register as a civil measure could start becoming a punishment.

Elsewhere other civil orders like the Sexual Offences Prevention Order or the Risk of Sexual Harm Order have been designed to transform into criminal proceedings should the subject of the Order breach its requirements. Already the House of Lords has ruled that the court must stop using civil procedures in deciding an original application and use criminal procedures (see above).

It is as though we believe the criminal sanctions we have are insufficient but instead of increasing them we prefer to take the parallel course of civil measures. The fear is that the two may get inextricably muddled as the civil measures come in to fill the 'incapacitation gap' (Janus, 2000).

If the overall aim is to have sex offenders either excluded from society or where we can see them (registers, Sexual Offences Prevention Orders and so on), there is also the possibility that we are only establishing them as 'others' against which we—the community—can identify and maintain our separate identities which we never have to question. In turn this leads to the danger of a 'jurisprudence of difference' whereby sex offenders become simply second class citizens, entitled to fewer rights than the rest of us, not just because they are offenders but because their 'bad behaviour flows inexorably from a being who is essentially different from the norm' (Janus, 2000).

QUESTIONS FOR DISCUSSION

1 Why is there so much concern about sex offending today compared to twenty years ago?

2 What forms does sexual offending take?

3 Why are we apparently prosecuting fewer and fewer sex offenders?

4 Should we punish or treat the sex offender?

5 How can we increase public protection from the sex offender?

GUIDE TO FURTHER READING

Brown, M. and Pratt, J. (eds) (2000) *Dangerous Offenders: Punishment and Social Order*. London and New York: Routledge.

A collection of essays with an international flavour looking at various aspects of 'managing' the dangerous offender, including sex offenders.

Matravers, A. (ed) (2003) *Sex Offenders in the Community*. Cullompton: Willan Publishing.

A collection of essays with a UK focus looking at various angles on protecting the public from sex offending in the community.

Silverman, J. and Wilson, D. (2002) *Innocence Betrayed: Paedophilia, the Media and Society*. Cambridge: Polity.

Written by a journalist and an academic it is an easy to read account of contemporary social responses to sexual offending; particularly good on the politics, public opinion and press side of the story.

Temkin, J. (2002) *Rape and the Legal Process* (2nd edn). Oxford: Oxford University Press.

Although written by a lawyer and with a clear legal perspective, this is an accessible book to the non-legal reader and presents a wider picture to contextualize the law in terms of contemporary society.

Thomas, T. (2000) *Sex Crime: Sex Offending and Society*. Cullompton, Devon: Willan Publishing.

A general history and descriptive account of penal and social responses to sex offending; contains detailed account of the parliamentary discussion on the proposals for a sex offender register.

WEB LINKS

http;//www.nota.co.uk/

National Organisation for the Treatment of Abusers (NOTA). A UK based organization for practitioners in a variety of professions working with sex offenders: contains policy papers, links to other organisations and conferences.

http://www.stopitnow.org.uk/

Stop it Now! An organization that sees sexual crime as a preventable public health problem and encourages offenders to come forward for treatment. It started in the USA and has now come to the UK.

http://www.atsa.com/

Association for the Treatment of Sexual Abusers (ATSA). The US equivalent of NOTA; an organization for practitioners in a variety of professions working with sex offenders; has details of publications, conferences etc.

http://www.medacad.org/iatso/

International Association for the Treatment of Sexual Offenders (IATSO). Takes a comparative view of global developments in working with sex offenders.

http://www.csom.org/

Center for Sex Offender Management (CSOM). A US based Center supported by the Department of Justice which started in 1997. Wealth of publications available on all aspects of sex offender management plus useful links.

REFERENCES

Barrett, D. (ed) (2000) *Youth Prostitution in the New Europe*. Lyme Regis, Dorset. Russell House Publishing.

Beech, A., Fisher, D., Beckett, R. and Scott-Fordham, A. (1998) An evaluation of the Prison Sex Offender Treatment Programme, Research Findings No. 79, Research, Development and Statistics Directorate. London: Home Office.

Bottoms, A.E. (1977) 'Reflections on the Renaissance of Dangerousness', *Howard Journal of Criminal Justice*, 16: 70–96.

Brown, A. and Barrett, D. (2003) *'Knowledge of Evil: Child Prostitution and Child Sexual Abuse in Twentieth Century England*. Cullompton: Willan Publishing.

Brown, M. and Pratt, J. (eds) (2000) *Dangerous Offenders: Punishment and Social Order*. London and New York: Routledge.

Bryan, T. and Doyle, P. (2003) *Developing Multi-Agency Public Protection Arrangements*, in A. Matravers (ed) *Sex Offenders in the Community*, Cullompton: Willan Publishing.

Carr, J. (2004) *Child Abuse, Child Pornography and the Internet*. London: NCH.

Cobley, C. (1997) 'Keeping Track of Sex Offenders—Part I of the Sex Offenders Act 1997', *Modern Law Review* 60: 690.

Cohen, S. (1973) *Folk Devils and Moral Panics*. St Albans: Paladin.

(CPSI) Crown Prosecution Service Inspectorate and (HMIC) H.M. Inspectorate of Constabulary (2002) A Report on the Joint Inspection into the Investigation and Prosecution of Cases Involving Allegations of Rape. London.

Department of Health (2002) Draft Mental Health Bill, Cm 5538–1. London: HMSO.

Department of Health (2003) Draft Mental Health Bill to Undergo Scrutiny (press release) 26 November.

Department of Health, Home Office, Department for Education and Employment, National Assembly for Wales (2000) Safeguarding Children involved in Prostitution. London.

Feeley, M. and Simon, J. (1994) *Actuarial Justice: the Emerging New Criminal Law*, in Nelkin D. (ed) *The Future of Criminology*. London: Sage.

Gallagher, B., Bradford, M. and Pease, K. (2002) 'The Sexual Abuse of Children by Strangers: its Extent, Nature and Victims' Characteristics', *Children and Society* 16: 346–59.

Garland, D. (2001) *The Culture of Control: Crime and Social Order in Contemporary Society*. Oxford: Oxford University Press.

Harris, J. and Gace, S. (1999) A Question of Evidence: Investigating and Prosecuting Rape in the 1990s, Home Office Research Study 196. London.

Home Office (1990) Crime, Justice and Protecting the Public, Cm.965. London: HMSO.

Home Office (1996) Sentencing and Supervision of Sex Offenders: a consultation document, Cm.3304. London.

Home Office (1999) Managing Dangerous People with Severe Personality Disorder, July. London.

Home Office (2000) Setting the Boundaries: reforming the law on sex offences, July. London.

Home Office (2002a) Achieving Best Evidence in Criminal Proceedings: guidance for vulnerable or intimidated witnesses, including children. London.

Home Office (2002b) Protecting the Public: strengthening protection against sex offenders and reforming the law on sexual offences, Cm.5668. London.

Home Office (2003a) Crime in England and Wales 2002/3. London.

Home Office (2003b) Government Proposals on the Issue of Sex Offenders who Travel Abroad. London.

Home Office/Scottish Executive (2001) Consultation Paper on the Review of Part I of the Sex Offenders Act 1997, July. London.

Hughes, B., Parker, H. and Gallagher, B. (1996) Policing Child Sexual Abuse: the View from Police Practitioners, Police Research Group, Home Office. London.

Janus, E. (2000) 'Civil Commitment as Social Control: managing the risk of sexual violence', in M. Brown and J. Pratt (eds) *Dangerous Offenders: Punishment and Social Order*. London and New York: Routledge.

Kane, J. (1998) *Sold for Sex*. Aldershot: Arena.

Knock, K. (2002) The Police Perspective on Sex Offender Orders: a preliminary review of policy and practice, Police Research Series, Paper 155, London: Home Office.

Lovell, E. (2001) *Megan's Law: does it protect children?* London: NSPCC.

Marshall, P. (1997) The prevalence of Convictions for Sexual Offending, Research Finding No. 55, Research and Statistics Directorate. London: Home Office.

Matravers, A. (ed) (2003) *Sex Offenders in the Community*. Cullompton: Willan Publishing.

Nash, M. (1999) *Police, Probation and Protecting the Public*. London: Blackstone Press Limited.

Nelkin D, (ed) (1994) *The Futures of Criminology*. London: Sage.

Plotnikoff, J. and Woolfson, R. (2000) Where Are They Now?: an evaluation of sex offender registration in England and Wales, Police Research Series, Paper 126. London: Home Office.

Power, H. (2003) Disclosing Information on Sex Offenders: the human rights implications, in A. Matravers (ed) *Sex Offenders in the Community*. Cullompton: Willan Publishing.

Silverman, J. and Wilson, D. (2002) *Innocence Betrayed: Paedophilia, the Media and Society*. Cambridge: Polity.

Sparks, R., Bottoms, A. and Hay, W. (1996) *Prisons and the Problem of Order*. Oxford: Clarendon Press.

Svedin, C.G. and Back, K. (1996) *Children Who Don't Speak Out*. Stockholm: Radda Barnen.

Temkin J. (2002) *Rape and the Legal Process* (2nd edn). Oxford: Oxford University Press.

Thomas, T. (2000) *Sex Crime: Sex Offending and Society*. Cullompton: Willan Publishing.

Thomas, T. (2002) Employment Screening and the Criminal Records Bureau, *Industrial Law Journal* 31(1): 55–70.

13 Corporate crime

Steve Tombs

INTRODUCTION

If you were to stop one hundred people in the street and ask them to list, in their opinion, the most five serious crimes in Britain today, it is a very safe bet that in the vast majority of responses no form of corporate crime would feature. Similarly, check today's newspapers for reports of political discussions or Home Office statements on law and order: again, corporate crime will be absent. Now scour those newspapers more thoroughly, and try to find corporate crime stories—corporate crime may be covered, but is unlikely to be given prominence, nor discussed in the language reserved for 'real' crime. Check your TV guide for today's viewing, and search for corporate crime coverage amongst what will no doubt be a great deal of fictional, real-life and documentary programmes on crime—and it would be a surprise to find much, if any. Open up your favourite (or most used!) criminology reader or textbook and look for corporate crime in the contents or even the index—and there is a very good chance you will not find it in either.

   The substance of this chapter is determined significantly by this relative invisibility of corporate crime from popular and academic views. It begins by examining the emergence of the concept of corporate crime, discussing what this term means, and then reviewing the extent to which corporate crime represents a crime problem. The main body of the chapter considers various dimensions of corporate crime, paying particular attention to issues of visibility, causation and control. The central aim of this chapter is to mark out corporate crime as a legitimate area of criminological concern.

BACKGROUND

In his famous Presidential Address to the American Sociological Association in 1939, and in various publications through the following decade, Edwin Sutherland (1940, 1945, 1983) introduced the idea of 'white-collar crime'—'a crime committed by a person of respectability and high social status in the course of his occupation' (Sutherland, 1983: 7). He thus challenged the stereotypical view of the criminal as lower class since 'powerful business and professional men' also routinely commit crimes. The main difference between the crimes of the upper and lower classes was in the implementation of the criminal laws that apply to them: 'upper class' criminals often operate undetected; if detected they may not be prosecuted; and if prosecuted they tend to receive relatively lenient (and overwhelmingly financial) penalties.

   Sutherland's 'clarion call' to criminologists to focus upon such crimes fell largely upon deaf ears—notwithstanding notable exceptions (for example, some of the work of Geis through the 1960s, notably Geis, 1967, 1968). It was not until the end of the 1960s/beginning of the 1970s that there occurred a re-emergence of interest in corporate crime as one aspect of a more general proliferation of both an academic concern with 'white-collar' crime and a popular and political concern with the socially harmful effects of corporate activity. More recently, however, some commentators, notably Snider (2000), have argued that this concern had diminished dramatically by the end of the twentieth century, as the social credibility of business had increased with the rise of right-leaning political regimes and commitments to market economics, to the extent that critical scrutiny of corporate activities—not least under the rubric of 'crime'—had become less feasible and/or less desirable.

In the UK, the level of academic attention to corporate crime has never reached that of some historical periods in the US. While there may be many reasons for this, one contributory factor has surely been the greater popular and political suspicion of 'big business' in the US. Yet there are signs, particularly with the emergence of post-privatization discourses around 'fat cats', demands for processes to ensure better accountability, probity and openness in organizational conduct ('corporate governance'), the sheer ineptitude of some privatized companies, as well as a series of national and international corporate 'scandals', that questions of corporate crime, or least the more effective regulation of corporate activities, may be re-emerging within political, social and even academic agendas.

Certainly one obstacle to the academic study of corporate crime can be traced back to Sutherland's path-breaking work. For, important as Sutherland's highlighting of 'white-collar' crime was, it generated significant theoretical and conceptual confusion, not least because having defined it in terms of people, Sutherland proceeded to study corporations (Cressey, 1989). To date, there remains considerable disagreement as to how to define this area of study (Friedrichs, 1996).

For the purposes of this chapter, corporate crime is viewed as 'illegal acts or omissions, punishable by the State under administrative, civil or criminal law, which are the result of deliberate decision making or culpable negligence within a legitimate formal organisation' (Pearce and Tombs, 1998, 107–10, following Box, 1983; Schrager and Short, 1977). Several aspects of this definition are worth emphasis. First, the term 'corporation' is used in its UK sense, so that this covers all companies registered under the Companies Acts, from the smallest limited liability company such as John Barr and Sons (the butchers involved in the E-Coli outbreak, below) to the largest multinationals such as ICI or BP. Second, while this definition may formally exclude some other kinds of organizations involved in the production of illegality—such as public sector bodies which carry out functions on behalf of the State (for example, health trusts, universities, the Strategic Rail Authority)—to the extent that these are involved in commercial activities then the modes of analysis set out below (notably in the section on causation) are mostly perfectly applicable to understanding illegalities produced by these. Third, through referring to 'legitimate formal organisation', the definition marks off corporate crime from organized crime, even if the two phenomena share some key characteristics (Ruggiero, 1996; Rawlinson, Chapter 14 below). Lastly, it incorporates Sutherland's insight that the distinctions between different forms of illegalities—that is, whether these are classed as criminal, civil, administrative—to a great extent reflect the ability of the powerful, including corporations, to have activities in which they may be implicated classified as less serious (Pearce and Tombs, 2003).

Dimensions of corporate crime

Corporate crime is a wide-ranging term, covering a vast range of offences of omission and commission with differing types of modus operandi, perpetrators, effects, and victims. For example, some crimes—such as the financial accounting offences associated with Enron (for a useful summary of this case, see extracts from Robert Bryce's book *Pipe Dreams*, at http://www.guardian.co.uk/enron/story/ 0,11337,834484,00.html)—can only emerge as a result of intentional, well-planned and systematic deception, not least on a scale amounting to widespread conspiracy; they are rendered possible by the multi-national structure of the company; and have both a wide range and large number of victims, including employees (loss of jobs), governments (loss of taxation revenue) and investors (loss of returns). In contrast, a breach of the Health and Safety at Work Act, a criminal offence, may emerge from somewhat different origins. At times, this may be caused by the prioritization of profit, which, though clearly very conscious, does not have as its intention the production of death, injury or illness; at other times, such a crime may lack intention, and occur more as the result of a complex chain of negligence and carelessness. Although either form of offence may end in large-scale disaster—such as the gas leak at Bhopal, India, which killed tens of thousands; see Pearce and Tombs, 1998: 194–219) or a multiple fatality train crash (Woolmar, 2001: 155–79)—more often the consequences of such an offence are very localized, if often tragic (such as the death of Simon Jones, a twenty-four year old student who died within hours of his first day at work at Shoreham docks; see http://www.simonjones.org.uk). Because 'corporate crime' refers to a wide range of events and processes, it is useful to seek to group its different types. Amongst various categorizations, four are used most frequently: financial offences; offences against consumers; crimes against employees and employment protection; and environmental offences.[1]

A number of academic studies have focused upon a range of financial crimes, including: illegal share dealings, mergers, and takeovers; various forms of tax evasion; bribery; and other forms of illegal accounting. Enron is the classic example of the latter and has joined a list of offenders—including Guinness (involved in illegal share dealings in the 1980s; see Punch, 1996: 167–80) and BCCI, a global bank which was systematically involved in fraud; money laundering and bribery (ibid.: 9–15)[2]—as symbols of what we mean by the term 'financial crime'.

A second general area of corporate crimes is those committed directly against consumers. Examples include illegal sales/marketing practices; the sale of unfit goods, such as adulterated food; conspiracies to fix prices and/or carve up market share amongst different companies, false/illegal labelling or information; and the fraudulent safety testing of products. A classic example of the last category was the outbreak of E-Coli amongst Lanarkshire residents in November 1996, resulting in eighteen deaths and almost 500 people ill. The poisoning was traced back to a local butchers which was eventually fined £2,500 for failing to ensure equipment was kept clean and that food was protected against contamination.

Third, we can identify crimes arising out of the employment relationship. These include cases of sexual and racial discrimination and other offences against employment law (including equal opportunities legislation); violations of wage laws; violations against rights to organize and take industrial action; and a whole range of offences against employee occupational health and safety. Such offences are widespread. For example, as Whyte (2004) has reported, it is estimated that there are up to two million school age children working in the UK (more than a quarter in food preparation and sales); around 75 per cent are thought to be employed illegally—employed without permits, in dangerous work, or in breach of working hours regulations.

The final category of offence, crimes against the environment, includes illegal emissions to air, water, and land; the failure to provide, or the provision of false, information; hazardous waste dumping; and illegal manufacturing practices. In 2002, the Environment Agency prosecuted 1,712 successful charges against businesses for a range of environmental offences (Environment Agency, 2003). This is an Agency hardly known for a prosecutorial ethos. For example, a 2001 Greenpeace report calculated that between 1999–2001 there were 533 *known* breaches of licences by the ten municipal waste incinerators operating in England. Most were likely to be emissions of dioxins, highly toxic, known cancer-causing substances—but only one of these breaches had been prosecuted (Brown, 2001; Whyte, 2004).

Beyond identifying the range of offences that fall within the general rubric of 'corporate crime', there are several observations, based on the available research evidence, which we can state with confidence regarding its impact and prevalence.

Corporate crime has economic, physical and social costs. Governments, taxpayers, consumers, workers, and other companies incur economic costs. Many forms of corporate crimes have physical costs—deaths, injuries, ill-health—arising out of dangerous workplaces, polluted environments, unsafe goods and services, and so on. Corporate crimes also have social effects. The economic and physical costs in general fall upon those in society who are already relatively disadvantaged: low paid workers are most likely to work in dangerous workplaces; poorer people are least able to relocate from polluted neighbourhoods; those on the tightest budgets are most vulnerable to purchasing goods and services which may lead them to be victims of corporate crime, such as the cheaper cuts of 'fresh' or processed meat, or cut-price electrical items. A further social cost of corporate crime is a diminution of social trust in the corporations upon whom we rely for the food we eat, the clothes we wear, the services we use and so on, and, by implication, the lack of trust in governments for their failure to regulate effectively the activities of these corporations.

Even if we confine ourselves to considering the economic costs of corporate offending, the best available evidence indicates that these far outweigh those associated with 'conventional' or 'street' offending. This conclusion is difficult to contest even whilst recognizing the difficulty faced by attempts to estimate the 'costs' of any form of crime. Even studies of 'single' examples or groups of corporate crime—such as the illegal activities of pensions companies in the so-called mis-selling cases of the 1990s, collectively said to have involved a sum of 'up to £11 billion' involving 2.4 million victims (*The Guardian*, 13 March, 1998)—are enough to support this general conclusion.

Finally, the range of work that now exists around corporate crime, such as case-studies either of particular offences or categories of offences by type or industry, as well as the more limited efforts at quantifying the scale and ubiquitousness of such crimes, indicates clearly that such offending is not a peripheral activity carried out by a marginal group of individuals and organizations, the so-called 'bad apples' of the business world. Rather, it is endemic within economic activity: corporate crimes are not simply widespread, they are routine and pervasive (Slapper and Tombs, 1999: 36–84).

The invisibility of corporate crime

Given its consequences, why is corporate crime almost entirely absent from 'crime, law and order' agendas? To address this question we need to recognize that there are many social processes that contribute to removing such offences from dominant definitions of 'crime, law and order' (Slapper and Tombs, 1999).

Both formal politics and the law play crucial roles in the production and maintenance of definitions that exclude corporate crime.

At the political level, both in particular policy decisions—such as resource allocations for various enforcement agencies—and in the political rhetoric of crime, law and order, corporate crimes are largely marginalized. Notice how 'zero tolerance', 'three strikes and you're out', mandatory sentences, being 'tough on crime and tough on the causes of crime', 'short sharp shocks', and protecting and furthering the rights of victims have all been deployed in the context of street or traditional crimes (Hale, Chapter 21) but not to corporate offending—even though they are perfectly applicable here as well (Etzioni, 1993; Geis, 1996; Lofquist, 1993).

Turning to the application of law and legal regulation, we find that, at every stage of the legal process, law tends to operate quite differently with respect to corporate crimes than in the context of 'conventional' crimes. Thus, in the very framing of the substance and parameters of legal regulation, its enforcement, the ways in which potential offences and offenders are investigated, the prosecution of offences, and the use of sanctions following successful prosecution, most forms of corporate and organizational offences are relatively decriminalized.

Related to the political and legal invisibility afforded to corporate crime is the poverty and paucity of official corporate crime data. Measures used to indicate the scale of the crime problem do not include corporate offences. Even a cursory examination of the notifiable offences for England and Wales reveals the extent to which they focus upon conventional as opposed to corporate crimes. If, as Maguire notes, 'a salient feature of almost all modern forms of discourse about crime is the emphasis placed upon terms associated with its quantification and measurement' (Maguire, 1994: 236), then it is hardly surprising that corporate crimes 'do not feature in . . . debates about the "crime problem" '(Nelken, 1994: 355; Green, 1990: 27).

Further, it is revealing that the Home Office's responses to problems in the official recording of conventional crimes, notably the sponsoring of the annual British Crime Survey (see Hope, Chapter 3), are not matched by any comparable energy to uncover the hidden figure of corporate crime. By contrast, it has, in recent years, been a key mover in developing a flourishing research area around crimes *against* business (Hopkins, 2002).

This latter point indicates the significance of ideologies surrounding business and the difficulties these pose for naming corporations as (potential) offenders (see Lacey, 1995: 21). Corporations are viewed differently to the objects of 'traditional' crime concerns; 'conventional criminals' tend to be represented as a burden upon society in a way that corporations will not be. Further, where business organizations engage in criminal activity, this is represented as an aberration from their routine, legitimate activities, while such offending tends to be cast as involving technical infringements of law, rather than real crimes.

These assumptions, and the general contrast with 'real' crime and 'real' criminals', are reflected in and reinforced by the media. Whether we survey fictional or documentary-style treatments of crime on TV, or newspaper and other print media coverage of the issues, we find that while there may be some attention to corporate crime, representations of crime converge to produce 'blanket' conceptualizations regarding 'law-and-order' that reinforce dominant stereotypes of crime and the criminal (Chibnall, 1977). Thus, where corporate crime is covered, its presence is vastly outweighed by treatments of conventional crime, it is treated in lesser profile outlets or formats, and is often represented in the rather sanitizing language of scandals, disasters, abuses and accidents rather than as criminal activity (Tombs and Whyte, 2001).

For many of us, then, corporate crime is far removed from our immediate experience. This is also partly an effect of the relationship between the offender and the victim in many corporate offences. In most forms of traditional crime there is, or must at some point be, a degree of proximity between offender and victim. By contrast, with corporate crimes, there are frequently enormous distances between offender and victim, in terms of both space and time. This has important implications in terms of awareness of, and then 'proving', victimization.

First, many victims of corporate crimes may never be aware of their status as victims (Croall, 1989; Meier and Short, 1995). That is, if we overpay for goods because of price-fixing between leading retailers in the market, or are duped into buying inappropriate pensions or mortgages due to illegal selling, we may never realize that we have been victimized. Even if people *are* aware of their status as victims, acting upon this awareness is often extremely difficult (Croall, 1989)—we may recognize that our health and those of neighbours is declining, but not be able to pinpoint the exact source of illegal pollution; or, if we can identify a factory or industrial process, we may feel they are too big, or that we lack support from public bodies (such as the Environment Agency), to make it worth our while acting upon this recognition.

None of the various mechanisms whereby corporate crimes are rendered relatively invisible are particularly remarkable in isolation. What is crucial, however, is *their mutually reinforcing nature*—that is, they all work in the same direction and to the same effect, removing corporate crime from 'crime law and order' agendas.

The 'causes' of corporate crime

One group to whom we might turn in order to bring to light issues which are rendered invisible through political and social processes are academic researchers. Yet one of the most intriguing characteristics of criminology is that it has focused relatively little energy upon bringing to light corporate crimes—historically, and to this day, the vast majority of criminological teaching and research tends simply to assume 'crime' as an activity engaged in by *individual* men (and sometimes women). Quite remarkably for a social science, one key feature of criminology is that it has taken the social construction of crime as its starting point![3] This applies to criminological theorizing with particular force (Cressey, 1989).

For example, classicism (on this and other criminological theories referred to below, see Hayward, Chapter 4, this volume) sought to develop a rational, just system of penality, albeit one aimed exclusively at conventional crimes. Its key claim was that the criminal is rational—s/he chooses, more or less freely, to commit crime. This choice is influenced through a form of calculative reasoning, a reasoning paying particular attention to the benefits of a criminal act on the one hand, and the costs (likelihood of detection and consequences of detection) of that crime on the other.

Now, if it is unlikely that most individuals are in a position to calculate rationally the benefits and costs of offending, this might be much closer to what corporations, or their directors and managers, actually do. For a corporation is an organization that claims to act rationally, to calculate, and to predict external responses to its actions in order to maximize its long run profits. To then add to this tendency to calculate the existence of relatively weak regulation (see below) produces exactly the combination of factors that, according to classicist logic, provides a fertile ground for criminality. There is genuine scope for considering the application of classicist forms of reasoning to the area of corporate crime control. This might entail, for example, a theoretical and empirical exploration of the potential for deterrent-based strategies for controlling corporate crime, even if such approaches have manifestly failed with respect to 'traditional' offenders (Pearce and Tombs, 1998: 292–305).

If we turn to the emergence of individual positivisms within criminology, here we find attempts to identify the abnormalities that either propel individuals into crime, or ensure that they are more predisposed to committing crime than the general population. To include corporate crime within these considerations would be illuminating, if only to undermine the very basis of individual positivism—for one of the most interesting features about individuals involved in corporate offending is their normality, there being an almost total lack of meaningful differences between these and non-offenders (Snider,

1993: 61; see also Virta, 1999; Waring and Weisburd, 2001). By contrast, where corporate offenders appear not to be 'normal', they are still unlikely to be cast negatively, in terms of pathology. Rather, their 'abnormality' is cast as a form of distinctiveness as they are held up as the type of individuals that we might all aspire to be—as successful, wealthy, hard-working, innovative, well-respected and connected, pillars of their local community, and so on—figures precisely such as Kenneth Lay, the extremely well-connected Chief Executive Officer of the now-defunct global energy giant Enron.

There have been some attempts to apply an individual positivist type analysis to corporate crime, though these have been marginal to criminology, conducted mostly within business or management studies. These have sought to identify those 'personality' factors associated with people who succeed in private companies, and have tended to highlight features such as being innovative, ambitious, shrewd, aggressive, impatient, and possessing a 'moral flexibility' (see Snider, 1993). It is clear why such qualities are likely to be valued within the corporate world; but it is also clear how such individuals may be more likely to be involved in corporate illegalities, either as leading figures or as individuals prepared to turn a blind eye.[4] And this latter observation tells us something about how we might explain many forms of corporate crime—if corporations seek to recruit people with these characteristics, and if the higher one goes in the corporate hierarchy the more likely are these to be accentuated, then we need to know something about the culture and functioning of the corporation itself, as well as the environments within which it operates, to understand how its employees, from the most senior downwards, act, think and rationalize. We shall return to this issue below.

If individual positivism failed to turn its attention to corporate offenders, then so too did the form of criminology that has dominated theorizing since the 1930s, namely sociological positivism. However, here there are some notable exceptions to this general failure to include corporate crime within theoretical frameworks.

As a member of the Chicago School, Sutherland himself attempted to develop a general, sociological, theory of crime causation, claiming that 'differential association' could explain how both upper-class and lower-class crimes: crime arises from an excess of definitions favourable to law violation over definitions unfavourable to law violation. Criminal activity—motivations, *post hoc* rationalizations and actual techniques of commission—is, like all behaviour, learnt. This learning, and exposure to different definitions regarding the appropriateness or otherwise of certain behaviours, emerges out of our various associations—and these associations vary by frequency, duration, priority and intensity.

This does seem to have some validity for understanding the willingness of individuals to engage in crime within and on behalf of corporations. Even with the demise of the so-called job-for-life in most western economies, it remains the case that our associations with individuals within a corporation are hardly fleeting; we spend a significant part of our week at work, and are likely to spend years working for the same company or in the same kind of industry. Further, most of us invest our work with significance—either instrumentally, seeing work as sheer necessity, or (for the lucky few) more expressively, as a means of realizing some ability or desire we possess.

Moreover, we know, either by experience or indeed by intuition, that within certain corporations or even industries, certain forms of activity are prevalent, both in terms of knowing how to engage in them and knowing why one must engage in them. Presumably, if this holds for legal activity, it holds for illegal activity too. For example, within the retail butchering trade it is common knowledge that frozen poultry can be defrosted in a particular way to make it resemble fresh poultry—so that it can be sold at a higher price, as if fresh, thereby defrauding the consumer. Further, there may also be generalized knowledge that 'everyone' in the trade is doing it—which not only provides a motivation, since not to do it is to place one's own shop or company at a competitive disadvantage, but also that to do it is so generalized that it is acceptable, not really criminal.[5]

Differential association has been subjected to stringent criticism (Taylor *et al.*, 1973: 125–30). It is of interest, however, precisely because it attempted to incorporate corporate crime within a general theory of crime. Other variants of sociological positivism have not sought to do so in such an explicit manner, yet some aspects may be utilized to explain corporate crime. Notable here is Mertonian strain theory and its central concept, anomie. Merton linked deviant behaviour to the disjunction between institutionalized aspirations and the availability of legitimate opportunity structures—albeit in terms of lower class crime. But Passas has argued that there is no compelling reason why anomie cannot apply to corporate deviance:

> As the meaning and content of success goals vary from one part of the social structure to another, similar difficulties in attaining diversely defined goals may be faced by people in the upper social reaches too; they are, therefore, far from immune to pressures towards deviance. (Passas, 1990: 158)

The pressures to succeed exist for business and organizations in terms of maximization of profit, growth and efficiency. These goals may have to be obtained *by all* or *any means* particularly when the continuation of the corporation is at stake and the corporate actors realize that the attainment of their own ends depends largely on the prosperity of the firm. Structural pressures and strains may be applied both to those at the top as well as employees, and the use of deviant methods may seem to be the only possible way of dealing with problematic situations (see Box, 1983).

Finally, those forms of criminology that have sought to place an understanding of power at the heart of their theorizing have also produced, or have the potential to produce, insights regarding the nature and incidence of corporate offending. Corporate crimes are, after all, made possible on the basis of relative power, or committed by the relatively powerful. Ironically, the labelling perspective, while it sought to examine how processes of criminalization operated with respect to individuals from certain social groups, failed to ask very obvious converse questions: why are certain kinds of crime *not* subject to social opprobrium, and why are certain kinds of offenders able successfully and consistently to resist the processes of criminalization to which lower-class offenders seem highly vulnerable? (Nelken, 1994)

Various forms of critical and radical criminologies—including Marxisms and feminism—have made important contributions to our knowledge of corporate crime causation. Notable here are: *Crimes of the Powerful* (Pearce, 1976), where it is argued that corporations, with the connivance of the American state, act systematically to control the markets within which they operate; Stuart Hills' edited collection on *Corporate Violence* (Hills, 1987), which consists of a series of empirical and theoretical case studies of the ways in which injury and death are produced systematically by the drive for profit; and Szockyj and Fox's (1996) anthology of analyses of the myriad ways in which corporations exploit constructions of gender to victimize female consumers, workers and recipients of health care.

Now, whilst there are clear differences between the labelling perspective, Marxisms and feminisms, one characteristic these share is the theoretical commitment to move beyond the narrowest confines of criminology, in particular to deconstruct dominant categories of crime and to view these constructions, and the criminal justice systems based upon them, as both an effect of and also a means of reproducing power.

From the preceding, it is becoming clear that to understand corporate crime causation we must take into account a series of factors ranging from the individual through to the structural. These will be set out here—albeit very briefly—in four analytically (though not of course empirically) distinct 'levels'.

At the level of the individual, we need to take account of individual personality and characteristics, not least in terms of the kinds of personalities that are recruited or encouraged within the organization, as well as 'individual' factors that are socially constructed as relevant, such as rank/position within hierarchy, age, gender, and ethnicity. For example it is relevant to enquire whether an organization is one where being female renders diminishes ones social power, or in which time served adds authority?

Moving to the level of the immediate work-group or sub-unit within the organization, we must take account of inter-personal dynamics, the culture of the work-group (and the extent to which this coheres or clashes with the culture of the wider organization), and its location within the overall organization, both structurally and geographically—that is, is it relatively autonomous or highly supervised, is it part of one large organizational complex, or is it geographically isolated?

There are also key sets of issues to be raised in relation to the organization itself. We need to understand something of its structure, its internal lines of decision-making and accountability, its geographical scope of operations, and the nature, volume and complexity of internal transactions. Issues of organizational culture must also be addressed: is the organization risk-taking or risk-averse; is it gendered; is it authoritarian; and is it one where a blame culture predominates? Of further relevance is to examine the very products or services that are the focus of the organization: are these opaque or transparent, are they sold to consumers or other organizations, is their production labour or capital intensive? Finally, and perhaps most obviously, we need to know something of the economic 'health' of the company, and of the organizational units within it, as well as the time-scale at which profitability is calculated.

Lastly, there are key sets of questions to be broached regarding the wider economic, political and social environments within which the organization operates. Amongst these extra-organizational features are: the nature of the market structure; the size and scope of the market; the material and ideological state of regulation; the more general nature of state-business relationships; the dominant form of political economy, and concomitant societal values, including the nature and degree of pro- or anti-business sentiment. Lastly, key information is to be gleaned in any understanding of the general 'health' of the economies in which the corporation operates.

This is only to summarize briefly what is an extensive, and complexly inter-related, set of factors. But the urgency of developing such a wide-ranging integrated explanatory framework has been raised by some commentators on corporate crime (Coleman, 1987; Punch, 2000; Vaughan, 1992). In truth, however, theoretical development here remains at an early stage, although there are now a number of book-length studies which attempt to use some of this range of factors. These include studies of safety crimes in the offshore oil industry (Whyte, 1999; Woolfson *et al.*, 1996), corporate crime in the asbestos (Tweedale, 2000), chemicals (Pearce and Tombs, 1998) and pharmaceutical (Braithwaite, 1984) industries, attempts to prosecute for corporate manslaughter (Slapper, 2000), corporate and state illegalities associated with the fateful launch of the Challenger space shuttle (Vaughan, 1996), and a national-case study in the micro/macro control of 'economic' crime (Alvesalo, 2003).

REVIEW QUESTIONS

1 How might we apply both classicism and individual positivism to an understanding of corporate crime causation?

2 What forms of sociological positivism have been turned towards the explanation of corporate crime?

3 What factors need to be incorporated into an adequate explanation of corporate crime?

'Controlling' corporate crime

Understandings of how corporate crime is caused inevitably influence claims regarding how it is to be controlled. And it is in the area of regulation that there is perhaps the most significant body of academic research around corporate crime. There are a number of studies—mostly nationally based, though with some useful cross-national comparative work—examining the practices of a whole range of regulatory bodies (for a review, see, for example, Clarke, 2000: 136–61). These allow several broad generalizations to be made about the practices and effects of regulatory enforcement agencies: non-enforcement is the most frequently found characteristic; enforcement activity tends to focus upon the smallest and weakest individuals and organizations; and sanctions following regulatory activity are light (Snider, 1993: 120–24).[6]

The most common finding of studies of regulatory enforcement, across business sectors and discrete areas of legislation, is that a cooperative regulatory approach is dominant. In short, regulators seek to enforce through persuasion—they advise, educate, and bargain, negotiate and reach compromise with the regulated (see Pearce and Tombs, 1998: 223–46). When violations become known to inspectors, they engage in a dialogue with management, prioritizing compliance with laws being violated in some areas (the most serious offences), usually on the basis of an agreed timetable, whilst accepting that others, deemed less serious, may take much longer to put right. This dialogue clearly takes into account the priorities of the inspectorate along with the commitment, motivation and resources of the regulated (see Hawkins, 2002).

There are, of course, important variations within this body of work not least about whether, or the point at which, compliance approaches should be abandoned and more punitive forms of regulation are invoked. This combination of cooperation and punitiveness is captured by the phrase 'the regulatory mix' The most sophisticated discussions of the appropriate 'regulatory mix' have been developed by John Braithwaite and colleagues. Their starting point is a consideration of the potential of self-regulation, on the basis that state regulators will never have the resources to enforce regulatory law effectively, and that internal regulators enjoy certain technical and social advantages over those on the outside (Braithwaite and Fisse, 1987). Self-regulation is described (and prescribed) on a 'carrot and stick' basis: where self-regulation proves ineffective, the next preferred regulatory tactic is to move to 'enforced self-regulation', this requiring a company to develop a tailored set of rules by which it intends to comply with law which, once approved by external regulators, would then be 'enforced' internally; where evidence of non-compliance emerges, the potential of punitive external intervention remains (Braithwaite, 2000: *passim*; Ayres and Braithwaite, 1992: 102–16; see also Gunnigham and Johnstone, 1999, on 'twin-track' and 'smart' regulation).

Strategies of enforcement are thus conceived of in terms of a pyramid, where non-compliance leads to the invoking of ever more interventionist or punitive modes of enforcement on the part of regulators (see, for example, Braithwaite, 2000: 78–82, 99–105). In essence, this is an incrementalist and compliance-oriented strategy based on the principle of deterrence.

By contrast there is a body of work that seeks to posit alternatives to cooperative approaches. This advocates a more punitive approach to enforcement—though not suggesting that each and every violation of law by corporations be prosecuted. A key argument of this work is that corporate crime becomes defined as *real* crime, and thus is subject to more adversarial, punitive and interventionist forms of regulation (Pearce and Tombs, 1998: 280–316). Such an approach *may* appear unproven and idealistic. However, there is evidence of the success this type of approach where it has been attempted in specific instances (Pearce and Tombs, 1990; Pearce and Tombs, 1998: 286–92). Moreover, under very specific social, political and economic conditions, it remains possible that such an approach towards the regulation of corporations can be generalized (Alvesalo, 2003).

In any case, it is incorrect to view cooperative and punitive approaches to regulation as alternative strategies: in practice, all forms of regulation reflect a mix of each approach, so that actual enforcement strategies are understood as lying somewhere on a continuum between these two ideal-typical polar opposites (see Figure 13.1).

However, what is at issue between the proponents of variants of 'cooperative models' of regulation and those who argue for a more adversarial strategy are a series of disputes

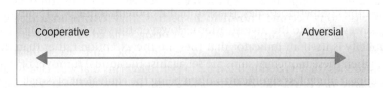

Figure 13.1 The regulatory continuum

which revolve around the extent to which corporate entities can and do act morally; can and do operate on the basis of some sense of social responsibility; can and do act upon some concern for their reputation, in the absence of bottom-line considerations. To answer such questions in the positive ultimately requires us to overlook the legal duties owed by managements to shareholders to maximize profits, to disregard the short-term horizons of those who own and control corporations and the realities of the stock market pressures upon them, and to under-estimate the intimate relationships between corporations and states.

Notwithstanding these disputes, a key issue remains—namely, that of sanctions that can be imposed once a violation has been taken to court and proven there.

By far the most common sanction is the monetary fine. Only in cases investigated by the Serious Fraud Office, unique amongst regulatory bodies in the UK in being established as part of criminal justice legislation, is imprisonment of individuals likely to be an outcome. But even here caution is needed. Thus, Fooks (2003) has noted that, after a short period in which a small number of financial crimes were subject to criminalization, the SFO has in recent years experienced retrenchment, with an increasing role being taken by the Financial Services Authority, which has an explicitly cooperative approach to regulatory enforcement (Spalek, 2001). Even during the 1990s, when the SFO received criticism for over-zealousness in terms of prosecution, it was taking an average of just fifteen cases to court per year (Fooks, 1999). Further, since the victims of serious fraud tend to be other corporations (banks and institutional investors), regulation in this sphere has been termed regulation *for* rather than *of* the City (Fooks, 2003).

More generally, following successful prosecution for corporate crime, fines are levelled at companies—and these are almost uniformly low. For example, an audit of Health and Safety Executive inspectors' activities (Unison/Centre for Corporate Accountability, 2002) found that in 1998/9: the average fine following a death was £67,000 (more than double the figure three years previously); a death of a member of the public resulted in an average fine of £33,000; and a major injury to a worker incurred an average penalty of £10,000. Such sanctions hardly appear significant, a conclusion reinforced when we turn to sentencing following environmental offences. In 2003, Barbara Young, the Chief Executive of the Environment Agency, criticized the 'weak' sentencing following environmental crime: 'Fines for environmental offences have struggled slowly upwards over five years, but still rarely exceed £20,000 . . . with irreparable environmental damage or serious risk to public health, penalties often fail to match up to the costs avoided' (cited in Brown, 2003).

Of course, at times large fines are imposed upon offending companies. For example, in February 2003, retailers Argos and Littlewoods were fined record amounts of £17.3m and £5.4m respectively by the Office of Fair Trading; they had, with manufacturer Hasbro, entered into agreements to fix the prices of Hasbro toys and games between 1999 and 2001, breaching competition rules. (Hasbro had its potential fine of £15.6m waived for providing key evidence to the investigation). However, the very fact that such large fines attract publicity is itself an indicator that they are the exception rather than the norm. Moreover, when these monetary sums are set against the annual turnover of companies, then they appear much less significant—often being the equivalent of 'small change'.

Whilst fines following successful prosecutions are low, it might be argued that, were they to be raised to sufficiently high levels to have a deterrent effect, this might be counter-productive: the company may pass the costs on to workers, consumers, or both, rather than to shareholders, who are the legitimate object of the sanction. Indeed, ultimately, fines that do impact too much upon a company may lead to its closure, thus affecting the innocent again—notably employees, but also other organizations (which, for example, may supply goods or services to the offending company) or consumers, who might find themselves buying goods or services in a less competitive market.

Of course, none of these are reasons why large fines should not be used in principle. Such factors do, however, indicate that fines need to be used sensitively—and also that they may take forms other than a direct monetary penalty, such as, for example, the use of an equity fine, which involves the confiscation of a block of shares by the government or a local authority (see http://www.corporateaccountability.org/ campaign.htm# Sentence). Moreover, even if we accept that there are problems with the use of monetary sanctions, sentencing of corporations and/or individuals involved in corporate crime is an area in which there now exists a range of imaginative proposals, some of which have been introduced in limited fashion, others of which remain at the proposal stage. Amongst these are:

- disqualification of individual directors, a sanction used in the case of financial crimes, but rarely beyond this context;
- the withdrawal of licences to operate and the barring of convicted companies from bidding for government-related contracts;
- the use of community service or restitution orders, whereby a convicted company is required to make good damage caused, or to use its resources and expertise to provide goods and services to a victimized community;
- the use of probation and rehabilitation orders, whereby a company is required to hire outside 'experts' to reform, for example, safety training or financial reporting systems;
- the use of adverse publicity and 'shaming', requiring a company to name itself, or be named, as an offender in appropriate media outlets.

All of these potential sanctions have their drawbacks, none is a panacea, and each is more or less appropriate for particular types of corporation and following specific forms of offence (Slapper and Tombs, 1999). Ultimately while there are clearly enormous difficulties in developing effective sanctions in the case of corporate crime these tend to be political rather than technical (Lofquist, 1993; Etzioni, 1993). Again, the key issue is the political refusal to treat corporate crime as real crime.

REVIEW QUESTIONS

1 What are the main problems associated with the use of fines as a sanction against corporations following conviction?

2 What are the strengths and weaknesses of alternative forms of sanctions?

CONCLUSION

The central aim of this chapter has been to mark out corporate crime as a legitimate area of criminological concern. To do this, it began by examining the emergence of the concept of corporate crime, before highlighting the extent to which it represents a (largely invisible) crime problem. The chapter then examined various dimensions of corporate crime, paying particular attention to issues of causation and control.

The fact that this chapter repeats a demand made by Sutherland over half a century ago—that corporate crime be given greater attention within the discipline of criminology—indicates the significance of the economic, political and social, obstacles to the task of taking corporate crime seriously. What is at issue here is power—for exposing corporate crime means exposing crimes associated with what are relatively powerful organisations, moreover organizations with which states (local, regional, national) have increasingly intimate relationships (Tombs and Whyte, 2003).

There has, of course, been progress within criminology since Sutherland's 'clarion call'—even if, as this chapter has indicated, this has been rather faltering. The very existence of this chapter in an introductory under-graduate text is, perhaps, one small manifestation of that progress. Yet, somewhat analogous to the demands made by feminist academics from the 1970s onwards, namely that issues of gender must be considered through all social science concerns rather than separated off for discrete consideration, the aim must be not for separate chapters or course units on corporate crime—rather, when academics speak of crime, whether they are seeking to measure, describe, explain or consider how to control more effectively this phenomenon, they need to recognize that the label 'crime' covers a range of acts and omissions beyond those associated with the relatively powerless individuals.

Corporate crime remains a problematic and contested area of inquiry. Notwithstanding the definitional, conceptual, methodological and theoretical disagreement and problems, it speaks to phenomena which on almost any criterion one chooses—the nature and extent of economic, physical, and social harms—are significant crime and social problems. Clearly, we need more research on corporate crime, not least because of a number of contemporary, pressing factors, including: the spread of the corporate form, as privatization has been championed across nation-states; diversification in the nature of corporate structures and organization; the increasingly international nature of much corporate activity; and associated claims regarding the growing power of corporations vis-à-vis national governments and their populations.

But corporate crime research—as research on the relatively powerful—faces enormous methodological difficulties, may be relatively unattractive to the funders of research, and is unlikely to produce immediately utilizable policy proposals, all of which may further explain its relative omission from dominant criminological agendas (Tombs and Whyte, 2003). And the force of these pressures changes over time. Thus, in the current era, corporate crime research may be more difficult, even if it is more pressing, not least because of the increasing valorization of business activity alongside the power of corporations to seek, via their political allies, the decriminalization of their activities through the introduction of various forms of self-regulation or through simple deregulation, each of which appear to be significant trends in contemporary capitalist nation-states (Snider, 2000).

Lastly, and taking us back to the discipline of criminology, corporate crime research remains worthwhile simply because it can perform an important role for the discipline. It encourages criminological reflexivity: a focus upon corporate crime entails continual scrutiny of the coverage and omissions of legal categories, the presences and absences within legal discourses, the social constructions of these categories and discourses, their underpinning of, treatment within and development through criminal justice systems, the ways in which particular laws are enforced (or not enforced), interpreted, challenged, and, of no little significance, the contours of the discipline of criminology itself. If the criminological imagination can shed important light upon corporate crime (White, 2003), then there is no doubting that the study of corporate crime is itself one means of reinvigorating that same criminological imagination.

QUESTIONS FOR DISCUSSION

1 The (In)visibility of corporate crime?

Select one broadsheet and one tabloid newspaper from the same day, then:

- find all stories related to: (a) conventional crime; and (b) corporate crime, and cut or photocopy;
- 'count' the stories devoted to 'conventional crime' and those devoted to 'corporate' crime;
- note the page (and/or section) of the newspaper on which they are found;
- list the titles of the corporate crime stories, and give a brief indication of, the 'corporate crime' stories;
- record any observations you have on the tone/nature of the corporate crime stories when compared with the conventional crime stories.

2 Explaining corporate crime?

Select a case study of corporate crime.

How might we apply the following criminological perspectives to understand the genesis and nature of this case?

- classicism;
- individual positivism;
- sociological positivism;
- labelling;
- marxist/critical criminologies.

    In what ways do the following factors help to understand the genesis of this case?

- individual/personality factors;
- organizational structure of the company/companies in question;
- organizational culture of the company/companies in question;
- wider political, social and cultural contexts within which the company/companies in question operated;
- the nature and level of regulation to which the company/companies were subject.

3 Compliance-oriented enforcement?

One of the arguments proposed on behalf of cooperative enforcement vis-à-vis business organizations is that to attempt to enforce the law strictly and punitively will lead to the 'stimulation of opposition and the destruction of cooperation' (Kagan and Scholz, 1984: 73).

Is it likely that business organization will react to strict and punitive enforcement in this way?

If it is likely, what weight does it carry as an argument against strict and punitive enforcement and in favour of cooperative enforcement vis-à-vis business organizations?

4 Sanctioning corporate offenders?

What are the advantages and disadvantages of the monetary fine as a sanction applied against convicted corporations and individuals?

What other sanctions might be applied?

What are the strengths and weaknesses of these other sanctions?

GUIDE TO FURTHER READING

Academic texts

Alvesalo, A. (2003) *The Dynamics of Economic Crime Control*. Espoo, Finland: the Police College of Finland.

Exploring the nature and interaction of the macro- and micro-processes and forces that characterize corporate crime control, using Finland as an empirical case, this book includes unique ethnographic and interview-based material on how corporate crime work is incorporated into policework.

Box, S. (1983) 'Corporate Crime', in Box, S., *Power, Crime and Mystification*. London: Tavistock, chapter 2.

Over sixty-plus pages, Box's classic introduction to this area of study explores the scale of corporate crime, its invisibility, ways in which it must be explained, and issues of regulation and control.

Pearce, F. and Snider, L. (eds) (1995) *Corporate Crime: contemporary debates*. Toronto: University of Toronto Press.

Across nineteen articles, this edited text covers a range of theoretical and empirical issues related to the incidence, nature, and regulation of corporate crime, including contributions by most of the leading corporate crime scholars across the English-speaking world.

Szockyi, E. and Fox, J.G. (eds) (1996) *Corporate Victimisation of Women*. Boston, Mass.: Northeastern University Press.

The eight articles here take a gendered view of corporate crime, covering theoretical debates around corporate crime, case studies of particular industries and forms of crime, and discussing the nature of regulation as well as prospects for regulatory reform.

Tweedale, G. (2000) *Magic Mineral to Killer Dust. Turner & Newall and the Asbestos Hazard*. Oxford: Oxford University Press.

Tweedale meticulously documents the asbestos scandal and the central role of Turner & Newall as its largest producer, highlighting the socially constructed boundaries between legality and illegality and the lengths to which corporations will go to evade their legal and moral obligations at the expense of thousands of lives.

Other material

Class Action (Director: Michael Apted, 1990)

Based upon one of the most infamous of all corporate crimes, the sale of the Ford Pinto, the movie follows legal efforts to secure compensation from a multinational car manufacturer for the victims of car 'accidents'.

Glengarry Glen Ross (James Foley, 1992)

A searing critique of the real estate industry in Reagan's America, this film examines the personal traumas and inter-personal conflicts generated by working in a business where lying, cheating, and stealing all are in a day's work.

The Insider (Michael Mann, 1991)

Based on a true story, this revolves around a former tobacco scientist violating contractual agreements to expose his ex-employer's inclusion of addictive ingredients in cigarettes, while a journalist struggles to report the story via the national media.

Michael M. (1998) *Adventures in a TV Nation. The stories behind America's most outrageous TV show*. London: Boxtree.

The story behind the show TV Nation, axed after seventeen episodes by the US TV network Fox, there is extensive coverage of corporate crime in this witty but savage indictment of American corporate politics, including the classic tale of 'Crackers, the Corporate Crime-Fighting Chicken'.

Wall Street (Oliver Stone, 1987)

A big budget Hollywood production with a predictably unrealistic ending, this is excellent at conveying the culture that surrounded the financial markets on both sides of the Atlantic during the 1980s, a culture captured in Gordon Gecko's catchphrase, 'Greed is Good'.

WEB LINKS

http://www.open.gov.uk/

The Open Government website, which contains links to all regulatory bodies in England and Wales.

http://www.corporatewatch.org/

A campaigning site, bringing together the work of activists and researchers seeking both to expose illegal and unethical corporate activity and to explore business-government relations in general.

http://www.essential.org/monitor/monitor.html

Documents unethical and illegal corporate activity, especially in the Third World, focusing particularly on public, worker and environmental health and safety issues.

http://www.corporatepredators.org

Here you will find the US-based 'Focus on the Corporation', a weekly column on illegal and unethical corporate activity.

http://paulsjusticepage.com/elite-deviance.htm

An excellent source of corporate crime material, and many links, maintained by Paul Leighton, co-author of Jeffrey Reiman's *The Rich Get Richer the Poor Get Prison*.

REFERENCES

Alvesalo, A. (2003) *The Dynamics of Economic Crime Control*. Espoo, Finland: the Police College of Finland.

Ayres, I. and Braithwaite, J. (1992) *Responsive Regulation. Transcending the Deregulation Debate*. Oxford: Oxford University Press.

Box, S. (1983) *Power, Crime and Mystification*. London: Tavistock.

Braithwaite, J. (1984) *Corporate Crime in the Pharmaceutical Industry*. London: Routledge and Kegan Paul.

Braithwaite, J. (2000) *Regulation, Crime and Freedom*. Aldershot: Ashgate.

Braithwaite, J. and Fisse, B. (1987) Self-Regulation and the control of corporate crime, in C.D. Shearing and P.C. Stenning (eds), *Private Policing*. Beverly Hills: Sage, pp. 221–46.

Brown, P. (2001) Incinerator Breaches Go Unpunished. Poisonous chemicals pumped into atmosphere, report reveals. *The Guardian*, 22 May.

Brown, P. (2003) Pollution still pays as firms shrug off fine. *The Guardian*, 31 July.

Chibnall, S. (1977) *Law-and-Order News. An Analysis of Crime Reporting in the British Press*. London: Tavistock.

Clarke, M. (2000) *Regulation. The Social Control of Business Between Law and Politics*. London: Macmillan.

Cressey, D. (1989) The poverty of theory in corporate crime research, in F. Adler and W.S. Laufer (eds), *Advances in Criminological Theory*. New Brunswick, NJ: Transaction, pp. 31–55.

Coleman, J.S. (1987) 'Toward an Integrated Theory of White-Collar Crime', *American Journal of Sociology* 93: 406–39.

Croall, H. (1989) 'Who Is the White-Collar Criminal?', *British Journal of Criminology*, 29, (2); 157–75.

Environment Agency (2003) *Annual Report and Accounts 2002/03*. http://www.environment-agency.gov.uk/commondata/105385/ar0203complete_569081.pdf

Etzioni, A. (1993) The US Sentencing Commission on Corporate Crime: a critique, in G. Geis and P. Jesliow (eds), *White-Collar Crime. Special Issue of the Annals of the American Academy of Political and Social Science*. 525, January. Newbury Park, Ca: Sage.

Fooks, G. (1999) The Serious Fraud Office: policing the City or policing for the City?, paper presented to the British Criminology Conference, Liverpool.

Fooks, G. (2003) 'Contrasts in Tolerance: the Peculiar Case of Financial Regulation', *Contemporary Politics*, 9, (2): 127–42.

Friedrichs, D.O. (1992) 'White-Collar Crime and the Definitional Quagmire: a Provisional Solution', *Journal of Human Justice*, 3, (2): 5–21.

Geis, G. (1996) A base on balls for white collar criminals, in D. Shichor and D.K. Sechrest (eds), *Three Strikes and You're Out. Vengeance as Public Policy*. Thousand Oaks, Ca: Sage.

Geis, G. (1967) White-collar crime: the heavy electrical equipment anti-trust cases, in M. Clinard and R. Quinney (eds), *Criminal Behaviour Systems*. New York: Holt, Rinehart & Winston.

Geis, G. (1968) *White Collar Criminal: The Offender in Business and the Professions*. New York: Atherton Press.

Green, G.S. (1990) *Occupational Crime*. Chicago: Nelson Hall.

Gunningham, N. and Johnstone, R. (1999) *Regulating Workplace Safety. Systems and Sanctions*. Oxford: Oxford University Press.

Hawkins, K. (2002) *Law as Last Resort. Prosecution Decision-making in a Regulatory Agency*. Oxford: Oxford University Press.

Hills, S. (ed) (1987) *Corporate Violence. Injury and death for profit*. Totowa, NJ: Rowman & Littlefield.

Hopkins, M. (2002) 'Crimes Against Businesses: The Way Forward for Future Research', *British Journal of Criminology* 42, (4), 782–97.

Kagan, R. and Scholz, J. (1984) 'The Criminology of the Corporation and Regulatory Enforcement Strategies', in K. Hawkins and J. Thomas (eds), *Enforcing Regulation*. Boston: Kluwer-Nijhoff.

Lacey, N. (1995) Contingency and criminalisation, in I. Loveland (ed), *Frontiers of Criminality*. London: Sweet and Maxwell, pp. 1–27.

Lofquist, W.S. (1993) Organisational Probation and the US Sentencing Commission, in G. Geis and P. Jesilow (eds), *White Collar Crime. Special Issue of the Annals of the American Academy of Political and Social Science*. 525, January. Newbury Park, Ca: Sage.

Maguire, M. (1994) Crime Statistics, Patterns, and Trends: changing perceptions and their implications, in M. Maguire *et al.*, (eds), *The Oxford Handbook of Criminology*, pp. 233–91.

Meier, R.F. and Short, J.F. Jnr. (1995) The consequences of white-collar crime, in G. Geis *et al.* (eds), *White-Collar Crime. Classic and Contemporary Views* (3rd edn). New York: The Free Press, pp. 80–104.

Nelken, D. (1994) White-Collar Crime, in D. Nelken (ed), *White-Collar Crime*. Aldershot: Dartmouth.

Passas, N. (1990) 'Anomie and Corporate Deviance', *Contemporary Crises* 14: 157–78.

Pearce, F. (1976) *Crimes of the Powerful: Marxism, Crime and Deviance*. London: Pluto.

Pearce, F. and Tombs, S. (1990) 'Ideology, Hegemony and Empiricism: Compliance Theories of Regulation', *British Journal of Criminology* 30, (4): 423–43.

Pearce, F. and Tombs, S. (1998) *Toxic capitalism: corporate crime and the chemical industry*. Aldershot: Dartmouth.

Pearce, F. and Tombs, S. (2003) Multinational corporations, power and 'crime', in Sumner, C. (ed.), *The Blackwell Companion to Criminology*. Oxford: Blackwell, pp. 359–76.

Punch, M. (1996) *Dirty Business. Exploring Corporate Misconduct. Analysis and Cases*. London: Sage.

Punch, M. (2000) 'Suite Violence: Why Managers Murder and Corporations Kill', *Crime, Law and Social Change*, 33, 243–80.

Ruggiero, V. (1996) *Organized and Corporate Crime in Europe. Offers that can't be refused*. Aldershot: Dartmouth.

Schrager, L.S. and Short, J.F. (1977) 'Towards a Sociology of Organisational Crime', *Social Problems*, 25: 407–19.

Slapper, G. (2000) *Blood in the Bank. Social and Legal Aspects of Death at Work*. Aldershot: Ashgate.

Slapper, G. and Tombs, S. (1999) *Corporate Crime*. London: Longman.

Snider, L. (1991) 'The Regulatory Dance: Understanding Reform Processes in Corporate Crime', *International Journal of the Sociology of Law*, 19: 209–36.

Snider, L. (1993) *Bad Business. Corporate Crime in Canada*. Toronto: University of Toronto Press.

Snider, L. (2000) 'The Sociology of Corporate Crime: an Obituary. (Or, Whose Knowledge Claims Have Legs?)', *Theoretical Criminology*, 4, (2); 169–206.

Spalek, B. (2001) 'Policing the UK Financial System: the Creation of the "New" Financial Services Authority and its Approach to Regulation', *International Journal of the Sociology of Law*, 29, (1); 75–87.

Sumner, C. (ed), *The Blackwell Companion to Criminology*. Oxford: Blackwell.

Sutherland, E. (1940) 'White-Collar Criminality', *American Sociological Review*, 5: 1–12.

Sutherland, E. (1945) 'Is "White-Collar Crime" Crime?', *American Sociological Review*, 10, 132–39.

Sutherland, E. (1983) *White-Collar Crime. The Uncut Version*, New Haven: Yale University Press.

Szockyj, E. and Fox, J.G. (eds) (1996) *Corporate Victimisation of Women*. Boston, Mass.: Northeastern University Press.

Taylor, I., Walton, P. and Young, J. (1973) *The New Criminology. For a Social Theory of Deviance*. London: RKP.

Tombs, S. (2002) 'Understanding Regulation? A Review Essay', *Social & Legal Studies*. 11, (1); 111–31.

Tombs, S. and Whyte, D. (2001) 'Media Reporting of Crime: Defining Corporate Crime Out of Existence?', *Criminal Justice Matters*, 43, Spring: 22–23.

Tombs, S. and Whyte, D. (eds) (2003) *Unmasking the Crimes of the Powerful: scrutinizing states ands corporations*. New York: Peter Lang.

Tweedale, G. (2000) *Magic Mineral to Killer Dust. Turner & Newall and the Asbestos Hazard*. Oxford: Oxford University Press.

Unison/Centre for Corporate Accountability (2002) *Safety Last? The Under-Enforcement of Health and Safety Law*. London: Unison/Centre for Corporate Accountability.

Vaughan, D. (1992) The Macro-Micro Connection in White-Collar Crime Theory, in Schlegel, K. and Weisburd, D. (eds) *White-Collar Crime Reconsidered*. 124–45.

Vaughan, D. (1996) *The Challenger Launch Decision. Risky Technology, Culture, and Deviance at NASA*. Chicago: Chicago University Press.

Virta, E. (1999) A thief is a criminal who has not had enough time to start a company, in A. Laitinen and V. Olgiati (eds), *Crime-Risk-Security*. Turku: University of Turku, pp. 91–128.

Waring, D. and Wesiburd, E., with Chayet, E.F. (2001) *White-Collar Crime and Criminal Careers*. Cambridge: Cambridge University Press.

White, R. (2003) Environmental Issues and the Criminological Imagination, *Theoretical Criminology*, 7, (4), 483–506.

Whyte, D. (1999) *Power, Ideology and the Management of Safety in the UK Offshore Oil Industry*. Unpublished PhD Thesis, Liverpool John Moores University.

Whyte, D. (2004) Regulation and Corporate Crime, in J. Muncie and D. Wilson (eds), *Student Handbook of Criminal Justice*. London: Cavendish.

Woolfson, C., Foster, J. and Beck, M. (1996) *Paying for the Piper: Capital and Labour in Britain's Offshore Oil Industry*, London: Mansell.

Woolmar, C. (2001) *Broken Rails. How Privatisation Wrecked Britain's Railways*. London: Aurum Press.

NOTES

1. Most work on corporate crime continues to emanate from the US, and many textbooks in this area understandably reflect this. This chapter aims to prioritize examples and work that derive from the UK.

2. See also 'BCCI's Criminality', section 4 of *The BCCI Affair. A Report to the Committee on Foreign Relations, United States Senate*, by Senator John Kerry and Senator Hank Brown (December 1992, 102d Congress 2d Session Senate Print 102–40), available at http://fas.org/irp/congress/1992_rpt/bcci/04crime.htm. This document further alleges: BCCI's support of terrorism, arms trafficking, and the sale of nuclear technologies; its management of prostitution; its commission and facilitation of income tax evasion, smuggling, and illegal immigration; and its illicit purchases of banks and real estate.

3. There are, of course, qualifications to this general observation. Notable exceptions are to be found within critical or radical criminologies. Further, one of the key contributions of feminist criminologies has been precisely to make more visible the myriad ways in which social institutions in general, and both the criminal justice system and 'malestream' criminologies in particular, obscure the peculiar experiences of women. Criminologically, this has particularly raised understandings of the peculiar (and often private) victimization of women, and the differential treatment of women through the criminal justice system. Feminist criminologies have had important impacts upon criminological theorizing and criminal justice practice.

4. *Wall Street* illustrates how the personality traits that helped to make Gecko a success were the same characteristics that allowed him, through a combination of intention and negligence, to break the law.

5. This is also one example of 'techniques of neutralisation', which are crucial to understanding motivation in the context of corporate crime: see Box, 1983: 54–7; Slapper and Tombs, 1999: 118–23.

6. These are, of course, generalizations: there are important national differences in enforcement strategies (Pearce and Tombs, 1998: 229–45) and important differences in enforcement strategies across different spheres of regulatory activity (Snider, 1991).

14 Understanding organized crime

Paddy Rawlinson

INTRODUCTION

Over the past decade, the topic of organized crime has become an increasingly popular addition to criminology courses in the UK, previously attracting little more than a passing reference. Its growing recognition as a subject for serious academic discussion has, in part, been provoked by a growing awareness of organized crime on an international scale, what is sometimes referred to as 'transnational' organized crime (TOC). Despite the so-called 'sexy' nature of the topic, organized crime is a complex and thought-provoking phenomenon, which too often finds itself subject to hyperbole and over-simplification. The chapter addresses some of the problems of understanding organized crime. It examines the major debates on definition and the role played by the media in influencing the public's perception of a form of crime rarely encountered directly. The chapter also includes a brief history of organized crime in the US, the country which has arguably exerted the greatest impact on crime fighting strategies worldwide. The section on transnational organized crime considers how global changes, such as the collapse of communism have affected the nature of organized crime and the way policy makers and law enforcement respond to it. Finally, the section on theory and methods discusses the various criminological explanations of organized crime and the different ways in which data are collected on a particularly elusive form of offending.

BACKGROUND

There can be few subjects, which provoke so much excitement and debate as that of organized crime surrounded as it is by a mystique made the more romantic by the diverse media representations. The majority of us identify organized crime with American gangsters, such as the Corleone family, the central characters of the Hollywood blockbuster films *The Godfather*, or more recently with the angst-ridden mobster, Tony Soprano, hero of the award winning TV series *The Sopranos*. These characters bear little resemblance to the evil minds behind human smuggling, drug trafficking and a whole gamut of international crime rings, we are told by governments, which represent national security threats to so-called targeted states and communities. The hugely diverse perceptions of organized crime make it difficult to get a handle on the reality of its operations, its structure, the threat it poses and so on.

In such an environment sound academic research takes on a highly significant role. However, criminologists who study organized crime are faced with problems less apparent or even absent from other areas of criminology. For obvious reasons data collection can prove difficult, although there are a growing number of ethnographies on the subject which serve to complement the more usual source of police records and media reports (Hobbs, 1988; Polsky, 1969; Rawlinson, 2000). Nor is it easy to define what exactly is meant by 'organized crime', a term which has become synonymous with other expressions such as mafia, criminal cartels, gangsters, the mob, to name but a few. Further complications arise when ethnic designations are used for example, La Cosa Nostra, the Russian Mafiya, the Yakuza, Triads, Yardies.

These difficulties aside, the diverse activities conducted by organized crime provide a broad field of enquiry some of which is relatively under-researched. These activities include illegal arms and drugs trafficking, people smuggling, the sex trade, protection rackets, contraband, the human organ trade, vehicle theft, loan sharking, fraud, and money-laundering. These sundry activities have broadened the study of organized crime beyond a criminological framework, often demanding a multidisciplinary approach. Collaborative research can involve political scientists, historians, economists, as well as security analysts and even former Cold War specialists. The definitional ambiguities of the term 'organized crime' (see section below) also encourage an intra-disciplinary approach, incorporating other areas of criminology such as corporate crime (see Chapter 13), white-collar crime, state crime (see Chapter 1) and terrorism (see Chapter 15).

Against such a varied and contentious background the promise by policy-makers to target organized crime primarily requires a greater effort in understanding the nature of this particularly elusive beast. The slow response by the academic community to engage in the study of organized crime prompted the comment by two American criminologists that: 'The field remains essentially in a state of intellectual atrophy . . .' (Rogovin and Martens 1997: 36). Whether this statement still remains the case is debatable. The recent participation of a new generation of academics, especially those indigenous to the so-called hot-spots of organized crime, particularly in Eastern Europe and Russia, would suggest the emergence of a renewed intellectual energy in understanding organized crime and its role in society (Markina, 1998; Backman, 1998). Cross-cultural collaborations also promise significant advances in the field. The recent surge of interest in organized crime, especially given its current high profile political status, provides greater opportunities for research. However this should not blind those who study organized crime to the possible constraints of officially funded projects which demand tangible policy-outcomes in favour of, as opposed to alongside, more intellectually critical research. As the rest of the chapter explains the study of organized crime has raised as many questions as it has provided answers, not just in terms of the subject itself but as a critique of these so-called 'experts' who study and work with it: academics, officials and practitioners alike.

What is this 'thing' called organized crime?

Legal definitions

Organized crime is broadly regarded as economically motivated offending involving more than two people. Unlike legally defined crimes or predicate offences such as murder, drug trafficking, money-laundering, and so on which refer quite clearly to a specific proscribed *acts*, any legal description of organized crime tends to be confined to its *structures* and *relationships* and the general nature of the crimes committed by such associations. Article 2 of the 'United Nations Convention Against Transnational Organized Crime' states that an organized criminal group must have at least three members operating in concert to commit a serious crime' as part of an internally structured organization which has been in existence over a period of time preceding and subsequent to the commission of the criminal act (United Nations, 2000). Such a definition, while it provides a general framework of understanding, can in practice undermine effective law enforcement responses. According to this definition an organized crime group can include anything from a four-person, low-level racketeering outfit to highly complex, international networks engaged in human smuggling or money laundering. Different criminal configurations will place varying pressures on police time and resources even though all are categorized as organized crime, leaving the police to prioritize cases according to the perceived threat at their local level, priorities which need not coincide with those of governments. The Netherlands based 'Fijnaut Group' contests the notion of stable structures and instead provides a working definition, which accounts for fluid networks in what it terms 'criminal 'co-operatives'. This revision of orthodox definitions was prompted by years of failing crime control strategies, which had pursued organized crime groups according to non existent hierarchical structures (Klerks, 2003).

Criminologists disunited

While there is a general consensus that organized crime involves a *multiplicity of actors*, the nature of its structures and operations, its relationship with legitimate bodies and the extent of its impact on society are just some of the fiercely debated issues in academic circles, particularly in the US. Certain interpretations, however, have dominated the official view. Alien conspiracy theory, which sees organized crime as an ethnically defined phenomenon, and comprising hierarchical, monolithic structures was given its first official airing in the early 1950s by the Kefauver Committee (see below). The findings of the committee were to make the term 'organized crime' and 'Mafia' synonymous and set the tone for US crime control strategies for decades. Its oversimplification of the organized crime problem through focusing on particular ethnic groups, a practice which has continued beyond the labelling of American-Italians and now includes Mexicans, Russian, the Chinese, and so on, helped to maintain the authority of the dominant values of American society by locating organized criminality *outside* the mainstream, that is, as alien elements conspiring to attack these values. This interpretation was largely endorsed by Donald Cressey (1969) whose *Theft of a Nation* was to provide academic credibility for Mafia-based theories.

It is hardly surprising that many counter this view. The criticisms levelled at alien conspiracy theory reflect the diversity of opinion on how to define organized crime per se. Some see this as a convenient political smokescreen used by governments as a means of detracting from failing policies or flawed ideologies (Smith, 1975; Albanese, 1989). Albini writes that 'rather than blame themselves for their desire to use drugs in the 1960s, Americans found it easier and more exciting to blame those foreigners from Sicily who brought the Mafia to America and addicted a drug-virgin country (Albini, 1997a: 69). Others argue that capitalism helps to deflect attention away from corrupt political and economic institutions, some of which willingly collaborate with organized crime (Block, 1993; Chambliss, 1988; Woodiwiss, 1993). The hierarchical, monolithic structure attributed to Mafia organizations are also frequently refuted. Ianni and Ianni's (1972) study found the mafia to be family based networks, active both in illegal and legal business. Gambetta's work on the protection industry, the major focus of the Sicilian mafia, identifies the protagonist(s) as 'a single person or a network of more or less organized agents' (1993: 17). Even if one acknowledges the predominance of ethnic minority members of organized crime groups, particularly in a multicultural society such as the US, some critics of alien conspiracy argue that it is not ethnic origin or nationality which determines criminality, but the socio-economic exclusion that immigrants often face because of their unfamiliarity with the dominant language and culture. As legal access to opportunities is blocked or made more difficult organized crime, described famously by Bell (1962) as 'the queer ladder of social mobility', provides an alternative means to success and integration. In other words, organized crime can be an alternative means of acquiring the requisite pecuniary success that is often required to get on and move up socially for those who do not have access to conventional means.

Business as usual

Organized crime is 'the ongoing activities of those collectively engaged in production, supply and financing for illegal markets in goods and services' (Gill, 2002:198) While an obvious generalization, the essential motivation of those engaged in organized crime is clear: business. Business takes many forms and involves different actors, but irrespective of which side of the legal divide it lies, its main preoccupation is seeking profit-making opportunities, in other words, enterprise. Even when organized crime is engaged in more politically motivated activities, such as the corruption of government officials, these relationships are underscored by entrepreneurial goals. However, academic opinion tends to be divided on the impact of these goals for society as a whole, and on whether the legal-illegal divide is too simplistic a way of representing a fluid, and often legally ambiguous world of commercial relations which link licit business and the underworld (Naylor, 1997).

As a provider of illegal goods and services, including drugs, a range of contraband, child pornography, human trafficking to name but a few, organized crime can be argued as primarily a *reactive* phenomenon, exploiting gaps in a diverse and lucrative market. Its clientele are, for the most part, 'ordinary' folk who seek, or are forced to seek, alternative routes to satisfying needs unmet or proscribed by the legislatures of the countries they inhabit or pass through (Caiden, 1985). In many cases clients are also victims, obliged or enticed into cooperation, as in the trafficking of women and children (Goodey, 2002). In areas of economic decline and acute social inequality organized crime can provide alternative employment and a reinstatement of status, a situation currently common in former communist states (Varese, 2001; Rawlinson, 2001). However, this tends to assume that organized crime is confined in its reach to the lower socio-economic stratum of society and that poverty is the major impetus for participation and victimization. Edwin Sutherland's famous study of white collar crime, looked at offences committed by those in employment, thus refuting the notion that crime was primarily caused by poverty, going as far as to describe crimes committed by corporations as being synonymous with organized crime (Sutherland, 1983). It was not just corporate crime he labelled in this way, but also professional theft, which he regarded as 'organized in the sense that it is a system in which informal unity and reciprocity may be found' (Sutherland, 1937: 209). Despite refocusing the debate onto crimes of the powerful, Sutherland has justifiably been accused of theoretical and definitional ambiguity, which can sometimes serve to undermine the importance of his work.

More recently, some studies have argued that even *legal* corporate activity should be regarded as organized crime insofar as its social and economic impact is as harmful, if not more, than that of organized crime (Slapper and Tombs, 1999; Pearce, 1976). These approaches focus attention away from the legal definition of criminality and instead regard the actions of corporate business according to the harm they inflict, such as the impoverishment or marginalization of vulnerable communities, particularly in Third World countries. Ruggiero's work locates criminality, including that of an organized nature, in any economic environment, but more importantly, it emphasizes that different environments provide different motivations for illegal acts. What he terms 'causality of contraries' explains why organized crime can thrive at any level of society, from the boardroom to the ghetto, that is, wherever opportunities exist. Importantly, he recognizes that opportunities for illicit behaviour more frequently arise for high-level legal business. While at one level of organized crime 'the absence of the State encourages the development of enterprise type criminality' on another level 'Access to the political and business financial elite has determined, rather than discouraged, the development of organized crime'. (Ruggiero, 2000: 9).

Hence this 'thing' we call organized crime, chimera, global threat, bad business, legal corporate exploitation, social climbing, unholy alliances between licit and illicit, organizations, associations, groups of networks, far from being a neatly packaged 'alien' evil, or comprising Hollywood anti-heroes is a phenomenon that is prepared to exploit opportunities provided *by* society, to produce goods and services required by the usually law abiding public, and can take many guises across a broad licit-illicit spectrum.

The following brief history of organized crime in America, the country which has undoubtedly exerted (and continues to do so) the greatest influence on worldwide perceptions of organized crime and whose crime fighting policies are being exported as enthusiastically as its Hollywood imagery, demonstrates the dangerous ambiguities and political minefields of a much misunderstood and misrepresented criminological genre.

REVIEW QUESTIONS

1 Why is organized crime so difficult to define?

2 How far is the ethnic label useful in our understanding of the term 'mafia'?

3 Discuss some of the similarities and differences between licit business and organized crime.

Organized crime in the USA

When America, home of legendary crime bosses Al Capone and John Gotti, and films such as *Scarface*, *The Godfather*, *Carlito's Way* and *Goodfellas* pronounces on organized crime, the world listens. The USA can boast over a hundred years of documented and colourful history of organized crime, a cornucopia of resources available to the English-speaking world. These resources and the story they tell reveal not just the American experience of organized crime, but also as Alan Block notes, 'the social history of the US', of which 'organized crime is but a part'. (1994: 57). Official and fictional representations of organized crime provide an insight into the political, social and economic climate of the country, its insecurities, real and imagined.

Arguably the origins of organized crime in America began in the pioneer days of the market, as a brutal form of capitalism conducted by nineteenth century so-called 'robber barons', speculators and railroad owners such as Drew and Vanderbilt, who with little regard for the law, ruthlessly pursued the creation of their business empires. Organized crime as gangsterism was especially prevalent in the mid-1800s with the political gangster antics of the Tammany Hall bosses who offered protection to Irish immigrants in return for votes. As we have seen above, how we define has an impact on perception, and in this case historical location. However, few would dispute, that while by no means the first instance of organized crime, it was the famous Volstead Act of 1919, more commonly known as Prohibition, that became the defining moment of the emergence of organized crime in America. In this new black market for illegal alcohol Italian immigrants were able to employ their winemaking skills to satisfy the unquenchable thirst of 'dry' America. This lucrative industry eventually shifted the balance of underworld power, placing ethnic Italians at the centre of organized criminal activity during, and for many years after, the Prohibition years.

The profusion of criminal activity in cities such as Chicago were to provide material for some of the first ethnographic studies of organized crime in the US most notably Thrasher's *The Gang* (1927) and Landesco's *Organized Crime in Chicago* (1968). This burgeoning of criminal entrepreneurship elicited sober and restrained official responses which recognized the source of much of the problem and genuinely desired to address an actual rather than imagined problem. The Wickersham Commission, set up by President Herbert Hoover to look at, amongst other things, the proliferation of organized crime, concluded in 1931 that the Volstead Act was unenforceable and largely responsible for the criminogenic environment. Significantly, it revealed misconduct in the criminal justice system across the country, political corruption and, as far as illicit entrepreneurship was concerned 'bound the businessman-gone-wrong and gangsters into a single category of organized crime' (Smith, 1991). Two years later the Volstead Act was repealed. The Commission's findings were to have little or no impact on future official investigations.

The Kefauver Committee, formed two decades later to look into interstate gambling, could hardly have been different in tone and content. It concluded that there existed a national and centrally run crime syndicate of Italian origin (Kefauver, 1951). Published during the height of the McCarthy anti-communist drive, the findings sat easily with a nation already fearful of Soviet communism. It was the McClellan hearings of 1963, which developed the Mafia theory further and provided the material for Cressey's highly influential *Theft of a Nation*. Central to the hearings (which were televised) was the confession of small-time gangster Joseph Valacchi who spoke of La Cosa Nostra (Our Thing), as bureaucratically structured crime families, run by a central organization known as the Commission. This interpretation became inculcated into policy responses to organized crime despite the methodologically unsound basis of giving such disproportionate credence to the testimony of one man (Block, 1994; Albini, 1997b). In 1970 the Racketeer Influenced and Corrupt Organizations Act, known as RICO, became the major legislative tool in fighting organized crime, owing much to Cressey's work. It made provision for prosecutors to try in one courtroom a number of defendants and their crimes, gave longer sentences for organized crime offences and allowed the seizure of the accused's assets. While it can boast trophies such as crime bosses Tony Salerno and John Gotti, RICO's general effectiveness as a deterrent against organized crime is debatable. Nevertheless, it has become a global model for legislation against organized crime.

In the 1980s the US government focused its attention more narrowly on organized crime and the illicit drugs business. The 'war' on drugs was to synthesize domestic and foreign policies and change the balance of power in the American underworld. The drugs war became a politically expedient means of engaging in an invasive foreign policy, under the guise of anti drug-trafficking operations, in Central and South America (Bullington, 1993). It also allowed the US to export its law enforcement policies on drugs, organized crime and other related areas to less experienced countries, thus creating a pan-American global police force (see below, Transnational Organized Crime). As far as the American Mafia, or so-called Cosa Nostra were concerned, the growing drugs trade was rapidly sidelining it as other crime groups indigenous to drug producing countries were able to carve out their own business networks in the US. 'By the later 1980s' writes Peter Reuter, 'the traditional circuitous route for South-east Asian heroin, through Sicily, southern Italy or France, had primarily been replaced by direction importation, via the West coast, by Chinese and Vietnamese entrepreneurs. The Mafia proved helpless to deal with any of these incursions on its traditional territories' (1995: 91). Thus, crime control needed to refocus away from the traditional hierarchy image to complex international networks if it was to have any impact on the illegal drugs trade. The appropriate response was tardy. For too long US policies towards organized crime had been entrenched in the Kefauver-Cressey model. With the final collapse of communism in 1991 and the rapid dispersal of Russian-speaking crimes groups beyond their hitherto confined national borders, the US found itself a new but ideologically familiar candidate for alien conspiracy theory, and with that stepped back into the limited horizons of the 1950s (Finckenauer and Waring, 1998).

Despite this, the impact of US policies towards organized crime has never been stronger. As new democracies emerge in Eastern Europe, crime control agencies, formerly the strong arm of the State, have been forced to confront soaring levels of organized crime and corruption, while lacking the proper resources, strategies and expertise. Under communism it was not possible to officially acknowledge the existence of organized crime, designated as it was 'capitalist crime'. Years of 'turning a blind eye' together with the negative social consequences of the rapid transition to the free market mean that struggling law enforcement agencies are grateful for any form of support. The US recognized this need and was generous in its financial support and willingness to provide the necessary training. However, the vital questions concerning the success rate of American policies domestically and whether these policies are appropriate for transition states have hardly been asked, never mind answered.

REVIEW QUESTIONS

1 What impact did prohibition have on organized crime in the US?

2 What do the different findings of the Wickersham Commission and the Kefauver Committee tell us about political attitudes to organized crime?

Transnational organized crime

With the rapid advance of technology, the extension of the so-called 'free market' and the seismic political shifts, which marked the end of the Cold War, national boundaries began to lose their significance. For example, the supranational state of the European Union, in a state of constant expansion, has provided a visa-free 'Schengen space' to allow the free movement of people and goods across a vast 'common' territory of member states. This world of shrinking frontiers, known as 'globalization' has had a huge impact on organized crime providing opportunities for the expansion of cross-border criminal activity. Popularly referred to as 'transnational organized crime' (TOC) the notion of 'crime without frontiers' provides a challenge not only to crime control and policy institutions but, on a less tangible basis, challenges a number of preconceived ideas on legitimacy, victimization, security, human rights and so on (Edwards and Gill, 2003).

Once again, the question of definition must be briefly examined, this time with the emphasis on the term 'transnational'. Meaning literally 'across nations' the term 'transnational' refers to crimes committed across a number of jurisdictions. But when looking at TOC in action and how it is policed, in contrast to that which we describe simply as 'organized crime', it has less credibility as a distinctive term. As Dick Hobbs (1998) points out, organized crime is 'local at all points', even when it involves international collaborations and operations. The execution of a crime, the demand for its goods and services, the victims, the benefactors, all these components exist in local space and not in a 'transnational' space. Even money laundering occurs at a series of 'local' points, albeit using 'virtual' means. So too is policing more likely to occur at a local level. Peter Stelfox, Head of Crime Investigation for Greater Manchester Police, is quite clear about the nature and response to so-called TOC:

> The fact remains, though, that most organized crime known about in England and Wales is not occurring in some virtual transnational domain, which remains un-policed in the absence of the sort of international treaties, legal instruments, data sharing protocols and cross-border policing structures . . . It is occurring, and being policed, locally'. (Stelfox 2003: 119)

In other words, while organized crime is increasingly exploiting opportunities offered on an international scale, such as drugs and human trafficking, these activities and the actors involved are locally based and will be affected by local conditions. The growing tragic trade in human trafficking, particularly involving women and children sold for sex, has arisen largely because of the increase in unemployment and poverty in certain parts of the world, and the rising demand for unprotected and underage sex in others (Hughes, 2002). Effective responses to this trade would include improving local socio-economic conditions as well as law enforcement strategies at the supply end.

The problem with TOC, even as an accepted concept, is that within its broad remit it throws up arbitrary designations of labels such as 'victim', or 'threat' which, in particular contexts, are reassigned contradicting meanings. A typical example of this is the issue of asylum seekers. The somewhat hysterical news coverage of so called large 'flows' of asylum seekers to Britain castigates a whole group of people who become threat rather than threatened. Further, because the majority of them have been forced to accept the services of organized crime as a means of escaping the often dire and dangerous conditions of their homeland, they form part of the broad TOC criminal picture, leaving them, as Goodey points out, in 'a "no man's land" between criminal and victim status' (2003: 168).

Policing TOC is now a major concern for many Western governments, especially in this post-September 11 era experiencing, as it is, a greater convergence between international and national security interests. The intensification of collaboration between organized crime and terrorism, and indeed the suspected merging of these activities has refocused attention onto centrally dispensed and intelligence-led policing. As all institutions face budgetary constraints this macro policy approach threatens to remove funds from local policing to these central agencies. Also in assessing the threat of TOC, the results of which will have a political impact as far as budgetary priorities are concerned, there are no standard methodologies for data collection (Burnham, 2003; Gregory, 2003). Different criminal codes, how and what types of crime are recorded and at what level all affect statistical outcomes and subsequent policy responses. And, of course, underlying all this is the ability and willingness of law enforcement agencies in the different jurisdictions to actually share intelligence and cooperate operationally.

The global environment of myriad cultures, different markets (regulated and unregulated) and numerous languages also require structural adjustments by organized crime. Traditional hierarchies and centrally managed structures, if they ever existed to the extent that they have been portrayed as doing, cannot survive in these conditions. The international market demands flexibility, short-term but effective collaborations, more complex forms of communication and safeguards against successful police operations and the engagement of an increasing number of different actors in different locations. Networks are therefore less likely to attract attention and can be disassembled and reconstructed quickly and in different forms. The most powerful position is no longer the head or leader of a structure, but with those who occupy certain 'nodal' points within the networks which give them the greater overall knowledge of an operation or series of operations. For this reason social network analysis is becoming an important methodological tool amongst law enforcement agencies, allowing them to identify who liaises with whom and the status of these interactions in terms of inflicting the greatest damage on the criminal networks (Coles, 2001; Klerks, 2003).

None of this, however, explains why organized crime has become such a global phenomenon, or what and whom exactly it threatens. Piling more resources into law enforcement and creating more punitive legislation historically has had little or no effect on the growth of organized crime and, in some cases, has had the adverse consequence of impinging on human rights. Locating some of the causes, or explanations for the proliferation of organized crime, requires a more self-critical assessment of the values and ideologies, which dominate the global society we inhabit. Different motivations assume different standpoints, how we explain, in other words, will be coloured by what Dwight Smith (1991) refers to as 'the entry point' of our discussion or investigation. The following section presents some of these explanations.

Theories and methods

The protean nature of organized crime, reflecting as it does the different environments in which it operates, opens up a broad field of theoretical approaches. Alien conspiracy theory, which as we have seen provided a popular ground of understanding, has been widely criticized for its inherent prejudices and ideological slant. It has the useful political function, however, of creating cohesion amongst disparate groups in its ability to locate threat and danger in a distinctive 'other'. This serves the purpose of reinforcing and further legitimizing the dominant culture. Underlying this approach is the notion that those involved in organized crime have freely chosen this career path and are fully conscious of the nature and effects of their actions (although it could be argued that this approach takes a more positivist line by attributing higher rates of crime to among certain social-cultural groups). This typical classical approach to criminal behaviour, as with the majority of crime, sees solutions to the problem in punitive-based measures doled out by the State such as greater investment in crime control and harsher sentencing.

As a social phenomenon organized crime can also be explained in terms of a variety of relationships that the individual forges, or not, with society (see Chapter 4). Sutherland (1983) explains his white-collar criminal as one who has learned his deviant behaviour because it becomes more favourable to violate the law than to uphold it. What he terms differential association describes a learning process where individuals are 'socialized' into deviant behaviour through their contact with or observation of role models, or influential figures in their immediate or close environment. A person is more likely to join an organized crime group if members of his/her family or friends live and work in a criminal milieu. What this explanation does not shed light on is the origins of this association, that is, what type of conditions encourages criminal behaviour in the first place in the absence of role models to emulate. Strain theory looks more at the 'why' than the 'how'. Developed from the work of Robert Merton strain theory explains criminal behaviour as a way of resolving the tension between achieving the dominant goals of society and the obstacles that prevent certain individuals and groups from achieving these goals legitimately. 'Crime and vice constitute a "normal" response to a situation where cultural emphasis upon pecuniary success has been absorbed, but where there is little access to conventional and legitimate means for becoming successful' (Merton, 1968: 198). Organized crime opens up possibilities for 'pecuniary success' (Bell's 'queer ladder') particularly for those whose circumstances do not provide opportunities, such as education, good connections, employment and so on, to 'get on' in the world. This explains why marginalized sections of society, such as ethnic minorities, might be more likely to engage in criminal enterprise.

Strain theorists stop short of criticizing the ideology of a society that places so much emphasis on wealth acquisition, the central feature of the Marxist critique. While Marx himself commented little on crime Marxist criminologists recognize the underlying assumptions that there exists 'a relationship between economic conditions and the amount of crime' and that its manifestation is in fact a ' "false consciousness", an adjustment to the society rather than an articulate striving to overcome it' (Taylor, Walton and Young, 1973: 218). Marxist theory offers explanations for different levels of organized criminal activity, whether involving the working classes or the powerful elites. Pearce (1976) in *Crimes of the Powerful* notes that gangs in the US helped to contain trade union activity, operating at the behest of employers who wanted to keep wages low and work conditions basic. This is organized crime as servant rather than partner, he concludes. Taylor's analysis of Merton's work describes the very system of capitalism as criminogenic: 'The enormous value placed on money as a value itself—without regard to the intrinsic value of the activity through which pecuniary success had been realized—was accompanied by no moral or legal qualification on such success' (Taylor, 1994: 478). In other words, in a capitalist society the law and morality are subservient to the pursuit of wealth acquisition, a viewpoint echoed by the famous gangster Al Capone in his alleged comment to a journalist on the State of corruption of American society, 'Lady, no-one's on the legit'.

The functionalist view would regard the increase in organized crime as an indication of emerging pathologies within those societies in which it is seen to be a problem. While describing the existence of crime as normal to society, it was the level of crime (too much or too less) which Durkheim (Giddens, 1972), the founding father of functionalism, regarded as the barometer for social cohesion and stability. The proliferation of organized crime in Russia after the break up of communism in 1991 was a classic indication of what Durkheim termed anomie, a state of lawlessness arising from the breakdown of social norms and the institutions that sustain them. The dramatic changes, such as the overnight move from a quasi-centralized to laissez-faire market and the collapse of communist state structures, left power vacuums which organized crime was quick to exploit, a pattern repeated in other transition states in the former Soviet Union, Eastern Europe and South Africa. Taking the functionalist paradigm a step further, there have been instances when organized crime has been seen to be an essential component of economic development. Echoing the role organized crime played in the containment of US trade unions, Luttwak attributes the success of much of Japan's building programme to the Yakuza (Japanese crime groups) who employed 'their colourful repertoire of threats and vandalism' to encourage inert householders to sell their economically impractical plots of land (1995: 7). And in their report on the chaotic state of the Russian economy in the 1990s, the Organization for Economic Cooperation and Development (1995) wrote that 'a degree of criminal activity . . . "could in a certain sense be thought of as providing a necessary service to business" '. This practical role of organized crime is, of course, only possible if, as Pearce observed, it remains subservient to the dominant structures.

Explaining organized crime is one thing, researching it is entirely another. Research into any areas of criminology is challenging, and even more so into the hidden and sometimes hazardous world of organized crime. A brief foray into how this research is carried out should simultaneously enlighten and dishearten.

REVIEW QUESTIONS

1 In your opinion which criminological theory best explains organized crime? Give reasons for your choice.

2 Discuss the differences between the functionalist approach to organized crime and the Marxist approach.

3 During the past couple of years Britain has reportedly seen an increase in armed gangs. Use one or more theories to try to explain this increase in violent tactics by organized crime groups.

Madness in their methods

There are a number of ways of gathering information on organized crime: the most popular being media reports, police files and ethnographic research. The quality of media reporting can vary enormously, from well researched articles and documentaries based on balanced interviews and all round impartiality, and occasionally, at the cost of a journalist's life to hearsay and the frenzied hysteria so often found in the tabloids. Police reports can afford a valuable insight into the type of offences and persons involved in organized crime, though as Anderson warns, the remit of law enforcement agencies 'is to identify and prosecute violations of the law, rather than to provide data banks for social scientists' (1979: 147). This leaves us with the ethnographic approach, going out into the field and observing first hand. For the student of criminology, ethnographic research into organized crime makes interesting reading although, as with any methodology, this type of research has its flaws.

Ethnographic research involves 'going out and seeing it for yourself', in other words, leaving the comfort of the study or library and acquiring information from inside the group or community being researched. As a method of inquiry it has its origins in cultural anthropology but was adopted as a serious form of sociological research by the Chicago School in the 1920s and 1930s under Robert Park. Urban sociology, as it is referred to, is qualitative research combining theory and fieldwork. It is especially favoured when researching the social relationships of deviant groups (Hobbs and May, 1993). There are obvious potential problems pitfalls, however, in researching sensitive subjects not least the responsibility of the researcher to those they are investigating (Lee, 1993) as well as the ethical considerations when the researcher has the option of becoming engaged in deviant activities as a means of continuing investigations (Whyte, 1972).

There is a growing literature on this type of research into organized crime. Landesco's (1968) study of organized crime in Chicago, Polsky's (1969) close encounters with poolroom hustlers, Ianni and Ianni's (1972) inclusion in the inner circle of the Lupollo crime family's social circle are all noteworthy examples of how first hand experience of the closed world of organized criminality can produce invaluable material. Nor has the subject matter deterred subsequent researchers. Hobbs' (1988) study of illegal entrepreneurship in London's East End, Rawlinson's (2000) work on organized crime in Moscow and

St Petersburg and Varese's (2001) study of protection rackets in Perm continue the tradition of ethnographic research across different time zones and varied geographies. 'Is it dangerous?' is a common and understandable, question. Hobbs refers to the murder of one researcher, Ken Pryce, who was looking into organized crime in the West Indian community in Britain (2000: 165). This fortunately is very much the exception. Collecting data on organized crime must have as top priority the security of the researcher and all of their contacts. Albini's work on organized crime in America led him to conclude that 'organized criminals, including my informants, couldn't care less what type of data academics usually collect' (1997a: 18). Academics are not out to expose organized criminals, and when they do get access to the underworld it tends to be on the conditions laid out by the criminals themselves. Does this colour the information received, the experiences observed? Undoubtedly, it must, thus emphasizing an important caveat for participant observers, that what you see is usually what you are allowed to get, unless of course, as some researchers have done, you do not reveal your academic identity, at which point the risk factor can increase dramatically.

So why engage in this type of research? Paradoxically, for the very reason that puts many people off: the inaccessibility of the topic and the abuses to which second and third hand data are subjected. Despite the possibility of unreliability and subjectivity, a danger in all types of research, there is arguably no better way of grasping the motivations and nuances of criminal society than 'being there'. Discussing the world of the illegal entrepreneur with its inhabitants in a London restaurant over a good meal and bottle wine, as Ruggiero (2000) did for his work on this subject, can open doors to information and contacts that no official records or media reports ever could, even if it does put a strain on the liver and the wallet. While answers to our questions might not be forthcoming, more importantly we are provided with other questions, ones we might never have realized needed to be asked. And in the ambiguous arena of organized crime, this has to be an important part of developing a more realistic understanding of it.

REVIEW QUESTIONS

1 While an ethnographic approach might have its advantages, there are obviously more problems than discussed here. What might these be?

2 Using one or more methodological approaches describe how you would conduct research into a local gang suspected of dealing in contraband cigarettes.

CONCLUSION

Organized crime as a serious component of criminology courses is long overdue, as too is its inclusion in current academic debates within, and beyond, the discipline of criminology. It deserves particular attention at the beginning of the twenty-first century not just because of its recent proliferation but because its very presence challenges the values of the societies in which it finds so many opportunities for exploitation. There can be few areas of criminology in which the debate on definition is so enduring and which, even now, shows no sign of reaching an adequate consensus. This, in itself, should alert us to the dangers of simplistic explanations and categorizations, to the problems of ring fencing activities and labelling them 'good' or 'bad' according to who is conducting them. Organized crime, we could argue, effectively reflects back on society the inadequacies and ills contained with it. Organized crime is not the pathology itself, but a symptom of it.

The definition debate also indicates how amorphous are the boundaries within which we surround other areas of criminology. Organized crime shares common ground with terrorism, violent crime, corporate crime; its huge inclusive remit embraces drugs and alcohol, race and ethnicity, it feeds off social exclusion and marginalization and has been influential in setting the agenda for a whole range of responses to crime. And yet despite this mutability it expresses features that are exclusive to this type of offending, most notably the economic drive underlying the actions of a number of people who have come together, whether as a clearly structured group or a complex, flexible network, to exploit and profit from discovered opportunities. In some cases, it can even create these opportunities itself.

Organized crime has had a rich history particularly in the US, which continues to exert a strong influence, not just on perceptions of organized crime but also on crime control strategies to contain it. Since the end of the Cold War the assumed status of the US as 'global policeman' has intensified this authoritative stance. Unfortunately, the predilection of a number of US administrations towards, what Hofstadter (1966) refers to as 'the paranoid style of American politics', has evolved a conspiratorial slant on organized crime. A number of successful Hollywood films have been made on the back of this monolithic, hierarchically structured, ethnic Italian Mafia image of organized crime, guaranteeing a large audience for this particular version. Not surprisingly, many criminologists have countered this view, and while there is no consensus on the definition of organized crime, there is general agreement that the alien conspiracy image is not appropriate and that greater emphasis should be placed on its entrepreneurial nature. The diverse aspects of organized crime as business have brought into focus, especially from a critical criminological perspective, the relationships between licit and illicit enterprise. The mutual benefits evident in some of these collaborations call into question the nature of legal business and demand a deeper critique of the economic status quo.

Operating across countries, on a transnational level, organized crime is able to exploit inequalities and injustices, which are increasingly in evidence as negative fall-out from globalization. Despite the ability of organized criminals to extend their links internationally, the actual implementation of their activities is at the local level. To effectively respond to organized crime, therefore, law enforcement should operate on a number of levels and not rely overly on intelligence-led centralized forms of policing. Further, crime control agencies have not been able to adapt at the same speed finding themselves caught up in political and financial straitjackets, as well as being hindered by traditional notions of what constitutes organized crime, though the latter is less of an issue as law enforcement adopts a broader and more realistic understanding of the problem.

Organized crime offers a challenge to practitioner and academic alike. For the student of criminology it demands a relinquishing of commonplace notions of crime and a willingness to think 'outside the box'. In some cases this will involve engaging in debates over the values and systems that have become integral to the way we live, an exercise that can be as disquieting as it can prove groundbreaking. For if, indeed, organized crime is but symptomatic of more entrenched problems in society at large it requires those who study it to look behind and beyond the symptom. Judge Falcone, Italy's most famous investigator into the Mafia's distinct brand of organized crime wrote: '. . . if we want to fight the Mafia organization efficiently, we must not transform it into a monster or think of it as an octopus or cancer. We must recognize that it resembles us' (1993: 70). It pays to take heed of a man who had first hand experience of organized crime, and was determined to bring a genuine understanding to the criminal phenomenon he dedicated his life to and died confronting.

QUESTIONS FOR DISCUSSION

1   Why do you think organized crime is so difficult to police? What new approaches could you suggest to address the problem?

2   Describe the character of any fictional mobster you might have read about or seen in films or on television. Why do you think the author/director created them in this particular way?

3   What are the advantages and disadvantages of transferring perceptions of organized crime and crime control strategies across cultures?

4   Should the actions of corporate business be compared to those of organized crime if, as a consequence of legal corporate activity, social or other harms result?

5   In the chapter a good deal of time is spent discussing how to define organized crime. Why, if at all, is it important to try and provide an appropriate definition?

GUIDE TO FURTHER READING

Ryan, P.J. and Rush, G.E. (eds) (1997) *Understanding Organized Crime in Global Perspective: A Reader*, California: Sage Publications.

This is a perfect introduction to American perceptions of organized crime and includes wide ranging debates about the nature of organized crime and how different American administrations have responded to it. Its contributors include some of the leading US specialists on organized crime.

Edwards, A. and Gill, P. (eds) (2003) *Transnational Organized Crime: Perspectives on Global Security*, London: Routledge.

One of the first books published in Britain dedicated solely to transnational organized crime. Its importance lies in the fact that it contains contributions from practitioners as well as academics from a number of different specialist backgrounds.

Hobbs, D. (1988) *Doing the Business*, Oxford: Clarendon Press.

One of the classic texts on professional crime in the UK based on ethnographic research into illegal business in the East End. Hobbs not only provides a unique insight into the penumbral world of business and informal relations between the police and the criminal fraternity, but describes the rewards and problems (the latter sometimes with wry humour) of ethnographic research (see also Hobbs, D. (1995) *Bad Business*, Oxford: Oxford University Press; Hobbs, D. (1997) 'Criminal collaboration: youth gangs, subcultures, professional crimials, and organized crime' in Maguire, M., Morgan, R. Reiner, R, (eds) *The Oxford Handbook of Criminology*, Oxford: Oxford University Press).

Howard Journal of Criminal Justice (Special Edition on Organized Crime), edited by Michael Levi. 37/4, 1998, Blackwell Publishing.

This special edition brings together a variety of perspectives on organized crime, including money-laundering, fraud, police strategies, media representations and geographies written by academics and practitioners.

Ruggiero, V. (2000) *Crime and Markets: Essays in Anti-Criminology*. Oxford: Oxford University Press.

Ruggiero's essays look at criminal activities within licit and illicit markets in a number of European countries. His discusses the 'causality of contraries', the notion that this type of crime is motivated by different causes involving a whole range of actors. This is an essential text for a critical perspective on the amorphous world of 'organized crime' (see also Ruggiero, V. and South, N. (1995) *Eurodrugs. Drug Use, Markets and Trafficking in Europe*, London: UCL Press).

WEB LINKS

www.iasoc.net

International Association for the Study of Organized Crime. This is aimed at academics and professionals. It includes the latest news on organized crime issues, reviews of publications on the subject and a members' list with their areas of expertise.

www.yorku.ca/nathanson

The Nathanson Centre for the Study of Organized Crime and Corruption is one of the leading research centres for this subject. It provides a wide range of perspectives on organized crime and related subjects.

www.ncis.co.uk

The National Criminal Intelligence Service is the UK coordinating intelligence body dealing with, amongst other areas, national and international organized crime. It is a particularly useful source of information for policy responses to organized crime in the UK.

www.unodc.org/unodc/en/crime_cicp_convention

The official UN website for organized crime, policing and other related areas. It provides a global view of strategies to fight transnational organized crime and is a useful starting point for investigating linked activities such as human and drug trafficking.

OTHER RECOMMENDED SOURCES

The following is a list of personal favourites, media depictions of the criminal underworld that do not succumb to the usual over dramatization of many Hollywood blockbusters. The strength of each is the social and personal context in which the main protagonists are placed.

The Sopranos (HBO)

Shown on Channel 4. A hugely successful television series, which tells the story of Tony Soprano, a middle-aged crime boss, who struggles to manage family traumas, work problems and his own neuroses.

Carlito's Way (1993) Director, Brian de Palma. Universal Studios.

A former drug-dealer, Carlito Brigante, attempts to go straight on his release from prison, but finds himself getting dragged deeper back into the only life he has ever known.

A Bronx Tale (1993) Director, Robert de Niro, HBO.

Narrated by the adult Calogero Anello, he tells of his childhood and adolescence as an Italian-American in the Bronx during the 1960s, and the effect that his father and the boss of the local mob had on his life.

Goodfellas (1990) Director, Martin Scorsese, Warner Studios.

Based on the novel *Wiseguys* by Nicolas Pileggi, the film tells the story of real life gangster, Henry Hill, whose increasing cocaine dependency leads him from successful 'entrepreneur' to desperation and a life saving Witness Protection Programme.

REFERENCES

Albanese, J. (1989) *Organized Crime in America* (2nd edn). Cincinnati: Anderson.

Albini, J. (1997a) The Mafia and the Devil in Ryan, P.J. and Rush, G.E. (eds) *Understanding Organized Crime in Global Perspective: A Reader*. California. Sage Publications.

Albini (1997b) Donald Cressey's contributions to the study of organized crime: an evaluation, in P.J. Ryan and G.E. Rush (eds) *Understanding Organized Crime: in Global Perspective: A Reader*. California: Sage Publications.

Anderson, A. (1979) *The Business of Organized Crime: a Cosa Nostra Family*. Stanford: Hoover Institution Press.

Backman J. (1998) *The Inflation of Crime in Russia: Paradoxes of a Threat Around the Baltic Sea* Paper given at a seminar organized by the Scandinavian Research Council for Criminology. Espoo, Finland (no pages given).

Bell, D. (1962) *The End of Ideology*. New York: P.F. Collier.

Block, A. (1993) Defending the mountaintop: a campaign against environmental crime in F. Pearce and M. Woodiwiss (eds) *Global Crime Connections*. Basingstoke: MacMillan.

Block, A. (1994) *Space, Time and Organized Crime*. New Brunswick: Transaction.

Bullington, B. (1993) All about Eve: the many faces of US drug policy in F. Pearce and M. Woodiwiss (eds) *Global Crime Connections*. Basingstoke: MacMillan.

Burnham, B. (2003) Measuring transnational organized crime in A. Edwards and P. Gill (eds) *Transnational Organized Crime: Perspectives on Global Security*. London: Routledge.

Caiden, G. (1985) 'Perspectives on organized crime' in H. Alexander and G. Caiden (eds) *The Politics of Organized Crime*. Massachusetts, Lexington.

Chambliss, W. (1988) *On the Take: From Petty Crooks to Presidents*. Bloomington: Indiana University Press.

Coles, N. (2001) 'It's Not What You Know—It's Who You Know That Counts: Analysing Serious Crime Groups as Social Networks', *British Journal of Criminology*, vol 41, Autumn.

Cressey, D. (1969) *Theft of the Nation: The Structure and Operations of Organized Crime in America*. New York: Harper & Row.

Falcone, G. (1993) *The Truth about the Mafia*. London: Warner Books.

Finckenauer, J. and Waring, E. (1998) *Russian Mafia in America*. Boston: Northeastern University Press.

Gambetta, D. (1993) *The Sicilian Mafia: The Business of Private Protection*. Massachusetts: Harvard University Press.

Giddens, A. (1972) *Emile Durkheim: Selected Writings*. London: Cambridge University Press.

Gill, P. (2002) Organized crime in (eds) E. McLaughlin and J. Muncie *The Sage Dictionary of Criminology*. London: Sage.

Goodey, J. (2002) Whose insecurity? organized crime, its victims and the EU in A. Crawford *Crime and Insecurity*. Cullompton: Willan Publishing.

Goodey, J. (2003) Recognising organized crime's victims: The case of sex trafficking in the EU in A. Edwards and P. Gill (eds) *Transnational Organized Crime: Perspectives on Global Security*. London: Routledge.

Gregory, F. (2003) Classify, report and measure: The UK Organized Crime Notification Scheme in A. Edwards and P. Gill (eds) *Transnational Organized Crime: Perspectives on Global Security*. London: Routledge.

Hobbs, D. (1988) *Doing the Business*. Oxford: Clarendon Press.

Hobbs, D. and May, T. (eds) (1993) *Interpreting the Field-Accounts of Ethnography*. Oxford: Oxford University Press.

Hobbs D. (1998) 'Going down the Glocal: The Local Context of Organized Crime', *Howard Journal*, 37/4, 407–22.

Hobbs, D. (2000) Researching serious crime in R. King and E. Wincup (eds) *Doing Research on Crime and Justice*. Oxford: Oxford University Press.

Hofstadter, R. (1966) *The Paranoid Style in American Politics and Other Essays*. London: Cape.

Hughes, D. (2002) *Trafficking for Sexual Exploitation: The Case of the Russian Federation*, IOM International Organization for Migration, Migration Research Series, No. 7.

Ianni, F. and Ianni, E. (1972) *A Family Business: Kinship and Social Control in Organized Crime*. London: Routledge & Kegan Paul.

Kefauver, E. (1951) *Crime in America*. New York: Doubleday.

Klerks, P. (2003) 'The network paradigm applied to criminal organizations: theoretical nitpicking or a relevant doctrine for investigators? Recent developments in the Netherlands' in A. Edwards and P. Gill (eds) *Transnational Organized Crime: Perspectives on Global Security*. London: Routledge.

Landesco, J. (1968) *Organized Crime in Chicago*. Chicago: University of Chicago Press.

Lee, R. (1993) *Doing Research on Sensitive Topics*. London: Sage.

Luttwak, E. (1995) 'Does the Russian mafia deserve the Nobel prize for economics?' *London Review of Books*, 3 August.

Markina, A. (1998) Organized crime in Estonia: a national and international issue, in K. Aromaa (ed) *The Baltic Region: Insights in Crime and Control*, Scandinavian Studies in Criminology, Vol. 15. Oslo: Pax Forlag A/S.

Merton, R. (1968) *Social Theory and Social Structure*. New York: Free Press.

Naylor, R.T. (1997) 'Mafias, Myths, and Markets: On the Theory and Practice of Enterprise Crime', *Transnational Organized Crime*, 3/3: 1–45.

Organisation for Economic Cooperation and Development (1995) 'Russian economy in line for boom' in *The European* 5–11, October.

Pearce, F. (1976) *Crimes of the Powerful*. London: Pluto Press.

Polsky, N. (1969) *Hustlers, Beats and Others*. New York: Anchor Books.

Rawlinson, P. (2000) 'Mafia, methodology and "Alien" culture' in R. King and E. Wincup (eds) *Doing Research on Crime and Justice*. Oxford: Oxford University Press.

Rawlinson, P. (2001) 'Russian Organized Crime and the Baltic States: Assessing the Threat' Working Paper 38/01, ESRC Research programme 'One Europe or Several'.

Reuter, P. (1995) 'The Decline of the American Mafia', *The Public Interest*, 120, Summer: 89–99.

Rogovin, C.H. and Martens, F.T. (1997) 'The evil that men do' in P.J. Ryan and G.E. Rush (eds) *Understanding Organized Crime in Global Perspective: A Reader*. California: Sage Publications.

Ruggiero, V. (2000) *Crime and Markets: Essays in Anti-Criminology*. Oxford: Oxford University Press.

Slapper, G. and Tombs, S. (1999) *Corporate Crime*. Harlow: Longman.

Smith, D.C. (1975) *The Mafia Mystique*. New York: Basic Books.

Smith, D.C. (1991) 'Wickersham to Sutherland to Katzenbach: Evolving an "Official" Definition of Organized Crime', *Crime, Law and Social Change*. 16(2):134–54.

Stelfox, P. (2003) Transnational organized crime: a police perspective in A. Edwards and P. Gill (eds) *Transnational Organized Crime: Perspectives on Global Security*. London: Routledge.

Sutherland, E. (1937) *The Professional Thief*. Chicago, Ill: Chicago University Press.

Sutherland, E. (1983) *White Collar Crime: The Uncut Version*. New Haven: Yale University Press.

Taylor, I., Walton, P. and Young, J. (1973) *The New Criminology: For a Social Theory of Deviance*. London: Routledge & Kegan.

Taylor, I. (1994) 'The political economy of crime' in M. Maguire, R. Morgan and R. Reiner (eds) *The Oxford Handbook of Criminology*. Oxford: Oxford University Press.

Thrasher, F. (1927) *The Gang*. Chicago: University of Chicago Press.

United Nations (2000) *Summary of the United Nations Convention Against Organized Crime and Protocols Thereto*. http://www.odccp.org/palermo/convensumm.htm

Woodiwiss, M. (1993) 'Crime's Global Reach' in F. Pearce and M. Woodiwiss (eds) *Global Crime Connections*. Basingstoke: MacMillan.

Varese, F. (2001) *The Russian Mafia: Private Protection in a New Market Economy*. Oxford: Oxford University Press.

Whyte, W. (1972) 'Street Corner Society' cited in (Lee, 1993) J. Douglas *Research on Deviance*. New York: Random House.

15 Terrorism and the politics of fear

Frank Furedi

INTRODUCTION

Since the destruction of the World Trade Centre in September 2001, terrorism has become one of the defining issues of the twenty-first century. Billions of dollars have been devoted to the so-called 'War Against Terrorism'. New technologies and laws have been created to assist the crackdown of what according to official accounts constitutes the gravest risk to our existence. Unfortunately, in the discussion of terrorism, what divides fact from fiction and information from propaganda is inexact. This chapter attempts to address this problem. It starts by casting doubt on simple, typically very narrow definitions of terrorism, before then going on to deconstruct the climate of fear currently surrounding the majority of research in this area. Finally, the chapter casts a critical eye on current counter terrorism measures and recently invoked anti-terrorist legislation, arguing that, if governments continue to adopt a cavalier attitude towards civil liberties, they will surely face the risk of playing into the very hands of those who promote and perpetrate political violence.

BACKGROUND

The inexplicable behaviour of apparently irrational terrorists is often tenuously linked to events whose causes are not known. Incomprehensible events are readily presented as the consequence of the actions of agents we do not understand. As Jenkins (2003) observes, even with the best will in the world, government officials are not in the position to inform the public of all the facts. When it comes to terrorism official agencies 'have a powerful vested interest in not revealing the full extent of the information available to them'. Indeed, transmitting misinformation is part of the job-description of anti-terrorist agencies. 'Since so much official action involves clandestine methods or sources, even the most reputable and responsible agencies will on occasion present less than the full truth, or actively give false information in order to protect their methods or sources' writes Philip Jenkins (2003: 6).

Of course, official statements that are designed to provide misleading information are not confined to the crime of terrorism. Information about crime statistics and specific crimes is often conveyed through statements that seek to gain political advantage through manipulating the facts. However, when it comes to conventional crimes, the questioning academic researcher is often in a position to demystify the official version of events and offer a plausible alternative. Matters are much more complicated when it comes to analysing terrorism. As Jenkins (ibid.) argues, it is easy to know when a particular act constitutes a crime such as robbing a bank. It is much more difficult to be certain that a particular deed is as an act of terrorism. For often, it is not the deed but the motives that inspired it that turns a particular event into an act of terrorism. A random shooting maybe the act of a psychopath or of a politically motivated activist, as Jenkins remarks, 'before we know whether the act falls within the scope of terrorism, we have to know both who did it, and why they did it' (ibid.: 6). These are very difficult questions to answer and unless we have direct access to the individual accused of a terrorist crime it is difficult to offer an alternative to the official version of events.

Interpreting terrorism

'Traditionalist' versus 'social constructionist' conceptions of terrorism

Although the terms 'terrorism' and 'terrorist' are widely used it is far from evident what these words actually mean. Until recently, terrorism tended to be associated with the tactics of individuals or organizations who were waging unconventional warfare against legitimate authority through targeting non-combatants and spreading fear through the populace (Wilson, 2003: 119). Since the turn of the century, the term terrorism is often used to connote a distinct identity or ideology of an individual or organization. Thus, the widely used phrase 'war on terrorism' suggests that there is more to this problem than the violent tactics carried out by illegitimate clandestine organizations. Implicit in this phrase is the idea that terrorism represents a way of life, a political outlook as well as a physical and military threat.

The unusual degree of controversy that surrounds the discussion on terrorism stems from the fact that acts of political violence encourage people to take sides. The vocabulary used to express acts of political violence is continually contested. It is not simply the case that 'one person's freedom fighter is another one's terrorist'. Are members of organizations like Hamas or ETA, militants, guerrillas or terrorists? And are they fighting a war or committing crimes? Most of the time the answers to these questions are influenced by one's attitude to the particular conflict. Whether or not an act of political violence is represented as a crime is linked to beliefs about its legitimacy.

The literature on terrorism is sharply divided between the 'traditionalists' who perceive it as a distinct form of violence that can be understood in its own terms and those who perceive it as the product of social construction. Paul Wilkinson's classic traditionalist account, *Political Terrorism* is devoted to the task of elaborating the fundamental features of this crime. According to Wilkinson the 'key characteristics common to all forms of political terror' are 'indiscriminateness, unpredictability, arbitrariness, ruthless destructiveness and the implicitly amoral antinomian nature of a terrorist's challenge' (Wilkinson, 1976: 17). Most supporters of the idea that terrorism is a distinct form of crime argue that its essential feature is the pursuit of violence for political ends. 'What distinguishes terrorism from both vandalism and non-political crime, is the motivated violence for political ends', writes Crozier (1974). Political motivation, randomness and the targeting of innocent non-combatants are the characteristics most often cited by contributors who seek to represent terrorism as a distinct form of violence (for a useful overview of these definitions see Thackrah, 2004: 66–71).

The main alternative to the project of representing terrorism as a distinct form of political violence that can be understood in its own terms is the social constructionist approach. This approach is oriented towards exploring how terrorism is constructed as a problem. As Jenkins argues a social constructionist perspective does not necessarily imply that terrorism does not exist and that it is an invented problem. Nor does it imply a particular political stance towards the question (Jenkins, 2003: 14–15). However, by suggesting that terrorism is not a self-evident concept most constructionist contributors tend to question the dominant consensus and representation of this subject.

Some constructionists claim that the attempt to portray terrorism as a distinct form of political violence represents an attempt to objectify it. Oliverio argues that 'terrorism as a construct is given an objective formation because it is accepted by most scholars as a special form of political violence' (1998: 27). According to Oliverio the objectification of the terrorist construct is inextricably associated with the imperative of legitimizing the authority of the State. She claims that the 'construct of terrorism is typically adopted discursively by the State to represent threats against its sovereignty' (ibid.). Many constructionist regard the problematization of terrorism as a self-serving attempt by the State to consolidate its power. For example, Tomis Kapitan appears to be more concerned with deconstructing the official rhetoric on terrorism than with the phenomenon of political violence itself. From this perspective it is difficult to avoid the conclusion that the promotion of the rhetoric of terrorism constitutes a problem that is at least as significant as the acts of political violence by those labelled as terrorist.

Problem of definition

Terrorism is an unusually controversial concept. Most leading contributions in this field recognize the difficulty that social scientists have had in defining this concept (See for example Gurr, 1979: 24, or Wilkinson, 1977: 52). One study reviewed 109 definitions of terrorism that covered twenty-two definitional elements (Schmid and Jongman, 1988: 5–6). Walter Laqueur, a well known expert on the subject has counted over 100 definitions. He has concluded that the only 'general characteristic generally agreed upon is that terrorism involves violence and the threat of violence' (Laqueur, 1999: 6). But of course the use and threat of violence is not confined to terrorism. The deployment and the threat of violence is also practiced by institutions that are deemed to be legitimate—particularly those of the State.

One reason why there may be so much confusion surrounding the definition of this term is due to the fact that it is not simply an objective analytical concept but also a moral statement on the behaviour of the terrorist. 'Thus in attempting to determine whether a specific action (or series of actions) is terroristic or not, the scholar should be aware that he is making a value judgement about the perpetrators of the alleged act, and about the circumstances of their actions', writes Wilkinson in his classic account of the subject (1974: 21). The normative dimension of this concept is evident in the political controversies that surround the issue of terrorism. Since so often debates about terrorism are linked to taking sides, the controversy that surrounds it is likely to be far more inflated than the kind of arguments that occur around other forms of deviant behaviour in the social sciences. The moral and political concerns that surround discussion on this subject means that the concept is rarely used consistently and objectively.

The term terrorist is a loaded one—highly subjective, with aggressive connotations. It has acquired extremely negative associations. In the West, only the crime of paedophilia can compete with the act of the terrorist as a symbol of evil (Filler, 2003). The terrorist label serves as a health warning, it suggests that those to whom it is attached are morally inferior individuals. 'To identify someone as a terrorist is to render judgement on them, not simply to make a discovery' writes Claudia Card (2003: 178). Frequently, the attempt to represent an individual or a movement as terrorist is part of a propaganda war designed to discredit opponents. Not surprisingly, academic discussion of terrorism is not entirely detached from the propaganda battle for hearts and minds.

Often the definition of terrorism that is adopted is self-consciously designed to undermine the legitimacy of those promoting political violence. According to the RAND Corporation, the aim of its definition is to criminalize the acts it deems to be terrorist. 'In separating terrorist tactics from their political context, the intent clearly was to criminalize a certain mode of political expression' (Jackson, 1999: v). Not surprisingly, when a definition serves in part as a political statement it is likely to become a focus for controversy.

Most serious contributions on the subject acknowledge that they have difficulty in defining terrorism. Often this difficult problem is side stepped through attempting to enumerate a list of features that distinguish this form of crime. However, the attempt to construct a list of characteristics that are specific to terrorism is undermined by the fact that they can be found in other areas of violent activities. For example Wilkinson (1974: 13) claimed that 'a major characteristic of political terror is its indiscriminate nature'. The insistence that the indiscriminate quality of terrorist violence is one of this phenomenon's distinct features is accepted by many specialists on the subject. Images of the Washington snipers terrorizing passers by during their killing sprees in the summer of 2002 or of pedestrians blown to bits in Tel Aviv by a hidden bomb lend weight to the argument that this form of violence is distinguished by its indiscriminate character. However, as the American sociologist Joel Best (1999) argues in his *Random Violence*, many of today's high profile crimes have a capacity to scare the public precisely because they are perceived to be carried out indiscriminately. It is random violence that characterizes the acts of the serial killer, the perpetrator of road rage or the paedophile preying on innocent children. Indiscriminate violence is not the sole property of terrorism. Indeed it is associated with many of the high profile crimes that excite the public's imagination.

The claim that terrorism is premeditated, politically motivated violence that targets innocent non-combatants is widely accepted by specialists as important features of this phenomenon. Those who object to this definition raise questions about the nature of political motivation or of the meaning of innocence. 'This definition, however, begs the question of who is innocent and by what standards is innocence determined' notes Record (2003). Record and others contend that innocent non-combatants are frequently the victims of state sponsored violence. He points to the firebombing of Japanese cities in 1945 and to the terrified inhabitants who were not involved in the war effort.

Many critics of conventional definitions of terrorism believe that its emphasis on the actions of non-state actors obscures the role of the State in promoting acts of political violence. In some cases, critics tend to represent political violence exercized by the State as another form of terrorism. Writing in this vein, Sterba (2003: 24) condemns the past misdeeds of the US and argues that 'the United States surely needs to take steps to radically correct its own wrongdoing if it is to respond justly to the related wrongdoing of Bin Laden and his followers. Likewise, Record criticizes the traditional definitions because 'they exclude state terrorism, which since the French Revolution has claimed far more victims—in terms of millions—than terrorism perpetrated by non-state actors' (Record, 2003: 7).

Whatever definition one supports it is difficult to make a fundamental distinction between the violence and attributes of terrorism and the acts of others. For example, the objective of terrorizing the enemy is widely practised by conventional military forces. 'Shock and Awe' was the term used by the Bush administration to describe its massive hi-tech air strike against the Iraqis during the Second Gulf War. Its aim was clearly to strike terror in the minds of the enemy population. But those who supported this campaign did not regard it as an act of terror for the simple reason that they believed that this was a legitimate operation against a legitimate opponent. Definitions of terrorism involve the making of judgements of value. They also involve an element of selection.

Definitions of terrorism are fluid because ideas are continually changing about what forms of acts are legitimate or illegitimate. For example, violence against abortion clinics in the US was not considered as an act of terrorism until 1994.

In the 1980s, Americans tended to view terrorism as a Middle Eastern phenomenon whereas in the 1990s the threat was perceived 'at least as much domestic as foreign' (Jenkins, 2003: 57; see also Hamm, 2002; 2004a). In recent years there has been a tendency on the part of Western Governments and institutions to widen the definition of terrorism. In Britain, until recently the official definition was based on the one contained in the 1989 Prevention of Terrorism (Temporary Provisions Act). According to this Act, terrorism 'means the use of violence for political ends and includes any use of violence for the purpose of putting the public or any section of the public in fear'. A review of

Figure 15.1 Fire trucks amid the rubble of World Trade Center

Source: © Reuters/CORBIS.

terrorism legislation carried out by Lord Lloyd in 1996, claimed that this definition was far too narrow since it did not encompass acts carried out by promoters of religious and single issue causes. The definition adopted in s. 1 of the Terrorism Act 2000 reflected these concerns and includes action that involves the 'use or threat of action' designed to 'influence the government or to intimidate the public or section of the public'. Violent acts committed against scientists conducting experiments on animals or in association with a hate crime are thus now frequently described as forms of terrorism.

State terrorism

One of the most frequent criticisms made against the mainstream definitions of terrorism is that by focusing on non-state actors it overlooks the far more important problem of state sponsored violence. Critics argue that the focus on the violence of the individual overlooks the fact that the real threat to humanity is destructive acts of state institutions. Gearty argues that the language of terrorism has become 'the rhetorical servant of the established order, whatever and however heinous its own activities are' (2002: 36–37). According to this perspective, the term terrorist is a label that the powerful use to stigmatize the activities of the powerless. 'It is easy for the politically satisfied and militarily powerful to pronounce all terrorism evil regardless of circumstance, but, like it or not, those at the other end of the spectrum are bound to see things differently' argues one critic (Record, 2003: 8). The belief that the promotion of the ideology of terrorism has helped minimize the crimes of the powerful has led many to insist that the political violence exercized by the State should be viewed as another form of terrorism. Some contributors to the debate emphasize the association of terrorism with the State because they believe that this powerful institution is responsible for far more violence than what has been perpetrated by non-state actors (see Morrison, 2004; and relatedly Cohen, 2001). According to one account 'state terrorism' should be given 'pride of place' because it 'has been responsible for more killings, more tortures, and more disappearances than all other forms' of crime (Williams, 2004: 499).

Historically, the terms terror and terrorism have been associated with both individuals and states. Regimes such as those of revolutionary France, Stalinist Soviet Union or Nazi Germany are just some of the states associated with terrorism. In more recent times Western government adopted the term 'state sponsored terrorism' to denounce regimes deemed to be responsible for supporting and promoting terrorist activities. Nevertheless, in recent decades 'the anti-state sense of the term has become paramount' (Thackrah, 2004). Today, the terrorist threat is predominantly associated with non-state networks of activists.

Although the problem of state violence is an important issue requiring serious analysis and deliberation, it does not follow that it should be characterized by the same label as the one that is used to describe the bombing of a nightclub in Bali in October 2002 or the indiscriminate killing of railway commuters in Madrid in March 2004. There are problems in using a single concept of terrorism to account for all forms of politically influenced violence or threat of violence.

State violence is of course widespread and is a subject in its own right (see Hagan, 1997 for a general criminological introduction). However, its context and social dynamics make it a very different type of activity to those pursued by non-state actors. States possess a monopoly over the means of coercion and apply force and violence against some of their citizens as well as those from other societies. Historically the right of the State to exercize force has rarely been questioned. In all societies a distinction is usually made between the use of violence by the State and by others. Unlike civilians, in certain circumstances police and military personnel are allowed to shoot and kill. Some may have ethical objections to this double standard regarding the application of violence. But it is worth remembering that this double standard is integral to the institutionalization of authority in the modern nation state.

Approaching the problem

The downside of conceptualizing terror as a form of violence associated with non-state actors is that it can easily be absorbed into an ideology that criminalizes individuals or groups who may have a legitimate cause to promote. However, the frequent manipulation of the terrorist label requires that we exercize care when we discuss the problem. Given the value laden and subjective character of the construction of the problem of terrorism it is tempting to avoid using the term altogether. This was the conclusion drawn by the BBC's World Service, when in the aftermath of 9/11 it decided not to use the word terrorist since to do so implied an 'improper value judgement' (cited in Jenkins, 2003: 18). Yet the problems that lead to the conceptualization of terrorism ought not be defined out of existence. Yes, there is a problem with the label terrorist—it is often used to mystify rather than clarify. But nevertheless there are a range of disturbing practices that need to be conceptualized through a distinct category. Twenty-first century terrorism has distinct features which will be discussed in the rest of this chapter.

Whilst any definition is unlikely to solve the problem of how to distinguish this form of political violence from others, it is possible to outline some of the significant features that are associated with contemporary terrorism. As many official and non-official definitions of this subject suggest, contemporary terrorism is self-consciously directed at non-combatants. These individuals are not hurt or killed by accident but are intentionally targeted. It is violence that is randomly directed at civilians. However, those who are killed are not the targets of terrorism. As Jackson notes, 'the identities of the actual targets or victims of the attack often were secondary or irrelevant to the terrorist objective of spreading fear and alarm or gaining concessions' (Lesser *et al.*, 1999: v). This form of violence is directed at civilians in order to create fear in others.

REVIEW QUESTIONS

1 Why are definitions of terrorism a continuous focus of contestation?

2 What do we mean when we say that 'terrorism is a social construction'?

Contemporary terrorism

Understanding the threat

Political violence has been around throughout most of history. Although often con-demned, politically motivated violence is not always considered to be a crime. The right to armed resistance against oppressive and coercive regimes is recognized by most polit-ical traditions. The case for a morally justifiable resort to political violence against a tyrannical regime is acknowledged within both the Christian and Western legal tradition and also within the Islamic worldview. Terrorism is a form of political violence that does not enjoy this legitimacy. Although terrorist tactics are sometimes linked to revolt and resistance, terrorism is generally regarded as a violation of prevailing moral norms. As Fred Halliday (2004) remarks, the stigma attached to terrorism has been 'remarkably resilient and universal'. He notes that 'the killings of women and children, of prisoners, or of groups of civilians are actions widely recognized in all cultures, religions and contexts as invalid in principle' (ibid. 6).

While non-state terrorist movements have been active since the nineteenth century, it is only in the recent period that they have been perceived as a significant if not principal threat to global stability. Since the end of the 1980s, the process of globalization has been experienced as one that encourages uncertainty, instability and the promotion of destructive forces. According to some accounts, global change has led to the disintegra-tion of previously stable countries and state systems. This development has stimulated the rise of religious, ethnic and other forms of internal conflicts, which in turn have helped consolidate a climate of global instability (Staten, 1999: 8). The fragmentation of the structural integrity of many societies has been linked to the rise of a variety of trans-national or non-state actors and to the emergence of a new breed of international terror-ists. It has been suggested that this new breed of 'postmodern' terrorists is particularly dangerous because for the first time such malcontents are able and are likely to access weapons of mass destruction (WMD) (see Laquer, 1996). The British House of Commons Select Committee on Defence has also expressed the view that society faces a new kind of terrorist. It noted, that:

> while the UK may be regarded as well geared up to deal with traditional terrorist threats in general, new forms of terrorism and other aspects of asymmetrical warfare such as the use of hostages, environmental degradation, cyberwar, black propaganda etc, may find us rather less well prepared (Select Committee on Defence 2002, para. 74).

The releasing of the nerve agent *sarin* in the Tokyo underground system in March 1995 marks an important watershed in the conceptualization of the global terorist. After Tokyo, terrorism 'was said to have made a qualitative leap' since for the first time a terrorist organization was prepared to discharge materials of mass destruction (Zanders, 1999). Yet, the impact of this experience on the conceptualization of asymmetric threat pales into insignificance in comparison to the way in which the events of 11 September have come to define the problem. The tragic events of 11 September have served to lend credence to the claim that terrorist threats represent the major challenge to global stability. As Delpech (2002) noted; 'to think that the leading world power would have found itself in the extraordinary position of needing to mobilize four aircraft carriers and 400 planes to oppose a non-state actor is astonishing' (Delpech, 2002).

There is a substantial body of opinion that equates the threat of terrorism with WMDs, particularly chemical and biological weapons (CBWs). This diagnosis of the problem clearly has an anticipatory character. The experience until now provides little evidence that non-state actors have the capability to deploy WMDs. It is in the sphere of information technology that new forms of techno-terrorism have been most successful. Although the significance of cyber-terrorism is often exaggerated, a variety of radical organizations have been successful in manipulating and destroying their opponents' information systems. More importantly, the easy availability of information technology has facilitated the mobility of networks devoted to the pursuit of political violence. 'The latest communications technologies are thus enabling terrorists to operate from almost any country in the world, provided they have access to the necessary IT infrastructure' argues an authoritative contribution on this subject (Zanini and Edwards, 2001: 38).

The characteristic feature of non-state terrorists

Although terrorist organizations are the product of a wide variety of circumstances and exist throughout the world, it is the Middle Eastern variety that appears to personify the problem. Frequently the threat posed by terrorism is ascribed to the power of religious ideology, especially that of Islam. 'Islamic fundamentalism represents a deep and coherent ideology stretching back fourteen centuries, and that is interiorized into the souls of millions of people' (Phillips, 2003: 101–102). The success of many Islamist movements notwithstanding, it is important not to interpret terrorism as an essentially religious phenomenon. As Halliday (2004) notes, the politics of terrorism has its roots in 'modern secular politics' and not in the distant past. It is both a product of and a revolt against modernity.

Unfortunately, the discussion and analyses of non-state actors is relatively underdeveloped and constitutes a weak link in the conceptualization of the problem. Many commentators cannot resist the temptation of using essentially moral or highly subjective categories to make sense of these individuals. Steele (1998) writes that 'when all is said and done, most men, and especially men from non-western cultures and less-developed areas, are capable of taking great pleasure in great evil' (ibid.: 79) Many other observers adopt the perspective of regarding 'them' as our moral opposites. Dunlap claims that 'likely future adversaries will be unlike ourselves'. He characterizes opponents as members of 'The New Warrior Class' 'who have acquired a taste for killing, who do not behave rationally, who are capable of atrocities that challenge the descriptive powers of language, and who will sacrifice their own kind in order to survive' (Dunlap, 1996: 2). Numerous observers promote the view that terrorists are behaving irrationally. For example it has been suggested that the great practitioners of terror—Stalin, Hitler, Pol Pot, Osama Bin Laden—what Robins and Post (1998) call charismatic terrorists suffer from a personality disorder. Apparently they have low self-esteem and end up blaming others.

It is difficult to ascribe a single cause or motive that can account for the pursuit of political violence. These acts are committed by a wide variety of individuals who often have very specific and sometimes very individual reasons for adopting this course of action. It is worth noting that that empirical research carried out on terrorists and suicide bombers does not support the idea that they are mentally unstable and irrational people. Scott Atran's (2003) research on the phenomenon of suicide bombers provides powerful evidence that suggests that these individuals are not irrational crazed people, but are frequently well-educated and stable members of their community.

From the previous analysis it should be evident that the abstract counterposition drawn between rational and irrational can lead to a miss-assessment of the dynamic of global terrorism. Even suicide bombing—which many in the West find incomprehensible—is motivated by the rational calculation that such tactics are likely to weaken the morale of the target population. As Sprinzak (2000) argues 'the perception that terrorists are undeterrable fanatics who are willing to kill millions indiscriminately just to sow fear and chaos belies the reality that they are cold, rational killers who employ violence to achieve specific political objectives' (ibid.: 4) Labelling such individuals as zealots and fanatics can lead to an underestimation or at least a misunderstanding of the problem. Sprinzak notes that the experience of 11 September indicates that 'some of the best and the brightest among the enemy would rather sacrifice themselves' for their cause. According to Sprinzak (2001) the people responsible for 9/11 can be seen as 'innovators' and 'developers' who are 'incessantly looking for original ways to surprise and devastate the enemy'.

One reason why the demonization of individuals engaged in political violence is counterproductive is that it helps transform them into omnipotent and unstoppable threats. Such an approach transforms them into a far more frightening and dangerous threat than is warranted by their capabilities. One possible consequence of this approach is to inflate public anxieties and thereby indirectly empower them.

Too great an emphasis on cultural differences—religion, value systems, morality—fails to take account of the fact that many individuals drawn towards terrorism are products of modern technologically advanced societies or have had considerable contact with life in western cultures. To take a few examples: members of the Rajneeshee cult, who employed biological agents to incapacitate many of the inhabitants of a small town in Oregon in 1984, were often American university-educated individuals; the *sarin* attack on the Tokyo underground in 1995 was carried out by a Japanese sect, whose members possessed considerable scientific and technological expertise. Likewise, some of the individuals involved in the first terrorist attack on the World Trade Centre were beneficiaries of American university education. Individual terrorists such as the 'Oklahoma bomber' Timothy McVeigh, an American Gulf War hero turned mass murderer, was no less prepared to inflict indiscriminate terror than his counterparts from different cultures. Similarly, the notorious 'una bomber', Theodore Kaczynski is a former university lecturer. Neither the British nail-bomber, David Copeland nor his fellow citizen Richard Reid, the alleged Al Queda operative, were brought up as members of a 'New Warrior Class'.

The problem of terrorism today is constituted through actors who are products of important changes within the global and domestic environment. One of the characteristic features of the so-called new terrorists is that they appear to be free of many of the constraints that curbed similar acts of violence in the past. The weakening of systems of state structures, the erosion of legitimate institutions and of shared values have played a significant role in the shaping of asymmetric threat. The process of globalization has provided new opportunities for non-state actors to develop powerful networks to sustain their operations. Halliday (2004) is right to draw attention to the fact that terrorism has emerged in 'rich and poor countries alike, as part of a transnational model of political engagement'. The global networks that underpin some of the terrorist organizations serve to enhance their influence. Hoffman claims that the problem is no longer confined to small groups of isolated individuals. The network associated with Osaman Bin Laden can mobilize 4,000–5,000 individuals scattered throughout the globe. He believes that 'the appearance of these different types of adversaries—in some instances with new motivations and different capabilities—accounts largely for terrorism's lethality in recent years' (Hoffman, 1999: 9).

Campbell (1997) believes that one of the distinguishing features of 'post-modern' terrorists is that they are 'free of constraints provided by sponsoring nation-states'. Many associated terrorist organizations have the character of free agents, whose activities transcend national boundaries and cultures. They are often mobile members of diasporic organizations who are unconnected to any formal state institutions. As a result they are freed from the geopolitical calculations that state actors are forced to make. These actors are not only less connected to formal institutions—they are often freed from accountability to a community and other forms of conventional networks. The erosion of a consensus around fundamental values about life also diminishes communal restraint. Throughout the world—and especially in the west—there has been a weakening of the prevailing value systems (see Hayward and Morrison, 2002: 146–50 for an account of this process in relation to contemporary terrorist activity). This has undermined many societies' ability to integrate and socialize its members. As a result many individuals drawn towards political violence are less restrained by such values and are therefore less accountable to conventional forms of behaviour than was the case in the past. The wider social and cultural disagreements about values actually free potential activists from having to justify their actions according to a specific ethos accepted by their community.

At a time of weakening state systems, the erosion of a sense of community and shared values, it makes little sense to attempt to label terrorists according to conventional political labels. In the past terrorist organizations could be labelled along ideological lines—conservative, revolutionary, religious or nationalist. Since the 1990s, as Sprinzak (2001) argues, this typology has been rendered, obsolete. Although these groups are 'not politically blind—they remain apolitical'. Since the end of the Cold War, the erosion of the distinction between left and right has rendered ideologically driven politics problematic. Tucker (2001) insists that because today's 'most pernicious terrorists are not motivated by political ideology on the far left or right' they are 'more likely to be extremists on the fringe of traditional religions or idiosyncratic cults with an apocalyptic mindset'. This shift of focus from political objectives is also stressed by Carter (2002). He argues that 'not in all cases, but at least in some important cases, the motivation for mass terror is a vengeful or messianic one, rather than a politically purposeful one'. As a result the actions of many radical movements has become less predictable and less oriented towards seeking political change. Instead of ideology, some movements have adopted a morally sanctioned worldview where ideas of evil and salvation influence behaviour. Such forms of behaviour often characterize movements involved in the so-called 'culture wars'. It also affects contemporary violent protest movements, for example, animal rights campaigners. What unites Western bred individuals like Timothy McVeigh and David Copeland with Islamic militants is the belief that their cause cannot be subject to conventional forms of restraint. As Tucker (2001) notes, today's terrorists 'experience fewer constraints on the use of violence to inflict indiscriminate casualties'. 'In these instances, the weakening of social capital lends individual grievances a cultural form'.

From research carried out by social psychologists, we know that individuals 'acting under the auspices of a group may feel that their personal accountability for the group's violent actions is diminished'. It is also suggested that, as a result, this diminished responsibility may lower individual thresholds of acceptability for violent behaviour' (Pynchon and Borum 1999: 345–6). What distinguishes some members of violent protest organizations from those of the past is that individual thresholds of acceptability for violent behaviour may become even lower in circumstances that prevail today (on this specific point see Chapter 11). With the intensification of social, institutional and community fragmentation, the actions of militants are less contained by conventional norms and sanctions. This reduction in accountability is particularly the case for mobile trans-national diasporic actors.

Finally, it is important to point out that the process of social fragmentation also encourages that of *individuation*. The general loosening of restraints also effects individual behaviour and may stimulate individual resentment to acquire a wider moral form. This may endow contemporary individual terrorism with a potentially more violent dimension. Developments in information technology help connect such individuals with one another and provide them with access to resources and ideas about how to conduct their affairs (See relatedly Chapter 8).

Conceptualizing the global problem of terrorism as the product of an estrangement from and rejection of modernity helps link this phenomenon to the wider social dynamic at work. The causes of individual cases of political violence are too numerous to be explained by a single set of variables. But it is not the existence of terrorism that represents a unique feature of the early twenty first century. Rather it is its ability to significantly destablize individual societies and the prevailing global order that constitutes the nub of the problem. And that is not merely the result of the actions of the terrorist but of the powerful forces of globalization that work to diminish the sense of common purpose in many societies.

REVIEW QUESTIONS

1 How do we account for the significance that contemporary society attaches to the problem of terrorism?

2 Discuss the concept of a 'post-modern' terrorist.

3 Is terrorism just politics pursued by other means?

4 Is state sanctioned violence just another form of terrorism?

CONCLUSION

The relationship between political violence and the criminal justice system has always been an uneasy one. It is important to note that not every form of political violence is criminalized and certainly not to the same extent. An analysis of the US media noted that the Irish Republican Army got a better press than the Puerto Rican FALN (Hewitt, 2003: 112). And while the Reagan Administration refused to describe anti-abortionist violence as terrorist, the Clinton one did. It is only in the past decade that the terrorist label has been applied to violent single issue campaigns such as the targeting of laboratories conducting animal experimentation or abortion clinics

Since terrorism is such a highly charged politicized concept there are considerable difficulties in treating it as a crime. Certainly, it is rarely treated as an ordinary crime. Since it is perceived as representing a threat to the security of society and the authority of the State, it is usually dealt with under special emergency powers. The official response to terrorism often exists in a state of tension between treating it as a crime—that is, as a normal law and order problem—or responding to this threat in a more militaristic fashion through the application of special anti-terrorist legislation (see Hamm 2004b for a recent critique of this approach in relation to the US Patriot Act). In fact almost every violent act associated with terrorism could be prosecuted through the normal laws of the criminal justice system. Since the stated aim of these laws is to protect the public from harm, it stands to reason that they ought to be applied in all circumstances. However, advocates of special anti-terrorist legislation claim that extraordinary powers are necessary for dealing with the unique threat posed by terrorism. But, it can be argued that the very act of treating terrorism as a special, unique and formidable threat serves to empower the terrorist as someone that cannot be dealt with through the normal institutions of society. It can also be argued that the use of special legislation serves to affirm the claim of those who argue that they are being persecuted for their beliefs rather than for their acts.

Although most governments and societies represent terrorism as a crime, they treat it as a problem that is quite distinct and one that requires special measures. Unlike a criminal who is seen to represent a threat to the wellbeing of the public, terrorism is perceived as a unique danger that threatens the very fabric of society. As a result organizations that are deemed dangerous are formally banned and membership in them is considered to be a criminal offence. For example, in February 2001, twenty-one international organizations were banned under the UK Terrorism Act 2000. These include organizations such as Al-Qaida, The Kurdistan Workers Party and Palestinian Islamic Jihad. One of the objectives of terrorist legislation is to curb the international activities of terrorists, particularly acts that transcend national boundaries. A variety of such acts—inciting terrorism abroad, financing terrorists overseas—are now prosecuted under special legislation on both sides of the Atlantic. Such legislation is frequently justified on the ground that the domestic criminal justice system is inappropriate for dealing with global threats to the functioning of society.

Anti-terrorist legislation is different to normal criminal legislation in that it actively seeks to pre-empt and not simply catch the perpetrators of a terrorist act. As a result such laws can turn into criminal offences people's beliefs, organizational affiliation, possession of certain literature and otherwise legal substances. Anti-terrorist legislation also allows authorities to detain and interrogate suspects in circumstances that are very different to what is acceptable under the criminal justice system. While such unusual powers appear to be necessitated by the extraordinary threat represented by the terrorist, the application of special anti-terrorist measures can be seen to represent a threat to civil liberties. Numerous commentators have pointed to the problem of enacting laws that have the potential for undermining the established liberties of a democratic society in the name of protecting freedom. As Wilkinson (1974: 109) noted:

if the government is provoked into introducing emergency powers, suspending habeas corpus, or invoking martial law, it confronts the paradox of suspending democracy in order to defend it. There is always the risk that by using heavy repression to crush the terrorist campaign the authorities may alienate the innocent mass of citizens caught up in the procedures of house-to-house searches and interrogations.

There is also the danger that a heavy-handed anti-terrorist policy could also end up repressing legitimate forms of dissent. Most governments have found it difficult to resist the temptation of adopting special powers to pre-empt and contain terrorism. Yet if governments adopt a cavalier attitude towards civil liberties they will surely play into the very hands of those who promote and perpetrate political violence.

QUESTIONS FOR DISCUSSION

1 Discuss the statement that 'Terrorism is in the eyes of the beholder'. Does the label terrorist necessarily represent a judgement of value?

2 How do we distinguish terrorism from other forms of violent crime?

3 What are the distinct features of twenty-first century terrorism?

4 Provide your definition of terrorism and explain the reasons for your choice.

5 Why and how could government over-reaction play into the hands of the terrorist?

GUIDE TO FURTHER READING

The following texts each provide interesting accounts of the debates and issues surrounding contemporary terrorism. They also, to varying degrees, attempt to confront the rhetoric and politics of fear that often surround these debates:

Arquilla, J. and Ronfeldt, D. (2001) *Networks and Netwars; The Future of Terror, Crime, and Militancy*, Santa Monica, CA: RAND.

Carter, A. Deutch, J. and Zelikow, P. (1998) 'Catastrophic Terrorism; Tackling the New Danger', *Foreign Affairs*, November/December.

Filler, D.M. (2003) 'Terrorism, Panic, and Pedophilia', *Journal of Social Policy and the Law*, Spring.

Hewitt, C. (2003) *Understanding Terrorism in America; From The Klan To Al Qaeda*, London: Routledge.

Jenkins, P. (2003) *Images of Terror: What We Can and Can't Know about Terrorism*, New York: Aldine de Gruyter.

Laqueur, W. (1999) *The New Terrorism: Fanaticism and the Arms of Mass Destruction*, New York: Oxford University Press.

Wilkinson, P. (1974) *Political Terrorism*, New York: Macmillan.

http://www.homeoffice.gov.uk/terrorism/index.html

The Home Office counter-terrorism website: these pages provide information for the public on the threat from international terrorism and accounts of what the Government is doing to protect, prevent and prepare for terrorist attacks.

http://www.terrorism.com

Website of the Terrorist Research Centre (see also http://www.terrorism.com/terrorism/documents.html for specific documents maintained by the Centre).

http://www.usinfo.state.gov/topical/pol/terror

US Department of State: Countering Terrorism.

http://www.hri.org/docs/USSD-Terror

US Department of State: Patterns of Global Terrorism Reports.

REFERENCES

Atran, S. (2003) 'Genesis of Suicide Terrorism', *Science* 299 March 7.

Best, J. (1999) *Random Violence; How we Talk about New Crimes and new Victims*. University of California Press: Berkely.

Campbell, J. (1997) *Weapons of Mass Destruction—Terrorism*, (www.interpactinc.com/home.html: Interpact press).

Card, C. (2003) 'Making War on Terrorism in Response to 9/11' in J.P. Sterba (2003) (ed) *Terrorism and International Justice*. New York: Oxford University Press, p.178.

Cohen, S. (2001) *States of Denial: Knowing About Atrocities and Suffering*. Oxford: Polity.

Crozier, B. (1974) *A Theory of Conflict*. London: Hamish Macmillan.

Delpech, T. (2002) 'The Imbalance of Terror', *The Washington Quarterly*, Winter 2002.

Dunlap, C. (1996) 'Sometimes The Dragon Wins; A Perspective on Information-Age Warfare' WebWarrior@Infowar.Com.

Filler, D.M. (2003) 'Terrorism, Panic, and Pedophilia', *Journal of Social Policy and the Law*, Spring issue.

Gearty, C. (2002) 'Terrorism and Morality', *European Human Rights Law Review*.

Gurr, T. (1979) *Violence in America*. New York: Sage Publications.

Hagan, F.E. (1997) *Political Crime*. Needham Heights, MA: Allyn and Bacon.

Halliday, F. (2004) 'Terrorism in historical perspective', *Open Democracy*, 22 April.

Hamm, M. (2002) *In Bad Company: America's Terrorist Underground*. Boston: Northeastern University.

Hamm, M. (2004a) 'Apocalyptic violence: the seductions of terrorist subcultures' *Theoretical Criminology* 8 (3) Special Edition: Cultural Criminology.

Hamm, M. (2004b) 'The US Patriot Act and the politics of fear' in J. Ferrell, K. Hayward, W. Morrison, and M. Presdee (eds) *Cultural Criminology Unleashed*. London: Glasshouse.

Hayward, K. J. and Morrison, W. (2002) 'Locating Ground Zero: caught between the narratives of crime and war' in J. Strawson (ed), *Law After Ground Zero*. London: Cavendish Press.

Hewitt, C. (2003) *Understanding Terrorism in America; From The Klan To Al Qaeda*. Routledge: London.

Hoffman, B. (1999) 'Introduction' in I.O. Lesser, B. Hoffman, J. Arquilla, D. Ronfeldt, M. Zanini and B. Jenkins (1999) *Countering The New Terrorism*. Santa Monica, Ca: RAND, MR–989.

Jackson, B.M. (1999) 'Foreword' in I.O. Lesser, B. Hoffman, J. Arquilla, D. Ronfeldt, M. Zanini and B. Jenkins (1999) *Countering The New Terrorism*, (RAND, MR–989 : Santa Monica, Calif.).

Jenkins, P. (2003) *Images of Terror: What We Can and Can't Know about Terrorism*. New York: Aldine de Gruyter.

Laqueur, W. (1996) 'Postmodern Terrorism', *Foreign Affairs*, Sept–October.

Laqueur, W. (1999) *The New Terrorism: Fanaticism and the Arms of Mass Destruction*. New York: Oxford University Press.

Lesser, I.O., Hoffman, B., Arquilla, J., Ronfeldt, D., Zanini, M. and Jenkins, B. (1999) *Countering The New Terrorism*. Santa Monica, CA: RAND.

Morrison, W. (2004) 'Criminology, genocide and modernity' in C. Sumner (ed) *The Blackwell Companion to Criminology*. Oxford: Blaclwell.

Oliverio, A. (1998) *The State of Terror*. Albany, NY: State University of New York Press.

Phillips, R.L. (2003) 'The war against pluralism' in J.L. Sterba (ed) (2003) *Terrorism and International Justice*. Oxford: Oxford University Press.

Pynchon, M.R. and Borum, R. (1999) 'Assessing Threats of Targeted Group Violence: Contributions from Social psychology', *Behavioral Sciences and the Law*, vol. 17.

Record, J. (2003) *Bounding The Global War On Terrorism*. Carlisle, PA: Strategic Studies Institute, available on http://www.carlisle.army.mil

Robins, R.S. and Post, J.M. (1998) *Political Paranoia: The Psychopolitics of Hatred*. New Haven, CO: Yale University Press.

Schmid, A. and Jongman, A. (1988) *Political Terrorism: A New Guide to Actors, Authors, Concepts, Data bases, Theories, and Literature*. New Brunswick, NJ: Transaction Books.

Select Committee on Defence (2001) *Eight-Report*, para.74. London: HMSO.

Sprinzak (2001) 'The Lone Gunmen', *Foreign Policy*, November.

Sprinzak, E. (2000) 'Rational Fanatics', *Foreign Policy*, September/October.

Sterba, J.L. (ed) (2003) *Terrorism and International Justice*. Oxford: Oxford University Press.

Thackrah, J.R. (2004) *Dictionary of Terrorism*. London: Routledge.

Williams, K.S. (2004) *Textbook on Criminology*. Oxford: Oxford University Press.

Wilkinson, P. (1977) *Terrorism and the Liberal State*. London: Macmillan.

Wilkinson, P. (1974) *Political Terrorism*. New York: Macmillan.

Wilkinson, P. (1976) 'Terrorism versus Democracy: The Problem of Response', *Conflict Studies*, no. 76.

Wilson N.B. (2003) 'Bibliographical Essay on Fear', *The Hedgehog Review*, Fall, vol.5, no.3.: 119.

Zanders, J.P. (1999) 'Assessing the Risk of Chemical and Biological Weapons Proliferation to Terrorists', *The Nonproliferation Review*, Fall.

Zanini, M. and Edwards, S. (2001) 'The Networking of Terror in the Information Age', in J. Arquilla, and D. Ronfeldt (eds) (2001) *Networks and Netwars: The Future of terror, crime, and militancy*. Santa Monica, CA: RAND.

Part Three

SOCIAL DIMENSIONS OF CRIME

16

Economic marginalization, social exclusion and crime

Chris Hale

INTRODUCTION

This chapter looks at a longstanding debate within criminology about the relationships between the economy, poverty and crime. Beginning with a review of what criminologists and others have to say about these factors it then considers the research evidence for links between unemployment, and more fruitfully the broader labour market, and crime. A more focused discussion of the links between poverty and crime follows, examining concepts such as the underclass and social exclusion. This will raise political issues of how to deal with these problems. For New Labour, integrating people into work is central to combating social exclusion and this links back to the discussion of the relations between the labour market and crime. At the centre of this debate lie not only matters of power and inequality, but also the need to question the nature of paid work and the position it takes within capitalist society.

BACKGROUND

'*The devil makes work for idle hands*'
'*Poverty is the mother of crime*'

These proverbs capture two strands of thought about the relationships between economic circumstances and crime. As with all folklore they contain a kernel of truth, but as with much 'common sense' they need interpreting with care.

The first suggests that work, gainful employment, is important in preventing crime. One take on this is that those who do not have jobs, the idle hands, are more likely to become involved in criminal pursuits, partly perhaps to provide resources for their daily needs and partly because they lack the discipline and structure going to work provides. As will be seen below, the relationship between unemployment and crime has been the site of much debate amongst criminologists. However, this is not the complete picture since it ignores the 'idle rich' and few suggest that they might benefit from the discipline of the workplace!

The second maxim suggests that poverty causes crime—that the poor will be more likely to be criminal. Again this seems sensible—those lacking in material resources may be forced into illegal behaviour to provide their daily bread, and further may have less to lose than the better off and so be less afraid of the consequences if their offending is discovered. Again it is silent about the crimes of the rich and the powerful where surely greed rather than need is more relevant. Space precludes examining the relationship between the economy and crimes of the powerful, but the interested reader is referred to Box (1987) and Tombs (Chapter 13 above).

So while this chapter will focus primarily on the debate around economic hardship and crimes such as burglary, vehicle theft and robbery, it should not be forgotten that this debate is a product of ideological emphasis on those types of crime that are more likely to be committed by the powerless than by the powerful.

There are theoretical arguments and empirical evidence to support the hypothesis that crime and the economy are related. Some, but not all, studies of the relationship between unemployment and crime have found a link. Other studies show that the poor and unemployed form a significant proportion of known offender populations. More broadly, work linking crime with wider economic changes in the structure of economy can be cited.

Critics of these positions will object that this is to label all the poor and unemployed as criminals, whereas most are upright law-abiding citizens. Further they will suggest that during the economic depression of the 1930s, when poverty was widespread and severe, crime was much lower than it has been throughout the period since 1945 when the standards of living of everyone in industrialized countries have improved considerably. Against this could be set the massive increase in recorded crimes in England and Wales during the severe recession between 1989 and 1992 and the fact that since 1992, the UK has had an unprecedented twelve years of steady economic growth accompanied by a steady decline in crime whether measured by police statistics or the British Crime Survey. This signals the danger of seeking a single explanation for crime. Social relationships are historically contingent; what may hold in one period may not in another because of broader social and cultural changes. In particular how problems related to economic hardship are dealt with, both formally and informally, how inequality and wealth are viewed will affect the relationship between crime and economic conditions.

REVIEW QUESTIONS

1 In what ways might being unemployed or poor increase the likelihood of engaging in crime?

2 In what ways might being in work or rich increase the likelihood of engaging in crime?

3 What were the differences between the 1930s and the 1960s in terms of crime and unemployment?

Why might economic conditions affect the level of crime?

What does social theory have to say about the relationship between economic conditions and crime? Despite being nearly twenty years old, Box (1987) still remains an excellent review of this area, so his approach is summarized and developed below. (See also Hayward and Morrison, Chapter 4 above for a wider discussion of the theories considered here.) As Box notes, many theories can be read in a way that predicts more crime when unemployment increases and income inequalities widen. What follows is a brief and selective look, at what some have had to say.

Strain theory

Strain theory tackles the question of motivation—why would anyone want to commit a crime? It argues people would conform to prevailing norms and laws were it not for stresses and contradictions in their lives. Two variations are identified, anomie leading to 'thwarted ambition' and relative deprivation caused by material inequalities in wealth.

Durkheim's concept of *anomie* (Durkheim, 1893 (1985)) describes a situation in society where rules are breaking down, or are blurred and confused so that people do not know what to expect of each other. This produces a feeling of isolation and a sense of meaninglessness in life. Durkheim was writing in the late nineteenth century after the massive upheavals of the Industrial Revolution that transformed predominantly rural agricultural societies into urban communities where manufacturing industry dominated. He was concerned with the problems of modernity and how society adapts to the increasing individualism accompanying it. For Durkheim, anomie—a state of normlessness—arises during periods of rapid social change and leads to dissatisfaction, conflict and deviance. Clearly this will happen during economic recessions, but it can also occur during periods of great prosperity. Many observers see changes in the late twentieth century, where industrialized countries have seen declining manufacturing industries and concomitant rises in the service sector, as producing similar effects.

Robert Merton adapted anomie as the basis of his strain theory (Merton, 1938). Unlike Durkheim, he does not argue the problem is sudden social change. Instead crime is one possible response to the strains produced by the unequal opportunities available for achieving success. Where the dominant culture values success in terms of material goods and economic status, crime would be expected to increase whenever legitimate opportunities to achieve such success are restricted. In a supposedly meritocratic society the major way for attaining material success is through education and hard work. During an economic recession, when unemployment rises and inequality widens, more people will experience a sense of failure to achieve these culturally defined goals and will be more likely to resort to illegal activities to achieve their aims. Note however that crime, termed by Merton as an innovative approach, is one of five possible responses to strain (see Hayward and Morrison, Chapter 4). Strain theory is a structural theory that posits disjuncture between culturally prescribed goals of success and the opportunity structure. There is a lack of fit between cultural goals and the means available to achieve them. More generally the theory would suggest crime would be a lower class phenomenon since they will have similar goals as middle and upper classes, but will lack the means to achieve them.

Relative deprivation is related to, but distinct from strain. As the name suggests it refers to relative, rather than absolute poverty, hence to the distribution of wealth and income across society. Wealth and income can be increasing for all individuals, but relative deprivation will also increase if the gap between rich and poor increases. For example, one objective measure often used is to compare the income of the top 10 per cent income earners with that of the lowest 10 per cent. To take an artificial example, if the income of the top decile triples while that of the bottom only doubles, then inequality has increased.[1] Clearly the UK is a richer society today than it was 100 years ago and that applies not just to economic wealth but also in matters such as health and education. However, whether or not it is a more equal society is a different matter. At an individual level it is possible to be well off and still feel relatively deprived. For example, I feel poor when I compare myself to Bill Gates but rich when I look at the homeless in my local town. As well as the objective situation, an awareness of one's position is also important. In modern society people are continually bombarded by media images and definitions of what constitutes the 'good life'. This usually involves consumption adding to the sense of unfairness of those unable to afford designer labels and expensive holidays. Similarly in urban areas the stratification of neighbourhoods is less marked than it used to be with the process of gentrification that follows the move of the middle classes into poorer neighbourhoods. Relative deprivation has become a popular explanation for crime, because for long periods in the second half of the twentieth century—in the industrialized economies at least—rising living standards have been accompanied by rising crime. Note that, unlike strain theory, relative deprivation does not necessarily suggest that crime is a lower class phenomenon, amongst societies' 'losers' since it accepts that discontent '. . . can be felt anywhere in the class structure where people perceive their rewards to be unfair compared to those with similar attributes' (Young, 2001). Nevertheless, a sense of relative deprivation is likely to be more pronounced for those whose economic position is least secure especially during periods of economic recession when unemployment increases and wage levels are likely to be depressed.

Social disorganization theory—The Chicago School

The Chicago School is famous for the links it established between environmental factors and crime (see Hayward and Morrison, Chapter 4 and Hayward, 2001 for more detail). An important part of this work is the idea of a zone of transition within cities, characterized by run-down housing, high residential mobility and high levels of poverty and poor health. It is the first home for immigrants who remain only long enough to become economically established before moving to more prosperous neighbourhoods. So the 'zone of transition' is a place of constant change, where communal ties are difficult to establish and most relationships impersonal. Such neighbourhoods were described as socially disorganized and as a consequence were likely to be low in informal methods of social control and high in crime. In Chicago, Shaw and McKay (1942) tested this hypothesis and found that delinquency rates were '. . . at their highest in run-down inner city areas and progressively declined the further one moved into the prosperous suburbs' (Hayward, 2001: 31). Generalizing these ideas, it seems a logical step to posit that in times and neighbourhoods where unemployment is high or economic prospects are poor it will be difficult to muster the necessary resources to combat social disorganization and maintain informal social control. Hence, again an argument suggests deteriorating economic conditions will lead to increasing levels of crime.

Economic theory: rational economic (wo)man

The economic model of crime posits individuals who choose between crime and legitimate work depending on the opportunities, rewards and costs of each. Thus, individuals choose to work or to commit a crime depending on the chances of getting a job and the wages in the legitimate market compared with opportunities for illegal earnings, the risk of being caught and the probability and severity of punishment if they undertake criminal activity (for an alternative to this calculating approach to crime that emphasizes its expressive attraction, see Ferrell, Chapter 7 above). Whilst originally this was posited as choice between legitimate and illegitimate work (Becker, 1968; Erhlich, 1973) more recently it has been extended to allow for individuals to engage in both crime and legitimate work during the same period of time. It will be argued below that this is particularly important in periods when many jobs are part-time, low quality, have little or no security, and are poorly paid. Again this theory suggests that as economic returns from paid employment deteriorate or disappear, crime will increase.

Control theory

Control theory avoids implicating social structure, its focus on individual responsibility appealing to those of a conservative political leaning. It asks not why do people commit crime, but rather how they are constrained not to offend, seeing offending as a natural human instinct. Individuals and their internalization of moral rules and codes become a key focus. One variant, Hirschi's social bond theory (Hirschi, 1969), emphasizes how social bonds to family, school, work, everyday activities and beliefs insulate people against deviant behaviour. The theory argues that those who:

- are high in *attachment*, with close emotional links to others;
- have a strong *commitment* to the future in that they believe conventional behaviour will lead to immediate or long-term rewards;
- have *involvement* so that they are kept busy in conventional activities such as school or work;
- hold the 'right' *beliefs* about what is permissible or not, that is beliefs that coincide with conventional rules and norms

are less likely to be involved in deviant or unlawful behaviour. At first sight this does not look hopeful for those seeking theoretical arguments relating unemployment and poverty to crime.

However, as Box (1987) argues, economic recession and unemployment might be expected to weaken social bonds and hence lead to increased levels of crime. Consider first *attachment*. Unemployment and increasing inequality are not likely to improve family relationships. Rather they will produce increased tension, anger and sullenness against society that may be transferred onto the family leading to its breakdown. This fracture of attachment within the family may lead some to become involved in crime as they care less about what others think of them. Turning to *commitment*, Box (1987: 45) suggests that unemployment 'casts a long shadow' over institutions that are supposed to prepare people for employment. Here he has in mind particularly schools, that risk being delegitimized if their role in preparing pupils for the discipline of work seems redundant as prospects of future employment appear reduced. Next he argues that individual *beliefs* in the legitimacy of conformity will weaken as recession undermines families and schools and this will damage the ability of one generation to impress its values on the next. Alert readers will have spotted that *involvement* has been skipped over. Surprisingly, Box does not consider this factor in his discussion, although it seems straightforward to integrate it in his approach. With more unemployment, shorter working hours and more part-time work, people will have less involvement in conventional activity and social bond theory would suggest that crime would increase.

Later work by Hirschi developed, or many would argue restricted, control theory most notably in his 1990 collaboration with Gottfredson under the rather grand title of *A General Theory of Crime* (Gottfredson and Hirschi, 1990). This rejected social bond theory conceiving of control instead as '. . . a permanent internal state' (Lilly *et al.*, 2002). As these authors note, this was part of a broader trend during the 1980s to prioritize individual, rather than structural, explanations of social problems. According to Gottfredson and Hirschi self-control, developed during early childhood, is the key factor that restrains people from engaging in crime. For them self-control depends on the quality of parenting during a child's early years. Ineffectual and neglectful parents will raise children who '. . . tend to be impulsive, insensitive, physical (as opposed to mental), risk-taking, short-sighted and nonverbal, and they will tend therefore to be engage in criminal and analogous acts' (Gottfredson and Hirshi, 1990). This somewhat depressing picture suggests that nothing can be done to correct traits already set firm in early years. And what of unemployment and recession? Harriet Wilson's work on socially deprived families in inner Birmingham (Wilson, 1980) looked at the degree of 'chaperonage' parents gave to their children. She found a:

> . . . very close association between lax parenting methods (and) severe social stress. Lax parenting methods are often the result of chronic stress, situations arising *from frequent or prolonged spells of unemployment* (emphasis added), physical or mental disabilities among members of the family and an often permanent condition of poverty . . . It is the position of the most disadvantaged groups in society, and not the individual which needs improvement in the first place.

So again, control theory is combined with a strong structural analysis. But the implications for the relationship between unemployment and crime are different. Parenting might be expected to deteriorate in times of recession. However, the effect on crime would not be immediate. Rather it would impact in perhaps eight to ten years time. Dealing with today's crime problems would have required action a decade ago.

Opportunity and routine activity theory

These argue that, in order for a crime to occur, three things are needed—a motivated offender, a suitable target and a lack of guardianship (see Hayward and Morrison, Chapter 4). Cantor and Land (1985) suggest rising unemployment will have two effects tending to increase the numbers of motivated offenders and the level of guardianship. The reasons behind the first effect have already rehearsed. According to Cantor and Land (1985: 350) the second arises because the increased numbers of unemployed means that more individuals will remain at home and hence both reduce the risks of their property being burgled and provide more informal social control within neighbourhoods. At the same time, the fact that the unemployed are not involved in daily travel to and from work may reduce their risk of becoming victims of street crime. Hence they argue unemployment has two opposite effects on crime. On one hand crime will tend rise as unemployment potentially causes the numbers of motivated offenders to rise. On the other hand, more unemployed will mean increased levels of guardianship that will tend to cause crime to fall.

Having swiftly reviewed theories that suggest crime is related to economic conditions—mainly the level of unemployment—the next step is to consider what, if any evidence exists to support of refute the hypothesis.

REVIEW QUESTIONS

1 What is meant by anomie?

2 What are the differences between relative and absolute deprivation?

3 Why might crime fall as unemployment increases?

What is the evidence for a relationship between crime and the economy?

It is worth beginning with some observations of Radzinowicz. In two classic papers looking at the economy and crime (Radzinowicz, 1939; 1971) he suggests that the more multifaceted the economic structure of society becomes, the harder it is to measure cycles of depression or prosperity. While relatively straightforward in a simple agricultural community in a complex industrial society measuring economic change is more complicated and relating these changes to trends in crime a more demanding task. Hence it will be necessary to use multiple economic indices rather than relying on single measures such as unemployment. Radzinowicz counsels that economic change may not influence crime at once but at some time in the future—there will be a lagged effect. Further, he makes the important point that economic conditions appear to affect certain types of crime more than others. He suggests property crime is the most sensitive and likely to decrease in times of prosperity. Conversely, crimes against the person seem to go up in times of economic growth.

Unemployment and crime

It has proved difficult to reach anything approaching a consensus on the unemployment-crime (U-C) relationship. As well as reviewing the evidence it is hoped to persuade the reader that a broader view of economic influences than just unemployment is needed. Others factors including the quality of employment, wage rates and the precariousness of employment also need considering.

Two major surveys of the statistical work on unemployment and crime are Chiricos (1987) and Box (1987). Both concluded that, while not consistent, the evidence was slightly in favour of there being a positive relationship, as unemployment increases crime will rise. However, as Chiricos comments, the period covered by most of the studies were dominated by the years up to the 1970s when unemployment was much lower than during the following two decades. Further, he also noted that the evidence for a positive relationship was stronger in studies that focused on property crimes.

As noted above, Cantor and Land (1985) use opportunity theory to explain why negative relationships may arise as unemployment leads to increased guardianship. Positive U-C relationships can be explained by the increased motivation to offend as unemployment grows. Hence in any particular study crime may rise, remain constant or fall as unemployment rises depending on the relative strengths of the two effects. Whatever the merits[2] of their argument Cantor and Land alert us to the need to take a more nuanced approach to unemployment and crime.

More recently, studies have questioned the focus on the U-C link when examining relationship between the economy and crime. Pyle and Deadman (1994) argue that unemployment may not be the best indicator of the State of the economy. At a practical level the definition of unemployment and its measurement underwent numerous revisions during the 1980s making it difficult to construct a consistent data series over a long period of time. (Unsurprisingly, the changes always reduced the numbers of unemployed entitled to benefit.) Further, they argue unemployment lags behind the business cycle by between six and twelve months. An economic recession will affect the labour market first through reduced overtime, more part-time work and falling wages. Unemployment will begin to rise only after the recession has been underway for some time. However if property crime increases in response to worsening economic conditions, to falling standards of living brought about by the aforementioned reduced overtime and so on, the time lag before unemployment rises suggests it may not capture the observed effect. Instead Pyle and Deadman suggest using other economic indicators that more closely track the business cycle, such as Gross Domestic Product or Consumers' Expenditure.

Other approaches to the relationship between the economy and crime

Field (1990) in a classic study found consumer expenditure was the best economic indicator for explaining crime. Twelve different categories of crime were examined using annual time series data for England and Wales. As well as economic variables, Field controlled for a wide range of demographic, criminal justice and environmental effects using multivariate statistical techniques. He concluded that economic factors have a major influence on the trends in both property crime (including burglary, theft, robbery, vehicle crime, criminal damage and fraud) and personal crime (including violence against the person, thefts from the person (excluding robbery) and sexual offences).

For property crime and consumption he found two opposite effects. In the short-run, year-on-year changes in consumption were negatively, or inversely, related to changes in crime. Field ascribes this to a motivational effect where individuals will switch in and out of criminal activity as their economic fortunes decline or improve. In the long-run, over a period of several years he found a positive or direct relationship between crime and the rate of growth of consumption. This he interpreted as an opportunity effect since in a growing economy there will be more goods and money available to steal.

Field's statistical models found that personal crime behaved quite differently from property crime. In both the short- and the long-term he found that personal crime is positively related to consumer expenditure. He suggests this is because increasing consumption leads to an increase in the amount of time spent outside the home and so increases the likelihood of being the victim of a personal attack. This is (probably) also linked to increased alcohol consumption as incomes rise (see Wincup, Chapter 10 above). Again care must be taken in interpreting these findings. In particular it might be asked whether domestic violence is likely to follow this pattern. Are decreasing incomes and increasing unemployment likely to lead to less spouse abuse?

Pyle and Deadman (1994) and Hale (1998) while improving on Field's statistical techniques confirmed his findings of short-run linkages between the economy and property crime: other things being equal it increases as economy declines. This held whether GDP, personal consumption or unemployment was used as the economic indicator. Moreover, for burglary and theft they found positive long-run relationships between crime and economic growth, indicating that for the period under consideration (1950–91), the growing economy led to increased crime.

Notwithstanding the mixed results on the U-C relationship it would seem foolish to ignore unemployment or more generally economic inactivity when attempting to explain crime. One issue that needs more consideration is how to measure unemployment. Aside from the problems of definitional and measurement change noted above, it is not clear that a single measure is appropriate. Chamlin and Cochran (2000) discuss various alternatives but argue that for property crime long-term or permanent unemployment is the best measure. Using UK data, Carmichael and Ward (2000) find that youth unemployment is positively related to criminal damage and robbery while adult unemployment is linked to theft. Their research found burglary to be positively related to both youth and adult unemployment.

The conclusion to which we are tentatively moving is that while the U-C relationship is likely to be important in many circumstances it is important to look at broader economic factors than unemployment.

Crime and the changing labour market

Hale (1999) uses data from England and Wales to explore the impact of broader labour market changes as well as unemployment on crime between 1946 and 1994. He argues that the UK economy, and particularly its labour market, has undergone fundamental changes in this period. There has been:

- a shift in employment from the manufacturing to the service sector;
- an increase in part-time employment and an accompanying increase in numbers employed in temporary and untenured jobs;
- a shift in the patterns of employment from men to women.

A dual labour market has developed with a primary or core sector and a secondary or peripheral sector. The primary sector consists of skilled workers usually working full-time for large organizations with good employment and benefit rights. On the other hand, those in the secondary sector are either unemployed or have a high propensity to be unemployed at some time. They have low skills, and when working, low wages. They are more likely to be employed part-time and have few rights to benefits with regard to sickness, holiday or pensions. The secondary sector is characterized by high labour turnover among the least skilled workers. For those at the margins:

Employment in the 1990s has become far more unstable. The penalties attached to job loss, jobless duration, and the reduced wages on return have risen. Hence, the secondary labour market has become far riskier. However this new insecurity has been concentrated on a minority for whom jobs for life will become the stuff of legends. (Gregg *et al.* 1996: 89)

In his empirical analysis Hale (1999) concentrated on de-industrialization, the shift from manufacturing to service sector jobs. This general approach was linked to the work of Allen and Steffensmeier (1989), on the relationship of youth crime to the quality of jobs available, and to that of Carlson and Michalowski (1999) which focuses on de-industrialization and crime. Allen and Steffensmeier show that for juveniles it is the availability of employment that matters whereas for young adults it is the quality of employment that is important: part-time work with low pay leads to higher rates of property crime. Braithwaite *et al.* (1992),[3] looked at the impact of the increased participation of women in the labour market[4] on crime in Australia. They contend that increased female employment may lead to increased crime in a patriarchal society if appropriate measures are not introduced to '. . . "take up the slack" in the traditional female role of guardianship' (Triggs, 1997). The mechanisms they identify for this link between crime and female employment include:

- supervision—women in traditional roles: (a) guard their own homes and those of neighbours during the day; (b) look after children who, if unsupervised, are more likely to be both offenders and victims;
- opportunity and motivation—women in the labour force may have more opportunity to commit crime; conversely of course their motivation might decrease. Victimization of working women might increase if they are out more or if domestic tensions increase. Conversely of course domestic tensions might decrease if the household economic situation improves via female wage contribution.

Similar results using US data may be found in Witt and Witte (1998) and for the UK Hale (1999). Hansen (2003) argues that increased female participation in the labour market is likely to have had two effects. First, increasing the supply of labour will tend to lower wages rates. Second, given that the increased employment of women is mainly in part-time unskilled work, this increased supply is likely to increase male unemployment. This will particularly be the case amongst young, less well-educated men most likely to commit property offences. Using cross-section data from England and Wales, she shows that areas with higher rates of female labour force participation are likely to have higher levels of recorded crime.

Crime and inequality

These changes in the labour market interact with broader household changes and have contributed to the growth in income inequality (McRae, 1997).[5] During the past three decades inequality in the UK grew more rapidly than in any other industrialized nation (Atkinson and Micklewright, 1992; Rowntree Report, 1995). This process accelerated during the 1980s. Since 1979, the lowest income groups have not benefited from economic growth and the proportion of the population receiving less than half the average income trebled (Rowntree Report, 1995). There was also a rapid growth in the numbers living in low-income families with children. Hale (1999) used two separate measures for inequality. The first was the Gini coefficient, which captures the level of income inequality in the whole population, and the second the ratio of the share of income going to the highest 10 per cent of earners with that going to the lowest 10 per cent. He found that the second measure was positively related to growth in burglary.[6]

The growing polarization between 'work rich' and 'work poor' households has reinforced patterns of poverty and inequality. For example, while employment is as plentiful as it was thirty years ago, the numbers of workless households has roughly quadrupled (Gregg *et al.* (1999)).[7] One in five children in Britain are growing up in workless households.

Wage inequality in the UK reached record highs for the twentieth century at the beginning of the 1990s. A key factor in this increased inequality was the rapid deterioration in the labour market position of less skilled workers at the bottom end of the wage distribution. The economic model of crime argues that individuals will choose between legal and illegal work on the basis of their relative rewards. Many individuals find that, whilst in work, their jobs are insecure, low-paid, and low-skilled. Often they are in part-time or temporary work and they are on the economic and social margins. Many of the theoretical arguments presented above for why unemployment and crime might be related apply equally well to that between low wage, low-skill employment. The importance of exploring these issues in any model of crime is underlined by the results of analyses by Reilly and Witt (1996), Witt, *et al.* (1998, 1999), Hansen and Machin (2004) and Machin and Meghir (2000). Witt *et al.* (1998) find a positive relationship between widening (male) wage inequality and crime (see also Borooah and Collins, 1995).

Recent work using US data has looked at the statistical relationship between crime and low wages. Gould *et al.* (2002) find significant negative relationships across areas between changes in wages and changes in recorded burglary, aggravated assault and robbery. Grogger (1998) shows that falling wages explain not only rising youth crime, but also age and ethnic differences. For England and Wales, Machin and Meghir (2003) analyse property crime (burglary plus theft and handling) at the police force area level from 1975 to 1996. They show that over this period falls in the wages of unskilled workers lead to increases in property crime.

In a similar vein Hansen and Machin (2005) examined the impact of the introduction of the minimum wage in England and Wales in April 1999. This gave a pay increase to an estimated two million low paid workers. Within an economic model of crime this would decrease the relative benefits of criminal as opposed to legal activity and so might be expected to persuade those on the margins not to engage in criminal activity and hence to reduce crime. Police force areas that gained most were those with the highest proportions of workers paid less than the new minimum prior to April 1999.[8] Hansen and Machin examined crime rates before and after its introduction. They looked at total crime, property crime, vehicle crime[9] and violent crime (violence against the person) and found that, on average, areas that benefited most from the minimum wage saw the greatest decreases in crime.

As well as wages, social security benefits might be expected to have an impact on crime levels by mediating the effects of unemployment and economic recession. If welfare payments are cut, or their eligibility criteria tightened, then the economic benefits from crime would increase. Machin and Marie (2004) consider the impact of the introduction of the Jobseekers Allowance (JSA) in Britain in October 1996. Replacing both unemployment benefit and income support, it brought about major changes in benefit entitlement. The period of non-means tested contributory benefits was reduced from twelve months to six and the requirements for job seeking tightened by stopping benefit where an individual was judged not to be actively seeking work. Although the idea behind the JSA is persuade people back to work, Machin and Marie point out unemployment may fall not by getting people back to work (or into education or training), but because they move off benefits and suffer an income cut. In such circumstances they are likely to find crime more attractive. They present evidence that crime rose by more in the areas more affected by JSA. Hence they argue that the benefits sanctions may have caused individuals previously on the margins to turn to crime.

Crime, the underclass and social exclusion

Crime and its relationship to poverty re-appeared in the last decades of the twentieth century as part of a politically right-wing response to the perceived failings of the welfare state. Cushioned by the welfare state so that they become 'welfare dependent', many were unable to stand on their own two feet.

Right realism saw crime and other social problems as the product of individual characteristics rather than the result of any structural factors. Criminality was voluntaristic, committed by individuals with no self-control who choose crime as well as unemployment and poverty.

Particularly relevant here is the work of Charles Murray (1984, 1990), who used the notion of the underclass.[10] For Murray the important distinguishing characteristic of the underclass is not that they are poor, although that is one characteristic but that they are not respectable. 'Their homes were littered and unkempt. The men in the family were unable to hold a job for more than a few weeks at a time. Drunkenness was common. The children grew up ill-schooled and ill-behaved . . .' (Murray, 1990: 1)

For Murray, the underclass has three main characteristics: illegitimacy; violent crime; and economic inactivity. Murray essentially sees a segregated society. On the one hand are those sectors upholding traditional values of hard work, sobriety and family; on the other the morally weak underclass who are unemployed, involved in crime, and drug addiction and have illegitimate children raised by single mothers living on welfare. For Murray this is a matter of choice and hence the solution is to reduce welfare payments for unmarried mothers to encourage the avoidance of pregnancy without working supportive fathers and the reduction of unemployment benefits to encourage those capable of work to seek employment. The problem of crime in Murray's view is that increasing numbers of young men are being brought up without positive male role models and are avoiding the civilizing institutions of marriage, family and work, preferring to live on welfare or illegal activities.

Murray sees the habitual criminal as a classic member of the underclass living off the mainstream society without contributing to it. Indeed the definitive sign that an underclass has developed is that '. . . large numbers of young healthy, low income males *choose* not to take job' (Murray, 1990: 17) [italics added]. The key word here is of course 'choose' as Murray believes that, as well as unemployed workers who are actively seeking work, there is a large group of 'economically inactive' people, some of whom have opted not to work.

The notion of the underclass is not unique to Murray and indeed under another name 'socially excluded' is prominent in the writings of those of the left and indeed central to much of New Labour thinking. The terms are different, but the people who Murray would include in his underclass are the same as those who are regarded as socially excluded. Social exclusion covers not just poverty but also political and spatial exclusion and the notion that the excluded are denied access to '... information, medical provision, housing, policing, security etc' (Young, 2002: 457). These factors interact and reinforce each other to the extent that those who experience the exclusion are denied the chance to participate fully as citizens. Whilst the symptoms of the underclass and the socially excluded are similar, the latter implies the issue is a structural problem rather than the fault of the individual. Hence there are here two variants of social exclusion: the weak and the strong (Veit-Wilson, 1998; Bryne, 1999). The 'weak' version, following Murray, emphasizes individual weaknesses that prevent full participation in society. The dysfunctional members of the underclass have chosen their lot and must be 'encouraged' to participate in the low wage labour market of poor quality work by attacking the dependency culture encouraged by the welfare state. The 'strong' version sees the problems at the structural level, driven by economic globalization that has led to the rapid changes in the labour markets of industrialized countries driven by the decline in manufacturing and the rise of precarious employment in the service sector discussed above. Young (2002) sees two approaches within explanations that see social exclusion as a result of structural problems. He distinguishes between on the one hand a 'passive' and active version. The first, most notably in the work William Julius Wilson (Wilson, 1987; 1996) sees the problems resulting from the failure of the system to provide jobs leading to '... "social isolation" wherein people lose not so much the motive to work but the capacity to find work because of lack of positive role models coupled with a spatial isolation from job opportunities' (Young, 2002: 458). The second emphasizes the active rejection of the underclass by society. In a story that should by now be familiar, it stresses the '... downsizing of industry, the stigmatization of the workless and the stereotyping of the underclass as criminogenic and drug-ridden with images that are frequently racialized and prejudiced' (Young, 2002: 458).

These distinctions are important when looking at the policies of New Labour. Whilst accepting the arguments that social exclusion is a structural problem, it has nevertheless adopted policies that blame the victim by locating solutions at the individual level. The Social Exclusion Unit (SEU) was set up in 1997 and has looked tackle a wide range of issues including deprived neighbourhoods, unemployment, drug use, teenage pregnancy, truancy, school exclusion—a list of the classic symptoms of social exclusion. To stress the interconnectedness of the problems and hence the need for 'joined-up' solutions it works across government departments and is the responsibility of the Deputy Prime Minister. The SEU is clear that social exclusion is a major factor in both crime and fear of crime, and that in turn these are part of the interlinked facets of the problem (Social Exclusion Unit, 2001). Whilst acknowledging the (global) economic and social changes that have taken place they see the problem of crime and social exclusion as related to issues of socialization and lack of control in young people related to poor parenting and inadequate schooling together with drug and alcohol abuse. Having first identified the problems at a structural level the emphasis, as Matthews and Young (2003) point out, shifts to an implicit control theory. Central to New Labour's strategy of combating social exclusion, and hence being tough on the causes of crime is entry into work. Any work is better than no work, and of course unpaid work is not proper work. So the focus has been persuading the unemployed and excluded back to work by threatening to cut benefits and offering re-training programmes. Evidence that suggested work per se is not the answer; that poorly paid work on part-time work with little security and sense of worth does not reduce crime in the long run was reviewed above. As Currie (1998) has shown inclusionary policies that focus on work as the mechanism where work involves long and inflexible hours serve to undermine the family and community and hence weaken rather than strengthen social control. As explored in Hale (Chapter 21 below) this has been coupled with a political emphasis on being tough on crime that has increased rather decreased social exclusion by pushing crime and disorder to the margins of society (see the references below to Trickett *et al.*).

Victims, inequality and crime

Thus far the focus has been on the economic circumstances of offenders and the relationship between crime and the business cycle. What of the economic situation of victims? In England and Wales the best source of information on this are the somewhat inappropriately named British Crime Surveys (BCS).[11]

The most recent information comes from the 2002/03 BCS (Simmons and Dodd, 2003). This examines how crime victimization risk varies according to neighbourhood. The highest risk areas for burglary are: (a) town and city areas whose residents are well off professional singles and couples; and (b) council estates with, elderly, lone parent or unemployed residents. For both the risk is 5 per cent compared to 3 per cent across households in England and Wales as a whole. Within the second group, households on estates with the greatest hardship have a burglary victimization risk of 6.9 per cent—over twice the national risk. For vehicle related thefts while 11 per cent of all vehicle-owning households were victims this rose to 21 per cent in the highest risk areas, described as multi-ethnic low-income neighbourhoods. Again the highest risk of violence, at 7 per cent, was to adults in multi-ethnic low income areas compared to the overall average of 4 per cent.

More generally the risk of crime victimization is unequally spread across society and follows the pattern suggested by Ulrich Beck in his book *The Risk Society*:

> The history of risk distribution shows that, like wealth, risks adhere to the class pattern, only inversely; wealth accumulates at the top, risks at the bottom. To that extent, risks seem to strengthen, not to abolish the class society. Poverty attracts an unfortunate abundance of risks. By contrast, the wealthy (in income, power or education) can purchase safety and freedom from risk (Beck, 1992: 35)

In a series of papers researchers from the University of Manchester Quantitative Criminology Group have analysed the unequal distribution of victimization across neighbourhoods. Their work, combining BCS and Census data, shows that around a fifth of the victims of household property crime in England and Wales live in the 10 per cent of residential areas with the highest crime rates and account for over a third[12] of the total of household property crime (see, for example, Hope, 2003; 2001). Twenty per cent of communities in England and Wales have over a third of all property crime victims and suffer over half of all property offences. At the other end of this crime spectrum, the least victimized 50 per cent areas suffer only 15 per cent of the crime and contain just 25 per cent of the victims. Moreover, when Census data on income and deprivation are considered a stark picture emerges of crime risk increasing markedly with area deprivation. Crime adds to the disadvantage suffered by the least well off groups in society and adds to their social exclusion. What is more, Trickett *et al.* (1995) show that during the 1980s, a decade when the long-term trend to greater equality of wealth, income and opportunity was rapidly reversed, inequality of victimization also became more marked.

This redistribution of crime victimization can also be seen in the regional figures. The North-South divide in terms of economic and demographic trends—with economic and population growth in the latter at the expense of the former, exacerbated by de-industrialization—was again inversely reflected in patterns of crime victimization. During the 1980s the North's disproportionate share of property crime increased relative to the South and to Greater London in particular (Trickett *et al.*, 1995: 353). Hence, crime contributes to the very inequality and social exclusion that are seen as its causes.

REVIEW QUESTIONS

1 Why might an increase in female employment cause crime to rise?

2 What are the differences between the concepts of the 'underclass' and 'social exclusion'?

3 Will creating more part-time, low paid jobs necessarily reduce crime?

CONCLUSION

This chapter has considered the impact of economic conditions on crime. Inevitably some topics of importance have been ignored. As noted earlier, the focus has been on crimes such as burglary and theft rather than those that might be described as corporate and white collar. That is not to imply that in times of economic downturn these will not also increase as competitive pressures increase the incentives for individuals and businesses to cut corners and bend and break the law in order to survive (see Tombs, Chapter 13 above). Indeed the notion that market economies based on competition and rewarding risk taking might encourage criminality has not been developed. Finally, violent crime might also have been considered, but for constraints on space. Again the evidence suggests that the long-term trend has been for violence to decline as countries' economies develop. Broadly speaking, comparative analysis suggests that rates of violence in industrialized countries are lower than in less wealthy economies. However, in the short run it seems that economic booms lead to increased levels of violence fuelled at least in part by increased alcohol consumption (see Ray, Chapter 11; Wincup, Chapter 10).

Turning to work, on balance both the theoretical arguments and the empirical evidence reviewed support the hypothesis that deteriorating economic circumstances will lead to increased property crime. Unemployment, poverty, inequality and low wages have all been found to be related to property crime in one study or another. Other work suggests that the quality of work available may also be key.

The growth in the secondary labour markets, with precarious employment in low paid, part-time work, that have been the consequence of the process of globalization and economic restructuring over the last thirty years have had an impact on crime similar to that of the nineteenth century when the Industrial Revolution caused major ruptures in the established structures of society. However, the work reviewed here also questions whether strategies to combat social exclusion based on encouraging people back to paid employment will necessarily succeed since it is not work per se that is important but its quality and the satisfaction it provides.

QUESTIONS FOR DISCUSSION

1 What do the main criminological theories have to say about the relationship between crime and the economy?

2 Compare and contrast the policy approaches of the New Right to the underclass with those of New Labour to social exclusion.

3 Is unemployment the main factor to consider when examining the relationship between crime and the economy?

4 Why might corporate crime increase during economic recessions?

GUIDE TO FURTHER READING

Box, S. (1987) *Recession, Crime and Punishment*, London: Macmillan.
This is as good a place as any to find a review of this field.

Gregg, P. and Wadsworth, J. (eds) (1999) *The State of Working Britain*, Manchester: Manchester University Press.
Provides a very useful discussion of labour market changes in the UK.

Hagan, J. and Peterson, R.D. (eds) (1995) *Crime and Inequality*, Stanford: Stanford University Press.
Another book that provides an overview of a wide range of issues.

Taylor, I. (1995) *Crime in Context: A Critical Criminology of Market Societies*, Cambridge: Polity Press.
Provides an excellent discussion of broader issues of crime in market economies.

Young, J. (2002) 'Crime and social exclusion' in M. Maguire, M. Morgan and R. Reiner (eds), *The Oxford Handbook of Criminology* (3rd edn), Oxford: Oxford University Press.
Jock Young's chapter is a good introduction to social exclusion.

WEB LINKS

http://www.cabinet-office.gov.uk/seu/
This provides information on the Government's Social Exclusion Unit.

http://www.jrf.org.uk/home.asp

The website for the Joseph Rowntree Foundation. This contains useful information.

http://www.poverty.org.uk/intro/index.htm

The Joseph Rowntree Foundation also supports this New Policy Institute site dedicated to monitoring poverty and social exclusion.

http://www.ifs.org.uk/

The site of the Institute of Fiscal Affairs. It has good reports on poverty and inequality and more generally on the economy.

http://www.tuc.org.uk

This is the website of the Trades Union Congress. It provides links to recent research and has discussion of labour market trends.

REFERENCES

Allen, E.A. and Steffensmeier, D.J. (1989) 'Youth, Underemployment, and Property Crime: Effects of the Quantity and Quality of Job Opportunities on Juvenile and Young Adult Arrest Rates', *American Sociological Review*, 54: 107–23.

Atkinson, A.B. and Micklewright, B. (1992) *Economic Transformation in Eastern Europe and the Distribution of Income*. Cambridge: Cambridge University Press.

Beck, U. (1992) *Risk Society, Towards a New Modernity*, London, Sage.

Becker, G. (1968) 'Crime and Punishment: An Economic Approach', *Journal of Political Economy*, 76: 175–209.

Borooah, V.K. and Collins, G. (1995) 'Unemployment and crime in the regions of Britain: a theoretical and empirical analysis', mimeo. University of Ulster: Ulster.

Box, S. (1987) *Recession Crime and Punishment*, London: Macmillan.

J. Braithwaite, B. Chapman, and C.A. Kapuscinski (1992) 'Unemployment and crime: resolving the paradox', mimeo, *American Bar Foundation Working Paper 9201*. Chicago: Illinois.

Bruegel, I. (2000) 'No more Jobs for the Boys? Gender and Class in the Restructuring of the British Economy', *Capital and Class*, 71, 79–102.

Bryne, D. (1999) *Social Exclusion*. Buckingham: Open University Press.

Cantor, D. and Land, K.C. (1985) 'Unemployment and Crime Rates in Post World War II United States: a Theoretical and Empirical Analysis', *American Sociological Review*, 50, 317–32.

Carlson, S.M. and Michalowski, R.J. (1994) Structural change in the economy, economic marginality, and crime, mimeo. Western Michigan University: CRIMINOLOGY.

Carmichael, F. and Ward, R. (2000) 'Youth Unemployment and Crime in the English Regions and Wales', *Applied Economics*, 32, 559–571.

Chamlin, Michael B. and Cochran, J. (2000) 'Unemployment, Economic Theory, and Property Crime: A Note on Measurement', *Journal of Quantitative Criminology*, 16, 443–455.

Chiricos, T.G. (1987) 'Rates of Crime and Unemployment: An Analysis of Aggregate Research Evidence', *Social Problems*, 34, 187–211.

Cohen, L.E. and Felson, M. (1979) 'Social Change and Crime Rate Trends: A Routine Activities Approach', *American Sociological Review*, 44, 588–608.

Currie, E. (1998) *Crime and Punishment in America*. New York: Metropolitan Books.

Durkheim, E. (1893) *The Division of Labour in Society*, 1984 edition translated by W.D. Halls, with an introduction by Lewis Coser. Basingstoke: Macmillan.

Ehrlich, I. (1973) 'Participation in Illegitimate Activities: a Thoertical and Emprical Investigation', *Journal of Political Economy*, 81, 521–63.

Felson, M. and Cohen, L.E. (1980) 'Human Ecology and Crime: A Routine Activities Approach', *Human Ecology*, 8, 389–406.

Field, S. (1990), 'Trends in Crime and their Interpretation: A Study of Recorded Crime in Post-war England and Wales', *Home Office Research Study No. 119*, Home Office, London.

Gogger, J. (1998) 'Market Wages and Youth Crime', *Journal of Labour Economics*, 16: 756–91.

Gottfredson, M. and Hirschi, T. (1990) *A General Theory of Crime*, Stanford: Stanford University Press.

Gould, D., Mustard, D.B. and Weinberg, B.A. (2002) 'Crime Rates and Local Labor Market opportunities in the United States: 1979–1997', *Review of Economics and Statistics*, 84, 45–61.

Greenberg, D.F. (2001) 'Time Series Analysis of Crime Rates', *Journal of Quantitative Criminology*, 17, 291–327.

Gregg, P., Hansen, K. and Wadsworth, J. (1999) 'Workless households', Chapter 5 in P. Gregg and J. Wadsworth (eds) *The State of Working Britain*. Manchester: Manchester University Press.

Grogger, J. (1998) Market Wages and Youth Crime, *Journal of Labor Economics*, 16 (4), 756–91.

Hagan, J. and Peterson, R.D. (eds) (1995) *Crime and Inequality*, Stanford: Stanford University Press.

Hale, C. (1998) Crime and the Business Cycle in Post-war Britain Revisited, *British Journal of Criminology*, 38 (4), 681–98.

Hale, C. (1999) 'The labour market and post-war crime trends in England and Wales', in P. Carlen and R. Morgan (eds) *Crime Unlimited: Questions for the 21st Century*. Basingstoke: Macmillan.

Hale, C. and Sabbagh, D. (1989) 'Testing the Relationship between Unemployment and Crime: A Methodological Comment and Empirical Analysis using Time Series data from England and Wales', *Journal of Research into Crime and Delinquency*, 28: 400–417.

Hansen, K. (2003) 'The Impact of Increasing female Labour Force Participation on Male Property Crime' Paper presented at the British Society of Criminology Conference, Bangor, July.

Hansen, K. and Machin, S. (2004) 'Crime and the Minimum Wage', *Journal of Quantitative Criminology*.

Hayward, K. (2001) 'Chicago School of Sociology' in E. McLaughlin and J. Muncie (eds) *The Sage Dictionary of Criminology*. London: Sage.

Hirschi, T. (1969) *The Causes of Delinquency*. Berkeley: University of California Press.

Hope, T. (2000) 'Inequality and the Clubbing of Society' in T. Hope and R. Sparks (eds) *Crime, Risk and Insecurity*. London: Routledge.

Hope, T. (2003) *Private Security and Crime Victimisation in Risk Society* Paper delivered at the conference *Per Una Società Più Sicura: il contributo conoscitivo dell.informazione statistica*, ISTAT, Rome, Italy, 3–5 December, 2003.

Kapuscinski, C.A., Braithwaite, J. and Chapman, B. (1998) 'Unemployment and crime: resolving the paradox', *Journal of Quantitative Criminology*, 14: 215–44.

Lilly, J.R., Cullen, F.T., Ball, R.A. (2002) *Criminological Theory: Context and Consequences* (3rd edn). London: Sage.

Machin, S. and Marie, O. (2004) 'Crime and Benefit Cuts', Paper presented to the Annual Conference of the Royal Economic Society, Swansea, April.

Machin, S. (1999) 'Wage Inequality in the 1970s, 1980s and 1990s', chapter 11 in P. Gregg and J. Wadsworth (eds) *The State of Working Britain*. Manchester: Manchester University Press.

Machin, S. and Meghir, C. (2003) 'Crime and Economic Incentives', *Journal of Human Resources*.

Matthews, R. and Young, J. (2003) *The New Politics of Crime and Punishment*, Cullompton, Willan.

McRae, S. (1997) 'Household and Labour Market Change: Implications for the Growth of Inequality in Britain', *British Journal of Sociology*, 48, 384–405.

Merton, R. (1938) 'Social Structure and "Anomie" ', *American Sociological Review*, 3: 672–82.

Murray, C. (1984) *Losing Ground*. New York: Basic Books.

Murray, C. (1990) *The Emerging British Underclass*. London Institute of Economic Affairs.

Pyle, D. and Deadman, D. (1994) 'Crime and the Business Cycle in Post-war Britain', *British Journal of Criminology*, 34, 339–357.

Radzinowicz, L. (1939), 'The Influence of Economic Conditions on Crime' *Sociological Review*, 33, 139–53.

Radzinowicz, L. (1971), 'Economic Pressures' Chapter 34 in Radzinowicz, L. and Wolgang, M.E., *Crime and Justice Volume 1: The Criminal in Society*. New York: Basic Books.

Reilly, B. and Witt, R. (1996) 'Crime, Deterrence and Unemployment in England and Wales: an Empirical Analysis', *Bulletin of Economic Research*, 48: 137–59.

Rowntree Report (1995) *Inquiry into Income and Wealth*. Joseph Rowntree Foundation: York.

Shaw, C.R. and McKay, H.D. (1942) *Juvenile Delinquency and Urban Areas*. Chicago: University of Chicago Press.

Simmonds, J. and Dodd, T. (2003) *Crime in England and Wales 2002/2003*.

Social Exclusion Unit (2001) *Preventing Social Exclusion*. London: Stationery Office.

Taylor, I. (1995) *Crime in Context: A Critical Criminology of Market Societies*. Cambridge: Polity Press.

Trickett A., Ellingworth, D., Hope, T. and Pease, K. (1995) 'Crime Victimisation in the Eighties', *British Journal of Criminology*, 35, 343–59.

Triggs, Sue (1997) *Interpreting Trends in Recorded Crime in New Zealand* www.justice.govt.nz/pubs/reports/1997/crime, New Zealand Ministry of Justice.

Veit-Wilson, J. (1998) *Setting Adequacy Standards*. London: Policy Press.

Wilson, H. (1980) 'Parental Supervision: A Neglected Aspect of Delinquency', *British Journal of Criminology*, 20,

Wilson, W.J. (1987), *The Truly Disadvantaged*. Chicago: Chicago University Press.

Wilson, W.J. (1996), *When Work Disappears*. New York: Knopf.

Witt, R., Clarke, A. and Fielding, N. (1998) 'Crime, earnings Inequality and Unemployment in England and Wales', *Applied Economics Letters*, 5: 265–67.

Witt, R., Clarke, A. and Fielding, N. (1999) 'Crime and Economic Activity: a Panel Data Approach', *British Journal of Criminology*, 39: 391–400.

Witt, R. and Witte, A.D. (1998), Crime, Imprisonment and Female Labour Force Participation: A Time Series Approach, *Journal of Quantitative Criminology*, 16: 69–86.

Young, J. (2001) 'Relative Deprivation' in E. McLaughlin and J. Muncie (eds) *The Sage Dictionary of Criminology*. London: Sage.

Young, J. (2002) 'Crime and Social Exclusion' in M. Maguire, M. Morgan and R. Reiner (eds), *The Oxford Handbook of Criminology* (3rd edn). Oxford: Oxford University Press.

NOTES

1. The definition of poverty used in UK policy refers to the numbers of families who earn less than 60 per cent of median income. Hence poverty here is a relative concept and tackling it requires reducing inequality as well as increasing low incomes.

2. See Hale and Sabbagh (1989) and Greenberg (2001) for methodological critiques of their statistical approach.

3. Published as Kapuscinski *et al.* (1998). This idea may be traced at least back to the papers of Cohen (1981), Cohen and Felson (1979) and Felson and Cohen (1980) who use a 'residential population density ratio' in their statistical work. This variable is defined as the sum of female labour force participants with husbands present plus the number of households that are non-husband-wife households divided by the total number of households. This ratio will increase as either of the terms in the numerator gets larger. A higher ratio in terms of the approach of these authors implies less 'guardianship' and hence is likely to lead to increased crime. On a technical note, the numerator is strange in that it adds individuals to households and hence is not bounded by 1.

4. The research was originally published as Braithwaite *et al.* (1992).

5. See also Breugel (2000) for a discussion of the feminization of employment in Britain.

6. See also amongst others Machin (1999) and the data and sources on wage inequality given therein.

7. Family Expenditure Survey estimates give 4 per cent households workless in 1968, 6.2 per cent workless in 1975 and 17.4 per cent workless in 1996. The Labour Force Survey estimates are comparable with 6.5 per cent workless in 1975 and 17.9 per cent workless in 1998 (Table 5.1, Gregg *et al.* (1999).

8. To take two (imaginary) extremes, in areas where everyone was paid more than the minimum wage to begin with, then no one would be better off when it was introduced. Conversely in areas where all workers earn less than the new minimum, then all will benefit.

9. Theft of a vehicle, theft from a vehicle, aggravated vehicle taking, vehicle interference and criminal damage to a vehicle.

10. As he himself pointed it was not a new idea. The Marxist notion of the lumpen proletariat is similar, but of course from a different political provenance. It also has resonance with Victorian notions of respectable and unrespectable, the deserving and undeserving poor—those who would try to help themselves and tried to maintain moral standards and those who did nothing to help and abandoned themselves to dissolution.

11. Similar information for Scotland can be obtained from the Scottish Crime Surveys (SCS).

12. The point being that some households are victimized more than once. See Hope, Chapter 3 for a discussion of area crime incidence (the number of crimes per head of population), area prevalence rate (the proportion of victims in the population) and area crime concentration (the number of victimizations per victim).

17

Gender and crime

Catrin Smith

INTRODUCTION

Crime is largely a male activity. Studies consistently show that males commit more crimes than females and their offences tend to be more serious and violent in nature. However, the 'maleness' of crime has, until recently, been taken for granted. While feminists have done much to make visible the experiences of women as offenders and victims and to highlight the gendered practices of the crime-processing system in relation to *women*, the important relationship between men, masculinity and crime has been somewhat neglected. The purpose of this chapter is to provide an overview of the issues around sex, gender and crime. It considers the contribution of feminist perspectives to the study of crime and criminal justice before providing an overview of the patterning of criminal behaviour and victimization according to sex. This leads to an analysis of the kinds of crimes men and women are involved in and the relationship between masculinity(ies), femininity(ies) and crime. The chapter then explores gendered differences in criminal justice at various stages of the system as well as the ways age, race and class may affect how males and females experience the criminal justice system. The chapter will conclude with a consideration of the implications of a 'gender agenda' for the discipline of criminology and for the criminal justice process.

BACKGROUND

The terms 'sex' and 'gender' are often used interchangeably as ways of categorizing the seemingly straightforward biological distinction between female and male. However, understanding the difference between sex and gender informs us that most differences between males and females are the result of complex social processes, not inborn necessity.

Sex differences are those based on biological criteria for classifying persons as male or female, including genital and hormonal differences and variations in reproductive capacity. In contrast, gender differences are ascribed by society and relate to expectations about appropriate social roles. Sex differences may determine an individual's ability to become pregnant, but gendered *assumptions* suggest that, because women have the reproductive capacity to bear children, it is women who should carry the burden of child-care responsibilities.

Most differences between men and women in terms of social roles, expectations and identities are gender differences not sex differences. They are often assumed to be 'natural'. However, they are learnt during the process of socialization where cultural definitions of 'masculinity' and 'femininity' and what it means to be a 'man' or a 'woman' are passed on.

Gendered constructions are historically diverse and different societies code 'manhood' and 'womanhood' in very different ways (Oakley, 1972). Moreover, there are differences not only between masculinity and femininity but also within them and diversity among men and masculinities and among women and femininities exist on the basis of various aspects of social experience (Connell, 1987). However, in most forms of societal organization some versions of masculinity and femininity are valued over others. In late modern societies the dominant form of masculinity, or what Connell (1987) defines as 'hegemonic masculinity', is possessed by those males who are *instrumentally* active, tough, risk-takers, breadwinners, who show no fear and emotion, and who give expression to 'normative heterosexuality'. In contrast, what society codes as feminine involves an *expressive* capacity for emotion, care, compassion, passivity, and subservience. In such a system, 'successful' masculinity and 'successful' femininity depend upon the extent to which one adopts the deeds and actions associated with the *idea* of being male (but not female) or female (but not male). Central to an understanding of the distinction between sex and gender is an understanding of the ways in which social value systems construct and legitimate differences between males and females and give tacit primacy to some definitions of masculinity and femininity over others.

To understand the current debates concerning sex, gender, crime and justice, it is first necessary to comprehend something of the relevant historical development of the discipline of criminology and the context into which feminist perspectives on crime and justice emerged.

Criminology is a diverse and fragmented discipline (see Chapter 4 above). In all its guises, however, academic criminology has tended historically to ignore females as both victims and offenders or, where included has done so in sexist and stereotypical ways. The work of Lombroso and Ferrero (1895), Thomas (1923), and Pollak (1961), for example, while different in certain ways, all expressed accepted views about female criminality, viewing females as 'driven' to crime because of biological and/or socio-sexual influences. In the main, however, female crime was seen as neither interesting nor important and, up until the 1970s, criminologists consistently left females out of their research models, questions and samples. For as long as systematic data on crime have been collated, males have far outnumbered females among known offenders, law-makers and law enforcers. Similarly, criminology as a discipline has been dominated by men and male perspectives. As Hearn (2003) points out, the history of criminology has been largely a history of men but one in which the 'maleness' of crime, crime control and crime analysis has been so taken-for-granted as to be rendered invisible.

The exclusion of females in criminological theorizing and empirical inquiry formed a key part of the critique developed by feminist writers, influenced by the growth of 'second wave' feminism and the women's movement (see Heidensohn, 1968; Smart, 1976). This work did much to expose the male dominance yet 'gender-blindness' of criminology and was formative in the development of what has become termed loosely as 'feminist criminology'.

Contrary to popular opinion, not all feminists think alike and, as in criminology, there are many different feminist perspectives. Despite the different stances, feminist theory is concerned generally with 'a woman-centred description and explanation of human experience and the social world' (Danner, 1989: 51). It asserts that gender and gender relations order social life and social institutions and it is directed towards social change and, in particular, towards negating the neglect and subordination of women. Inherent to many strains of feminist thought are the concepts of sexism and patriarchy. Sexism refers to oppressive attitudes and behaviours directed towards either sex but, in particular, the concept has been used to refer to discriminatory practices aimed primarily at women. Patriarchy, on the other hand, refers to a system of social structures and practices in which men dominate.

The influence of feminist thinking is evident in the large body of writing on the subject of women, gender and crime. While there is no one set of perspectives which define 'feminist criminology', the main contributions to knowledge include:

- a more central focus on women as offenders and victims;
- a critique of earlier (male) criminological studies of, and theories about, (male) crime and the advancement of more rigorous research methodologies and theory-building around gender and crime;
- the deconstruction of the sexist and stereotypical images of female offenders and victims within much criminological theorising;
- the identification of institutionalized sexism not only within academic criminology, but also within criminal justice policy and practice;
- an understanding of the effect of gender constructs on the propensity for women to offend and a recognition that inequalities between the sexes can differentially shape male and female experiences and behaviours, including criminality;
- an insight into the interrelationship between prior victimisation and offending;
- an increasing concern with examining how constructs of class, race and sexuality affect the gender dimension of crime.

In making the 'woman question' central, feminist work has been accused of partiality and has been criticized for not including considerations of gender and male crime. However, it is wrong to assume that feminist work has ignored men and masculinity. Rather, feminist theories have examined masculinity and men's lives in order to more fully understand women's, especially the acts of force and violence committed *against* women. More recently, feminist research has also influenced the development of critical studies of male criminality and has helped understand the risk factors for offending for *both* males and females. The discipline of criminology has also benefited from more gender-specific crime courses and texts and through the academic production of more feminist scholars (women and men). Moreover, feminist thinking has also had an influence on criminal justice policy and practice. For instance, legal reform (especially in relation to sexual and domestic abuse) and developments in crime prevention have resulted from a feminist focus on women and crime. In summing up the achievements of feminists working within criminology, Naffine (1996: 29) argues that feminist criminologies have helped us to 'see crime differently' and many aspects of feminists' thinking will be developed throughout the sections to follow.

Sex and crime

Students of criminology and criminal justice will learn at an early stage to be critical of the main sources of data on crime—recorded statistics, self-report studies and victim surveys (see Chapter 3 above). Despite their limitations, each source includes information on sex and, as such, is worthy of consideration.

Recorded statistics

The most commonly referred to sources of information on offending are the 'official statistics' on *known* offenders. These statistics are compiled annually in England and Wales by the Home Office and offer us the following picture of male and female offending in 2002 (Home Office, 2003a):

- Eighty per cent of known offenders were male.
- The peak age of known offending was nineteen for males and fifteen for females.

- Between 85 and 95 per cent of offenders found guilty of burglary, robbery, drug offences, criminal damage or violence against the person were male.
- Ninety-eight per cent of people found guilty, or cautioned for, sexual offences were male.
- For indictable offences, 57 per cent of female offenders were found guilty of, or cautioned for, theft and handling stolen goods compared with 34 per cent of male offenders.
- In the ten years between 1992 and 2002, the numbers of male and female offenders found guilty or cautioned for indictable offences have generally decreased.
- However, between 2001 and 2002, the numbers of male offenders found guilty for all offences rose by 5 per cent. For females, the rise was 9 per cent.
- Between 2001 and 2002, offences of violence against the person rose by 9 per cent for males and 18 per cent for females; burglary offences rose by 3 per cent for males and 14 per cent for females; robbery offences rose by 7 per cent for males and 22 per cent for females; drug offences rose by 10 per cent for males and 9 per cent for females.
- In 2002, the proportionate use of immediate custody for males aged twenty-one or over was 30 per cent. This compares with 18 per cent in 1992. For females in this age group, the proportionate use of immediate custody was 17 per cent. It was 6 per cent in 1992.

These statistics paint a somewhat complex picture. First, they seem to confirm that crime is a 'male problem'. Males seem to commit more crime than females and are typically prosecuted for more serious offences. However, the statistics also suggest that, in recent years, the share of female criminality has increased, with percentage increases for burglary, robbery, drug offences and offences of violence against the person. Second, it seems that while the longer-term trend suggests that offending is on the decrease, 'youth' remains the most criminogenic age for *both* males and females (see Chapter 19 below). Third, it seems that while females tend to commit less crime and their offences are, in the main, less serious, they are being sentenced to immediate custody at a far greater rate proportionately than males. Indeed, the number of women in prison has risen steadily since the early 1990s. In 1993, for instance, the female prison population stood at 1,580. On 26 March 2004, there were 4,589 women in prison, representing about 6 per cent of the total prisoner population in England and Wales (HM Prison Service, 2004, online).

Self-report studies

Most self-report studies suggest that offending is far more widespread than the official statistics would imply and that the sex gap in relation to offending is narrower. Muncie (1999), for example, casts some doubt on the lack of offending by young women, suggesting that, up to the age of seventeen, male and female offending rates are similar but that female offending decreases thereafter while male offending increases. Heidensohn (1996), similarly, points to American and British self-report studies that claim that girls report more offending than conviction rates would suggest. However, even here, criminal activity remains predominantly male and predominantly more serious (Coleman and Moynihan, 1996).

Victim surveys

Victimization surveys such as the British Crime Survey (BCS) have been conducted since the early 1980s and have revealed that the extent of crime may be much greater than that detailed in the official statistics. In 2002/2003, for instance, only 43 per cent of crimes were reported to the police (Home Office, 2003b). In terms of sex differences, the BCS has also revealed that:

- men are more likely to be the victims of violent crime than women, with those in the sixteen to twenty-four age group being most at risk;
- domestic violence is the only category of violence where the risks for women are higher than for men;
- risks of stranger violence remain substantially greater for men than for women;
- despite being more likely to be the victim of crime, men are less worried than women about most types of crime. Moreover, females are less likely than males to go out alone at night and are more likely to feel unsafe either outside or when home alone at night (see Home Office, 2003b).

Women, femininity(ies) and crime

There is now a large body of work on women and crime and this section provides an overview of the main debates.

Female conformity

The relative lack of offending by females has been explained in various ways. Some writers suggest that the observable differences in the extent and nature of offending between males and females (and unquestioned by many criminological theories) are non-existent. Pollak (1961), for instance, maintained that women commit as many crimes as men, but rarely find their way into the official statistics.

Other writers point to the socially constructed nature of official statistics to account for the seeming relationship between sex and offending. Crime statistics, as we know, represent the end product of a series of decisions: including whether or not to *report* a crime and, if so, whether it is *recorded* as such. Moreover, changes in policing priorities and changes in legal definitions of what counts as crime will affect statistical representations. For example, sexual assault and domestic violence are both examples of events whose measurement has been susceptible both to changing cultural norms and measurement methods.

Murgatroyd (2004, online) argues that official statistics are not gender-neutral. She suggests that, in areas such as crime, while the statistics include information on sex, there may be a tendency for the gender dimension to be hidden through measurement and/or conceptual difficulties, leading to gaps in information. Such gaps may result from cultural norms and assumptions regarding male and female characteristics and behaviours. This view leads to the suggestion that it is the *perception* of crime as a male activity that may affect the overall picture of men and women as perpetrators of crime. This perception may lead to female offending going unreported to the police and, where reported, not recorded, allowing females to evade the formal criminalization processes.

Heidensohn (1996) suggests that data on female offending may also be complicated by gender assumptions about what is 'typically' female crime. She argues that stereotypical assumptions about women's lives affect assumptions about the crimes they commit. Take shoplifting, for example. Because stereotypes link women with shopping, shoplifting is viewed as an extension to women's 'normal' role (Morris, 1987). Hence, shoplifting is regarded typically as *the* female crime, despite the evidence that males still account for the vast majority of arrests and convictions. Similarly, prostitution, in law and in practice, has been constructed as a 'typically' female crime (see Walkowitz, 1980). Here, stereotypes which view sex work as an extension of the female role (to service male sexual desire) may serve to render male offenders invisible whilst sanctioning female prostitutes more rigorously than their clients, who are typically male. This suggests official statistics reflect not patterns of offending but a double standard in the construction and enforcement of the law.

Naffine (2003) suggests that the criminal law and its enforcement is about male patterns of behaviour and about male standards of acceptable conduct. She points to the construction of laws on anti-social violence which are significantly about men and what men do. Similarly, McIntosh (1978) suggests that there are *more* laws concerning male behaviour than female behaviour and that this explains why men are convicted of more crimes than women. She argues that female behaviour tends to be 'policed' in other contexts by informal, non-criminalizing means. This theme is picked up by Heidensohn (2002) who argues that in order to understand female conformity—what it is about women that makes them more law-abiding—it is important to understand something of the social construction of femininity and of the disciplinary forces that act *upon* women at various levels including:

- *The media*: where cultural representations of 'appropriate' female appearance and behaviour serve to objectify the female body and exhort women to identify with, and mould their bodies into, a state of 'feminine excellence' (Dines and Humez, 1995).

- *The domestic sphere*: where women are constrained by, on the one hand, the responsibilities of motherhood and housewifery (Oakley, 1981) and, on the other hand, through the exercize of male power (Carlen, 1983).

- *In public*: where fear of crime and of reputation damage effectively constrain women's public behaviour (especially after dark), relegating women to the context in which they are, in fact, most at risk: the home (Stanko, 1990).

- *In education and the workforce*: where ideas about the physical and emotional frailty of women have historically kept women uneducated and unemployed and where women are still constrained through social hierarchies and sexual discrimination (Benjamin, Mauthner and Ali, 2003).

- *In medicine and psychiatry*: where illness labels may reflect social ideas about women's bodies (as more *naturally* unstable than men's) and where various aspects of women's lives have become defined as problematic requiring intervention and control (Reiss-man, 1998).

- *In legislation*: where models of femininity inform social policies around 'cash and care', determining the choices open to women (Heidensohn, 1996).

Such approaches imply that the *techniques* of control and surveillance may be different for males and females. Heidensohn (2002) suggests that this provides some explanation for sex differences in offending and may help to explain why, in similar circumstances, women are less likely to offend than their male counterparts. This is not to suggest, however, that Heidensohn (2002) sees women as the passive recipients of informal control directives. On the contrary, she describes a complex process in which the 'norms of femininity' serve as a form of social control and where women themselves, often contradictorily, learn to discipline their own bodies and police themselves. Not *all* women, however, and not all the time and variety of disciplines despite the seeming success of the system of gender imperatives, *some* women are unable or unwilling to conform.

Gender-convergence

There has been much political and popular debate in recent years in relation to the perceived increase in female crime and, in particular, female violence. Batchelor (2002), for instance, points to news stories of so-called 'girl gangs'—ladettes—who have been associated with a 'rising tide' of lawlessness. Such stories have been bolstered by wider concerns about, for example, 'binge drinking' and the increase in female alcohol consumption. Female offending, it seems, has achieved not only greater visibility as a women's issue, but also status as a 'social problem'.

Heidensohn (1996: 154) points out that 'moral panics' about female offending are not new and have been linked recurrently to concerns about female emancipation and liberation. She cites the work of Pike (1876) and Bishop (1931) who both argued that female criminality was linked to sexual equality. Pollak (1961), similarly, drew parallels between increased female offending and the progressive emancipation of women. However, it was in the 1970s that the patterns of female offending rates over time received increased attention with the advent of Adler's (1975) and Simon's (1975) so-called 'liberation hypothesis'. Adler (1975) and Simon (1975) both made links between the women's 'liberation' movement and the female crime rate, arguing that as women become more equal to men, offending rates will converge.

While liberation theories have been heavily criticized (Smart, 1982; Box and Hale, 1983; 1984), the main crime data sources provide some evidence in support of convergence. The official statistics, for instance, point to a change in the ratio between male and female crime over time. They also suggest an upward shift in the pattern of convictions of women for robbery, burglary, drug and violent offences (Home Office, 2003a). Taken in the context of a longer-term decrease in the number of known offenders over the past ten years or so, the more serious offences seem to represent an increasing proportion of those crimes for which females are arrested, cautioned or convicted (Burman, 2003). The dramatic and unprecedented increase in the female prison population in

England and Wales in recent years also lends some support to a narrowing of the gap between male and female offending.

On closer examination, however, the hypothesis that women's crime rates are catching up with men's is questionable. Numerically, males far outnumber females in all offence categories and percentage rises for female crime, therefore, represent small increases to low base numbers. Furthermore, the largest numerical increases tend to be in less serious offence categories. The rise in female offenders in 2002, for example, was partly due to increased numbers of women convicted of television licence evasion (Home Office, 2003a). Similarly, with regard to violent crime, the proportional increases, tend to be in the less serious offence categories such as common assault, rather than serious assault or homicide (Burman, 2003). Females account for a small percentage of violent crime and most research has found that the female violent crime rate has, in fact, remained relative stable (Burman, 2003) and, while violence remains a predominantly male activity, the long-term pattern suggests that violent crimes are decreasing for both sexes (Home Office, 2003a). Discussions over whether female crime is increasing (or indeed decreasing) are, of course, complicated by changes in criminalization processes such as police recording procedures and priorities and the general patterns of sentencing over time.

Overall then, there is limited evidence for convergence theses and most researchers agree that women's crime rates have more or less stayed the same, with some marginal increases in the areas of less serious property offences and alcohol and drug use (Belknap, 2001). Where gender convergence seems to exist it may be understood in terms of inflation in the small base of women's crimes, changes in data collection methods and in law enforcement processes (see, for example, Smart, 1982; Belknap, 2001). At the end of the day, males still make up the majority of known offenders for even those offences where there seems to be a convergence.

Female criminality

Most discussions of female criminality are grounded in the context of women violating socially prescribed gender roles as well as criminal laws; what has become known as 'double deviance'. While it is clear that *some* women offend and, indeed, women can be found in all offence categories from the most serious to the least serious, male and female criminal behaviour tends to be interpreted differently. For men, it is more likely to be viewed as 'normal' behaviour or as a rational response to such factors as boredom, peer pressure, necessity, greed and so forth. In contrast, female offenders are so few so as to present something of an anomaly, in need of explanation. Female offending challenges the dominant scripts of femininity and, hence, is commonly explained, on the one hand, as a consequence of individual women failing to conform to their innate biological tendencies (masculinized, sexualized, pathologized) or, on the other hand, it is redefined as evidence of what Showalter (1987) refers to as the 'female malady' (irrationality, psychological instability). Positioning women's criminal behaviour in such a way effectively dismisses it. It removes any element of agency from the woman herself and any onus on society to reflect upon why it occurred.

Modern analyses of women and crime have done much to challenge stereotypical assumptions about female motivation and have highlighted the rational and purposeful nature of much female offending. Carlen (1985, 1988), for example, has argued that female criminality involves conscious decision-making processes and can, often, be understood in terms of women's socioeconomic circumstances. Similarly, studies of girl gangs and of females charged with robberies and aggravated assault have found few differences in the motivations between males and females. Crimes of violence were most often committed to get money for material goods and/or to support a drug habit (Miller, 1998, 2001; Sommers and Baskin, 1993).

There is, of course, no monolithic female experience and female motivations for crime are likely to depend upon a number of factors. As we have seen, criminological theories have tended to be sex-blind, either ignoring females or viewing them in a stereotypical manner that usually distorts real-life experiences. Any analysis of gender must avoid a similarly restricted view by accounting for difference *among* females. Here, it is important to consider the ways in which sex interacts with other variables such as age, race and class.

REVIEW QUESTIONS

1 Are women more law-abiding than men?

2 Are women becoming more criminal?

3 Do women commit crimes for the same reasons as men?

Men, masculinity(ies) and crime

If, as Heidensohn (1996) suggests, a central question for criminology concerns female *conformity*, then the issue of male *criminality* should be equally, if not more, pressing. All the available evidence suggests that men outnumber women among offender (and victim) populations. Men are more likely than women to be repeat offenders and more likely than women to engage in the most serious offence categories. So what is it about men that makes them so much more predisposed to criminality?

The 'man question' in relation to crime has, until relatively recently, been overlooked by criminologists. Historically, (male-dominated) criminology has focused attention on men and male offending without tackling the issue of masculinity head on (Winlow, 2004). The 'maleness' of crime has been so taken-for-granted as to be rendered invisible. As Sim (1994) suggests, studies have tended to be on men as *offenders* rather than offenders as *men*. However, the relationship between men, masculinity and crime has been the focus of increased academic attention over the last ten years, influenced, not least, by feminist criminological work; but also by scholars in gender and gay studies and in critical, pro-feminist studies of men as gendered subjects (see, for example, Connell, 1987; Morgan, 1992).

Analyses of masculine identity and masculinity became increasingly important within criminology during the 1990s with a number critical studies focusing specifically on men and crime (see, for example, Newburn and Stanko, 1994; Bowker, 1998; Messerschmidt, 1993, 1997). This work provides an attempt to explain why men are more criminal and, in particular, more violent than women, whether it be at the inter-personal or collective level; and why *some* men are more criminal and more violent than others (Bowker, 1998). In what follows, some of the main issues raised by this and earlier work are summarized under the themes of *gender learning processes, power and control models, masculinities and masculine identities*, although it is recognized that there is much overlap.

Gender learning processes

Discussions of male criminality cannot be divorced from the social construction of gender and gendered subjectivities. Here, male offending is often explained in terms of the socialization processes where, on the one hand, boys experience a relative lack of informal control and, on they other hand, they learn that 'femaleness' is something to be avoided and that to be a 'man' involves being tough, fearless and non-emotional (Walklate, 2001). Male crime is thus linked to cultural notions of 'manhood' and to the prescribed and gendered social roles that are learned and legitimated in various arenas, including:

- *The family*: where male offending can be correlated with prevailing social stereotypes about male behaviour, on the one hand, and with parental models, on the other hand (Oakley, 1972). According to this argument, boys learn what 'men do' and, in the pursuit of 'authentic manhood' and its approved forms of expression, boys are more likely to engage in anti-social behaviour than girls. In terms of parenting models, various risk factors for male offending have also been highlighted, including a parental deprivation of love and childhood experiences of witnessing and/or suffering violence (Farrington and Painter, 2004).

- *The media*: where society's approved definition of male and female sex roles are reflected, reinforced and exploited (Surrette, 1998).

- *Sport and leisure*: where being seen to be 'tough' is celebrated and where male violence (usually directed towards other men) comes with its own rewards (Jefferson, 1998; Williams and Taylor, 1994).

- *Social policies*: where models of 'fatherhood' and 'breadwinning' determine and constrain the choices open to men (Hobson, 2002).

- *The law*: where certain male behaviours have been condoned historically (for example, wife battering and rape) whilst those behaviours that deviate from the sex-typed model (for example, homosexuality) have been subject to sanction (Weitz, 1998).

Sex role analyses point to the processes, extending through childhood and into adult life, through which individuals become not only conscious of their gender roles but also, through years of learning, internalize them and make them part of their own personalities.

While this approach constitutes an important first step towards an understanding of gender relations and the gendered nature of criminality, it has been criticized for an under-emphasis on the inequalities between males and females and, in particular, the forms of power that men exercise *over* women (Stoltenberg, 2000; Walklate, 2001).

Power and control models

Stoltenberg (2000) argues that male and female roles are not equal. He highlights the social construction of masculinity as the main source of societal injustice and discrimination. Here, it is suggested that an understanding of male criminality depends upon an understanding of gendered power and power relationships and, in particular, men's use and abuse of women and women's bodies.

Power and control models of male crime owe much to radical feminists' analyses of patriarchal systems of exploitation and oppression and of the techniques for 'doing gender'. That is, the ways in which male domination is made real through acts of force and 'sexual terrorism' (Stoltenberg, 2000: 27). According to this argument, male superiority is constituted through power and control tactics such as rape, battery, prostitution and pornography, but also through the exploitation of women's labour (at home and in the workplace) and through sexist language and harassments—acts in which women are subordinated whilst men are affirmed in their 'manhood' (Messerschmidt, 1993). Male superiority is thus not seen as 'natural'. Rather, men learn to experience their lives and, in particular, their sexuality, in terms of conquest and power (Biddulph, 1994; Seidler, 1989). So, masculine 'excellence' in this sense is based on force and anger, the one expression of emotion associated with the notion of masculinity. Moreover, it has been bolstered and legitimated by a whole range of laws and cultural norms (Weiz, 1998).

Of course, not *all* men are the same and not *all* men commit crime or are violent or sexual predators and, indeed, the victims are not *all* female. As we know, violence and sexual violence are not uniquely masculine behaviours, for women can also use power in this way, albeit to a much lesser extent. Power and control models that posit two opposing categories—men and women—overlook the complex nature of power and the power relations *among* men and *among* women. For example, they cannot fully explain female violence or the changing position of women in patriarchal discourses. Nor can they fully account for the contradictory experiences of male power (for example, in the home) and powerlessness (for example, in the workplace) or the impact of power imbalances on subjective feelings and identities (Walklate, 2001). To this end, such approaches to understanding male crime and violence have been much criticized. However, they provide a useful context for the emerging focus on power relations *between* men and masculinities (Hearn, 2003).

Masculinities and masculine identities

There has been an increasing recognition in the field of 'masculinities studies' of the plurality of masculinities, masculine identities and, indeed, patriarchies. Here, it is argued that there is no universal male experience. Rather, there is diversity among men and, similarly, there are many different types of masculinity and forms of patriarchal organization. Connell's (1987, 1995) work, in particular, has made a significant contribution to an understanding of the relationships between different types of masculinity and masculine identity. That is, how males see themselves as 'men'. Connell (1995) identified a range of masculinities and highlighted the cultural and historical variations. However, he argued that, in any given era, a broad delineation can be made between hegemonic, or dominant, masculinity (white, heterosexual and middle class in contemporary western societies) and other types of subordinated masculinities.

Hegemonic masculinity, according to Connell (1995), represents the culturally dominant ideal of 'manhood', which serves to provide individual men with a sense of self while downgrading other types of masculinity and femininity(ies). 'Successful' male identity requires a distancing from that which is perceived to be 'non-male' (Stoltenberg, 2000). Thus, 'real men' dispense with inferior feminine emotions such as compassion, fear or distress (Mosher and Thomkins, 1988). Stoltenberg (2000) argues that there is, however, no such thing as a 'real man'. There is only the *idea* of it and the *consequences* of trying to make it seem real: the subordination of women and others identified as 'non-male'. Consider, for example, the way in which being 'a girl' is viewed in pejorative terms and the rich linguistic taunts used to define and demean so-called 'effeminate' men. While the sanctions applied to those who deviate from the hegemonic ideal may take the form of social ridicule, they may also be forced institutionally, economically and through law. For instance, heterosexual masculinity has traditionally kept homosexual masculinity subordinate through social stigma *and* legal sanctions.

Connell's (1995) work suggests that, at any given time, the social structure produces numerous masculinities and femininities and different ways of *being*, and of *seeing oneself as*, male and female. It also produces sets of relationships between masculinities and femininities based on degrees of domination and subordination and stratified by age, social class, racial difference and sexuality. Together, these practices create a gender order characteristic of the society at that particular stage. However, the gender order can be challenged, can change and can sometimes undergo periods of 'crisis' (Connell, 1995).

In criminology, the work of Connell has been drawn upon in an increasing body of work examining the relationship between masculinities and crime (but see, in particular, Messerschmidt, 1993, 1997, 1998, 2000). This work points to the importance of understanding male crime and victimization and, indeed, male involvement in crime control, in terms of the *idea* of hegemonic masculinity; the social *context* (where different constructions of masculinity are produced); and the *power relations* between different groups of men.

While hegemonic masculinity's power over subordinate masculinities and femininity(ies) may negatively affect the lives of those perceived to be 'non-male', the non-identification with that which is perceived to be feminine (such as powerlessness) also has consequences for those men who are violently and/or sexually victimized. Here, gendered assumptions regarding the 'typical victim' may lead to problems for men not only in understanding themselves as 'men' but also in terms of their experiences in the criminal justice and victim support systems (see Stanko and Hobdell, 1993; Goodey, 1997; McMullan, 1990; Gadd *et al.*, 2002).

Messerschmidt (1993, 1994, 1998) argues that men construct and maintain their own masculine identities in the context of their position in society and, in particular, their access to power and resources. Here, he identifies the importance of understanding male social positioning in relation to other key variables such as age, socioeconomic status and racial difference. For example, he points to the complex way in which race and class interact in the social construction of youthful masculinities and crime (Messerschmidt,

1994). He also identifies the social conditions and practices that have not only led to the construction of 'racial masculinities', but have also sought to keep black masculinities subordinate, whilst affirming white-supremacist masculinity (Messerschmidt, 1998). In his work, we can see the ways is which socially organized power differences between men produce different constructions of masculinity.

In a similar vein, various studies have shown how men who lack societal power may create a sense of themselves as men through 'compensatory' measures including crime, violence, drugs and 'risk' behaviour (see Katz, 1995; Hobbs *et al.*, 2003; Winlow, 2004). Katz (1995), for example, points to the socio-cultural challenges to male hegemony in post-industrial capitalist societies and, in particular, the increasing economic instability and dislocation of working-class, white males. He suggests that, in response to these pressures, we have seen the development of different and exaggerated forms of masculine expression involving the physical body as a mode of aesthetic and actual power (also see Bloor *et al.*, 1998). Other writers have also suggested that socio-economic changes have led to a white, working-class culture of 'hyper-masculinity', expressed through forms of violent and abusive behaviour (see Surette, 1998; Winlow, 2004). Winlow (2004), for instance, argues that the involvement of predominantly young men in crime and violence needs to be seen as a product of their economic positioning *and* their need for masculinity validation.

Such analyses of 'underclass masculinities' (Winlow, 2004: 19) provide an important contribution to an understanding of male criminality. However, while the nature of the economy may explain why *some* men resort to crime, it cannot be applied to all male offending. As Katz (1988) suggests, crime can be attractive for males and it can be exciting. Campbell (1993), similarly, highlights the fun and risk elements of male involvement in crime. Here, it is important to consider the gratifications and pleasures derived from crime, which may themselves be linked to aspects of masculinity and masculine expression. Moreover, as Walklate (2001) suggests, the focus on working class masculinities may well serve, on the one hand, to legitimate the targeting of the crimes of the socially powerless and, on the other hand, to deflect attention away from the structural and political context in which offending behaviour is expressed and without which 'manhood' has no social or subjective meaning. Here, it is important to consider the processes through which certain forms of masculinity-validating power are condoned while others are condemned and criminalized.

REVIEW QUESTIONS

1 Why do you think there has been a 'masculinity turn' in criminology?

2 Can masculinity be used to explain all crimes?

3 What are some of the difficulties of explaining crimes in terms of masculinity?

Gender and the criminal justice system

It has been suggested that the organizational structures of criminal justice are highly 'gendered'. That is, practices and procedures are patterned by distinguishing between males and females. Here, concerns about the sex-neutrality of the system are bolstered by its overwhelming 'maleness': official agents at every level of the system are predominantly male. What is less clear, however, is whether this has a discriminatory impact on decision making and, if so, in whose favour?

A common assumption is that women are treated more leniently than men simply because they *are* women—the 'chivalry hypothesis'. Here, it is suggested that paternalistic decision makers extend chivalrous treatment to women and that males are discriminated against (see Farnworth and Teske, 1995). To a certain extent, this view is supported by the official statistics—males are more likely than females to be arrested, convicted and, if convicted, given a custodial sentence. However, when the defendant's previous record and the nature of the offence are taken into account, the evidence for chivalry is less clear-cut and studies which have controlled for legal variables have found that males and females are treated similarly—the 'equal treatment hypothesis' (Farrington and Morris, 1983).

Both of these hypotheses have been challenged by feminist writers, who describe the process in a very different way, viewing the system as sexist and discriminatory against women. They argue that females are treated more harshly than males for similar offences and are punished for breaching the criminal law and sex role expectations—the 'double-deviance thesis' (see Howe, 1994, for an overview). Other writers still argue that there is no monolithic male or female experience and *some* men and *some* women are dealt with in a discriminatory manner—the 'selectivity hypothesis'. This view considers the interaction of gender with other aspects of social experience and points to the ways in which constructions of age, race, class and sexuality affect how males and females are treated.

It is questionable whether any of the above hypotheses can ever be 'proved' empirically (Gelsthorpe, 1996). However, a large body of research has been conducted at many different stages of decision making to establish whether discrimination exists in criminal justice. In what follows, some of the major issues are examined in relation to policing, punishment and sentencing.

The culture of policing

The police occupy a crucial role in determining *who* enters the criminal justice process and, while there are statutory anti-discrimination requirements, it is suggested that 'extra-legal' factors frequently affect police decision making. For example, it seems that males and females are treated differently: women are more likely than men to be cautioned rather than prosecuted and are less likely to be stopped and searched (Hough, 1995). This would seem to support the 'chivalry hypothesis'. However, the greater proportion of women cautioned by the police does not necessarily demonstrate preferential treatment. Rather, it may be that women commit less serious offences than men. Indeed, studies that take the nature of the offence into account find little evidence of leniency and instead point to equal treatment (Laycock and Tarling, 1985).

In contrast, it is suggested that, in some circumstances, females are treated more harshly than males and are more likely to be prosecuted. Gelsthorpe (1989), for example, argues that female promiscuity has, historically and contemporarily, been treated more harshly than male. Hudson (1989), similarly, suggests that girls are judged by the police in terms of their 'femininity' and are treated differently to boys for identical behaviours (such as running away, sexual activity, alcohol consumption). Such research dispels the notion that females are treated chivalrously and, instead, provides evidence in support of the 'double deviance hypothesis'.

It has been well documented that socialization into a police 'culture' influences the way in which officers go about their work and relate to those with whom they come into contact (Smith and Gray, 1985; Jefferson, 1990; Reiner, 1992; Fielding, 1994). Here, it has been suggested that a pivotal feature of police culture is the ethos of 'masculinity'. Policing, like offending, is numerically dominated by men and can been seen as a form of masculine expression (Hunt, 1984). Hunt (1984) suggests that police officers routinely employ stereo-types to make sense of the world they police and tend to associate women with 'morality' and with the domestic domain. As a consequence, those few women who are processed as offenders are not considered 'real women'. This distinction between female offenders and 'real' women has been seen most clearly in relation to female prostitutes, the group of women with most regular contact with the police (see Edwards, 1987; Heidensohn, 1996).

Horn (1995) suggests that police treatment of women is more complex than simple support for the 'equal treatment', 'chivalry' or, indeed, 'double-deviance' hypotheses. She argues that police officers tend to categorize women offenders in terms of their personal characteristics and the nature of the offence. So, while *all* women offenders may be perceived more negatively than women who do not offend, not *all* women offenders are treated the same and chivalrous treatment may be reserved for those women who act in ways consistent with hegemonic assumptions of femininity. Horn (1995) proposes that essentially 'decent' women are thought to be those who have temporarily offended due to circumstances. In contrast, women who are physically violent and/or involved in drug offences or who show antagonism to the police, are thought to be 'non-women' and actually 'worse' than male offenders.

In a similar vein, there is evidence that police discretion works against young, poor minority males. As Fielding (1994) suggests, 'cop culture' is also a 'white', 'heterosexual' culture and any evaluation of policing must recognize that there are different life experiences *among* men and *among* women, depending on such factors as race, class, age and sexuality. Moreover, opportunities for the operation of selectivity based on assumptions, value judgements, stereotypes and prejudices are not just confined to policing but run throughout the criminal justice process.

Punishment and sentencing

As with policing, there is a general assumption that women are sentenced and punished more leniently than men. This is often attributed to a 'courteous' attitude on the part of sentencers who may *explain* female offending in very different terms to male offending and who may be reluctant to send women to prison, especially if they have children (Morris, 1987). The idea of chivalrous treatment as an example of 'reverse discrimination' has been evidenced in sentencing statistics that reveal that women are far less likely than men to receive a custodial sentence, are more likely than men to receive probation or discharges and, if given a custodial sentence, are generally given shorter sentences (see Hedderman and Hough, 1994; Gelsthorpe, 1996). However, chivalrous treatment, if it exists, is likely to be far more complex than the simple lenient treatment of *all* women. Belknap (2001: 132) argues that chivalrous treatment is part of a 'bartering system' or exchange relationship in which lenient treatment is extended only to certain kinds of females, according to the nature of the offence but also according to adherence to 'proper' gender roles.

The theme of punishment for breaching sex role expectations has been identified in much of the literature on women and crime and it has been argued that the sentencing of women reflects notions of the 'ideal' woman, related to family and domestic consider-ations, leading to differentiation between women. Thus, being married, having depend-ent children and being a 'good' home-maker may all afford women lenient treatment.

Studies of sentencing, therefore, suggest that while chivalry might well be extended to *some* women—whose behaviour conforms to approved stereotypes—leniency will not be shown to those women who 'deviate' from notions of appropriate sex-role behaviour, who may be dealt with more harshly than other women and, indeed, men. Research on women and punishment also suggests a differential *impact* of sentences on men and women (see, for example, Carlen, 2002). It has, for instance, been suggested that many aspects of imprisonment which, in principle, apply equally may have different implica-tions for men and women. On the one hand, this may be due to the relative invisibility of female prisoners in penal policy and practice—women remain a minority of the prison population and, in a system where women emerge as 'deviations', their needs and experi-ences have been often misunderstood (Morris *et al.*, 1995). On the other hand, it has been suggested that women find prison life harder than their male counterparts because regimes for women have been based on stereotypical assumptions about women's role in society and about the needs of women prisoners. This view suggests that regimes for women prisoners have been dominated by oppressive forms of 'patriarchal control' (see, for example, Sim, 1990; Morris, 1990; Eaton, 1993; Edwards, 1994). Thus, women prisoners experience a harsher disciplinary regime than men and the impact of, and responses to, imprisonment may be more severe (Smith, 2002).

In summary, there is evidence that some women are dealt with in a discriminatory manner in sentencing and punishment procedures. As Gelsthorpe (1996) concludes, those women who conform to stereotypical conceptions of 'ladies' seem to receive differ-ent sentences to those who breach these expectations. Moreover, there is no monolithic female experience that can be defined independently of other factors such as race, class and sexuality. In this respect, distinctions are similarly drawn between *different* men and it would be wrong to suggest that men are treated in non-discriminatory ways. For example, poor, black, young men are over-represented in our prisons and there is evi-dence of discriminatory treatment of some men in some situations, even when control-ling for legal variables (Hood, 1992). This leads to the suggestion that the criminal justice system is grounded upon deeply embedded discourses around hegemonic femininity *and* masculinity and where other variables interact with sex to provide a different pattern for criminal justice for male and female offenders.

REVIEW QUESTIONS

1 Which hypothesis do you find the most convincing?

2 Identify as many factors as possible other than gender which influence the way in which offenders are treated?

CONCLUSION

This chapter has outlined some of the key issues in relation to sex, gender and crime. Despite the many contributions of feminists working within criminology and, more recently, the developing criminological thinking about masculinities, many questions about the relationship between gender and crime remain unanswered. For example, the 'real' extent of male and female offending is probably unknowable. And yet, there is a need to develop more adequate *gender statistics* on crime and justice, not least where statistics are used to measure the impact of policy on both women and men. In addition, some areas remain relatively unexplored such as the concept of violence as a form of feminine expression and there is scope to develop further work on femininities and crime.

What seems clear, however, is that a consideration of gender has had an influence on academic criminology, although the precise nature of that influence is debatable. Heidensohn (2003) and Naffine (2003), for example, both suggest that questions of gender remain peripheral to mainstream criminology and criminological theory. Hearn (2003), similarly, points to the resilience of patriarchy in the discipline. It remains, after all, a discipline dominated by men studying men. Here, there is a real need to address the fundamental gender flaws in much criminological theorizing and empirical work as well as the academic gendering of the discipline itself (see also Scraton, 1990).

Finally, politicians and policy makers, like criminologists, have been slow in considering crime as 'gendered work'. While there has been an increased recognition of the need to adopt anti-discriminatory procedures in recent years and there have been developments in risk-focused prevention and interventions in relation to violent, sexist masculinities, the social structures which frame how individuals experience themselves as men or women and in which offending behaviour is expressed remain largely intact.

QUESTIONS FOR DISCUSSION

1 What impact has feminism had on criminology?

2 How far is the problem of crime a problem of men and masculinity?

3 To what extent is the criminal justice system composed of gendered institutions?

4 Has criminology explained gendered patterns of offending in an adequate manner?

5 Compare and contrast the different ways in which male and female offenders have been represented in: (a) criminological theories; (b) media representations; and (c) criminal justice processes.

GUIDE TO FURTHER READING

Chesney-Lind, M. and Pasko, L. (2004) *The Female Offender: Girls, Women and Crime*, Thousand Oaks, Ca.: Sage.
This US text provides a detailed look at the lives of women offenders and the treatment they receive from criminal justice agencies. Gender issues are explored alongside social class and racial inequalities.

Heidensohn, F. (1996) *Women and Crime*, Basingstoke: Macmillan.
This is a second edition of a classic text written by one of the pioneers of feminist perspectives in criminology. It explores women's criminal behaviour, provides a critique of conventional theories of women's criminality, offers alternative feminist explanations and describes women's experiences of the criminal justice system.

Newburn, T. and Stanko, E. (1994)(eds) *Just Boys Doing Business: Men, Masculinities and Crime*, London: Routledge.
This edited collection explores the relationship between masculinity and crime. The chapters describe the ways in which masculinity is essential to understanding men's involvement in crime, their experiences of victimization and dynamics within criminal justice agencies.

Walklate, S. (2004) *Gender, Crime and Criminal Justice*, Cullompton: Wiilan Publishing.
This student text provides an accessible introduction to gender issues in crime and criminal justice. Divided into three sections, it explores theory, practice and policy respectively.

Winlow, S. (2001) *Badfellas: Crime, Tradition and New Masculinities*, Oxford: Berg.
This research monograph brings complex debates around masculinity and crime to life. It draws upon covert research with professional criminals and violent men and explores the ways in which male identity is expressed each day though a range of activities including criminal ones.

WEB LINKS

www.criminology.fsu.edu/dwc
The American Society of Criminology has a Division on Women and Crime. It developed out of the growing interest in the study of gender and women as offenders, victims and criminal justice professionals. The website provides access to copies of their newsletter and other publications plus a chance to join an e-mail discussion list.

www.crimeinfo.org.uk
Developed by the Centre for Crime and Justice Studies, this website contains an abundance of material about crime and responses to it. It includes factsheets on women and crime, girls and crime and domestic violence plus autobiographical accounts by male and female offenders.

www.fawcettsociety.org.uk
The Fawcett Society is a leading organization campaigning for equality between women and men. The website describes its commission on women and the criminal justice system, details the work of its gender and justice policy network and provides information on women's experiences of the criminal justice system.

www.womeninprison.org.uk
Women in Prison was set up in 1983 by a ex-prisoner The website outlines the work it does providing welfare and education advice to women in prison.

www.homeoffice.gov.uk
The Home Office website includes research studies on gender, crime and criminal justice and policy documents. It is also possible to access the annual publication: *Statistics on Women and the Criminal Justice System*. Despite its title, it brings together data on men's *and* women's experiences of crime and criminal justice.

REFERENCES

Adler, F. (1975) *Sisters in Crime: The Rise of the New Female Criminal*. New York: McGraw-Hill.

Belknap, J. (2001) *The Invisible Woman. Gender, Crime and Justice* (2nd edn). Belmont, Ca: Wadswoth/Thomson Learning.

Benjamin, S. and Mauthner, M. and Ali, S. (eds) (2003) *The Politics of Gender and Education: Critical Perspectives*. Basingstoke: Palgrave Macmillan.

Biddulph, S. (1994) *Manhood*. Sydney: Finch.

Bloor, M. *et al.* (1998) 'The body as a chemistry experiment: steroid use among South Wales bodybuilders' in S. Nettleton and J. Watson (eds.) *The Body in Everyday Life*. London: Routledge.

Bowker, L.H. (ed) (1998) *Masculinities and Crime*. London: Sage.

Box, S. and Hale, C. (1983) 'Liberation and Female Criminality in England and Wales', *British Journal of Criminology*, 23 (1) 35.

Box, S. and Hale, C. (1984) 'Liberation/Emancipation, Economic Marginalisation, or Less Chivalry: The Relevance of Three Arguments to Female Crime Patterns in England and Wales, 1951–1980', *Criminology*, 22, 473–98.

Burman, M. (2003) 'Girls Behaving Violently', *Criminal Justice Matters*, 53, 20–21.

Campbell, B. (1993) *Goliath: Britain's Dangerous Places*. London: Virago.

Carlen, P. (1983) *Women's Imprisonment*. London: Routledge and Kegan Paul.

Carlen, P. (1985) 'Law, Psychiatry and Women's Imprisonment: A Sociological View', *British Journal of Psychiatry*, 146, 618–21.

Carlen, P. (1988) *Women, Crime and Poverty*. Milton Keynes: Open University Press.

Carlen, P. (2002) *Women and Punishment. The Struggle for Justice*. Uffculme: Willan Publishing.

Coleman, C. and Moynihan, J. (1996) *Understanding Crime Data*. Milton Keynes: Open University Press.

Connell, R.W. (1987) *Gender and Power*. Oxford: Polity Press.

Connell, R.W. (1995) *Masculinities*. Oxford: Polity Press.

Danner, M.J.E. (1989) 'Socialist Feminism: A Brief Introduction' in B.D. MacLean and D. Milovanovic (eds) *New Directions in Critical Criminology*. Vancouver: The Collective Press.

Dines, G. and Humez, J. (eds) (1995) *Gender, Race and Class in Media*. London: Sage.

Eaton, M. (1993) *Women After Prison*. Milton Keynes: Open University Press.

Edwards, S. (1987) 'Prostitutes: Victims of Law, Social Policy and Organized Crime' in P. Carlen and A. Worrall, (eds) *Gender, Crime and Justice*. Milton Keynes: Open University Press.

Edwards, S. (1994) 'The Social Control of Women in Prison', *Criminal Justice*, 12, 9–10.

Farnworth, M. and Teske, R.H.C. (1995) 'Gender Differences in Felony Court Processing', *Women and Criminal Justice*, 6 (2), 23–44.

Farrington, D. and Morris, A. (1983) 'Sex, Sentencing and Reconviction', *British Journal of Criminology*, 23 (3), 229–48.

Farrington, D. and Painter, K. (2004) *Gender differences in risk factors for offending*. Home Office Findings 196. London: Home Office.

Fielding, N. (1994) 'Cop canteen culture' in T. Newburn and E.A. Stanko (eds) *Just Boys Doing Business? Men, Masculinities and Crime*. London: Routledge.

Gadd, D. *et al.* (2002) *Domestic Abuse against Men in Scotland*. Edinburgh: Scottish Executive.

Gelsthrope, L. (1989) *Sexism and the Female Offender*. Aldershot: Gower.

Gelsthorpe, L. (1996) 'Critical Decisions and Processes in the Criminal Courts' in E. McLaughlin and J. Muncie (eds) *Controlling Crime*. London: Sage.

Goodey, J. (1997) 'Boys don't cry: Masculinities, fear of crime, and fearlessness', *British Journal of Criminology*, 37 (3), 401–18.

Hearn, J. (2003) ' "Just Men Doing Crime" (and Criminology)', *Criminal Justice Matters*, 53, 12–13.

Hedderman, C. and Hough, M. (1994) *Does the Criminal Justice System Treat Men and Women Differently?* Home Office Research and Statistics Department, 10. London: Home Office.

Heidensohn, F. (1968) 'The Deviance of Women: A Critique and an Enquiry', *British Journal of Sociology*, 19 (2).

Heidensohn, F. (1996) *Women and Crime* (2nd edn). Basingstoke: Macmillan.

Heidensohn, F. (2002) 'Gender and Crime' in M. Maguire, R. Morgan and R. Reiner (eds).*The Oxford Handbook of Criminology* (3rd edn). Oxford: Oxford University Press.

Heidensohn, F. (2003) 'Changing the Core of Criminology', *Criminal Justice Matters*. 53, 4–5.

HM Prison Service (2004) *Female Prisoners* [online]. HM Prison Service. Available from: http://www.hmprisonservice.gov.uk/adviceandsupport/prison_life/femaleprisoners/ [Accessed 14 May, 2004].

Hobbs, D. *et al.* (2003) *Bouncers: Violence and Governance in the Night-time Economy*. Oxford: Oxford University Press.

Hobson, B. (ed.) (2002) *Making Men into Fathers: Men, Masculinities and the Social Politics of Fatherhood*. Cambridge: Cambridge University Press.

Home Office (2003a) *Criminal Statistics for England and Wales 2002*. London: HMSO.

Home Office (2003b) *Crime in England and Wales, 2002/2003*. London: HMSO.

Hood, R. (1992) *Race and Sentencing*. Oxford: Oxford University Press.

Horn, R. (1995) 'Not Real Criminals: Police Perceptions of Women Offenders', *Criminal Justice Matters*, 15–16.

Hough, M. (1995) 'Scotching a Fallacy', *Criminal Justice Matters*, 19, 17–18.

Howe, A. (1994) *Punish and Critique*. London: Routledge.

Hudson, B. (1989) 'Justice or welfare? A comparison of recent developments in the English and French Juvenile Justice System' in M. Cain (ed) *Growing up Good: Policing the Behaviour of Girls in Europe*. London: Sage.

Hunt, J. (1984) 'The development of rapport through the negotiation of gender in fieldwork among the police', *Human Organisation*, 43 (4).

Jefferson, T. (1990) *The Case Against Paramilitary Policing*. Milton Keyens: Open University Press.

Jefferson, T. (1998) 'Muscle, "Hard Men" and "Iron" Mike Tyson: Reflections on Desire, Anxiety and the Embodiment of Masculinity', *Body and Society*, 4.

Katz, J. (1988) *The Seductions of Crime*. New York: Basic Books.

Katz, J. (1995) 'Advertising and the construction of violent, white masculinity' in G. Dines and J.M. Humez (eds) *Gender, Race and Class in Media*. London: Sage.

Laycock, G. and Tarling, R. (1985) 'Police Force Cautioning: Policy and Practice', *Howard Journal*, 24 (2), 81–92.

Lombroso, C. and Ferrero, W. (1895) *The Female Offender*. London: Unwin.

McIntosh, M. (1978) 'The State and the Oppression of Women' in A. Kuhn and A. Wolpe (eds) *Feminism and Materialism*. London: Rutledge and Keegan Paul.

McMullen, R.J. (1990) *Male Rape: Breaking the Silence on the Last Taboo*. London: Gay Men's Press.

Messerschmidt, J.W. (1993) *Masculinities and Crime: Critique and Reconceptualization of Theory*. Totowa, NJ: Rowman and Littlefield.

Messerschmidt, J.W. (1994) 'Schooling masculinities and youth crime by white boys' in T. Newburn and E.A. Stanko (eds) *Just Boys Doing Business? Men, Masculinities and Crime*: Rowman and Littlefield.

Messerschmidt, J.W. (1997) *Crime as Structured Action*. London: Sage.

Messerschmidt, J.W. (1998) 'Men Victimizing Men: The Case of Lynching, 1865–1900' in L. Bowker (ed) *Masculinities and Violence*. London: Sage.

Messerschmidt, J.W. (2000) *Nine Lives*. Boulder, Col.: Westview.

Miller, J. (1998) 'Up it Up: Gender and the Accomplishment of Street Robbery', *Criminology*, 36 (1), 37–66.

Miller, J. (2001) *One of the Guys: Girls, Gangs and Gender*. Oxford: Oxford University Press.

Morgan, D.H.L. (1992) *Discovering Men*. London: Routledge.

Morris, A. (1987) *Women, Crime and Criminal Justice*. Oxford: Basil Blackwell.

Morris, A. (1990) 'Women in the Criminal Justice System', *Prison Service Journal*, 2–5.

Morris, S. *et al.* (1995) *Managing the Needs of Female Prisoners*. London: Home Office.

Mosher, D.L. and Tompkins, S.S. (1988) 'Scripting the macho man: Hypermasculine socialization and enculturation. *Journal of Sex Research*, 25, 60–84.

Muncie, J. (1999) *Youth and Crime. A Critical Introduction*. London: Sage.

Murgatroyd, L. (No date) 'Developing gender statistics in the UK', *Radical Statistics* [online]. Available from: http://www.radstats.org.uk/no074/article2.htm [Accessed 8 May, 2004].

Naffine, N. (1997) *Feminism and Criminology*. Oxford: Polity Press.

Naffine, N. (2003) 'The "Man Question" of Crime, Criminology and Criminal Law', *Criminal Justice Matters*, 53, 10–11.

Newburn, T. and Stanko, E.A. (eds) (1994) *Just Boys Doing Business? Men, Masculinities and Crime*. London: Routledge.

Oakley, A. (1972) *Sex, Gender and Society*. Aldershot: Gower.

Oakley, A. (1981) *Subject Women*. Oxford: Martin Robertson.

Pollak, O. (1961) *The Criminality of Women*. New York: A.S. Barnes.

Reiner, R. (1992) *The Politics of the Police* (2nd edn). Hemel Hemstead: Harvester Wheatsheaf.

Reissman, C.K. (1998) 'Women and Medicalization: A New Perspective' in R. Weitz (ed) *The Politics of Women's Bodies*. Oxford: Oxford University Press.

Scraton, P. (1990) 'Scientific knowledge or masculine discourses? Challenging patriarchy in criminology' in L. Gelsthorpe and A. Morris (eds) *Feminist Perspectives in Criminology*. Buckingham: Open University Press.

Seidler, V. (1989) *Rediscovering Masculinity: Reason, Language and Sexuality*. London: Routledge.

Showalter, E. (1987) *The Female Malady*. London: Virago.

Sim, J. (1990) *Medical Power in Prisons*. Milton Keynes: Open University Press.

Sim, J. (1994) 'Tougher than the rest? Men in prison', in T. Newburn and E.A. Stanko (eds) *Just Boys Doing Business? Men, Masculinities and Crime*. London: Routledge.

Simon, R. (1975) *Women and Crime*. London: Lexington.

Smart, C. (1976) *Women, Crime and Criminology*. London: Routledge and Kegan Paul.

Smart, C. (1982) 'The New Female Offender: Reality or Myth?' in B.R. Price and N.J. Sokoloff (eds) *The Criminal Justice System and Women*. New York: Clark Boardman.

Smith, C. (2002) 'Punishment and Pleasure: Women, Food and the Imprisoned Body', *Sociological Review*, 50 (2), 198–214.

Smith, D.J. and Gray, J. (1985) *Police and People in London*. Aldershot: Gower.

Sommers, I. and Baskin, D.R. (1993) 'The Situational Context of Violent Female Offending', *Journal of Research in Crime and Delinquency*, 30 (2), 136–62.

Stanko, E.A. (1990) *Everyday Violence: How Women and Men Experience Sexual and Physical Danger*. London: Pandora.

Stanko, E.A. and Hobdell, K. (1993) 'Assaults on Men: Masculinity and Male Violence', *British Journal of Criminology*, 33 (3), 400–15.

Stoltenberg, J. (2000) *Refusing to be a Man. Essays on Sex and Justice*. Revised Edition. London: UCL Press.

Surette, R. (1998) *Media, Crime and Criminal Justice* (2nd edn). London: West/Wadsworth.

Thomas, W.I. (1923) *The Unadjusted Girl*. Boston: Little Brown.

Walklate, S. (2001) *Gender, Crime and Criminal Justice*. Uffculme: Willan Publishing.

Walkowitz, J. (1980) *Prostitution and Victorian Society*. Cambridge: Cambridge University Press.

Weitz, R. (1998) 'A History of Women's Bodies' in R. Weitz (ed) *The Politics of Women's Bodies*. Oxford: Oxford University Press.

Williams, J. and Taylor, R. (1994) 'Boys keep swinging: masculinity and football culture in England' in T. Newburn and E.A. Stanko (eds) *Just Boys Doing Business? Men, Masculinities and Crime*. London: Routledge.

Winlow, S. (2004) 'Masculinities and Crime', *Criminal Justice Matters*, 55, 18–19.

18 'Race', ethnicity and crime

Olga Heaven and Barbara Hudson

INTRODUCTION

The aim of this chapter is to explore the relationships between 'race', 'ethnicity' and 'crime', and we shall examine how these conflated and complex terms are used interchangeably. There is a considerable body of empirical research in the UK and elsewhere that illustrates the extent to which people from minority ethnic communities are disproportionately subject to criminal justice intervention and penal sanction. It is by situating the discussion in the plight of female foreign nationals caught in the criminal justice system of England and Wales that we can demonstrate the fractures, disharmonies and contradictions between the rule of law and practice. The first section of the chapter will examine how terms such as 'race', 'ethnicity', 'discrimination' and 'crime', are used in criminology, the 'race' relations industry, and in the criminal justice system. We will show that categorizing individuals according to race/ethnicity is by no means unproblematic. The next section looks at some of the penal policies that are associated with the disproportionate imprisonment of black people. We will suggest the ways in which theory and policy interact in shaping the criminal justice system and produce discriminatory outcomes. Finally, it is by deconstructing the relationships between race, ethnicity and crime through the work of Hibiscus and in turn the experiences of foreign nationals, that you, the reader will begin to see how bias in the criminal justice system operates.

In particular this chapter is based on the experiences of the principal author (Olga Heaven) as Director of the Female Prisoners Welfare Project/Hibiscus, a charity that works with foreign national women prisoners. The goal of FPWP/Hibiscus is to improve the conditions of female foreign nationals who find themselves locked in the criminal justice system. Her first experience of working with foreign nationals in prison began when working as a social worker in Tower Hamlets. Many of the women she encountered led chaotic life-styles. Many had spent time in 'care', where itinerants, were often in poor health, suffered from some form of mental illness or substance abuse, and experienced extreme poverty. A disproportionate number were black, mainly foreign nationals, and this became the focus of FPWP/Hibiscus's work.

The second author (Barbara Hudson) has also been a social worker in south east London, and has worked as a research officer for the probation service. She became involved with issues of race and criminal justice because the area probation service for whom she worked covered Broadwater Farm in Tottenham. After the disturbances there in the mid-1980s, questions of possible discrimination in the criminal justice system became urgent. Trying to face up to the issue of how it could deal with minority offenders in a genuinely non-discriminatory manner, the probation service became aware that many dearly held principles—such as cooperating with police and other agencies, demanding written evidence from offenders alleging racist treatment in young offenders institutions—might have to be rethought.

Since FPWP/Hibiscus works mostly with women in prison, we need to understand the concept of 'crime' and the causal factors responsible for sending some of them to prison, in some cases for up to fifteen years. Is 'crime' a contested, socially constructed concept like 'race', or ethnicity, or is it a scientific concept like an 'atom' or a 'molecule'? This book is about 'criminology', which translates into ordinary English as the 'science of crime'. Yet, like other textbooks, the chapters here demonstrate that the concept of crime is historically and culturally variable (see Chapters 2 and 7). For example, homosexuality was decriminalized with the 1967 Sexual Offences Act. However, it is still criminal in Saudi Arabia. In most countries cocaine use and supply is illegal, although people in the Andes have been chewing coca leaves for over 3,000 years to avoid altitude sickness. Less than a hundred years ago opium was the main ingredient in most patent medicines. Today heroin, cocaine, and cannabis are classified as illicit substances, and that classification is responsible for millions of people being imprisoned all over the world. Thinking about women's crime, in some countries criminology students would have to include abortion among the crimes for which they seek causes, and of course the laws surrounding prostitution vary widely from place to place and time to time. The concept and debate about 'moral panics' (see Chapter 19) illustrates the construction of crime and the linking of 'race' with 'crime'.

Finally, we will use FPWP/Hibiscus as a case study to show how a flawed policy of 'deterrence', based on outmoded theories of crime and punishment, results in disproportionate sentences for thousands of foreign national women. We will also look at the methods of advocacy used to influence policy.

Unlike previous chapters in criminology textbooks on 'race', ethnicity and crime (for example, Croall, 1998; Phillips and Bowling, 2002), we will not attempt to explore fully the question of whether members of minority ethnic groups face discrimination at every stage of the criminal justice system. Adopting the approach outlined above inevitably imposes some editorial boundaries. Most significantly, by focusing on the ways 'race' and 'ethnicity' shape the punishment of offenders, we are conscious that debates about race and policing do not get the attention they deserve. There is a growing literature on this topic and readers are directed to Rowe (2004) for an introductory overview of the issue.

BACKGROUND

'Race' is a controversial concept, which explains why it is put in quotation marks. Despite developments in population genetics, which show that humans are over 99.9 per cent the same, some people still persist in dividing human beings into 'races', based on such superficial aspects as skin colour, thickness of lips, straightness of nose and hair, head and eye shape. Popular programmes on BBC, Channel 4, and the 'Discovery Channel' show that even these superficial differences conceal more similarities between than within these 'races', but bad habits of thought are hard to break, and we speak of Africans from Namibia and Ethiopia as members of the 'black' or 'Negro' 'race', even though they might be genetically more different from each other than from Norwegians, who are almost stereotypes of the 'white' race with thin noses and lips, pale skin, and long, straight, blond hair (see Cohen, 1999; Malik, 1996).

Such pseudo-scientific concepts of 'race' may not seem relevant in the modern world. Even anthropologists, who used to classify humans on supposed physical differences such as head size and shape (see Lombroso, 1876), now recognize that there is greater diversity within than between the 'races', and have sought new labels for dividing people such as 'culture'. But again residues of bad thinking persist and people speak of 'black', 'white', or 'mixed'-'blood' or 'race' even though there is no correlation between blood type and 'race', so you cannot tell whether someone is: 'A Negative' or 'O Positive' from the colour of his or her skin. It is a well-known fact that people inherit their characteristics not through 'blood', but through their genetic make-up.

The question is why do we still use race in our discussion of the causes of crime? Is it because criminologists no longer look for criminal 'types' by measuring the shape of their cranium (a pseudo-science called phrenology), or try to predict criminal behaviour from people's physiques? For example, if this were the case, what type of man would Arnold Schwarzenegger's build be? The answer is that some social scientists are already looking for genes that supposedly 'cause' crime and low IQs, even though studies have shown the nature of IQ tests are highly questionable (Herrnstein and Murray, 1994). If one looks back at the history of theories of crime over the past two centuries one finds that biological terms were used by people to 'explain' the criminal tendencies of the 'poor', the 'Irish', 'Catholics', 'Jews' or other disadvantaged people, whether majority or minority (Solomos and Back, 1994; Solomos, 1993). In the US and UK the Irish were once considered a separate 'race' and stigmatized with characteristics remarkably similar to those assigned to black Britons and African-Americans today: such as lazy, dissolute, purposeless, promiscuous, unintelligent and prone to crime. These discourses are a reflection of how a dominant social group ascribes negative, stereotypic characteristics to construct a hierarchy of discrimination in society.

Several points should be noted from this discussion. The first is that despite the claims by some that 'race' is a scientific concept which suggests commonality, it is in fact a socio-political construct. However, it should be noted, in certain counties, such as in apartheid South Africa, it is possible for siblings of the same parents to belong to different 'races' if they looked sufficiently different in terms of colour. Such outcomes were possible under apartheid, a system based on racial segregation instituted in 1948, and ended when Nelson Mandela was elected as the first President in post-apartheid South Africa in 1994.

Because of the confusion surrounding the concept, 'race' and its association with unpleasant terms such as 'racism', 'genocide' (literally 'murder of a race'), 'apartheid' and 'eugenics' (literally 'science of race'), most modern societies prefer to use 'ethnicity' (Miles, 1989). However, this is not clear cut; a person's ethnic identity may be complex and multi-layered and the individual's self-definition of their ethnicity may differ from the standard categories. A 'black' Londoner may consider herself 'West Indian' or 'African', while an 'Asian' may consider himself 'Indian', 'Bangladeshi', 'Hindu', or 'Muslim', or a white Londoner as Welsh with Jewish and Afro-American heritage. Our society is made up from a proliferation of different cultures and different influences.

'Racial' or 'ethnic' classification may appear comparatively straightforward; however, the above discussion demonstrates that it is really highly complex. Here in the UK, that complexity is reflected by the way in which categorization changes. In the 1980s, one of the difficulties confronting researchers was that classifications varied among different government departments and agencies (for example, research on mentally disordered offenders was made difficult because the Department of Health and the Home Office used different systems). More recently, although there has been some standardization across departments, there have been changes at various times, making year-on-year evaluation of the extent of over-representation of minority offenders in prisons problematic. The category 'Asian' is now 'South Asian'. This may not seem a big difference, but it may mean that earlier prison statistics included Chinese and other far-Eastern groups, whereas 'South Asian' excludes them and reserves the category for those from the Indian sub-continent. Importantly for the case study presented here, the way in which foreign nationals are categorized has changed in the last few years.

One thing we can be sure of when considering the construction of 'race' identities and the constructions and divisions used in criminal justice systems around the world is that the groups over-represented in prison statistics, and the race/ethnic identities associated with criminality, are characterized by poverty. In all countries for which statistics are available, it is impoverished groups who fill the prisons: African/Caribbeans in the UK; African-Americans in the US, aboriginals in Australia; Lapps and Inuits in Scandinavia; guest-workers from former Yugoslavia and Turkey in Germany; Filipino workers throughout Europe and the Gulf states; the Romany in former Eastern Europe; Romany and north Africans in southern Europe.

The US has the highest prison population in the world. More than half of the two million inmates are African-American or Hispanic; the majority are convicted for drugs offences, despite the fact that they represent less than a quarter of the population and less likely to be drug takers than whites (Tonry, 1995). The same is true, though to a lesser extent, in the UK where a disproportionate number of ethnic minority people are in prison for drugs offences, despite consistent surveys showing that young white people are more likely to be taking, or have taken drugs than non-whites. The explanations for these anomalies, and their effects on society and on the criminal justice system, will be explored in the next section.

REVIEW QUESTIONS

1 Using local newspaper reports consider the extent to which crime has been racialized in your own local area?

2 Why do many view biological explanations of crime as problematic?

Getting tough on crime?

In the decade between 1992 and 2001, the number of inmates in prison in England and Wales rose by 45 per cent from 45,486 to 66,403 (see Table 18.3). This was due to 'tougher' sentencing policies as Home Office ministers declared a 'war on drugs'. However, Table 18.1 reveals that this increase was not uniform.

Table 18.1 Percentage increase in number of prisoners by sex and race for the years 1992–2001

	% Increase
All prisoners	45
All males	43
All females	141
All whites	38
All blacks	93
White males	35
Black males	89
White females	151
Black females	155

Source: Prison Statistics England and Wales 2001 (Cm 5743). The Stationery Office, London.

Table 18.2 Percentage increase in no. of prisoners by sex and race for the years 1997–2001	
	% Increase
All prisoners	7.40 per cent
All males	6.6
All females	39
All whites	4.3
All blacks	21.6
White males	3
Black males	19.4
White females	35.5
Black females	50.7

Source: Prison Statistics England and Wales (Cm 5743). The Stationary Office, London.

The black prison population constituted 10 per cent of the prison population, compared to less than 2 per cent of the general population in 1992; but while their percentage of the general population remained constant, the percentage in prison rose to 13 per cent in 2001. Within the prison population the numbers of black women were more disproportionate, rising from 20 per cent of all female inmates in 1992 to 21 per cent in 2001 and 25 per cent in 2003. The male prison population (94 per cent of the total in 2001) increased by 43 per cent, females went up by 141 per cent; whites by 38 per cent, blacks (see Tables 18.1 and 18.3 for Home Office ethnic classification) by 93 per cent; white males increased by 35 per cent, black males by 89 per cent, white females by 151 per cent and black females by 155 per cent. Afro-Caribbeans (constitute less than 1.5 per cent of the general population) are, as we can see from the Tables 18.1–18.5, over-represented in the criminal justice system (see also Home Office, 2002; HM Prison Service, 2004; Hudson, 1989).

By comparing Tables 18.1 and 18.2, we can see that since New Labour came to power in 1997, the rate of imprisonment has slowed. Overall the prison population increased from 58,795 in 1997 to 66,403 in 2001, a rise of 7 per cent compared to 22 per cent for the similar five-year period under the Conservative Party. The breakdown by 'race' and 'ethnic' group shows a similar decline while the differentials remained: white male increased by 3 per cent, black male by 19 per cent, all females by 39 per cent, white females by 35 per cent, and black females by 51 per cent.

Since these figures were published (see Tables 18.1 and 18.2), there appears to have been acceleration in the numbers again: in 2003 there were 73,091 inmates, an increase of over 10 per cent in less than two years. This number is expected to rise to 91,000 by 2006 and possibly 110,000 by 2009, if the present trends continue. Since the absolute capacity of the system is for 77,500 inmates, the government will have to build new prisons (see NACRO, 2003, 2004).

Table 18.3 Population in prison by sex and ethnic group*

England and Wales 30 June

Sex of prisoner	Total		White		Black**		South Asian***		Chinese Other****	
	No	%	No	%	No	%	No	%	No	%
Males and females										
1992	45,486	100	37,705	81	4,773	10	1,388	3	1,043	2
1993	44,246	100	36,855	83	5,013	11	1,356	3	926	2
1994	48,879	100	40,754	83	5,606	11	1,347	3	1,102	2
1995	51,084	100	42,207	83	5,982	12	1,497	3	1,318	3
1996	55,256	100	45,029	81	6,986	13	1,654	3	1,524	3
1997	61,467	100	50,164	82	7,585	12	1,865	3	1,795	3
1998	65,727	100	53,677	82	7,976	12	2,007	3	2,046	3
1999	64,529	100	52,377	81	7,964	12	1,929	3	2,225	3
2000	65,194	100	52,581	81	8,287	13	1,837	3	2,457	4
2001	66,403	100	52,303	79	9,223	14	1,993	3	2,835	4
Males										
1992	43,950	100	36,616	83	4,464	10	4,464	3	981	2
1993	42,666	100	35,691	84	4,690	11	4,690	3	854	2
1994	47,075	100	39,399	84	5,236	11	5,236	3	1,050	2
1995	49,086	100	40,697	83	5,592	11	5,592	3	1,247	3
1996	52,951	100	43,280	82	6,538	12	6,538	3	1,441	3
1997	58,795	100	48,151	82	7,062	12	7,062	3	1,684	3
1998	62,607	100	51,304	82	7,416	12	7,416	3	1,889	3
1999	61,322	100	49,961	81	7,355	12	7,355	3	2,081	4
2000	61,839	100	50,059	81	7,644	12	7,644	3	2,304	4
2001	62,690	100	49,475	79	8,435	13	8,435	3	2,678	4
Females										
1992	1,536	100	1,089	71	309	20	309	2	62	4
1993	1,580	100	1,164	74	323	20	323	1	72	5
1994	1,804	100	1,355	75	370	21	370	1	52	3
1995	1,998	100	1,510	76	390	20	390	1	71	4
1996	2,305	100	1,749	76	448	19	448	1	83	4
1997	2,672	100	2,013	75	523	20	523	1	111	4
1998	3,120	100	2,373	76	560	18	560	1	157	5
1999	3,207	100	2,418	75	609	19	609	1	144	4
2000	3,355	100	2,522	75	643	19	643	1	153	5
2001	3,713	100	2,728	73	788	21	788	1	157	4

* Prior to 1993 coding of ethnic group was similar to that used in the EC Labour Force survey. In 1993 a new ethnic classification system was adopted by prisons which is congruent with that used for the Census of population. The change in coding means that figures for 1998, 1992 and 1993–96 are not directly comparable.
** Between 1988 and 1992 ethnic group classification was 'West Indian, Guyanese, African'.
*** Between 1988 and 1992 ethnic group classification was 'Indian, Pakistani, Bangledeshi'.
**** Between 1988 and 1992 ethnic group classification was 'Chinese, Arab, Mixed Origin'.

Source: HM Prison Statistics England and Wales 2001 (Cm 5743). The Stationery Office, London.

Table 18.4 Prison population: selected countries

Country	Prison population	Inmates per 100,000 population
USA	1,993,503	700
Lebanon	7,296	220
Portugal	13,106	130
England and Wales	67,056	125
Scotland	6,172	120
Spain	45,633	115
Turkey	71,860	110
Germany	79,348	95
France	46,376	80
Greece	8,343	80
Denmark	3,279	60
Northern Ireland	863	50

Source: The Times 6 December 2003.

The prison capital of the world is the USA, which, with over two million inmates, jails nearly 700 of every 100,000 of its population (see Sim, 2004). How are we to make sense of, or explain the increasing numbers of people imprisoned, and their variation in terms of gender, 'race' and 'ethnicity'? What policies or theories lay behind this surge in incarceration compared to Europe and the developing countries? Since both the Conservatives and New Labour seem to take their cue from the US in many areas of penal policy, it would be useful to look at how policy has developed in the USA.

The USA penal policy agenda unleashed on the criminal justice system of England and Wales

Under the influence of far-right ideologues such as Charles Murray (1990) and Richard Hernstein (1995), conservative US administrations from the time of Ronald Reagan (1981–89) to George Bush (2001—current at the time of writing) have supported earlier theories of the causes of crime such as biology, physiology and now genetics. These theories also concentrate on the individual rather than society, ignoring the influence of structural factors. It was argued that the propensity for criminal behaviour lay in a person's genetic make-up. If this was the case, change could only take place through medical treatment. The emphasis of current penal policy is on punishment and retribution rather than the rehabilitation of the offender. Consequently, this rise in a punitive and retributive discourses on both sides of the Atlantic from the Clinton Administration to the Labour party in the UK through to the Bush Administration justifies harsher measures against offenders.

Crime policy is not made in isolation but is part of a political conception of society, which drives economic and social policies and that mutually reinforce each other. In this chapter it is important to refer back to earlier periods of social philosophy. The role of the government has changed from an interventionist stance most clearly seen with the birth of the welfare state to a more laissez-faire approach. This is most evidently seen, with the shift of resources from social welfare, education, and public housing to the military, business subsidies, and the expansion of prisons. Criminologists have drawn on political/ social theory to explain this shift from social policy to penal policy. Highlighting crime as the problem of the times connects with people who are not suffering from unemployment or other social ills, and it creates demands for ever more punishment, ever more government intervention. Several criminologists have suggested that new right economics is the most important explanation for the war on crime policies, which are directed at the most marginalized and disadvantaged groups (this idea goes some way to explaining the differences between the USA/UK and northern European countries) (see O'Malley, 2000).

New Labour arresting the problem

The questions of policing, discrimination in the criminal justice system raised in the Scarman Report entered the political arena in mid-1990s. The focus this time was the murder of Stephen Lawrence, an eighteen year-old black man stabbed to death whilst waiting for a bus on 22 April 1993. In response to the then Home Secretary, Jack Straw, set up the Mcpherson Commission in 1998. The report found that the criminal justice system and, by implication, other aspects of British society, was 'institutionally racist', which according to Dr Robin Oakley, 'can influence police service delivery ... not solely through the deliberate actions of a small number of bigoted individuals, but through a more systematic tendency that could unconsciously influence police performance generally' (Macpherson, 1999; Chapter 6, section 6.31). When Labour came to government in May 1997, the prison population was 60,131. Previously it took four decades (1954–94) for the prison population to rise by 25,000. On 5 March 2004, there were 4,549 women in prison, an increase of 151 per cent in the last ten years (Prison Reform Trust, 2004, 3). Over the last year, prison overcrowding has been at its highest level and there are some prisons, which are not only overcrowded, but have also exceeded their safe maximum capacity. Out of the 138 prisons in England and Wales, 85 were overcrowded. England and Wales has the highest imprisonment rate in the European Union and women's prisons rank among the worst in the country (ibid.). Over a quarter of this number are from ethnic minorities, including many foreign nationals who have been given long 'deterrent' sentences for smuggling drugs. The policies of the subsequent Home Secretary, David Blunkett, of longer, mandatory sentences, and the abolition of the right to jury trials for some categories of crimes, are opposed by the judicial establishment, as they watch the numbers of prisoners spiralling out of control (*The Times*, 6 August 2003).

The Labour government did, however, commission a major report into sentencing policy, the Halliday Report, which laid the framework for the Criminal Justice Act 2003.

Its recommendations, however, continued the trend evident from the mid-1990s of emphasizing persistence, redefining proportionality in sentencing from 'proportionality of punishments to the seriousness of the current offence', to 'proportionality to seriousness of offence plus record' (see www.homeoffice.gov.uk/docs/halliday.html).

Under this Labour government, there has been a re-emergence of rehabilitation, under the Home Office's 'what works' programme. All persons under sentence, whether in prison or in the community, are to be offered courses and treatments designed to help them refrain from re-offending. While this is an improvement on the previous Conservative government's emphasis on incarceration with little thought to rehabilitation, there are some causes for concern. First of all, the programmes are based on crime patterns, motivations and causes associated with the male criminal majority: special female programmes do exist, but they deal with stereotypical female 'needs' rather than being rooted in the circumstances surrounding female offending.

Moreover, assessment of offenders for the programmes and for suitability for community rather than prison sentences (custody-minus rather than custody-plus, as the new sentencing terminology puts it), or for early release still include the racially correlated risk-of-reoffending factors first used in the USA.

Home Office ministers, and the government more generally, express commitment to eradicating discrimination in criminal justice. Ethnic monitoring, inspections and race/gender awareness training have been introduced in all criminal justice agencies, and yet the figures of over-representation of black offenders—particularly black female offenders—in prison continues. Whatever the penal policy in fashion (rehabilitation, just deserts, incapacitation, risk management), it is the poor, especially the poor from ethnic minorities, who are at the hard end of penal policies. There has been a shift in the nature of discrimination from direct to indirect, that is, from discrimination based blatantly on gender and/or race prejudice to discrimination which results from policies which are intended to be gender/race neutral in fact disproportionately affecting certain groups. It is the embedding of this form of indirect discrimination in the routines and processes of criminal justice which is only just beginning to be acknowledged as institutional racism.

REVIEW QUESTIONS

1 How useful is the concept of institutional racism?

2 What evidence is there of racial discrimination in the criminal justice system?

3 Can racism, where it occurs in the criminal justice system, be explained best by examining discriminatory acts of criminal justice practitioners, the cultures of organisations, or institutional racism?

The tabloid press: creating moral panics

Hall *et al.*, in the book, *Policing the Crisis: Mugging the State and Law and Order* (1978) criticize what they saw as the exaggerated and racist reporting of black criminality in the British tabloids. In taking the example of the dramatic increase in 'mugging' in the 1970s, Hall *et al.*, suggested that official crime figures were used as political cannon fodder during times of economic crisis to justify a failing capitalist economy. In this way, a myth or illusion of black street crime was created to act as a scapegoat, to draw the public's attention away from the real social problems of the time. A more recent moral panic was witnessed with public reaction over the Bulger case (1993), the Soham Murders (2002) and the death of Sarah Payne (see Chapter 12). Vigilante groups formed and in some incidents paediatricians were attacked because people confused the word paediatrician with paedophile.

By labelling mugging as a crime of young, black males (see Hall, 1978) the mass media constructed the image of the archetypical mugger, the black male. There are three key positions when studying the relationship, if any, between 'race', ethnicity and crime. The idea espoused by Stuart Hall and Paul Gilroy of the neo-Marxist Centre for Contemporary Cultural Studies, argues that higher levels of criminality amongst the British Black population are 'mythical', the illusion being created as the result of distorted media attention. The second position also connected with Gilroy, goes further to suggest that the above population do not commit more crime, but that the supposed level of criminality is the effect of selective police practices arising from 'police racism'. Third, the New Left Realist perspective argues that the anti-colonial political struggle, media exaggeration and police racism may all exist, but this does not adequately explain the over representation of certain groups in official figures and in prison. Instead, it is the increased levels of marginalization experienced by this group that can explain their use of crime as a response to their situation.

In most cases of murder, both victim and perpetrator are from the same race and ethnic group. But in the majority of murders committed by white against white, race or ethnicity fails to be an issue. When Afro-Caribbeans commit murder, however, especially with guns, it becomes a sensational issue of black-on-black crime. When certain crimes become racialized, political pressure builds to target the offending community, rather than the individual perpetrator. Thus, stereotyping or stigmatizing means that all members of a particular group or type of people are assumed to be guilty. One of the reasons for the failure of the police to solve the murder of Stephen Lawrence in 1993 was that the police assumed that it was gang related, because he was young, black and male. The stereotypes of the young African/Caribbean male as criminal are so strong that it was initially taken for granted that Stephen Lawrence must have been part of the trouble, not an innocent victim.

The absence of racialized discourse for certain crimes is illustrated in the portrayal of paedophilia, which is almost exclusively a crime of white males (Chapter 12). The tabloids never identified them as such, and this is not fixed in the minds of the public. Public hatred and suspicion may be directed at all paedophiles, and suspected paedophiles, but this label is not attached to all white men, or all white men living in the same neighbourhood as a convicted paedophile, in the way that the label 'mugger' is applied to young black men. Similarly, the labels joy riding, serial killing, arson, corporate manslaughter, football hooliganism, racial violence, and professional assassination do not attach to white males, although their perpetrators are almost exclusively from this group.

REVIEW QUESTIONS

1 Give examples of the form of discrimination that exists in the courtroom/sentencing or the prison setting?

2 Why is it so difficult to assess the extent of police racism or discrimination?

3 Write from the perspectives of a Labour and a Conservative Home Secretary explaining why a disproportionate number of prisoners are from ethnic minorities.

FPWP/HIBISCUS: A case study in the social construction of crime

This section focuses on the role of Hibiscus in its work with female foreign nationals who find themselves locked in the criminal justice system of England and Wales. At present there are over 3,000 Jamaicans in UK prisons, most of them for attempting to import drugs (Heaven, 1996). In 2002, 20 per cent of women in prison were foreign nationals; the majority, 60 per cent, had West Indian Nationalities (Prison Reform Trust, 2004: 10). Jamaica is a Caribbean island which had a population of 2.7 million in 2002 (http://www.cia.gov/cia/publications/factbook). If these prisoners were in their own country, Jamaica would then have one of the highest prison populations (120 per 100,000) in the world. Male Jamaicans constitute less than 5 per cent of the total UK prison population, but 600 Jamaican women constitute 15 per cent of the 4,000 inmates in women's prisons here. Table 18.5 shows that Jamaican women in prison for drugs offences increased from

Table 18.5 Number of Nigerian and Jamaican women in UK prisons for the years 1990–2003

Year	Nigerian	Jamaican
1990	83	30
1991	66	42
1992	70	43
1993	62	54
1994	59	56
1996 (JUN)	20	40
1996 (Dec)	16	52
2001	16	329
2003*		800

Source: Crown Copyright. Data provided by the Research, Development and Statistics Directorate of the Home Office.

* Figures at the time writing were not available.

30 in 1990 to 800, which is an increase of almost 2000 per cent. These numbers explain to some extent the record rise in the female population to over 4,000. Table 18.5 also shows that the number of Nigerian couriers peaked at 83 in 1990, and declined steadily to 16 in 2001.

For over twenty years Olga Heaven has worked with the Prison Service to address the needs of female foreign nationals in prison in the UK and the following section will outline who foreign nationals are, where they come from and what happens to them once in prison. As a result of the war on drugs policy, the government responded with 'tough' measures (Heaven, 1996; Hood, 1992). Lord Lane, the Lord Chief Justice in 1986, introduced the idea of long, 'deterrent' sentences, based on the quantity and purity of drugs, disallowing any inclusion of mitigating circumstances to be used as a defence (see McKoy, 1991). The effect of this new policy has led to longer sentences in the UK and under the Nigerian law, it is possible for couriers who had completed their sentence in the UK to be punished and imprisoned again.

The mule

According to the tabloid stereotype, the 'mule' is a young, sophisticated, beautiful woman who deals in large quantities of heroin and cocaine to fund a jet-set lifestyle. The reality unearthed by FPWP is far more mundane. In reality the courier is poorly educated, from the lowest socioeconomic group, in her late twenties to mid-thirties, a single mother of two to three children and living in absolute poverty. In many cases women come from the slums of Jamaica or Columbia, from the cities of countries in economic crisis. It is these women who find themselves locked in the UK prison system. Many of the women Hibiscus has encountered claimed they were tricked or forced into carrying drugs, and others were driven by desperation and poverty. The Misuse of Drugs Act 1971 distinguished between the possession of drugs and trafficking drugs. The law stipulates that trafficking in a Class A drug carries a maximum penalty of fourteen years, while possession of a Class B drug carries a maximum of seven years. Sentencing is based on the weight and the purity of the drug. For example: a quantity of 500g at 100 per cent purity attracts a sentence of ten years and 1kg a length of between 10 and 14 years.

One in ten passengers on some flights from Jamaica are couriers holding small quantities of drugs. This view supports anecdotal evidence that some women now in prison are used as decoys to divert attention from middle class couriers carrying larger quantities of cocaine. When these decoys are caught, these women have no way of coping with the situation. These women arrive in the UK without appropriate clothing for the British climate, far from their children and unaware of their rights. They find themselves competing for survival in an alien and hostile prison culture, where the food and language is different and even basic cosmetics for skin and haircare are in some prisons unavailable or far too costly.

Ninety per cent of female foreign nationals are first offenders who had never been in the UK before, and are sole providers for several dependent children. They become victims of a sentencing policy which refuses to take their circumstances into account. Sentencing a man to prison punishes one person, while a woman's sentence must be multiplied by the children she has left behind. In prison the women suffer constant anxiety about their children, left behind without a family or a state to care for them. Furthermore, without a structure of care many of the children are thrown out of squalid rented accommodation onto the streets. In some cases, family members are shot or recruited into the drug trafficking trade. These are just some of the effects of imprisoning a female foreign national for an average of ten years.

Hibiscus is an independent charity founded in 1991. We have offices in London, Lagos and in Kingston. The primary functions are to locate and inform dependent children and other family members of the woman's situation. This helps to ensure that contact with the prisoners and their family are maintained. Moreover, our role is to inform and advise the women of their rights, provide interpreters, counselling, social, legal and welfare assistance. Advocacy is central to our role. It is through media interviews, participating in documentaries, campaigning and writing a chapter such as this that the charity attempts to raise awareness of the plight of female foreign nationals. It is by informing and advizing government policy, the female prison estate and educating public opinion about the nature and conditions that lead women into this type of crime that we can begin to address the needs of female foreign nationals.

In 1991, Hibiscus and the BBC produced a highly successful documentary entitled *Mules*. The 30-minute documentary provided a graphic display of the poverty faced by Nigerian women in their own country and the social conditions and experiences endured whist imprisoned at HMP Holloway. Audiences in the UK were horrified to see the level of social deprivation that foreign nationals faced as they found themselves in British gaols. Moreover, this documentary had a huge impact on dispelling myths about women drug couriers both in the UK and in Nigeria, while at the same time exposing the flaws in the 'deterrent' policy discussed earlier on in the chapter.

In Nigeria the impact was even more dramatic: the High Commission in London taped the programme and sent it to Lagos where it was shown on prime-time national TV. Like the British tabloids, they had created the Mule as a woman driven by money rather than a women driven by desperation. Faced with the images of dilapidated houses and malnourished children that were left behind, the Nigerian public demanded that the government should tackle this social problem.

The transmission of the documentary in Nigeria showed potential Mules the reality of prison life in the UK. Dealers could no longer convince them that they would not be caught, or that they would be deported on the same flight that they came in on. The pool of couriers dried up; the numbers arrested or imprisoned began to fall, and there is anecdotal evidence that Nigerian drug dealers shifted attention to other West African countries and to South Africa.

As the Jamaican numbers approached crisis proportions, Hibiscus, with the assistance of the UK High Commission organized a conference in Kingston in September 2001, to address the issues and find solutions to the problem. Experts, professionals, charities and others involved with the operational needs of the Criminal Justice System and the welfare of prisoners in both countries gathered to share ideas on what could be done to reverse this growing trend.

Since the Conference in 2001, there has been a huge publicity campaign in Jamaica supported by the media and government officials to spread the message that carrying drugs or acting as Mule is not the road out of poverty. This publicity campaign has led to government-based training programmes on a local level but has also led to the use of sniffer dogs and scan machines at airports. In addition, both governments have introduced legislation to seize the assets of dealers. After these measures were introduced, just one Jamaican courier was arrested in the UK over a period of months compared to three a day previously. But our work is still unfinished as thousands of foreign nationals choke the prison system. The 3,000 Jamaicans in the UK prison system, costs the tax payer over £150 million per year. Hibiscus has therefore much the following recommendations:

(a) amnesty for less serious offenders of good behaviour coming to the end of their sentences;

(b) parole and reduced time for those serving longer sentences;

(c) an arrangement with the Jamaican government to let offenders serve part of their sentences in their country or to supervise released prisoners on parole;

(d) a system of cash incentives for those of good behaviour who make the fullest use of educational and employment opportunities in prison;

(e) the Jamaican and the UK government to collaborate on a prison building programme in Jamaica.

REVIEW QUESTIONS

1 Use the experience of Hibiscus to suggest a role for the voluntary sector in the criminal justice system.

2 How does imprisonment impact differently on foreign nationals?

3 Is there a relationship between ethnicity and crime? Give reasons for your answers.

CONCLUSION

This chapter has examined how theory, ideology, rhetoric, politics and the media have combined to influence the policies that have resulted in foreign national women being over-represented in prisons in the UK. Moreover, we have shown that 'race', 'ethnicity' and 'crime' are social constructs that vary from society to society, within societies and over time. Earlier theorists concentrated on genetic 'defects', physical characteristics, on 'blood', inherited characteristics, 'race' or national origin as the causes of crime. More modern theories have looked to structural causes in society, such as deprivation, unemployment, and inequality. Foreign national women prisoners are over-represented amongst ethnic racial minorities and the work of Hibiscus has brought to the fore of prison policy in various countries the plight of foreign nationals. It is only through advocacy and challenging outmoded typifications of femininity and ethnicity, that we can address the inhumanity, ineffectiveness and counter-productivity of a 'deterrent' policy that suffuses penal policy today. Furthermore, it is an indictment of the English criminal justice system that justice and equality before the law as highlighted here and in other parts of the book are so unevenly distributed.

QUESTIONS FOR DISCUSSION

1 How can we explain the disproportionate number of ethnic minorities in the prison population?

2 Write a letter to the Home Secretary with recommendations on how to tackle racial discrimination in the criminal justice system.

3 Discuss the relationship between gender, ethnicity and crime.

4 Have recent penal polices impacted differentially on ethnic minorities?

5 Explain the reasons for the increase of political attention on ethnicity and crime.

GUIDE TO FURTHER READING

Bowling, B. and Phillips, C. (2002), *Racism, Crime and Justice*, Harlow: Longman Criminology Series.

This is a lucid presentation of the relations between racism and crime as they develop and interact in the Criminal Justice System. The critical analyses of 'race', 'ethnicity', 'prejudice' and 'discrimination', and how they affect the social constructions of 'crime' are particularly valuable, especially when placed in their historical contexts.

Cohen, P. (ed), *New Ethnicities, Old Racisms* (1999), London: Zed Books.

This book analyses these concepts from a post-modern perspective which rejects essentialist notions of race and ethnicity. This edited collection shows how a post-modernist account explains how identities develop, within the context of cultural transformation in modern Britain.

Green, P. (ed), *Drug Couriers* (1996), Quartet Books: London.

This collection is part of the Howard League Handbooks series. It combines the work of scholars and practitioners who reject the popular prejudices and stereotypes propagated by the media and politicians. By fostering a more objective and rational explanation of the problem it gives policy makers the opportunity to be truly 'tough on the causes of crime'.

Ramsbotham, P. *Prisongate* (2003), Simon and Schuster: London.

The book by Her Majesty's former Chief Inspector of Prisons is a severe indictment of the policies of successive governments which fail in their statutory duties to care for their imprisoned population.

Tonry, M. *Malign Neglect* (1996), Oxford University Press: New York, Oxford.

The book examines how certain policies develop that would appeal to middle-class voters. Under Presidents Reagan, Clinton and Bush, certain policies had the effect of increasing numbers of young black males in prison, whilst the actual crime rate remained constant. He addresses the nature of policy making, hidden agendas and whether male Afro-Americans are expedient to the voting system as reflected in the execution of certain policies.

WEB LINKS

http://www.homeoffice.gov.uk/rds

Is a useful website to find statistics on almost every aspect of the criminal justice system. The site includes sections on community policy, crime reduction, criminal justice, drugs prevention, immigration and nationality, race equality and diversity. An important report pertinent to this chapter is the report titled Statistics on Race and The Criminal Justice System (2002).

http://www.statistics.gov.uk/census2001

The National Census is the most complete source of information about the population that we have.

http://www.liberty-human-rights.org.uk

Liberty is an independent human rights organization which works to defend and extend rights and freedoms in England and Wales.

http://fpwphibiscus.mysite.wanadoo-members.co.uk/index.jhtml

Hibiscus is an independent organization that campaigns and provides advice for the families of foreign national women who are in prison in England and Wales.

http://www.womeninprison.org.uk

Women in Prison is a charitable organization that campaigns and provides advice for women who are in prison and who are on release.

REFERENCES

Carmichael S. and Hamilton C.V. (1968) *Black Power: The Politics of Liberation in America*. London: Penguin.

Cashmore, E. (1996) *Dictionary of Race and Ethnic Relations* (4th edn). London: Routledge.

Cohen, P. (ed) (1999) *New Ethnicities, Old Racisms*. London: Zed Books.

Croall, H. (1998) *Crime and Society in Britain: An Introduction*. London: Longman.

Green P. (eds) (1996) *Drug Couriers: The Construction of a Public Enemy in Drug Couriers: A New Perspective*. London: Quartet Books.

Hall, S. (ed) (1997) *Representation: Cultural Representations and Signifying Practices*. London: Sage.

Hall, S., Clarke, J., Critcher, C., Jefferson, T. and Roberts, B. (1978) *Policing the Crisis: Mugging, the State and Law and Order*. London: Macmillan.

Heaven, O. (1996) 'Hibiscus: working with Nigerian women' in P. Green (ed) *Drug Couriers : A New Perspective*. London: Quartet.

Herrnstein, R.J. (1995) 'Criminogenic Traits, in J.Q. Wilson and J. Petersillia (eds), *Crime*. San Francisco, CA: ICS Press.

Herrnstein, R.J. and Murray, C. (1994) *The Bell Curve: Intelligence and Class Structure in American Life*. New York and London: Free Press.

HM Prison Service (July 2004) *Foreign Nationals*. London: Home Office.

Hood, R. (1992) Race and Sentencing. Oxford: Clarendon Press.

Home Office (2002) Prison Statistics England Wales 2001, Cm 5743. London: Home Office.

Hudson, B. (1989) 'Discrimination and Disparity: The Influence of Race on Sentencing'. New Community, 16, 1: 23–34.

Macpherson, W. (1999) The Stephen Lawrence Inquiry, of an Inquiry by Sir William Macpherson of Cluny. Advised by Tom Cook, The Right Reverend Dr John Sentamu and Dr Richard Stone. Cm 4262–1. London: Home Office.

Malik, K. (1996) *The Meaning of Race*. London: Macmillan.

McKoy, A.W. (1991) *The Politics of Heroin*. New York: Lawrence Hill.

Miles, R. (1989) *Racism*. London: Routledge.

Murray, C. (1990) *The Emerging British Underclass*. London: Institute for Economic Affairs.

NACRO (2003) Race and Prisons: Where are we now? London: NACRO.

NACRO (2004) Barriers to Equality—Challenges in tracking black and minority ethnic people through the criminal justice system. London.

O'Malley, P. (ed) (2000) *Crime and the Risk Society*. Aldershot: Ashgate.

Phillips, C. and Bowling, B. (2002) 'Racism, ethnicity, crime, and criminal justice' in M. Maguire *et al.* (ed) *The Oxford Handbook of Criminology*. Oxford: Oxford University Press.

Prison Reform Trust (2004) Many Forgotten Prisoners—The Plight of Foreign National Prisoners in England and Wales.

Prison Statistics England and Wales 2001, Cm 5743. London: The Stationery Office.

Ramsbotham, D. (2003) *Prisongate*. London: Simon and Schuster.

Rowe, M. (2004) *Policing, Race and Racism*. Cullompton: Willan Publishing.

Sim, J. (2004) 'Thinking about imprisonment' in J. Muncie and D. Wilson (ed) *Student Handbook of Criminal Justice and Criminology*. London: Cavendish.

Solomos, J. and Back, L. (1994) *Race, Politics and Social Change*. London: Routledge.

Solomos, J. (1993) *Race and Racism in Contemporary Britain*. London: Macmillan.

The Times, 6 September (2003) 'Prison Crisis as Foreign Inmates Soar'.

The Times, 3 September (2003) 'Imprisoned in the Iron Cage of Vengeance'.

Tonry, M. (1995) *Malign Neglect: Race, Crime and Punishment in America*. New York: Oxford University Press.

19 Young people and crime

Derek Kirton

INTRODUCTION

There are many reasons for examining the relationship between young people and crime. One of the more obvious is that the peak ages for involvement in criminal activity, whether judged by official statistics or self-report studies, lie in the teenage years. Crime statistics for England and Wales show peak ages for offending as eighteen to twenty for males and fifteen to seventeen for females, while the corresponding figures from self-report studies have been eighteen to twenty-one and fourteen (Home Office 2003a; Flood-Page *et al.*, 2000). Official statistics also indicate that in 2002, 38 per cent of those cautioned or sentenced for indictable offences were aged between ten and twenty. A second reason is that childhood and youth are commonly seen as times when patterns for later life are being set. Effective intervention or the lack of it, may decide whether young offenders become 'hardened criminals' and moral panics regarding the 'youth of today' have recurred throughout history (Pearson, 1983).

In this chapter, the focus will be on analysing both youth crime and responses to it. The latter are concentrated largely on the youth justice system, but may also involve initiatives relating to parenting, schooling or social inclusion. In the main body of the chapter, we will discuss the key principles around which youth justice has evolved and how the balance between them has changed over time. This will be followed by examination of some of the main theories and models that have been put forward to explain youth crime, including patterns linked to social divisions such as those based on class, ethnicity and gender. Finally, a review of recent developments and future directions in youth justice is provided. First, however, the context will be set with an overview of some key concepts and debates relating to young people and crime.

BACKGROUND

Before looking at what is distinctive about young people and crime, it is important to acknowledge that there are many similarities with the treatment of adult offenders. For example, in both instances there are debates regarding the appropriate balance between punishment, rehabilitation and deterrence and that between the rights and responsibilities (including to victims) of offenders. Similarly, there is a broad range of sentencing options from fines and discharges to custody. Within the field of criminology, the tensions between crime as an act of free will or as a product of other (psychological, sociological, biological) factors apply to young and adult offenders alike. It should be noted here that 'young' has different meanings depending on context. Within the criminal justice system in England and Wales, those aged between ten and seventeen are dealt with through a distinctive youth justice system with its own courts, custodial institutions, professional personnel and in many cases, sentences. Young adulthood is also marked through separate custodial facilities, with Young Offender Institutions catering for those up to the age of twenty-one. In research, young has sometimes been taken up to the age of twenty-five or even thirty, largely in order to explore further the process of 'growing out of crime'.

Despite the similarities, however, there are also important differences between the domains of young and 'adult' offenders, differences that in broad terms can be taken as reflecting perspectives on childhood and youth as life stages. Crucially, they are seen as periods of evolving understanding and morality, rendering children and young people less responsible than adults for their actions. This is generally embodied within criminal justice systems in four main ways. First, there is a minimum age of criminal responsibility (currently ten in England and Wales), below which the child cannot legally commit a crime. The rationale for this is that they lack the *mens rea* (or 'guilty mind') required. Second, even above the age of criminal responsibility, children and young people tend to be treated differently from adult offenders in various ways. Typically, these will include separate courts (or alternatives to courts) and certain sentencing options that are specific to young offenders. A third feature is that of parental responsibility, either directly for their children's behaviour or failure to control their offspring. Finally, the State is usually regarded as having responsibilities, to address the behaviour of young people but also to protect their rights and ensure their 'welfare'. As will become apparent, these seemingly straightforward features of youth justice systems hide great complexity and often fierce controversy. One example of this is that the age of criminal responsibility has varied significantly over time and between countries—currently ranging in Europe from seven to eighteen.

As will be seen below, understandings and responses to youth crime were transformed during the nineteenth century and much of the twentieth. A growing sense of childhood 'innocence' was reflected in separation from adult offenders and other corrupting influences. Links were increasingly drawn between childhood deprivation and later involvement in crime. This gave rise to what is generally referred to as a welfare model for dealing with youth crime, in which offending is taken to by a symptom of psychological or social deprivation. The response rests with providing expert-led treatment in order to meet the child's needs and so reduce offending. The high spot of the welfare model occurred in the late 1960s but thereafter, its core assumptions were largely rejected, and replaced by what became known as the justice model. Rather than focusing on deprivation and needs, the justice model places the offence at the centre, regarding it as an act of will, with the offender to be punished in line with the seriousness of the crime.

The shift from welfare to justice highlighted a crucial aspect of responses to youth crime, namely that intervention can sometimes be seen as counter-productive. This may occur through the effects of labelling (see Chapter 5 above) young people as criminals but also because any re-offending tends to provoke more severe ('high tariff') sentences. This may accelerate young offenders' paths towards custody and deepen their involvement in offending. Interventions for minor offences or even 'risk' of offending are often characterized as net widening, to describe the way they draw young people into the youth justice system, perhaps unnecessarily and with negative consequences. In the case of young offenders, attempts to avoid the effects of net widening are underpinned by the notion that young people generally 'grow out of crime' and that diversion from the youth justice system is more effective. The strategy of diversion describes efforts to minimize young offenders' involvement with the formal youth justice system, steering them away from the more punitive sentences such as custody, and where possible keeping them out of the system entirely.

While debates on welfare, justice, diversion and net widening focus on the perceived effectiveness of particular interventions, some analysts have argued that the youth justice system is driven by other considerations, notably concern with management of the system and its 'value for money'. The concept of corporatism was developed by Pratt (1989). Its main elements are those of centralization, government intervention and cooperation of agencies and professionals working towards common goals. Typically, it has also been associated with the use of targets, and prescribed ways of working.

The development of youth justice in England and Wales

A specific focus on young offenders is generally traced to the early years of the nineteenth century when organizations emerged to highlight the issue and campaign for reform (Muncie, 2004). At the heart of their work was a plea for a move away from harsh, generally physical punishment towards more subtle means. A growing sense that children and young people could be moulded heightened awareness of the potential for both rehabilitation and corruption.

The rise of the welfare model

During the nineteenth century, there was increasing separation from adult offenders through the establishment of juvenile prisons and the Reformatory and Industrial Schools of the 1850s. The latter, developed by the reformer Mary Carpenter, emphasized strict discipline and training for modest but respectable trades (usually domestic service in the case of girls), but also sought to offer children a more caring environment. Such developments can, in turn, be seen as part of a wider movement to regulate childhood through protective legislation, removal from the streets, compulsory schooling and organized leisure (Hendrick, 1994).

In line with ideas of childhood as a period of 'natural innocence', stronger links were drawn between deprivation and involvement or risk of offending. Establishment of juvenile courts and separate custodial institutions (known as 'Borstals') under the Children Act 1908 marked a clearer separation from adult criminal justice, while the Children and Young Persons (CYP) Act 1933 highlighted the need to protect children from bad company, moral danger and neglect and strengthened the legal powers to remove children from their families. Young offenders were now more likely to be seen as victims of circumstance, and in principle to be treated more sympathetically. However, the changes also brought closer surveillance of families and intervention aimed at preventing future offending (Donzelot, 1980).

These trends continued after World War II, with growing faith in child psychology and psychiatry. John Bowlby's (1946; 1955) work, attributing a range of anti-social behaviour and criminal behaviour to lack of a consistent maternal figure in the lives of children, was particularly influential. In a period of rising affluence, responsibility for crime was increasingly laid at the door of 'problem families' and a role developed for social workers to address their inadequate parenting. This welfare based strategy was buoyed by the failure of approved schools and custody to reduce re-offending (Minty, 1987).

The CYP Acts of 1963 and 1969 enshrined a new orthodoxy that youthful offending had to be understood and addressed within a broader framework of child welfare. Under this welfare model (see above), responsibility for young offenders was to be significantly relocated from the criminal justice system to welfare agencies. The goal of decriminalization was embodied in the CYP Act 1969 which raised the age of criminal responsibility (already raised from eight to ten in 1963) to fourteen. Another key measure was the introduction of the care order, where offending was one of the possible grounds, along with abuse, neglect and non-school attendance, for transferring parental rights to the local authority. The message seemed clear, namely that young offenders were to be seen as children first, their problems as those of child welfare.

The return to justice

In hindsight, the CYP Act 1969 can be seen as the high point of the welfare model, as it quickly came under attack from the political right and left. The emerging 'new right' blamed 'permissiveness' for a rising crime rate (Hall *et al.*, 1978) and portrayed the welfare model as 'soft on crime', making excuses and undermining individual responsibility. The incoming Conservative Government declined to implement the new age of criminal responsibility, leaving it at ten. There was also opposition from police and magistrates, and a sharp rise in custodial sentences seemed to reflect the latter's desire to ensure punishment and retain greater control over the treatment of young offenders.

While the welfare model attracted predictable hostility from the political right, it also came under fire from the left, arguing that whatever the intentions behind the model, its effects were often harsh (Thorpe *et al.*, 1980). For example, care orders could last many years (until age eighteen), effectively creating indeterminate sentences. Net widening occurred as those committing relatively minor offences or even adjudged 'at risk' of offending could be drawn into supervised activities and treatment regimes. In addition to raising civil liberties questions, this could lead to harsher sentences if a young person (re-) offended while taking part, a phenomenon known as 'raising the tariff'. The dangers of net widening were greater because, as Thorpe *et al.* (1980) suggest, the welfare model had effectively been grafted onto the existing system, rather than replacing it. These pressures led to the development of what became known as the justice model (see above) (Morris *et al.*, 1980). For those who worked with young offenders, the model was to bring a focus on 'offending behaviour' rather than the background of the offender.

Diversion in the 1980s: a quiet revolution

The 1980s present something of a paradox in relation to youth justice. The Conservative Government elected in 1979 was strongly committed to taking a tough stance on crime. Yet during the following decade there was a very sharp fall in the number of young offenders sentenced to custody, the figure for fourteen to sixteen year olds dropping from 7,700 in 1981 to 1,400 in 1991 (Smith, 2003: 20). Although the figures remain subject to debate, it is clear that declining custody cannot be explained by a corresponding fall in the crime rate (Pitts, 2001). Rather, explanation may be found in an accommodation between different interpretations of the newly adopted justice model. On the one hand, the Conservative government's commitment to 'law and order' was reflected in punitive measures, notably tougher regimes in detention centres to provide a 'short, sharp, shock' for young offenders. Yet, government was also keen to contain costs and sought ways of marrying 'toughness' with relative economy. In broad terms, the answer was to be found under the slogan 'punishment in the community', with sentences that could be pre-sented as alternatives to custody (Bottoms *et al.*, 1990). Within the new community programmes, youth justice workers were able to develop a strategy of 'diversion'.

At its heart, diversion meant pursuing the 'least restrictive alternative' for offenders, avoiding custody at the higher end of the tariff and using cautions and warnings at the lower end. The number of cautions rose significantly, from 36 per cent of young male and 60 per cent of young female offenders in 1984, to 59 and 80 per cent respectively in 1994 (Ruxton, 1996). The underpinning rationale for diversion was that most young offenders 'grow out of crime' and that strong intervention from the criminal justice system tends to be counter-productive. The success of the diversionary strategy rested partly on 'systems management', the capacity of youth justice workers to exert influence on decision-making at all stages of the process from arrest to sentencing (Haines and Drakeford, 1998). Youth justice workers were able to develop programmes that proved acceptable to the courts, largely by emphasizing responsibility on the part of offenders, including making reparation to victims or to the wider community.

Despite high youth unemployment, withdrawal of benefits and numerous inner city disturbances in the 1980s, offending by young people generated few moral panics. It was thus that the 'quiet consensus' (Haines and Drakeford, 1998: 32) developed in support of the diversionary strategy and its principles were enshrined in the Criminal Justice Act 1991. This stressed custody as a last resort and introduced measures to reduce its use, while community sentences were promoted as 'tough alternatives' and the responsibilities of parents for their children were strengthened. Despite its 'success', however, some critics argue that the diversionary model and its fit with a 'just deserts' model meant that there was often little engagement with the personal difficulties experienced by offenders or wider issues of inequality and social justice (Brown, 1998; Pitts, 2001).

The punitive turn

Repeating in many respects the earlier fate of welfarism in the 1970s, the diversionary philosophy of the Criminal Justice Act 1991 was soon undermined due to mounting opposition and a series of moral panics. Pitts (2001: 11) suggests that there was a growing realization both that many young people were not 'growing out of crime' and that some youth crime was 'serious'. Combined with increased awareness of victimization, especially in economically deprived areas, this called into question the relatively 'hands off' approach embodied in the Act. Equally influential, however, was a string of moral panics. Debate on an emerging 'underclass' in Britain (Murray, 1990; Dennis and Erdos, 1992) was augmented by a series of folk devils, both individual ('rat boy' and 'safari boy') and collective (the 'joyrider', 'bail bandit' and 'persistent young offender') (Hagell and Newburn, 1994). The common thread, however, was that of growing lawlessness and dangerous young criminals who had become 'untouchable'. Into this volatile situation came the tragic murder of toddler James Bulger by two boys barely above the age of criminal responsibility, an event which seemed to signify the demise of 'childhood innocence' (Jenks, 1996).

Responding to John Major's call to 'condemn a little more and understand a little less' (*The Mail on Sunday* 21 February 1993), the government introduced a wide-ranging set of 'get tough' measures. The use of cautions was restricted and bail conditions tightened. The anti-custodial emphasis of the 1991 Act was overturned by changes that allowed longer custodial sentences and for these to apply to younger offenders. Secure Training Centres (widely characterized as 'junior prisons') were introduced for persistent young offenders aged twelve to fourteen. The changes prompted a 40 per cent rise in custody for young offenders between 1992 and 1997 (Audit Commission, 2004). To further emphasize toughness, custodial regimes were to be modelled on US style 'boot camps' and use of the army's 'glass house' was proposed.

This punitive turn went hand in hand with what Pitts (2001) has referred to as 'dejuvenilization', that is, eroding the principle of treating children and young people separately from adults. Electronic tagging was extended to those under sixteen, and the Crime (Sentences) Act 1997 allowed young offenders to be publicly named. Dejuvenilization brought the UK into increasing conflict with those who monitor the United Nations Convention on the Rights of the Child (UNCRC), ironically signed by the UK government very shortly before the punitive turn took place. This conflict will be discussed further later in the chapter.

New Labour—'tough on crime and tough on the causes of crime'?

Tony Blair's famous soundbite indicated that New Labour would attempt to match the Conservatives in terms of 'toughness' but also outflank them with a wider approach to preventing crime. Once in government, New Labour launched an ambitious new programme, with the provisions contained in the Crime and Disorder Act 1998 and subsequent legislation. The main measures can be summarized as follows:

- removal of *doli incapax*;
- custody and tough community sentences;
- strengthening warning systems;
- reparation and restorative justice;
- anti-social behaviour orders;
- curfews;
- child safety orders;
- parental involvement;
- establishing a national Youth Justice Board and local Youth Offending Teams.

The ancient presumption of *doli incapax* (literally 'incapable of evil') meant that for offenders under fourteen, courts had to establish clearly that they understood the consequences of their actions. Its removal was intended to symbolize the government's rejection of 'excuses' but was controversial in its implication that children of this age held an 'adult' understanding of their behaviour. The aims of punishment and reintegration were enshrined in a new Detention and Training Order (DTO), allowing sentences to be split between custody and the community, the latter operating close monitoring alongside supervized activities. In 2001, the 'Intensive Supervision and Surveillance Programme' (ISSP) was introduced to provide a tough community based intervention for persistent or serious offenders. Programmes involve a minimum of twenty-five hours per week supervised activity aimed at reducing offending behaviour, while the surveillance component includes measures such as tracking, tagging, voice recognition and police intelligence. The ISSP can be used at various stages of the criminal justice process, as a bail condition, as part of a community sentence or as the second part of a DTO.

The Labour government was also keen to promote the use of restoration within youth justice, with the offender through word, deed or by other means making direct restoration to the victim (or community) for the offence. Restorative youth justice was enshrined in measures such as the reparation order and subsequently the referral order (made under the Youth Justice and Criminal Evidence Act 1999). The latter entailed first time offenders being referred to a Youth Offender Panel whose main focus would be to consider how restoration could be made. Membership of Panels comprises two volunteers from the local community and one representative from a Youth Offending Team.

While anti-poverty programmes such as Sure Start were seen as contributing to crime reduction, being 'tough on the causes of crime' focused above all on preventing it through early intervention. Such intervention, however, entailed controversial extension of legal powers. Drawing on principles of 'zero tolerance', young people could be made the subject of anti-social behaviour orders (ASBOs). These orders can be made in cases where someone's behaviour is causing distress or harassment to others, and may prohibit that person from going to particular places or doing particular things. Similarly, local curfews (originally for those under ten but later under sixteen) could be imposed to keep all children off the streets at particular times. The child safety order was introduced to allow intervention in cases where children under the age of ten engaged in behaviour that would constitute an offence if they were older. For critics, this provision represents a way of effectively lowering the age of criminal responsibility by the back door. Another key element in the strategy of early intervention lay in addressing perceived deficiencies of parenting, including the introduction of the parenting order, obliging parents to attend classes to improve their skills (Drakeford and McCarthy, 2000). It is debateable, however, whether this extensive range of state interventions is likely to promote the desired responsibility on the part of young people and their parents.

Corporatism and managerialism: an alternative explanation?

Thus far, this historical review has been couched largely in term of competing principles or philosophies relating to youth crime—welfare and justice, diversion and intervention. However, some writers argue that better explanations can be found by examining the ways in which youth justice services have been organized and managed. 'Corporatism' (described earlier), with its emphases on management, performance and cost-effectiveness, became more prominent during the 1980s. In the 1990s, these concerns were reflected in the growing influence of the Audit Commission, which produced a series of reports on the operation of youth justice services (1996; 1998). These reports highlighted organizational inefficiencies such as delays in taking offenders to court, but also promoted the idea of early 'preventive' interventions as a means of saving public money in the longer term. For its critics (Smith, 2003) corporatism is seen as a repressive force, using state power to increase surveillance and control over those who deliver and receive services. For supporters, however, it offers potential for 'joined up' responses, with agencies working together towards the common goal of reducing offending. This view was readily apparent in the Labour Government's establishment of a Youth Justice Board and local Youth Offending Teams, with representation from police, probation, social services, health and education (Burnett and Appleton 2004).

REVIEW QUESTIONS

1 How would you explain the rise and fall of the welfare model in youth justice?

2 Can the diversionary strategies pursued during the 1980s be regarded as successful?

3 Is Pitts right to say that recent decades have seen a process of 'dejuvenilisation' in youth justice?

Understanding youth crime

As noted earlier, explanations advanced for youth crime are similar in many ways to those within criminology more generally, but are also significantly influenced by perspectives on childhood and youth as life stages, including questions as to whether and how young people may 'grow out of crime'. These issues along with consideration of parenting and schooling are rarely applied to older offenders! It is not our intention here to offer a review of theoretical explanations, including those addressing the ways in which youth crime has been defined and 'constructed' as a social problem (for discussion see, for example Muncie, 2004). Rather, our focus rests with the relationship between explanations and policy and practice in youth justice. Earlier, it was seen how ideas about deprivation influenced the rise of the welfare model and how interactionist accounts of 'labelling' effects and stigma (Becker, 1963; Lemert, 1967), helped to underpin diversion strategies. Similarly, the influences of realist perspectives can be seen from the 1980s onwards. For 'right realism' this meant emphasizing personal responsibility and moral culpability while for 'left realism', a focus on social causation had to be tempered by 'taking crime seriously'. In both instances, a stronger focus on victims supported the growing interest in restorative justice.

Risk factors: the new orthodoxy

For most of the past decade, the dominant paradigm for understanding and addressing youth crime has been provided by the concept of risk factors, particularly associated with work from the Cambridge Institute of Criminology (West, 1973; Farrington, 1996). During a period of some pessimism regarding youth crime, the risk factor approach appeared to point a way forward, identifying a range of factors associated with youth crime, which might then be targeted for intervention, singly or in combination. Farrington and West's research was based on a longitudinal study, following a group of 411 working class boys from the age of eight in 1961 through to 32. Its obvious strength was the potential to track offending careers over many years and to identify factors associated with their progression. Farrington (1996) highlights the following major risk factors:

* low income and poor housing;
* living in 'deteriorated' inner city areas;

- high degree of impulsiveness and hyperactivity;
- low intelligence and low school attainment;
- poor parental supervision and harsh and erratic discipline;
- parental conflict and broken families;

to which might be added:

- the influence of delinquent friends;
- use of drugs or alcohol.

(Smith and McVie, 2003).

For New Labour, while these factors could readily be linked to wider initiatives in respect of social exclusion and education, arguably the most influential to be taken up was the notion of parenting deficit. Not only were family stability and parental supervision directly important in lowering the risk of offending, but they could also be seen as relevant to reducing those that stemmed from material deprivation or educational failure (Utting *et al.*, 1993). This research seemed to point towards the value of early intervention and was supported by other studies suggesting that potential persistent offenders could readily be identified from their early behaviour (Chief Secretary to the Treasury, 2003: 19).

The risk factors approach and supporting research have been criticized, however, especially for their lack of social and political context (Haines and Drakeford, 1998; Smith, 2003). For example, risk factors identifiable from the 1960s and 1970s may be less applicable to today's society, with its different ethnic make-up, family structures and lifestyles. Moreover, risk factors cannot be assumed to work in a similar fashion irrespective of social context. Pitts (2000: 11) cites US research by Wikstrom and Loeber showing that individual risk factors can be significantly outweighed by neighbourhood factors. A recently launched longitudinal study in Edinburgh will attempt to make links between individual and wider social risk factors (Smith and McVie, 2003)(www.law.ed.ac.uk.cls/esytc/). It may also be argued that in practice, the risk factors approach gives very limited recognition to wider social factors associated with offending, and allows the locus of 'responsibility' to rest firmly with young people and their families. Offending behaviour has been explained in terms of the way young people 'think' and their lack of self-control rather than as a product of the situations in which they find themselves. Similarly, Smith (2003: 152) suggests that poor parents are treated as 'shock absorbers', charged with instilling self-control in their children regardless of the effects of unemployment, poverty or homelessness. A further difficulty with the risk factors approach is that it may be stigmatizing, labelling those who fall into the risk categories as 'potential offenders' and often targeting them for intervention.

Profiling youth crime: lessons from self-report surveys

In recent years, knowledge of youth crime has been boosted by a series of self-report studies, typically sampling around 5,000 young people of varying ages. The 'Youth Lifestyle Survey' (Graham and Bowling, 1995; Flood-Page *et al.*, 2000) involved young people from age twelve up to thirty, while the age range for the later Youth Justice Board surveys was eleven to sixteen (MORI 2003). Collectively, these self-report studies provide a useful complement and counterweight to official statistics. In particular, they generate useful data on young people's involvement in 'crime' (bearing in mind that in most cases there have been no convictions). The surveys show a fairly consistent pattern over recent years (at a time when officially recorded youth crime has been falling) and tend to confirm a number of key aspects of youthful offending. One of these is that it is by no means uncommon. A recent MORI survey (2003: 4) found that 26 per cent of mainstream school students and 60 per cent of those excluded admitted at least one offence in the previous year. A second is that a relatively small number of young people account for a significant proportion of crime, Flood-Page et al., (2000: 14) finding that 2 per cent of their overall sample were responsible for 50 per cent of offences. Surveys also show that only a minority of offenders are 'caught', with only 12 per cent of self-confessed offenders reporting a caution or court appearance during the past year (2004: 17). Another key finding is that the vast majority of those involved in youthful offending do indeed 'grow out of crime', the peak age for young women being fourteen and for young men of ages eighteen to twenty-one. The surveys confirm the importance of the risk factors cited above, with statistical analysis suggesting drug use to be the strongest predictor, followed by school-related factors such as truancy and exclusion (Flood-Page et al., 2000: 43). Statistical association does not of course show that such factors 'cause' crime, and complex questions remain about how they interact. It should also be noted that self-report studies raise important methodological issues, not least in terms of reliability, and data from them must be interpreted with caution (Coleman and Moynihan, 1996).

Young people as victims: a neglected story?

When young people and crime hit the headlines it is almost invariably when 'they' (young people) are perceived as a threat to 'us' (respectable, 'adult' society). Young people have not been included in the British Crime Survey and until some studies carried out in the 1990s, there was little focus on them as victims of crime, whether perpetrated by adults or by other young people (Anderson et al., 1994; Brown, 1995; Hartless et al., 1995). One of their most striking findings was that young people suffered higher levels of victimization than adults, including from 'normal crimes', such as theft, violence or harassment as well as abuse within the family (Brown, 1998: 90). Surveys have also shown how widespread 'fear of crime' is by no means restricted to adults (MORI, 2003: 7).

Another important finding to emerge is that levels of victimization are higher among those who are involved in offending or excluded from school (MORI, 2003: 49; Smith and McVie, 2003). To some extent, this may reflect the higher incidences of crime and victimization found in particular areas, peer groups or from time spent in public places. However, it is also the case that many offenders have themselves been victims. Boswell (1995), for example found that 72 per cent of young offenders committing the most serious crimes, had themselves been the victims of abuse. Child welfare campaigners might broaden this argument, claiming that young offenders are almost invariably victims, if only in the sense of having been failed by (adult) society.

Young people, crime and social divisions

In discussing youth crime, it is important to remember that the term 'youth' brings together those with widely differing backgrounds and circumstances, not least those arising from major social divisions. In respect of both social class and ethnicity, there is a long-established pattern of over-representation in official crime statistics of those from less powerful, privileged groups. Debate, however, has often raged as to whether this reflects levels of participation in crime or is generated by discriminatory policing and processes within the criminal justice system (Muncie, 2004).

Findings from self-report studies suggest that both factors are present to a degree. The importance of socio-economic deprivation as a risk factor has already been noted and self-reported offending rates in Social Class V have been found to be roughly twice those in Class I (Flood-Page et al., 2000: 22; Smith and McVie, 2003: 185). Flood-Page et al., found no significant differences according to ethnicity, although a more recent study (MORI, 2003) found higher levels of self-reported offending among black respondents than for white or Asian counterparts. The difference however, was fairly modest, particularly in comparison to figures which show that black (and mixed parentage) offenders are roughly twice as likely to be sentenced to custody and less likely to receive low tariff sentences (Audit Commission, 2004).

Explaining 'over-representation' is arguably as difficult and controversial as gauging its extent. Concepts such as class and ethnicity are notoriously slippery and have their own complex relationships with factors such as education, unemployment, drug use and neighbourhood. Additionally, they are open to cultural/behavioural and structural interpretations which provide very different explanations for involvement in crime. Discussion of these factors is beyond our scope here but readers may wish to consult Chapters 16 and 18.

Gender inequalities raise a qualitatively different set of issues from those associated with class or ethnicity. Young women are far less likely than young men to appear in criminal statistics, although self-report studies suggest that they under-estimate female involvement in youth crime. Nonetheless, the studies show that young male offenders outnumber females by ratios in the range of 2–3:1, and even higher for persistent or serious offenders (Graham and Bowling, 1995; MORI, 2003; Smith and McVie, 2003). There are many competing explanations for such difference (see Chapter 17 for fuller discussion) but part of the answer clearly lies with different patterns of socialization, where conformity is highly valued for girls and young women and their behaviour more tightly monitored and controlled. Feminist writers highlight that girls are already 'policed' heavily, especially in terms of sexuality, prior to any contact with the criminal justice system (Hudson, 2001). Gender stereotypes tend to portray offending as relatively 'normal' for young men, while running counter to the 'nature' of women. Yet, as Brown (1998) argues, these norms may be so taken for granted that the relationship between masculinity and crime is rarely scrutinized.

Stereotyping appears to produce mixed results for young female offenders. On the one hand, beliefs that they are less likely to become persistent or serious offenders may lead to more lenient treatment. Cautioning rates lend some support to this, with 71 per cent of young women compared with 49 per cent of young men receiving cautions in 2002 (Home Office, 2003a). However, it is also the case that female offenders, especially when they commit violent crimes, may be 'doubly damned', having transgressed the bounds of femininity as well as the criminal law (Brown, 1998: 103). Custodial sentences for young women have risen rapidly in recent years, a rise attributed by some to backlash against women's liberation (Worrall, 2001) and moral panic regarding women becoming more violent, even though there is little evidence to support this (Bachelor *et al.*, 2001).

REVIEW QUESTIONS

1 What are the most likely explanations for the over-representation of working class and minority ethnic young people in the official crime statistics?

2 How do gender stereotypes affect responses to youth crime?

Contemporary youth justice and future directions

In this section, we will seek to review the main characteristics of current youth justice policy in England and Wales and consider the principal debates surrounding its future direction. Since its election in 1997, the Labour Government has continued to emphasize 'toughness' in sentencing, promotion of responsibility on the part of young offenders and their parents and a wide range of early intervention measures. A major concern has been to 'take crime seriously' in order to limit their political vulnerability when public and media opinion are generally seen as punitive. This stance has, however, set the government at odds with penal reform groups, major children's charities, children's rights bodies and many youth justice professionals who claim that it treats young people as 'offenders first, children second'. In seeking to reverse this priority, the pressure groups are in many ways drawing upon ideas associated with the welfare model, suggesting that rumours of its death have been exaggerated. We will return to these arguments below, but first consider how the current Government's youth justice policy has evolved.

A key element in 'taking crime seriously' has been to ensure that 'something happens' as a consequence of crime. This is reflected in attempts to cut delays in the youth justice system, but above all in sentencing. During the first five years of Labour Government, there was a sharp fall in low tariff sentences, such as cautions, fines and discharges and a rise in those (especially community sentences) perceived as having greater consequences for young offenders (Tables 19.1 and 19.2).

Table 19.1 Percentage of male offenders (aged 10–17) cautioned or found guilty by type of sentence received

	Cautions	Fines/ discharge	Community sentences	Custody	Total (thousands) (100 per cent)
1997	57	18	19	6	95.6
2002	49	9	33	7	82.4

Source: Home Office (2003a, Table 4.5B).

Table 19.2 Percentage of female offenders (aged 10–17) cautioned or found guilty by type of sentence received

	Cautions	Fines/ discharge	Community sentences	Custody	Total (thousands) (100 per cent)
1997	77	12	9	1	24.4
2002	71	6	20	2	23.3

Source: Home Office (2003a, Table 4.5B).

The modest increases in custody hide significant rises among those groups, notably female offenders and younger (ten to fourteen) male offenders, for whom custody was rarely used in the past.

Whatever the debates about the appropriateness of custody and whether it 'works', concerns for cost-effectiveness tend to militate against its use. The Audit Commission argues for greater use of community sentences, observing that ISSP programmes provide twice the level of constructive activity compared with Young Offender Institutions at one third of the cost (2004: 4). The high cost of custody is also relevant to a broader preventive strategy where it is argued that modest early expenditure may produce savings on individual offenders of £70,000 or even £140,000 in the longer term (Scott *et al.*, 2001; Audit Commission 2004: 93). Despite its persuasive logic, however, this argument makes bold assumptions regarding the ability to identify future offenders and divert them from criminal careers. Equally, it appears to gloss over the negative consequences that may arise from intervention. Nonetheless, prevention and early intervention continue to play important parts in youth justice policy. This includes activity-based programmes such as SPLASH, Positive Activities for Young People, and the Youth Inclusion Programme introduced in 2000 for 'at risk' thirteen to sixteen year olds in high crime areas. Younger children and their families have also been targeted, initially through the On Track programme for four to twelve year olds and more recently Youth Inclusion and Support Panels for those aged eight to thirteen. In line with a 'joined up' approach to crime reduction, panels may refer children and parents to a range of activities, advice, mentoring or counselling services. (For a review of On Track see Hine and Harrington (2004) and for details of other initiatives, www.youth-justice-board.gov.uk/YouthJustice Board/Prevention/). Restorative justice has established a prominent place in youth courts, with referral orders accounting for 20 and 29 per cent of sentences for young male and female offenders respectively in 2002 (Home Office, 2003a: 17). However, it has proved difficult to engage victims directly in the process. Newburn *et al.* (2002) found victims attending Youth Offender Panels in only 6 per cent of cases.

Children first?

The proposition that young offenders should be treated as 'children first' draws significantly upon discourses of children's rights as set out in the United Nations Convention on the Rights of the Child (UNCRC) 1989 and domestically in the Children Act 1989. Monaghan *et al.* (2003) set out six key requirements for a child-centred youth justice, which should:

(a) be in line with the principles of the UNCRC;

(b) be distinct and separate from the adult criminal justice system;

(c) have children's 'best interests' as its guiding principle;

(d) raise the age of criminal responsibility;

(e) treat offenders as children first, that is, in line with children's legislation;

(f) use secure accommodation only as a last resort and ensure it provides a safe and caring environment.

In policy terms, the two most important elements are support for decriminalization and opposition to custody. Decriminalization is partly a matter of raising the age of criminal responsibility (fourteen is typically the preferred age) but also entails moving away from the 'adversarial' court towards more welfare-focused settings, such as the Scottish hearings system. 'Children first' opposition to custody focuses strongly on the failure of custodial regimes to protect and meet the needs of vulnerable young people. As noted earlier, young offenders have often experienced troubled and abusive childhoods and around half may have spent time in care (Welsh and Williams, 2001). Mental health problems are estimated to affect between 46 and 81 per cent of those in custody (Hagell, 2002), with significant incidence of (attempted) suicide (Downey, 2002). Penal reform groups, most notably the Howard League, have waged a long, and at least partially successful, campaign to prevent young offenders being remanded to adult prisons and to establish that the protections of the Children Act 1989 apply to Young Offender Institutions (YOIs). They have also sought to promote the use of local authority secure accommodation over YOIs, the former being generally regarded as providing better care and education, albeit at greater expense (Audit Commission, 2004).

Some supporters of a 'children first' position also oppose restorative justice measures when they take place within a framework of threats and sanctions and are grafted onto a system based on very different principles (Pitts, 2001). Haines (2000) argues that pressuring young offenders to apologize and make reparation can be very one-sided in situations where they may be more sinned against than sinners. From this perspective the pendulum has swung too far towards emphasizing young people's responsibilities at the expense of their rights and the responsibilities of others to them (Haines and Drakeford, 1998).

REVIEW QUESTIONS

1 Has New Labour's approach to youth crime been successful?

2 Assess the arguments for and against treating young offenders as 'children first'.

CONCLUSION

In this chapter we have reviewed key aspects of the relationship between young people and crime, whether as offenders, victims or recipients of youth justice. We have seen how, through the many changes taking place over the past two centuries, certain enduring questions can be identified. These relate to whether young offenders should be treated differently from adults, and if so, in what ways? Responses have been shaped by the need to effectively address (youth) crime while also dealing appropriately with offenders as children and young people. It is important here to remember that 'childhood' and 'youth' are socially constructed terms and can vary according time and place. Different constructions may point to different approaches, such as those based on welfare and justice principles respectively. Competing perspectives on whether young people 'grow out of crime' may support diversion or early intervention strategies. Following a long period of growing separation between the respective treatment of young and adult offenders, recent decades have witnessed a reversal of this trend. It is clear that successive governments have felt obliged to take a 'tough' stance on youth crime to meet media and public demands, but by doing so they have tended to amplify moral panics surrounding youth crime, while reinforcing the image of youth justice as 'too lenient'. Yet as the Audit Commission (2004: 48) notes, the public perception of leniency fades significantly when people are better informed about sentencing. To its supporters, the Blair government's approach has much to commend it, combining a tough stance on persistent and serious offending while reaching out to prevent those 'at risk' becoming involved in crime. There is, however, mixed evidence on its success with constant levels of self-reported crime casting doubt on the reductions shown in official crime statistics, a politically sensitive issue given significant recent rises in expenditure (Audit Commission, 2004: 15).

While successive UK governments have looked to the US for inspiration, 'children first' advocates favour European models as the way forward. These remain more rooted in welfarist ideas, with much lower rates of custody, higher ages of criminal responsibility (the European average being fourteen–sixteen), investigative enquiry into the offender's circumstances and emphasis on promoting social inclusion (Pitts, 2001). Although transplanting ideas from one culture to another is a difficult process, it seems strange that policy makers look towards the US with its high crime rate and vast prison population rather than to Europe where these are generally much lower.

At the time of writing, the government is proposing further changes to youth justice through its *Next Steps* paper (Home Office, 2003b) and legislation such as the Anti-Social Behaviour Act 2003. Essentially these can be characterized as consolidating and extending recent measures, maintaining a strong focus on anti-social behaviour, community sentences, restorative justice and parenting. The *Next Steps* document was issued alongside but clearly separate from the Government's Green Paper

Every Child Matters (Chief Secretary to the Treasury, 2003) dealing with reforms to child protection in the wake of the Victoria Climbié case (for details see www.victoria-climbie-inquiry.org.uk) For children's advocates and penal reformers, the separation implied continuation of an 'offenders first' stance, a case of 'every child matters unless they are an offender'.

Although currently the main political parties appear only to offer variations on a theme of 'toughness', there remains a significant liberal opposition advocating a response to youth crime based on children's rights and welfare. While marginalized in many respects, this opposition draws strength from the wider framework of children's rights and the persistence of welfare concerns in the lives of young offenders. A youth justice system in England and Wales based on 'children first' appears very unlikely at present, but it would be unwise to assume that this cannot change in the future.

QUESTIONS FOR DISCUSSION

1 Should the age of criminal responsibility be raised to fourteen?

2 Do young offenders have too many rights and too few responsibilities?

3 Based on this chapter and Chapter 8, to what extent do you consider that the moral panics surrounding youth crime can be blamed on media coverage?

4 Is legislation on anti-social behaviour likely to help reduce offending by young people?

5 'Reducing social inequalities such as those based on class and "race" is a vital part of the fight against youth crime'. Discuss.

GUIDE TO FURTHER READING

Muncie, J. (2004), *Youth and Crime: a Critical Introduction (2nd edn),* London: Sage.
This book is probably the most useful of the overview texts in the field of youth crime and youth justice. It provides a good historical account of youth crime and locates discussion in a wider context of theorizing about youth and youth culture(s).

Smith, R. (2003), *Youth Justice: Ideas, Policy, Practice,* Cullompton: Willan Publishing.
The main strength of this book is its very detailed analysis of the workings of youth justice, making it complementary to Muncie's book in many respects.

Youth Justice
This journal is produced by the National Association for Youth Justice and offers many topical articles on the workings of the youth justice system.

Muncie, J., Hughes, G. and McLaughlin, E. (eds) (2001), *Youth Justice: Critical Readings*. London: Sage.
This edited collection covers a very wide range of topics relating to youth justice. It combines many 'classic' articles with more contemporary analyses.

Goldson, B. (ed) (2000), *The New Youth Justice*, Lyme Regis: Russell House Publishing.
Within this edited collection, various aspects of New Labour's approach to youth justice are explored, including its emphases on responsibility, restoration and parenting.

WEB LINKS

www.youth-justice-board.gov.uk/YouthJusticeBoard/

The website for the Youth Justice Board provides an excellent guide to the workings of the youth justice system, including information on sentences, courts, and custody. It also highlights the YJB's publications and research and provides links to relevant legislation and reports.

www.nayj.org.uk/

The National Association for Youth Justice broadly advocates an approach to youth justice based on the rights of children and young people. It publishes a newsletter and the journal *Youth Justice*.

http://society.guardian.co.uk/youthjustice/

This section within the *Guardian's* Society website provides useful links to other relevant sites and details of recent articles dealing with youth crime and youth justice.

http://www.howardleague.org/lawdept/lawdeptindex.htm

Along with other penal reform groups such as NACRO, the Howard League runs various projects and campaigns linked to youth justice in addition to producing publications and reports.

www.barnardos.org.uk

Like other major children's charities, Barnardo's takes a keen interest in youth justice issues. The website provides details of the project work undertaken and of relevant research.

REFERENCES

Anderson, S., Kinsey, R., Loader, I. and Smith, C. (1994) *Cautionary Tales: Young People, Crime and Policing in Edinburgh*. Aldershot: Avebury.

Audit Commission (1996) *Misspent Youth: Young People and Crime*. London: Audit Commission.

Audit Commission (1998) *Misspent Youth '98: the Challenge for Youth Justice*. London: Audit Commission.

Audit Commission (2004) *Youth Justice 2004: A Review of the Reformed Youth Justice System*. London: Audit Commission.

Bachelor, S., Burman, M. and Brown, J. (2001) 'Discussing Violence: Let's Hear it from The Girls', *Probation Journal*, 48 (2): 125–34.

Becker, H. (1963) *Outsiders: Studies in the Sociology of Deviance*. New York: Free Press.

Boswell, G. (1995) *Violent Victims*. London: Princes Trust.

Bottoms, A., Brown, P., McWilliams, B., McWilliams, W. and Nellis, M. (1990) *Intermediate Treatment and Juvenile Justice: Key Findings and Implication from a National Survey of Intermediate Treatment Policy and Practice*. London: HMSO.

Bowlby, J. (1946) *Forty Four Juvenile Thieves: Their Characters and Home Life*. London: Baillière, Tindall & Cox.

Bowlby, J. (1955) *Child Care and the Growth of Love*. Harmondsworth: Penguin.

Brown, S. (1995) 'Crime and Safety in Whose "Community"?', *Youth and Policy*, 48: 27–48.

Brown, S. (1998) *Understanding Youth and Crime: Listening to Youth?* Buckingham: Open University Press.

Burnett, R. and Appleton, C. (2004) 'Joined-Up Services to Tackle Crime: A Case-Study in England', *British Journal of Criminology*, 44, 1, 34–54.

Chief Secretary to the Treasury (2003) Every Child Matters (Green Paper), Cm 5860. London: Stationery Office.

Coleman, C. and Moynihan, J. (1996) *Understanding Crime Data*. Buckingham: Open University Press.

Dennis, N. and Erdos, G. (1992) *Families Without Fatherhood*. London: Institute of Economic Affairs.

Donzelot, J. (1980) *The Policing of Families*. London: Hutchinson.

Downey, R. (2002) 'Youth Crimes and Punishment', *Community Care* (14–20 February): 30–2.

Drakeford, M. and McCarthy, K. (2000) 'Parents, responsibility and the new youth justice' in B. Goldson (ed), *The New Youth Justice*. Lyme Regis: Russell House Publishing.

Farrington, D. (1996) *Understanding and Preventing Youth Crime*. York: York Publishing Services.

Flood-Page, C., Campbell, S., Harrington, V. and Miller, J. (2000) *Youth Crime: Findings from the 1998/99 Youth Lifestyles Survey*. London: Home Office.

Graham, J. and Bowling, B. (1995) *Young People and Crime*. Home Office Research Study no. 145. London: HMSO.

Hagell, A. (2002) *The Mental Health Needs of Young Offenders*. London: Mental Health Foundation.

Hagell, A. and Newburn, T. (1994) *Persistent Young Offenders*. London: Policy Studies Institute.

Haines, K. (2000) 'Referral orders and youth offender panels: restorative approaches and the new youth justice' in B. Goldson (ed), *The New Youth Justice*. Lyme Regis: Russell House Publishing.

Haines, K. and Drakeford, M. (1998) *Young People and Youth Justice*. Basingstoke: Macmillan.

Hall, S., Critcher, C., Jefferson, T., Clarke, J. and Roberts, B. (1978) *Policing the Crisis: Mugging, the State and Law and Order*. London: Macmillan.

Hartless, J, Ditton, J, Nair, G. and Phillips, S. (1995) 'More Sinned Against Than Sinning: a Study of Young Teenagers' Experiences of Crime', *British Journal of Criminology*, 35 (1): 114–33.

Hendrick, H. (1994) *Child Welfare, England 1872–1989*. London: Routledge.

Hine, J. and Harrington, V. (2004) *Delivering On Track*. Development and Practice Research Report 12. London: Home Office.

Home Office (2003a) Criminal Statistics England and Wales 2002. London: Stationery Office.

Home Office (2003b) *Youth Justice—the Next Steps: Companion Document to Every Child Matters*. London: Home Office.

Hudson, A. (2001) ' "Troublesome girls": towards alternative definitions and policies', in J. Muncie, G. Hughes and E. McLaughlin (eds), *Youth Justice: Critical Readings*. London: Sage.

Jenks, C. (1996) *Childhood*. London: Routledge.

Lemert, E. (1967) *Human Deviance, Social Problems and Social Control*. Englewood Cliffs: Prentice-Hall.

Minty, B. (1987) *Child Care and Adult Crime*. Manchester: Manchester University Press.

Monaghan, G. Hibbert, P. and Moore, S. (2003) *Children in Trouble: Time for Change*. Ilford: Barnardo's.

MORI (2003) *Youth Survey 2003*. London: MORI.

Morris, A., Giller, H., Geach, H. and Szwed, E. (1980) *Justice for Children*. London: Macmillan.

Muncie, J. (2004) *Youth and Crime: a Critical Introduction* (2nd edn). London: Sage.

Murray, C. (1990) *The Emerging British Underclass*. London: Institute of Economic Affairs.

Newburn, T., Crawford, A., Earle, R., Goldie, S., Hale, C., Hallam, A., Masters, G., Netten, A., Saunders, R., Sharpe, K. and Uglow, S. (2002) *The Introduction of Referral Orders into the Youth Justice System: second interim report*. London: Home Office.

Pearson, G. (1983) *Hooligan: a History of Respectable Fears*. London: Macmillan.

Pitts, J. (2000) 'The New Youth Justice and the Politics of Electoral Anxiety', in B. Goldson (ed), *The New Youth Justice*. Lyme Regis: Russell House Publishing.

Pitts, J. (2001) *The New Politics of Youth Crime: Discipline or Solidarity*. Basingstoke: Palgrave.

Pratt, J. (1989) 'Corporatism: the Third Model of Juvenile Justice', *British Journal of Criminology*, 29 (3): 236–54.

Ruxton, S. (1996) *Children in Europe*. London: NCH Action for Children.

Scott, S., Knapp, M., Henderson, J. and Maughan, B. (2001) 'Financial Costs of Social Exclusion: Follow up Study of Antisocial Children into Adulthood', *British Medical Journal*, 323: 191–94.

Smith, D. and McVie, S. (2003) 'Theory and Method in the Edinburgh Study of Youth Transitions and Crime', *British Journal of Criminology*, 43 (1): 169–95.

Smith, R. (2003) *Youth Justice: Ideas, Policy, Practice*. Cullompton: Willan.

Thorpe, D., Smith, D., Green, C. and Paley, J. (1980) *Out of Care: the Community Support of Juvenile Offenders*. London: Allen & Unwin.

Utting, D., Bright, J. and Henricson, C. (1993) *Crime and the Family: Improving Childrearing and Preventing Delinquency*. London: Family Studies Policy Centre.

West. D. (1973) *Who Becomes Delinquent*. London: Heinemann.

Welsh, M. and Williams, G. (2001) 'Securing the Future', *Community Care* (26 July–1 August): 22–3.

Worrall, A. (2001) 'Girls At Risk?: Reflections on Changing Attitudes To Young Women's Offending', *Probation Journal*, 48 (2): 86–92.

20 Older offenders, crime and the criminal justice system

Azrini Wahidin

INTRODUCTION

This chapter will review what is known about older people and crime. We will start by defining the term 'older offender', and then critically explore why older people in the criminal justice system have been constructed as victims rather than perpetrators and why crimes committed by elders are absent from the criminological agenda. Work in this area has been led by American researchers and it is only in the last ten years, that researchers in the UK (see Phillips, 1996; Manthorpe, 1983; Wahidin, 2004) have examined the relationship between ageing and crime. I will identify the key issues and current debates in criminology surrounding older people and crime and will focus on the specific issues an ageing population poses to the criminal justice system (with reference to the prison system in England and Wales). The first section offers an exploration of why when we think about elders and the criminal justice system, we equate the stereotypical image of a vulnerable frail person as being the victim rather than the offender.

The chapter will provide an introduction to the area, contextualize the age demographics of the prison population, discuss age specific theories of crime, raising epistemological questions about the nature of imprisonment, and finally, examine the role that age-specific programmes can play in reducing the pains of imprisonment. I will argue that it is only by systematically addressing the needs of elders in prison rather than reacting to them, that can we begin, 'to look after them with humanity and help them lead law-abiding and useful lives in custody and after release'. (This statement may be seen displayed at the entrance of every prison. Go to http://www.hmprisonservice.gov.uk/ to enter HM Prison Service website.)

We are unaccustomed to thinking about people in later life as criminal offenders. Usually, when the elderly receive publicity, they are represented as the victims of crime, not its perpetrators. Some women and men in later life, nevertheless, do commit crimes, some are arrested, some are convicted, some are sent to prison, and some grow old in prison. A decade ago we would never imagine it possible that people were committing crimes in later life, growing old behind bars and that prison nursing homes would be a feature of the prison landscape. This section will address the relationship that criminology has to the study of age and crime.

BACKGROUND

It is difficult to draw precise conclusions about the extent of crimes committed by persons in later life. The first problem arises with the definition of the 'elder', which can produce information that at first appears contradictory. Social scientists who have researched older persons and their criminal behaviour have failed to come to a uniform agreement on what age constitutes 'old'. Although there is no definitive, nationwide or international standard for what constitutes an 'older offender', most researchers identify fifty as the threshold age. The inability to agree on what constitutes an older offender is one of the most troubling issues involved in comparing research outcomes on both sides of the Atlantic. For the purpose of this chapter, the term 'older' or offender in later life will be used to denote a person aged fifty or over.

Age and crime: the usual suspects?

Criminal behaviour and criminological studies have focused predominantly on young people's activities. While young people have for long been associated with crime, it appears that, as is the case with social class, different age groups commit different types of crime. Yet many theories deal almost exclusively with juvenile delinquency. It has been stated that '[o]ne of the few facts agreed on in criminology is the age distribution of crime' (Hirschi and Gottfredson, 1983: 552). A series of moral panics have 'demonized young people, from the teddy boys, mods and rockers of the 1960s, through to punks, skinheads, muggers, joyriders, "rat" boys' (Curtis, 1999: 28), girl gangs and mobile phone snatchers of 2000 (see for example, Cohen, 1973; Pearson, 1983). However, the assumption that crime is overwhelmingly a young person's activity must be called into question (see Chapter 19).

Victimology and old age

In popular and political discourses the 'problem of crime' is associated with 'youth crime' as if they were synonymous. As a result, all manner of myths and stereotypes about 'troublesome' people and spaces have come into play. The vast majority of research on youth and crime in the UK has focused on young people as offenders rather than as victims of crime (Williams, 1998; Wahidin and Powell, 2005). They have long been positioned outside the boundaries of the 'ideal victim'; they are, as Presdee (1994) argues, 'invaders of space' (see Chapter 19). 'Youth' and 'old age', and much that we can connect with these categories can be viewed as cultural and historic constructs, the meaning they carry varies over time and space. Conditions often associated with older people are more a result of how society constructs them rather than as a product of the biological ageing process.

The elderly population should be a source of concern if only because it is a growing population. The United Nations estimates that by the year 2025, the global population of those age sixty years and over will have doubled from 542 million in 1995 to around 1.2 billion people (Krug, 2002: 125). In 2002 there were 19.8 million people aged 50 and over in the UK. The number is projected to increase by a further 41 per cent by 2031, when there will be close to 28 million people aged 50 and over (National Statistics Online, November 2004: http://www.statistics.gov.nk/).

Fear of crime

Victims and offenders are constructed in opposition to each other: good and evil, innocent and guilty, predators and prey, and so on. This is important when we come to think about older people as victims of crime. However, this is not just an oversimplification of a complex phenomenon but a deliberate attempt to ignore or at least to overlook the striking similarities, affinities and overlap between these two populations (see Brian Williams' chapter). Within the literature on the fear of crime, older people are usually discussed as experiencing a high level of fear. However, the high-fear/low-risk equation has been questioned in a number of studies that suggest that elders are not in fact any more fearful of crime than younger people (Ferraro, 1995: Crawford *et al.*, 1990; Pain, 1995; Holloway and Jefferson, 2000). Studies from the British Crime Survey have shown that the elderly are less at risk from both violent crime and burglary, and that young men are the group most at risk from assault.

If older people are characterized by an overall low degree of victimization, then why have they been singled out as a specific group in research into the impact of crime? Although the aged are among the least victimized with regard to many serious crimes, there is evidence to suggest that this is not true for certain specific crimes. Second, why do elderly victims of crime provoke such a public outcry? Two possible answers can be found in the portrayal and construction of old people. The image of the older victim as vulnerable wins votes and sells newspapers; neither criminal activity nor the inhumane denial of the special needs of elders in prison are easily squared with this attitude of paternalistic concern. Moreover, the literature suggests that, irrespective of age, those more concerned with the problem of crime and expressing most fear of crime are not necessarily the most likely to have experiences of victimization. In terms of actual rates of victimization, older people are at relatively low risk from crime (although elder abuse, which is not considered here due to the lack of space and nature of discussion, is certainly underreported (Mawby and Walklate, 1994). As with other characteristics which make people vulnerable to victimization, it is difficult to disentangle the age factor from others, which means that older people figure prominently among those for whom victimization has a high impact. However, while the aged may be relatively unlikely to become victims of crime, their fears are understandable: if they are poor, in poor health, live in bad neighbourhoods, isolated, house-bound, and if they feel vulnerable, the risk of victimization substantially increases (Zedner, 1997). Moreover, one must stress that the experience of *fear* is very real to the individual and thus makes measuring degrees of fear an impossibility. Sparks (1992) rhetorically asks, 'What is a rational level of fear? In other words, if *fear* is *experienced*, then ultimately, it is *real*.

A hidden minority

When thinking about elders as perpetrators of crime we associate them with relatively minor offences such as: breach of the peace, shoplifting or driving under the influence of alcohol. We are unlikely to associate this group with crime serious enough to result in prison sentences continuing into old age. Ageing, in criminological literature, is not seen to be an issue, which in itself reflects how the age and crime relationship has been constructed. Contrary to popular belief, the most common offences for the older female age group are not perpetrated by the menopausal shoplifter; they are not theft and handling or fraud and forgery, but violence against the person and drug offences. By comparison, the most common offences for men in this group are sexual offences, violence against a person, and drug offences.

Too few to count?

Women in prison of all ages form only a very small proportion of the total prison population 5 per cent (Home Office, 2004) and women over fifty represented only 5 per cent of the total female prison estate in 2003. Out of the total prison population 13 per cent are over the age of fifty (see Figure 20.1) (Wahidin, 2005).

Men in prison constitute 94 per cent of the total prison population and men over fifty represent 8 per cent of the male estate (see Figure 20.2). In terms of actual numbers, there were 170 women and 4,513 men in prison who were over the age of fifty in January 2005

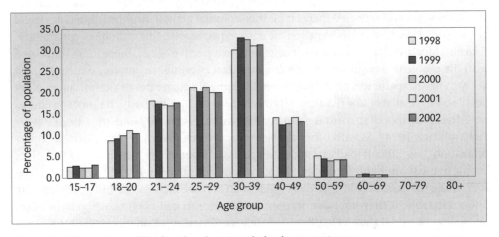

Figure 20.1 Percentage of the female prison population by age category

Source: Wahidin 2004.

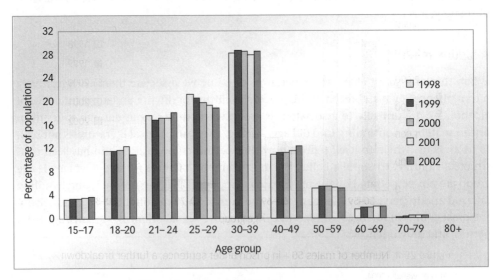

Figure 20.2 Percentage of the male prison population by age category

Source: Wahidin 2004.

(ibid). From 1995 to 2003, the female over fifty population rose by 87 per cent and for men by 113 per cent (Wahidin, 2004). From 1999 to 2004, the older prison population doubled from 3,000 to almost 6,000 (see Wahidin, 2004).

Figures 20.3 and 20.4 show that the highest older age range for both males and females in prison is the 50–59 cohort. Prison personnel and prisoners were interviewed at four older male units in the UK (Wahidin, 2005a). At one of the prisons, the 50–59 cohort represented 15 per cent of the prison population but consumed 60 per cent of all bed-watches, and findings show that the 50–59 age group was the most costly group to maintain.

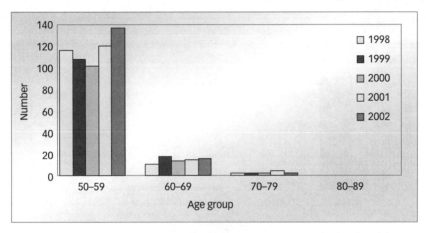

Figure 20.3 Number of females 50 + in prison under sentence: a further breakdown

Source: Wahidin 2004.

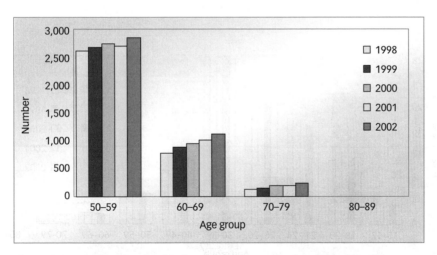

Figure 20.4 Number of males 50 + in prison under sentence: a further breakdown

Source: Wahidin 2004.

Ethnicity

Figures 20.5 and 20.6 show the percentage breakdown of men and women over the age of fifty on the basis of ethnicity.

The Figures show that the most significant difference between male and female older prisoners is in the proportion of black and white offenders.

The Home Office Prison Department in England and Wales has no overall policy or strategy for dealing with older females in prison, although the Home Office does have four elderly units for men. To date, there has been no discussion or plans for similar arrangements to be made for women.

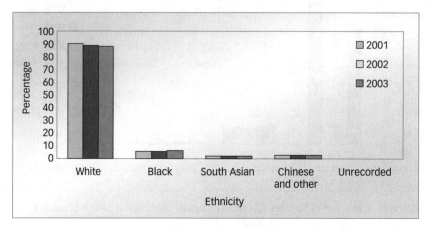

Figure 20.5 Males over 50 in prison by ethnicity, years 2001–2003

Source: Wahidin 2004.

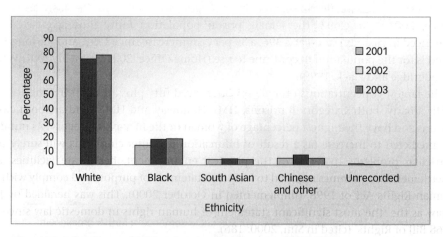

Figure 20.6 Females over 50 in prison by ethnicity, years 2001–2003

Source: Wahidin, 2004.

REVIEW QUESTIONS

1 How and why are elders portrayed as victims of crime rather than perpetrators of crime?

2 Discuss the idea that a decade ago we would never have thought it possible that prison nursing homes would become a necessity.

Lost offenders in forgotten places

The elderly prison population is likely to increase because our population is ageing (Newman, Newman and Gerwitz 1984: xvii), more and more people are being incarcerated, and the times served by people subject to mandatory sentences (the mandatory life sentence is the only sentence available to the courts for persons over the age of twenty-one found guilty of murder), are getting longer (Flynn, 1992; James, 1992; Steffensmeier and Moti 2000). In 1984, the mean time served by females serving a mandatory life sentence was three years and, by 1994, the time served went up to thirteen years (see Home Office 2001, 2001a, NACRO 1992a). If more and more people are receiving longer mandatory sentences, this will mean that some will remain imprisoned until they are old. This phenomenon is known as the 'stacking effect' (Aday, 2003). A related fact is that those serving life sentences in general are older than the average age of the prison population as a whole. From 1996 to 2000, the over-fifty lifer female population rose by 45 per cent and by comparison the lifer male population rose by 66 per cent.

Age breakdown of prison population

The population of women prisoners in England and Wales has features that distinguish it from that of men (Home Office: 1994, 1999, 2002; HMCIP 2001, 2002a; HMIPP, 2001). Between 1993 and 2001, the female prison population rose 140 per cent as against 46 per cent for men, reflecting sentencing changes (Home Office, 1999: 4; see also Home Office, 2001b). In 2002, the female prison population (only those convicted and sentenced to custody) stood at 3,396, a 39 per cent increase since 1999, and the long-term trend is for the population to continue to rise (Home Office, 2001c; HMCIP, 2001; White, Woodbridge and Flack, 1999).

The largest concentrations of male prisoners aged fifty-plus are at HMP Kingston and HMP Albany, both Category B prisons. HMP Holloway and HMP Send are both closed prisons and have the highest percentage of women in the fifty-plus category. As numbers are predicted to increase (as a result of bifurcation in sentencing), this will surely pose particular problems in terms of the physical environment, healthcare facilities, and resettlement programmes required to fulfil the statement of purpose and comply with the Human Rights Act of 1998, (implemented in October 2000). This was heralded by Jack Straw as the 'the most significant statement of human rights in domestic law since the 1968 Bill of Rights' (cited in Sim, 2000: 186).

Old age and crime

'Old criminals offer an ugly picture and it seems as if even scientists do not like to look at it for any considerable amount of time . . . On the other hand, if the thesis of the interrelationship between age and crime is to hold, an investigation of all its implications has to yield results, and with the tendency of our population to increase in the higher age brackets, a special study of criminality of the aged seems to meet a scientific as well as a practical need'. (Pollak 1941: 212)

The absence of elders in the criminological imagination mirrors where the study of female offenders in criminology was thirty years ago. The lack of research in this area is an implicit form of ageism that implies that the problems of this group can be disregarded, or that ageing criminals are simply not worth discussing. The explanation frequently given for the lack of statistical information on this topic is that at present the numbers involved are too small to yield significant information, with the implication that this justifies excluding and ignoring the rights of elders in prison. Yet there has been no assessment of the implications of this, or recognition that England and Wales, like the US, are facing an ageing prison population. This phenomenon has become known as the 'geriatrification' of the prison population.

If Pollak's view was accurate in 1941, it is even more so today, over sixty years later. With the elder prison population representing the fastest growing age group in our prison system, we have reached an important juncture in the disciplines of gerontology and criminology.

A historical view of older offenders

The literature available on elder offenders is restricted to predominantly American-based research (Newman, 1984). It was in the 1980s in America, that there was renewed interest in ageing offenders (Ham, 1976; Rubernstein, 1984). However, research interest in criminal behaviour among the elderly dates back to the end of the nineteenth century—the phenomenon was first discussed at a criminology conference in Budapest in 1899 (Pollack, 1941: 213 cited in Gewerth, 1988: 15). The work of Aday (1994, 1994a, 2003) has been instrumental in raising the profile of older offenders in the US and he identifies a void in the literature regarding the ageing prison population in general. In contrast to Aday's work there has been only one study in the UK that addresses the needs of the older male and female prison population (Wahidin, 2004; Wahidin and Cain, 2005b).

Types of offenders

We know that there are different types of offenders, ranging from the:

- older first time offender currently serving a term of imprisonment;
- the older offender who has had previous convictions but not served a prison sentence before;
- the recidivist who may have spent a significant amount of her or his life in and out of prison;

- prisoners fulfilling a life sentence and who have grown old in prison;
- long-term inmates.

Typically, the crimes committed by the above mirror those of young offenders. However, in all five groups, the ageing prison population is a special one in terms of health and social care needs, individual adjustment to institutional life, maintaining kinship networks, and end of life issues (Gallagher, 1990). This group challenges the structure of the prison system regarding purposeful activity, rehabilitation, and resettlement needs of offenders in later-life.

Theories of crime

The search for causes of crime at any age has been the principal concern of criminologists from Cesare Lombroso and Guglielmo Ferrero in 1895 to Richard Herrnstein and Charles Murray in 1994 (see Chapter 6). The literature on crime in later life has largely been descriptive, with little attempt to provide a theoretical perspective to account for growing numbers of older offenders encountering the criminal justice system.

What this chapter attests to is that women and men across the life course engage in crime for very different reasons. We know that women's experiences of incarceration are qualitatively different to the experiences of men (Carlen, 2002). In the same way, one can argue that older offenders may engage in criminal activities for different reasons to young offenders. Moreover, their experience of incarceration is qualitatively different to the younger able-bodied prison population. The non-age-specific theories of crime emphasize either of two primary influences in illegal behaviour. These are the 'gains' derived from legitimate versus illegitimate activities and the extent to which an individual undergoes social integration and internalization of conventional norms (Hirschi, 1969).

Although non-age-specific theories may differ with respect to the emphasis placed on a particular independent variable, a summary of the crucial predictors would probably include at least some of the following factors:

(a) age;

(b) ethnicity;

(c) gender;

(d) marital/partnership status;

(e) socio-economic status (occupation, education);

(f) criminal associations.

Those few theories that focus on older persons identify the same causes and correlations as more general theories of lawbreaking. Indeed, in most cases, the explanations offered for elders engaging in illegal behaviour might better qualify as 'speculation' than 'theories'. What one can ascertain from the literature is that there are causes and correlates of illegal behaviour that influence:

    (a) all age groups equally;

    (b) elders and non-elders differentially;

    (c) and/or elders uniquely.

Elders in prison

The increase in the proportion of elders is having far reaching effects on all components in the criminal justice system. This section will examine how prisons can begin to address the need of the older prison population. Once in prison, the vulnerabilities of age are exacerbated by the lack of adequate facilities to enable elders to lead 'law abiding and useful lives in custody and after release' (this statement can be found at every prison in England and Wales). The lack of facilities catering for individual need increases the pain of imprisonment where the prisons focus resources and facilities, such as training and educational programmes, on the young and able-bodied. This is a good example of how the discourse of ageism and the idea of less eligibility operate when faced with limited resources. Prison officers/prison personnel fail to place elders on educational or training programmes, assuming that, due to their age, they are less likely to find employment.

    The lack of help and rehabilitation renders elders a 'hidden minority'. Once prisoners are released, the effect of the discontinuity of pension contributions will leave them with insufficient contributions and consequently they will be in receipt of either a partial pension or none at all. The current wave of anti-social legislation,[1] such as the Housing Act of 1988, (reducing the housing available for ex-prisoners), the Criminal Justice and Public Order Act of 1994 and the Crime and Disorder Act of 1998, the diminishing value of the basic retirement pension and the complexity of the forms that need to be completed, have in turn led to low take-up rates of benefits by elders in the wider society (Phillipson and Walker, 1986).

    A useful initiative would be to introduce independent advice centres in prisons, ensuring that the prisoners had information about available benefits and access to legal resources. A network of employment schemes, linking offenders across the life-course to jobs, would provide occupational skill, an employment record, and promote self-esteem. The continuation of National Insurance contributions whilst in prison is an obvious necessity for offenders across the life-course. Furthermore, a network of halfway houses needs to be established, and facilities/schemes comparable to those at Grendon Underwood[2] and Latchmere House.[3] Such schemes have already been successfully introduced, but far more is needed to ensure that all eligible prisoners are able to access this kind of support.

    Women and men in later life need improved health services, better pensions, different types of housing, age-sensitive regimes, and a variety of aids when they become disabled. We have to recognize that the elderly inmate, due to the effects of ageing, has far different needs and places far different demands on a system that is designed for the younger inmate. But they also need a reason for using these things. 'In our society the purpose of life in old age is often unclear . . . Old age is seen as a 'problem' with the elderly viewed as dependants; worse still, they are often described as a non-productive burden upon the economy' (Phillipson, 1982: 166). It is not surprising then that elders experience isolation and alienation when they are denied access to the sources of meaning valued by the society in which they live (Phillipson and Walker, 1986; Turner, 1988).

Although little research has been undertaken in England and Wales into the health of older female and male prisoners, I found that women prisoners compared to men over fifty considered themselves disadvantaged in preventative health and wellness schemes (Wahidin, 2000: 55–6). Similarly, in the USA Kratcoski and Babb (1990), (cited in Kerbs, 2000: 219), found that older female prisoners were less likely than men to participate in recreational programmes, and reported significantly higher levels of poor or terrible health (46 per cent versus 25 per cent), with depression and generalized 'worry' being the two most persistent health problems they experienced. McDonald's (1995) study identified several conditions that have forced prison health care costs in the US to rise. A similar pattern is emerging in the prison system in England and Wales. The factors influencing the increase in expenditure are the following:

(a) the rising cost of health care in society at large;

(b) the increasing number of prisoners in the prison system;

(c) the general ageing of the prison population;

(d) the higher prevalence of infectious diseases among prison populations.

As long as these trends continue, prison health-care costs will continue to increase. Like prisoners in general, ageing prisoners have not had proper access to health care on the outside. They often come into the prison system with numerous chronic illnesses and consume multiple medications. Jonathan Turley, Director of the Project for Older Prisoners (POP'S), noted that: 'the greatest single contributor to the high costs of older prisoners is medical expenditures' (Turley, 1990: 26). On average, prisoners over the age of fifty suffer at least three chronic health problems, such as hypertension, diabetes and emphysema (Acoca, 1998; Turley, 1990). Prisoners, as a population, traditionally have medical and social histories that put them more at risk for illness and disease than their non-inmate peers (Marquart et al., 1997, 2000). As the number of older prisoners increases, the prison system will be even more challenged to provide adequate health and social care provision.

The health needs profile of the ageing offender is hard to map in the absence of statistical information relating to health care costs in prisons in England and Wales. We know that in the US, daily medical care for the general prison population costs $5.75 per offender. On average, for an offender over fifty years of age, the cost of incarceration is approximately three times as much as a prisoner aged under fifty (Neeley, Addison and Craig-Moreland, 1997; Fazel et al., 2001). Statistics for 2001 provided by the Florida Corrections Commission, support the above findings and demonstrate that prisoners over fifty, despite making up only 9 per cent of the total prison population, were responsible for 19 per cent of the costs paid for ambulatory surgery episodes, 17 per cent of costs for non-emergency room episodes, 31 per cent of costs for ancillary care episodes, 20 per cent of costs for specialty care episodes, and 29 per cent of costs for inpatient care episodes.

With a predicted rise in the number of offenders who are older, sicker, and serving longer sentences, coupled with institutions' stretched resources, it is reasonable to argue that if we fail to address the needs of elders in prison, we will be facing an inevitable crisis (Prison Reform Trust: 2003). As more cohorts enter the latter stages of life, the age revolution will significantly affect all facets of the criminal justice system.

REVIEW QUESTIONS

1 How might we define ageism? Give three examples of ageist behaviour or language.

2 What are the effects of growing medical costs on the prison system and what strategies can be employed to improve healthcare in the prison system?

3 Is there much point in providing a rehabilitation programme for a fifty, sixty, seventy year old offender serving a five to ten year sentence? Please give reasons for your answers.

Age-sensitive policy recommendations

To alleviate some of the pains of imprisonment, the prison authorities should be turning their attention to literature relating to residential homes (Atherton, 1989; Coleman, 1993; Hockey, 1989). There are many simple measures that could be taken which would allow elders control over their immediate physical environment, for example, installing doors and windows which they could open easily, and radiators which they could adjust themselves, replacing the harshness of the prison corridors with appropriate carpet tiles, use of electricity sockets which would allow all elders the opportunity to listen to the radio, and replacing the glare of the strip light with something less harsh.

Such measures would at once make prison a less hostile and more accessible place. In addition, due to the impairment of sight, hearing, memory and reflexes, and also the general slowing of movement and mental responsiveness, elders need to be cared for by staff members who are specifically trained in the needs of elders in prison.

Segregation versus integration

The American criminal justice system has been at the forefront of delivering special programmes for older offenders (Krajick, 1979; Aday and Rosenfield, 1992). 'Special programmes', here constitute the distinctive treatment of the elderly prisoner housed in an age-segregated or in an age-sensitive environment. Segregation provides a concentration of specialized staff and resources for the elderly, thereby reducing costs (Florida Corrections Commission, 2001).

Previous research supports the notion that participation in a specific group increases self-respect and increases capability to resume community life once released. A choice of age segregation or age integration provides older prisoners with the opportunity for forming peer networks, while at the same time reducing vulnerability and violence they may encounter in the mainstream of prison life. Fattah and Sacco state:

> Concern for their safety and the need to protect them against victimisation, exploitation and harassment outweigh any stabilizing effect their integration may have. (1989:101)

It is imperative that the prison system provides not only comprehensive opportunities whilst in prison and appropriate resettlement programmes, but also alternatives to the traditional custodial framework in which elders find themselves growing old. What is needed is the flexibility of having accommodation and provision reserved for elders, without creating a separate prison or excluding elders from the main prison environment. Aday succinctly states: 'Like the elderly in the free world, they are familiar with life in the general population and perceive that it has a mark of independence' (2003: 146). The criminal justice system in England and Wales, unlike the American criminal justice system, is still operating without a comprehensive plan to respond adequately to a pending crisis. The needs of elders in prisons are substantial, and can include physical, mental and preventative health-care; custody allocation to special housing, educational, vocational or recreational programmes, physical exercise, and rehabilitation programming; dietary considerations and long-term geriatric and nursing care.

An overriding theme within the integration versus segregation debate is that the way forward is to provide flexible accommodation, not through segregation, but through integration, within a framework of tolerance, understanding and adaptability. The ageing prison population poses a true dilemma, and deserves recognition both among those interested in the wellbeing of those in later life and those executing prison policy. Age, in time, will be considered as one of the biggest issues that will continue to affect the criminal justice system and prison health care in the future. With the continued increase in criminal activity among the elderly population as a whole, learning more about crime and ageing, and about institutional adjustment, recidivism and release, seems imperative.

Today, we have family courts, juvenile courts, and a large variety of special courts to handle specific problems (Wahidin and Cain, 2005b). Along with the medley of juridical experts, from child psychiatrists to social workers, in the future, will we see court reports and parole boards informed by gerontologists? Could we be accused of infantilizing the older offender if we were to advocate a court that deals specifically with the elder offender? The literature suggests the following initiatives. This is not by any means an exhaustive list, but it does raise various policy questions:

- Should we change our sentencing structure to reflect probable years remaining in the offender's life?
- Should older prisoners be segregated from the general prison population or should they be integrated into the mainstream of prison life?
- What are the alternatives to imprisonment for this cohort (dependent on risk, nature of offence and time served)?

The limited knowledge concerning elders and crime and the absence of relevant policies and planning in this area, lead one to suggest that the criminal justice system should be turning its attention to:

- an examination of existing formal and informal practices regarding elders, as the first step in developing an explicit and integrated set of policies and programmes to address the special needs of this group;

- developing a comprehensive and gender sensitive programme for elders, which fosters personal growth and accountability and value-based actions that lead to successful reintegration into society;

- preparing all personnel of the criminal justice system to understand and appropriately address elder-specific topics and issues.

In terms of being able to address the needs of elders in the criminal justice system, the Prison Policy Unit for England and Wales should be able to institute the following:

- adopting the age of fifty as the definition of an older offender;

- compiling comprehensive data on the over fifties in the criminal justice system from arrest to custody, through to re-entry to wider society;

- introduction of specific programmes geared towards the needs of the elderly;

- identification of the costs of long-term incarceration of infirm prisoners and the potential risks of early release or extended medical leave for this population.

Elders in prison are less likely to be a risk to society, and less likely to re-offend, and this allows for the possibility of designing future prisons/alternatives to prisons with the older person in mind (see Table 20.1). In a report produced by the Florida Corrections Commission (1999), it was found that elderly prisoners have the lowest recidivism rate of any group examined (see Table 20.1).

In England and Wales, the only figures that compare release by age are in relation to the Home Detention Curfew (HDC was introduced across England and Wales in 1999). It allows short-term prisoners to spend up to the last two months of their custodial sentence subject to an electronically-monitored curfew for at least nine hours per day). Figures suggest that the release rate on HDC tends to increase with age and it is more likely to be used for the fifty-plus groups. The association here is that there is a higher risk of reconviction for younger offenders (Home Office, 2001c; Johnson and Alozie, 2001; Long, 1992).

Whilst further research is needed to ascertain how these figures break down for the female and male prison population, one could certainly imagine a future in which imprisonment of elder females and males is a rarity, reserved for those who are convicted of truly heinous crimes of a nature indicating a continuing risk to society. Male and female prisoners are not comparable; they have different criminal profiles, in terms of types of offences committed, previous offending history and reconviction rates. It has

Table 20.1 The correlation between age and re-offending

Age	Percentage
16–18	>70
45–49	27
50–64	22
65 and older	7

Source: http://www.fcc.state.fl.us/fcc/rep[orts/final1909/1eld.html cited in Wahidin, 2004.

been suggested that a gender-specific policy based on substantive equality will improve the plight of women in prison across the life-course (Carlen, 2002; NACRO, 1993, 1994). It can be argued that women in later life compared to older men who are in prison are a low-risk group in terms of repeat offending and nature of offence. Thus, it can be argued that a pilot group from this age cohort, who are assessed as low risk, could be used to explore alternatives to imprisonment. This could lead to savings being made on both a humanitarian and fiscal level.

A good example of diverting or reducing custodial sentences for elders is an early release scheme orchestrated by The Project for Older Prisoners in the US. Candidates must be over fifty years of age, have already served the average time for their offences, and have been assessed as low risk and thus unlikely to commit further crimes. Another unique requirement of this programme is that the victim, or the victim's family, must agree to early release. As a result of these strict standards, no prisoner released under the Project for Older Prisoners has ever been returned to prison for committing another crime (Turley, 1992). The programme helps them find employment and housing, and ensures that they receive their full entitlement to benefits. Such a scheme could beneficially be extended to England and Wales, to include a large number of older prisoners and, if successful, could foster a willingness within the penal system to consider shorter or non-custodial sentences for this low-risk group.

REVIEW QUESTIONS

1 Explain why prison nursing homes have become a necessity.

2 Can we use old age as a bona fide legal defence as a mitigating factor in the court of law?[4]

3 What are the advantages and disadvantages of holding elderly offenders?

CONCLUSION

Traditionally, questions concerning discrimination in criminal processing have focused on the effects of factors such as gender, ethnicity, disability, sexuality, socio-economic status and age (for those between ten and eighteen), but have neglected later-life issues (Dimensions of Crime we consider these areas). It has been argued throughout this chapter that crimes committed by elders are of sufficient importance to warrant increased research, better reporting of the age of offenders once released, and research into where they go after serving their sentence. Research is required to investigate their domestic responsibilities prior to imprisonment and the possibility of designing future prisons with elders in mind. Their experiences have remained marginalized in the debates around policy, and how the criminal justice system responds to these changes remains yet to be seen.

In light of this growing population, we have to begin to re-evaluate fundamental theories of punishment, deterrence, retribution and rehabilitation for this particular group. One also has to consider the types of offence, risk and need in relation to the above. This hidden minority will pose challenges to the jurisprudence and due process system. It is because of the failure to provide adequate facilities in prison that elders are unable to have a reasonable quality of life behind and beyond the walls.

Professionals in the field of criminology and gerontology can provide a greater awareness and understanding of the problems facing persons who encounter the criminal justice system in later life. For it is only in the context of heightened understanding of ageing in general that the problems of offending, prison adjustment, and successful re-entry to society of the aged can be fully addressed. Policymakers will have to address the special needs of prisoners who will spend the remainder of their lives in prison as well as those who will be released in late old age.

For many years, both gerontologists and criminologists have concentrated their attention exclusively in their respective fields (Malinchak, 1980). In this chapter, I have tried to make the case for a combined criminological and gerontological approach to the area. Both disciplines bring a richness to understanding the experiences of older men and women who find themselves lost in the criminal justice system that treats adults the same, be they twenty-five or seventy-five. It is only by having an integrated approach that we can begin to fully understand the complexity of ageing in the criminal justice system and, in turn, put the needs of elders firmly on the research and penal policy agenda.

If society has little place for elders in general, it has even less place for the elderly prisoner or ex-convict. Some have served an extremely long sentence in prison and find that they have no family or social networks on the outside and it is on this basis release can be denied. So what happens to the elderly offender who has nowhere to go? Prison does not stop at the prison gates (see Social Exclusion Unit, 2002; Halliday Report, 2001, HMIP 2002a). Women and men who leave prison bring with them the effects of a custodial sentence and, on release, they encounter suspicion, rejection and hostility as they make this transition from prison to a society which discriminates against the elderly.

Figure 20.7 State Prison #4017
Source: Sandy Campbell, Tennessean, 10 April 1994. Copyrighted, *The Tennessean*.

1   From the statistics provided in Figures 20.1 and 20.2 describe the trends they show across the life-course.

2   What are the advantages and disadvantages of having separate prisons for older offenders?

3   What are the advantages and disadvantages of having an integrated elderly unit for older offenders?

4   What would be the advantage of setting up a similar early release scheme such as, The Project for Older Prisoners in the UK?

5   Give three examples of the future challenges an older prison population will pose for the criminal justice system.

GUIDE TO FURTHER READING

Aday, R.H. (2003), *Aging Prisoners: Crisis in American Corrections*, Westport CT: Praeger.

This is an excellent introduction to the profile of older offenders in US prisons. It provides a comprehensive view of the needs of offenders in later life, and recommends policy initiatives to address this growing population.

Biggs, S. (1993), *Understanding Ageing—Images, Attitudes and Professional Practice*, Buckingham: Open University Press.

Simon Biggs examines theoretical approaches to understanding old age. His book provides new insights into how older age is imagined, defined and experienced. By studying self-perception, communication and power relations, and applying his conclusions to the helping professions, institutions and community care, Biggs offers a new framework for constructive social gerontology and reflexive praxis.

Bond, J., Coleman, P. and Peace, S. (eds) (1993), *Ageing in Society—An Introduction to Social Gerontology*, London: Sage.

This book provides a comprehensive coverage of gerontological issues while capturing the complexity inherent in the processes of ageing. The book emphasizes diversity in the experience of ageing as a function of cultural, social, racial/ethnic, and individual variability.

Rothman, M.B., Dunlop, B.D., and Entzel, P. (2000), *Elders, Crime and the Criminal Justice System* New York: Springer.

The Rothman collection *et al.*, is the only book that provides an international perspective on ageing offenders. This edited book examines the relationship between old age and crime and the criminal justice system.

Wahidin, A. (2004), *Older Women in the Criminal Justice System: Running out of Time*, London: Jessica Kingsley.

This book introduces the reader to key debates and issues surrounding the needs of the older prison population in England and Wales. In particular, this book is based on a national study of older women and their experiences of imprisonment. The author uses her recent work on older men in prisons and the management of the older prison population in the US and the UK to highlight implications for older offenders.

Wahidin, A. and Cain M. (eds) (2005), *Age, Crime and Society*, Cullompton, Willan Press.

The starting point of this book is that 'age' is under-theorized and viewed as unproblematic in criminology. There is very little material on 'elder' or later life crime, little on the victimization of elders except in relation to the presumptively irrational nature of their fears. The book examines some of the issues and concerns in the field of elder abuse and neglect and argues the case that criminology as a discipline must address issues of ageing and its complex relationship with crime. This book is the first comprehensive text to tackle these issues.

WEB LINKS:

http://www.gwu.edu/~commit/law.htm

This website details the largest volunteer prison assistance project for older offenders.

http://www.elderabuse.org.uk

Action on Elder Abuse is a site giving information about conferences and news as well having a special link page for students who are researching the topic of elder abuse.

http://www.howardleague.org

The Howard League is the oldest penal reform charity in the UK. The site gives access to publications, conferences, and information pertaining to the criminal justice system in the UK.

http://www.hmprisonservice.gov.uk/

An extremely useful site, this includes a range of link pages to government departments, statistical information and is the official site of HM Prison Service.

REFERENCES

Acoca, L. (1998) 'Defusing the Time Bomb: Understanding and Meeting the Growing Healthcare Needs of Incarcerated Women in America', *Crime and Delinquency*, 44, 49–70.

Aday, R.H. (1994) 'Aging in Prison: A Case Study of New Elderly Offender', *International Journal of Offender Therapy and Comparative Criminology*, Vol.1, Part 38: 79–91.

Aday, R.H. (1994a) 'Golden Years Behind Bars: Special Programs and Facilities for Elderly Inmates', in *Federal Probation* 58: 2: 47–54.

Aday, R.H. (2003) *Aging Prisoners: Crisis in American Corrections*. Westport USA: Praeger.

Aday, R.H., and Rosefield, H.A. (1992), 'Providing for the Geriatric Inmate: Implications for Training', *Journal of Correctional Training*, 12, 14–16, 20 Winter.

Atherton, J.S. (1989) *Interpreting Residential Life—Values to Practice*. London, Tavistock: Routledge.

Biggs, S. (1993) *Understanding Ageing—Images, Attitudes and Professional Practice*. Buckingham: Open University Press.

Bond, J., Coleman, P., and Peace, S. (eds) (1993), *Ageing in Society—An Introduction to Social Gerontology*. London: Sage.

Bowling, B., and Phillips, C. (2002), *Racism, Crime and Justice*. London: Longman.

Bytheway, W.R., and Johnson. J. (1990), 'On Defining Ageism', *Critical Social Policy*, Vol. 27.

Carlen, P. (2002) *Women and Punishment: The Struggles for Justice*. Cullompton: Willan.

Cohen, S. (1973) *Folk Devils and Moral Panics*. Oxford: Martin Robertson.

Coleman, P. (1993) 'Adjustment in later life' in J. Bond, P. Coleman, and S. Peace (eds) (1993), *Ageing in Society—An Introduction to Social Gerontology*. London: Sage.

Crawford, A., Jones, T., Woodhouse, T., and Young, J. (1990) *Second Islington Crime Survey*. Middlesex: Middlesex Polytechnic.

Curtis, S. (1999) *Children Who Break the Law* London: Waterside Press.

Devlin, A. (1998) *Invisible Women*. Winchester: Waterside Press.

Fattah, E.A. and Sacco V.F. (1989) *Crime and Victimisation of the Elderly*. New York: Springer-Verlag.

Fazel, S., Hope, T., O'Donnell, I., Piper, M. and Jacoby, R. (2001), 'Health of Elderly Male Prisoners: Worse than the General Population, Worse than Younger Prisoners', *Age and Ageing* 30: 403–407.

Featherstone, M. and Hepworth, M. (1993) 'Images of ageing', in J. Bond, P. Coleman, and S. Peace (eds), (1993) *Ageing in Society—An Introduction to Social Gerontology*. London, Sage.

Ferraro, K. (1995), *Fear of Crime: Interpreting Victimisation Risk*. New York: State University of New York Press.

Florida Corrections Commission (1999) Elderly Inmates Annual Report, http://www.fcc.state.fl.us/fcc/reports/final99/1eld.html

Florida Corrections Commission (1999) Annual Report Section 4: Status Report on Elderly Offenders. Florida Corrections Department.

Flynn, E. (1992), 'The greying of America's prison population', in the *Prison Journal*, Vol. 72 Nos. 1 and 2 77–98.

Gallagher, E. (1990) 'Emotional, Social, and Physical Health Characteristics of Older Men in Prison', in the *International Journal of Aging and Human Development*, Vol. 31 (4): 251–65.

Genders, E. and Players, E. (1995) *A Study of a Therapeutic Prison*. Oxford: Oxford University Press.

Gewerth, K. (1988) 'Elderly Offenders: A Review of Previous Research', in B. McCarthy, *Older Offenders*. New York: Praeger.

Government Actuary's Department, http://www.gad.uk/Population=

Halliday, J. (2001) *Making Punishments Work: Report of a Review of the Sentencing Framework for England and Wales*. London: Home Office.

Ham, J. (1976) *The Forgotten Minority an Exploration of Long-Term Institutionalized Aged and Aging Prison Inmates*, PhD. Diss., University of Michigan.

Her Majesty's Chief Inspector of Prisons (1997) *Women in Prison: A Thematic Review*. London: The Home Office.

Her Majesty's Chief Inspector of Prisons (2001) Annual Report 1999–00, Inspector's Report via http://www.homeoffice.gov.uk/hmipris/ch2.pdf.

Her Majesty's Chief Inspectors of Prisons (2001a) Report on a Full Announced Inspection of HMP Kingston: 12–16 February 2001. Inspection Reports via http://www.homeoffice.gov.uk/hmipris/inspects/kingston01.pdf (Accessed 3 August 2004).

Her Majesty's Inspectorate of Prisons for England and Wales (2002a) Report of HM Inspectorates of Prison and Probation Conference: *Through the Prison Gates*. London: The Stationary Office.

Her Majesty's Inspectorates of Prisons and Probation (2001) *Through the Prison Gate: A Joint Thematic Review*. London: HMIP.

Herrnstein, R., and Murray, C. (1994) *The Bell Curve—Intelligence and Class Structure in American Life*. London: The Free Press.

Hirschi, T. and Gottfredson, M. (1983) 'Age and the Explanation of Crime', *American Journal of Sociology*, 89: 552–84.

Hirschi, T. (1969) *Causes of Delinquency*. Berkeley: University of California Press.

Hockey, J. (1989) 'Residential Care and the Maintenance of Social Identity: Negotiating the Transition to Institutional Life', in M. Jefferys (1989), *Growing Old in The Twentieth Century*. London: Routledge: 201–218.

Holloway, W. and Jefferson (2000) 'The Role of Anxiety in Fear and Crime', in T. Hope and R. Sparks (eds), *Crime, Risk and Society*. London: Routledge.

Home Office (1994) *Does the Criminal Justice System Treat Men and Women Differently?* Research Findings No. 10. London HMSO.

Home Office (1999) *Statistics on Women and the Criminal Justice System—A Home Office Publication Under Section 95 of The Criminal Justice Act 1991*. London: HMSO.

Home Office (2001) *The Halliday Report: Making Punishment Work: review of Sentencing Framework for England and Wales*. London: HMSO.

Home Office (2001a) *The Government's Strategy for Women Offenders: Consultation Report*. London: HMSO.

Home Office (2001b) *Home Office Prison Population Brief*. London: HMSO.

Home Office (2001c) *Prison Statistics of England and Wales*. National Statistics Cm. 5743.

Home Office (2002) *Statistics on Women and the Criminal Justice System: A Home Office Publication Under Section 95 of the Criminal Justice Act*. London: HMSO.

Home Office (2004) Prison Statistics obtained on special request from the Research, Development and Statistics Directorate of the Home Office.

James, M. (1992) 'Sentencing of Elderly Criminals', *American Criminal Law Review* Vol. 29: 1025–44.

Johnson, W. (1989) 'If only, the Experience of Elderly Ex-Convicts', *Journal of Gerontological Social Work*, 1989 Vol. 14: 191–208.

Johnson, W., and Alozie, B.O. (2001) 'The Effect of Age on the Criminal Processing: Is there an Advantage in Being "Older"'? *Journal of Gerontological Social Work*, 35, 47–62.

Jones, G.M. (1987) 'Elderly People and Domestic Crime', *British Journal of Criminology*, Vol. 27, 191–201.

Kerbs, J. (2000) 'The older prisoner: social, psychological and medical considerations' in M. Rothman, B. Dunlop, and P. Entzel (2000), *Elders, Crime and The Criminal Justice System—Myth, Perceptions, and Reality in the 21st Century*, New York: Springer Publishing Company.

Krajick, K. (1979) 'Growing Old in Prison'. *Corrections Magazine*, 5(1), 32–46.

Krug, E.G. (2002) *World Report on Violence and Health*. Geneva: World Health Organisation.

Lombroso, C. and Ferrero, G., (1895) *Female Offender*. London: Appleton.

Long, L.M. (1992) A Study of Arrests of Older Offenders: Trends and Patterns in the *Journal of Crime and Justice*, 15, 157–75.

Malinchak, A.A. (1980) *Crime and Gerontology*. Englewood Cliffs, NJ: Prentice Hall.

Manthorpe, J. (1983) 'With Intent to Steal in the New Age', *Journal of Offending Counselling Services and Rehabilitation*, 13 (Spring) 25–28.

Marquart, J.W., Merianos, D.E., Herbert, J.L., and Carroll, L. (1997) 'Health Condition and Prisoners. A Review of Research and Emerging Areas of Inquiry' in the *Prison Journal* 77, 184–208.

Marquart, J.W., Merianos, D.E., and Doucet, G. (2000) 'The Health Related Concerns of Older Prisoners: Implications for Policy', *Aging and Society* 20, 79–96.

Mawby, R and Gill, M. (1987) *Crime Victims: Needs, Services and the Voluntary Sector*. London: Tavistock.

Mawby R. and Walklate S. (1994) *Critical Victimology: The Victim in International Perspectives*. London: Sage.

Mcdonald, D.C. (1995) *Managing Prison Health Care and Costs*, Washington, DC: National Institute of Justice, US Department of Justice

NACRO, (1992a) *Women and Criminal Justice: Some Facts and Figures*: NACRO Briefing No. 91, (August). London: NACRO.

NACRO (1993) *Women Leaving Prison*. London: NACRO.

NACRO (1994) *Prison Overcrowding—Recent Developments*. NACRO Briefing No. 28 (July). London: NACRO.

Neeley, L.C., Addison, L., and Moreland-Craig, D. (1997) 'Addressing the Needs of Elderly Offenders', *Corrections Today, August, 59*, 120–24.

Newman, E. (1984) 'Elderly Offenders and American Crime' in E. Newman, D. Newman,. M. Gewirtz (eds), *Elderly Criminals*. Oelgeschlager, Massachusetts: Gunn and Hain, Publishers Inc., Cambridge.

Newman, E,. Newman, D,. and Gewirtz, M. (eds), (1984) *Elderly Criminals*, Oelgeschlager, Massachusetts: Gunn and Hain Publishers Inc. Cambridge.

Pain, H.R. (1995) 'Elderly Women and Fear of Violent Crime: the least likely Victims', *British Journal of Criminology*, 38 (4), 584–98.

Pearson, G. (1983) *Hooligan: A History of Respectable Fears*, London: MacMillan.

Pertierra, J.C. (1995) 'Do the Crime: Do the Time: Should Elderly Criminals Receive Proportionate Sentences?' *Nova Law Review*, Winter: 1–25.

Penal Affairs Consortium (1996) *The Imprisonment of Women: Some Facts and Figures*. London: (March).

Phillips, J. (1996) 'Crime and Older Offenders', *Practice*, Vol. 8, 1, 43–55.

Phillipson, C. (1982) *Capitalism and the Construction of Old Age*, London: Macmillian.

Phillipson, C., and Walker, A. (eds) (1986) *Ageing and Social Policy, A Critical Assessment*. Aldershot: Gower.

Pitts, J. (1988) *The Politics of Juvenile Crime*, London: Sage.

Pollak, O. (1941) 'The Criminality of Old Age', *Journal of Criminal Psycho-theraphy*, 3, 213–35.

Presdee, M. (1994) 'Young people, culture and the construction of crime: doing wrong versus doing crime' in G. Barak (ed), *Varieties of Criminology*. Westport CT: Praeger.

Prison Reform Trust (2003) *Growing Old in Prison: A Scoping Study on Older Prisoners*. London.

Rothman, M.B., Dunlop, B.D., and Entzel, P. (2000) *Elders, Crime and the Criminal Justice System*. New York: Springer.

Ruberstein, D. (1984) 'The Elderly in Prison: A Review of the Literature' in E. Newman, D. Newman, M. Gewirtz *et al.*, (1984), *Elderly Criminals*. Oelgeschlager, Cambridge, Massachusetts: Gunn and Hain, Publishers Inc., 153–68.

Sim, J. (2000) 'One Thousand Days of Degradation: New Labour and Old Compromises at the Turn of the Century', *Social Justice* Vol. 27 (2), 168–92.

Social Exclusion Unit (2002) *Reducing Re-offending by Ex-prisoners*. London: Office of Department of Prime Ministers.

Sparks, R. (1992) 'Television and the Drama of Crime—Moral Tales and the Place of Crime' *Public Life*. Buckingham: Open University.

Steffensmeier, D., and Moti, M. (2000) 'Older Women and Men in the Arms of Criminal Law; Offending Patterns' *The Journal of Gerontology*: 5141–51.

Turley, J. (1990) 'Long-Term Confinement and the Aging Inmate Population', US Department of Justice, Federal Bureau of Prisons, Form on Issues in Corrections, 'Alternative Solutions'. Washington DC: US Government. Printing Office.

Turley, J. (1992) 'A Solution to Prison Overcrowding' *USA Today Magazine*, November 12, 80–81.

Turner, B. (1988) 'Ageing, Status Politics and Sociological Theory' in *The British Journal of Sociology*, Vol. 40, No. 4: 589–605.

Wahidin, A. (2000) 'Life Behind the Shadows: Women's Experiences of Prison in Later Life' in *Issues in Forensic Psychology, Positive Directions for Women in Secure Environments*, R. Horn and S. Warner (eds). The British Psychological Society.

Wahidin, A. (2004) *Older Women in the Criminal Justice System: Running Out of Time*. London: Jessica Kingsley.

Wahidin, A. (2005) 'No Problems: Old and Quiet: Older Prisoners Unleashed' in D. Scott, A. Barton, I. Corteen and D. Whyte, *The Criminological Imagination: Readings in Critical Criminologies*. Cullompton, Willan Press.

Wahidin, A. (2005a) Managing the Needs of Older Male and Female Offenders, 'Re-Awakening the Criminological Imagination', British Society of Criminology Conference, Leeds University. Unpublished paper.

Wahidin, A. and Powell, L.J. (2005) 'Age, victimisation and crime' in P. Davis, P. Francis and C. Greer (ed), *Crime, Violence and Victimisation*. London: Sage.

Wahidin, A. and Cain, M. (eds) (2005), *Age, Crime and Society*, Cullompton, Willan Press.

White, P., Woodbridge, J., and Flack, K. (1999) *Projections of Long Term Trends in the Prison Population to 2006:* Home Office Statistical Bulletin Issue1/99: 20th January 1999.

Williams, B. (1998) *Victims and the Criminal Justice System*. London: Longman.

Zedner, L. (1994) 'Victims' in M. Maguire, R. Morgan and R. Reiner (eds.) *The Oxford Handbook of Criminology*. Oxford: Oxford University Press.

NOTES

1. The Housing Benefit, Council Tax Benefit and Income Support (Amendments) Regulations 1995 ended the previous practice of using housing benefit to meet rent payments of convicted prisoners serving up to a year in custody. Assistance is now confined to prisoners serving sentences of up to six months who receive conditional discharge subject for good behaviour after thirteen weeks in custody. These changes have increased homelessness among released prisoners by causing a substantial number of prisoners to lose their homes during periods in prison, from between thirteen and fifty-two weeks. A report, *Housing Benefit and Prisoners*, (Penal Affairs Consortium, November 1996), estimates that 5,000 additional prisoners could be released as homeless each year as a result of this change (Devlin, 1998: 42).

2. Grendon prison was opened in 1962, as a unique experiment in the psychological treatment of offenders whose mental disorder did not qualify them for transfer to a hospital under s. 72 of the Mental Health Act 1959. Grendon is a category B training prison and may be described as a multi-functional establishment, accommodating three adult therapy wings which operate as therapeutic communities, an assessment and induction unit, and a treatment wing designed specifically for sex offenders (see Genders and Players, 1995).

3. HMP Latchmere House is a resettlement prison, which holds male adult prisoners serving a sentence of four years or more, including up to twenty life-sentenced prisoners, and assists them to prepare for release.

4. Cristina Pertierra (1995) presents a series of cases brought to the American Court of Appeal in which elderly offenders, under the 18th Amendment, have claimed that, given their ages and life expectancies, the sentences imposed amount to life imprisonment, and are thus disapropriate to the crimes committed. For further details, see *United States* v *Angiulo*, 85 2F.Supp. 54, 60 (D.Mass. 1994); see also *Alspaugh v State*, 133, So. 2d 597, 588 (Fla. 2d dist. Ct App.1961).

Part Four
RESPONSES TO CRIME

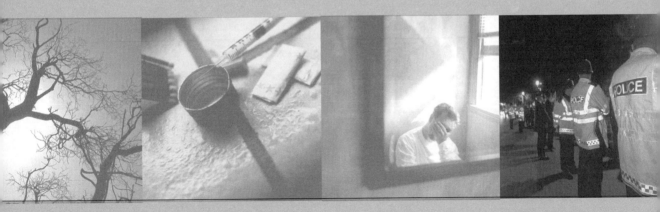

21 The politics of law and order

Chris Hale

INTRODUCTION

In the UK, public statements on crime and criminal justice from representatives of both main political parties, the Conservatives on the right and Labour on the left,[1] seem driven by the need to appear tough, to avoid seeming soft on criminals and to promise they will be treated severely and taught a lesson. This approach has been characterized as 'punitive populism' (Bottoms, 1995) since politicians are following what they believe to be electorate's wishes as expressed and reinforced by the media (see Greer, Chapter 8 above). Courts are urged not to shrink from using custodial sentences despite record numbers in gaol, and expensive prison building programmes are planned. Politicians are wary of being thought of as unsupportive of the police. All must claim they have, or will, increase the numbers of officers on the beat. The Prime Minister, Tony Blair (Blair, 1993) coined the famous phrase 'Tough on crime, tough on the causes of crime' when he was the shadow Home Secretary in the early 1990s and it has dominated New Labour thinking on law and order ever since. This linked firm treatment of offenders—being tough on crime—with the more traditional Labour concerns with social and economic conditions—being tough on the causes of crime. The New Labour Government has indeed introduced policies aimed at both parts. But its main public statements have concentrated on promises to deal with offenders quickly and have played down the impact on crime rates of its strategy on social inclusion. Why has this happened? Why after ten years of more or less continuous drops in recorded crime levels is the government still emphasizing the need to make individuals take responsibility for their actions whilst remaining virtually silent, in the context of law and order policy, on attempts to reduce poverty and tackle social exclusion and on the success of its economic policies that have led to steady growth and falling unemployment (see Hale, Chapter 16 above). To understand how this situation has arisen we need examine the history of law and order policies since the end of World War II. But these cannot be understood in isolation. They developed against the background of recorded crime rates that reached historically high levels in the early 1990s having risen seemingly inexorably since the mid-1950s. This period also saw the development of the welfare state where the guarantee of minimum standards of income, health and education was initially supported across the political spectrum. Within this there was also broad consensus on approaches to tackling crime. By the 1970s however the Welfare State was regarded by some as both a cause of the UK's economic problems and a reason for the growth in crime. The 1970s is a key decade in this story. It marks the beginning of the period of ascendancy of Thatcherism in the UK, a political creed that emphasized individual responsibility and economic market forces and saw welfarism as undermining both. The accomplishment of Margaret Thatcher in pushing through her reforms had a dramatic effect on the economic and political landscape. Law and order did not escape, and while in practice the policies did not change as dramatically as the rhetoric, the impact of that rhetoric is still evident today.

BACKGROUND

One function of the modern State is to guarantee the safety and wellbeing of its citizens. We expect government to protect us from threats both external and internal. Historically, the external threat was invasion by other, rival foreign, states, now more commonly it is terrorist attack. Internally we require the State to minimize our risk of becoming crime victims and, if we are victimized, to deal with the offenders. Internally the Criminal Justice System (CJS) has taken responsibility for our safety. The main institutions of the CJS are the Police, the Crown (soon to be Public) Prosecution Service, the Courts, and the Probation and Prison services (see Uglow, Chapter 22 below). How these operate, the strategies they adopt and how effective they are in ensuring our safety and sense of security, has been over time, to a greater or lesser extent, the subject of much political and public debate. In what follows we introduce the reader to the complex intertwining of politics and crime, punishment and social order. As Downes and Morgan (1994) note, this is a vast subject and here we can only introduce some of the main issues.

At a general level crime is always political since the government, through its control of parliament, has the power to determine which acts are criminal. Further, since limited resources imply choices about which crimes are prioritized by the CJS, the political nature of law enforcement is again apparent. The political debate has focused on property crimes such as burglary, theft and mugging and crimes of violence.[2] Conversely, political rhetoric has given little attention to crimes committed by businesses even though they undoubtedly have a much greater impact in terms of the damage they inflict (see Tombs, Chapter 13 above). Pursuing this argument would then raise the question of whose interests are served by the State and the rule of law. Whilst this perhaps paints too stark a picture, since it is by no means clear that these 'interests', are unambiguously clear and uncontested it is important to remember that what acts are seen as 'crimes' is not fixed and given but changes over time, across cultures and political ideologies (see Morrison, Chapter 1 above).

On the other hand an enduring belief about the justice system in the UK is that the operation of the law is free from political interference. The judiciary particularly guard their independence from interference from government ministers. While Parliament makes the laws, it should not interfere in how they are applied. Judges and magistrates may be encouraged, exhorted, informed and reasoned with, but never instructed. Douglas Hurd, Conservative Home Secretary from 1985 to 1989, put this succinctly:

> It is not for the Home Secretary, Government or the House to lay down to the courts how many people they send to prison. It is our job to provide places for them. (*Hansard*, 5 November 1987, column 1055)

Whilst true of individual cases we will see below that governments have had significant influence on how punitive courts are in dealing with offenders and have increasing control over how the police have targeted their resources (see Jones, Chapter 25).

The important symbolic role crime and its control plays in broader political debates around the type of society we want is one of the themes that will emerge from this chapter. If protection from criminal victimization has long been one of the commitments governments have made to the electorate, the large increases in recorded crime levels since the 1950s have raised serious questions about their ability to deliver on this promise. More widely, crime is often an indicator, a metaphor, as Hall *et al.* (1978) suggest for a more general feeling of social anxiety and apprehension, a theme pursued historically by Pearson, who sees preoccupation with disorder by the respectable as serving:

> . . . an ideological function within British public life, as a convenient metaphor for wider social tensions which attend the advance of democratization. (Pearson 1983: 230)

Whether it is just the advance of democratization or whether it is a more wide-ranging response to a sense of powerlessness and unease produced by economic globalization, or simply a straightforward response to increasing levels of recorded crime, there is no doubt that concern about crime in general, and fear of crime in particular, has become a major political issue. It may seem surprising, given the prominent place occupied by crime and disorder within political debate in the last thirty years, that prior to the UK general elections of 1974 and 1979, the approach to law and order by the Conservative and the Labour Parties was essentially bi-partisan. Whether in government or opposition they shared an understanding of the problems of crime and offending and a belief that solutions lay in policies combining elements of both punishment and welfare, the 'penal-welfare state' (Garland, 2001) whose central institutions are the police, courts, prisons, probation and so on. This consensus stood in stark contrast to other policy areas such as economic management, foreign affairs, health or education where political debate was always intense. After briefly discussing the meaning of 'penal welfare state', we will examine why this consensus broke down.

Loader and Sparks (2002: 84) see the penal-welfare state as being organized around 'mutually reinforcing axioms':

- a conception of crime as conceptually unproblematic and geographically and socially delimited;
- a causal theory of crime that understood crime as a presenting symptom of more deep-seated social problems;
- an attachment to the idea of crime control policy as the province of 'experts' and expert knowledge.

By conceptually unproblematic and socially delimited they mean there was a belief that it was known what crime was, where it happened and who did it. Given that prior to the 1970s, crime was not a political issue nor of major media concern, this meant that the emphasis was on identifying and reforming the individual 'delinquent'. There was acceptance of the 'rehabilitative ideal', part of the broader modernist agenda that looked to apply scientific knowledge to reform individuals and improve social conditions. The second axiom produced policies aimed at improving housing, increasing social welfare and family support coupled with '. . . "correctionalist" treatment programmes oriented at returning individual offenders to the fold of social democratic citizenship' (Loader and Sparks, 2004: 84). This was part of the broader welfare state focused on meeting a range of the basic needs of its citizens including education, work, housing and health. Loader's and Sparks's final axiom refers to the view that the direction of crime policy could, and should, be left to a small group, of civil servants and senior practitioners with minimal input from politicians or the general public. Again this fits with the idea that dealing with crime was a technical scientific issue and hence best left to experts.

As noted this consensus around the belief in the effectiveness of rehabilitative measures coupled with the amelioration of social conditions was to end in the 1970s with the growing awareness that these policies had not had the anticipated impact. The expected reduction in crime had not occurred. On the contrary, recorded crime had begun to grow at an increasing rate. Loader and Sparks (2002), amongst others, identify structural changes at the level of economic, social and cultural relations[3] as responsible for the end of this consensus. Some of these will be discussed below while others, particularly economic changes, are considered in more detail in Chapter 16. The four that Loader and Sparks list are: (a) transformation in capitalist production and exchange (production—the shift from economies predominantly based on manufacturing industry to ones based on the service sector and the related impact on the labour market with the creation of core, secondary and periphery sectors; exchange—the rise of consumerism); (b) changes in family structure (the proliferation of dual career households along side those with no working adults, increased numbers of single parent households and rising divorce rates) and changes in the ecology of cities particularly suburbanization; (c) the universal presence of electronic mass media; and (d) a 'democratization' of everyday life '. . . as witnessed in altered relations of between men/women, parents/children and so on, and a marked decline in unthinking adherence towards authority.

We begin with a broad overview of changes in crime and politics post-1945 before embarking on a more detailed review.

REVIEW QUESTIONS

1 What is meant by punitive populism?

2 Give two key features of Thatcherism.

3 What distinguishes being 'tough on crime' from being 'tough on the causes of crime'?

4 In what senses is crime political?

5 What were the main characteristics to the bi-partisan approach to law and order that operated in the UK until the 1970s?

6 What reasons have been suggested for the end of the consensus around the penal welfare state?

A brief introduction to recorded crime and the politics of law and order in the UK since 1945

No discussion of the (party) politics of law and order can ignore the large growth in recorded crime since 1945. This growth itself needs to be located within broader social and economic developments.

Figure 21.1 shows how crime in England and Wales changed from an exceptional experience to one that is relatively normal. From a low of around 430,000 in 1954, recorded offences increased nearly thirteen-fold to peak at over 5.5 million in 1992. Criminal victimization moved from the margins to '. . . become a routine part of modern consciousness a standing possibility that is constantly to be "kept in mind" ' Garland (2001). Some idea of the magnitude of the shift may be taken from the fact that the *increases* in recorded crime from both 1989 to 1990 and 1990 to 1991 were larger than the total level of crime in any year until 1959.

Within this overall trend of increasing crime risks there are variations. Building on Hale (1999) and McClintock and Avison (1968) it is possible to identify four distinct periods in post-war trends of recorded crime:

   (a) Crime period 1: 1945–54—recorded crime fluctuates around low level;

   (b) Crime period 2: 1955–72—recorded crime begins to grow steadily;

   (c) Crime period 3: 1973–92—recorded crime growth accelerates;

   (d) Crime period 4: 1992 to the present: levels of recorded crime stabilize and fall.

The important periods in terms of their influence on policy and politics are periods 2 and 3. Taken with wider changes noted earlier these periods were to see major shifts in attitudes to crime and crime control that still reverberate today. What of the major political

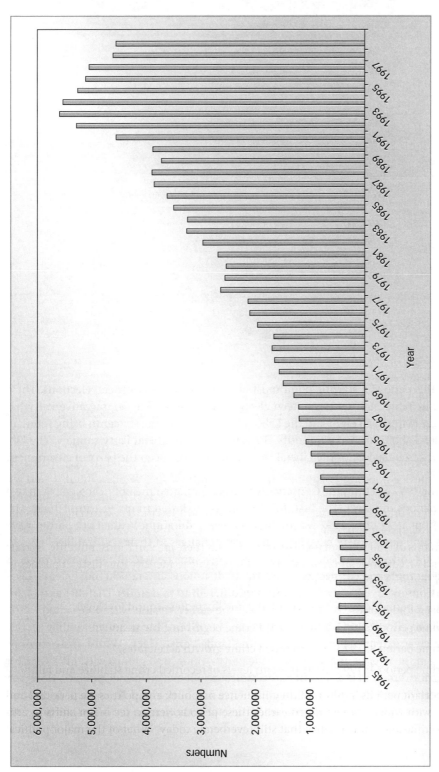

Figure 21.1 Recorded crime in England and Wales

Source: Home Office Criminal Statistics.

Table 21.1 Post-1945 general elections in the United Kingdom	
Date	**Result**
1945	Labour victory
1950	Labour victory
1951	Conservative victory
1955	Conservative victory
1959	Conservative victory
1964	Labour victory
1966	Labour victory
1970	Conservative victory
1974 (Feb)	Labour government but only with liberal support
1974 (Oct)	Labour victory
1979	Conservative victory
1983	Conservative victory
1987	Conservative victory
1992	Conservative victory
1997	Labour victory
2001	Labour victory

shifts in this period? A starting point must be with the post-war general elections. These are listed in Table 21.1. Of the sixteen elections since 1945, the Conservative Party has won a clear majority in eight and the Labour Party in seven, the sixteenth being February 1974 when Labour formed a minority Government with Liberal Party support. The Liberal Party, and its successor the Liberal Democrats, has not been the party of government since 1945.

Until the 1997 election, the Conservative Party dominated the political scene with two lengthy periods in power. The first, for thirteen years, lasted from 1951 until 1964. The second, from 1979 until 1997 was of eighteen years' duration. While both parties have kept the same names there have been significant changes in their political ideologies in this period.[4] Indeed New Labour adopted the 'New' precisely to distance itself from its 'old' Labour roots and connections with the trade unions and radical movements. Likewise the Conservative Party of the 1950s was different to that under Thatcher and Major in the last decades of the twentieth century. The earlier version was more suited to the label 'conservative' being based around ideas of tradition, hierarchy and public service and to a great extent still dominated by the landed aristocracy. Whilst these factions remained in the later period, control of the party belonged to groups with little time for looking backwards and a commitment to radical neoliberal economic policies. However, their moral views and approaches to crime were not in the least libertarian. In government, this combination of economic liberalism and authoritarian moralism had dramatic effects.

Downes and Morgan (2002) identify three distinct phases in the political debates around law and order

(a) Politics phase 1: 1945–70—political census around support for penal-welfare approach. A liberal progressive agenda based on ideas of rehabilitation.

(b) Politics phase 2: 1970–92—political division and sharp disagreements between the main political parties. Initially the Thatcher Conservative Government focused on more resources for the police and prisons linked to a punitive political rhetoric. When crime numbers continued increasing, the emphasis shifted to individual and community self-help and a 'softer' approach to dealing with offenders.

(c) Politics Phase 3: 1992—present a new consensus based around 'populist-punitiveness' with New Labour successfully challenging the Conservative's claim to be the party of law and order.

The first of these political phases roughly coincides with the first two of our crime periods. At the risk of over-simplification, we suggest that the gradual increases in the second crime period were at least in part the cause of the political divisions and sharp disagreements that characterized the second political phase. Political phase 2 coincides with our third period for crime where the rate of increase in recorded crime accelerated rapidly. It was a period of increased social tension, growing unemployment and increased inequality. The Conservative Government's crime policy fluctuated from an initial tough punitive stance to a more tolerant approach and back to the 'prison works' philosophy of Michael Howard when Home Secretary in the mid-1990s. Uniquely the final political period saw sustained drops in recorded crime. There was steady uninterrupted economic growth, falling levels of unemployment and, particularly in the latter years, decreasing inequality. However, so keen was New Labour to lose its reputation for being soft on crime it adopted a strategy of 'out-toughing' the Conservatives on law and order. Hence falling crime and an improving economy were accompanied by an increasingly hard-line rhetoric from both parties, a new consensus around punitive populism.

Having sketched out the major post-war periods for both recorded crime and the politics we now examine each in more detail.

REVIEW QUESTIONS

1 Describe the major trends in recorded crime in England and Wales since 1945.

2 What were the key political phases in the UK since the end of World War II?

Crime, economy and the politics of law and order: 1945–70

After a period from 1930 to 1948 of deepening economic crisis and political unrest including World War II and its immediate aftermath, when crime grew at around 7 per cent annum, from 1949 until 1954, recorded crime was at a low level fluctuating around

500,000 offences per year. Indeed crime levels per head were actually about 18 per cent lower in 1954 than 1948, a reduction that until recently later governments could only dream of. The immediate post-war period was one of economic reconstruction influenced by Keynesian economic theory. Whilst unemployment was low, the rationing introduced in the war continued and levels of consumption grew only slowly. The major economic crises of the 1920s and 1930s had led to greater economic intervention by governments, a trend reinforced by experiences of the economic planning during the war. Meanwhile the Beveridge Report (Beveridge, 1942) laid the foundations for the wideranging system of social security that became the Welfare State. Government would help promote social progress by improving health, housing and diet, thereby attacking Beveridge's five great evils Want, Disease, Ignorance, Squalor and Idleness. The Labour Government of 1945 to 1951 was committed to full employment and improved living conditions for the working class. This interventionist 'welfarist' approach was accepted by the Conservative governments of the 1950s becoming part of the consensus of British political life, a bipartisanship that we have seen also extended to crime and punishment. As McClintock and Avison (1968: 19) note, the expectation at this time was that crime had stabilized and indeed would begin to fall.

This expectation was soon dashed. From 1955 recorded crime levels began a steady, and seemingly inexorable growth of around 10 per cent each year. This rate of growth, twice that of the 1920s and from a much higher base, was an early warning that the welfare state might not deliver the peaceful pleasant land its advocates had hoped.

After the years of post-war austerity, the late 1950s saw beginning of the consumer boom. According to then Prime Minister Macmillan Britons had '. . . never had it so good'. However the continuing prosperity enjoyed by many through these decades could not hide the relative decline in the UK global economic position. The post-war expansion began to falter in the early 1960s and the Labour Government effectively abandoned its commitment to full employment in 1967 by implementing policies to restrain earnings, devalue sterling and encourage industrial rationalization. Rising unemployment led to a major upsurge in industrial unrest that intensified during the 1970–94 Conservative Government under Edward Heath. The 1960s was also a time when the post-war baby boom generation reached their teenage years and as well as the political upheavals around the globe, particularly in 1968, the decade witnessed moral panics around the behaviour of increasingly rebellious youth.

Historians regard the years from 1945 to 1970 as a period of relative social harmony where a political consensus between the Conservatives and Labour Parties held sway. In particular, debates over crime and punishment were muted in comparison with that was to follow. Downes and Morgan (1994, 1997, 2002) examine the main party manifestos for general elections since 1945. Not until 1959, when the Conservatives promised to review the Criminal Justice System, did any refer to law and order. In 1964, adopting themes still familiar today, the Conservatives promised to strengthen the police, to introduce tougher measures against hooliganism and to counter delinquency by supporting family ties. The Labour Party remained silent, even though with a Conservative Government in power since 1951 crime rates had risen significantly. This changed in 1966 when for the first time, after two years in power, Labour devoted as much space as the Conservatives to crime issues. However, as Downes and Morgan (1994: 187) point out in this election as previously '. . . no party manifesto suggested that the level or form of crime was itself attributable to the politics of the party in government.'

Crime, economy and the politics of law and order: 1970–92

In this period, 1970 to 1992, increases in the numbers of offences recorded were very large by historical standards. With accelerating crime growth, the temperature of the debate on law and order rose bringing to an end the post-war consensus and lack of party political debate on law and order. The 1970 election campaign saw all parties devote more words than ever before to the issue. Significantly, for the first time, the Conservatives suggested that the Labour Government was not entirely blameless for the worsening crime problem. They also made clear links between crime, protest and industrial disputes and picketing. The law needed modernizing '. . . for dealing with public order—peculiar to the age of demonstration and disruption' (Conservative Party, 1970). Labour deplored the 'cynical . . . attempts of our opponents to exploit for Party Political ends the issue of crime and law enforcement' and reassured the voters that the streets of British cities were as safe as any in the world. This did not prevent it losing the election.

Anticipating the 1980s, the Conservatives won the 1970 election on a platform that included radical economic reform and a commitment to allowing market forces to operate. Wages were allowed to find their own level and no longer would governments protect traditional manufacturing industries struggling to survive in the global economy. However trade union resistance forced it to discard its non-interventionist policies and turn once more to income policies and Keynesian demand management.

There were two elections in 1974, in February and October. The first resulting in a hung Parliament with Labour returned to power only with Liberal support led to a second in October. In their February manifesto the Conservatives claimed success in fighting crime (rates were fairly constant between 1970 and 1973) and attributed this to the growth in police numbers, tougher penalties for offences involving firearms and the ability of the courts to impose compensation orders (Downes and Morgan, 1994: 91). The Labour Party returned to its strategy of silence on both the Conservatives record and their own plans. In the October election, the Conservatives returned to the attack with the critical change that now they explicitly criticized Labour's record on crime and questioned their integrity. In particular the government was linked to the support some Labour MPs and shadow cabinet members had given to the use of mass picketing in the 1973 miners' strike. By so doing they were able to accuse Labour of failing to support the 'rule of law'. This was to become a key part of the Conservative 1979 election strategy when they successfully presented themselves as the party of law and order that alone had the moral authority and practical ideas to deal with problems of disorder.

The late 1970s saw increasing fluctuations in levels of unemployment and widening divisions between those in relatively secure full–time work and those with unskilled, often part-time, but certainly insecure, jobs. By 1975 the Labour Government was arguing that high unemployment was part of the price to be paid for combating high inflation. It began to restrict money supply and to cut public expenditure hoping that this policy linked to increasing unemployment would produce wage constraint. In 1976, after a series of currency crises and visits from the International Monetary Fund (IMF), further major cuts in public expenditure were announced. Whilst the Labour Government presented this abandonment of welfarism and adoption of monetarism as an IMF imposed pragmatic necessity, the Conservative Party embraced them as core parts of their ideology. They were elected in 1979 on a platform committed to monetary discipline and reductions in government borrowing and spending. In winning the general election, the Conservatives used law and order as a central unifying theme. Industrial militancy and public protest was aligned with a general decline in morality and breakdown of respect for law and order. This in turn was blamed on the dependency culture fostered they argued by the Welfare State. The mugger became symbolic of the moral and economic decline of the nation:

> In their muddled but different ways, the vandals on the picket lines and the muggers in our streets have got the same confused message—'we want our demands met or else' and 'get out of the way give us your handbag'. (Margaret Thatcher 1979)

This laid the foundation for their success in marshalling the police and the courts to break organized working-class resistance to their economic and social programme. For the new Conservative Government, law and order meant new forms of social discipline leading, they hoped, to self-discipline. It was a metaphor for certain forms of morality emphasizing individual effort and endeavour. Their criminology had several distinctive features. First, social conditions were irrelevant to criminality; it was the individual who was basically bad. Second, punishment and retribution were central to policy. This was reinforced by the view that with offenders 'nothing works';[5] that programmes aimed at rehabilitation and reform of individuals were having no impact (see Worrall, Chapter 26 below). From these was to develop a pessimistic emphasis on crime prevention through greater vigilance and awareness of the individual citizen.

It set out its, stall clearly in its election manifesto:

> The next Conservative Government will spend more on fighting crime even while we economize elsewhere . . . Britain needs strong efficient police forces with high morale. (Conservative Party 1979)

In the early years it certainly met this pledge. Between 1979 and 1988 the number of police officers increased by 11 per cent, there was a 12 per cent increase in civilians employed and a 64 per cent increase in real terms in total police expenditure. At the same time it planned and implemented a major prison building programme and oversaw an increase in the numbers imprisoned from an average population of 42,220 in 1979 to 47,200 in 1986–87. This last figure was 13 per cent above the capacity of the prison system (Brake and Hale, 1992). Whilst punitive tactics helped their industrial strategy (for example, the 1984 miners' strike) it became apparent that strong policing and tough sentencing were having little impact on the crime levels.[6] Set against the additional resources given to the police, these rises could not escape notice within a government committed to reducing public expenditure. Conservative utterances showed subtle shifts in the 1983 election and subsequently. It was no longer just a matter of extolling the virtues of strong police powers and tougher sentencing to curb crime. Now:

> Dealing with crimes, civil disobedience, violent demonstrations and pornography are not matters for the police alone. It is teachers and parents—and television producers too—who influence the moral standards of the next generation. There must be close co-operation and understanding between the police and the community they serve. (Conservative Party 1983)

Between 1983 and 1987 recorded offences increased by just under 20 per cent. From being an electoral asset, law and order risked becoming the Conservatives' biggest failure. A cost-conscious government could not continue repeating the same refrain when faced with such a stark picture of ineffectiveness. Pragmatically the emphasis shifted, playing down the role of the police, and increasingly stressing the importance of 'community' and the 'active citizen'. The Conservatives were not alone in this. Crime prevention was endorsed by all the major parties in the 1987 election. But while for the Labour Party the approach was to be a collective one through the local authorities, the Conservatives placed responsibility on individual householders and voluntary neighbourhood schemes.

Home Office research backed the growing feeling that increasing police resources had little impact on crime, that more generally there were:

> . . . limitations in what the criminal justice system can do: that the burden of crime prevention cannot be carried solely by the police, the courts and the penal system. As well as citizens themselves, those responsible for housing, for schools, for employment and leisure provision also have a more crucial role in crime prevention than has been acknowledged previously. (Hope and Shaw 1988: 11)

These considerations led to two inter-related approaches to the problem: multi-agency policing and partnership and citizen involvement.

> At the very centre of our ideas on how to control crime should be the energy and initiative of the active citizen. (John Patten, Minister of State Home Office, Foreword to Hope and Shaw, 1988)

The cornerstone of the Conservative approach to community crime prevention was the 'active citizen' and his or her involvement particularly in Neighbourhood Watch (NW) schemes that encouraged residents to keep a vigilant eye on their local area and report anything suspicious to the police. Another concern for a cost conscious government were the numbers in prison. During the 1980s there was a schizophrenic approach to the issue of punishing prisoners. While Home Office Ministers argued consistently that prison was only to be used for violent and serious offenders, they were also clear that the government role was to provide prison places not to interfere with the judicial process. So, despite various measures introduced during the 1980s to reduce the numbers imprisoned, the punitive rhetoric dominated. As with the police expenditure on the prison service rose considerably—by 36 per cent in real terms between 1979 and 1989. This led to the growing awareness that prison was an expensive way of making bad people worse.[7] There began another attempt to persuade courts and the public that non-custodial community sentences (see Worrall, Chapter 26) were not soft options but properly applied would be tough measures. The culmination of this was the 1991 Criminal Justice Act (CJA). At its core the Act had the principle that the sentencing decision should focus on the seriousness of the offence; that normally the offender's previous convictions were not to be taken into account. It was a clear statement that the 'Just Deserts' theory of punishment outlining a clear hierarchy of sentences of increasing severity from discharge through fines to community-based sentences to custodial sentences should be used with increasing seriousness of offence. Custodial sentences were only to be imposed if the offence was sufficiently serious, or in the case of violent or sexual offences if necessary to protect the public. However, as we shall see after an initial positive impact, a mixture of circumstance and political opportunism thwarted it.

In 1991 there were riots in several British cities and media-fuelled anxiety over joy-riding and ram raiders. Recorded crime in 1992 was 50 per cent more than 1988. This increase can be attributed to the severe economic recession of 1989–92, itself a reaction to the deliberately constructed boom prior to the 1997 election. Despite these problems, Labour was unable to gain political advantage and it lost the 1992 election.

REVIEW QUESTIONS

1 What links did the Conservative Government elected in 1979 make between crime and industrial unrest?

2 What did the Conservative Government of the 1980s believe had been the effect of the welfare state?

3 What happened to crime between 1979 and 1992?

4 What factors caused Conservative policies on crime to change?

5 What changes occurred in Conservative policies on law and order?

Crime, economy and the politics of law and order: post 1992

If the recession of 1988–92 dented the Conservative reputation for sound economic management, a further blow fell in September 1992 when currency speculation forced Sterling out of the European Exchange Rate Mechanism (ERM).[8] As Faulkner (2001: 122) notes, a fundamental and dramatic change in the Conservative government's political style occurred during 1993. He traces this in part to rising crime figures and difficulties within the Conservative Party following the ERM withdrawal and the accession to the Maastricht Treaty.

These events created an urgent need for the Government to re-unite the Party around a suitable populist issue, and crime and law and order were a natural choice. (Faulkner, 2001: 122)

Faulkner also points out that the change was not unsupported by the other parties since none could easily oppose such a populist based campaign once it had gathered impetus. As we shall explore below there must in any case be some doubt as to whether the Labour Party would have wished to do so. On 12 February 1993, the toddler James Bulger was abducted and brutally murdered by two ten-year-old boys. This was to have a major impact on public perceptions of youth crime:

> The Bulger case has become a powerful symbol of our collective helplessness, of a malaise that goes beyond a single case, beyond even crime figures. (*Independent on Sunday*, 28 February 1993)

As part of this populist strategy the Conservatives made a dramatic and rapid U-turn over the 1991 CJA that came into operation in October 1992 following a lengthy training programme to ensure its smooth introduction. Its diversionary impact was clear. The monthly prison population figures peaked at 47,605 in April 2002 and thereafter showed a continuous downward drift to 40,722 by the end of December. The *Independent on Sunday* (IOS) referred to this reduction as the '. . . largest and swiftest decline in living memory'. With the government now seeking to regain lost ground by emphasising a (re)new(ed) commitment to toughness it quickly abandoned the liberal thinking behind the 1991 CJA. In his speech to the 1993 Conservative Party Conference, Home Secretary Howard jettisoned the view that prison was an expensive way of making bad people worse by baldly asserting 'prison works'. Unsurprisingly this led to a further increase in the prison population. More broadly the Conservatives sought re-establish electoral credibility by returning to the punitive authoritarian approach of the 1970s with a call to go 'back to basics'. This moralistic campaign was soon undermined as several senior conservatives were engulfed by revelations of extra-marital affairs and allegations of sleaze.

Meanwhile, Labour began a major overhaul of its policies. Central to this process were moves to counter the belief that the Conservatives were *the* party of law and order. Although between 1993 and 1996 the Party was to produce several policy papers that linked crime with social problems, publicly it focused on criticizing the operation of the criminal justice system under the Conservatives (Downes and Morgan, 1997).

Their attack on the 1991 CJA and Conservative policy generally was in terms of criticisms of Just Deserts, the inadequacies of the CJS, falling conviction rates, and delays in dealing with juvenile offenders rather than on the economic and social consequences of the Conservative policies. The clear resolve to break the link in the minds of the electorate between Labour and soft responses to crime was encapsulated by Tony Blair, then Shadow Home Secretary in the phrase 'tough on crime, tough on the causes of crime'. As Downes and Morgan (2002: 296) point out this slogan resonated with the public fear of, and anger about rising crime, in several respects:

- crime tackled more toughly, *but* crime, not the criminal;
- however, this does not rule out being tough on the criminal;
- and being tough on the causes of crime captures traditional Labour concerns with inequality and social problems;
- it implicitly condemns the Conservatives for failing to make these connections since 1979.

Unfortunately, in terms of public rhetoric the emphasis was firmly on tough measures to deal with offenders. This had immediate headline catching power compared to the more long-term tackling of the causes of crime.

Michael Howard fought hard to win this battle of toughness. He doubled the maximum custodial sentence for fifteen/seventeen year olds, introduced new custodial sentences for twelve to fourteen year olds, and drawing on the US experience, established military style boot camps and proposed mandatory minimum sentences for serious repeat offenders.

Blair and his successor as shadow Home Secretary, Jack Straw not only dogged all Howard's attempts to put clear blue water between the Conservatives and the Labour opposition on these issues, but often led the way. Straw's admiration for the New York Police Department's zero tolerance policing (see Jones, Chapter 25 below) and his attacks on beggars and car washers at traffic lights were grist to the headline writers' mills. We were treated in Newburn's words to the '. . . unedifying spectacle of the Home Secretary and his Labour Shadow fighting to out-tough each other' (Newburn, 2003).

Not that New Labour ignored wider social issues. In this period they produced several papers that formed the basis of the policies implemented after their 1997 Election victory. In particular *Tackling the Causes of Crime* (Labour Party, 1996a) linked crime with problems of parenting, schools and truancy, drugs and alcohol abuse, unemployment and recession, care in the community, homelessness and the inadequacies of the Youth service. Key to this and other New Labour strategies was the idea of social exclusion and how to combat it (see Young and Matthews, 2003; Hale, Chapter 16 above). Indeed, as Newburn, (2003: 206) amongst, others notes in adopting the 'tough on crime, tough on the causes of crime' mantra, the Labour Party was seeking to move the argument about crime away from the dichotomy of personal and social responsibility away from 'the notion that there are only two sides to the "law and order" debate—those who want to punish the criminal and those who point to the poor social conditions in which crime breeds' (Blair, 1993). But in the run up to the 1997 election, the emphasis from Labour was on the need for more secure places for juveniles, proposals for lengthy periods of imprisonment for breaches of community safety orders and the new idea of Anti-Social Behaviour Orders (ASBOs) as a way of tackling 'neighbours from hell', and support for zero tolerance policing. ASBOs in particular have been criticized for producing the very social exclusion New Labour is trying to end.

Since coming to power, the New Labour Government has continued with this two-track attitude to law and order. On the one hand, there is much to applaud in the changes it has made. On the other, it seems unable to take the opportunity presented by the more or less continuous decline in crime rates since 1992 to move away from the punitive populism it did so much to create whilst in opposition.

The Crime and Disorder Act (CDA) 1998 was the first fruit of New Labour approaches to criminal justice and showed clearly the tensions in its approach. As Newburn (2003: 121) points out, it is an amalgam of preventative, ameliorative and punitive elements. At its preventative core were provisions for the fulfilment of its manifesto promise to implement measures to deal with community safety and crime prevention. The Act placed statutory duties on both local authorities (LAs)—covering social services, education and youth services—and the police to form partnerships and develop local strategies to help prevent and reduce crime and disorder. The partnerships, now termed Crime and Dis-order Reduction Partnerships (CDRP) were also to include probation committees and health authorities. The aim was to enshrine in legislation the belief that crime prevention could not be left to the police alone. Community safety became the new buzz-words signalling a broader, more holistic approach to crime prevention. Crawford (1998) sees three key elements in the approach, it tends to be localized, it looks at social problems beyond just crime and disorder and it is delivered by 'partnership'. The latter two in particular are central to much of New Labour's thinking. Social problems are seen as interrelated with various causes that cannot be treated in isolation but need joined up solutions and partnership working. The Government backed this commitment to crime prevention with a £400 million Crime Reduction Strategy. The money was to be spent on crime reduction initiatives and their evaluation. The more punitive aspects of the Act are seen in the toughening of sentences for offenders. It introduced new court orders, min-imum mandatory sentences for repeat offences of burglary, drug trafficking violence and sexual offending, curfews for juveniles, electronic monitoring, and did away with *doli incapax*.[9] The Act also introduced the promised ASBOs to tackle 'anti-social behaviour' and had provisions to require parents of young offenders to attend classes to improve their parenting skills.

Labour also moved rapidly to reform the youth justice system. It had published its plans in 1996 in *Tackling Youth Crime, Reforming Youth Justice* (Labour Party, 1996b) Within six months of taking office it published six consultation documents that developed these ideas. The proposals they contained were also incorporated in the 1998 CDA. As with the CDRPs the Act placed a responsibility on LAs, again in consultation with others, for formulating 'youth justice plans'. At the same time, New Labour sought to impose central control by establishing the national Youth Justice Board to monitor the youth justice system and the provision of youth justice services. At the local level, again reflecting the search for joined-up solutions, Youth Offending Teams were established in all areas in 2000. Their two main roles were to coordinate the provision of youth justice services locally and to carry out the functions specified for them in the LA youth justice plan. These had to include a probation officer, a social worker, a police officer, a represen-tative of the local health authority and someone nominated by the chief education officer. For children and young people, the negative aspect of the New Labour approach to justice is the numbers locked up. By spring 2002 this had reached the highest level since the youth justice system was introduced in 1908 (Pitts, 2003). In January 2004 there were 10,645 under twenty-one year olds in prisons (Prison Reform Trust, 2004), an increase of nearly 82 per cent since 1995. Recorded crime peaked in 1992 and then declined steadily until the late 1990s (see Figure 21.1). Changes in the recording rules in 1998 and 2002 make comparisons of recent years more complex (see Hope, Chapter 3). The British Crime Survey (BCS) showed a decline in crime of 23 per cent between 1995 and 1999, following a 14 per cent drop between 1995 and 1997 (Kershaw *et al.*, 2000). This was a remarkable change from the previous four decades and as Young (2003) points out, the New Labour Government has been fortunate in the law and order stakes. He queries why this has not led to celebration of their policies. They might have linked the decline in property crime to their successful economic policy, or to investment in crime reduction strategies. They could have pointed to a range of projects aimed at social inclusion (Young and Matthews, 2003). Instead they have chosen to focus publicly on violent crime and social disorder and underline their commitment to provide more police officers and to expand prison capacity to accommodate more convicted offenders. The UK is not alone in having experienced a sustained decline in levels of crime; indeed this is common to many countries.

Young (2003) suggests this continued focus on more police and increased imprisonment, rather than on economic and demographic factors, crime reduction and target hardening as explanations for the downturn in crime, has four reasons. First, he suggests the mass media has consistently taken a pessimistic even alarmist view of the crime problem that has reinforced the pessimism of politicians. Second, the police by successful lobbying have promoted the widespread view that there is a crisis in police numbers. Third, the ideas that New Labour has assimilated with regards to crime control are those of the American Right (see Hale, Chapter 16). Fourth, he suggests that there is a simple populism at work—giving the public what they want.

REVIEW QUESTIONS

1 Why did the Conservative government return to a punitive penal policy in 1992?

2 What happened to recorded crime after 1992?

3 Why did the Labour Party seek to be tough on both crime and the causes of crime?

4 How do the New Labour policies on law and order fit with those on social exclusion?

CONCLUSION

In this chapter we have looked at how the politics of law and order have changed since 1945 and particularly since 1970. We have seen how crime was linked in the Thatcherite lexicon with industrial unrest and the de-moralization brought about by welfare dependency. The success of this strategy was one of the factors in the continuing conservative hegemony during the 1980s. Despite pragmatic liberal measures, the Tory party turned once again to populist punitiveness when faced with an economic crisis in the early 1990s. From this, Labour took the lessons that it could not be seen as soft on crime, that it had to out-tough its political opponents. This approach has led to it its current contradictory position. Despite ten years of falling levels of crime and a commitment to social inclusion, New Labour has maintained its punitive rhetoric with dire consequences in particular for those imprisoned. In 1992, as we have seen, the prison population fell to just over 40,000. At the time of writing, the latest available figures on the Prison Service website show that as at 12 December 2003, this had risen to just over 74,000. Despite spending over £2 billion on providing 15,200 additional places since 1995[10] overcrowding in 2003 was at its highest ever level with over 16,000 prisoners sharing cells designed for one. England and Wales have become the prison capitals of the European Union (*The Guardian*, 2 February 2004) imprisoning 141 people per 100,000 of the population and putting it ahead of countries such as Libya, Burma and Turkey as well as all other EU states Walmsley (2003). This despite the fact that even with increased severity of sentencing re-offending rates remain high. Nearly 60 per cent of offenders return to crime within two years of being released (Prison Reform Trust, 2004); something the Government's Social Exclusion

Unit estimates costs £11 billion per year. And despite the fact that a report by the Prime Minister's own Strategy Unit (Carter, 2003) says that a 22 per cent increase in the prison population since 1997 is estimated to have reduced crime by around five per cent during a period when, overall, crime fell by 30 per cent. The report states: 'There is no convincing evidence that further increases in the use of custody would significantly reduce crime'. In the current climate of punitive populism, it is depressingly unlikely that such findings will be heeded.

QUESTIONS FOR DISCUSSION

1 In what senses are crime and responses to it always political?

2 When and why did crime become a party political issue?

3 What were the main characteristics of the bi-partisan approach to law and order?

4 Compare and contrast 'penal welfare' and 'punitive populist' approaches to crime and punishment.

5 Has New Labour been 'tough on crime' and 'tough on the causes of crime'?

GUIDE TO FURTHER READING

Brake, M. and Hale, C. (1992) *Public Order and Private Lives: The Politics of Law and Order*, London: Routledge.
Covers the impact of Conservative policies through the 1970s and 1980s.

Downes, D. and Morgan, R. (1992, 1997 and 2002) in M. Mauire, M. Morgan and R. Reiner (eds), *The Oxford Handbook of Criminology*, Oxford: Clarendon Press.
Downes and Morgan provide the most comprehensive reviews of the politics of law and order in the period since 1945.

Garland, D. (2001) *The Culture of Control: Crime and Social Order in Contemporary Society*. Oxford: Oxford University Press.
Provide a broad review of all of these issues.

Young, J. and Matthews, R. (2003) 'New Labour Crime Control and Social Exclusion' in J. Young and R. Matthews (eds) *The New Politics of Crime and Punishment*. Cullompton: Willam.
Includes chapters covering various aspects of New Labours Law and order policies.

WEB LINKS

There are no websites dedicated to the politics of law and order. You should check out the websites of the main parties to see how their views and policies are developing.

http://www.conservatives.com/
The website of the Conservative Party

http://www.labour.org.uk/
The website of the Labour Party

http://www.libdems.org.uk
The website of the Liberal-Democrat Party

For helpful information and critiques of current policies the websites of the campaigning groups are useful as follows:
http://www.nacro.org.uk/
The website of NACRO

http://www.prisonreformtrust.org.uk/
The website of the Prison Reform Trust

http://www.howardleague.org/
The website of the Howard League for Penal Reform

REFERENCES

Beveridge, W. (1942) *Social Insurance and Allied Services*, London: HMSO.

Blair, T. (1993) 'Why Crime is a Socialist Issue', *New Statesman*, 29(12), 27–8.

Bottoms, A.E. (1995) 'The philosophy and politics of punishment and sentencing' in C. Clark and R. Morgan (eds) *The Politics of Sentencing Reform* Oxford: Clarendon Press.

Brake, M. and Hale, C. (1992) *Public Order and Private Lives: The Politics of Law and Order*. London: Routledge.

Carter, P. (2003) *Managing Offenders, Reducing Crime: A new approach*. London: Prime Minister's Strategy Unit.

Conservative Party (1970) *A Better Tomorrow*. London: Conservative Party.

Conservative Party (1979) *Conservative Party Manifesto*. London: Conservative Party Central Office.

Conservative Party (1983) *Conservative Party Manifesto*. London: Conservative Party Central Office.

Crawford, A. (1998) *Crime Prevention and Community safety: Politics, Policies and Practices*. Harlow: Longman.

Downes, D. and Morgan, R. (1994) ' "Hostages to Fortune"? The Politics of Law and Order in Post War Britain' in M. Maguire, M. Morgan and R. Reiner (eds), *The Oxford Handbook of Criminology* (1st edn). Oxford: Clarendon Press.

Downes, D. and Morgan, R. (1997) 'Dumping the "hostages to fortune"? The politics of law and order in post war Britain' in M. Maguire, M. Morgan and R. Reiner (eds), *The Oxford Handbook of Criminology* (2nd edn). Oxford: Clarendon Press.

Downes, D. and Morgan, R. (2002) 'The skeletons in the cupboard: The politics of law and order at the turn of the Millenium' in M. Maguire, M. Morgan and R. Reiner (eds), *The Oxford Handbook of Criminology* (3rd edn). Oxford: Clarendon Press.

Faulkner, D. (2001) *Crime, State and Citizen: A Field Full of Folk*. Winchester: Waterside Press.

Garland, D. (2001) *The Culture of Control: Crime and Social Order in Contemporary Society*. Oxford: Oxford University Press.

Hale, C. (1999) 'The labour market and post-war crime trends in England and Wales' in P. Carlen and R. Morgan (eds) *Crime Unlimited? Questions for the 21st Century*. Basingstoke: Macmillan.

Hall, S., Critcher, C., Jefferson, T., Clarke, J., and Roberts, B. (1978) *Policing the Crisis: Mugging, the State and Law and Order*. London: Macmillan.

Hope, T. and Shaw, M. (1988) 'Community approaches to reducing crime' in T. Hope and M. Shaw (eds) *Communities and Crime Reduction*. London: HMSO.

Kershaw, C., Budd, T., Kinshott, G., Mattinson, J., Mayhew, P. and Myhill, A. (2000) *The 2000 British Crime Survey, England and Wales*. Home Office Statistical Bulletin 18/01. London: Home Office.

Labour Party (1996a) *Tackling the Causes of Crime*. London: Labour Party.

Labour Party (1996b) *Tackling Youth Crime, Reforming Youth Justice*. London: Labour Party.

Loader, I. and Sparks, R. (2002) 'Contemporary Landscapes of Crime, Order and Control: Governance, Risk and Globalization' in M. Maguire, M. Morgan and R. Reiner (eds), *The Oxford Handbook of Criminology* (3rd edn). Oxford: Clarendon Press.

McClintock, F.H. and Avison, N.H. (1968) *Crime in England and Wales*. London: Heinemann.

Martinson, R. (1974) 'What Works? Questions and Answers about Prison Reform', *The Public Interest*, 35, 22–54.

Newburn, T. (2003) *Crime and Criminal Justice Policy* (2nd Edn). London: Pearson Longman.

Pearson, G. (1983) *Hooligan: The History of Respectable Fears*. London: Macmillan.

Pitts, J. (2003) 'Youth Justice in England and Wales' in J. Young and R. Matthews (eds) *The New Politics of Crime and Punishment*. Cullompton: Willan.

Prison Reform Trust (2003) *Briefing from Prison Reform Trust February 2004*. London: Prison Reform Trust.

Social Exclusion Unit (2002) *Reducing Re-offending by Ex-prisoners*. London: Office of the Deputy Prime Minister.

Walmsley, R. (2003) *World Prison Population List* (5th edn) Home Office Research Development and Statistics Directorate Findings 234 London: Home Office.

Young, J. (2003) 'Winning the fight against crime? New Labour, populism and lost opportunities' in J. Young and R. Matthews (eds) *The New Politics of Crime and Punishment*. Cullompton: Willan.

Young, J. and Matthews, R. (2003) 'New Labour crime control and social exclusion' in J. Young and R. Matthews (eds) *The New Politics of Crime and Punishment*. Cullompton: Willan.

NOTES

1. Any attempt to summarize political beliefs in a short endnote is bound to distort and miss important nuances. Broadly speaking, the Conservative Party emphasizes individual freedoms and responsibilities and with its belief in the benefits of allowing market forces free rein is often seen as the party that represents the interests of business and landowners. The Labour Party, while moving some way recently from its roots in the Trade Union movement, is still more willing to acknowledge structural factors as causing social problems even if in practice they do not always seek their solution in collective rather than individual responses. The Liberal Democrats are closer to New Labour than the Conservatives and in many respects offer a more radical perspective on many issues than either of the main parties.

2. It should be noted that many crimes that are recorded as violent are in fact relatively minor.

3. It is worth emphasizing that quite dramatic changes have taken place leading many to talk about a new era of 'late' or 'post' modernity distinguishable from the era of modernity.

4. Perhaps dominant political ideologies would be more accurate since both parties are made up of competing factions who have held internal sway at different times. For example, the pro- and anti-Europeans in the Conservative party and the modernizers and old guard within New Labour.

5. See Martinson (1974) for a clear statement of this view. Although by 1979 Martinson was to recant his pessimistic view, the 'nothing works' slogan was to become very powerful and contribute to the crisis of confidence in treatment programmes for offenders.

6. Especially, cynics might observe, when set alongside economic policies that had led to increased unemployment and tightening welfare support

7. For example, in 1989 NACRO (the National Association for the Care and Resettlement of Offenders) published figures showing the annual cost in 1986–87 of keeping an offender in prison was £14,976 compared to £900 for Probation Orders and £520 for Community Service Orders. See Chapter 26 for further discussion of the use of non-custodial sentences.

8. This devaluation led to a period of sustained and steady economic growth that still continued in 2004. Ironically this improving economic situation has arguably had at least as much to do with declining crime over this same period as punitive approaches to dealing with offenders or crime prevention initiatives.

9. the presumption that a child between the age of ten and thirteen is incapable of committing a criminal offence.

10. Eighty-one of 138 prisons in England and Wales were overcrowded (Prison Reform Trust, 2004).

22 The criminal justice system

Steve Uglow

INTRODUCTION

Within civil society, it is criminal justice that most highlights the coercive nature of the State—detaining people against their will and punishing them brings into sharp relief the beliefs and principles about how we live with one another. To interfere with such fundamental rights requires clear principles about why we should make certain sorts of conduct criminal but not others, about those whose behaviour requires investigation, about the limits of state investigation of private life and about the objectives of any punishment. Any examination of criminal justice requires consideration of the extent of individual freedom, the nature of common interests and the problems of fair treatment. There are no simple answers and criminal justice is a complex process with many dimensions, ethical, political, constitutional and economic, all of which affect criminal justice policy making (see Hale, Chapter 21).

This chapter examines the adult[1] criminal justice system in England and Wales.[2] We devote significant public resources on the criminal justice system—the Treasury's Spending Review in 2002 concluded that, in 2005–2006, we would spend £18.336bn on police forces, prosecution and defence lawyers, courts, probation and prisons. Despite this investment, the briefest survey reveals that 'system' is perhaps the wrong, albeit convenient, word. A system implies clear and consistent objectives, transparent demarcation of responsibilities and lines of management, understood procedures and good communication between the different elements. Some public services, such as education or health, are characterized by such unifying purposes and principles, clear organizational structures, identifiable lines of management and recognized and effective means of accountability, normally ending with ministerial responsibility to Parliament. Such a description may be seen as a rose-tinted view of our education or health systems, but it is basically accurate. It is difficult to identify any of these characteristics within the English and Welsh criminal process.

The reason for this is that criminal justice is a collection of autonomous and semi-autonomous agencies, such as the police, the Crown Prosecution Service (CPS), the Crown and magistrates' courts and the correctional services. Each has its own objectives, principles and core responsibilities—prosecuting and punishing offenders, reducing crime, maintaining community safety, caring for victims as well as protecting the rights and interests of the accused. The perspective of the probation officer may be poles apart from that of the prison officer; the police investigator sees the defence solicitor as an opponent; the volunteer supporting the victim seeks to protect the witness while the barrister[3] sees her as simply a means to an end. It is as if the whole system is contaminated by the competitive, adversarial nature of the criminal trial itself.

The extraordinary fact is that there is no overarching ministry of justice with parliamentary responsibility for the whole structure. Different government ministers assume responsibilities for different parts of the system—the Lord Chancellor is responsible for the magistracy and judiciary; the Home Secretary for the police, prisons and probation service; and the Attorney General for the CPS. The police and the courts, avoid even this direct constitutional accountability, having no government minister answerable in parliament for day-to-day operational matters. Such a structure invariably affects the extent of mutual cooperation and shared coherence of policy objectives. Recently there have been two Royal Commissions in this area—in 1981 the Royal Commission on Criminal Procedure (RCCP) and in 1993 the Royal Commission on Criminal Justice (RCCJ). Neither considered the manner in which we manage criminal justice: yet the critical flaw is the lack of overall structure.

After a short overview of the system as a whole there follows individual sections on the main components of the system—police, prosecution, legal representation, the courts.

BACKGROUND

This chapter aims to describe and analyse the key elements of the criminal justice system—from arrest to trial and appeal. The following is an outline of the building bricks of criminal justice:

- *Substantive criminal laws*—the police and the courts require legal authority to exercise their powers of investigation and trial. These are all based upon the existence of criminal offences— laws that forbid particular conduct and lay down punishments. Such offences must be created in a constitutionally proper fashion, normally through legislation passed by Parliament. The vast majority of offences are created and defined in this way. These statutory offences can be contrasted with 'common law' offences which are based on the decisions of courts. Originally the courts themselves were able to create criminal offences and some crimes, such as murder and manslaughter, are still based on common law. Nowadays the courts no longer have the capacity to create new crimes, although their decisions and interpretations inevitably shape the boundaries of offences.

- *Procedural criminal law*—procedural laws empower and constrain law enforcement agencies in their investigation of crime, providing them with the legal powers for arrest, detention and trial of suspects, but also ensuring that suspects are treated with due respect. Pre-trial procedures affect the investigation and prosecution of crime—the work of the police and the CPS. Their powers and procedures are primarily governed by such statutes as the Police and Criminal Evidence Act 1984 or the Criminal Procedure and Investigations Act 1996. The trial procedures themselves deal with the manner in which the accusations are put to the defendant, the selection and function of the jury, the functions of the judge, the roles of the prosecuting or defending lawyers, the presentation of evidence, the questioning of witnesses or the taking of verdicts. The trial itself is not an inquiry into truth where the judge calls and questions witnesses with the aid of lawyers, but an adversarial process where the prosecution and defence present conflicting accounts, call their own witnesses and critically examine the other party's evidence and witnesses. Procedure is a highly technical area but the rules reflect key ethical principles and are underpinned by the key concept of a 'fair' trial, a right reinforced by Article 6 of the European Convention on Human Rights.

- *Law enforcement agencies*—the police service (Jones, 2004) is the key agency responsible for the investigation of criminal offences, but other agencies are also involved in law enforcement such as the Inland Revenue or Customs and Excise. The role of the police is not narrowly circumscribed. While they have many specific responsibilities for investigating crime, gathering of evidence, interviewing witnesses and suspects and preparing the case for the prosecuting authorities, their functions also include such matters as the maintenance of public order, the prevention of crime and the regulation of traffic. Recently, the police and local authorities were given joint responsibility for community safety in local crime and disorder partnerships under the Crime and Disorder Act 1998.

- *Prosecution of offenders*—the preparation of a case for trial and the presentation of that case at magistrates' and Crown Courts is predominantly undertaken by the CPS, although Customs and Excise and Inland Revenue may take responsibility for mounting their own prosecutions.

- *Legal representation of offenders*—the criminal justice system also provides for defendants to be assisted by lawyers, paid out of public funds. From April 2000, the Legal Services Commission has been responsible for the public funding of defence work. The Commission established the Criminal Defence Service—this is introducing a mixed system by which criminal defence will be organized through, on one hand, contracted private practitioners and on the other, public salaried employees.

- *Trial and sentencing of the accused*—magistrates' and Crown Courts are responsible for making the initial decision of guilty or not guilty as well as for imposing penalties. These range from the financial to community-based sanctions to imprisonment (see Chapters 26 and 27 below). These decisions are subject to appeal, either on the question of the conviction itself or the appropriateness of the sentence. The initial appeal is normally to the Court of Appeal with the possibility of a further appeal to the House of Lords. These courts are responsible for examining whether the law has been properly applied and that the sentence guidelines have been followed.

- *A correctional system*—there are three different sorts of sentence laid down by a court: fines are administered by the magistrates' court; community sentences are the responsibility of the National Probation Service and custodial sentences are in the hands of the Prison Service Agency. The enforcement of sentences passed by the Youth Court is locally in the hands of Youth Offending Teams, overseen nationally by the Youth Justice Board (see Chapter 19 above).

- *Policy formulation*—this is undertaken by a range of government departments responsible for differing parts of the criminal justice system. The Home Office (police and prisons), the Department for Constitutional Affairs (the court service), the Attorney General (the prosecution system) all play a role as do executive agencies such as the Youth Justice Board and the Audit Commission. In recent years, local authorities have played an important role in local community safety policies. Local policy is also influenced by the criminal justice consultative committees that have been set up in all forty-two criminal justice areas.

A criminal justice system is concerned first and foremost with 'crime'. This immediately raises difficult issues about what is or should be designated as criminal within a society (see Chapter 1 above). Similar questions arise about when criminal laws are enforced and against whom (see Chapter 13 above). This chapter avoids these debates and takes 'crime' for granted as acts which are forbidden by law—we all have seen crimes being committed and we all have committed them. But even here, mapping the extent of crime throws up problems (see Chapter 3 above). Before any incident is recorded as a crime, the criminal justice system needs to be mobilized and this is usually done by a member of the public, who is a victim or a witness, who defines the event as a crime and who reports it to the police. The police must agree that an offence has taken place and may choose to record the incident as a crime. From these figures, the Home Office publish the official criminal statistics annually (Home Office, 2003a).[4]

Table 22.1 Recorded crime 1950–2002/3

Year	Number of offences	Offences per 100,000
1950	479,400	Na
1980	2,520,600	5,119
1990	4,363,600	8,630
1992	5,383,500	10,535
2002/2003	5,899,450	11,327

Source: Home Office Criminal Statistics.

Table 22.2 BCS estimates of crime for selected years

Year	Number of Offences
1981	11.045m
1991	15.075m
1993	18.561m
1995	19.152m
1997	16.486m
2002/03	12.308m

Source: Home Office: British Crime Survey.

Table 22.1 shows that recorded crime increased dramatically since the 1950s but particularly in the 1980s, peaking in 1992. It has declined by over 30 per cent since that time. This is not apparent in the figures, but the apparent rise has been due to changes in recording practice (Simmons *et al.*, 2003).

The police record of crime is not complete—they recorded nearly six million incidents as crimes in 2002/3. This does not represent the totality of crime as the public may not report incidents, or the police may choose not to record the incident as an offence. The generally accepted measure in recent years has been the British Crime Survey (BCS).[5] The survey shows crime peaking in the mid-1990s, but significantly declining. The survey's estimate of criminal offences in 2002/03 is 12.3 million, over twice that of the official figures gathered by the Home Office (Home Office, 2003b), but over 30 per cent less than the figure in 1995 (for further discussion see Table 22.2 and Chapter 3 above).

Once an offence has been recorded by the police, the legal process that operates is set out in straightforward terms in the Figure 22.1:

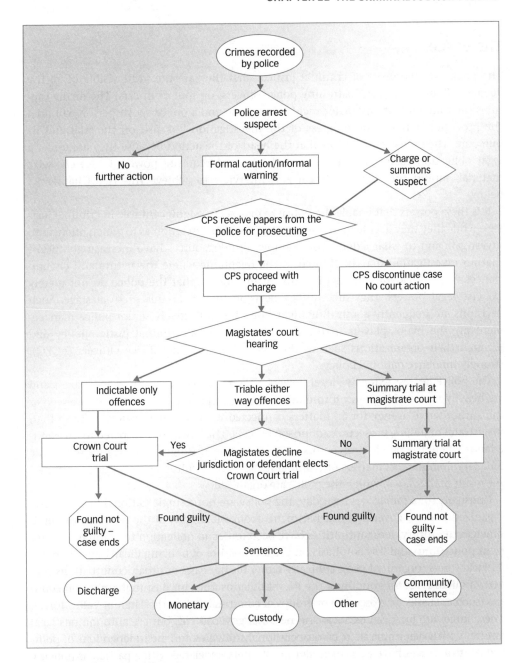

Figure 22.1 The prosecution process

Source: CJS Online 2004; © Crown Copyright.

REVIEW QUESTIONS

1 Identify the major agencies of the criminal justice system.

2 Outline the steps in criminal justice prison process from commission of the offence to prison.

The police

The police are the pivot of criminal justice—first they are the most visible of all the agencies. Routinely we see patrolling police officers, on foot or in cars. The media captures their presence at any major incident or crime and a police spokesperson will brief the press not only on the progress of the investigation but also on the trial and its outcome. The police are positioned at the heart of the action because they are under a legal obligation to investigate crime and have the requisite powers to search, seize material, mount surveillance, detain and interview to achieve this (see Chapter 23 below).

It is these powers that enable the police to play such a significant role in criminal justice—while they may decide to investigate, they possess discretion as to which offences to investigate and to what extent. For example, finite resources have increasingly meant that an investigation may be limited to the telephone where the nature and circumstances of the incident warrants it. This in turn means that the police do not merely exercise legal powers, they are the key decision makers at this pre-trial stage. Such decisions are frequently about individual cases, but collectively senior police management are the major players in the formulation of local criminal justice policy and through their organizations such as the Association of Chief Police Officers (ACPO), strongly influence national policy.

The police possess extensive legal powers, they are autonomous decision makers and are heavily involved in policy formulation. It is unsurprising that the police are seen as the authoritative agency for all matters connected with criminal justice, more so than magistrates or judges, prosecutors or prison officers. This might be compared to the Netherlands where the public prosecutors are perceived in this light or to France where the judiciary dominate all matters of criminal justice. These cultural perceptions are in part the result of the way in which the police are organized.

Unusually for a public service today, the police are not a single national force directly organized under a government department. From the origins of the police in the mid-nineteenth century, local authorities have been under an obligation to maintain an efficient police force and this emphasis on the local nature of policing means that there are 43 local forces, organized geographically either on the basis of urban conurbations (the Metropolitan force for London or the West Midlands force for Birmingham) or on counties (such as Sussex or Worcester) or groups of counties (such as the Thames Valley force). These forces are financed by local and national government, but are autonomous legal entities which determine their own operational strategies and are independent of political control. Forces have their own identities, often associated with a particular policing strategy such as community or geographic policing, problem-oriented policing or intelligence-led policing (Tilley, 2003).

Although there is no political control, there is considerable political influence. Conventionally, the management of the police service is seen as having a tripartite structure:

- The Chief Constable of each force—this officer has the legal power to direct and control the force. This is the power of day-to-day operational management.

- Local government—this is exercized through a separate police authority, independent of the local council, that has the duty to maintain an efficient and effective force. This involves appointing senior officers, supervizing finances and keeping a watching brief over the quality of local policing as well as carrying out 'best value' assessments.[6] They have no power to influence police operational decisions.

- National government through the Home Office. The Home Secretary has no operational control but has the statutory duty to promote efficiency and effectiveness. This is done through setting national objectives and performance targets as well as publishing a national policing plan. Furthermore, the Home Office influences forces by a system of circulars which advise chief officers on all aspects of running a force, be that financial management, best practice on operational matters or criminal justice strategy. Because government provides 75 per cent of police funding, the Home Secretary is in a position to make such interventions count. A minister can now require police authorities to take specific remedial action and exerts considerable influence over all aspects of policing—while remaining unaccountable to Parliament for any operational matters. The Home Office monitors the quality of policing through the Inspectorate of Constabulary and the Police Standards Unit.

In the criminal justice process, the police have the responsibility to investigate crime, to gather the evidence and to initiate action against the suspect. It is usually a member of the public who will report matters to the police. The police have a certain discretion whether to record the incident as a crime and whether to invest resources into an investigation. This may involve forensic examination of the scene, house-to-house inquiries, tracking down and questioning witnesses, the use of informants, covert surveillance and the interviewing of suspects. However, most crimes are not resolved—the detection rate was 24 per cent in 2002/03 (Home Office, 2003b: ch. 7; Hope, 2004). Those that are resolved, resolve themselves—the suspect is still at the scene or is clearly identified by a witness; a suspect arrested for one offence admits to committing other crimes.

When the police are satisfied that a suspect has committed the offence and that they have gathered sufficient evidence, they have various options. They may decide:

- to take no further action;
- to issue a formal caution about future conduct with the threat that next time there will be a prosecution;[7]
- to charge the individual with a view to a prosecution in the magistrates' court or Crown Court.

The police will now hand the prosecution of the case to the CPS.

REVIEW QUESTIONS

1 What is the structure of the police service?

2 What functions do the police perform?

3 What mechanisms exist to make the police accountable?

Prosecution

For much of the twentieth century, the police acted not only as investigators but also as prosecutors. Police forces developed prosecuting solicitors' departments which employed barristers to appear in the Crown Court on behalf of the police while, until the late 1980s, in magistrates' courts, in many cases it was a uniformed police inspector who was the prosecutor. The system was inefficient, especially in the preparation of cases; unfair because, in principle, investigation and prosecution should be separate processes, and lacked any executive or democratic accountability (Royal Commission on Criminal Procedure, 1981). In 1985, an independent prosecuting body, the CPS, was set up, organized on a regional basis—there are forty-two CPS areas so that each is co-terminous with the police. Each has a Chief Crown Prosecutor who is answerable to the national executive director, the Director of Public Prosecutions (DPP), who in turn answers to the Attorney General who is responsible to Parliament.

Has the new system addressed the problems? There is now a clear distinction between the processes of investigation and prosecution as well as proper systems of accountability. But the government still regards the criminal justice system as inefficient—of the estimated 12.9 million offences in 2002/03, only 670,000 cases were heard in court (Home Office, 2002). This attrition rate is the product of many factors, but the prosecution process is one of them. One aspect of this is that the relationship between the police and CPS remains ill-defined, particularly in relation to charging and the gathering of further evidence. CPS lawyers increasingly play a role at the investigative stage. Under the Criminal Justice Act 2003, the CPS have been given more responsibility for determining the charge in cases other than for routine offences or where the police need to make a holding charge. By involving the prosecutor at an earlier stage, after a suspect has been identified, but before a charge is preferred, investigators are in a better position to ensure that relevant and sufficient evidence is obtained and that the suspect is charged with the appropriate offence. A further problem is that when suspects are brought to court, the CPS often choose to offer no evidence so that the accused is immediately discharged by the judge or present such a weak case that the judge directs the jury to acquit. There are many factors that can lead to a non-jury acquittal but one of these is the adequacy of the preparation of contested cases.

In other jurisdictions such as the Netherlands or the USA, the prosecutor is the lynchpin of the criminal justice system. In the UK, the two symbolic reference points are instead the police officer and the judge. The CPS is a relatively anonymous office, reflected by public ignorance of their function. What, after all, do prosecutors do? The functions of the CPS are to:

- Advise the police at the investigatory stage and in some cases be responsible for framing the charge.
- Review prosecutions started by the police to ensure the right defendants are prosecuted on the right charges before the appropriate court.
- Prepare cases for court and prosecute people in England and Wales who have been charged by the police with a criminal offence. The CPS lawyer will always present the

case in magistrates' courts and more occasionally will act as advocate in Crown Court.

- Work with other agencies such as the police and the courts to improve the effectiveness and efficiency of the criminal justice system.

The decision to prosecute

The files of individual cases will be assigned to a prosecutor for review. They will ask questions such as:

- Is the nature and level of charge appropriate given the evidence?
- What mode of trial (magistrates' court or Crown Court) would be suitable?
- What is the quality of the evidence—is it relevant, credible and substantial?
- Is there a realistic prospect of conviction?
- Is there any reason in the public interest why this prosecution should not proceed?

We have seen that the police act as a preliminary filter, removing cases from the conveyor belt of justice, by decisions either to take no further action or to caution. The CPS acts as a second filter using their power to discontinue prosecutions. The criteria they use are to be found in the Code for Crown Prosecutors (CPS, 2000). There are two basic issues:

(a) Whether there is sufficient evidence—namely if there is a realistic prospect of conviction. This is an objective test, namely whether a court would be more likely than not to convict the defendant of the charge alleged. The prosecutor must consider whether there is admissible, substantial and reliable evidence to support the accusation.

(b) Whether a prosecution is in the public interest—the prosecutor should then consider whether the public interest requires a prosecution. Not every suspected crime should automatically be prosecuted but reading the Code suggests that there is a presumption in favour of prosecution. The Code's constant refrain is the 'seriousness' of the offence and the prosecutor is enjoined that, broadly speaking, the graver the offence, the more likelihood that the public interest requires prosecution. Factors against prosecution include the trivial nature of the incident and the likelihood of a nominal penalty, any delay in bringing proceedings and the health and age of the accused.

There is also the possibility of negotiation—discontinuance of all charges is not the only option since the defendant may well wish to plead guilty to a lesser charge while maintaining a plea of not guilty to more serious charges. There are often hidden negotiations known as 'plea bargaining'. The CPS can accept such 'deals', but the Code's strictures are that the overriding consideration in considering acceptance of guilty pleas is that the court must not be left in the position where it is unable to pass a sentence consistent with the gravity of the actions. The danger in such practices is that administrative convenience is taking precedence over interests of justice.

Legal representation for the defendant

Defendants were not permitted professional assistance to examine witnesses or to speak on their behalf until 1836, but it is now taken for granted that the right to a fair trial includes legal representation, not only in court but also in the police station and for other pre-trial procedures. For most defendants, the cost of legal advice and representation would be prohibitive. The legal aid scheme allows for the costs of conducting the defence to be borne by the State and not by the defendant. The scheme includes the right of a suspect in police custody to the advice of a lawyer, usually one provided under a 'duty solicitor' scheme organized by local solicitors.[8] At court, the scheme provides for legal representation in most criminal proceedings.

The management of this has been recently reformed—the Legal Services Commission took over the public funding of defence work from the Legal Aid Board in April 2000.[9] The Commission established the Criminal Defence Service (CDS) which is introducing a mixed system by which criminal defence will be organized through, on one hand, contracted private practitioners and on the other, public salaried employees. There will be a contractual scheme by which private solicitors will be accredited and publicly funded.

The radical departure is the introduction of salaried public defenders. The scheme in England and Wales is currently being piloted. Such schemes are common in North America and Australia and a review of research (Scottish Office, 1998) found that the average case costs of staff lawyers are cheaper than private lawyers and that, despite the lower average costs, staff lawyers were found to achieve broadly similar or slightly better outcomes for their clients than private lawyers.

It is only in magistrates' courts that defendants will be unrepresented. Recent reforms (Home Office, 1997) have provided for an enhanced court duty solicitor scheme and defendants who might formerly have been unrepresented are now getting advice. For those who remain unrepresented, magistrates' courts are much less adversarial than higher courts and both the bench and the clerk often question the defendant to obtain the information that they need, whether for the purpose of the plea itself, mitigating circumstances before sentence or working out a suitable payment plan for the fine. In provincial courts, this may come over as benevolent paternalism (McBarnet, 1981).

REVIEW QUESTIONS

1 What is the structure of the prosecution service?

2 What does the Crown prosecutor do?

3 What are the key elements in the decision whether to prosecute?

4 By what means do we ensure that a defendant will be legally represented?

The courts

There are currently two systems of courts that hear and decide criminal cases: the magistrates' courts for minor, summary, cases (discussed below) and the Crown Courts for more serious cases heard on indictment (discussed below). Decisions in these courts can be challenged through a number of channels. These structures can be seen in Figures 22.2 and 22.3.

Quantitatively 95 per cent of all criminal cases will be dealt with in the magistrates' courts. Some 1.93 million defendants were dealt with in magistrates' courts in 2002 (Home Office, 2003b: 16) whereas there were only 81,776 cases disposed of in the Crown Court (Department for Constitutional Affairs (2003), Table 6.1: 68).

In magistrates' courts, the justices of the peace who hear cases are local people with no legal background, taking time from their jobs to serve as unpaid judges. There are paid and legally qualified magistrates in major conurbations. In contrast the Crown Court has a judge who will have been a lawyer of some experience before being appointed to the judiciary. The trial takes place in front of a jury, a body of twelve people randomly selected from the local community.

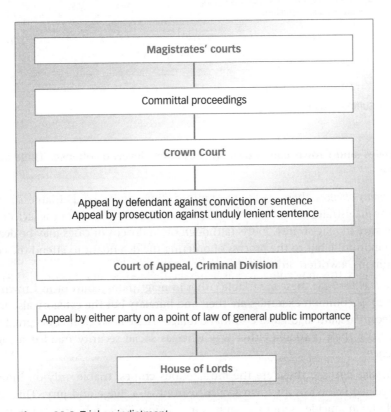

Figure 22.2 Trial on indictment

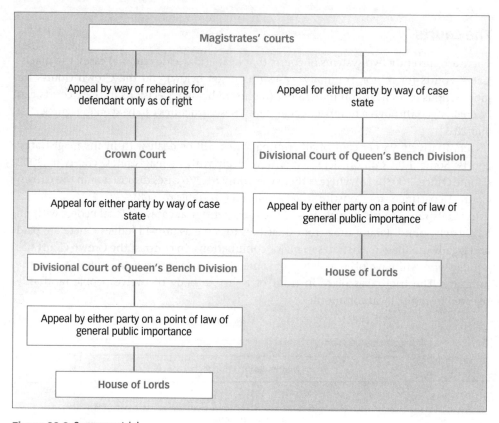

Figure 22.3 Summary trial

Magistrates' and Crown courts deal with different levels of offence. There are three categories:

(a) *Summary offences:* these are the most minor crimes and are only triable 'summarily' in the magistrates court. 'Summary' does not refer to the speed or the lack of quality of justice in magistrates' courts (although often dozens of cases may be dealt with in a morning), but to the process of ordering the defendant to attend the court by summons, a written order usually delivered by post.

(b) *Triable either way:* these are triable either in magistrates' court or in Crown Court. The most common examples are theft and burglary but the category also includes indecent assault, arson and criminal damage. There is no clear conceptual boundary here: theft is triable either way whereas social security fraud is a summary offence.

(c) *Indictable offences:* these are the most serious crimes, triable only on indictment (discussed below) in a Crown Court in front of a judge and jury. This category includes homicide, serious assault, rape, kidnapping, robbery, conspiracy and Official Secrets Acts offences.

Where an offence is triable either way, summary trial is only possible if both the accused and the magistrates assent to it. The defendant has the right to insist on jury trial and if the magistrates consider summary trial inappropriate, they too can elect for trial on indictment. Most defendants opt for summary trial, not least because of the speed of the proceedings and the ceiling placed on the punishments that magistrates' courts can impose.

Magistrates and clerks

The unqualified, unpaid magistrates' justice of the peace (JP) may be seen, alongside the jury, as an exemplar of the 'active community' with the ordinary citizen's input into the processes of justice. In 2003, there were 28,344 JPs in England and Wales (Department for Constitutional Affairs (2003) Table 9.4: 98).

Magistrates are normally appointed by the Lord Chancellor acting on the advice of local advisory committees (Department for Constitutional Affairs (2003a)). There are over one hundred of these and each is left to devise its own methods of generating applications. Individuals and organizations can put forward candidates for consideration. Local political parties often nominate candidates. The magistrates' bench should 'reflect the community it serves', but the problem that occurs is one of balance, less in terms of gender than of age, race and class. It has proved very difficult to appoint sufficient working class or ethnic minority magistrates. Magistrates are unpaid, receiving only a modest allowance for financial loss and subsistence. They are also not qualified, although there is compulsory training before they are allowed to adjudicate as well as continuing refresher courses—JPs will spend about a week a year on training activities. Typically, they serve for between ten and twenty years. They are required to sit for a minimum of twenty-six half-day court sittings each year, but on average sit forty or more times a year.

Sitting part time and normally in benches of three, magistrates deal mainly with criminal matters, but also with some civil cases, in the main family and licensing matters. In many conurbations, a legally qualified and paid magistrate often takes the place of the lay magistrates. Once called stipendiary magistrates, they are now known as district judges. They are drawn from the ranks of practising lawyers and normally sit alone.

There is also the youth court dealing with criminal offences by defendants aged seventeen or under. The magistrates who sit in the youth court are specially selected and the rules and procedures are different from the adult court as is its philosophy, based as it is on the welfare of the child (see Chapter 19 above).

The 'clerk to the court' assists the magistrates. The clerk, a fully trained and paid lawyer, is the focal point of the court. They are responsible for legal advice tendered to the justices and for the administration of the courthouse: listing cases for hearing; summoning witnesses; handling adjournments; collecting the fines; as well as managing the personnel of the court. In court, the legal adviser has the duty to provide justices with any advice they require to properly perform their functions, but must not play any part in making findings of fact although they may ask questions of witnesses and the parties. The overall duty is to ensure that every case is conducted fairly. Problems can arise when clerks are seen to be too involved in the decision making.

Unlike trial in the Crown Court, an accused does not have to be present for summary trial. Cases can take place in the absence of the accused who may have pleaded guilty by post or simply have failed to turn up. The CPS will normally conduct the prosecution. The accused may be legally represented, either by a barrister or solicitor, although one may choose to represent oneself. The clerk should assist an unrepresented defendant in explaining the procedure and perhaps suggesting the sort of questions that may be asked in cross-examination.

Where there is a 'not guilty' plea, the prosecution and defence will call and examine their witnesses, who will be subject to cross-examination by the other party's lawyer. Both sides have the opportunity to address the court although the defence does have the right to the last word. The magistrates listen to the evidence, but will play no part in calling or examining witnesses. At the conclusion of a contested case, they will reach a verdict. If they find the accused 'guilty' (or where the defendant has pleaded 'guilty'), they proceed to sentence. There is a range of penalties from discharges to fines to community penalties to imprisonment. The maximum penalty will be specified in the statute creating the offence, but a magistrates' court cannot imprison anyone for more than six months for any single offence or for more than one year where they are dealing with more than a single offence. Where the magistrates have tried a case summarily but have decided that their sentencing powers are insufficient, they can commit the defendant to the Crown Court for sentence. Crown Courts also hear appeals against conviction or sentence from the magistrates' courts.

The Crown Court

When an offence is too serious for the magistrates' court, an indictment is drawn up for trial in Crown Court. The Crown Court is more formal and traditional than magistrates' courts—at the front of the court will be the raised bench where the judge sits beneath the Royal coat-of-arms. A private door will lead to the judge's room. Below the judge sits the clerk to the court, a less qualified and influential figure than the justices' clerk. Facing the judge will be the dock where the accused stands and in front of the dock will be the benches for the lawyers. At one side is the jury box with two rows of six seats and on the other is the witness box where witnesses enter to testify. There will be a public gallery at the back. There may be an area for probation officers or police officers.

A trial in Crown Court is based on an indictment, a formal document containing the alleged offences. This document supersedes all other accusations (the police charge or the information laid before the magistrates) and it is to the indictment that the accused pleads guilty or not guilty. It is the indictment that should provide the starting point for the judge and the jury. Presiding in the Crown Court is a single 'professional' judge who will be a lawyer of at least ten years' experience. He or she sits with a randomly selected jury. There are different categories of judge—the most senior are High Court judges, normally attached to the Queen's Bench Division in London; the routine work will be handled by a circuit judge or recorder—the latter are equivalent to circuit judges but their appointment is only part time. Circuit judges and recorders handle 95 per cent of the work of the Crown Court.

The jurisdiction of the Crown Court is less varied than the magistrates—the major work is hearing criminal trials on indictment, both for offences that are indictable only and for those that are triable 'either way'. The court has exclusive jurisdiction over such trials. There is a wide diversity in the complexity and seriousness of cases and this is reflected in the division of work between High Court judges and circuit judges.

Guilty pleas are less common in the Crown Court—approximately 60 per cent of defendants will plead guilty (Home Office, 2003a). The course of a contested trial is very similar to that in a magistrates' court with both the prosecution and defendant examining their own witnesses and cross-examining those of the other side. However, after the closing speeches, the judge will address the jury, explaining the legal issues that have to be decided, summarizing the evidence and explaining the burden of proof. After the judge's summing up, the jury retire to consider their verdict.

REVIEW QUESTIONS

1 What is the structure of the criminal courts?

2 Describe the work of the magistrates' courts and the Crown Court.

3 Who are the magistrates and how do you become one?

4 What is the job of the clerk to the magistrates' court?

Sentencing and the correctional system

If the magistrates or jury acquits an accused, they are free to leave the court. If they are convicted, the court proceeds to the sentencing stage. This is the imposition of a punishment of some kind. For the Crown Court judge, the maximum penalty will specified in the statute creating the offence but, as mentioned above, a magistrates' court has a maximum of one year's imprisonment.

Courts have a certain freedom in what punishment to impose—the only mandatory sentence is a life sentence for those convicted of murder.[10] In general, a statute that creates an offence will specify a maximum rather than minimum penalty. A court can choose from the range of penalties from the minimum (an absolute discharge) to the maximum specified for the particular offence (Dickson, 2002). The possible punishments include:

- absolute and conditional discharges;
- fines;
- community punishments including community rehabilitation orders and community punishment orders (see Chapter 26 below);
- prison (see Chapter 27 below).

But a court cannot exercise an unfettered discretion in imposing a sentence—there is a statutory sentencing framework, originally introduced in 1991 but now contained within the Criminal Justice Act 2003. This conceives of sentencing as a two-stage process:

(a) The primary decision is the type of penalty, namely fine, community penalty or custody. The fine is the presumptive penalty and the court must be satisfied, if it wishes to move from a fine to a community penalty or from there to custody, that the offence is sufficiently serious to warrant this.

(b) The secondary decision is that of the tariff. Having decided on the type of penalty, the court must decide on the size of the fine, the content of the community sentence or the length of the prison sentence.

The sentencing court's discretion is also subject to other controls and influences. Defendants have the right to appeal against sentence (discussed below) and this means that the Court of Appeal exercises a significant oversight and regularly issues guideline judgements as to the appropriate level of sentencing for particular offences. For example, in *Billam*[11] the court provided sentencing guidelines for offences of rape, including aggravating and mitigating factors. Another recent influence has been the creation of the Sentencing Advisory Panel that has produced research reports on sentencing in offences such as domestic burglary (Russell, 2001).

The enforcement of the sentence will rest with different agencies—fines are administered by the magistrates' court;[12] community sentences are in general the responsibility of the National Probation Service and custodial sentences are in the hands of the Prison Service Agency. For those prisoners serving more than four years, the decision to release is in the hands of the Parole Board whose function is to make decisions on the release and recall of prisoners on the basis of risk assessments.

The organization of the probation and prison services is in the process of change. As a result of the Carter Report (Carter, 2003) and the subsequent White Paper (Home Office, 2004), the latter two agencies will be amalgamated into a single organization, the National Offender Management Service, from June 2004. The expectation is that integrating the management of offenders whilst in custody or under supervision in the community is the most effective and efficient way forward. NOMS will be organized managed at regional level where '. . . effective links can be forged and joint strategies developed with complementary services, including health, education, and employment.' (Home Office, 2004: 10)

REVIEW QUESTIONS

1 Describe the range of sentences available to a court.

2 What is the sentencing framework?

3 What limits are put on the sentencing powers of a magistrates' court?

4 What controls exist over the court's discretion in passing sentencing?

Appeals

The right of appeal is an essential element of any criminal justice system. The review of decisions allows justice to be done to individual defendants, to bring finality to the process and enhance public confidence. But the appellate system in England and Wales is far from straightforward and has mixed and overlapping routes. The process of appeal from a magistrates' court demonstrates this. A defendant can appeal in two ways from the decision of a bench of justices:

(a) *to Crown Court*—the defendant can appeal as of right against conviction or sentence. The appeal takes the form of a complete re-hearing of the entire case, calling the original witnesses and hearing the legal arguments again. The circuit judge is assisted normally by two JPs and they can uphold or quash the conviction or vary the sentence;

(b) *to Divisional Court of Queen's Bench*—either the prosecution or the defence can appeal by way of 'case stated' to the Divisional Court of the Queen's Bench Division. This is an ancient jurisdiction by which the Queen's Bench controls the decisions of inferior judicial bodies. But this is an appeal on the law—there is no rehearsing of the evidence and the hearing will consist of legal argument that the magistrates applied the law wrongly.

If convicted in the Crown Court, a defendant may appeal against conviction or sentence to the Criminal Division of the Court of Appeal. Appeal against conviction is governed by s. 2 of the Criminal Appeals Act 1995. The appellant must establish that the conviction should be quashed according to the sole criterion that it was 'unsafe'. The 'safety' of a conviction is a difficult concept. The court's practice is not to review the evidence in order to substitute their judgement for that of the jury. Nor is it a re-hearing of the case although the court can receive fresh evidence and is free to assess the evidence as it sees fit. An 'unsafe conviction' exists where the judge has made an error, in explaining the law to the jury, in allowing the introduction of inadmissible evidence or in some other significant procedural fashion. Where the appeal is successful, the court can quash the conviction, vary the sentence or order a re-trial.

The final court of appeal in criminal matters in this country is the Judicial Committee of the House of Lords. A panel will consist of five senior judges. Appeals must involve a point of law of general public importance. It deals with little criminal work—from 1998–2000, it dealt with ten criminal appeals only.

The Criminal Cases Review Commission

Wrongful convictions can stem from police malpractice, from the prosecution withholding evidence, from trial judge bias, from faulty forensic evidence. It is the job of the Court of Appeal to ensure that such errors are rectified. They have frequently been proved inadequate for this task. In the 1980s there was growing anxiety about the performance of the Court of Appeal. Again and again cases have had to be referred back to the court by the Home Secretary. The Birmingham Six were men of Irish origin who were convicted of the Birmingham pub bombings that occurred in 1974. They appealed against conviction originally in 1976 (Mullin, 1986). This appeal was rejected, but the Home Secretary referred the case back to the Court of Appeal in 1987 and the appeals were dismissed again. Referred again in 1990, the DPP decided not to resist the appeal, thus pre-empting the court. However, the court went ahead with the hearing and quashed the convictions in 1991. The 'fresh' evidence was that the confessions had been obtained by coercion and that there were flaws in the expert forensic testimony which stated that they had been handling explosives. In its essentials that evidence had been heard by the court in 1987, but at that time the convictions were still upheld. It is hard to understand why the Lord Chief Justice, Lord Lane, and his colleagues were unable to discover a 'lurking doubt' that was patently obvious to most.

It was clear that the Court of Appeal were unlikely to ensure that wrongful convictions would always be rectified. What was often required was an organization to instigate and supervize further investigation, a function which is ill-suited to a court. For many years, it was a department in the Home Office that undertook this function and occasionally referred cases to the Court. In 1995 an independent Criminal Cases Review Commission was set up to take over this work and be responsible for referring cases back to the Court of Appeal. It deals with all miscarriages of justice, and refers them to the appropriate court where it considers that there is a 'real possibility' that a conviction would not be upheld. It is an investigative body and reports to the Court of Appeal on any matter in an appeal referred to it by the Court.

Prosecution appeals

The English common law never allowed the prosecution any right to appeal against acquittal or sentence. This was the rule against 'double jeopardy'—once the jury had acquitted, that was the end of the matter as far as the State was concerned. But there are now a series of mechanisms that give the prosecution a limited right of appeal. The case stated procedure discussed earlier allows the prosecution to appeal on a point of law to the Divisional Court of Queen's Bench. This can be from the magistrates Court, Recent statutes gave a right of appeal regarding 'tainted acquittals' where a person has been convicted of intimidating or interfering with a juror or witness that has led to an acquittal. The Attorney-General's Reference system, introduced in 1972 by the Criminal Justice Act permits the Attorney-General to refer to the Court of Appeal any point of law even though the defendant was acquitted—this does not affect the status of the original verdict. Finally there can be an appeal against sentence where a defendant has been convicted, but in the eyes of the prosecution has been given an 'unduly lenient' sentence.

The Criminal Justice Act 2003, in allowing retrial for a number of serious offences where new evidence has come to light, has undermined the rule against double jeopardy itself. Further this legislation allows the prosecution to appeal rulings before trial, during the hearing of the prosecution case and of no case to answer as well as other 'terminating rulings'.

The European Court of Human Rights

A final port of call for those who feel that they have been mistreated by the UK criminal justice system is the European Court of Human Rights. The basis of any individual application to the Court is that a State has acted in breach of its obligations under the European Convention on Human Rights, such as by denying a person a fair trial (under

Article 6) or by infringing a person's right to liberty, privacy or freedom of expression. A judgement upholding such an application is an embarrassment for the government, but does not overturn a domestic judgement or invalidate government action. There is a moral pressure for the government to amend the domestic law so that it is compatible with the European Convention on Human Rights. Mostly, the government does pass amending legislation.

To an extent, applications to Strasbourg will become less significant with the passage of the Human Rights Act 1998. Although this does not make the European Convention part of English law, it obliges public authorities, including the courts, to act in a manner which is compatible with Convention rights. It requires courts to interpret all legislation in a way that is compatible with Convention rights, if this is possible. Courts must take account, not merely of the Convention itself, but of the body of jurisprudence that has been built up through the decisions of the European Court of Human Rights. If it is not possible to interpret the law in this way, a superior court may make a 'declaration of incompatibility'. But it is still a matter for the government to amend the law—or not! The impact of this for the criminal justice system is considerable—these guarantees have already compelled the government to make amendments to laws which allowed inferences to be drawn from silence or the use as evidence of answers obtained under compulsion.

REVIEW QUESTIONS

1 Describe the process of appeal from conviction in magistrates' court.

2 To whom do you appeal from conviction in Crown Court and on what grounds?

3 When can the prosecution appeal?

4 By what means do we aim to prevent miscarriages of justice?

CONCLUSION

As we have seen, the criminal justice system in this country is a complex amalgam of different agencies, pursuing their own aims. The key unifying principle to which all should subscribe is that the accused has the right to a fair and just process, from investigation to arrest, to trial and sentencing through to release from prison. In most areas, the criminal justice system in this country measures up to this yardstick. In many ways, this is a creation of history, notably through the decisions of courts and judges and Parliament. Out of these decisions came a number of checks and balances on the power of the State which, when put together, can be seen as ensuring that an accused person has the right to a fair trial: the presumption of innocence, the burden of proof resting on the State, the strict rules governing the admissibility of evidence, the principle that penal legislation should be narrowly interpreted, among many others. Such safeguards have been reinforced by the passage of the Human Rights Act 1998.

But judges and juries, as well as parliaments, have assaulted individual rights as often as they have protected them. In 1791, Thomas Paine wrote *The Rights of Man* arguing for equal political rights. It was a jury that convicted him of seditious libel, although Paine had already fled to France. The institutions of criminal justice provide the State with the most coercive powers in civil peacetime society: people under arrest lose their freedom of movement until it is restored by the police or by a court; they are under an obligation to account for their actions and behaviour either to police officers or to a court; on conviction they are liable to lose their property through fines, their leisure through community punishments, or their liberty through imprisonment. States frequently seek to expand these powers, seeking greater control over the population. Recently, Parliament has passed legislation that has permitted indefinite detention without trial (Terrorism Act 2001), abandoned the double jeopardy rule (Criminal Justice Act 2003) and considered the possibility of reducing the standard of proof to be applied in criminal trials from 'beyond reasonable doubt' to 'on the balance of probabilities'. Perhaps a concluding point to emphasize is that the burden should always be on the State to demonstrate the necessity for the existence of such powers rather than on individuals to justify their freedom of movement and action.

QUESTIONS FOR DISCUSSION

1   What should be the principal objectives of a criminal justice system?

2   What would be the advantages and disadvantages of a 'Minister for Justice' responsible for all aspects of criminal justice?

3   To what extent should the police be subject to local or national political control?

4   Should investigation and prosecution be dealt with separately?

5   What elements (procedures, personnel, rights and so or) are necessary for a 'fair trial'?

6   What factors should a court consider in sentencing an offender?

7   Should the prosecution have a right to appeal against conviction and/or sentence?

8   Is the system of appeal too complex? How could it be simplified?

GUIDE TO FURTHER READING

Ashworth, A. (1998) *The Criminal Process* (2nd edn). Oxford: Oxford University Press.

Home Office *Justice for All* (Cm 5563) (2002). London: Home Office.

McConville, M. and Wilson, G. (2002) *The Handbook of the Criminal Justice Process*. Oxford: Oxford University Press.

Padfield, N. (2004) *Text and Materials on the Criminal Justice Process* (3rd edn). London: Butterworths).

Sanders, A. and Young, R. (2001) *Criminal Justice* (2nd edn). London: Butterworths.

Uglow, S. (2002) *Criminal Justice* (2nd edn). London: Sweet & Maxwell.

Wasik, M. *et al.* (1999) *Criminal Justice: Text and Materials*. Harlow: Longmans.

WEB LINKS

The following websites contain links to most official criminal justice system webpages:

www.homeoffice.gov.uk
Home Office

www.dca.gov.uk
Department for Constitutional Affairs

www.cjsonline.org
Criminal Justice Online

More specialist webpages include:
www.courtservice.gov.uk
The Court Service

www.ccrc.gov.uk
Criminal Cases Review Commission

www.criminal-courts-review.gov.uk
Criminal Courts Review (the Auld Report)

www.cps.gov.uk
Crown Prosecution Service

www.leeds.ac.uk/law/ccjs/ukweb.htm
Leeds Centre for Criminal Justice weblinks

www.magistrates-association.org.uk
Magistrates' Association

www.paroleboard.gov.uk/
Parole Board

www.police.uk
Police Service

www.hmprisonservice.gov.uk/
Prison Service

www.probation.homeoffice.gov.uk
Probation Service

www.sentencing-advisory-panel.gov.uk/
Sentencing Advisory Panel

www.victimsupport.com
Victim Support

www.youth-justice-board.gov.uk
Youth Justice Board

REFERENCES

Carter, P. (2003) *Managing Offenders, Reducing Crime*. London: Home Office.

CJSOnline (2004): www.cjsonline.org/citizen/defendants/prosecution.html (accessed April 2004).

CPS (2000) *Code for Crown Prosecutors* (with addendum 2004; available at www.cps.gov.uk/home/CodeForCrownProsecutors/).

CPS (2003) *Crown Prosecution Service Annual Report* 2002–03. HCP 03/870.

Department for Constitutional Affairs (2003) *Judicial Statistics 2002* accessible at www.dca.gov.uk/judicial/jsar02/judicial_stats6.pdf.

Department for Constitutional Affairs (2003a) *National Strategy for the recruitment of Lay Magistrates* accessible at www.dca.gov.uk/magist/recruit/magrecruit.htm.

Dickson, L. (2002) 'Issues in sentencing' in S. Uglow, *Criminal Justice* (2nd edn). London: Sweet & Maxwell.

Duff P. and Hutton, N. (1999) (eds) *Criminal Justice in Scotland*. Aldershot: Dartmouth.

Home Office (1997) Review of Delay in the Criminal Justice System. London: Home Office.

Home Office (2002) Narrowing the Justice Gap—A Framework Document. London: Home Office.

Home Office (2003a) *Criminal Statistics 2002* (Cm 6054). London: Stationery Office.

Home Office (2003b) Crime in England and Wales 2002/2003 (Home Office Statistical Bulletin 07/03). London: Home Office.

Home Office (2004) *Reducing Crime—Changing Lives*. London: Home Office.

McBarnet, D. (1981) *Conviction*. London: Macmillan.

Mullin C. (1986) *Error of Judgement*. London: Chatto and Windus.

Royal Commission on Criminal Procedure (1981) *Report* Cmnd 8092. London: HMSO.

Royal Commission on Criminal Justice (1993) *Report* Cm 2263. London: HMSO.

Russell, N. and Morgan, R. (2001) *Sentencing in Domestic Burglary*. London: Sentencing Advisory Panel.

Scottish Office (1998) *A Literature Review of Public Defender or Staff Lawyer Schemes*. Legal Studies Research Findings 19. Edinburgh: Scottish Office.

Simmons, J., Legg, C. and Hosking, R. (2003) *National Crime Recording Standard: an analysis of the impact on recorded crime*. Home Office Online Report 31/03. www.homeoffice.gov.uk/rds/pdfs2/rdsolr3103.pdf

Tilley, N. (2003) 'Community policing, problem-oriented policing and intelligence-led policing' in T. Newburn (ed) *Handbook of Policing*. Cullompton: Willan.

NOTES

1. The youth justice system deals with offenders who are seventeen or under. A description of the system can be seen at the Youth Justice Board website at www.youth-justice-board.gov.uk (Kirton, 2004).

2. An account of the Scottish system can be found in Duff (1999) or on the Scottish Executive website at www.scotland.gov.uk. Information on the system in Northern Ireland can be found in Northern Ireland Office: 'A Review of the Criminal Justice System in Northern Ireland' (March 2000), available at www.nio.gov.uk/pdf/mainreport.pdf. Recent developments can be followed at www.cjsni.gov.uk.

3. There are two categories of lawyer in England and Wales: the solicitor is the general practitioner, available to the public for legal advice and limited representation; the barrister is the consultant and advocate (only available through a solicitor) who will provide specialist advice and represent clients in court.

4. The 2002 criminal statistics can be accessed at www.official-documents.co.uk/document/cm60/6054/6054.htm.

5. The BCS is best accessed through www.homeoffice.gov.uk/rds/bcs1.html.

6. Best value reviews of performance arise from the duty of continuous improvement for local authorities as set by the Local Government Act 1999.

7. There is a separate statutory scheme involving reprimands and final warnings for young persons under the Crime and Disorder Act 1998.

8. This is provided for by ss 58 and 60 of the Police and Criminal Evidence Act 1984.

9. Access to Justice Act 1999; www.legalservices.gov.uk/

10. There are other mandatory sentences under the Crime (Sentences) Act 1997 although these are rarely applied.

11. [1986] 8 Crim App Rep (S) 48.

12. There are other financial penalties such as compensation orders. Confiscation of assets is also possible under the provisions of the Proceeds of Crime Act 2002.

23 Surveillance

Richard Jones

INTRODUCTION

In this chapter I will discuss the topic of surveillance. The aims of this chapter are: to introduce and discuss what is meant by surveillance within criminology; to introduce key theories relating to the concept of surveillance; and to identify certain contemporary developments relating to surveillance, particularly new surveillance (or related) technologies. The topic is now fairly broad and extensively researched within criminology, so by necessity any introduction has to be selective.

BACKGROUND

The Oxford English Dictionary (OED) 2nd edition (1989) defines 'surveillance' as, 'a. Watch or guard kept over a person, etc., [especially] over a suspected person, a prisoner, or the like; often, spying, supervision; less commonly, supervision for the purpose of direction or control, superintendence. [. . .] b. [an attribute, especially] of devices, vessels, etc., used in military or police surveillance.' The term 'surveillance' seems to imply practices of watching or listening not merely briefly, but rather over an extended period of time.

Within criminology, areas in which some form of surveillance might be practised include: the visual, telephone, and eavesdropping surveillance of suspected offenders by police, customs or immigration services; neighbourhood watch schemes; CCTV systems, including in city centres, banks, shops, hotels and restaurants, at airports, and on public roads; in prisons; in relation to Internet usage; and the electronic monitoring of offenders ('tagging'). Applications of surveillance falling outside usual criminological boundaries but nevertheless conceptually related to it include military surveillance; surveillance (of various types) carried out by intelligence agencies; satellite surveillance both military and civilian (of weather patterns, crop status, and so on); and medical surveillance of individuals and populations (epidemiological monitoring of the spread of the SARS or HIV/AIDS viruses, for instance).

A term appearing to be related to surveillance is 'monitoring'. In the course of providing a definition of 'monitor', the OED notes that senior pupils may be assigned as 'monitors' and entrusted with special duties including that of keeping order that a monitor may be a 'device which monitors or displays performance, output, etc.; or a monitor may be 'One who admonishes or gives advice or warning to another about his conduct' (OED 2nd edition). Moreover, a monitor may be, 'Any instrument or device for monitoring some process or quantity'. Apparently originating in the 1940s in the field of nuclear science, air monitors were devices used to detect dangerous levels of radiation. A 1973 text advises that: 'There are situations in which a portable monitor can with advantage be replaced by a *permanently-installed* instrument which performs a *"watch-dog"* function and gives *warning* if the radiation level rises above a pre-set value (or alternatively warns if any radiation is present at times when none should exist)' (*Biomed. Engin.* VIII. 255/3, cited in OED 2nd edn, emphases added). In this chapter I will focus on criminological understandings of *surveillance*, but I will argue towards the end of the chapter that the concept of monitoring may be a better term to characterize the operation of certain contemporary information-gathering practices and technologies, particularly because 'monitoring' seems to capture both the 'hands-off' approach characteristic of these practices and technologies ongoing use, and their alarm function once a certain threshold of behaviour or conditions is reached.

Academic and political attention to the topic of surveillance, as it is familiar to UK criminology today came to the fore in the 1980s, following a combination of interest in (and concern regarding) urban policing tactics, the policing of various workers' strikes and political marches and demonstrations; the 'Zircon' spy satellite saga; the emergence of the 'personal microcomputer'; the presence of CCTV cameras in some central London streets; the suspected wiretapping and 'bugging' by the security services of certain politicians and activists; and renewed public interest in George Orwell's novel *1984* (despite the fact it is actually about a fictional 1948). Public and political concern regarding surveillance centred on the powers of the new technologies, on their possible political uses, and on the consequent threat to civil liberties, a perspective that is still strong today. Criminological interest in surveillance theory was stimulated partly by Marxist criminology and sociology (especially from the 1960s and 1970s), and also by the publication in the UK of Michel Foucault's (1979) *Discipline and Punish* (see below). The topic of surveillance thus has many aspects, and would seem to have links with many other topics, including policing, the politics of law and order, punishment in the community, prisons, terrorism and state crime, and media images of crime. In the following section, key theoretical perspectives on surveillance will be introduced and discussed.

Theories of surveillance

Marxism, social control and surveillance

Following Karl Marx (1818–83), Marxists emphasize the repressive nature of social control, and of social control's class basis. It is convenient to distinguish between two types of social control, namely formal social control and informal social control. Formal social control refers to the criminal law, the police and the criminal justice system. Informal social control, on the other hand, refers to compliance with social norms (such as that people should obey the law) demanded by an individual's own family, friends, teachers, neighbours, workmates, or fellow citizens. The concepts of formal and informal social control are used by Marxists and non-Marxists alike. Marxists offer a particular interpretation of these two forms of social control, seeing them as key means by which the ruling class maintain their dominance over the working class. Marxists argue that both forms of social control represent the implementation of ruling class ideology (either explicitly, in the criminal law and criminal justice system (formal) or implicitly in social norms (informal)).

Both informal and formal social control may involve forms of surveillance. In the case of informal social control, the form of surveillance involved would seem to be primarily of an interpersonal kind. In the case of formal social control, though, it may be that along with surveillance at the local, human level (by police officers out walking the beat, for example), specific surveillance technologies are also employed in order to gain additional or alternative quality surveillance information (via CCTV, for example). In all cases, Marxists would interpret the surveillance employed in terms of its social control 'role' or even 'function' within society. Various studies on social control were published during the 1980s which, while not necessarily Marxist, shared Marxists' vision of social control as one that was essentially controlling or repressive, whether intentionally or unintentionally so (see, for example, Cohen 1985; and Cohen and Scull, 1983). Marxist analyses can be complex, sophisticated and subtle, and can offer interpretations of a variety of surveillance practices including state-sanctioned surveillance, by intelligence agencies (they are protecting the State, which is said principally to serve ruling class interests); CCTV schemes (they are said, for example, to be directed primarily at protecting retailers' profits, or against working class public order disruption); and informal, peer surveillance (which may be a key mechanism by which bourgeois norms are upheld).

Foucault, 'discipline' and surveillance

Many contemporary accounts of surveillance remain strongly influenced by Michel Foucault (1926–84) and his work on discipline, set out in closest detail in his book *Discipline and Punish*. The original title of the book on its publication in France in 1975 was *Surveiller et Punir*. On its translation into English, the publishers discussed with Foucault what English title to give the book; he thought 'discipline' a better word to use than 'surveillance' perhaps because the latter usually has a more detached meaning in English, usually implying only the watching rather than the correcting of behaviour, thus failing to capture the interactive quality of 'corrections' that Foucault's book sets out to describe. Nevertheless, surveillance, optics, observation, and knowledge, are all central themes of Foucault's book, and it has made a distinctive contribution to a certain type of critical sociological criminology, particularly in the areas of the sociology of punishment and the study of social control.

At the same time, it is important to realize that Foucault was not a criminologist, that his book is not intended as a criminology book as such, and that his interest ultimately is in the study of the Western 'subject' (person) in modern societies. It makes a certain sense to think, at least in the first instance, of the criminological topic of *Discipline and Punish* as one Foucault happened by chance to use as the case study for his book; he could have written the same book, he once noted, instead about the school, factory, hospital or army.

Discipline and Punish (Foucault, 1979) famously opens with brief descriptions of two, very different, forms of punishment from French history: the brutal execution of Damiens the regicide in 1757, and a prison timetable from about 1838. The public execution is gory and brutal, taking place in public before a large crowd, and today seems quite barbaric to us. The prison timetable, in contrast, appears infinitely more civilized and modern and, in its specifications of when and where prisoners should be doing things at different times of the day, in its form strikes us as familiar today, even if its content is now somewhat old-fashioned. Foucault notes that these two very different types of punishment are separated by a period of only about eighty years. How, he asks, did the change from one to another come about? His answer rejects the obvious liberal explanation that the change is attributable to French society becoming more civilized and humane. Instead, and controversially, he suggests that modern prisons evolved not because they are *kinder* ways of punishing but because they are more *efficient* ways of punishing; to use Foucault's terminology, modern prisons are based on a more efficient technology of power.

A technology of power, Foucault writes, is a particular, historically specific way by which humans exercise power over one another. A technology of power is comprised both of *knowledges* and of *practices*. Different technologies of power are dominant during different phases of history. Foucault's model of history is reminiscent of Rusche and Kirkheimer's (1968), in that it characterizes history as being composed of a succession of phases (each phase lasting for decades or centuries). During each phase, social organization follows certain patterns. But social life changes dramatically at certain points, as one phase gives way to another. (As such, Foucault rejects the conventional liberal understanding of history as a process of continual and gradual change.)

According to Foucault, technologies of power are be found within all areas of social life, including health and medicine, education, the military, and factories. *Discipline and Punish* is concerned specifically with the role that three, historically successive, technologies of power play within the spheres of punishment and of social control: monarchical power, juridical power, and disciplinary power. Monarchical punishment is the spectacular, brutal, public form of punishment being carried out in the execution of Damiens. It is a display of the monarch's absolute power, and typically involves some sort of visible marking or disfiguring of the offender's body; but it is also, says Foucault, an unstable, hard to control, form of punishment: its use of brute force and heady emotions can backfire, and the impassioned crowd turn on the executioner and the State. Juridical punishment is the punishment of classical criminology ('let the punishment fit the crime') from the late eighteenth century. Punishment is to be proportionate, with length of time spent in prison supposed to reflect the gravity of the offence committed. It is not particularly interested in the offender as such, who is readmitted as a full citizen once the prison sentence has been served.

Disciplinary punishment began towards the beginning of the nineteenth century, according to Foucault, when 'discipline' (an older set of techniques that had been used in places such as monasteries for several centuries) took root in the newly formed modern prisons, and began guiding penal practices and knowledges. Discipline is based on supervision, training, correction of unwanted behaviour, and the continual examination and testing of each individual person. (The plates in the middle of the book *Discipline and Punish* provide perhaps the best illustration.) Rather than seek to crush an offender (as had monarchical punishment), or merely incarcerate them for a time but do little more (as juridical punishment had done), disciplinary punishment seeks to rehabilitate. Discipline utilizes measures of time and space to bring order to the social world. Groups of soldiers can be taught to march in step in orderly rows and columns, the sick can be assigned one hospital bed each, schoolchildren a desk each, and prisoners their own cell. By individualizing each person in this way, abnormal or incorrect behaviour becomes easier for a supervisor to identify, study and address. Foucault argues that this is what surveillance is; a system by which a small number of supervisors can exercise dominance over a larger group. The aim is to 'normalize' each person, by identifying and dealing with any abnormal behaviour, however small. Once this has been done, the individual can successfully and safely be handed over to a different, less intensive part of the surveillance apparatus. But remember that it is a very specific form of dominance, in that its aim is not violent repression, but rather the detailed study of each individual's behaviour, record, and history, with a view to reforming and rehabilitating them, at least in part. Foucault notes that 'experts' have an important role to play here (particularly in the more problematic cases) because of their role in generating and applying specific knowledges within each field, but that equally important are the specific practices facilitated by each institution's architecture. In the case of the modern prison, Foucault sees Jeremy Bentham's 'Panopticon' prison design as epitomizing the role that surveillance plays inside the prison. The circular prison design, featuring a central guard's tower from which a guard can see into every single prison cell while themselves remaining hidden, separates out the prisoners (one to each cell), thus helping control order in the prison, but also generates knowledges and practices relating to the prisoners through facilitating study of them as individuals.

Foucault argues that the social scientific study of people, and in particular in disciplines such as psychology and criminology ('the disciplines') emerges at this time, alongside the birth of the modern prison. But the maximum security prison is not the only place in which discipline and surveillance (in Foucault's sense) are to be found within the criminal justice and crime control system. Disciplinary punishment, Foucault claims in his 'dispersal of discipline' thesis, underpins not only all other, less secure prisons, but also probation work, diversion schemes, half-way houses, and outreach work—a network that he terms the 'carceral archipelago'. Moreover, disciplinary surveillance penetrates deep into the social body, with various professions exercising implicit watching-and-judging powers through their specialized forms of surveillance: the teacher-judge, the lawyer-judge, the police officer-judge. Further still, this judging (surveillance and normalization) is exercised to some extent by us all. In this way, disciplinary punishment and social control are 'genetically' related to one another, as it were, with discipline (active surveillance) being their shared characteristic.

As David Garland (1990) has noted, Foucault's account of discipline and surveillance practices constitutes an original and thought-provoking reinterpretation not only of punishment in modern society but also of the connections between punishment and social control. As Garland has also noted, there are certain problems with Foucault's account. Garland (1985) has argued that in England, at least, disciplinary punishment actually appears to have begun almost a century later than Foucault claims. Moreover, Foucault's 'power perspective' (his insistence that social relations and historical change must be understood only in terms of power and domination), and his related 'anti-humanist' approach, are highly questionable as analytic frameworks. They also beg certain questions: Is power really as one-sided as Foucault portrays? Is resistance to power possible? Are people really primarily motivated by, and is history really explicable in terms of power alone? To some extent, Foucault addresses these and other criticisms in interviews and essays after *Discipline and Punish* was first published (see for example, Gordon 1980), though in other respects they remain fundamental objections to his whole approach dating from the early to mid-1970s.

There is a certain limited connection between Marxist accounts of social control (both types) and Michel Foucault's account of disciplinary surveillance—and indeed some Marxist accounts have been influenced by Foucault's work—but there are also differences. (See Sumner (1990) for an approach that draws both from Marxism and Foucault.)

What is important to us here, however, is to recognize that although Foucault (1979) was clearly very interested in the topic of surveillance, and indeed built this whole book around a particular, unique interpretation of this term, he was less concerned with alerting his readership to the 'Big Brother' nature of the State (despite the fact that his work sometimes gives this impression) and instead more concerned with trying to say something about the individualizing practices of surveillance—about the *creation* of the modern individual, rather than the *repression* of the individual as Marxists would have it. Foucault was interested in this greater issue, namely of the history of Western subject, about how this particular subject formation came about, about knowledge-production, and relations between knowledge formations and power formations (note however that Foucault does not say 'knowledge is power') (see Dreyfus and Rabinow (1982)). Nevertheless, Foucault's work continues to be influential within the study of surveillance today, because of his particular interpretation of surveillance, and though the suggestiveness of his discussion of the Panopticon and its potential application to electronic surveillance technologies: 'the electronic Panopticon' (see Lyon, 1993; 1994).

'Post-disciplinary' theories of surveillance

In the early 1990s, Feeley and Simon (1992) claimed that a new guiding logic was emerging within punishment which they termed 'The New Penology'. They suggested that this new logic was a historical successor to disciplinary punishment, or at least that it stood in sharp contrast to it. The characteristics of the new penology were said to involve an interest in aggregates rather than individuals; use of actuarial analysis; and incapacitation rather than rehabilitation as a sentencing rationale. In a subsequent article, Feeley and Simon (1994) extended the new penology argument and argued that practices informed by those identified with the new penology could be seen emerging in various different parts of criminal justice and crime control systems: they termed this actuarial justice. The relevance of their work to the study of surveillance lies in their identification of a crime control approach that utilizes a form of surveillance seemingly rather different to the involved, individualizing approach modelled by Foucault. In a discussion of screening techniques being used in airport security checks of passengers, Feeley and Simon (1994: 177) argue that such screening is now often based on identifying typical offender characteristics, and utilizing this information in risk identification systems. In the busy world of the airline business, where it is important to maintain security but not delay the majority of passengers unduly, a risk factor system is said to be able to flag-up certain passengers as being 'high risk' based on a simple calculation. By using basic information such as a passenger's age, nationality, transit origin and destination, and so on, a risk instrument can quickly derive an initial risk 'score' for each passenger. Passengers scoring above a certain threshold score can be searched, questioned or investigated further, or discreetly put under surveillance within the airport terminal. Even the proponents of such systems do not claim that they are foolproof; rather the aim is to help allocate the scarce resources of airline security (equipment, personnel and their time) in focusing on potentially higher risk individuals. So an important point is that it may not be the actual immediate behaviour of certain passengers that draws the attention of the surveillance system but instead various prior factors.

Critics of such risk checklists claim that they may involve stereotypes (of race, religious faith, nationality, gender, for example); that sometimes there is little social scientific research underpinning them; and that there could be a circularity involved, in that risk factors may simply reflect outcomes of past practices and beliefs (which may be biased or partial); or that even in the absence of actual bias, the resulting decisions can still seem somehow profoundly unfair (see also Simon, 1988). Alternatively, it could be argued that the aforementioned are only present in poorly researched and implemented screening systems, and that properly researched, evidence-based screening systems that have been properly evaluated and revised as necessary are a useful additional tool. However, the key sociological point for us is that to the extent that such checklists and other risk factor-based screening systems are used in various crime control and criminal justice 'surveillance' systems, it could be argued that their usage may represent a move *away* from Foucauldian surveillance practices and *towards* a new, 'post-disciplinary' form of surveillance (a historical shift which seems to have been hinted at, at least, by Feeley and Simon (1992) in the title of their original article).

However, it could be that the risk-based practices Feeley and Simon identify are indeed historically fairly novel and sociologically significant, but that these newer practices overlay and complement existing (and more Foucauldian) surveillance practices rather than simply replace them. Such an interpretation would avoid the inherent implausibility of a claim that one form of surveillance has relatively suddenly replaced another form wholesale, yet retain the insight as to the significance of the new practices.

Another approach, similar in certain respects to Feeley and Simon's, involves a particular reading of Michel Foucault's (1991) notion of 'governmentality'. Governmentality is a neologism of Foucault's used to describe particular techniques and practices of government used to nurture the economic, social, and medical health of the population as a whole (a good introduction and discussion can be found in Garland (1997)). These 'arts of governing' were developed over the centuries, but are particularly associated with the development of the disciplines of economics and public health. On one reading, adopted by a number of commentators particularly from the UK, US and Australia (see Barry *et al.*, 1996), Foucault's work on governmentality is used to analyse neo-liberal politics (as emerging in the mid-1970s, around the time at which he began studying governmentality), and to be suggesting that governmentality somehow comes to supplant discipline. On this reading, in respect of the specific fields of crime control and criminal justice, individualizing surveillance is said to be gradually replaced, as from about the 1980s, by aggregating, actuarial surveillance or monitoring, of the kind on which Feeley and Simon focus. However, while Foucault undoubtedly was interested in the then rise of neo-liberalism, his discussion of governmentality makes it clear that he himself envisaged the State practices to which it refers as augmenting discipline, not replacing it. If this is correct, then Foucault's concept of governmentality should not be regarded as in any way *post*-disciplinary. Governmentality may possibly have some utility in analysing surveillance and classification practices at the level of the State, for instance in relation to national identity cards of the sort the UK government has been considering introducing. However, from the perspective of governmentality, such ID cards would be seen less as an historical innovation indicative of something distinctly 'new' happening, and more as merely the latest in a long series of historical measures, including letters of passage, passports, national insurance numbers, visas, driving licences, and birth certificates.

Rather different 'post-disciplinary' perspectives can be found in two separate essays by French post-structuralist writers Jean Baudrillard (1929–) and Gilles Deleuze (1925–95). In a short, critical book entitled *Forget Foucault*, Baudrillard (1987) claims that Foucault's work in *Discipline and Punish* gives too much credence to the concept of power, and that Foucault's book was itself part of a fading era; as such, Baudrillard seems to reject Foucault's power perspective, and the concept of 'technologies of power'. Baudrillard (1983; 1993) instead argues that contemporary Western societies are societies of 'simulation' (of surface, image, appearance, digitization, and perfect replicability, an era in which the electronic or genetic 'copy' is indistinguishable from the 'original'). From this perspective, the imagery produced by CCTV cameras, for instance, should not be theorized in terms of attempts to 'know' the truth about the person under surveillance, but more in terms of the odd combination of visual proximity and emotional distance that the electronic image produces, or the voyeurism or even the banality of its reality TV. Although Baudrillard sees himself as standing in stark opposition to Foucault, others see certain potential linkages between their work. Bogard (1996) has argued that Foucault's work on surveillance can be combined with Baudrillard's work on simulation, helping us recognize that today electronic forms of surveillance may involve elements both of Foucauldian surveillance and of Baudrillard's simulation in their (electronic) representation of the person under surveillance. With the emergence of electronic forms of surveillance producing electronic representations of the person or thing under surveillance, we also enter an era in which those representations can be electronically recorded, analysed and replayed. For Bogard, the possibilities that various electronic surveillance systems offer in terms of their enabling surveillance to begin to escape from the ties of the here-and-now are tied into the wider emergence not just of an information society but of 'the conversion of persons and social relations into the universal ether of information, which is their simulation' (1996: 69).

Deleuze, too, has contributed (albeit in brief) to post-disciplinary perspectives in an essay suggesting that Foucault's third 'technology of power' (disciplinary power) may presently be being replaced by a fourth, which he terms 'control'. Deleuze's (1995) essay is more than a little opaque, but he seems to be suggesting that contemporary capitalism, with its electronic communications, dynamic consumer economy, geographic mobility, and fluid organizational techniques, gives rise to a cultural form in which disciplinary institutions become superseded by life-long flow control systems (see Jones, 2000; Haggerty and Ericson, 2000; see also Lyon, 2003). Deleuze might point to electronic tagging of offenders (particularly involving satellite tracking) as an example of this form of control—rather than being detained in a prison, today's society is able to punish and control even while 'setting free'. Tracking tags, like electronic access cards, can permit/disallow (cards) or warn against (tags) entry to a particular zone or place, possibly at a particular time or day. In this way, such tags 'modulate' a given offender's daily routine, rather than simply restricting it or subject it to traditional surveillance supervision. Moreover, tracking tags themselves from this perspective appear just another instance of a greater system of electronic access controls, swipe cards, RFID cards (see below), PIN numbers, biometric recognition systems, login names and passwords, and so on—each with their own 'access privileges' and limitations. In a suitably equipped apartment block, an RFID card waved at the shared entrance can grant all residents access to the foyer, but waved at a sensor in one of the lifts, allows each resident access only to the floor on which their apartment is situated. (There's a certain analogy with users logging on to a computer system and being able to access certain shared folders, but only their own private folders, on a shared network server.) As such, if there's surveillance at work, it is less the tracking of individual users, and more simply the granting of electronic keys, which allow users to lead their lives just as with any other sort of keys. In some cases, such keys may be enabling or even liberating. Yet they also are likely to leave a little digital record somewhere in a digital archive each time they are used. From the point of view of the key issuer, day-to-day surveillance of the vast majority of users probably is not necessary; the archived record is a way to reconstruct events should something go awry. But nevertheless, the potential to combine this mass of stored data and to build up a 'picture' of a person's activities, communications, interests, financial transactions, and so on, seems to bring us back toward the intensive, person-centred focus of Foucauldian surveillance.

REVIEW QUESTIONS

1 What does Foucault mean by 'discipline' and 'surveillance'? For Foucault, what is the relationship between punishment and social control?

2 What are 'post-disciplinary' theories of surveillance, and why might there be a need for such theories today?

Surveillance technologies

Having considered some of the main theoretical *perspectives* within sociological criminology on the topic of surveillance, this section will discuss various different surveillance *technologies*.

Surveillance cameras

Perhaps one of the best-known forms of surveillance today is closed-circuit television (CCTV) camera surveillance. In the UK, CCTV camera usage expanded dramatically during the 1990s, partly as a result of Home Office backing of CCTV city street schemes. The number of CCTV cameras also increased over this same time period in shopping centres and malls, on roads and highways, within private premises (homes, offices, shops) and in institutions such as prisons. Their increase in popularity over this time is probably due to the technology becoming more affordable, a belief that CCTV cameras would somehow 'deter' crime, and a wider shift toward usage of situational crime prevention measures generally on the part of individuals and organizations (see Garland, 2001).

CCTV is often thought of as being a form of situation crime prevention (SCP), following Clarke's (1995) classic classification of situational crime prevention techniques. Clarke identifies 'increasing the risk of detection' as one of the three main ways in which

SCP can work. During the 1990s it was often presumed that the appearance of CCTV cameras in a place or area would 'deter' offenders from offending because of the offender's perception of the greatly increased risk of getting caught. Much of the research into CCTV during this time were evaluations of schemes (whether in a city centre, or certain shops or institutions), trying to establish whether schemes did indeed have such an effect; whether they were having no effect; whether they were instead merely 'displacing' criminal activity to other areas nearby lacking CCTV; or whether they were not only working but were also 'diffusing' benefits to other areas nearby lacking CCTV (Brown, 1995; Tilley, 1993; Ditton and Short, 1999). Research findings are mixed, but seem to suggest that in many cases CCTV schemes do not seem nearly as effective at crime reduction as their early proponents had hoped, and indeed research suggests that something as simple as improving street lighting may be more effective. It should be noted that a scheme's effectiveness may depend on various factors, and that effectiveness may vary over time. In a study comparing the effectiveness of the crime preventive effects of CCTV surveillance cameras and improved street lighting both in Britain and in America, Welsh and Farrington 'found that they are equally effective in reducing crime ... that improved street lighting was more effective in reducing crime in city centers, that both were more effective in reducing property crimes than violent crimes, and that both measures were far more effective in reducing crime in Britain than in America' (Welsh and Farrington, 2004: 497). They also noted that in Britain city centre CCTV cameras generally appear popular with the public.

However, in addition to (or in place of) any deterrent effect achieved, an attraction of CCTV surveillance is that even if it does not deter an offence, if the camera is pointing in the correct direction and the images are being recorded then a visual record of the offence is made which could be used to apprehend the offender and/or secure conviction in a court. (Issues relating to (poor) image quality and recording quality seem likely to become less significant as technology improves.) During the commission of an offence, CCTV surveillance cameras may prove useful in coordinating police or security staff deployment, with a central operator able to radio staff on the ground as to the exact location(s) they should go, the nature of the offence(s), and the appearance of the offender(s). It may be that these applications of CCTV, involving their combination with recording and communications technologies, which lend them evidential and resource-allocation applications respectively, eventually take over as the 'justification' for CCTV. Norris *et al.* (1998) raise a third possible way in which CCTV can be combined with other technologies, namely, the connecting of camera output to a computer running facial recognition software. The computer can attempt to match facial image data from CCTV live feeds with facial image data stored on a database of known individuals (known or suspected offenders, for example). The software uses techniques which in theory can match images even where an offender has sought to disguise themselves. A city-centre scheme using the technology is in use in Newham, East London. Norris *et al.* (1998) characterize such systems as 'algorhythmic surveillance', and suggest that they represent an intensification of surveillance and a step toward intensified social control. It seems possible however that CCTV visual recognition systems will turn out to have one of two specific uses. The first is as a technical assistant to busy CCTV operators, flagging up 'known offenders' as they appear on a street. There are various privacy objections to such practices, yet they may still become integrated into traditional policing practices. A second role is likely to be as part of a biometric identity validation device, for entry control systems (such systems are presently being introduced at certain European airports, for restricted personnel areas, or at passenger security gates).

Two important aspects of the development of surveillance cameras seem likely to shape their usage over the next decade. The first is miniaturization, leading to the increasing possibility of concealed cameras (whether such surveillance is being carried out lawfully or not). This is likely to have social ramifications as areas previously hidden from public view become more visible, with the attendant social consequences (in Goffman's terms, the 'backstage' becomes 'frontstage'). Areas increasingly subjected to such surveillance might include police stations and prisons themselves. A second (related) aspect seems likely to be the connection of miniature cameras to mobile communications. Already being produced and marketed for their 'picture messaging' and 'video call' features, suitably equipped phones can send or receive images from one place to another. Both aspects enable the surveillance of areas of social life that may already have been accessible but whose activities had previously been undocumented. Both developments have the potential to contribute to social change.

Finally, it is important to note that although in terms of CCTV applications, we are most familiar with city-centre CCTV schemes and with CCTV in and around private properties (offices, shops, homes, and so on), there are various other possible applications of CCTV in relation to crime control and criminal justice. Among these are the use of CCTV in prisons, on roads and highways in conjunction with (excess) speed detectors, in ATM bank teller machines as a check against bank and credit card fraud, in courts as a way of linking proceedings between remote sites, and in the custody suites in police stations. On this last topic, Newburn and Hayman (2002) conducted detailed sociological research on the effects of the introduction of CCTV in the custody suite in a police station in London, England. Their study shows how the functions the CCTV system performed were not always as had been anticipated, and that to understand how it was used and its effects one needs to understand the social dynamics of the police custody suite itself. Such studies thus suggest that CCTV does not have some generic or intrinsic 'function', but rather that the uses to which it is put depend on various contingent local factors.

Electronic monitoring of convicted offenders

Research into the possibility of 'electronically tagging' convicted offenders can be dated back to the early 1960s, and may even have been considered earlier. In 1964, four Harvard University academics published an article on 'behavioural electronics', one of whom by 1970 had developed a prototype electronic system for tracking a person's movements within a city (Schwitzgebel et al., 1964; Schwitzgebel, 1970). Bulky, cumbersome, and impractical, their device was essentially experimental. By 1983, however, the advent of the silicon chip permitted smaller devices to be developed, and in the US a New Mexico judge is said to have pioneered the introduction of the electronic monitoring of convicted offenders as a feasible sentencing option for the courts. The first time a person in England was electronically tagged in a criminal justice context was in 1989, when a man was granted bail on condition that he 'voluntarily agreed' to have a device attached to him (Lilly and Himan, 1993: 1). Various pieces of legislation were introduced by the then Conservative government in the UK during the late 1980s and 1990s. Tagging schemes were opposed on moral and ethical grounds by various groups, though once in power the Labour government has since sought to expand rather than contract such schemes, and opposition to them on political or ethical grounds, though still occasionally voiced, is presently much less pronounced.

In formal terms, from the 1980s through to today, courts and the law have presented the 'tagging' of offenders with electronic 'tags' not as a punishment in and of itself, but rather as a device by which compliance with a specific other penalty can be monitored. In the 1980s and 1990s, the most common application of the electronic monitoring of offenders was alongside a home detention curfew order. The 'first generation' of electronic tags do not in fact have any capability of 'tracking' an individual tagged offender's movements as such. Rather, the limited radio transmitter technology used in the tags—which is similar to that found in short range (thirty to one hundred metres) domestic cordless telephones—is exploited to ensure that an individual is in fact at home in compliance with their curfew order (typically 6 p.m.–6 a.m. or similar). The tag is attached to the offender after sentencing, usually in the form of a smallish plastic anklet in which the transmitter is encased, and a base unit is installed in the offender's home and connected to a dedicated telephone line. During the pre-arranged curfew hours, the base unit 'listens' out for an intermittent signal pulse transmitted by the anklet. As long as it hears the pulse, nothing happens. But if no pulse is detected—because the offender has moved out of the receiving range of the base unit, and hence must therefore no longer be at home—the base unit automatically dials a monitoring centre, which can then alert a member of their staff (or potentially a probation or police officer) and request they investigate the breach. Electronic monitoring using this technology has now been implemented in a number of jurisdictions including England and Wales, Scotland, several US states, Canada, Sweden, New Zealand and Australia (see Black and Smith, 2003; Scottish Executive, 2000). Courts in England and Wales seem to have been relatively reluctant to adopt electronically monitored curfew orders as an initial disposal, possibly because of uncertainty as to its severity as a punishment or appropriateness for particular offences or offenders. In England and Wales today, many offenders being electronically monitored at any given moment are not in fact offenders whom a court has so sentenced, but are actually prisoners who have been granted early conditional release from their medium-term prison sentences, the conditions including that they must not re-offend and that they must abide by an electronically-monitored home detention curfew order for the remainder of the time that would have been their prison sentence duration (see Home Office, 2001). Many prisoners have now passed through this scheme.

While the electronic monitoring of offenders' compliance with a home detention curfew order is surveillance of sorts, it is also in certain respects only of a fairly limited kind. The tag does not 'know' the location of the tagged offender as such, merely whether they are or are not at home. Nor does it know what the offender is doing while they are at home, nor where they are of what they are doing during non-curfew hours. As such, and while this practice bears some relation to Foucauldian disciplinary surveillance, it also appears somewhat different, being much more limited and superficial in kind.

Recent years, however, have witnessed the emergence of a 'second generation' of electronic tags, which look set to supersede and replace the earlier generation tags. These newer 'tracking' tags (currently being trialled in England) incorporate a combination of mobile cellular phone technology and Global Positioning System (GPS) technology. The GPS technology enables the tag to identify its (and hence its wearer's) exact geographical position, while the mobile cell phone technology enables the tag to relay this positional data back to a monitoring centre. Whilst the initial application of such tags is likely to be in monitoring compliance with home detention curfew, attendance, or exclusion orders, it is not hard to see how these 'tracking tags' could permit a far more continual and detailed form of surveillance, at least in terms of monitoring an offender's geographical location (and hence even possible activity or intent). Advocates of such tags argue that a possible benefit of their implementation could be that tags could provide additional geographical evidence linking the tagged offender with any subsequent offences in their known whereabouts (or indeed exonerating them of these offences), and that they might provide further reassurance to the public while contributing to a reduction in reliance on custodial sentences. Critics argue that, as with the earlier tags, tagging itself does nothing meaningful by way of addressing an offender's offending behaviour; and that the continual, detailed geographical monitoring of a person's movements (even if they are a convicted offender) is a worrying development within liberal democratic societies. On the latter criticism, while such tags would indeed represent an escalation in the intensity of surveillance in certain respects, it is hard to see the argument winning the day so long as the alternative to such electronic monitoring of curfew/attendance/exclusion orders remains a prison sentence, which would seem to be even more restrictive in terms of curtailment of freedom of movement and privacy.

Internet surveillance

Internet 'surveillance' can take many forms, but arguably can be reduced to one of two main types. The first type involves gathering information about a specific user. The second type, on the other hand, involves gathering data about a large group of Internet users (for example, all visitors to a particular website) which is then aggregated as a data set and analysed for patterns or for time trends. Surveillance of the first kind (a specific user's Internet usage) might be carried out, for example, by an employer who suspects an employee of improper Internet usage, or of betraying commercial secrets to a rival company. Internet surveillance of an individual might also be carried out by the police (for example, investigating an individual suspected of downloading or trading in computer images of child pornography), or indeed by state intelligence agencies seeking to gather information on a specific individual's communications, activities and associates. Monitoring of groups of people's usage of the Internet, on the other hand, might be conducted by an Internet Service Provider interested in patterns of usage by their customers, or by a computer security chief tracking the changing methods used by the many hackers trying to hack into their organization's network.

The technical methods used to gather the information might be similar for both types, but they might be different. Surveillance (if this is the proper term) of individual Internet users can be carried out by a computing officer in a company or institution simply by examining log files routinely generated by network servers, which record which user logged on from which computer, at what time, and for how long; by examining proxy servers which may reveal which websites an individual visited; or e-mail servers to establish what e-mails a user has sent, when, to whom, and what information these contained (Casey, 2000). In addition, a computing officer can also obtain considerable information by examining the hard disc drive of individual computers or, where this is not possible, by capturing a 'snapshot' of network traffic as it passes through a network. Additional means of tracking an individual user's computing activities include keystroke monitors; spyware installed on the computer; and remote screen-view software, enabling remote viewing of an individual's computer screen in real time. Most computer activities leave an electronic 'trace' of some sort, on a hard disc or on a network server or both, and virtually all network activity is traceable back to specific network addresses and ultimately back to specific computers. However, as with all forms of surveillance, the more knowledgeable the person (potentially) under surveillance is about the surveillance practices likely to be used against them, the more strategies they can employ to try to evade surveillance.

In practice, 'surveillance' of employees' Internet usage is likely to remain at a general background level, at least until a case of improper Internet usage comes to the attention of someone in computing security, company management, or law enforcement. Their attention may be drawn by a complaint from someone within or outside their company; by the police; by a routine sweep of log files by a computing officer looking for suspect sites visited or files downloaded; or by a piece of monitoring software set to run in the background on a network, looking out for certain suspicious network activity. When one of these events alerts an organization to a potential problem, they can then proceed with a forensic investigation in search of data, which may or may not involve surveillance of particular individuals or computers.

Lastly, it is worth mentioning briefly, as another form of the second kind of internet 'surveillance', the practice of using 'cookies'. Often used to add functionality to a website by tracking individual users' preferences (by storing a small 'cookie' data file on the user's own hard disk), cookies can also be used by the website owners to analyse user visits to their sites (which links were followed, how long users looked at each page, and so on). In practice, such data is likely to be of interest to the website owners only as an aggregate of all visitors. Moreover, visitors can choose to disable/reject cookies on their computer should they wish. As forms of surveillance such practices thus appear quite limited. However, cookies remind us that companies (especially retailers and media providers) are often keen to obtain as much information about their customers (or potential customers) as they can, and may exploit new technological features to obtain such information.

Surveillance of wireless communications

Wireless communication can take many forms, including voice or data transmissions over mobile cellular telephones, wireless Internet connections ('WiFi'), short-range wireless connection technologies such as 'Bluetooth', micro radio tags such as RFIDs, and microwave or satellite links. In many respects, the surveillance of wireless communications is conceptually no different to the surveillance of telephone data, or other landline telecommunications. Nevertheless, certain differences exist as between landline and wireless communications. The first is that wireless communications involves the broadcasting of data (even if this is very low power and hence over a very short range), and as such it has a certain intrinsic 'openness' theoretically leaving it susceptible to eavesdropping. With wireless communications of all kinds seemingly likely to become ever more ubiquitous, this would seem to present various additional opportunities for communications to be subjected to surveillance. The second is that insofar as wireless communications enable an increased user-mobility, they seem to attach more closely to a person (or persons) rather than to a locale. As such, the wireless transmission seems more likely to relate directly to a given person (and their life), and hence its surveillance may be particularly revealing as to a person's activities. Finally, while ironically wireless technologies permit greater geographical freedom of communication, freeing users from geographically fixed communications points, the combination of the need for network addresses to manage communications together with the likely future ubiquity within mobile communications devices of geographic location technologies such as GPS, means that in future there may be potential not only to conduct surveillance on a user's communications but on their physical location too.

A form of surveillance of sorts is presently emerging in respect of the tagging of goods in retail stores with miniature identifier tags. These tags potentially can be concealed within a product's packaging or indeed within the product itself. These RFID (Radio Frequency Identification) tags transmit data which identify such things as exact details of the product (which might be anything from a carton of milk, to a DVD, to a pair of shoes), its price, and the name of the retail store in question. RFID tags have short transmission range, but are sufficient for a store to use the tags' movements in order quickly to calculate the total price of a basket of groceries at a supermarket; to track points of interest for marketers such as which goods are picked up, examined, but ultimately put back on the shelves by consumers; and as a means of combating shoplifting, the idea being that the tiny tags are hard to find and remove. The nature of the tags appears to be that to track them, a sensor needs to be in very close proximity; thus, an individual's clothes cannot easily be tracked walking down the street, but should they move through a scanning gateway (of a similar sort to that already installed at entrances/exits to shops to combat shoplifting), their passage through the gateway could in theory be recorded. Indeed, civil liberties groups have already suggested that stores may not bother to remove RFID tags from products at point of sale, opening up the possibility not only that the product's movements could be tracked in the future using the tag, but that other stores may track each other's tags entering and leaving their stores (which marketers may find useful in understanding patterns of consumption, for example, Store X finding that some people who shop at their store have also bought Brand Y designer clothes from Store Z). RFID tags could thus potentially usher in a new era of the monitoring of product movements and consumer behaviour.

Other technologies used in surveillance

The above represent just some of the many different surveillance (and related) technologies in use today. A few additional types are worth mentioning. The first is computer databases. The development of computer technology, especially since the 1980s, has meant that large amounts of data can be stored on and recalled from computer databases. The difference between such databases and former paper-based archives is essentially the ability to search records very quickly, giving databases a quality that paper archives never had. An example of a database in the UK is the Police National Computer. However, it is not entirely clear whether computer databases are themselves actually 'surveillance technologies', or whether they are merely technologies that can be used in conjunction with other surveillance practices, in order to store and retrieve surveillance information obtained. Having said that, such a distinction is less clear in instances where the surveillance practice and the database appear one and the same, such as in the case of computer activity log files.

A second surveillance technology worth mentioning briefly, not least because of its likely expansion over the coming years, is the biometric sensor (see Lyon, 2001: Chapter 5; van der Ploeg, 2003). Biometric sensors can be used in conjunction with computer databases to identify individuals. Such sensors work by obtaining various measurements of biological features unique to each individual, such as iris pattern, fingerprint or handprint, and comparing this data to previously recorded data of the same type in a database. The first of the two most obvious applications for biometric devices is as part of access control systems, such as at airport check-in desks, immigration desks, or in order to log on to a computer. However, as with any such access control information, the information about who has passed through the access control could be used for surveillance purposes, either of a generalized kind (aggregate information) or for conducting surveillance of a specific individual. The difference between biometric access control systems and other types (such as using passwords, identity documents, or electronic cards) is that it is much harder for an individual to use a false identity. The second application of biometric sensors is in terms of surveillance of a person's recent use of drugs or alcohol, or of their medical condition. Alcohol 'breathalysers' have been used for several decades in countries around the world, principally in the area of motoring, though they appear increasingly to be used in other areas of transportation, such as to ensure that airline pilots are not intoxicated prior to flight. Drug testing of arrestees at police stations is another application of such testing technology, in this case principally in order to try to gather data on patterns and trends in illegal drug use among the arrestee population.

REVIEW QUESTIONS

1 What are some of the surveillance technologies in use today? How does each work, and what information do they gather?

2 What difference, if any, is there between surveillance technologies, and technologies that can be used for surveillance?

The 'architecture' of surveillance and monitoring

In this penultimate section, I will present my own interpretation of surveillance practices and technologies, and in so doing attempt to contribute to existing theoretical models of surveillance.

Table 23.1 is an attempt at a typology of different kinds of surveillance. The aim of the typology is to distinguish between the various different types of surveillance discussed in this chapter, and to help compare and contrast between them. (Incidentally, the typology applies both to surveillance in the real world and on the Internet (one can imagine each of the types in the context of the Internet) and thus provides us with a model for interpreting surveillance on the Internet generally.) However, Table 23.1 also serves another purpose. Because it distinguishes between different surveillance practices by distinguishing between practices in different social contexts (by whom, of whom, to what end), my argument is that it is possible to use a similar typology to analyse monitoring practices. (Monitoring was defined at the beginning of the chapter as a system designed to warn individuals about their conduct or to warn or alert the authorities that something untoward had happened or was about to happen.) In terms of Table 23.1 surveillance

Table 23.1 A typology of surveillance

By whom	Of whom or what	Overt or covert	Method	Comments
1. Intelligence agencies	Political or criminal threats to state security	Covert	Human and/or technological	
2. Law enforcement agencies	Suspected (serious) criminals	Covert	Human and/or technological	
3. Employers, private detectives, individuals	Specific individuals suspected of wrongdoing	Covert	Human and/or technological	
4. Public sector staff or private sector management	Institutionalized or employees	Overt	Mostly human, some technology	Foucauldian surveillance, 'discipline'
5. Guardians of places, people, or things	A place, person(s), or thing(s)	Overt, but may be covert	Human and/or technological	Police, neighbourhood watch, private security guards, CCTV, 'tags'
6. Anyone	Behaviour of family, friends, workers, public	Overt	Human	Informal social control

types, we could thus distinguish between intelligence agencies' (type 1) use of surveillance practices (i.e. spying) and their use of ongoing monitoring systems designed to alert them to certain circumstances of interest or concern, such as intense bursts of communications between foreign embassies and their home nations, or certain movements by another nation's armed forces. Similarly, in terms of the (type 5) guarding of the private space of a shop and its stock, for example, the shop owners could employ a store detective to conduct surveillance of known or suspected shoplifters, but could also tag their stock with magnetic strips or RFID tags as part of a system of monitoring stock (an alarm only sounds when an attempt is made to remove goods from the store without having paid for them).

In this final section I will argue that while a key factor in determining the effectiveness of all types of surveillance is the effectiveness of mechanisms of ensuring that the person under surveillance complies with the system of surveillance, it is also precisely the inescapability of surveillance and the compliance with surveillance so demanded that lends surveillance its peculiar quality, and one that many people find so objectionable. This formulation may sound odd at first glance, but it is important to understand that there are many reasons why a person may not wish to be subjected to surveillance (for example, loss of privacy, autonomy, trust, or control) and may thus actively resist or seek to subvert it. Given this, it may be useful for surveillance studies to borrow from research in areas such as on compliance in the context of criminal justice. Bottoms (2001) has pioneered work on the specific topic of compliance and community penalties, and has distinguished between various ways in which compliance can be sought, including threats of penalties for non-compliance, affective attachment, perceived legitimacy and others. Although of likely relevance to the study of surveillance, there is insufficient space to explore all these ways in this present chapter, so I will focus on just one, namely a compliance mode which Bottoms terms 'constraint-based compliance' and which I term 'architectural' (following Lessig, 1999). The particular aspect of interest of the architectural/constraint mode of compliance is that it refers to the 'designing in' of features or systems such that (in theory, anyhow) a person has no choice but to comply. (Within the field of crime prevention, situational crime prevention can be seen as the 'architectural' mode of crime prevention.) The architectural mode typically exploits physical, real-world properties, or virtual, software properties in order to try to ensure compliance.

On reflection, we can see that the exploitation of physical properties lies at the very heart of surveillance. Human surveillance is based on proximity, lines of sight, observing, and hearing what another has to say. Foucault's disciplinary surveillance is centrally concerned with the observable, with the capacity of the human body to be trained, with physical segregation and isolation, and in the figure of the Panopticon we find Bentham's ingenious exploitation of architecture and optics, such that the central prison guard can see all the prisoners but not vice versa. More recently, we can see that biometric sensors exploit certain unique identifiers of our bodies and our inability to escape from our given body; CCTV cameras exploit optics, but are also themselves constrained by lines of sight; contemporary telephone surveillance can exploit features of digital telephone exchanges to obtain lists of numbers dialled and calls received, and can make electronic recordings of calls; websites can use information automatically received by the web server about each visitor to the website to identify the approximate geographical location of the visitor; RFID tags seem a classic example of an architectural solution to the problem of keeping track of stock movements; and lastly, and perhaps most centrally, the covert surveillance practices of types 1–3 in the typology rely on their hidden nature to obtain information. However, resistance to surveillance also typically exploits physical properties and the limits of the surveillance practice in question, as in the case of political activists, football hooligans or bank robbers who conceal their identity from CCTV cameras by the simple device of wearing a mask or even merely a hat.

A key possibility here, and one that Lessig (1999) is particularly good at identifying and discussing, is the way in which states and hardware and software manufacturers sometimes try to 'design in' features that will enable them to conduct surveillance of one kind or another on the users of computer, electronic or network systems. The concept of architecture is useful here, because, as Lessig explains, what may appear merely a technical question of system design often (intentionally or unintentionally) masks political and social choices and the implementation of certain preferred social and political values. This sometimes happens without any prior social or political debate. (Lessig gives the example of user anonymity in online forums; anonymity may encourage freedom of speech but also facilitate antisocial behaviours (verbal attacks on other users, or hate speech), whereas forbidding anonymity may restrict antisocial behaviour but also inhibit freedom of expression.) An implication of this is that it is important to recognize that architecture and constraint-based compliance systems are not homogeneous, but are instead quite diverse, and that society has a choice as to what *sort* of architectures it wants for its surveillance systems. Moreover, although architectures constrain, they also always simultaneously enable certain practices. In the case of surveillance architectures, the least objectionable today may precisely be those technologies that are sufficiently effective while remaining as unobtrusive, uninvasive, and speedy as possible. However, there may well be a strong linkage with another of Bottoms' factors underpinning compliance mechanisms, namely legitimacy, in that this acceptability may only hold good so long as the information so obtained is recognized as being legitimate information for the surveillance system to obtain given the circumstances. In the absence of such legitimacy the public may deeply resent a given surveillance practice, particularly if it is powerful and rapidly executed.

The penultimate point to make about architecture is that it may be exploited both by surveillance practices and by what are in fact better characterized as monitoring practices. Whereas surveillance practices are concerned with obtaining ongoing detailed information about certain specific individuals, monitoring practices could be said to involve the implementation of ongoing warning systems running 'in the background'. In this regard, it can be seen that the two can be mutually complementary, and that insofar as they rely on technological systems the effectiveness of their practices may depend on how cleverly they utilize architectural properties.

In summary then, the concept of 'architecture' provides a way of analysing both how surveillance works (and in particular its technological dimension, or the way it utilizes physical or virtual properties) and what its limits may be. The architectural dimension is nevertheless just one aspect of surveillance and other features such as legitimacy and social norms are also important. Finally, the concept of architecture is useful because it also helps draw attention to the relationship between technical design and political values.

REVIEW QUESTIONS

1 What difference, if any, is there between 'surveillance' and 'monitoring'?

2 Why might citizens not wish to comply with surveillance or monitoring systems? In what circumstances do you think people are more likely to find surveillance or monitoring acceptable?

CONCLUSION

This chapter has covered a number of topics, including definitions of surveillance and monitoring, some of the key theoretical models, and some particular contemporary technologies of surveillance and monitoring. Foucault's theoretical work on disciplinary surveillance remains influential, but Foucault's understanding of surveillance was originally targeted not so much at the 'Big Brother' state, as at our everyday institutions. Critical (civil libertarian, or Marxist) approaches to surveillance technologies reveal some of the political abuses to which they can be put. Today, however, we live with a spectrum of technologies (with new technologies emerging all the time) whose applications vary from intentional, covert surveillance at one extreme, to CCTV cameras in shops in which we shop every day, through to systems whose everyday applications seem not really designed for surveillance purposes at all, but which could possibly be put to such ends (CCTV cameras on motorways, entrance swipe cards, RFID chips in retail products). Many issues regarding surveillance then ultimately come back to issues to do with security, convenience, privacy, and the adequacy of theories of social control.

QUESTIONS FOR DISCUSSION

1 What is Michel Foucault's contribution to the study of surveillance, and what are the similarities and differences between his approach and that of Marxists?

2 What are some of the different types of surveillance that could be carried out? What sort of technologies could this surveillance use, and what information would these technologies help gather?

3 Compare and contrast surveillance carried out directly by people, with surveillance using technology. From the point of view of the person or organization conducting the surveillance, what are the strengths and weaknesses of the two?

4 Where should society decide to draw the line between surveillance and privacy? How should this line be decided?

5 Why might someone try to counteract surveillance, and how might they try to do this?

GUIDE TO FURTHER READING

Bogard, W. (1996) *The Simulation of Surveillance: Hypercontrol in Telematic Societies*.
Cambridge: Cambridge University Press. A suggestive postmodern exploration of contemporary and future surveillance.

Foucault, M. (1979) *Discipline and Punish: The Birth of the Prison*, London: Penguin.
While primarily concerned with punishment, and not always an easy read, this book nevertheless remains an essential part of the repertoire for anyone interested in surveillance. See especially centre illustrative plates, pp. 3–8, Parts 3.2, 3.3 and 4.3.

Lyon, D. (2001) *Surveillance Society: Monitoring Everyday Life*, Buckingham: Open University Press.
An interesting discussion of contemporary surveillance theories, technologies, and political issues.

WEB LINKS

http://www.queensu.ca/sociology/Surveillance/intro.htm
The Surveillance Project. Run by David Lyon and colleagues at the sociology department of the Queen's University, Canada.

www.surveillance-and-society.org
Surveillance and Society. A peer-reviewed transdisciplinary online surveillance studies journal.

www.liberty-human-rights.org.uk
Liberty. Website of a leading UK civil liberties pressure group. Includes information on their privacy concerns regarding various surveillance policies and technologies.

www.wired.com
Wired. US-based website containing a wide range of news stories and features on the latest technological developments, including cultural, governmental, and privacy issues.

www.homeoffice.gov.uk
Home Office. Website of a UK ministry responsible for dealing with crime, policing, criminal justice, counter-terrorism, and immigration.

REFERENCES

Barry, A., Osborne, T. and Rose, N. (eds) (1996) *Foucault and Political Reason: Liberalism, Neo-Liberalism and Governmentality*. London: UCL Press.

Baudrillard, J. (1983) *Simulations [aka 'Simulacra and Simulations']*. New York: Semiotext(e).

Baudrillard, J. (1987) *Forget Foucault*. New York: Semiotext(e).

Baudrillard, J. (1993) *Symbolic Exchange and Death*. London: Sage.

Black, M. and Smith, R.G. (2003) 'Electronic Monitoring in the Criminal Justice System', *Trends and Issues in Crime and Criminal Justice* No. 254. Canberra: Australian Institute of Criminology.

Bogard, W. (1996) *The Simulation of Surveillance: Hypercontrol in Telematic Societies*. Cambridge: Cambridge University Press.

Bottoms, A.E. (2001). 'Compliance and community penalties', in A.E. Bottoms, L. Gelsthorpe and S. Rex (eds), *Community Penalties: Change and Challenges*. Cullompton: Willan.

Brown, B. (1995) *CCTV in Town Centres: Three case studies (Crime Detection and Prevention Series: Paper 68)*. London: Home Office, Police Department.

Casey, E. (2000) *Digital Evidence and Computer Crime*. London: Academic Press.

Clarke, R.V. (1995). 'Situational crime prevention', in M. Tonry and D. Farrington (eds), *Building a Safer Society: Crime and Justice: A Review of Research*, Vol. 19. Chicago: University of Chicago Press.

Cohen, S. (1985) *Visions of Social Control: Crime, Punishment and Classification*. Cambridge: Polity.

Cohen, S. and Scull, A. (eds) (1983) *Social Control and the State*. Oxford: Martin Robertson.

Deleuze, G. (1995) 'Postscript on control societies', in *Negotiations: 1972–1990*. New York: Columbia University Press.

Ditton, J. and Short, E. (1999) 'Yes, it works—no, it doesn't: Comparing the effects of open-street CCTV in two adjacent town centres', *Crime Prevention Studies*, Vol. 10: 201–23.

Dreyfus, H. and Rabinow, P. (1982) *Michel Foucault: Beyond Structuralism and Hermeneutics*. Hemel Hempstead: Harvester Wheatsheaf.

Feeley, M. and Simon, J. (1992) 'The New Penology: Notes on the Emerging Strategy of Corrections and its Implications', *Criminology*, Vol. 30 (4): 449–74.

Feeley, M. and Simon, J. (1994) 'Actuarial justice: the emerging new criminal law', in D. Nelken (ed) *The Futures of Criminology*. London: Sage.

Foucault, M. (1979) *Discipline and Punish: The Birth of the Prison*. London: Penguin.

Foucault, M. (1991) 'Governmentality', in G. Burchell *et al.* (ed) *The Foucault Effect: Studies in Governmentality*. Hemel Hempstead: Harvester Wheatsheaf.

Garland, D. (1985) *Punishment and Welfare: A History of Penal Strategies*. Aldershot: Gower.

Garland, D. (1990) *Punishment and Modern Society: A Study in Social Theory*. Oxford: Clarendon.

Garland, D. (1997) ' "Governmentality" and the Problem of Crime: Foucault, Criminology, Sociology', *Theoretical Criminology*, 1(2): 173–214.

Garland, D. (2001) *The Culture of Control: Crime and Social Order in Contemporary Society*. Oxford: Oxford University Press.

Gordon, C. (ed) (1980) *Power/Knowledge: Selected Interviews and Other Writings*. Hemel Hempstead: Harvester Wheatsheaf.

Haggerty, K. and Ericson, R.V. (2000) 'The surveillant assemblage', *British Journal of Sociology*, 51 (4): 605–22.

Home Office (2001) *Electronic monitoring of released prisoners: an evaluation of the Home Detention Curfew scheme: Home Office Research Studies 222*. London: Home Office.

Jones, R. (2000) 'Digital Rule: Punishment, Control and Technology', *Punishment and Society*, 2 (1): 5–22.

Lessig, L. (1999). *Code and Other Laws of Cyberspace*. New York, NY: Basic Books.

Lilly, J.R. and Himan, J. (eds), (1993). *The Electronic Monitoring of Offenders: Symposium Papers, Second Series*. Leicester: De Montfort University Law School Monographs.

Lyon, D. (2003) 'Surveillance as social sorting: Computer codes and mobile bodies', in D. Lyon (ed) *Surveillance as Social Sorting: Privacy, Risk and Digital Discrimination*. London: Routledge.

Lyon, D. (1993) 'An Electronic Panopticon? A Sociological Critique of Surveillance Theory', *Sociological Review*, 41 (4): 653.

Lyon, D. (1994) *The Electronic Eye: The Rise of Surveillance Society*. Cambridge: Polity.

Lyon, D. (2001) *Surveillance Society: Monitoring Everyday Life*. Buckingham: Open University Press.

Newburn, T. and Hayman, S. (2002) *Policing, Surveillance and Social Control*. Cullompton: Willan Publishing.

Norris, C., Moran, J. and Armstrong, G. (1998) 'Algorithmic surveillance—The future of automated visual surveillance', in C. Norris, J. Moran and G. Armstrong (eds) *Surveillance, Closed Circuit Television and Social Control*. Aldershot: Ashgate.

Rusche, G. and Kirchheimer, O. (1968) *Punishment and Social Structure*. New York: Russell & Russell.

Schwitzgebel, R.K. (1970) 'Behavioral Electronics Could Empty the World's Prisons', *The Futurist*, April 1970: 59–60.

Schwitzgebel, R.K., *et al.* (1964) 'A Program of Research in Behavioral Electronics', *Behavioral Electronics*, 9: 233–8.

Scottish Executive (2000) *Tagging Offenders: The Role Of Electronic Monitoring In The Scottish Criminal Justice System* (Consultation paper), Edinburgh: Scottish Executive.

Simon, J. (1988) 'The Ideological Effects of Actuarial Practice', *Law and Society Review*, 22: 772–800.

Sumner, C. (ed) (1990). *Censure, Politics and Criminal Justice*. Buckingham: Open University Press.

Tilley, N. (1993). *Understanding Car Parks, Crime and CCTV: Evaluation Lesson from Safer Cities (Crime Prevention Unit: Paper 42)*. London: Home Office.

Van der Ploeg, I. (2003). 'Biometrics and the body as information', in D. Lyon (ed) *Surveillance as Social Sorting*. London: Routledge.

Welsh, B. and Farrington, D. (2004). 'Surveillance for Crime Prevention in Public Space: Results and Policy Choices in Britain and America', *Criminology and Public Policy*, 3(3) 497–526.

24 'Victims'

Brian Williams

INTRODUCTION

This chapter introduces the reader to the study of victims of crime and to the political and social changes which have brought victims increasingly to the centre of debates about crime. Academic research has helped to change our understanding of victimization, assisted by the insights and pressure of a growing victims' movement. The criminal justice system has itself gradually changed to reflect increased under-standing of victims' needs, and they have been accorded greater entitlements and rights—at least on paper. Some of the difficulties which prevent victims from taking up these rights are considered, and the effectiveness of particular approaches to meeting victims' needs in different countries is discussed. The greater centrality of victim issues is not necessarily reflected in greater sensitivity on the part of politicians or criminal justice practitioners, and the links between policies and practice are considered.

BACKGROUND

The academic study of victims of crime is a comparatively recent phenomenon, and the importance of victimology as a discipline has increased along with the growing social and political attention to issues of criminal victimization and how the criminal justice system should respond to victims. Since the 1970s, at first in North America and then elsewhere, the emergence of a vocal victims' movement has helped to increase the momentum for change in criminal justice policies affecting victims. In turn, this has increased the demand for research and knowledge about the effects of crime upon victims and the best ways of responding to their needs.

However, the first systematic study of victims was in the late 1940s, and its approach was extremely influential. It sought to understand the victimization process by examining the relationships between victims and offenders and classifying victims according to the degree to which they could be regarded as 'prone' to victimization (von Hentig, 1948). This attempt to produce a typology of victimization was emulated by a number of subsequent studies which tried to place victims on a spectrum from the randomly chosen to those who in some way helped to precipitate the crime (Mendelsohn, 1956; Wolf-gang, 1958; Amir, 1971; Gottfredson, 1984). In the process, the authors of these studies were perpetuating the idea that there are 'innocent' victims and others who—to a greater or lesser extent—contribute to their own victimization (Elias, 1993). Politicians, policy makers and criminal justice practitioners based their beliefs about victims on an understanding that there was a spectrum of blameworthiness, with some types of victims less deserving of credence and support than others.

It was only with the increasing influence of feminist criminologists that this stereotype (or ideal type) was challenged as a form of victim-blaming (see Mawby and Walklate, 1994; Williams, 1999). The early victimological studies used questionable research methods (often not involving any direct contact with victims themselves) and in many cases it was not difficult for critical criminologists from the 1970s onwards to challenge them on an intellectual level (Temkin, 1987; Radford, 2001). The damage in terms of the social and political influence of their publications had already been done, however, and there remains work for criminologists to do in terms of challenging commonsense beliefs about victims ('if you drive a Vauxhall Astra, it's bound to get stolen'; 'this fire seems suspicious—was it an insurance job?'; 'she asked for it, going out dressed like that').

This is not to deny that commonsense beliefs may have some foundation in reality, but rather to suggest that often they may not have the explanatory power necessary to justify giving them greater credence than hard evidence. The Vauxhall Astra *is* a relatively easy car to steal, but being told this does little to help the person reporting its theft, and may make her feel that the police are blaming her for her own victimization (Curry *et al.*, 2004). Perhaps the manufacturers should do something about the car's security systems. People undoubtedly do set fire to unsuccessful businesses in order to escape their debts, but this is not the only possible explanation for a pub catching fire, and the residents who narrowly escape a fire may not take kindly to being treated as arson suspects. The concept of 'contributory negligence', based upon a belief that women can provoke men to rape them by dressing in particular ways, depends upon particular beliefs about male sexuality which are not justified by the facts (Mullender, 1996; Kennedy, 1993). It also ignores the power dynamics involved— and this is a common theme in the more recent victimological writing which questions victim-blaming approaches and links them to hate crime against, for example, black people, people with disabilities and lesbian and gay people (Bowling, 1998; Shakespeare, 1996; Moran, 2001). For women, too, issues of power are central in relation to the criminal justice system. As senior barrister Helena Kennedy put it in the context of defence lawyers' tactics sometimes used in the case of 'domestic' murders by men (1993; 69), 'within the male stronghold of the court it is all too easy to create the feeling that a women had it coming to her'.

The academic and policy challenges posed by the women's movement (and subsequently by campaigns against other forms of discrimination) led to a number of different approaches to studying victims of crime. Rather than relying heavily upon statistics and case records compiled by criminal justice agencies, as the early victimologists did, researchers began to ask victims themselves about what had happened. This occurred both in the form of victim surveys (on local, national and international levels), and in a change of approach towards research methods which increasingly relied upon victims' own detailed accounts. Thus, victimology began to embrace both large scale empirical work aimed at producing reliable statistics on the prevalence and distribution of victimization, and smaller scale qualitative work which tried to hear and understand victims' experiences (for examples of survey methodology see Koffman, 1996; O'Mahony *et al.*, 2000; Kershaw *et al.*, 2001; MVA Consultancy, 2000; van Dijk, 2000; for qualitative studies see for example Boswell, 1999; Bowling, 1998; Temkin, 2002; Curry *et al.*, 2004). In the process, questions began to be raised about whether some people who had suffered criminal victimization were ever officially defined as victims, and about the processes which led to the systematic exclusion of some types of victims from the statistics. Where particular offences are less likely to be reported, there is a larger 'dark figure' of victims as well as of offenders. Some offences which are not generally accepted as such are particularly unlikely to yield large numbers of victims seeking help (obvious examples being so-called domestic violence, crimes committed against residents of institutions, and crimes with victims with difficulties in expressing their views, for example people with severe learning difficulties or communication problems). Increasingly in the UK, research since the 1990s has also taken the form of evaluative studies assessing the impact of criminal justice policies and practices on victims and the effectiveness of particular forms of victim services.

In the UK, the initial move in the late 1970s towards crime surveys which took victims' perceptions seriously was largely motivated by local government concerns about fear of crime and the concentration of some types of crime in poorer areas (see Williams, 1999: 47–8; Zedner, 2002: 421–5), as well as a desire to bring 'hidden' crime such as violence within the home out into the open. Crime surveys made a major contribution to increasing awareness of the real risks of criminal victimization, and they also had an impact upon the ways in which academic research was subsequently done (as had happened earlier in the USA). More recently, an international crime victimization survey has made it much easier to make reasonably valid comparisons between countries (van Dijk, 2000). Increasingly, victim surveys include questions about victims' views on the treatment they receive at the hands of the criminal justice system as well as their victimization rates. Survey methodology is usually designed to reveal unreported crimes as well as more obvious offences, which is important in increasing understanding of the consequences of crime, given that the criminal justice system largely ignores victims who do not come forward for assistance. (The great majority of referrals to victim support agencies come via the police, who clearly cannot refer people for assistance if crimes go unreported.)

As legislation and policies make greater demands upon the criminal justice and related professions in terms of how they deal with victims of crime, research attention has increasingly turned to service delivery and victims' perceptions of the ways in which they are treated. Impassioned debates are taking place about such issues as:

- the effectiveness of Victim Impact Statements (Victim Personal Statements in England and Wales) in meeting victims' need to make their views known to sentencers (see for example Erez and Rogers, 1999; Sanders *et al.*, 2001);

- the possible dangers and benefits of restricting defendants' right to cross-examine alleged rape victims in court (see for example Temkin, 2002);

- the benefits and pitfalls of restorative justice, which involves victims and offenders in direct contact or indirect discussion of how best to resolve the problems caused by a crime (see for example Johnstone, 2002; Home Office, 2003);

- how much, if anything, victims should be told about the sentencing and subsequent treatment of 'their' offender, and how much help criminal justice agencies should provide to victims in the process of eliciting their views (see for example, Williams, 2002, 2005; Newton, 2003).

These debates, and the extent to which research into victims' needs and views inform them, demonstrate the relevance and the applied nature of much recent victimological research. This chapter now turns to consider the needs of victims of crime and the extent to which the criminal justice system has responded appropriately in its increasing anxiety to be seen to meet such needs.

REVIEW QUESTIONS

1 In what ways did the early development of academic victimology impact upon attitudes to and policy about victims of crime?

2 How did the rise of the women's movement and of an organized victims' movements alter the academic approach to the study of victims in the 1970s?

3 Are some victims guilty of 'contributory negligence', bringing their victimization upon themselves by their own behaviour or status?

The reactions and needs of victims of crime

Individual victims experience crime in very different ways, and this is an important consideration when it comes to meeting their needs within the framework of criminal justice. A 'one size fits all' approach is unlikely to succeed. However, criminal justice agencies are not necessarily very good at responding flexibly to individual needs.

Some victims—particularly in serious cases—will be sufficiently traumatized by what has happened to them, that they need expert help. This is a small minority of cases, but the system has found such needs hard to accommodate. In cases where a victim is in need of psychiatric treatment or counselling before the trial of the accused takes place, it has only recently been agreed in England and Wales that the victim's needs should take priority even if this puts the prosecution at risk (CPS *et al.*, 2002). After sentencing, victims in more serious cases are routinely put in touch with Victim Support and (less systematically) with other agencies which may be able to help them such as Rape Crisis, the NSPCC and Women's Aid (Newton, 2003). There is, however, a degree of selectivity on the part of the police in some parts of the country in relation to which types of victims' details are passed on to the helping agencies (Spackman, 2000: 19). This means that victims only receive services if they are aware of their existence and have the confidence to make contact with the agencies concerned. In many cases, particularly less serious ones, victims do not need specialist help of this kind, but they may still welcome the opportunity to give vent to their feelings with a neutral person: those who are closest to the victim may quickly tire of discussing an incident repeatedly, and an independent person such as a Victim Support volunteer can provide a welcome listening ear.

There is a good deal of research evidence that victims of crime benefit from being kept informed about the progress of the criminal cases in which they are involved, and that failure to provide this information can make life more difficult for them (Mawby and Walklate, 1994; Tudor, 2002). Since the early 1990s, the probation service has been responsible for giving victims of serious crime in England and Wales a choice about whether they wish to be kept informed about the outcomes of their cases and, where an offender is sentenced to custody, about the subsequent treatment and eventual release of the person concerned. Since 2000, this has applied to all cases in which the offender is sentenced to twelve months or more in custody, and after some teething problems the requirement is now being implemented successfully in the great majority of cases (HMIP, 2003). Particularly where the shorter sentences are concerned, rates of take-up of the offer of information are lower than might be expected, however—and male victims are much less likely to make contact with the probation service than their female counterparts (Newton, 2003).

In more general terms, it is clear that victims feel better about the criminal justice system when its agencies have made serious efforts to keep them properly informed, and they are correspondingly dissatisfied when this is not done (Reeves and Mulley, 2000; Curry *et al.*, 2004). Victims are often having their first contact with the criminal justice system, and hardened professionals who are familiar with its workings need to bear this in mind (but do not always do so).

Reactions to victimization may include seemingly irrational responses such as guilt and shame: helping agencies can often assist by providing reassurance that such reactions are not unusual. Victims may also benefit from an opportunity to express their anger, anxiety or depression in a safe environment.

A frequently expressed, and hardly unreasonable, desire on the part of victims is to be treated with respect by the criminal justice system and its various staff. To meet this need, the agencies concerned need to provide their staff with appropriate training and resources. Police officers, in particular, tend to underestimate the impact of some types of crime upon their victims (Mawby and Walklate, 1994; Williams, 1999; Reeves and Mulley, 2000; Curry *et al.*, 2004). Some of the agencies have frequently also failed to respond sensitively to the varying needs of victims arising from their membership of different racial groups, their gender, sexuality, age, religion or disability. The most glaring example is the failure of the Metropolitan Police to provide a professional or even non-racist service to Duwayne Brooks, who was with black murder victim Stephen Lawrence when he died (Bowling, 1998; Brooks, 2003). The inquiry report on this case has had a considerable influence upon practice within a number of criminal justice agencies (Chouhan, 2002; Downes and Morgan, 2002). Other criminal justice agencies have also been criticized for their insensitivity towards victims of hate crimes (McManus, 2002), where apparently minor incidents may build up into almost intolerable patterns of harassment and discrimination (Bowling, 1998; Sanders *et al.*, 1997).

Victims often simply want practical help, which may include:

- compensation/reparation for damage;
- protection from further victimization and advice about crime prevention;
- assistance in giving evidence in court;
- making their premises safe after a break-in.

Obstacles to victim take-up of services and entitlements

As already noted, one problem for victims in obtaining services is that they are frequently unfamiliar with the workings of criminal justice and may not even know of the existence of agencies which could offer them help. Substantial efforts have been made to remedy this problem, and the level of victims' awareness of the services of Victim Support (for example) is steadily increasing (Maguire and Kinch, 2000). Initiatives such as the *Victim's Charter* (Home Office, 1996), however, have been criticized for failing to provide victims with the information they need to access a range of appropriate services. Some voluntary organizations have been supported and promoted by central government while others have not received such support to anything like the same extent (Williams, 1999).

The ways in which services are delivered may also create a barrier. For example, in a Scottish survey, victims of commercial crime welcomed the crime prevention advice they received from the police, but some victims of personal crime found it patronizing or alarming. In particular, advice about the likelihood of repeated offences needs to be delivered with some sensitivity (Curry *et al.*, 2004). Some victims contacted by the probation service, particularly when the implementation of the responsibility to keep victims of more serious crimes informed first began, found such approaches insensitive and unwelcome (Williams, 1999: 110–16). Low response rates by victims to contacts from the probation service may be explained in a number of ways,[1] but no research has so far been undertaken to find out victims' own views (Newton, 2003).

There is considerable evidence that victims of sexual offences frequently find the process of reporting such crimes, attending court and giving evidence extremely distressing, despite a number of improvements made to the system since the 1970s (Temkin, 2002; Williams, 2005). A significant proportion of such victims interviewed about their experiences refer to the criminal justice process as a re-victimisation, and reporting rates for some offences are believed to be artificially low as a result.

The issue of the 'ideal victim' discussed earlier also has a bearing upon access to and take-up of services. For example, a young Albanian woman who has been abducted, raped and trafficked, and forced to work as a prostitute in this country, is likely to be treated by official agencies first as an illegal immigrant and only secondly, if at all, as a victim of crime. She is far from the stereotypical victim of crime: she has no right to be in the country in the first place, and she works in the sex trade, albeit under duress. She is, nevertheless, in need of protection and access to services—both of which are in very short supply for people in these sorts of circumstances in the UK. Power and the lack of power are important determining factors here.

The distinction between the ideal and the guilty victim also has less dramatic effects. For example, it can mean that people with criminal convictions are frequently refused criminal injuries compensation, even when they suffer the most serious assaults. The likely success of efforts to 'put victims at the heart of the criminal justice system' (Criminal Justice Online, 2002) depends to a large extent upon the breadth of the definitions of victims employed.

Advances in the treatment of victims of crime

The law and agencies' policies in England and Wales have been changed a good number of times since the 1960s with a view to improving the treatment of victims of crime, and there is insufficient space here to go into great detail (see Williams, 1999; Williams, 2002; Zedner, 2002). However, it is worth noting the broad areas in which significant changes have been made:

- criminal injuries compensation for the victims of violent crime was introduced in 1964 and the UK system is among the most generous in the world, despite its limitations;
- in legislation since the 1970s, the arrangements for court-ordered compensation of victims by offenders have been strengthened;
- women's aid refuges and rape crisis centres have been established by voluntary organizations and in recent years they have begun to receive some State financial support;
- Victim Support, established in the 1970s, soon achieved national coverage and now receives substantial financial support from the State for a volunteer-based service;
- the identity of complainants in rape cases has been increasingly protected, and they

have gradually been shielded from aggressive questioning by investigating police officers and cross-examination in court (although more needs to be done);

- victim-offender mediation and other forms of restorative justice which offer choices to victims have increasingly been introduced, in youth justice in the 1990s and in relation to adult offenders more recently (see the final section of this chapter, below);

- international organizations including the United Nations and the Council of Europe have been active since the 1980s in highlighting states' responsibilities towards victims of crime, and policy and legal changes have followed (see www.victimology.nl for some of the relevant international agreements);

- telephone advice services such as Childline and the Victim Supportline have been introduced;

- programmes confronting offenders with their crimes' consequences for victims have become increasingly common and comprehensive;

- vulnerable witnesses have received increasing legal protection and opportunities (for example) to give evidence via video links, with major legislation in 1999 gradually coming into effect in subsequent years;

- provisions for keeping victims informed at various stages of the criminal justice process have been introduced (although this is another field where much more could still be done).

REVIEW QUESTIONS

1 Given that some victims need assistance from outside their own circle of family and friends, what obstacles currently prevent them from obtaining access to this help?

2 What are the main needs expressed by victims of crime, and how does the criminal justice system go about responding to these?

3 What forces have driven the increased emphasis upon victims of crime in UK policy-making?

Effectiveness and international comparisons

It can be instructive to compare the ways in which different legal systems respond to the demands of new pressure groups. In this section, a small number of specific examples of innovation in relation to the rights and needs of victims of crime will be briefly considered in a comparative perspective.

In various jurisdictions, changes have been made in response to consistent research findings about victims' desire to be kept better informed about the progress of cases. One of the key questions is which agency is in the best position to undertake such work. The police have the necessary information and they have direct contact with victims at an early stage. The prosecution service has information about every stage of the case but has no tradition of direct contact with victims. The probation service has no such experience either, but it has staff with relevant training in supporting people at difficult times. In different countries, each of these agencies has been entrusted with the responsibility for making and sustaining contact with victims who require information.

In the Netherlands, the police were given this role and it is clear that when they implement the policy which requires them to keep victims informed, this increases victims' overall satisfaction with the criminal justice system. Sadly, implementation is inconsistent and according to several research studies in the 1990s fewer than 40 per cent of those entitled to information were actually provided with it (Wemmers, 1996). Victim satisfaction with their treatment is likely to be adversely affected by offers of help which do not actually materialize, and this is clearly the case when the police offer to keep people informed and then fail to follow this through in practice (Curry *et al.*, 2004).

Given the difficulty of delivering this service by adding it to the duties of hard-pressed police officers, there is a good deal to be said for approaching the problem in a different way. In England and Wales, the problem was recognized in the *Victim's Charter* (Home Office, 1990; 1996) which added this task to the responsibilities of the probation service, initially only in respect of victims whose offenders were sentenced to lengthy terms of imprisonment. Over subsequent years, the scheme has been extended to cover most victims in cases where the offender is imprisoned (that is, the victims of more serious offences). There were considerable problems in implementing the new arrangements, not least because the probation service was initially provided with no additional resources with which to do so. Many staff also found the idea of working with victims unattractive, and this was a considerable cultural obstacle to change. Over a period of years, these difficulties were overcome (Williams, 2002), but victim take-up of the service remains relatively low: under 40 per cent overall, and a little over 50 per cent in the case of sexual offences, according to one study (Newton, 2003). It seems likely that victims' attitudes towards the probation service, which remains primarily concerned with the surveillance of offenders, are a key factor in this low response to offers of a service which victims consistently demand when asked about their expectations of the criminal justice system.

A different approach has been taken by the criminal justice system in Scotland, where in more serious cases the provision of information to victims has been entrusted to a Victim Information and Advice Service within regional offices of the Procurator Fiscal Service. This is a relatively recent development which has yet to be evaluated, but it will be interesting to see how the experience of delivering the service in this way compares to the successes and difficulties encountered elsewhere. It seems likely that the perceived independence of the people offering the service may encourage higher take-up rates.

It would appear that there is a recognition that victims do need to be provided with information, and in some countries this has been made into a firm entitlement, but implementation can be problematic. If the necessary resources are not made available, policy changes may actually make matters worse by raising victims' expectations but not meeting them in more than a minority of cases.

Another need expressed by victims is that for financial compensation. Many criminal justice systems have responded to the evidence by establishing state compensation schemes, and this is often the first legislative attempt to accommodate victims' needs, but there are considerable differences between these arrangements. In most jurisdictions, state-funded compensation is restricted to victims of violent crime.[2] The extent to which offenders can (additionally or alternatively) be required to pay compensation to their victims through the courts varies considerably from country to country. In England and Wales, such payments can now be made by the court to the victim and recovered from the offender, which is an improvement on the previous system under which offenders often made small and infrequent payments by instalments.

While the UK criminal injuries compensation arrangements are among the best-funded in the world (Brienen and Hoegen, 2000), they have been consistently criticized by victims' organizations (see for example Victim Support, 1995). The lowest levels of award (currently starting at £1,000) can be perceived as belittling victims' injuries: an award of £1,000 for what is seen by the victim as a serious offence can feel insultingly small. Restrictions on claims by victims who happen to have criminal convictions themselves, or who delayed reporting offences to the police, or who are claiming state benefits, have been seen as discriminatory (Williams, 2005). The administration of the scheme is often slow and it is certainly bureaucratic, involving the completion of complex forms and the provision of extensive evidence, especially where claims involve compensation for psychological injuries. Perhaps most importantly, many victims simply are not told that they can claim. Victims' organisations thus find themselves in the position of promoting the scheme, although they have reservations about its operation, and advising individual claimants about how to appeal against decisions. Nevertheless, the UK scheme was set up as long ago as 1964 (a year after the first such system in New Zealand). As such, it has provided a model for similar arrangements elsewhere, and perhaps some lessons have been learnt from its advantages and disadvantages. Unlike discretionary schemes in countries such as Italy, the UK compensation fund is on a statutory basis and it covers domestic violence offences (which are specifically excluded from some European countries' schemes: see Brienen and Hoegen, 2000).

Victims also want direct services, as shown by the high levels of take-up of such services where they are provided. The type and extent of service provision varies enormously between countries, as Mawby (2003) has shown. In the US, there is a strong emphasis upon providing victims with professional counselling, whereas a self-help model prevails in western Europe, where volunteers are more likely to be deployed to provide neighbourly support to victims and referral on to professional services where required. In the UK, Victim Support prioritized property offences for many years (particularly burglary, although this has since changed) while North American victim agencies concentrated upon victims of violent offences.

In the Netherlands, services to support victims were originally set up by the probation service, and there has always been a strong emphasis upon victim–offender mediation (which is viewed with suspicion in many other countries) and referral to professional counselling agencies (which is beyond the resources of other jurisdictions). The Dutch victim support arrangements have always covered victims of road traffic accidents, while in England and Wales this has not formally been the case—although extending services to such victims is now under discussion here. While victim support services in countries such as the Netherlands, England and Wales and Scotland are provided on a national, fairly standardized basis, this is far from being the case in countries with federal systems such as the US or Belgium. In other jurisdictions such as Germany and most eastern European countries, provision is much more patchy, depending upon locally available resources. German victim support agencies tend to concentrate upon providing legal and financial rather than emotional support. Services for victims are generally not well-developed in countries with no tradition of voluntary activity by non-governmental organizations. Engagement with the victims of more serious crimes is the exception rather than the norm internationally, and appears to be at its most sophisticated in western Europe and North America—which is to say, in the richer countries—although it is also developing in response to unmet needs in countries in violent transition such as South Africa.

As a final case study, this section concludes with a discussion of the introduction of victim impact statements in a variety of countries (VIS, known in England and Wales as Victim Personal Statements). First introduced in the USA, VIS were intended to improve victims' position in the criminal justice system by creating an opportunity for them to give information about the loss and damage suffered as a result of the offence, and express their feelings about this. Not only would this involve victims in a system which had traditionally marginalized them (and it might thus to some extent empower them), it was also intended to alter the culture of the system by allowing case-hardened practitioners to obtain a victim perspective.

In the US, the use of VIS ran into constitutional problems from a fairly early stage: emotive victim statements were being read to courts, even in capital cases, and inflaming emotions in a way which made decision-making more difficult. As a result, the higher courts ordered restrictions on the use of the statements in the most serious cases—which also happened for different reasons in the UK (Doerner and Lab, 2002; Zedner, 2002). Take-up rates were relatively low among victims in the US and, later, elsewhere, although it was initially unclear what reasons lay behind this (Doerner and Lab, 2002; Hoyle *et al.*, 1998). Possible explanations included difficulty in tracing victims, failure to inform them of their right to make a statement, and victims choosing, for a variety of reasons, not to take part. Research established that these reasons included fear of retaliation by offenders, general dissatisfaction with and distrust of the criminal justice system, and a disinclination to expose themselves to further emotional distress (Erez and Tontodonata, 1992). There was also a belief on the part of some participants that no notice would be taken of what they said, a feeling also observed when Victim Personal Statements were piloted in England (Hoyle *et al.*, 1998). There was considerable controversy among researchers and practitioners about the extent to which participating in the VIS process made victims feel any better or made judges feel better-informed (Sanders *et al.*, 2001; Erez *et al.*, 1997), and low levels of participation made the argument that VIS empowered victims ring somewhat hollow. Nevertheless, as so often in criminal justice policy, the American arrangements were adapted or emulated in a number of other jurisdictions, including Australia, Canada, England and Wales, Ireland and Scotland.

Some authors have suggested that US politicians introduced VIS primarily for political reasons—to show that 'something was being done' for victims (Garland, 2001; Ashworth, 2000). Given the ambiguity of the research evidence briefly reviewed above, it does seem difficult otherwise to explain the enthusiasm of legislators in other jurisdictions for undertaking similar experiments in their own countries. While it is true that (for example, in Ireland, England and Wales and Scotland) some of these VIS schemes were explicitly designed to avoid some of the pitfalls observed in the US, they all derive from the same principles and they are likely to face at least some of the same problems

(Walklate, 2002). New ideas spread rapidly in criminal justice, and politicians do not always take sufficient (or any) notice of research evidence. The careful, measured evaluation of the pilot VIS scheme in England and Wales by Hoyle *et al.* (1998) in which evidence for not introducing VIS in England and Wales was provided, was swiftly followed by the Home Office decision to 'roll out' Victim Personal Statements nationally, and the authors became somewhat more impassioned in their subsequent discussions of the issues (Sanders *et al.*, 2001).

CONCLUSION

A number of general issues emerge from this brief exercise in international comparisons. While more comparative research is needed (Mawby, 2003) it seems clear that the extent to which victim services exist in a particular country has less to do with levels of need than with the availability of resources and the existence or otherwise of voluntary organizations willing to take on the task.

Whereas some services are introduced in response to research evidence about victims' wishes and needs, other reforms are carried out despite what is known about victims' wishes and responses to experimental projects.

Legislation is not always effectively implemented—which is generally true in a number of fields, but seems to apply particularly to laws and policies relating to victims of crime. This being the case, a number of authors have expressed the suspicion that politicians are particularly prone to making rhetorical statements about the need to assist victims of crime and accordingly putting forward what might be called rhetorical legislation, which looks good but is not properly brought into effect (Williams, 2005; Walklate, 2002). Whether sufficient resources are allocated to ensure the success of new initiatives is one test of the seriousness of those who bring forward the legislation, and a recurrent theme in the discussion above (and in the literature generally) is the failure to make adequate resources available to allow effective implementation of reforms in this area of policy. A linked issue is that of publicity: a number of the initiatives described have been less successful than they might have been due to inadequate publicity. The cynical observer might say that one way to limit take-up of services is to ration the knowledge of the public about their availability (Williams, 1999).

Internationally, there is a growing tendency to experiment with—and in some cases even to replace traditional adversarial criminal justice approaches with—restorative methods. There is insufficient space here to debate the merits of restorative justice (see Johnstone, 2002) and there has not yet been enough research on the merits or otherwise of the experimental projects in the UK to be clear about how successful they are. However, such approaches have been remarkably successful in other jurisdictions (notably in Austria and New Zealand) and they appear to show considerable promise in terms of keeping victims of crime better informed, involving them and giving them a say in the criminal justice process if they so wish, and ensuring that the victims who do decide to take part in such approaches are treated respectfully and get something out of their involvement (see Williams, 2005).

Finally, and perhaps most importantly, many reforms in the area of services for victims have been initiated by people whose primary concern is the welfare and fair treatment of offenders, and praiseworthy as this is, it tends to make victims somewhat wary.

QUESTIONS FOR DISCUSSION

1   Whose interests, apart from those of the victims themselves, are served by legislation and policies which purport to meet the needs of victims of crime?

2   What prevents legislation and policy on victims of crime from being effectively implemented—and what reasons might help to explain this?

3   Why did services for victims of crime only begin to emerge in the 1960s, and why have policy initiatives and legislation in this area become so much more common in recent years?

4   Why are some groups of victims seen as more 'deserving' than others? Which groups does this particularly apply to? What are the practical consequences?

5   Many services for victims of crime have been initiated by groups whose primary focus is upon offenders (for example, the restorative justice movement, Victim Support, Victim Impact Statements). What possible explanations are there for this, and what consequences might it have?

GUIDE TO FURTHER READING

Doerner, W.G. and Lab, S.P. (2002) *Victimology* (3rd edn), Cincinnati: Anderson.

Although it fails to consider most of what is happening outside North America, this is a useful textbook, providing evidence about the growth of victim services and the victims' movement in North America which is based upon research.

Goodey, J. (2005) *Victims and Victimology: Research, Policy and Practice*, Harlow: Longman.

An up-to-date textbook on victims policy internationally; particularly strong on gender issues.

Johnstone, G. (2002) *Restorative Justice: Ideas, Values, Debates*, Cullompton: Willan.

A carefully argued critique of some of the central claims of restorative justice, including the issues affecting victims of crime. This book also gives examples of what restorative justice involves in practice and how it is implemented. Draws upon philosophical evidence but is clearly and accessibly written.

Mawby, R.I. and Walklate, S. (1994) *Critical Victimology: International Perspectives*, London: Sage.

Although now somewhat dated, this remains the key text on the victims' movement, the needs of victims and provision for them across the western world. It introduces a critical approach to the study of victims of crime, questioning many of the previously prevalent orthodoxies.

Williams, B. (2005 forthcoming) *Victims of Crime: Justice Rebalanced?* London: Jessica Kingsley.

An up-to-date account of policy and research relevant to the position of victims of crime, paying particular attention to community justice and restorative justice.

Zedner, L. (2002) 'Victims' in Maguire, M., Morgan, R. and Reiner, R. (eds) *The Oxford Handbook of Criminology* (3rd edn), Oxford: Oxford University Press.

This chapter succinctly summarizes current academic knowledge about victims and witnesses of crime and their place in the criminal justice system.

WEB LINKS

http://www.victimology.nl

An extremely useful site, which provides two databases, one on research and the other on victim services. It also includes a wide range of documents such as international conventions, a news section and links with other victimological websites worldwide.

http://www.natiassoc03.uuhost.uk.uu.net/

The combined sites of the UK's national Victim Support organizations. In each case, the site gives access to leaflets, publications, links, press releases and contact details for the national and local VS schemes.

http://www.restorativepractices.org

A US-based site giving information about conferences and news as well as access to an online library and an e-forum on restorative justice.

REFERENCES

Amir, M. (1971) *Patterns of Forcible Rape*. Chicago: University of Chicago Press.

Ashworth, A. (2000) 'Victims' rights, defendants' rights and criminal procedure' in A. Crawford and J. Goodey (eds) *Integrating a Victim Perspective within Criminal Justice*. Aldershot: Ashgate.

Boswell, G. (1999) 'Young offenders who commit grave crimes: the criminal justice response' in H. Kemshall and J. Pritchard (eds) *Good Practice in Working with Violence*. London: Jessica Kingsley.

Bowling, B. (1998) *Violent Racism: Victimisation, Policing and Social Context*. Oxford: Clarendon.

Brienen, M.E.I. and Hoegen, E.H. (2000) *Victims of Crime in 22 European Criminal Justice Systems*. Nijmegen: Wolf Legal Publications.

Chouhan, K. (2002) 'Race issues in probation', in D. Ward, J. Scott and M. Lacey (eds) *Probation: Working for Justice* (2nd edn). Oxford: Oxford University Press.

Criminal Justice Online (2002) *Justice for All—CJS White Paper Published—the Executive Summary*, http://www.cjsonline.org/publications/whitepaper_2002/cjs_white_paper_summary4.html

Curry, D., Knight, V., Owens-Rawle, D., Patel, S. and Semenchule, M. (2004) *Restorative Justice in the Juvenile Secure Estate*. London: Youth Justice Board.

Doerner, W.G. and Lab, S.P. (2002) *Victimology* (3rd edn). Cincinnati: Anderson.

Downes, D. and Morgan, R. (2002) 'The politics of law and order' in M. Maguire, R. Morgan and R. Reiner (eds) *The Oxford Handbook of Criminology* (3rd edn). Oxford: Oxford University Press.

Crown Prosecution Service, Department of Health and Home Office (2002) *Provision of Therapy for Vulnerable or Intimidated Witnesses Prior to a Criminal Trial: Practice Guidance*. London: Home Office.

Elias, R. (1993) *Victims Still: the Political Manipulation of Crime Victims*. London: Sage.

Erez, E., (1997) 'Victim Harm, Impact Statements and Victim Satisfaction with Justice: an Australian Experience', *International Review of Victimology* 5 (37): 37–60.

Erez, E. and Rogers, L. (1999) 'The Effects of Victim Impact Statements on Criminal Justice Outcomes and Processes: the Perspectives of Legal Professionals', *British Journal of Criminology* 39 (2): 216–39.

Erez, E. and Tontodonato, P. (1992) 'Victim Participation in Sentencing and Satisfaction with Justice', *Justice Quarterly* 9: 393–417.

Garland, D. (2001) *The Culture of Control: Crime and Social Order in Contemporary Society*. Oxford: Oxford University Press.

Gottfredson, M.R. (1984) *Victims of Crime: the Dimensions of Risk*. London: Home Office (Research Study XX).

Her Majesty's Inspectorate of Probation (2003) *Valuing the Victim: an Inspection into National Victim Contact Arrangements*. London: Home Office.

Home Office (1990) *Victim's Charter: a Statement of the Rights of Victims*. London: Home Office Public relations Branch.

Home Office (1996) *The Victim's Charter: a Statement of Service Standards for Victims of Crime*. London: Home Office Communications Directorate.

Home Office (2002) *A Better Deal for Victims and Witnesses*. London: Home Office.

Home Office (2003) *Restorative Justice: the Government's Strategy*. London: Home Office Communications Directorate.

Hoyle, C., Cape, E., Morgan, R. and Sanders, A. (1998) *Evaluation of the One Stop Shop and Victim Statement Pilot Projects*. London: Home Office Research and Development Directorate.

Johnstone, G. (2002) *Restorative Justice: Ideas, Values, Debates*. Cullompton: Willan.

Kennedy, H. (1993) *Eve was Framed: Women and British Justice*. London: Chatto & Windus.

Kershaw, C., Chivite-Matthews, A., Thomas, C. and Aust, R. (2001) *The 2001 British Crime Survey: Home Office Statistical Bulletin 18/01*. London: Home Office.

Koffman, L. (1996) *Crime Surveys and Victims of Crime*. Cardiff: University of Wales Press.

Maguire, M. and Kynch, J. (2000) *Public Perceptions and Victims' Experiences of Victim Support: Findings from the 1998 British Crime Survey*. London: Home Office RDSD.

Mawby, R. (2003) 'The provision of victim support and assistance programmes: a cross-national perspective' in P. Davies, P. Francis and V. Jupp (eds) *Victimisation: Theory, Research and Practice*. Basingstoke: Palgrave Macmillan.

Mawby, R.I. and Walklate, S. (1994) *Critical Victimology: International Perspectives*. London: Sage.

McManus, J. (2002) 'Systems not Words? Some Organisational Response to Hate Crimes', *Criminal Justice Matters* 48, Summer, 44–5.

Mendelsohn, B. (1956) 'Une nouvelle branche de la science bio-pyscho-sociale: victimologie', *Revue Internationale de Criminologie et de Police Technique*: 10–31.

Moran, L.J. (2001) 'Affairs of the Heart: Critical Reflections on Hate Crime', *Law and Critique* 12 (3) 1–15.

Mullender, A. (1996) *Rethinking Domestic Violence: the Social Work and Probation Response*. London: Routledge.

MVA Consultancy (2000) *The 2000 Scottish Crime Survey*. Edinburgh: Scottish Executive.

Newton, E. (2003) 'A study of the policies and procedures implemented by the probation service with respect to victims of serious crime', *British Journal of Community Justice* 2 (1) 25–36.

O'Mahony, D., Geary, R., McEvoy, K. and Morison, J. (2000) *Crime, Community and Locale: the Northern Ireland Communities Crime Survey*. Aldershot: Ashgate.

Radford, J. (2001) 'Feminist research' in E. McLaughlin and J. Muncie (eds) *The Sage Dictionary of Criminology*. London: Sage, 121–3.

Reeves, H. and Mulley, K. (2000) 'The new status of victims in the UK: opportunities and threats', in A. Crawford and J. Goodey (eds) *Integrating a Victim Perspective within Criminal Justice*. Aldershot: Ashgate.

Sanders, A., Creaton, J., Bird, S. and Weber, L. (1997) *Victims with Learning Disabilities: Negotiating the Criminal Justice System*. Oxford: University of Oxford Centre for Criminological Research.

Sanders, A., Hoyle, C., Morgan, R. and Cape, E. (2001) 'Victim Impact Statements: don't work, can't work', *Criminal Law Review* 447–58.

Shakespeare, T. (1996) 'Power and prejudice: issues of gender, sexuality and disability' in L. Barton (ed) *Disability and Society: Emerging Issues and Insights*. Harlow: Longman.

Spackman, P. (2000) (ed) *Victim Support Handbook: Helping People Cope with Crime*. London: Hodder and Stoughton.

Temkin, J. (1987) *Rape and the Legal Process*. London: Sweet and Maxwell.

Temkin, J. (2002) *Rape and the Legal Process* (2nd edn). Oxford: Oxford University Press.

Tudor, B. (2002) 'Probation work with victims of crime' in B. Williams (ed), *Reparation and Victim-focused Social Work*. London: Jessica Kingsley.

Van Dijk, J. (2000) 'Implications of the International Crime Victims Survey for a victim perspective' in A. Crawford and J. Goodey (eds) *Integrating a Victim Perspective within Criminal Justice*. Aldershot: Ashgate.

Von Hentig, H. (1948) *The Criminal and his Victim*. New Haven: Yale University Press.

Victim Support (1995) 'The Rights of Victims of Crime', policy paper. London: Victim Support.

Walklate, S. (2002) 'Victim Impact Statements' in B. Williams (ed) *Reparation and Victim-Focused Social Work*. London: Jessica Kingsley.

Wemmers, J.-A. (1996) *Victims in the Criminal Justice System*. Amsterdam: Kugler.

Williams, B. (1999) *Working with Victims of Crime: Policies, Politics and Practice*. London: Jessica Kingsley.

Williams, B. (2002) 'Justice for victims of crime' in D. Ward, J. Scott and M. Lacey (eds) *Probation: Working for Justice* (2nd edn). Oxford: Oxford University Press.

Williams, B. (2005 forthcoming) *Victims of Crime: Justice Rebalanced?* London: Jessica Kingsley.

Wolfgang, M. (1958) *Patterns in Criminal Homicide*. Philadelphia: University of Pennsylvania Press.

Zedner, L. (2002) 'Victims' in M. Maguire, R. Morgan and R. Reiner (eds) *The Oxford Handbook of Criminology*, (3rd edn). Oxford: Oxford University Press.

NOTES

1. One might speculate that male victims in particular tend to wish to avoid a fuss and put the incident behind them. Some victims will not want contact with the probation service because they view it as an offender orientated service. Others will view the incident as relatively minor, and still others may lack confidence in the criminal justice system as a whole.

2. A notable exception is South Africa, where there are insufficient resources available to set up a general compensation scheme, but the near-defunct arrangements to compensate victims of terrorism cover property as well as personal injuries.

25 Policing

Trevor Jones

INTRODUCTION

The last four decades have seen a huge increase in academic, media and political interest in policing. During this time, 'police studies' has emerged as a major sub-field within criminology. This chapter provides an overview of the key themes that have been explored by the large and growing body of work on the police and policing. Given the volume of this material, the chapter can only provide a broad introduction to the main concepts and some of the key debates within the field. The chapter is divided into four main sections. The first explores the meaning of 'policing', and outlines how the study of policing has become such an important area of concern within criminology. The second section examines some of the key functions of modern policing organizations. The third section explores some important contemporary debates in policing, before the final section provides concluding thoughts. Because of space restrictions, the focus will be upon policing in England and Wales. For more information about the policing arrangements in Scotland and Northern Ireland, the reader is referred to Walker (2000), and Ellison and Smyth (2000) respectively.

BACKGROUND

Until relatively recently, criminological studies of policing focused exclusively upon the specialist state agency—'the police'—tasked with law enforcement and peace-keeping. Recent years, however, have seen a growing body of work exploring a broader range of 'policing' activities carried out by a range of individuals and organizations other than the police (Bayley and Shearing 1994, Johnston 1992, 2000; Jones and Newburn 1998). This work has extended our gaze beyond the police and highlighted the fact that regulation, order maintenance, and law enforcement activities are increasingly 'pluralized'—that is, provided by complex networks of individuals and agencies (Johnston and Shearing, 2002). Various elements to this pluralization have been identified including the expansion of the commercial security sector (Johnston, 1992; Jones and Newburn, 1998), new forms of public sector policing provision such as local authority patrol forces and municipal police forces (Loader, 2000), the hiring of commercial security by local authorities; the alleged increase in incidence of informal policing forms such as vigilantism (Johnston, 1996), and the emergence of new transnational policing forms above the State (Sheptycki, 1998). As Shearing (2000) argues, security provision is now shared within a network of 'agencies, groups and collectivities, both within and outside the public sector'.

It is important not to overstate the novelty of some of these developments and automatically conclude that a dramatic transformation in policing arrangements is occurring. Regulatory policing bodies attached to national and local government have been in operation for well over a century, and there has been a smaller (but still significant) commercial security industry operating in Britain since the early twentieth Century (Jones and Newburn, 2002). Thus, we should be careful not to conflate 'new ways of thinking about things' with 'new things to think about' (Crawford, 2003). Nevertheless, there are clearly significant things happening. Not least amongst these is the substantial growth of the commercial security industry and the emergence of other forms of non-police patrol provision, such as local authority patrol services and neighbourhood wardens (Crawford, 2003).

Thus, in thinking about 'policing' we must take care not to simply conflate this with 'what the police do'. However, broader definitions do risk blurring 'policing' with the broader processes of formal and informal social control operating in society. Perhaps the definition that best captures the distinctive contribution of policing within the wider notion of social control is that of Reiner (1997). He suggests that policing involves 'the creation of systems of surveillance coupled with the threat of sanctions for discovered deviance' (1997: 1005). Given the current space restrictions, and the fact that state-organized policing arrangements are likely to remain central to the formal provision of security in England and Wales, at least for the foreseeable future, the focus of the current chapter will be upon public forms of policing, or 'policing by government' (Loader, 2000).

Prior to the 1960s, the police—and the wider criminal justice system—were rather invisible within criminology (Reiner, 1997). The central focus of the 'criminological enterprise' for the first part of the twentieth century was 'criminals', and the challenge was, broadly, to identify them, discover what was different about them, and later, to develop interventions to address offending behaviour. The police and criminal justice system were simply regarded as providing institutional responses to the more sociologic-ally interesting concepts of crime and criminality. From the late 1960s onwards, however, this approach was increasingly challenged by the emergence of 'labelling' perspectives that highlighted the socially constructed nature of crime and criminality (Becker, 1963; Lemert, 1964). These new approaches ana-lysed crime and deviance as the product of complex interactions between individuals and the social audience. From this 'interactionist' viewpoint, the operation of criminal justice agencies—and particularly the police—was absolutely vital. In order to fully comprehend the problem of crime and its construction, criminologists needed a more detailed knowledge of police interactions with members of the public, the factors that shape police attitudes and behaviour, and the ways in which organizational policies are formed and translated (or not) into practice (Reiner, 1997).

Outside the world of academia, wider social and political developments contributed more generally to a growing focus upon policing (Newburn, 2003). From the 1950s onwards, there were large and sustained increases in recorded crime. The sporadic outbreak of serious urban disorders fuelled political and public concern about law and order. From the 1970s onwards, major industrial disputes brought the police service into controversial and sometimes violent conflict with pickets, with perhaps the 1984 miners' strike being the key example here. More generally, during the latter part of the twentieth century and the early years of the new millennium, wider public concerns about law and order have been stimulated by politicians of all parties who have adopted a strategy of 'talking tough' on crime in order to enhance their electoral popularity (Downes and Morgan, 2002). A host of other developments have kept policing at the top of the political agenda. Growing inequality and social divisions have continued to highlight the uneven impact of adversarial policing on different social groups, most visible in the arena of race relations (Bowling and Phillips, 2003). A series of high profile miscarriages of justice during the 1980s and 1990s damaged public confidence in the police, and focused attention on police corruption and malpractice (Rozenberg, 1992). Of particular importance in recent years has been the growing focus on police per-formance and effectiveness. All these developments have led to much more critical scrutiny of policing, and a decline in levels of public confidence in the police from the high water mark of police legitimacy in the 1950s (Reiner, 2000). Nevertheless, it is clear that the police institution retains a significant, perhaps unique, cultural and symbolic significance in England and Wales (Loader and Mulcahy, 2003). Though public support for the police has declined, it remains high relative to public confidence in other institutions such as the press and government. Public demands for increased levels of policing, typified by the call for 'more bobbies on the beat', are growing (Loader, 1997; Morgan and Newburn, 1997). Furthermore, representations of the police remain a central part of our popular culture, with crime and policing stories providing a core part of both news reporting and popular fiction on film and television (Reiner, 2000, 2003; Leishman and Mason, 2003; Clarke, 2001). Thus, despite the increasing criticism and scrutiny of the police over recent decades, we retain a peculiar attachment to, and fascination with, the police institution.

Policing functions

The characteristic of being an 'omnibus' or 'catch-all' public service remains one of the core features of the public police service (Jones and Newburn, 1998). One of the founding fathers of police studies, the American sociologist Egon Bittner, highlighted two core defining characteristics of the police (Bittner, 1974). The first concerned this broad functional mandate. Such is the breadth of this mandate that it is 'all but impossible to imagine a human problem which could not be their proper business' (Jones and Newburn, 1998: 248). The second key feature highlighted by Bittner was the fact that the police bring to this broad mandate a distinctive legal capacity—access to the legitimate use of force. Despite the broad functional mandate, certain core police functions can be identified. In particular, past research has explored the degree to which police officers spend their time engaged in crime-fighting (in the form of law enforcement and criminal investigation), crime prevention, and order maintenance.

Crime fighting

The police are the primary law enforcement agency in all contemporary industrial democratic societies. 'Crime-fighting' is central to the occupational self-image of many police officers, as well as the wider representations of policing in media and public debate. However, the overwhelming conclusion of research on what police officers actually do is that crime-related activities account for a relatively small proportion of everyday police-work (PA Consulting Group, 2001; Morgan and Newburn, 1997). Typical of this kind of approach was Skogan's (1990) analysis of the British Crime Survey, which concluded that broader 'service' functions are the staple diet of everyday police work, and that 'most public-initiated encounters reflected the integration of the police into the routines of everyday life'. The police are called upon to preserve tranquillity, ease the flow of traffic, serve as a clearing house for reports of a variety of community problems, assist in civil emergencies, and help people find their way. However, this view has been challenged in a number of ways in recent years. For example, Shapland and Vagg (1988) analytical calls to the police and their study suggested that 'potential crime' accounted for over half of all calls. Whether or not a call is a 'crime' depends not only whether an offence has taken place, whether an offender is present and so on, but also, on whether the attending officer(s) decides—in negotiation with others—that the incident be recorded as a crime. In addition, Reiner (2000) suggests that recent changes in the organization of police forces have increased the number of specialists with a law-enforcement function, and increased the involvement of uniformed officers in the investigation of routine crime. The central drive of many government reforms to the police from the 1990s on administrations has been to improve levels of police performance. Much of this has focused, explicitly or implicitly, on crime-related work. Thus, while the view of the police as 'crime-fighters' remains somewhat distanced from the reality of everyday police work, dealing with crime remains not only symbolically important to policing, but a key part of what the police actually do.

Crime prevention

Within the police service, specialist crime prevention departments began to grow from the mid-1960s onwards, although crime prevention specialists have remained rather marginal within the police organization. Traditionally, this aspect of police work has included providing information to the general public about physical security, giving crime prevention advice to designers and planners, inputs into the training of new police recruits, and the collection and analysis of information. This rather narrow approach to crime prevention has placed the primary emphasis on technical or hardware expertise. In recent decades, a broader approach to crime prevention has emerged in England and Wales. The language of the community-based or multi-agency approach has permeated police discourse about crime prevention, which increasingly emphasizes community involvement and inter-agency cooperation (Crawford, 1998; Hughes, 1998).

A central feature of central government policy since the late 1980s has been the advocacy of the 'partnership' approach. This is based upon a growing recognition that the police alone can in practice have only a limited impact on levels of crime. There is a need for integrated approaches involving the range of agencies that can influence community safety including housing, environment, education, transport, planning, as well as the police and other criminal justice agencies (Hughes *et al.*, 2002). Although since the mid- to late–1980s, the partnership approach has been widely hailed as a key to successful community crime prevention, in practice it has proved extremely difficult to implement. Research has suggested a number of reasons for this including unequal power relations within partnerships, the lack of a natural lead agency to coordinate projects, differences in the structure and culture of organizations, and the lack of real community involvement (Rosenbaum, 1988; Sampson *et al.*, 1988; Saulsbury and Bowling, 1991). Despite these difficulties with multi-agency working, there have been significant examples of success, and studies have highlighted some significant improvements brought about by community safety partnerships in which local authorities have taken the lead (NACRO, 1996).

Following the recommendation of the Standing Conference on Crime Prevention (Standing Conference on Crime Prevention, 1991), it was increasingly accepted that effective crime prevention and community safety work in local areas should be coordinated by local authorities. However, it was not until the Crime and Disorder Act 1998 that this became a reality. The role of the police in crime prevention is now developing within the broader context of statutory Crime and Disorder Reduction Partnerships established under the Act. These involve the local authority, police, probation service, a range of voluntary and statutory agencies, plus local commercial organisations and community groups. In three yearly cycles each partnership must conduct and publish an audit of local crime and disorder problems, consult locally on the basis of the audit, and publish a strategy for tackling issues identified in the audit. The framework established by the Crime and Disorder Act 1998 has thus further entrenched a multi-agency approach to crime prevention, and underlined the changing police role in crime prevention that has been developing since the 1970s.

Order maintenance

Although the crime-related aspects of police work often take primacy in police and public debate about policing, the consensus of most academic research on the police is that the primary police task is peace-keeping, or 'order maintenance'. For example, Reiner (2000) has argued that in practice, the majority of what police officers actually do from day to day involves settling of disputes without recourse to their formal legal powers. This arises from the wide level of discretion that police officers on the ground retain. It is now a well-established feature of sociological discussions of the police that the scope for discretion increases for officers the further they are down the police hierarchy (Manning, 1977). Police officers will not invoke the law in every situation where a crime has been committed, but in circumstances where they believe that a crime has been committed and they deem it appropriate to apply their legal powers. Decisions to enforce the law are often made in pursuit of the broader objective of 'peacekeeping'. This was recognized by Lord Scarman in his 1981 report on the Brixton riots, when he argued that in situations where law enforcement may conflict with maintaining the public peace, it is the latter that must take priority (Scarman, 1981).

Of course, order maintenance activities range in size and complexity. Such activities include mediating in relatively minor neighbour disputes, providing a visible police patrol presence at public events such as football matches or demonstrations, as well as major 'paramilitary-style' interventions of organized force to major outbreaks of public disorder (Waddington, 2003). It is this last category that places public order policing in its most morally ambiguous position, because it inevitably involves the upholding and maintenance of a particular order. Ultimately, this involves protecting the vested interests that benefit from a continuation of the status quo. This kind of 'order maintenance' policing is highly contentious, as reference to media discussions of particular examples from recent years will demonstrate (for example, the major public disorder in Bradford in July 2001). On the one hand, Waddington has argued that modern professional police responses to major disorder require a degree of paramilitary organization, equipment and tactics. In particular, strong central 'quasi-military' forms of command and control in these situations enable a more directed and therefore effective application of force than tactics that would allow individual officers to take *ad hoc* defensive action. Furthermore, officers who are acting as part of a disciplined group under the direct command of a senior officer are, he argues, less likely to commit acts of individual over-aggression or other kinds of indiscipline. Finally, lines of accountability in such situations are much clearer in that it is the commanding officer who is clearly responsible for the officers' behaviour (Waddington, 1993). Against this, Jefferson has argued that the development of paramilitary public order policing tactics has transformed the nature of policing in

England and Wales (Jefferson, 1993). In particular, it has encouraged police forces to prepare for the worst-case scenario in their public order planning strategies, thus building in expectations of trouble. All too often, this expectation becomes a self-fulfilling prophecy when aggressive police tactics provoke similar responses from crowds, and spirals of disorder develop. In sum, Jefferson argues that the equipment, tactics and mindset of paramilitary public order policing actually generates crowd violence and disorder, rather than controlling it (Jefferson, 1990, 1993).

REVIEW QUESTIONS

1 What are the core policing functions?

2 What kinds of things do police officers actually spend most of their time doing?

3 How does the reality of police work compare with popular views about what the police do?

Key debates in contemporary policing

This section will focus upon a selected number of issues that have formed the subject of important contemporary debates about policing. Space restrictions inevitably mean that a number of important debates will not be discussed and the reader is referred to other key works for further information. In particular, there is no discussion of the historical development of policing institutions (Rawlings, 2002), the emergence of transnational policing arrangements (Sheptycki, 2000), or the legal powers of the police (Sanders and Young, 2003). However, the following areas are felt to have occupied a particularly important place within recent debates about British policing.

Police occupational cultures

As noted above, police constables operate with a considerable degree of discretion, a situation that arises from the practical realities of policework (such as its relatively 'invisible' nature) and from established common law traditions ('constabulary independence'). It is clear that the law and organizational rules can only set broad parameters for police behaviour, and certainly do not determine the pattern of policing on the ground (Smith, 1986). A key debate within police research concerns the degree to which informal working cultures within the police organization shape the ways in which officers use their discretion.

Occupational police cultures can be defined as beliefs, norms, working practices and informal rules that help police officers to make sense of their world (Reiner, 2000). The early observational studies of policing—mainly focused on uniformed patrol officers—suggested there was a relatively stable set of dimensions that appeared to characterize 'cop culture' in a range of different societies. Skolnik (1966) highlighted how common tensions associated with policing in liberal societies appeared to foster a common set of cultural responses. Police officers face the problem of constant pressure for results, combined with the difficult position of being symbols of social authority in a way which sets them apart from their fellow citizens. Skolnik argued that these structural problems tend to generate a series of traits within a shared police sub-culture, and highlighted in particular suspicion, social isolation/group solidarity, and conservatism. More recent studies have added other elements to the standard 'list' of features that are said to characterize 'cop culture'. These include the sense of mission, cynicism/pragmatism, machismo and racial prejudice (Reiner, 2000). Although as Waddington (1999) points out, notions of cop culture have tended to be used in pejorative terms, it is important to understand how far these features are linked with the structural realities of policing, and cannot necessarily be considered wholly negative. For example, police officers are trained and socialized to suspect that things are not always as they seem. Though this may have positive aspects, of course, it can also lead to the unfair stereotyping of particular groups or individuals. Group solidarity can be related to the vital interdependence between police officers, who are in many incidents outnumbered by, sometimes hostile, members of the public. The need to rely upon one's colleagues helps to foster a strong sense of group loyalty, which again cannot always be seen as entirely negative. However, this strong group identification brings with it the danger of negatively stereotyping 'outsiders', and also a marked tendency to close ranks in the face of investigations of police malpractice. Though racial prejudice and machismo can never be regarded as positive, it is also important to understand the complex dynamics via which these traits also arise and are perpetuated in the police organization. Crucially, they are linked to the experience of 'doing policing' in societies characterized by structural inequalities of race and gender. They are also connected to the practical realities of new recruits 'learning on the job' in the company of more experienced officers (Jones, 1998).

An important question is how far can these cultural tendencies be explained with reference to the individual dispositions that police recruits bring to the job? Some research has suggested that police recruits tend to be more authoritarian than other comparable groups in the population (Coleman and Gorman, 1982). However, most research on this matter suggests that occupational police subcultures are better understood as a collective cultural adaptation to the everyday realities of police work, rather than being the product of individual personality traits (Reiner, 1997). Thus, whilst reforming the police organization in order to eliminate the negative aspects of police culture has been seen as a prerequisite for better policing, this is a far more difficult task than simply weeding out individual officers with inappropriate attitudes. For example, once we accept occupational culture as a complex collective phenomenon, we can begin to understand the limitations on traditional approaches to changing the culture. Interventions such as better recruitment practices or improved 'cultural awareness' training tend to individualize problems such as prejudice, and not allow for the fact that much policing is learned on the streets.

More recent work has presented a more sophisticated notion of occupational police culture. In particular, it has highlighted the fact that too often 'cop culture' is discussed as if it is a universal and homogenous phenomenon (Chan, 1996). Indeed, it is more accurate to talk about 'police cultures', given the noted differences within police forces. For example, there appear to be significant contrasts in occupational cultures between different functional specialisms, officers of different ranks, and urban and rural force areas (Foster, 2003). In addition, the notion that cop culture provides a straightforward explanation of deviant police behaviour has been challenged. Waddington (1999) argues that 'canteen culture' is primarily an oral phenomenon that involves the telling of 'war stories' away from the front-line of policing. Many of these verbal accounts of policing as told by one officer to another bear little relation to the more mundane reality of police-work. For Waddington, this demonstrates that the oral culture provides a number of functions for the officers who participate within it. It helps bolster occupational self-esteem, and mutually reassures officers that they are doing a dangerous and valuable job. It helps provide a gloss that enables officers to practically and emotionally deal with the depressing, difficult and messy situations that they are often faced with (Reiner, 2000). Waddington (1999) has further argued that although many elements of this oral culture are unpalatable, it cannot be related to practical police behaviour in a straightforward causal way. For example, individual officers are not helpless in the face of an all-pervasive culture, but actively interpret and react to it. We therefore need to understand the ways in which individual officers resist and rework the occupational cultures in which they find themselves.

Policing a diverse society

During recent decades, Britain, along with most western industrial societies, has experienced increasing social and cultural diversity. For example, social differences along lines of religion, age, gender, region, nationality, ethnicity, sexuality, and lifestyles are becoming more important as a source of individual and group identity. At the same time, social and economic inequality has increased substantially over the past twenty years (Morgan and Newburn, 1997). An important challenge for contemporary policing is to balance and respond to conflicting demands from an increasingly diverse society. However, a central finding of much policing research is that the adversarial aspects of policing have always been experienced disproportionately by those at the lower end of the social hierarchy (Reiner, 2000). The unemployed, the poor, people living in inner-city areas, immigrants and ethnic minorities consistently find themselves more likely to be on the end of police powers (see also Chapters 11 and 18). We will focus here on the arena of race relations, although it should be noted that similar arguments have applied with regard to the policing experiences of other social groups. In particular, concerns have been raised about the experiences of women and LGB (lesbian, gay and bisexual) people both as police officers, and also as receivers of policing services (Heidensohn, 2003; Williams and Robinson, 2004). In addition, as society has become more diverse during the latter half of the twentieth century, police relations with a range of other minority groups have come under scrutiny (Jones and Newburn, 2001).

The subject of crime, ethnicity and policing remains highly controversial and explanations have too-often been reduced to those entirely related to police racism, or alternatively, to alleged higher offending rates among minority ethnic groups. Recent work has provided a more sophisticated understanding of the different forms of racial discrimination that operate within the police organization and in wider society (Bowling and Phillips, 2002). It has also highlighted the important impact of wider structural patterns of disadvantage that disproportionately place some ethnic minority communities in the geographical places and social groups that are more likely to be on the end of adversarial policing. The research also continues to demonstrate that, despite over twenty years of official attention to the issue, it is clear that relationships between the police and minority ethnic communities remain problematic in a number of respects (Bowling and Phillips, 2003). First, considering the dimension of suspects/offenders, it is clear that ethnic minority people (and especially black people) are substantially over-represented in police stop and arrest statistics. Recent data at the national level shows very stark differences, with black people about eight times as likely as whites (on average) to be stopped by the police, and about five times as likely overall to be arrested (Home Office, 2003). Second, there is strong evidence that ethnic minorities remain 'under-protected' as well as 'over-policed'. Levels of victimization overall remain higher amongst ethnic minorities (Mirlees-Black *et al.*, 1996). In particular, concerns have been raised about levels of racist harassment and violence (Bowling, 1998). The police service has come under strong criticism for failure to deal effectively with such crimes, although it is accepted that significant improvements have been made in recent years. However, the British Crime Survey still shows lower levels of satisfaction with the police expressed by crime victims from some ethnic minority groups (Clancy, *et al.*, 2000). Finally, despite over two decades of official attention, ethnic minorities remain markedly under-represented among police officers. The most recent figures show that ethnic minority officers account for less than 3 per cent of total police strength, compared to 7 per cent of the working population (Home Office, 2003). Difficulties in attracting sufficient numbers of ethnic minority recruits, and the relatively high level of ethnic minority resigners, have been related to the experience of racism from colleagues and the general public (HMIC, 2000).

There are a number of possible explanations for these different experiences of policing. Direct discrimination by individual police officers is certainly a contributory factor, given what we know about the pervasive nature of racial prejudice within occupational police cultures (see above). Direct discrimination is also suggested by the fact that racial dis-proportions are widest for the offence categories in which police officers have the greatest discretion to target, such as drugs possession or minor public order offences (Smith, 1997). However, questions have been raised about the degree to which levels of stated prejudice within the oral police culture are put straightforwardly into practice in police behaviour (Smith and Gray, 1985; Waddington, 1999). More recent official attention has been applied to the concept of 'institutional discrimination' highlighted in the MacPherson Report into the racist murder of the black teenager Stephen Lawrence. MacPherson defined institutional racism, as unwitting and unintentional discrimination that is built into organizational policies and practices, with the (sometimes unintended) effect of disadvantaging members of particular ethnic groups. This clearly moves us towards a more sophisticated notion of discrimination, one in which discriminatory practices arise out of the everyday functioning of an organization rather than being equated simply with examples of individual racial discrimination. However, the concept as outlined by MacPherson has itself come under criticism for its lack of specificity, and its failure to identify the particular policies, and the organizational dynamics that underpin them, that lead to discriminatory outcomes (McLaughlin and Murji, 1999; Lea, 2000).

On the other hand, there is evidence that factors other than police discrimination (direct and institutional) contribute at a more fundamental level to problematic relationships. For example, although definitive conclusions cannot be drawn, there is some evidence that there are disproportionately high numbers of some ethnic minority groups involved in crime and disorder (Smith, 1997). This should not be a contentious finding given what we know about wider patterns of racial disadvantage, and associations with offending of socio-economic problems such as unemployment and poverty (Dickinson, 1993). In addition, as mentioned above, these wider structural features often work to place ethnic minorities at greater risk of police attention, in a very practical sense. For example, a number of factors, including higher levels of unemployment and more school exclusions among young black people, mean that they are disproportionately 'available' in public places for police stops (MVA and Miller, 2000). Most commentators would probably accept the position of Left Realist criminologists, who argued that socio-economic disadvantage contributes both to higher offending and greater targeting by the police. This, in turn, helps further generate mutual hostility between the police and some ethnic minority groups, which fosters resentment on the part of the community and prejudice within the police organization. These processes then feed back into the wider patterns of wider ethnic disadvantage (Lea and Young, 1984). Thus, as Reiner (2000) has stated, 'the police are reproducers rather than creators of social injustice, although their prejudices may amplify it'. It is to these amplification effects that police reformers must turn their attention in order to bring about improvements within the framework of policing policy (Jones, 1998).

Police effectiveness and performance

In recent years, the issue of police performance has been the central concern of political interest in policing in England and Wales. By the early 1990s there was heightened official concern that, despite ever-increasing amounts of public expenditure devoted to the police, crime rates had continued to rise, whilst detection rates had fallen substantially (Jones and Newburn, 1997). Since this time, however, there have been substantial falls in crime as recorded by the British Crime Survey, although it is unclear what contribution policing has made to these falls. Despite the recent evidence of decreasing victimization, an obsession with promoting police effectiveness remains central to government attempts to reform the police service. The roots of the current raft of reforms aimed at improving the performance effectiveness of the police service could be detected during the early 1980s, when the then Conservative government began to apply market disciplines to a range of public services. The process began when the government's 'Financial Management Initiative' (designed to promote economy, efficiency and effectiveness in public services) was extended to the police service in 1983. This was the first significant attempt to bring about more central budgetary control of policing by linking increases in police staffing levels to evidence that police forces had 'civilianized' posts. Since the mid-1980s the Audit Commission has been increasingly influential, promoting 'value for money' within police forces. By the end of the 1980s, however, senior Conservative politicians were becoming frustrated by the apparent lack of results following major increases in public expenditure on the police (Baker, 1993). During the early 1990s, a succession of government reports began to frame a radical programme of reform for the police service. Government reforms during the 1990s were underpinned by a 'rigorous instrumentalism' (Walker, 2000: 98), with the key focus being to promote efficient and effective service delivery. The reforms embodied in the Police and Magistrates Courts Act 1994 contained a substantive element of marketization that was to be confirmed and accelerated under later governments. Of particular importance were the following: the introduction of a 'purchaser-provider' split between police authority and force; the development of national policing objectives and key performance indicators; the introduction of costed local 'business plans' for policing; the appointment of independent members to police authorities to make them more 'businesslike'; charging for police services and promoting sponsorship and the devolution of budgetary controls to the local level (Jones, 2003).

Concerns about improving police performance have particularly focused upon the arena of crime investigation and control, which have increasingly been shaped by economic forms of thinking (Maguire, 2003). The Audit Commission has promoted a more 'proactive' strategy in contrast to more traditional case-based methods of detective work (Audit Commission, 1993). This includes a more calculative and risk-oriented approach towards crime investigation, including crime management, case screening, the increasing use of surveillance technologies, and more systematic quantitative methods of crime analysis (Johnston, 2000). These developments are currently being systematically introduced across all police forces in England and Wales with the development of the National Intelligence Model (NIM), which provides a 'business model' for the organization of police crime control activities (Maguire, 2003).

These policy trends have been further encouraged by Labour administrations since 1997. Two of the most significant developments within this are the stringent national planning framework introduced by the Police Reform Act 2002, and the establishment of the Police Standards Unit—a Home Office Unit with a brief to promote improvements in 'under-performing' police force areas—in the same year. These specific developments have been accompanied by an ever more strident rhetoric on the part of government ministers expressing frustration at levels of police performance and the need for more radical reform (Travis, 2002). Another example of this heightened political concern with police performance was the Street Crime Action Group that was established in March 2003. This involved direct central intervention in day-to-day policing by senior government ministers, with senior officers in ten target force areas required to report on a regular basis to government ministers on progress towards targets (Home Office, 2002).

Police governance and accountability

Whilst debates about police governance and accountability have been less salient in recent discussions of British policing, the issue remains of central importance in a democratic society. A key part of the debate on police accountability has concerned the governance of policing policies concerned with overall priorities, resource-allocation and policing styles. A central theme within the literature on police governance has been the progressive centralization of control over policing policy in England and Wales (Jones, 2003). The 1964 Police Act divided responsibility for the framing and monitoring of police policy between a 'tripartite structure' comprising chief constables, the Home Office, and local government (in the form of police authorities). It is clear that the local element of this structure became increasingly weakened over the latter part of the twentieth century. This was related to a variety of factors. For example the Home Office has taken a much more proactive role in promoting central government priorities and has exerted greater control over the training and promotion of senior police officers (Reiner, 2000). Local police authorities have traditionally been weak in terms of legal powers, and rather reluctant to use the few powers that they do have (Jones and Newburn, 1997). The autonomy of local forces has been constrained by the emergence of national level policing institutions during the late 1990s, including the National Criminal Intelligence Service (NCIS) and the National Crime Squad (NCS) (Johnton, 2000). In addition, the senior officers' professional association—the Association of Chief Police Officers (ACPO)—has emerged as a significant policy-making and lobbying body at the national level (Savage *et al.*, 2000). Whilst many of these developments have been visible over the longer term, there is no doubt that the embrace of a rigorous 'performance model' by successive governments from the 1990s onwards has contributed significantly to the erosion of local democratic controls and the greater influence of national institutions (see above). Most recently, there have been indications from both main political parties that they wish to enhance the local electoral input into the governance of policing. A Conservative policy document called for a return to localized police forces, but responsible to elected sheriffs (based on the system in certain parts of the USA). The Labour Party also remains enamoured with US-style solutions, and has recently floated the idea of placing local police services under the control of directly elected mayors, or introducing direct election to police authorities (to replace the current system of appointment from constituent local authorities).

The pluralization of policing poses significant challenges for the development of effective systems of governance and accountability. Loader (2000) has proposed the establishment of local, regional and national 'Policing Commissions' with a statutory responsibility to monitor and control *policing* policy as exercised by a wide range of policing agencies and institutions. This kind of institutional approach was adopted by the Patten Commission on reforming policing in Northern Ireland (Patten, 1999). The Commission recommended that local policing units be answerable to 'District Policing Partnership Boards'—a committee of the local authority that would have the power 'buy-in' extra local policing resources from providers other than the public police. It also recommended that at force level, a 'Policing Board' (and not a 'Police Board') should be established that would have substantially more powers than the existing police authority (Walker, 2000). This would have responsibility for regulating all policing providers including the commercial security industry, and coordinating provision across policing networks.

Police accountability can also be considered in terms of the accountability and control of police officers as they go about their day-to-day activities. There have been significant developments regarding the regulation of police behaviour in particular cases. Two of the most significant involve the regulation and control of police powers in dealing with suspects in criminal investigations, and the development of effective complaints mechanisms for the police. Although space prevents a detailed discussion, the Police and Criminal Evidence Act 1984 introduced a number of regulations over the powers held by the police over suspects in custody. These included things such as the introduction of a custody officer to monitor visits to suspects detained in police cells, time limits for how long a person can be held without charge, the right to legal representation, and tape-recording of interviews. Although a number of criticisms have been raised regarding the impact of PACE (Sanders and Young, 2003), the balance of research does suggest that there has been a significant effect on police behaviour within the police station, and possibly on wider detective culture (Maguire, 2002). Whatever the ongoing problems about controlling police discretion via the imposition of rules, it seems fair to say that the police are certainly more accountable than they were for their use of powers in particular investigations. Turning to the areas of police complaints mechanisms, until recently a major criticism of the arrangements has focused upon the independence (or rather the perceived lack of it) of the complaints process from the police organization. Ultimately, police officers have investigated serious complaints against other officers, although there was an independent element in the supervision of such investigations in the form of the Police Complaints Authority (PCA) (Maguire and Corbett, 1991). The Police Reform Act 2002 established the Independent Commission for Police Complaints (ICPC), staffed entirely by non-police officers and with a greater remit and more powers than the old PCA. It remains to be seen exactly what impact these new arrangements will have on the individual dimension of police accountability, but it is likely to be significant.

CONCLUSION

This chapter has presented a broad overview of some of the key themes surrounding policing and the provision of security in Britain today. It has demonstrated how the study of the policing emerged from a position of relative invisibility during the 1960s, to the forefront of debate in the latter years of the twentieth century. The chapter has clear links with some of the themes explored elsewhere in this volume including the chapters on Criminological Theory, Surveillance, Race and Ethnicity, the Politics of Law and Order, and Violence. For much of the past forty years, this renewed academic and political interest in policing has focused on the State institution known as 'the police'. Recent years, however, have seen a growing focus upon the idea of fragmentation and pluralization of policing. This has even led some to question the relevance of a continued focus on public constabularies. This chapter has taken a somewhat different approach. Although there have been some highly significant developments within the policing systems of the UK (such as the growth of commercial security), it still seems that for the forseeable future, state-organized policing arrangements will remain central to security provision. Thus, the primary focus has been on traditional police forces, what they do, how they do it, and what key debates have arisen in relation to them. These include the issue of the nature, sources and dimensions of police occupational cultures, and how they might relate to problematic behaviour by police officers. Also important is the challenge of providing equitable policing services to an increasingly diverse society in which a range of groups make contrasting demands upon the police. A central theme in recent government policy has concerned police performance and effectiveness and, finally, there is the challenge of how best to make the police accountable to the publics they serve. Although the policing landscape has undoubtedly become considerably more complex in recent decades, these areas of debate—and others connected with the police and policing—are likely to remain hot topics of discussion for some time to come amongst students, academics and the police themselves.

QUESTIONS FOR DISCUSSION

1 What is 'cop culture' and where does it come from?

2 How and why do some ethnic minority groups experience difficult relationships with the police?

3 What ways have the government tried to improve police effectiveness in recent years?

4 In what ways is control over policing policy becoming more centralized in England and Wales? Are the police becoming more or less accountable for what they do?

GUIDE TO FURTHER READING

Bowling, B. and Foster, J. (2002) *'Policing and the police'* in M. Maguire, R. Morgan and R. Reiner (eds) *The Oxford Handbook of Criminology*, Oxford: Oxford University Press.
This chapter provides a useful review of the key themes of recent British policing research and a helpful guide for further reading in the field.

Jones, T and Newburn, T. (2002) 'The Transformation of Policing? Understanding current trends in policing systems', *British Journal of Criminology* 42(1): 129–46.
This paper addresses the central issue of the pluralization of policing, and questions the degree to which such developments signify a dramatic transformation in the policing systems of western industrial countries.

Newburn, T. (ed) (2003) *The Handbook of Policing*, Cullompton: Willan.
This Handbook provides an authoritative and comprehensive overview of British policing, and draws on the expertise of both academics and senior police practitioners.

Reiner, R. (2000) *The Politics of the Police*, Oxford: Oxford University Press.
This is the third edition of a widely praised book that provides a detailed review of the history, politics and sociology of the police in England and Wales. This edition remains a key text for students, and is now comprehensively updated with a wealth of research data published during the past decade.

Johnston, L. (2000) *Policing Britain: Risk, Security and Governance*, Harlow: Longman.
An extremely useful text on British policing that provides a wealth of factual detail about contemporary developments in policing and the provision of security in the UK. In particular, this work pays significant attention to developments in policing outside of the police, and provides some extremely useful theoretical insights on how best to understand these changes.

WEB LINKS

http://www.crimereduction.gov.uk
A government-run website with a wealth of information on crime reduction, community safety and policing, including up-to-date statistics on the criminal justice system, on-line reports on policing and community safety, and details of the latest policy initiatives.

http://www.homeoffice.gov.uk/hmic/hmic.htm
HMIC has a statutory responsibility to promote the efficiency and effectiveness of police forces in England and Wales via a programme of regular force inspections and reports. It has become increasingly influential in recent years in promoting the Home Office agenda on performance improvement, as well as producing influential thematic reports on such matters as race relations and equal opportunities. This website includes a range of useful information and statistics on policing in England and Wales, and also provides online access to HMIC reports.

http://www.homeoffice.gov.uk

The Home Office is the central government department with responsibility for policing in England and Wales, and this website allows access to a wide range of relevant material for students interested in research and current policy developments on policing. In particular, students can access online a large body of Home Office research studies on policing, dating back to 1995.

http://www.policereform.gov.uk

A key website for students interested in the major programme of police reform introduced by the current Labour government. It includes key official publications such as consultation documents and summaries of recent legislation, and also the influential National Intelligence Model (NIM) for policing, and the most recent National Policing Plan.

http://www.police.uk

A police service website with important details and contact addresses for all the police forces (and related organizations) in the UK. This includes a range of relevant service-related information about current issues of concern, as well as details of police recruitment processes.

REFERENCES

Audit Commission (1993) *Helping with Enquiries: Tackling Crime Effectively*. London: Audit Commission.

Baker, K. (1993) *The Turbulent Years: My Life in Politics*. London: Faber and Faber.

Bayley, D. and Shearing, C. (1996) 'The Future of Policing', *Law and Society Review* 30(3): 585–606.

Becker, H. (1963) *Outsiders: Studies in the Sociology of Deviance*. New York: Free Press.

Bittner, E. (1980) *The Functions of the Police in Modern Society*. Cambridge, MA: Olgeschlager, Gunn and Hain.

Bowling, B. (1998) *Violent Racism*. Oxford: Clarendon Press.

Bowling, B. and Phillips, C. (2002) *Racism, Crime and Justice*. Harlow: Longman.

Bowling, B. and Phillips, C. (2003) 'Policing ethnic minority communities' in T. Newburn (ed) *The Handbook of Policing*. Cullompton: Willan.

Chan, J. (1996) 'Changing Police Culture', *British Journal of Criminology* 36(1): 109–34.

Clancy, A., Hough, M., Aust, R. and Kershaw, C. (2000) *Crime, Policing and Justice: The Experience of Ethnic Minorities*. London: Home Office.

Clarke, J. (2001) 'The pleasures of crime: interrogating the detective story' in J. Muncie and E. McLaughlin (eds) *The Problem of Crime* (2nd edn). London: Sage.

Clarke, R. and Hough, M. (1984) *Crime and Police Effectiveness*. London: Home Office Research Unit.

Coleman, A. and Gorman, L. (1982) 'Conservatism, Dogmatism and Authoritarianism in British Police Officers', *Sociology* 16(1): 1–11.

Crawford, A. (1998) *Crime Prevention and Community Safety: Politics, Policies and Practices*. London: Longman.

Crawford, A. (2003) 'The pattern of policing in the UK: policing beyond the police', in T. Newburn (ed) *The Handbook of Policing*. Cullompton: Willan.

Dickinson, D. (1993) *Crime and Unemployment*. Cambridge: Institute of Criminology.

Downes, D. and Morgan, R. (2002) 'Dumping the "hostages to fortune"? the politics of law and order in post-war Britain', in M. Maguire, R. Morgan and R. Reiner (eds) *The Oxford Handbook of Criminology*. Oxford: Oxford University Press (3rd edn).

Ellison, G. and Smyth, J. (2000) *The Crowned Harp: Policing Northern Ireland*. London: Pluto Press.

Foster, J. (2003) 'Police cultures', in T. Newburn (ed) *The Handbook of Policing*. Cullompton: Willan.

Heidensohn, F. (2003) 'Gender and policing', in T. Newburn (ed) *The Handbook of Policing*. Cullompton: Willan.

Her Majesty's Inspectorate of Constabulary (2000) *Winning the Race: Embracing Diversity. Consolidation Inspection of Police Community and Race Relations 2000*. London: Home Office.

Home Office (2002) *Delivering the Street Crime Initiative: Partnership in Operation*. London: HMSO.

Home Office (2003) *Race and the Criminal Justice System 2003*. London: Home Office.

Hughes, G. (1998) *Understanding Crime Prevention: Social Control, Risk and Late Modernity*. Buckingham: Open University Press. Chapter 6.

Hughes, G. McLaughlin, E. and Muncie, J. (2002) *Crime Prevention and Community Safety*. London: Sage.

Jefferson, T. (1990) *The Case Against Paramilitary Policing*. Milton Keynes: Open University Press.

Jefferson, T. (1993) 'Pondering Paramilitarism', *British Journal of Criminology* 33(3): 374–81.

Johnston, L. (1992) *The Rebirth of Private Policing*. London: Routledge.

Johnston, L. (1996) 'What is Vigilantism?', *British Journal of Criminology*, 36:2: 220–36.

Johnston, L. (2000) *Policing Britain: Risk, Security and Governance*. London: Longman.

Johnston, L. and Shearing, C. (2002) *Governing Security: Explorations in Policing and Justice*. London: Routledge.

Jones, T. (1998) 'Police and race relations', in R. Chadwick (ed) *The Encyclopedia of Applied Ethics*. San Diego, CA: Academic Press.

Jones, T. (2003) 'The governance and accountability of policing', in T. Newburn (ed) *The Handbook of Policing*. Cullompton: Willan.

Jones, T. and Newburn, T. (1997) *Policing After the Act: Police Governance After the Police and Magistrates' Courts Act 1994*. London: Policy Studies Institute.

Jones, T. and Newburn, T. (1998) *Private Security and Public Policing*. Oxford: Clarendon Press.

Jones, T. and Newburn, T. (1999) 'Urban Change and Policing: Mass Private Property Reconsidered', *European Journal on Criminal Policy and Research* 7: 225–44.

Jones, T. and Newburn, T. (2001) *Widening Access: Improving relations with 'hard to reach groups'*. London: Home Office.

Jones, T. and Newburn, T. (2002) 'The Transformation of Policing? Understanding Current Trends in Policing Systems', *British Journal of Criminology*, 42:1: 129–46.

Kinsey, R., Lea, J. and Young, J. (1986) *Losing the Fight Against Crime*. Oxford: Blackwell.

Lea, J. and Young, J. (1984) *What is to be Done About Law and Order?* Harmondsworth: Penguin.

Lea, J. (2000) 'The Macpherson Report and the Question of Institutional Racism', *Howard Journal of Criminal Justice* 39(3).

Leishman, F. and Mason, P. (2003) *Policing and the Media: Facts, Fictions and Factions*. Cullompton: Willan

Lemert, E. (1964) 'Social structure, social control and deviation', in M. Clinard (ed) *Anomie and Deviant Behaviour*. New York: Free Press.

Loader, I. (1997) 'Private security and the demand for protection in contemporary Britain', *Policing and Society*, Volume 7: 143–62.

Loader, I. (2000) 'Plural policing and democratic governance', *Social and Legal Studies*, 9:3: 323–45.

Loader, I. and Mulcahy, A. (2003) *Policing and the Condition of England: Memory, Politics and Culture*. Oxford: Oxford University Press.

Lustgarten, L. (1986) *The Governance of Police*. London: Sweet and Maxwell.

McLaughlin, E. and Murji, K. (1999) 'After the Stephen Lawrence Inquiry', *Critical Social Policy* 19(3): 371–85.

Maguire, M. (2002) 'Regulating the police station: the case of the Police and Criminal Evidence Act 1984', in M. McConville and G. Wilson (eds) *The Handbook of the Criminal Justice Process*. Oxford: Oxford University Press.

Maguire, M. (2003) 'Criminal investigation and crime control, in T. Newburn (ed) *The Handbook of Policing*. Cullompton: Willan.

Manning, P. (1977) *Police Work*. Cambridge, MA: MIT Press.

Mirlees-Black, C., Mayhew, P. and Percy, A. (1996) The 1996 British Crime Survey: England and Wales.

Morgan, R. and Newburn, T. (1997) *The Future of Policing*. Oxford: Oxford University Press.

MVA and Miller, J. (2000) *Profiling Populations Available for Stops and Searches*. Police Research Series Paper 131. London: Home Office.

NACRO (1996) *Crime, Community and Change*. London: National Association for the Care and Resettlement of Offenders.

Newburn, T. (2003) 'Introduction: understanding policing' in T. Newburn (ed) *The Handbook of Policing*. Cullompton: Willan.

PA Consulting Group (2001) *Diary of a Police Officer*. Police Research Paper 149. London: Home Office.

Patten, C. (1999) *A New Beginning for Policing in Northern Ireland: The Report of the Independent Commission on Policing for Northern Ireland*. Belfast: HMSO.

Punch, M. (1979) 'The secret social service', in S. Holdaway (ed) *The British Police*. London: Edward Arnold.

Rawlings, P. (2002) *Policing: A Short History*. Cullompton: Willan.

Reiner, R. (1997) 'Policing and the police', in M. Maguire, R. Morgan and R. Reiner (eds) *The Oxford Handbook of Criminology*. Oxford: Oxford University Press (2nd Edn).

Reiner, R. (2000) *The Politics of the Police* (3rd Edn). Oxford: Oxford University Press.

Reiner, R. (2003) 'Policing and the media', in T. Newburn (ed) *The Handbook of Policing*. Cullompton: Willan.

Rosenbaum, D.P. (1988) 'Community Crime Prevention: A Review and Synthesis of the literature', *Justice Quarterly* 5(3): 323–96.

Rozenberg, J. (1992) 'Miscarriages of justice', in E. Stockdale and S. Casale (eds) *Criminal Justice Under Stress*. London: Blackstone Press, pp. 91–117.

Sampson, A., Stubbs, P., Smith, D., Pearson, G., and Blagg, H. (1988) 'Crime, Localities and the Multi-Agency Approach', *British Journal of Criminology*, 28(4), pp.478–93.

Sanders, A. and Young, R. (2003) 'Police powers', in T. Newburn (ed) *The Handbook of Policing*. Cullompton: Willan.

Saulsbury, W. and Bowling, B. (1991) *The multi-agency approach in practice: the North Plaistow racial harassment project*. Research and Planning Unit Paper No. 64. London: Home Office.

Savage, S., Charman, S. and Cope, S. (2000) 'The policy-making context: Who shapes policing policy?', in F. Leishman, *et al.* (eds) *Core Issues in Policing*. Harlow: Longman.

Scarman, Lord (1981) *The Brixton Disorders 10–12 April 1981: Report of an Inquiry by Lord Scarman*. London: HMSO.

Shapland, J. and Vagg, J. (1988) *Policing by the Public*. London: Routledge.

Shearing, C. (2000) 'A "new beginning" for policing', *Journal of Law and Society* 27(3), pp. 386–93.

Sheptycki, J. (ed) (2000) *Issues in Transnational Policing*. London: Routledge.

Skogan, W. (1990) *The Police and Public in England and Wales: A British Crime Survey Report*. London: HMSO.

Skolnik, J. (1966) *Justice Without Trial: Law Enforcement in a Democratic Society*. New York: Wiley.

Smith, D.J. (1986) 'The framework of law and policing practice', in J. Beynon and C. Bourn (eds) *The Police: Powers, Procedures and Proprieties*. Oxford: Pergamon Press.

Smith, D.J. (1997) 'Ethnic origins, crime and criminal justice', in M. Maguire, R. Morgan and R. Reiner (eds) *The Oxford Handbook of Criminology*. Oxford: Oxford University Press (2nd Edn).

Smith, D.J. and Gray. J. (1985) *Police and People in London*. London: Policy Studies Institute.

Standing Conference on Crime Prevention (1991) *Safer Communities: The Local Delivery of Crime Prevention Through the Partnership Approach*. London: Home Office.

Travis, A. (2002) 'Met Police Get Six Month Deadline To Tackle Crime'. *Guardian*, 15 February.

Waddington, P.A.J. (1993) 'The Case Against Paramilitary Policing Considered', *British Journal of Criminology* 33(3): 352–66.

Waddington, P.A.J. (1999) 'Police (Canteen) Sub-Culture: An Appreciation', *British Journal of Criminology* 39(2): 286–308.

Waddington, P.A.J. (2003) 'Policing Public Order and Political Contention', in T. Newburn (ed) *The Handbook of Policing*. Cullompton: Devon.

Walker, N. (2000) *Policing in a Changing Constitutional Order*. London: Sweet and Maxwell.

Williams, M. and Robinson, A.L. (2004) 'Problems and Prospects with Policing the Lesbian, Gay and Bisexual Community in Wales', *Policing and Society*, 14(3), pp. 213–232.

26 Punishment in the community

Anne Worrall

INTRODUCTION

When the topic of punishment is discussed, many people think first about prison. Yet the vast majority of people who commit crimes and are detected are dealt with by measures that do not involve imprisonment. Approximately 1.6 million offenders were found guilty or were cautioned in 2001 (Home Office, 2002a) and, of these, approximately 106,000 were sent to prison. The remainder were cautioned, discharged, fined or placed on community sentences. This chapter explores and explains the history, philosophies, current practices and policy debates surrounding those measures which are, often mistakenly, frequently referred to as 'alternatives to prison'. In this chapter, it will be argued that non-custodial sentences should not be viewed merely as 'alternatives' to prison but should be understood as representing a different sphere of penal regulation which is based on enabling and requiring offenders to take responsibility for changing their own lives and behaviour without the physical constraints of imprisonment. The following section will provide a brief introduction to the terminology and key concepts of punishment in the community. There will then follow a more detailed description of the range of sentences available to courts, the relevant legislation and the extent to which these sentences are used. A brief history of the Probation Service—the agency responsible for most community sentences—will follow, concluding with the creation of the National Probation Service in 2001. The chapter then proceeds to an analysis and discussion of the main issues and problems presented by punishment in the community, culminating in an exploration of the impact of the 'What Works' agenda, which has dominated developments in this area over the past decade. The concluding section of the chapter will summarize the key facts, concepts and debates relating to this topic.

BACKGROUND

There is no single generic term for punishment that does not involve imprisonment. The most commonly used terms are 'alternatives to custody' or 'non-custodial sentences', but ' community punishment', 'community corrections', 'community penalties' and 'community sentences' are now widely recognized terms, though the word 'community' in this context means little more than 'not in prison'. The term 'community' is difficult to define because it has different meanings in different contexts. It conjures up images of neighbourliness, mutual aid and a positive sense of belonging, while, at the same time, blurring the boundaries of responsibility between the State and the individual. In relation to crime, it is not clear whether 'the community' is tolerant, resourceful and healing or intolerant, fearful and punitive (Worrall and Hoy, 2005). The extent to which the 'community' is involved in community sentences in practice is generally very limited and the implication that such sentences enhance social inclusion, rather than exacerbating social exclusion, is also debatable (see Chapter 16). The phrase 'punishment in the community' entered penal vocabulary in a government discussion paper in 1988 (Home Office, 1988) and was an attempt to dislodge prison from its central position in penal thinking. It became integrated into legislation in the Criminal Justice Act 1991, which remains the overarching legal framework for sentencing until the Criminal Justice Act 2003 is fully implemented.

It is possible to classify community sentences in three ways: self-regulatory, financial and supervisory (Worrall and Hoy, 2005). Self-regulatory penalties involve some form of public admonition or reprimand which is assumed to be sufficiently shaming of itself to deter the offender from further law-breaking. Financial penalties are of two kinds: fines are both retributive and deterrent (see Chapter 22) in purpose and are paid to the central administration of a criminal justice system; compensation is paid (through the courts) to the victim of a crime and is intended to provide reparation. Supervisory sentences are imposed when courts believe that the offender is unable to stop committing crimes without support or surveillance and they may contain one or more of three elements: (a) rehabilitation (through education, therapeutic programmes, counselling and welfare advice); (b) reparation (through unpaid work for the community); and (c) incapacitation (through curfews and electronic monitoring).

Some community sentences have long histories, while others have been introduced more recently. For example, the origins of probation (the main form of supervision) can be traced back to the late nineteenth century, whereas community service (unpaid work) was introduced in the 1970s and electronic monitoring in the 1980s, initially as a mechanism for reducing the numbers of offenders being remanded in custody to await trial or sentence. Expansion in the use of supervisory sentences since the 1970s has been due to the desire of governments to be seen to be finding less expensive, but equally demanding, alternatives to imprisonment. This has been termed the 'decarceration' debate and resulted from a loss of confidence in the 1950s and 1960s in the 'rehabilitative ideal' (based on the discredited therapeutic possibilities of institutions). In reality, such expansion has been an accompaniment, rather than an alternative, to a rising prison population (Scull, 1984; Cohen, 1985).

It could be argued that community sentences might have several advantages over imprisonment. They allow offenders to retain family, work and social ties while, at the same time, giving them the opportunity to repair the damage they have done to the community and resolve the personal and social problems which may have led to their offending in the first place. They enable offenders to avoid the stigma of imprisonment and the risk of becoming embedded in a criminal culture as a result of constant association with other criminals in prison. Community sentences are also less costly to administer than imprisonment (Home Office, 1990; Raynor *et al.*, 1994; Smith, 1995; Walker and Beaumont, 1985; Worrall and Hoy, 2005).

Despite these apparent advantages, community sentences have an 'image' problem. Although many more offenders receive some form of community punishment than are imprisoned, penal debates and policies focus overwhelmingly on prisons and neglect other forms of punishment (Windlesham, 1993). Attempts to raise the profile of community sentences encounter a number of obstacles.

First, and of most significance, is the public and media perception that community punishment is but a poor substitute for the 'real punishment' of prison. Viewed as 'soft options', community sentences are often represented in policy documents as weak and undemanding 'let offs', which do not command public confidence. There is, therefore, a constant search among advocates of community sentences to include more and more demanding conditions which distinguish 'intermediate sentences' (as they are sometimes called) from traditional welfare-oriented supervision (Byrne *et al.*, 1992). Second is the obstacle of unfair and inconsistent sentencing. Despite increasingly sophisticated guidelines on the use of community sentences, there remain concerns that certain groups of offenders are over-represented in prison for reasons that may have little to do with the seriousness of their offences. Community sentences tend to be available only to the relatively advantaged socially—those with sufficient money to pay a fine, those who are employed and those who are perceived to be able to benefit from supervision. Third is the obstacle of 'net-widening', a term which entered criminal justice vocabulary in the 1960s in the wake of labelling theory (see Chapter 4). With the proliferation of alternatives to custody comes the danger that instead of keeping people out of prison, community sentences will simply draw more and more people into the 'net' of the criminal justice system (Cohen, 1985) and thereby increase the likelihood that they will eventually end up in prison. The fourth obstacle is that of enforcement. Ensuring compliance with community sentences is notoriously difficult and courts have the right to send to prison any offender who fails to pay a fine or who breaches the conditions of a supervisory order. In this way, community sentencing always functions 'in the shadow' of imprisonment.

Types of community sentences and sentencing trends

We have already seen that there is no agreement on a collective name for penalties that do not involve imprisonment. It is also the case that there is no agreement on whether or not the term 'community sentences' should include sentences that do not involve some form of supervision by the Probation Service (see next section). For the purposes of this exercise and in order to provide a comprehensive introduction to the full range of non-custodial sentences, we will use the term in this broader sense.

Self-regulatory sentences are those which do not impose any immediate sanction on an offender. They assume that the very act of being detected, arrested and, in some cases, taken to court, will cause sufficient shame to either deter or reform the offender, without need of further penalty. Formal police cautions, reprimands and warnings are used very widely for juvenile offenders, especially those committing first or minor offences. They are also available for adults but are used less frequently. Overall, the cautioning rate fell from 40 per cent of all known offenders in 1995 to 32 per cent of all known offenders in 2000 (Johnson, 2001). For adults, the most common self-regulatory sentence is known as a 'conditional discharge'. This involves a court appearance but the offender is put 'on trust' for a period of time. If they re-offend during that period, they are liable to be re-sentenced for the original offence, as well as for the new one. The use of conditional discharges has also declined steadily over the past decade (Johnson, 2001). Other self-regulatory sentences are available for special situations but are used less frequently than those described here. For example, it is possible for a prison sentence to be suspended, but this disposal is used infrequently nowadays.

Financial penalties remain the most commonly imposed sentences in the courts of England and Wales, although their use has reduced over the past decade (Johnson *et al.*, 2001). The two main types of financial penalty are fines and compensation. Advocates of the fine argue that it is a very flexible sentence which can take account of the offender's ability to pay as well as the seriousness of the offence. Thus, it combines elements of retribution (reflecting the seriousness of a crime), deterrence (convincing the offender that crime, literally, 'does not pay') and reparation (paying society and/or the victim back for harm done). However, many people are either unable or unwilling to pay fines and they are then sent to prison 'in default'. In an attempt to resolve this problem, in the early 1990s, courts experimented with 'unit fines' which involved a specific formula for matching an offender's disposable income with the seriousness of their offence (Home Office, 1990). But it was unpopular with sentencers, who believed that it was fettering their sentencing discretion, and the experiment was discontinued in 1993. There are large numbers of offenders who go to prison for 'fine default' but, because they spend only a few days there on average, their numbers are underrepresented in prison statistics (Home Office, 2003). Aware of this problem, courts have become more reluctant to impose fines, especially on unemployed offenders and on women, who often do not have an independent source of income and who are responsible for the care of children (Hedderman and Gelsthorpe, 1997). Compensation to a victim can be ordered as a separate sentence or as an adjunct to any other sentence. It is also possible for courts to confiscate the proceeds from serious drug offences.

Supervisory sentences come in many forms and it is confusing that, since the creation of the National Probation Service in 2001, the traditional names for the main sentences have been changed. Probation Orders are now called Community Rehabilitation Orders (CRO); Community Service Orders (unpaid work) are now called Community Punishment Orders (CPO); Combination Orders (which combine probation and community service) are now called Community Punishment and Rehabilitation Orders (CPRO). In addition to these main orders, there are also Curfew Orders (with or without electronic monitoring) and Drug Treatment and Testing Orders (DTTO). For juveniles, the standard sentence is now a Detention and Training Order (DTO—not to be confused with a DTTO!), which involves some time spent in custody (in a Young Offender Institution) and some time spent under supervision in the community. It is important to note that supervision is being used increasingly as an addition to prison, rather than as an alternative to it. Traditionally, supervisory sentences have aimed to reform or rehabilitate offenders through advice, counseling, treatment and constructive activity. Community Service Orders also contain strong elements of reparation to the community. Increasingly, however, the term 'supervision' is accompanied by the terms 'intensive' and/or 'monitoring', reflecting a change of ethos towards the principle of 'incapacitation'. Restricting offenders' liberty, checking on their whereabouts and gathering ever more information about them, are routine features of contemporary supervision. The use of electronic monitoring to ensure compliance with Curfew Orders is but an extreme example of current trends towards 'incapacitation in the community'.

Every year the Home Office produces *Probation Statistics for England and Wales* and these are now available on the Home Office website (www.homeoffice.gov.uk/rds/pdfs2/probation). Figures 26.1–26.3 show the trends in supervisory sentences over the past decade. They indicate the numbers of people starting the different kinds of supervision ordered by courts.

The increase in all orders for men has been steady, with over 100,000 starting an order during 2001. The slight decline in orders in 2000 and 2001 may be accounted for by the introduction of Drug Treatment and Testing Orders in 1998. In 2001, 4,400 DTTOs were made on males and females combined. On a much smaller scale, the same pattern can be seen in CPOs and CPROs for women. But the trend is slightly different for CROs for women. The lowest figure of 7,104 comes in 1993 and this represents a decline from nearly 12,000 probation orders a decade previously. At that time probation orders on women represented 33 per cent of all such orders compared with 16 per cent in 1993. Despite an increase since then, they still represent only 18 per cent of all CROs. The implication is that sentencers have shifted from placing women on CROs (with their

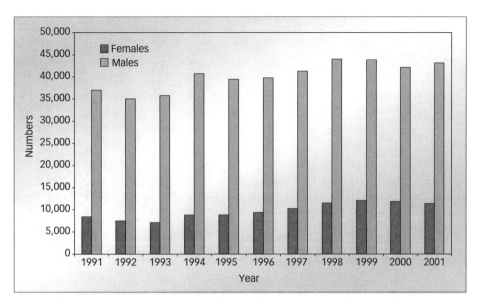

Figure 26.1 Persons starting community rehabilitation order by gender

Source: Based on data from Table 3.3, Probation Statistics England and Wales 2001, Home Office (2002b).

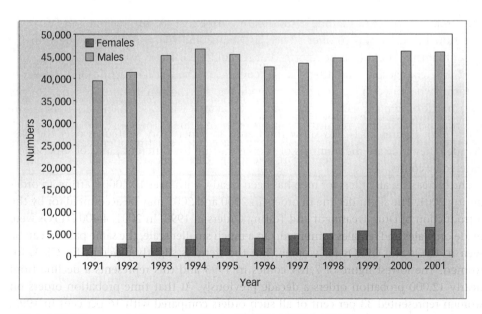

Figure 26.2 Persons starting community punishment orders by gender

Source: Based on data from Table 3.3, Probation Statistics England and Wales 2001, Home Office (2002b).

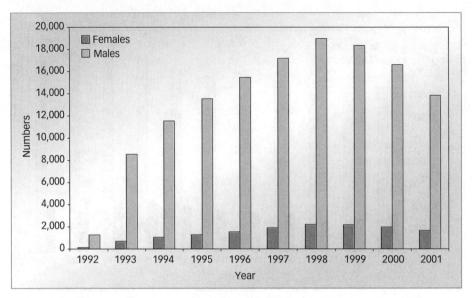

Figure 26.3 Persons starting community punishment and rehabilitation orders by gender

Source: Based on data from Table 3.3, Probation Statistics England and Wales 2001, Home Office (2002b).

welfare connotations) to placing them on CPOs, CPROs and, of course, prison. Overall, just under 20,000 women were given community sentences in 2001.

Community rehabilitation orders (formerly probation orders)

The probation order has a long history dating back to 1907 in England and Wales. Its traditional purpose was to offer advice, assistance and friendship to offenders, in the belief that they could thus be reformed or rehabilitated. These two terms are frequently used interchangeably and there is no consensus about their definitions. However, 'reform' (when used in relation to an individual rather than an institution) tends to refer to a change of mind or will (as in 'reformed character'), whereas 'rehabilitation' has more deterministic overtones, requiring a change of circumstances (personal, social or medical) (Worrall and Hoy: 11). More emphasis is now placed on restricting offenders' liberty, protecting the public and preventing re-offending. Offenders are selected for probation through a process of assessment by a probation officer who advises, or writes a report for, the sentencing court. Probation orders, which can be between six months and three years in length, require the offender to maintain contact with their supervising officer and to tell their supervisor about changes in their circumstances. Failure to comply with these conditions constitutes a breach of the probation order and the offender can be re-sentenced, usually to a period of imprisonment.

It is also possible for courts to add conditions to a basic order requiring an offender to live at an approved residence (which can include bail and probation hostels, now known as Approved Premises) or to undergo psychiatric treatment. More recently, courts have been able to require an offender to attend treatment programmes or other activities. Since

1991, it has been possible for courts to combine probation orders with community service orders (see below) to produce combination orders which are intended to fulfil both rehabilitative and reparative penal purposes.

Community punishment orders (formerly community service orders)

Community Service was introduced in England and Wales in 1973 (although its predecessor, hard labour, has a very long history) and requires offenders to undertake unpaid work in the community for a period ranging from sixty to 240 hours. It was introduced because of concern about rising prison populations and the apparent ineffectiveness of probation orders to reduce re-offending. It has a chameleon-like ability to adapt its aims and objectives to fit almost every traditional justification of punishment—retribution (visible hard work), reparation (unpaid work for the community), deterrence (working for no reward), incapacitation (restriction of liberty) and rehabilitation (learning skills and/or achieving something of worth). This has made it very popular with sentencers, who see it as having the flexibility of a fine but without its disadvantages. It has been described as a fine on time. Offenders typically work in groups on projects involving land restoration, painting, decorating and woodwork, or in individual placements with charity shops, voluntary organizations and so on.

Curfew orders with electronic monitoring

Electronic monitoring was introduced on an experimental basis in England and Wales in the 1980s for a number of reasons. It was seen as a way to reduce prison overcrowding and prison costs. It was also seen as a way to introduce privatization to punishment in the community as well as to prisons. Finally, it was seen as a sophisticated way to subject offenders to some of the restrictions of prison without inflicting on them the damage of being removed from their home environment.

Electronic monitoring requires offenders to be fitted with a special bracelet or anklet which is connected electronically to a telephone which is, in turn, connected to a call centre, whence regular checks are made on the offender's whereabouts. Offenders have individualized schedules requiring them to be at home between certain hours. There are now two distinct ways in which electronic monitoring is used to enable offenders to live in the community. First, courts can sentence offenders to curfew orders with electronic monitoring. Second, prisoners may be released several weeks before the end of their sentence, on condition that they are monitored. Both measures have been available nationally since 1999 and are likely to be incorporated increasingly into a number of community sentences in order to provide a stronger element of surveillance (Nellis, 2003). In 2001, around 6,000 curfew orders with electronic monitoring were made. In the same year, around 14,000 prisoners were released on HDC and 90 per cent successfully completed their curfew (Home Office, 2003).

Although most of the early technological problems relating to 'tagging' have now been overcome, there remain other matters of concern. Some people argue that it is an infringement of civil liberties and encourages 'net-widening' (resulting in more minor offenders being tagged who would not have gone to prison anyway). Others point to the visible stigma of the tag (or, alternatively, the danger that it becomes a 'badge of honour' for some young offenders). Yet others have suggested that confining certain offenders to their homes may place a strain on other members of their family.

Drug treatment and testing orders

Drug Treatment and Testing Orders were introduced with the Crime and Disorder Act 1998 in three pilot areas. Since 2000 they have been available nationally and 4,400 orders were made in 2001, of which 83 per cent were made on men (Home Office, 2003). They constitute a government response to the increasing number of offenders who appear to commit crimes to finance their drug addictions and they are aimed at those offenders who are willing to cooperate with treatment, supervision and urine testing (Turnbull *et al.*, 2000). DTTOs have been criticized for making drug treatment compulsory and for over-simplifying the link between drug use and crime. As with other penal innovations, they have also been criticized for being used for 'petty' offenders (net-widening), for not taking sufficient account of the needs of women and minority ethnic offenders, and for not providing sufficient social support to ensure that rehabilitation is sustained (Fowler, 2002).

REVIEW QUESTIONS

1 What different types of community penalties are there?

2 What principles of sentencing underpin these different sentences?

3 What have been the main features of trends in community sentencing over the past decade?

The National Probation Service and National Offender Management Service (NOMS)

There is a broad consensus that the earliest recognizable 'probation officers' were the 'police court missionaries' who worked in London courts in the last quarter of the nineteenth century. Their job was to rescue and befriend drunken offenders, setting them on the path to redemption. Secular probation officers have been a presence in all criminal courts since the early twentieth century, and from the 1930s, they were trained as social workers, influenced by 'welfare' and 'medical' models of delinquency (Chui and Nellis, 2003). From the 1970s, however, such models became discredited and probation officers became increasingly influenced by 'non-treatment paradigms' (Bottoms and McWilliams, 1979) and increasingly exercised about securing the correct balance between 'care' and 'control' in their work with offenders. By the end of the twentieth century, probation officers had to accept that their role was to 'confront, control and monitor' and not merely to 'advise, assist and befriend' (Worrall and Hoy, 2005; Brownlee, 1998). Organizationally, until 2001, each of over fifty area Probation Services was managed autonomously, although most of the Service's funding came from the Home Office. Each Probation Service had its own Chief Probation Officer and, like the police, there was no centralized organization or spokesperson for the Service. Until the 1980s, the Home

Office did not really interfere at all with the running of local Probation Services, but in 1984, it produced a Statement of National Objectives and Priorities. The content of SNOP was not particularly contentious, but the fact that it had been produced at all certainly was and it proved to be the start of a debate lasting almost two decades on the management of the Probation Service. By the 1990s, all area Services were required to meet National Standards of practice and policy and, by the middle of the decade, training for probation officers (which had previously constituted a specialism within social work training courses) had been separated completely from social work training. By the end of that decade, the government was mooting the abolition of the name 'Probation' altogether and considering the merger of probation and prisons into one correctional service (Home Office, 1998; Raynor, 2002). This caused much protest and the eventual compromise was the creation in 2001 of a centralized National Probation Service with a Director. The number of areas was reduced from fifty-four to forty-two and, as we have already seen, the names of the main court orders were changed. These changes both reflected and confirmed a major change of ethos for the Probation Service and, as Chui and Nellis muse, 'continuity with the past may be less than meets the eye' (2003: 1). The National Probation Service now views itself, first and foremost, as a law enforcement agency delivering community penalties (National Probation Service, 2001). However, this was not to be the end of the restructuring story and in 2003, the Carter Review (Carter, 2003) and subsequent government response (Home Office, 2004a) proposed a new National Offender Management Service (NOMS) which would finally bring together the Prison and Probation Services (from June 2004) to provide 'end-to-end management of all offenders, whether they are serving sentences in prison, the community or both.' (Home Office, 2004b). As we shall see later in this chapter, this has implications for work with offenders, where the focus is no longer on the welfare of the offender (with some ill-defined hope that this will lead in some way to reform) but on clearly defined goals of reducing re-offending and protecting the public. Central to this approach is the concept of enforcement—ensuring that offenders meet the requirements of their orders. Returning an offender to court for non-compliance with an order (known as 'breaching'), which was seen in the past as an admission of failure by the probation officer, is now viewed as essential to the credibility of orders and an act of strength (Hedderman, 2003).

REVIEW QUESTIONS

1 In what ways has the Probation Service changed since its early days in the late nineteenth century?

2 What are the priorities of the National Probation Service?

Ways of understanding the politics of punishment in the community

In this section we consider three different ways of explaining and understanding (or theorizing) about the development of community penalties. We draw on Stan Cohen's analysis of the history of 'social control talk' (1983) which juxtaposes three models of correctional change: 'uneven progress', 'benevolence gone wrong' and 'it's all a con' (1983: 104–106).

Uneven progress

Accepting that, in an imperfect world, progress will never be unimpeded, Cohen describes, first, an optimistic conservative rhetoric which argues that penal reform has been steady and that alternatives to custody represent the enlightened values of an ever more civilized society. Before the end of the nineteenth century, the only non-custodial sentences (apart from the death penalty) used regularly by courts were fines and release on recognizances (the equivalent of cautions, binding over and discharges—see below). Most histories of the probation service place it within the humanitarian considerations of Victorian and Edwardian penal reformers, but Raynor and Vanstone (2002) provide a more critical summary which emphasizes the dimension of 'moral training'. An increasing confidence in both their material wealth and their scientific knowledge led reformers to believe that crime was a social disease for which a cure was possible through 'specific practices of normalization, classification, categorization and discrimination between criminal types' (Garland 1985: 32). Social control could now be achieved 'through attention to the material, social and psychological welfare of criminals' (Worrall and Hoy, 2005: 4) without the need for physical incarceration. Throughout the twentieth century a range of non-custodial penalties developed, adding increasing numbers of conditions and restrictions on offenders' freedom, while stopping short of incarcerating them. Courts are now able to require offenders to reside in certain places, to receive psychiatric or drug treatment, to attend therapeutic programmes, to perform unpaid work or to observe curfews that are monitored electronically. The aim of all these measures is to prevent offenders from re-offending without resorting to sending them to prison. In this way, it is argued, the public is more likely to be protected in the longer-term because imprisonment protects the public for only a short while and, by cutting offenders' social ties and fuelling their resentment, may make them more likely to re-offend in the future (Hagan, 1994; Maruna, 2000; Farrall, 2002).

Benevolence gone wrong

But the rehabilitative ideal came increasingly under attack in the 1960s and 1970s for both ideological and pragmatic reasons. Ideologically, attempts at offender rehabilitation were regarded as, on the one hand, intrusive and an infringement of civil liberties and, on the other hand, as a 'soft option'—an indulgence of middle-class liberals out of touch with the 'real' world of crime victimization. Pragmatically, it seemed that rehabilitation just did not 'work' and, in some cases, made matters worse (Worrall and Hoy, 2005: 24).

Cohen's second account of penal change reflects this disillusion with rehabilitation which characterized much of the symbolic interactionist literature on the sociology of deviance and the 'nothing works' approach to punishment. Rather than seeking reform, this model suggests, we should be looking for ways to manage both the system and individual criminal careers so as to cause the least damage, cost and inconvenience to the rest of society. However, after a decade of defensiveness and soul-searching in the 1980s,

CHAPTER 26 PUNISHMENT IN THE COMMUNITY 537

advocates of rehabilitation slowly regained confidence with the discovery of what is now termed the 'What Works'—or 'evidence-based'—approach, which we will consider in more detail later in this chapter. For Cohen, however, these developments (though he wrote before the term 'what works' was coined) represented a process of official mystification.

It's all a con

Cohen's third model presents a conspiracy of the powerful to mystify and obfuscate. He argued that humanism, good intentions, professional knowledge and reform rhetoric did not simply result in change 'for the better'. They also involved the exercize of power and the social construction (see chapter 1) of offenders as certain 'types' of people (objects of knowledge) about whom it is both possible and desirable to accumulate information and make judgements. The decarcerated criminal is one such new object of knowledge about whom new bodies of information must be accumulated. Community programmes, far from reducing the restrictions on criminals who might otherwise have been sent to prison, create a new clientele of criminals who are controlled or disciplined by other mechanisms. The boundaries between freedom and confinement become blurred. The 'net' of social control is thus thrown ever wider into the community, its thinner mesh designed to trap ever smaller 'fish'. Once caught in the net, the penetration of disciplinary intervention is ever deeper, reaching every aspect of the criminal's life.

REVIEW QUESTIONS

1 How might we explain the historical development of community penalties?

2 Which explanation do you find the most convincing and why?

Diversity and punishment in the community

Traditionally, the probation order was the sentence 'of choice' for women. They were considered ideally suited to being 'advised, assisted and befriended' (to adapt the former mission statement of the probation service). But the influence of feminist perspectives on criminal justice led many probation officers to be concerned that too many women were being placed on probation and, more significantly, too early in their criminal careers. The good intentions of probation officers in recommending supervizory sentences for women appeared to result in 'net-widening' and ultimately accelerating a woman's journey to custody. There was an assumption (informed by theories of labelling and deviancy amplification) that diverting women from probation would automatically reduce the numbers in prison. As Eaton (1986) and Worrall (1990) demonstrated, probation officers' court reports (known then as social inquiry reports, now pre-sentence reports) constructed women within the ideological constraints of the family and inadvertently reinforced sentencers' stereotyped views on 'good' and 'bad' women. This emerging gender awareness among probation officers resulted in a concerted effort to write non- or anti-discriminatory reports which strove to avoid collusion with such stereotyping.

The effort was partially successful in that fewer women were placed on probation for minor offences, and for a while in the early 1990s, there was some cause for optimism. The Criminal Justice Act 1991, based on the principle of 'just deserts', *should* have resulted in a fairer deal for women criminals. If sentencing was to depend predominantly on the seriousness of the current offence, the implication *should* have been that fewer women would go to prison for relatively minor offences, however frequently committed. But as the prison population rose (see Cheney, Chapter 27), this did not seem to happen. As the female prison population rose steadily from 1,500 in 1992 to 4,300 in 2002, it became clear that the traditional probation order was seen as insufficiently punitive for women who were no longer regarded as in need of 'help'. So the focus turned to community service orders and combination orders (now CPOs and CPROs).

There is nothing in theory or in law to debar women from doing community service, but sentencers have always had ambivalent feelings about giving such orders to women (Worrall and Hoy, 2005: 129). Research has suggested that there is greater inconsistency in the use of community service for women than for men and that women are more likely than men to receive such orders for their first offence (Hine and Thomas, 1995). It has always been viewed by courts as not quite an appropriate sentence for women and the practicalities have always been an obstacle—the absence of childcare facilities being the main problem (Howard League, 1999). There is debate about what constitutes appropriate work for women on such orders. Should they be encouraged to broaden their horizons and do 'male' work or should they stick to what they know in order to get through the hours?

The problems surrounding community service for women are well-known but by no means unresolvable. What is required is a change in the attitude that regards community service as predominantly a punishment for 'fit, young men' (Worrall and Hoy, 2005: 133). Better child-care arrangements, more female supervisors and consideration for the kind of working environments most suitable for women would also result in greater use. Whatever the perceived disadvantages to women of doing community service, they cannot possibly outweigh the disadvantages of imprisoning those same women.

The use of community sentences for black and Asian offenders has also been controversial (Durrance and Williams, 2003). It is well-established that black offenders, in particular, are over-represented in prison in relation to their distribution in the general population—24 per cent of the male and 30 per cent of the female prison population was from a minority ethnic group in 2002 (Home Office, 2003). What is less clear is whether or not this over-representation is due to discrimination (either direct or indirect) within society and/or the criminal justice system and what contribution, if any, the Probation Service makes to that discrimination. Research literature is inconclusive (Powis and Walmsley, 2002) but there is widespread concern that community sentences are not meeting the needs of black and Asian offenders. This may be because the theoretical underpinnings of contemporary rehabilitative programmes (see below) fail to take sufficient account of the particular experiences of poverty, racism and exclusion of many black and Asian offenders. Projects which seek to combine the cognitive behavioural approaches that characterize contemporary Probation intervention with approaches that emphasize issues of identity and empowerment are in the process of being evaluated and interim findings are promising (Durrance and Williams, 2003). One further problem is that, as with all criminal justice professions, the proportion of probation officers from minority ethnic groups is relatively small in comparison with the proportion of offenders from those groups (Home Office, 2003).

REVIEW QUESTIONS

1 What issues arise when considering the appropriateness of community sentences for women?

2 Why might the use of community sentences discriminate against black and Asian offenders?

Soft options? community sentences and populist punitiveness

The policy of 'bifurcation' (separating out the 'minor' from the 'dangerous' criminals) has been a feature of the politicization of crime in the past two decades and has allowed successive governments to sustain a paradoxical rhetoric of supporting alternatives to prison while arguing that there are many 'dangerous' criminals for whom alternatives are simply not 'suitable'. Since 'dangerousness' (as politically defined) is very much 'in the eye of the beholder', this line of official rhetoric has given rise to the concept of 'populist punitiveness', which has resulted in the chronic under-use and under-resourcing of alternatives to custody. Raynor and Vanstone (2002) discuss populist punitiveness and its impact on the use of community sentences. They argue that 'crime-related issues [are] defined by political elites as problems of insufficient punishment or as being "soft" on criminals' (2002: 69). By playing on understandable public concerns about crime, supporting biased media coverage and fuelling moral panics, it is argued that politicians use crime-related issues to manipulate public opinion. Within this discourse, the only acceptable kind of community sentence is a 'tough' one, the implication being that most community sentences are far from 'tough'. The dialogue between probation or community corrections officers and governments (for a detailed account of one such dialogue, see Worrall and Hoy, 2005) has been one centred on the so-called 'strengthening' of community sentences by means of increasingly unrealistic 'conditions' that have to be met by offenders. Carlen (1989) has referred to this process as being one which disregards 'sentencing feasibility'. Practitioners often refer to it as 'setting an offender up to fail'.

This 'toughness' has resulted in a range of penalties known in the USA as 'intermediate sanctions'—penalties that 'fit' between traditional probation orders and prison. Intermediate sanctions involve a greater intensity of supervision, coupled with greater monitoring or surveillance (Byrne, Lurigio and Petersilia, 1992). In England and Wales, the government's Green Paper *Punishment, Custody and the Community* (Home Office, 1988) and subsequent Action Plan for dealing with young adult offenders led to eight pilot Intensive Probation schemes which ran between 1990 and 1992 and were evaluated by the Home Office (Mair, *et al.* 1994; Mair, 1997). Underpinned by the penal philosophies of specific deterrence and incapacitation, rather than rehabilitation (Byrne, Lurigio and Petersilia, 1992), these schemes involved targeted 'serious' offenders in multiple weekly contacts with their probation officer.

Evaluations of Intensive Probation projects England and Wales were consistently discouraging in terms of their impact on recidivism. Programmes also varied greatly in terms of frequency of contact, size of caseload, extent of surveillance, type of offender accepted, practices of supervision and responses to violations (Mair *et al.*, 1994) and the evaluators bemoaned the 'lack of innovation' in the schemes. In their favour, it was clear that offenders themselves spoke very positively of the projects, enjoying the additional attention. The projects were also successful in providing greater control or structure for offenders and thus making it more likely that they would persevere with—and possibly benefit from—treatment programmes.

Towards the end of the twentieth century partnerships between the police and Probation Services have resulted in prolific (or persistent) offender projects in England and Wales, which represent an extension of the theoretical underpinnings, policy objectives and multi-agency practices of previous intensive supervision schemes. Combining penal philosophies of deterrence, incapacitation and rehabilitation, they seek to provide a mix of frequent contact, access to treatment (particularly drugs treatment) and community facilities, and constant monitoring. They also seek to demonstrate cost-effectiveness and increased public safety.

The major departure from previous projects, however, is their avoidance of the pitfall of relying on offenders to reduce their own rates of re-offending. This was always the weakest link in the chain and the one which consistently undermined claims of success. Instead, it is now accepted that prompt re-arrest (resulting from increased intelligence and monitoring) is also a measure of success. There is, however, a serious flaw in this logic. The possibility that a project could claim success entirely on the basis of arrests and order breaches does seem to be somewhat at odds with the spirit of the exercise. Nevertheless, the reality of modern corrections demands that those who do not respond promptly to the 'carrot' of rehabilitative efforts should experience the 'stick' of enforcement (Worrall and Walton, 2002; Worrall, *et al.*, 2002).

REVIEW QUESTIONS

1 What is meant by the term 'populist punitiveness' in relation to community sentences?

2 In what ways have community sentences been 'strengthened' in response to calls for greater public protection?

Community sentences and the 'What Works' agenda

The nature of probation intervention has changed radically in the past two decades. Personal counselling, based on psychotherapeutic approaches, has been replaced by cognitive behavioural programmes, based on social learning theory. Rather than attempting to change the whole personality or circumstances of an offender, cognitive behavioural programmes focus on specific unacceptable behaviours and seek to modify these by correcting distortions in the way offenders think about their crime. Offenders are required to accept full responsibility for their actions (instead of blaming the victim or their circumstances), empathize with the victim of their offences and expand their reper-toire of responses to those situations which have previously triggered a criminal response. Programmes may focus on generic cognitive skills or cover a range of specific problem behaviours such as anger management, drink-impaired driving and sex offending.

These programmes collectively form the 'What Works?' agenda. The etymology of this phrase lies in a famously pessimistic remark made in 1974 by a criminologist called Robert Martinson (1974) to the effect that 'nothing works' in penal interventions. The disillusion which followed this conclusion (supported by research findings at the time) led to a loss of confidence in probation which lasted until the early 1990s when the 'discovery' of cognitive behavioural programmes (initially in North America) gave rise to a series of conferences entitled 'What Works?' (McGuire, 1995). The phrase caught the imagination of politicians and professionals and now dominates probation intervention in the English-speaking world. Evaluation research gives cause for cautious optimism in respect of the effectiveness of such programmes in reducing re-offending (Vennard and Hedderman, 1998) but critics have argued that enthusiasm for the cognitive behavioural approach should not result in the neglect of other provision such as basic literacy skills and social skills. Nor should the wider social problems that may lead people into crime be overlooked (Bottoms, Gelsthorpe and Rex, 2001).

REVIEW QUESTIONS

1 What are the main components of contemporary rehabilitative interventions with offenders?

2 What criticisms have been made of the 'What Works' agenda?

CONCLUSION

In this chapter we have explored the range of punishments which do not involve incarceration that are available to courts. The aim of the chapter has been to demonstrate that, despite the overwhelming focus of the media, penal policy and academic literature on prison and imprisonment, the vast majority of people who commit crimes and are detected are punished in ways that require them to self-regulate, pay money or cooperate with some form of supervision or monitoring of their behaviour—within their own communities. We have identified a number of advantages to dealing with offenders in this way. Apart from the high cost of imprisonment, allowing offenders to remain in conditions of freedom enables them to retain family, social and employment ties, all of which may reduce the likelihood of re-offending. It also avoids the stigma of imprisonment, which is a major contributor to persistent offending. We have also demonstrated the ways in which community penalties can meet the conventional requirements of the principles of punishment, providing opportunities for retribution, deterrence, incapacitation, rehabilitation and reparation.

The chapter has provided an overview of the historical and political development of community penal-ties, suggesting a number of different ways of theorizing (or explaining) that development. It has traced the main features of the Probation Service over the past century and the changes which have taken it from its religious origins, through to a secular social work profession and its culmination in the twenty-first century as a law enforcement agency concerned primarily with public protection.

However, we have also discussed a number of issues and problems related to community penalties. These include the 'image' of community sentences as being 'soft options' and poor substitutes for imprisonment. The recent history of community penalties has been characterized by the need to respond to populist punitiveness by making such sentences 'tougher'. This has involved a proliferation of additional requirements, combinations of orders, increased intensity of contact and even close collaboration with the Police Service. Ultimately, it has involved the Probation Service in accepting physical restrictions on an offender's liberty, such as electronic monitoring, compulsory drug treatment and even prompt re-arrest and incarceration, as being measures of success, rather than measures which undermine the fundamental values of the Service.

The chapter has also explored the issue of diversity and the potential for discrimination in the implementation of community penalties. The particular needs of women offenders and those from minority ethnic groups have been highlighted. Finally, some of the ideas that are central to the 'What Works' agenda for offender rehabilitation have been introduced.

Although it remains the case that research into community sentences is overshadowed by research into prisons, there now exists an interesting and accessible body of research literature in this area (Mair, 2000; 2004). Much of the recent research can be found on the Home Office website and the details of some key recent books are set out at the end of this chapter.

QUESTIONS FOR DISCUSSION

1 What are the advantages and disadvantages of dealing with offenders in the community rather than sending them to prison?

2 To what extent do community sentences meet the requirements of punishment for retribution, deterrence, incapacitation, rehabilitation, and/or reparation?

3 Which of the existing community sentences are most suitable for women and why?

4 What are the central principles of the 'What Works' agenda and what are its implications for the treatment of offenders?

5 How, if at all, should community sentences contribute to the reduction of the prison population?

GUIDE TO FURTHER READING

Chui, W.H. and Nellis, M. (eds) (2003) *Moving Probation Forward: Evidence, Arguments and Practice*. Harlow: Pearson Longman.

An up-to-date summary of recent developments and the changing context of offender management in the community.

Mair, G. (ed) (2004) *What Matters in Probation*. Cullompton: Willan Publishing.

A very lively, critical and controversial examination of the 'What Works' agenda for offender rehabilitation.

Raynor, P. (2002) 'Community Penalties: Probation, Punishment and "What Works" ' in M. Maguire, R. Morgan and R. Reiner (eds) *The Oxford Handbook of Criminology*, Oxford: Oxford University Press, pp. 1168–1206.

A comprehensive and balanced resume of the key issues and debates surrounding community penalties.

Raynor, P. and Vanstone, M. (2002) *Understanding Community Penalties*. Buckingham: Open University Press.

An accessible introductory text that, amongst other things, provides a detailed history of the ideas and policies of probation.

Ward, D., Scott, J. and Lacey, M. (eds) (2002) *Probation—Working for Justice* (2nd edn), Oxford: Oxford University Press.

Contains a number of interesting chapters written by probation practitioners and managers as well as academics.

Home Office (annual) *Probation Statistics England and Wales*, London: Home Office—available on the Home Office website.

Contains all relevant statistics about both community penalties and the National Probation Service workforce.

WEB LINKS

www.homeoffice.gov.uk

The Home Office website provides a wealth of information and statistics about criminal justice policy, practice and research. It also provides links to many other relevant websites.

www.probation.homeoffice.gov.uk

The National Probation Service website provides useful information about various aspects of policy and practice relating to the management of offenders in the community.

www.official-documents.co.uk

The Official Documents website provides all relatively recent (last ten years) criminal justice statistics and government papers.

www.rethinking.org.uk

The Rethinking Crime and Punishment website is funded by the Esmee Fairbairn Foundation (an independent grantmaking organization) and encourages informed debate among the general public about alternatives to imprisonment.

REFERENCES

Bottoms, A. (2001) 'Compliance and community penalties' in A. Bottoms, L. Gelsthorpe, and S. Rex (eds) *Community Penalties: Change and Challenges*. Cullompton: Willan.

Bottoms, A., Gelsthorpe, L. and Rex, S. (eds) (2001) *Community Penalties: Change and Challenges*. Cullompton: Willan.

Bottoms, A. and McWilliams, W. (1979) 'A Non-treatment Paradigm for Probation Practice', *British Journal of Social Work*, 9, 2, 159–202.

Brownlee, I. (1998) *Community Punishment: a Critical Introduction*. Harlow: Longman.

Byrne, J.M., Lurigio, A.J. and Petersilia, J. (1992) *Smart Sentencing: the Emergence of Intermediate Sanctions*. London: Sage.

Carlen, P. (1989) 'Crime, inequality and sentencing' in P. Carlen and D. Cook (eds) *Paying for Crime*. Milton Keynes: Open University Press.

Carter, P. (2003) *Managing Offenders, Changing Lives*. London: Home Office.

Chui, W.H. and Nellis, M. (eds) (2003) *Moving Probation Forward: Evidence, Arguments and Practice*. Harlow: Pearson Longman.

Cohen, S. (1979) 'The Punitive City: Notes on the Dispersal of Social control', *Contemporary Crises*, 3, 339–63.

Cohen, S. (1983) 'Social control talk: telling stories about correctional change' in D. Garland and P. Young (eds) *The Power to Punish*. London: Heinemann.

Cohen, S. (1985) *Visions of Social Control*. Cambridge: Polity Press.

Durrance, P. and Williams, P. (2003) 'Broadening the agenda around what works for black and Asian offenders', *Probation Journal*, 50, 3, 211–24.

Eaton, M. (1986) *Justice for Women?* Milton Keynes: Open University Press.

Farrall, S. (2002) *Rethinking what Works with Offenders: Probation, Social Context and Desistance from Crime*. Cullompton: Willan Publishing.

Fowler, L. (2002) *Drugs, Crime and the Drug Treatment and Testing Order*, Issues in Community and Criminal Justice Monograph 2. London: NAPO.

Garland, D. (1985) *Punishment and Welfare: A History of Penal Strategies*. Aldershot: Gower.

Hagan, J. (1994) *Crime and Disrepute*. Thousand Oaks: Pine Forge.

Hedderman, C. (2003) 'Enforcing supervision and encouraging compliance' in W.H. Chui and M. Nellis (eds) (2003) *Moving Probation Forward: Evidence, Arguments and Practice*. Harlow: Pearson Longman.

Hedderman, C. and Gelsthorpe, L. (1997) *Understanding the Sentencing of Women* Home Office Research Study 170. London: HMSO.

Hine, J. and Thomas, N. (1995) 'Evaluating work with offenders: Community service orders' in G. McIvor (ed) *Working with Offenders*, Research Highlights in Social Work 26. London: Jessica Kingsley.

Home Office (1988) *Punishment, Custody and the Community*, Cm 424. London: HMSO.

Home Office (1990) *Crime, Justice and Protecting the Public*, Cm 965. London: HMSO.

Home Office (1998) *Joining Forces to Protect the Public: Prisons-Probation—A Consultation Document*. London: Home Office.

Home Office (2002a) *Criminal Statistics England and Wales 2001*, Cm 5696. London: Home Office (also available at www.official-documents.co.uk).

Home Office (2002b) *Probation Statistics England and Wales 2001*. London: Home Office.

Home Office (2003) Prison Statistics England and Wales 2001, Cm 5743. London: Home Office.

Home Office (2004a) *Reducing Crime, Changing Lives*. London: Home Office (also available at www.homeoffice.gov.uk).

Home Office (2004b) *Reducing Crime, Changing Lives* (press release 5/2004). London: Home Office.

Howard League (1999) *Do women paint fences too? Women's experience of community service*. London: Howard League for Penal Reform.

Johnson, K. and colleagues (2001) *Cautions, court proceedings and sentencing, England and Wales 2000*, Home Office Statistical Bulletin 20/01. London: Home Office.

McGuire, J. (ed)(1995) *What Works: Reducing Reoffending*. Chichester: John Wiley.

Mair, G. (1997) 'Evaluating intensive probation' in G. Mair (ed) *Evaluating the Effectiveness of Community Penalties*. Aldershot: Avebury.

Mair, G., Lloyd, C., Nee, C. and Sibbitt, R. (1994) *Intensive Probation in England and Wales: an Evaluation*, Home Office Research Study 133. London: HMSO.

Mair, G. (2000) 'Research on community penalties' in R. King and E. Wincup (eds) *Doing Research on Crime and Justice*. Oxford: Oxford University Press.

Mair, G. (ed)(2004) *What Matters in Probation*. Cullompton: Willan.

Martinson, R. (1974) 'What works? Questions and answers about prison reform', *The Public Interest*, 35, 22–54.

Maruna, S. (2000) *Making Good: How Ex-Convicts Reform and Rebuild their Lives*. Washington DC: American Psychological Association.

National Probation Service (2001) *A New Choreography: An Integrated Strategy for the National Probation service for England and Wales—Strategic Framework 2001–2004*. London: Home Office.

Nellis, M. (2003) 'Electronic monitoring and the future of the Probation Service' in W.H. Chui and M. Nellis (eds) (2003) *Moving Probation Forward: Evidence, Arguments and Practice*. Harlow: Pearson Longman.

Powis, B. and Walmsley, R. (2002) *Programmes for black and Asian offenders on probation: lessons for developing practice*, Home Office Research Study 250. London, Home Office.

Raynor, P. (2002) 'Community penalties: probation, punishment and "what works" ' in M. Maguire, R. Morgan and R. Reiner (eds) *The Oxford Handbook of Criminology*. Oxford: Oxford University Press, pp.1168–1206.

Raynor, P., Smith, D. and Vanstone, M. (1994) *Effective Probation Practice*. London: Macmillan.

Raynor, P. and Vanstone, M. (2002) *Understanding Community Penalties*. Buckingham: Open University Press.

Scull, A. (1984) *Decarceration: Community Treatment and the Deviant*. Cambridge: Polity Press.

Smith, D. (1995) *Criminology for Social Work*. London: Macmillan.

Turnbull, P.J., McSweeney, T., Webster, R., Edmunds, M. and Hough, M. (2000) *Drug Treatment and Testing Orders: Final Report* Home Office Research Study 212. London: Home Office.

Vennard, J. and Hedderman, C. (1998) 'Effective interventions with offenders' in P. Goldblatt and C. Lewis (eds) *Reducing Offending: an Assessment of Research Evidence on Ways of Dealing with Offending Behaviour*, Home Office Research Study 187. London: Home Office.

Walker, H. and Beaumont, B. (eds) (1985) *Working with Offenders*. London: Macmillan.

Windlesham, Lord (1993) *Responses to Crime*, Vol. 2. Oxford: Oxford University Press.

Worrall, A. (1990) *Offending Women: Female Lawbreakers and the Criminal Justice System*. London: Routledge.

Worrall, A. and Hoy, C. (2005) *Punishment in the Community: Managing Offenders, Making Choices* (2nd edn). Cullompton: Willan.

Worrall, A. and Walton, D. (2002) 'Reducing volume property crime: targeted policing and case management', *Vista*.

Worrall, A., Dunkerton, L. and Leacock, V. (2002) 'Targeting and treatment: do prolific offender projects have a future?' *Probation Journal*.

27

Prisons

Deborah Cheney

INTRODUCTION

With the click of a computer mouse, anyone can enter the prison world. A virtual tour provided by HM Prison Service website, allows you to accompany a prisoner through reception, sit with them in their cell and view their preparation for release. At each stage of the process pre-set questions and answers provide a seamless trip, one of reassurance that all needs are met and all problems dissolved by immediate attention. So why is the re-offending rate so high, why were there seventy-five self-inflicted deaths amongst prisoners in 2002 (PRT, 2004; see also HMCIP, 1990) and why have inspectors of prisons walked out of establishments in protest at conditions?

The purpose of this chapter is to expand the virtual world to include different perspectives, including those of the Chief Inspectorate of Prisons and Probation (HMCIPP), Prisons and Probation Ombudsman (PPO), academics, government and statutory agencies, pressure groups and, not least, prisoners themselves.

BACKGROUND

Historically places of mere containment, prisons have evolved into establishments with high ideals to provide constructive regimes and improve education and skills, within a safe and decent environment, in order to promote law-abiding behaviour in custody and on release (Muncie, 1996; see also Morris and Rothman, 1995). These ideals must be situated within the theoretical purposes of punishment, to: rehabilitate; deter; incapacitate, and deliver retribution. Debate upon these purposes of punishment, and thus the way in which punishment is meted out in prisons, has been the subject of political and academic debate for many years (Cavandino and Dignan, 2002). Indeed whether prison itself can actually achieve any or all of these aims, and the price to be paid in achieving them, remains an unresolved argument (Bottoms, 1995; Sim, 2004).

What is clear is that the Prison Service (PS) is a key player in improving outcomes for the Criminal Justice System (Morris and Rothman, 1995). How a prisoner is treated whilst serving sentence and what that sentence involves to prepare them for release, has a direct effect upon protection of the public and the reduction of reconvictions, and therefore, crime levels (HMIPP, 2001). As such it is necessary to examine how present day prisons work toward delivering these results (Woolf Report, 1991; Morgan, 1991).

Until the eighteenth century places of confinement, houses of correction and prisons were essentially 'warehouses' for those condemned to death or transportation, and centres of corporal punishment for transgression of the laws. Practices differed across the country, but all were characterized by the profiteering practices of unwaged jailers driven to exploit prisoners for their own survival (McConville, 1981; Morgan 2003; Priestly, 1995). Thus, when in 1777 John Howard published 'The State of the Prisons', following an exhaustive survey of every prison in the country, the squalor of prison conditions and a two-tier system based on wealth to purchase release from irons or extra food, was revealed. Howard advocated a more sensitized system to encourage 'amendment of the mind', and this ideal was advanced by reformers in the nineteenth century. The Gaol Act of 1823 established basic rules and salaried positions for jailers, while statute in 1835 introduced prison inspectors (Priestley, 1999). An emphasis on securing penitence through solitary confinement, yet within a regime providing physical and spiritual care, was embraced by the first penitentiary, Pentonville. The first major investigation into the practices of imprisonment, undertaken by the Gladstone Committee in 1895, identified shortcomings which resulted in sweeping changes to regimes and placed the Home Secretary at the head of adminis- tration of the prison service. Here were the beginnings of the present-day multi-faceted approach to prisoners. Physical 'assault' of the body, mind and senses, was replaced with a positive move toward seeing prisoners as individuals, via classification, reward of good conduct, separation of male and female prisoners, and some foresight of how to 'improve' them prior to release. Resignation was replaced by optimism. In 1991 the Woolf Report into the riots at HMP Manchester, the most significant analysis of the penal system in one hundred years, became the catalyst for further changes (Woolf Report, 1991).

Much of this historical movement, continuing through to the establishment of the Prison Department of the Home Office in 1963 and granting of agency status to the service in 1992, was a result of the changing debates in criminological theory, the sociology of deviance and the psychology of crime. For example, the idea of the 'born criminal' was challenged and, as such, the 'writing off' of the prisoner re-thought. Today, similar theories thread their way throughout how a sentence is served. Political pressures, public con- cerns, media representation and research findings on the social background of crime, inform what input is needed before a prisoner is returned to society. In the latter category, findings of the government's Social Exclusion Unit have informed debate in regard to resettlement programmes and even sown the seeds for reform of the Rehabilitation of Offenders Act 1974, on grounds that the requirements may undermine any progress made within the prison setting (Social Exclusion Unit, 2002; HMCIP, 2001).

Given that all prisoners are sentenced 'in our name' it behoves everyone to be informed of what takes place behind prison walls. Given that, out of a current prison population of 73,735 (HM Prison Service, 2004), all but circa twenty-five will be released back into the community, it is equally important that we inform ourselves of, and are satisfied with, the input into rehabilitation of those offenders (see also Home office, 2003).

Prison service structure and accountability

In 2003 a Correctional Services Board was established together with a new Permanent Secretary level post of Commissioner of Correctional Services, a post with direct responsibility for the Director Generals of both the Prison and Probation Services. The Director General of the Prison Service chairs the Prison Service Management Board (PSMB) made up of the seven Directors of the various areas of PS responsibility, such as Personnel, Resettlement and Health, and each of these Directors in turn, is responsible for a chain of command consisting of specific groups and units. One of the seven Directors is also Deputy Director General and Director of the High Security Estate. The PSMB is the body through which policy is translated into practice at ground level, through Area Managers responsible for geographical clusters of prisons, and thence to prison gov- ernors. It is the PSMB which decides upon, and monitors, performance targets set for individual establishments. Each prison has a governing governor who is assisted in the day-to-day running of the prison both by a senior management team made up of various management grades, and uniformed officers.

Private prisons were introduced to the UK in 1992 in a move to deal with overcrowding problems. In practice the Government enter into a Service Level Agreement with the companies, determining the services and standards for each establishment, and the State employs a Controller within each prison to authorize the use of control and restraints and to ensure the contractual specifications are complied with. In the event that standards are not met, the contractor is fined. Critics of privatization argue that there are problems of accountability, not least because standards specified in contracts are confidential.

Individual prisons are designated via security category according to the risk posed by the prisoners housed there. Adult males, who form the largest number in the prison population are categorized security A to D, with Category A prisoners categorized further as Exceptional, High or Standard risk, and housed in the nine high or maximum security prisons, and Category D prisoners who can be trusted in open prisons. Women are categorized within the system differently from men, as Open, Semi-Open, Closed and Local, with the only exception to this being sharing the highest security risk in Category A status (Home Office, 1993).

Internal prison service accountability

Accountability within the prison setting is generated by the PS itself, through their measurable headquarters targets and standards. The PS publish Performance Standards, currently covering seventy-two areas of prison life, each of which include measurable audit baselines. Prison Service Orders are the main route through which Performance Standards are elaborated upon in more detail and directions are sent to prisons giving guidelines and advice on the implementation of policies and strategies, and amendment of previous Orders. Governors must strive to ensure that at the time of auditing the outcome required for each standard is met, or face an audit report that deems the prison deficient, marginal or unacceptable. Failure to meet standards has a direct relation to funding of establishments. It is worth comparing the standards in specific areas designated by the PS with the 'expectations' in these areas outlined by HMCIPP in the annual report of 1999/2000. The then Chief Inspector, Sir David Ramsbotham, had been outspoken against Key Performance Indicators themselves on the grounds they measured quantity rather than quality and reflected goals that could have been replaced by others more meaningful. In his 'expectations' document he reflects this preferred emphasis on quality, over outcome quantity, in the area of assessing prisoner treatment and conditions.

HM Chief Inspectorate of Prisons and Probation

This input by HMCIPP is just one of the ways in which their office in itself can hold the PS to account, as too can the office of Prisons and Probation Ombudsman. The drawback with both offices is that neither can 'insist' on something being done. Both are offices which are restricted to recommending actions be taken, their only other route being to rely upon publicizing PS shortcomings in the hope this will prompt action being taken. Thematic Reviews published over the years by the Inspectorate have drawn attention to areas such as suicide and self-injury, young offenders and the remand population and, certainly in respect of the review of women prisoners, has proven to be a catalyst for change (Home Office, 1995, 1999, 2001, 2002).

An overview of the effectiveness of thematic reviews demonstrates the disappointing response by the PS to some significant findings. The 1996 review of prison healthcare recommended the NHS take over responsibility and although they assumed funding responsibility in 2003, standards of provision have yet to reach NHS equivalent (DoH, 1999; HM Prison Service, 1999). The investigation into suicides, undertaken in 1999, recommended adoption of a US system proven to be efficient in reduction of the numbers of suicides, yet these methods have not been introduced and the number of suicides continues to rise. The study, action-plan and funding recommended by the 2000 review of treatment and conditions of the remand population, have all failed to materialize. Similar lack of action has characterized the recommendations in 2000 regarding casework information needs in the Criminal Justice System; 'Expectations', a guidebook on consistent quality assurance for a healthy prison, was resisted by one Home Secretary (although subsequently published by Sir David Ramsbotham as an appendix to his Annual Report HMCIP for England and Wales 1999–2000), and a planned review on minority groups in prison entirely suspended by another. Consistent observations and recommendations in reports are, in the end, subject to the political will to make them happen.

Prisons and Probation Ombudsman

The Prisons Ombudsman shares the fate of the Inspectorate in not being on a statutory footing and thus, again, fettered to recommending action on the part of prisoners' complaints. However the creation of the post in 1994 was an important development, arising directly from the Woolf Report undertaken following the riots in Manchester prison. This in-depth exploration of the causes of the riots established the origins of the disorders as an imbalance between security, control and justice (Woolf Report, 1991). Whilst the report identified many elements which led to the riots, specifically relating to Manchester itself, these three factors and the areas of prison life in which they should be paramount, set the PS a nationwide agenda. Most particularly they relate to the processes of complaints and discipline (Morgan, 1991). The complaints system is a relevant consideration with regard to accountability of the Prison Service.

Prior to the creation of the Ombudsman's post the avenues for prisoners' complaints lay solely in the PS internal complaints system and recourse to Boards of Visitors (now called Independent Monitoring Boards, explained below). The internal complaints system, by its very nature seen as partisan, was regarded by prisoners with suspicion. The Ombudsman presented as an entirely independent and objective avenue for complaints to be dealt with. Recourse to the Ombudsman is only open to prisoners who have exhausted the in-house complaints' avenues. Correspondence between prisoner and Ombudsman is 'in confidence', as is communication between prisoner and legal representative, and after full investigation of a complaint the Ombudsman takes the decision to uphold the complaint or not. In the former instance s/he will make recommendations to the Prison Service.

This system has uncovered many injustices in PS dealings with prisoners, as evidenced by the contents of the Ombudsman's Annual Reports, where a large selection of complaints and outcomes are catalogued. That said, there remain many weaknesses, not least that as the post carries no statutory authority, like the Chief Inspectorate, recommending action be taken in a specific case is the extent of his/her powers. Also, if complaints give rise to identification of a pattern of unacceptable practice in a number of cases, this does not give rise to blanket change of practice, merely action taken to benefit an individual prisoner. This weakness is demonstrable when looking at Annual Reports from the office of the Ombudsman over a period of time, where similar complaints arise again and again. In particular, highlighting PS practices with regard to handling prisoner property and categorization of prisoners has not led to any proactive steps to eradicate the problem across the board. Similarly the Ombudsman's office has itself questioned their own accessibility to women prisoners and young offenders from whom complaints remain rare.

Current consideration of placing the post on a statutory footing may resolve such problems, as too could the extension of the ambit of the Ombudsman to undertake investigation of complaints by the families of prisoners. Certainly the spirit of extending the ambit is alive, with the recent extension of his sphere of investigation to that of deaths in custody. This will ensure greater engagement with families and, as a result of his commitment to public openness, better quality investigation, although the lack of a statutory base remains an inherent weakness of the office.

Other agents of accountability

The Prison Service is also effectively 'policed' by different statutory and voluntary bodies, each with differing degrees of influence. Interested pressure groups have formed across the years, not least the Howard League for Penal Reform which had its genesis in the work of John Howard in the eighteenth century (Muncie, 1996). Others include Prison Reform Trust and New Bridge, and a host of agencies directing their energies to specific groups of prisoners or aspects of prison life such as young offenders, women in prison, foreign prisoners and deaths in custody.

The Prison Rules include provision for the appointment, by the Secretary of State, of Independent Monitoring Boards to all prison establishments. The Boards are made up of members of the public, their appointment subject to triennial review, whose duties are to oversee the 'state of the prison premises, the administration of the prison and the treatment of prisoners'. They are required to produce an Annual Report for submission to the Secretary of State, commenting upon their findings in respect of how the prison is run. Their unfettered access to the prison, on unannounced rota duties, allows this group a unique perspective and insight to life in their establishment; as too does their daily handling and investigation of complaints by prisoners. That said, there has been much criticism of the effectiveness of Boards. Not least of these is that the nature of the duties makes it essential that they have a great deal of free time at their disposal and this has generated large numbers of retired members which, together with relatively small numbers of members from minority ethnic groups, renders them non-representative of the prison population. There have also been instances of concerns raised in Annual Reports being consistently ignored and coming to light only after tragic results or intervention by HMCIPP.

REVIEW QUESTIONS

1 How could the roles of the Prisons' Ombudsman and HM Chief Inspector of Prisons and Probation be improved?

2 Is there any other accountability which should be introduced in respect of PS practice, if so, why?

3 Students should investigate what support and campaigning groups for prisoners exist, and the extent of their influence.

Who are the prisoners?

It is important to identify specific groups of prisoners in order to appreciate the diverse demands the Prison Service must meet. The young and older offenders in prison are at each end of a 'needs spectrum', and what of the disabled in prison, the foreign prisoners, women with babies beside them in their sentence, the remand versus the sentenced?

A pen-picture of the 'average prisoner' across the whole population reveals much in common. Low educational levels and a history of truanting or exclusion from school early is a characteristic shared across all groups of prisoners, with some two-thirds not having the basic literacy skills of an average fourteen-year old. Males and females alike have a background of mental health and drug and alcohol problems, with 80 per cent of women prisoners entering prison with a drug dependency. It is estimated that 20 per cent of men and 40 per cent of women have attempted suicide prior to reception into the system, and the suicide rate of women prisoners has now reached the highest number on record. Poor standards of health are common throughout the population, the poorest being found within the unsentenced remand population, and social and economic deprivation is a standard background amongst all prisoners. The majority of prisoners are parents, with an estimated 125,000 children having a parent in custody, and by far the majority of women prisoners have suffered physical and sexual abuse (Social Exclusion Unit, 2002).

The young offender population is both volatile and vulnerable. Coming from backgrounds with poor prospects and self-esteem lowered by lack of parental interest, they invariably take into prison their own 'street culture' that has been their only sense of identity in a disruptive family life. This culture is often reinforced within the prison setting where their poor sense of a future combines with immaturity and impulsiveness to lead them to respond to frustration with violence. Suicide amongst young prisoners remains a cause of concern, with sixteen young people under twenty-one dying by their own hand in 2002 (Go to http://www.inquest.org.uk).

In sum, the majority of the prison population have been, in many ways, failed by and excluded from society prior to incarceration. What then must the prison setting offer them to be able to rejoin society?

Adult male prisoners

By far the largest number of prisoners in the existing 138 prison establishments are adult males. At the time of writing they number 59,722 out of a total population of 73,735, compared with 10,312 young males. A large proportion of this group will have poor standards of literacy and numeracy and previous convictions, making them a particular challenge to the prison service in respect of rehabilitation. A great deal has been done in recent times to improve the lot of the adult male prisoner, with investment being made into basic education, skills and vocational training courses, lifestyle re-education and improving family ties.

The area of family ties has been a particular focus of the PS through the Family Man Course. This is an intensive parenting/relationship course having its impetus in the statistic that 43 per cent of sentenced prisoners are recorded as having lost contact with their families since beginning their sentence (Social Exclusion Unit, 2002). Piloted at HMP Wandsworth, and successfully evaluated, the course is to be extended across all prisons. Reduction of re-offending through developing a positive and responsible attitude to parenting lies not just in encouraging ambitions for a law-abiding life in the prisoner himself, but also in their communicating this message to their children. This Course, together with the Storybook Dad Scheme, pioneered in HMP Dartmoor (to be extended to other prisons) are the first initiatives in many years to recognize in tangible terms the importance of family ties in reducing re-offending. Since inception the Storybook Dad Scheme has reached over 275 families and is unique in being accessible to all prisoners regardless of their reading abilities.

Women prisoners

The first step in meeting the needs of the female population was taken in 2001 when women were officially identified by the PS as a distinct group, through the establishment of a Home Office Women's Policy Team and the appointment of an Operational Manager of Women's Prisons. As of April 2004, the women's estate will be managed geographically with a dedicated senior manager and staff. This is a massive step forward in dealing with the problem areas raised by HMCIPP and will put in place a structure which will facilitate greater opportunities to address female prisoners' rehabilitation and resettlement needs.

Whereas the Prison Rules continue to apply to males and females alike, and key-performance indicators and targets remain non-gender specific, there is nonetheless now a distinct ethos of recognition of the needs of female prisoners. The Policy Group was the direct response of the Prison Service to a Thematic Review of women prisoners undertaken by the Chief Inspectorate of Prisons in 1997. A follow-up review undertaken by HMCIPP in 2001 identifies which of the original recommendations made for change have been met, and which remain outstanding. Not least of the latter is the fact that young women continue to be held alongside adults, there being no Young Offender Institutions for females.

There are currently seventeen prisons for women, two female-dedicated wings at male prisons, and four Mother and Baby Unit (MBUs). These house 3,836 adult females and 505 female young offenders. The MBUs accommodate babies up to nine or eighteen months and the capacity country-wide is circa ninety places. Given that it is estimated that some 30,000 children per year are affected by the imprisonment of their mother, the availability of MBU places, the criteria for mothers applying for places, and the age ceiling for children remaining there with their mothers, remain subjects of debate. However, in 2003, new PS Orders and Performance Standards were implemented with a view to improvement of mother/baby relationships in these units.

Given the paucity of women's prisons, despite their growing numbers, women are more likely to be held further from their children than males; something affecting both the maintenance of family ties and the re-housing of them with their children after sentence. Another concern which has been raised about this section of the population is the security surrounding women prisoners. As the least problematic and violent of prisoners, the relaxation of security recommended by HMCIP in 1997 has yet to be achieved. The fact that women do not pose a major risk is not reflected in ground level practices.

Young offenders

According to the HMCIP Thematic Review undertaken 1997, the youthful population requires a specific approach be adopted. Their number, currently standing at 10,935, includes juveniles of seventeen and under, and young adults aged eighteen to twenty-one (see Home Office, 2000). In common with concerns voiced by HMCIP regarding holding female young offenders alongside adults, there is also concern over the housing of juvenile males in similar circumstances. The argument runs that, given their disruptive background, positive adult-role models are essential and the provision of this by Prison Service staff may be undermined by a preference for the significant adult to be an offender sharing their own experience. With a background of social dysfunction, the main challenge of this section of the prison population is to address problematic behaviour, whilst enabling them to be normal adolescents. This means replacing bravado with self-confidence, impulsiveness with assumption of responsibility and, throughout all, giving them a sense that a crime-free future is possible and employability a reality. This difficult task is largely dealt with by programmes incorporating psychologists, probation officers and prison officers.

The PS has, in recent years, taken positive steps to be youth-conscious in service delivery to young offenders, not least as a result of the Children's Act 1989 being recognized, in 2002, as applicable to the under eighteen estate housed in nine establishments. Working together with the Youth Justice Board the Prison Service have been identified by HMCIPP as providing better care to those under eighteen than in previous times. Improvement of skills and a focus on education is the cornerstone of how the juvenile estate should operate, with specific planning for release. Recognition of their being adolescents, but largely also parents themselves (a quarter of young offenders currently held are parents), has led to innovations such as teaching parenting skills, and involving families in sentence progress. However, the ideal is not always the reality and both the HMCIPP and Ombudsman have identified failings in the system.

Remand prisoners

As an unconvicted body within the prison population remand prisoners are entitled to vote, wear their own clothes (in all but those categorized security risk C), and generally enjoy more generous quality and quantity of contact and communication. That said, within the prison setting there is often in reality less tangible evidence to the prisoners themselves that they are favoured. A thematic review by HMCIP in 2000, which investigated the remand experience, uncovered findings that led them to entitle the report 'Unjust Deserts'. Despite the fact their number were characterized prior to entry into prison as being without work, it was found they are half as likely as the sentenced population to have undertaken work in prison, and half as likely to receive help in resettlement. Housed mainly in local prisons, acute overcrowding and lack of facilities renders them also less likely to benefit from physical exercise, time out of cell and purposeful activity, despite the generous PS Statement of Principle in respect of this group.

Particularly worrying is the high levels of suicide and self-harm amongst this group, with over a quarter of the male remand population having attempted suicide in their lifetime, and the whole identified by HMCIP as having a higher level of psychiatric morbidity than the mainstream population. Over the period 1990 to April 2003, 358 remand prisoners have died by their own hand. Of the fifty three self-inflicted deaths by prisoners in 1999, twenty-six were remanded and in 2000, of forty-eight such deaths, twenty were by prisoners on remand (http://www.inquest.org.uk/). In these circumstances, the plan of HMCIP to complete a follow-up report on the remand population within two years and particularly to monitor the unsentenced population during this interim period, is to be welcomed.

Foreign prisoners, the disabled and the older offender

Although diverse groups in themselves, prisoners who fall within these groups share a double incapacitation. Foreign prisoners, many of which are serving sentence for drug smuggling, are invariably a long way from home (see Chapter 18). In addition to suffering from cultural deprivation, contact with families by phone or visits is either fraught with difficulty or, in the main, impossible. Communication difficulties, together with lack of enjoyment of a full regime, are just a few of the problems that many disabled prisoners face, whilst older offenders are ill-catered for in the majority of prisons (see Chapter 20).

REVIEW QUESTIONS

1 Considering one of the pen pictures, students should design a regime that best meets the needs of the selected group.

2 Has the Prison Service gone far enough in addressing the needs of women and babies in prison?

3 Do remand prisoners pose particular problems for the Prison Service and, if so, how should these problems be resolved?

How prisons are run

Today prisons are as much a wall of paper as they are of brick. At ground level Governors and officers must work within boundaries provided by Delivery Plans, Key Performance Indicators and Targets and Performance Standards. At every level, extensive paperwork characterizes all prisoner movements behind prison walls and during vehicular transportation.

Beginning a sentence

Reception into prison poses one of the most vulnerable times for a prisoner, the moment of all control being ritually stripped away. Research shows that the majority of prisoners will be at the greatest risk of committing self-injury or suicide on the first night, and between the first week and three months of a sentence. Property is logged and stored, and only those items permitted in-cell returned to the prisoner, religion and dietary needs are identified, together with any disabilities or language requirements. Prisoners are security categorized and photographed, strip-searched and undertake health checks, and it is at this time that officers must identify the most vulnerable of prisoners. Those regarded as a risk to themselves should be housed in the healthcare unit and prisoners who are at risk from others within the prison, accommodated in a vulnerable prisoners' wing. Such textbook processing is not always carried out to the letter, as has been revealed by many reports by the offices of the Ombudsman and Chief Inspectorate, and pressure groups.

Every prisoner should follow induction into the establishment they have been sent to. This involves being informed of prison rules, regimes and routines and having a clear sentence plan explained, which might incorporate drug and/or alcohol rehabilitation or programmes such as anger management or cognitive skills. Those who require specific offending behaviour courses, for example the sex offender treatment programme should, at the earliest opportunity, be enrolled on the programme or moved to a prison where one is available. Lifers will be provided with a Life Sentence Plan, annually reviewed and updated, and triennial progress reports will be prepared to assess progress and raise areas of concern to the Life Management Unit (Home Office, 1993; Sapsford, 1983).

This is in an ideal world. Property is often poorly recorded, pressures on staff can lead to inadequate identification of, and provision of programmes, and some vulnerable prisoners may fall through the safety net. Whilst officers may identify religious needs or language and disability requirements, the majority of prisons are ill-equipped to meet these needs on immediate demand.

Purposeful activity

The Prison Service Key Performance Indicators, which translate into expected targets for establishments, include ensuring prisoners spend, on average, 24 hours of purposeful activity per week. There are also targets for delivery of accredited behaviour programmes, including sex offender treatment programmes, and achievement of basic skills awards. Regretably, in the past eight years the service has failed to meet its own standard of providing twenty-four hours per week purposeful activity and in some prisons this has fallen as low as eleven hours. Sex offender treatment programmes are only available in twenty-six prisons and there is even greater paucity of provision of courses such as anger management and cognitive self-change, and all serve those best who have a good educational standard. Equally the running of courses is subject to the vagaries of getting onto the programme in an overcrowded prison where pressure on staff is acute.

A goal within the 2003–4 list of PS targets is ensuring 30,690 prisoners have a job, education or training outcome within one month of release. Work and training, addressing behaviour (including drug and alcohol problems), achieving educational goals and the learning of life skills, such as parenting, form part of how a prisoner will fill his or her day. Of course the average day for a prisoner is fixed: when they rise, when they eat, when they work, when they exercise and associate and when they are locked in cell. This routine varies between establishments and according to the categorization of the prisoner in terms of security risk. However such goals benefit most those prisoners serving a lengthy sentence and short-stay prisoners are unlikely to benefit from such intensive input toward rehabilitation.

Education and the achievement by prisoners of at least basic educational skills, such as reading, writing and mathematics, during their sentence is an important goal when viewed in the light of the poor literacy and numeracy levels of the prison population. However, attending education classes is not compulsory for the adult population and thus their benefiting from this is solely reliant upon personal motivation or, more cynically, the boredom threshold of being faced otherwise with empty in-cell hours (Social Exclusion Unit, 2002). For many adult prisoners the preferred option is pursuing vocational training courses, such as bricklaying, carpentry, tailoring and hairdressing, and working within the prison and earning a wage. Whilst remand prisoners are not required to work, convicted prioners must engage in up to ten hours per day 'useful work'. The availability of work and training varies between prisons both in quantity and quality and, in accordance with the National Minimum Wage Act 1998, prisoners do not qualify for the national minimum wage and, on average, will receive circa £7 per week for any work undertaken. That said, HMCIPP reports on individual establishments continue to highlight too many prisoners unemployed, patchy availability of education and training and lack of resettlement strategies.

Additionally, the concept of a therapeutic community prison, pioneered at HMP Grendon Underwood, has been embraced by the PS. Grendon is premised on democracy and respect for the individual and day-to-day routines differ considerably from the mainstream estate. The focus is less on education and training and more on intensive therapeutic intervention on an individual basis, and the PS are now planning a limited expansion of the Grendon model elsewhere. However, it is worthy of note that it has taken forty years of success in Grendon before such action being taken.

Contact with the outside world

Traditionally, the maintenance of prisoners' family ties has been channelled via communication through letters, telephone calls and visits and the importance of these to prisoners should not be underestimated. Imprisonment has moved a long way from isolating the 'penitent' in order that s/he has the maximum time in which to reflect on their crimes and repent. In 1895 the Gladstone Committee recommended that, if visits and communications would be beneficial to making a prisoner 'a better man', they were indeed a desirable part of a prison sentence (Priestley, 1999).

That said, minimizing the socially harmful effects of removal from normal life, by maintaining contact with the outside world, must be balanced with regulation of prisoners' communications on grounds of the demands of security and good order. The quality and quantity of visits, letters and telephone calls thus varies according to issues such as the security category of the prisoner concerned, suspicion of involvement with drugs, and child protection measures.

Despite the fact that visits are not a privilege, but a right, there remain concerns about the quality of provision across establishments. The Prisons and Probation Ombudsman has recorded complaints about the use of closed visits, where no physical contact can be made, and of arrangements for accumulated visits, for which there are long waiting lists. To these complaints are added those of various conditions imposed on visits, the power of staff to terminate, and varied criteria on what can be exchanged between prisoner and visitor.

The sentiments of the Gladstone committee recognizing the importance of prisoners' links with family and community were echoed by the Woolf Report in 1991, which itself saw visits and the opportunity to have them as a significant incentive to responsible behaviour. This link to responsible behaviour was the impetus behind the PS making visits one of the key earnable privileges within the Incentives and Earned Privileges Scheme introduced in 1995. The scheme operates on the levels of Basic, Standard and Enhanced and is premised on earning incentives such as additional or longer visits. Theoretically this is an excellent idea, encouraging better behaviour through reward, but in practice, it has posed difficulties, and one valid criticism is that, arguably, it punishes families themselves. Not least, the offering of extra/longer visits relies entirely upon availability of staff and space in an establishment and, more worrying than this, the Ombudsman has identified instances where the scheme has been used as a punishment rather than incentive.

Table 27.1 Visits for convicted prisoners

	Disc. minimum	Basic	Standard	Enhanced
Visits—quantity	Restrictable to basic level for 42/21 days. PR 55, YOI 53	2 half hour or one hour per 28 days	At least 3 per 28 days	4 or 5 one hour visits per 28 days
Visits—quality	As above	Visits area	Visits area with additional facilities	Element of choice over times, days, finishing times, use of enhanced visits area

Source: M. Leech and D. Cheney (2000) *The Prisons Handbook*. Waterside Press.

Table 27.2 Visits for unconvicted prisoners

	Disc. minimum	Basic	Standard	Enh anced
Visits—quantity	As convicted	1.5 hours per week	Higher than basic	Higher than standard
Visits—quality	As above	Visits area	As convicted	As convicted

Source: M. Leech and D. Cheney (2000) *The Prisons Handbook*. Waterside Press.

How the prison service deals with letters and telephone calls recalls the balance that must be achieved between basic human rights such as freedom of expression and right to respect for family life, and security. Unconvicted prisoners can send and receive as many letters as they wish; however, for the convicted regulations govern the kind of letters allowed and amount permitted, to whom they may be sent and from whom received, and the extent of control of length and content. Also, in certain circumstances letters are read routinely. These include where the prisoner is Cat A, where there are grounds to believe content poses a threat to security or good order and discipline of the prison, if letters are written in a foreign language, and if it is believed the prisoner is at risk of escape. Confidentiality in respect of correspondence with legal representatives and the Ombudsman should be strictly adhered to; indeed even when prisoners are on dirty protest such correspondence can only be destroyed if there is obvious contamination. This confidentiality mirrors how in legal visits, the prisoner's legal advisor has the right to visit in sight, but out of hearing, of prison staff. However, findings of a survey undertaken by HM Chief Inspectorate in 2000 of the percentage of unsentenced prisoners reporting whether their legal correspondence was received sealed or open revealed that the reality of confidentiality can be somewhat different.

One of the findings of the Woolf report was that access to telephones increases links with the outside world and the prospects of prisoners taking and accepting their responsibilities. All prisoners are therefore given access to telephones to maintain their family ties, calls being made during periods of association, and staff must again respect the privacy of calls made as far as is practicable without compromising the security and good order and discipline of the prison. Improvements have been made in recent years with the introduction of a PIN-phone system which, although having its impetus in the

Table 27.3 Sealed/opened legal correspondence

	Adult men	Adult women	Young men	Young women
Always sealed	52	31	27	17
Sometimes sealed	26	33	26	33
Always opened	22	36	47	50

Source: M. Leech and D. Cheney (2000) *The Prisons Handbook*. Waterside Press.

protection of victims from harassment, achieved the added benefit of removing the reliance upon phone cards which had been elevated to 'currency' on prison landings and was a source of bullying and intimidation of the more vulnerable prisoners to obtain them.

Under the new scheme each prisoner has a list of approved numbers, entering a personal PIN number before calling, and the cost of the call is debited from the monies available to the prisoner in their 'spends account'. The added benefit of the system is a pre-recorded message that warns the recipient the call is being made from a prison, allowing them the opportunity to accept or reject it. Most prisons undertake random call monitoring, with prisoners categorized as high or exceptional risk having their calls routinely monitored. Again confidentiality is required for legal contacts and the same must be applied to calls to such as the Samaritans, which cannot be monitored or recorded. That said, frustration does exist amongst prisoners in respect of telephone access to legal contacts. Not least, the timing of calls during prisoners' association rarely coincides with the availability of solicitors and, where a daytime call does so, the expense of calls means that those prisoners with limited funds must choose between calling home or calling their legal representative. For foreign prisoners, problems of telephone contact with families abroad—so important because visits are unfeasible—are even more acute given time zones and prohibitive expense.

REVIEW QUESTIONS

1 Has concentration on quantity rather than quality of provision outcomes led the Prison Service to a position from which it cannot retreat in improving services to prisoners?

2 Is current provision of visits, letters and telephone calls adequate to meet the needs of both prisoners and their families?

3 Should elements of the therapeutic community prison be introduced into mainstream establishments?

What about justice in prison?

The need for 'justice' in the prison setting is a requirement that covers a number of areas. Those who regard incapacitation as a solution to the crime problem often do not give a thought to the fact that crimes do indeed take place behind prison walls. There are murders, assaults and thefts, bullying and intimidation amounting to harassment, bribery and extortion, and crimes that extend into the world beyond prison walls. Incarceration, per se, does not itself prevent crime. It is therefore a role of the prison service to ensure that a law-abiding life is led by prisoners whilst in custody.

There is, however, also the concept of standards of justice for the prisoners, something that was identified by the Woolf Report of 1991 when one of the recommendations was the improvement of standards of justice in the prison setting (Player and Jenkins, 1994). This concept includes facilitating prisoners' access to the Ombudsman, operating a fair grievance and disciplinary procedure and, most importantly, communicating to a prisoner reasons for any actions taken which might affect them.

The introduction of the post of Prisons' Ombudsman has greatly assisted prisoners' who, hitherto, were frustrated by the internal complaints procedure as their last resort to resolving grievances. The disciplinary system has also, in recent times, undergone enormous change, which points to a future with an improved justice model at the point of operation of disciplinary procedures. The changes, brought about by a decision in the European Court of Human Rights in 2002, overhaul a system criticized by many over the years as, not least, lacking in access to justice and fairness of trial. An overview of trends identified in the Annual Reports of the Ombudsman since 1995 consistently places disciplinary adjudications as the largest single category of complaints, above loss of property and security categorization. Recurring complaints catalogue incorrect procedures, sketchy records of evidence, refusal of witnesses without reason given, failure to examine defences and findings of guilt falling short of the test of proof beyond reasonable doubt. Changes in disciplinary procedures, not least the guaranteed right to legal representation and an opportunity for prisoners to appear before an independent adjudicator, should considerably improve the fairness of hearings.

The intervention of a Human Rights focus on the lives of prisoners has been beneficial to prisoners in the past although, given the necessity for them to appeal to Strasbourg, lengthy procedures have led to most successes benefiting the long-term prisoner population and lifers in particular. With the coming into force of the Human Rights Act 1998, the potential for prisoners to improve the justice and fairness of their treatment has increased considerably. In addition to access to justice and proportionate punishment, the PS must heed protection of life and physical safety. They must also consider the effect of prison conditions on their physical and mental health. Facilities such as Close Supervision Centres, the quality of prisoner transport, how the service deals with bullying and intimidation and the handling of overcrowding and segregation must all be managed to avoid degrading treatment or punishment. Contact with the outside world must meet the right to respect for private and family life and religious freedom must be ensured. Perhaps most importantly the disadvantaging of certain groups within the enjoyment of rights is of particular significance in the prison setting, not least in respect of the disabled and minority ethnic groups whose equality of treatment in the prison setting has fallen far short of acceptable standards.

REVIEW QUESTIONS

1 In which areas of prison life is the Human Rights Act 1998 likely to make the most difference?

2 Should the disciplining of prisoners be solely one of independent regulation?

3 Is the focus on justice and fairness, as promulgated by the Woolf report, the key to a safe and effective prison system?

CONCLUSION

The job of the Prison Service is a taxing one extending far beyond mere housing of prisoners. To them falls the responsibility of attempting resettlement into the community of some of the most damaged and disadvantaged members of our society. As the 'pen pictures' of the average prisoner illustrates, they are a needy group who have been failed time and again by the system prior to entering a prison establishment.

A central tenet of Lord Woolf's 1991 report was that justice in prisons is a precondition for order, order a precondition for rehabilitation, and that rehabilitative efforts were the aim of crime prevention. A prison fails if it leads to deterioration of the prisoners' ability to act as an effective member of society on release, if it leaves prisoners' embittered by the experience (King and McDermott, 1989). Indeed, as work at Grendon has shown, if prisoners are marginalized within the system itself they are likely to consider themselves 'victims' rather than consider the victims of their crimes and thereby change their ways. In sum then, prisons should be a positive experience that inputs to improving the quality of a prisoner's life and, from the start of a sentence, contributes to his/her resettlement (Shine, 2000). At present, the reality is that in too many cases a sentence can make factors associated with re-offending worse: a third of prisoners lose their homes whilst in prison, two-thirds lose their jobs and two-fifths contact with their families.

The PS have in place many very good initiatives in the fields of education and training, offending behaviour courses and maintaining family ties. These are, however, consistently undermined by problems of overcrowding in prisons which affects time out of cell and purposeful activity. In the last twelve months alone, the prison population increased by 2,381 and the continued steep rise in the female population, with few prisons to house them, makes it difficult to offer the women's estate a full purposeful regime (Home Office, 2000). In the final event, it may be that resolution of some of the problems, lies at the point of sentencing. This could include the housing of those large numbers with psychiatric problems else-where than in a prison setting, and increased use of community punishment. Equally, reform of the archaic Rehabilitation of Offenders Act 1974 is another proactive possibility. Over a quarter of the working population in this country have a previous conviction. Yet serving a prison sentence can seriously under-mine employment opportunities. The Act should reflect an ethos of assisting those who want to lead law-abiding lives post-release, rather than undermining their efforts.

Equally, there is the problem of political will. There exists good, well-founded research, from the offices of the HMCIPP and government, from prisons themselves and from non-governmental bodies, offering solutions. However political will to act, and therefore impetus to provide funding to a population of 70,000 plus with no votes to be won, is poor. If prisoners could vote, would things change?

The experience of working with prisoners, and reading writings from prison, reveals what the majority of prisoners want most is respect and to be treated as individuals, within a system where demands of security and good order render individualization impossible. The only route to some semblance of this goal lies in increasing prisoners' self-esteem, allowing them some responsibility and providing the tools and strong family ties that render a law-abiding future a distinct possibility. Thus, even in the face of acute overcrowding, it is essential the PS must make good education and training and offending behaviour programmes more widely available. Low self-esteem and a poor sense of future prospects feed into those feelings which lead to self-harm and suicidal acts. Too many parents who sigh with relief if a drug dependant child is taken into a custodial setting, where they expect care and treatment to be given, have had to face a death in custody.

As the government's Social Exclusion Unit has pointed out, work with prisoners' is less about resettling them in society than settling them for the first time. The Unit identifies factors which reduce re-offending and it is these factors that the prison setting must address. The most obvious are education and employment and, for the majority, drug and alcohol misuse, housing, finances and debt problems. Pre-existing mental and physical health problems and inadequate institutional and life skills are factors which the prison must not only address, but must ensure do not deteriorate as a result of conditions of imprisonment. Finally, attitudes and self-control must be worked on and family networks strengthened, with the maintenance of the latter possibly the major route to encouraging the former personal changes.

The PS may never get it 'completely right', because perhaps there is nothing which will make prison 'work' for everyone, but just because it is not perfect should not stop the Service trying to make it better.

QUESTIONS FOR DISCUSSION

1 Examine the current PS Key Performance Indicators and suggest how they can be improved.

2 Are the theories of punishment reflected in how the day-to-day life of prisoners is managed?

3 What are the advantages and disadvantages of holding young offenders alongside adult prisoners?

4 Critically evaluate Prison Service efforts to reduce suicide and self-injury in prison.

5 Critically evaluate the impact of the Woolf Report 1991 on the development of the Prison Service and its establishments.

GUIDE TO FURTHER READING

The Rt Hon Lord Justice Woolf and His Honour Judge Stephen Tumim, (1991) *Prison Disturbances April 1990*, Cm1456, London: HMSO.

The first major investigation of prison practices since the Gladstone Committee of 1895 the Woolf Report, while investigating the prison disturbances of April 1990, had a major impact in the development of the modern prison.

Bryans, S. and Jones, R. (2001) *Prisons and the Prisoner: an introduction to the work of Her Majesty's Prison Service*, London: The Stationery Office.

A basic description of the structure and work of the prison system in England and Wales, with insights into all aspects of prison life.

Leech, M. and Shepherd, J. (eds) (2003) *The Prisons Handbook 2003–2004*, Manchester: MLA Press.

A comprehensive account of all aspects of prison life, updated annually. This edited work brings together full details of all prison establishments, details of publications relevant to prisons by both government and non-governmental bodies and précis of PPO reports and HMCIPP inspection reports and thematic reviews.

Ramsbotham, D. (2003) *Prisongate: the shocking state of Britain's prisons and the need for visionary change*, London: The Free Press.

A critique of the State of prisons today by a former HMCIPP, based on his extensive experience in investigating prison conditions, together with proposals for improvement.

Cheney, D. (2001) Prisoners' Rights in D. Cheney *et al.* (eds) *Criminal Justice and the Human Rights Act 1998*, London: Jordans, pp. 193–36.

Commentary on the relevance of the Human Rights Act 1998 to elements of the prison regime, together with details of cases which have challenged the PS and which are relevant to prisoners.

WEB LINKS

hmprisonservice.gov.uk

The official site of HM Prison Service offering a virtual prison tour, library of publications, PS documents, links to relevant government departments and organizations and details of all aspects of prison life.

homeoffice.gov.uk

For a link to the site of HM Chief Inspectorate of Prisons and Probation, which contains inspection reports and thematic reviews.

ppo.gov.uk

The site of the office of Prisons and Probation Ombudsman which offers full details of their work, publications and frequently asked questions.

prisonreformtrust.org.uk

A long-standing non-governmental organization, the site of the Prison Reform Trust offers current news, publications and research briefings.

Prisonhandbook.co.uk.

Site of the comprehensive annual publication. The Prisons Handbook, which has been published since 1995, offers e-book extracts of the publication, news releases and details of the Institute of Prison Law.

REFERENCES

Bottoms A. E. (1995) 'The philosophy and politics of punishment and sentencing', in C. Clarkson and R. Morgan (eds) *The Politics of Sentencing Reform*. Oxford: Oxford University Press.

Cavadino, M. and Dignan, J. (3rd edn, 2002) *The Penal System: An Introduction*. London, Sage.

Department of Health, HM Prison Service/NHS Executive (1999), The Future Organisation of Prison Health Care. London: The Stationary Office.

Her Majesty's Chief Inspector of Prisons (1990) Suicide and Self-Harm in Prison Service Establishments in England and Wales, Cm 1383. London: HMSO.

Her Majesty's Inspectorate of Prisons for England and Wales (2001), *Follow-up to Women in Prison*. London: The Stationary Office.

Her Majesty's Inspectorate of Prisons for England and Wales (2002a), Report of HM Inspectorates of Prison and Probation Conference: *Through the Prison Gates*. London: The Stationary Office.

Her Majesty's Inspectorate of Prisons for England and Wales (2002b), *Annual Report of HM Chief Inspector of Prisons for England and Wales*. London: The Stationary Office.

Her Majesty's Inspectorate of Probation, (1991), *Women Offenders and Probation Service Provision: A Thematic Report*. London: The Home Office.

HM Inspectorates of Prisons and Probation (2001), *Through the Prison Gate: A Joint Thematic Review*. London: HMIP.

HM Prison Service (2004) Prison Population and Accommodation Briefing, 27 August.

Home Office (1993) Lifer Manual—A Guide For Members of The Prison and Probation Services Working With Life Sentence Prisoners. London HMSO.

Home Office (1995) *Managing the Needs of Female Offenders*. London: Home Office.

Home Office (1999) *Statistics on Women and the Criminal Justice System*—A Home Office Publication Under Section 95 of the Criminal Justice Act 1991.

Home Office (2000) Prison Population Findings: A Statistical Review. Home Office: London.

Home Office (2001a), *The Government's Strategy for Women Offenders: Consultation Report*. Home Office: London.

Home Office Prison (2003) Population Brief England and Wales Nov. London: Home Office.

Home Office, (1994), *Does the Criminal Justice System Treat Men and Women Differently?* Research Findings No. 10. London: HMSO.

King and McDermott, K. (1989) 'British Prisons 1970–1987: The Ever Deepening Crisis' *British Journal of Criminology*, 29: 107–28.

Leech, M. and Cheney, D. (2000) *The Prisons Handbook*. Winchester: Waterside Press.

McConville, S. (1981) *A history of English Prison Administration*, Vol. 1: (1750–1877). London: Routledge.

Morgan, R. (2003) 'Imprisonment: current concerns and a brief history since 1945' in M. Maguire, R. Morgan and R. Reiner (eds) (2002) *The Oxford Handbook of Criminology*. Oxford: Oxford University Press.

Morgan, R. (1991) 'Woolf: In Retrospect and Prospect', *Modern Law Review, 54*: 713–25.

Morris, N. and Rothman, D. (eds) (1995) *The Oxford History of the Prison*. Oxford: University Press.

Muncie, J. (1996) 'Prison Histories' in E. McLaughlin and J. Muncie (eds) *Controlling Crime*. London: Sage.

Player, E. and Jenkins, M. (eds) (1994) 'Prisons after Woolf: Reform through Riot'. London: Routledge.

Prison Reform Trust Annual Report 2004: A Measure of Success. Prison Reform Trust: London.

Priestley, P. (1999) *Victorian Prison Lives*. Pimlico: London.

Sapsford, R. (1983), *Life Sentence Prisoners—Reaction, Response and Change*. Milton Keynes: Open University Press.

Shine, J. (ed) HMP Grendon: A Compilation of Grendon Research. Aylesbury.

Sim, J. (2004) 'Thinking about imprisonment' in J. Muncie and D. Wilson (eds) *Student Handbook of Criminal Justice and Criminology*. London: Cavendish.

Social Exclusion Unit (2002) *Reducing re-offending by ex-prisoners*. London.

Woolf Report (1991) Prison Disturbances April 1990: Report of an inquiry by the Rt. Hon. Lord Justice Woolf (part I and II) and His Honour Judge Stephen Tumin (Part II), Cm 1456. London: HMSO.

GLOSSARY OF TERMS

Abolitionism A political and criminological perspective that advocates the radical transformation/replacement of modern punishment forms with a more reflexive and multifaceted approach capable of better understanding dominant ideological constructions of crime.

Accountability The ways in which organizations and individuals are rendered answerable for their policies and day-to-day activities, exerted by internal and external mechanisms.

Acquisitive crime A term used to categorize economically motivated crimes.

Actuarial justice A term coined by Malcolm Feeley and Jonathan Simon to try to characterize a possible emerging aspect of criminal law and criminal justice. The term derives from 'actuary', meaning a statistician who works for an insurance company to calculate risks, premiums and pay-outs. Actuarial justice thus suggests a form of justice based on calculation of risks, and the statistical use of past data to predict the likelihood of future events.

Administrative criminology A form of practical policy-relevant criminology that focuses almost exclusively on the nature of the criminal event and the particular setting in which it occurs. Under this perspective, the offender is considered only as a 'rational actor' who makes calculated decisions about the costs and benefits of criminal action. Administrative criminologists seek to reduce the opportunities for crime, thus making the costs/risks of crime outweigh the potential benefits.

Aetiological crisis The majority of post-war criminology was predicated on the basis that poor social conditions caused crime. Consequently, if a meaningful reduction in crime was to occur, then governments needed to implement a series of social democratic policies specifically aimed at reducing unemployment and raising general living standards. Despite substantial improvements in the Western world in these and other areas during the years 1950–70, recorded crime soared to unprecedented levels. This refutation of the then major thinking in the social sciences has been described by Jock Young as the 'aetiological crisis'.

Aetiology The philosophy of causation; the study of causes.

Ageism Discrimination or prejudice against people because of their age or presumed age.

Appeal The initial decisions made by magistrates' or Crown Courts can be challenged by a convicted defendant (or in some cases by the prosecution). This is known as an 'appeal' and can be either on the question of the correctness of the conviction itself or the appropriateness of the sentence. The appeal will be to a higher court—this will normally be to the Crown Court from the magistrates' or to the Court of Appeal from the Crown Court.

Atavism The recurrence of certain primitive characteristics that were present in an ancestor but have not occurred in intermediate generations.

Behaviourism A psychological approach (first promoted by J.B. Watson in 1913) that stresses that the only proper subject matter for scientific study in psychology is directly observable behaviour.

Bifurcation A dual-edged approach to the problem of offending differentiating between serious and not-so-serious offenders; it also involves a more punitive approach across the whole range of punishments. In this way, a bifurcated policy allows governments to get tough and soft simultaneously.

Binge drinking There is no universally accepted definition of binge drinking. In general terms, it refers to the consumption of large amounts of alcohol in a single drinking session.

Business cycle (or economic) cycle The ups and downs often seen simultaneously in most parts of a country's economy. They tend to repeat at fairly regular time intervals. This involves shifts over time between periods of relatively rapid growth of output (recovery and prosperity), alternating with periods of recession or relatively slow economic growth.

Civilizing process Concept developed by Norbert Elias (1897–1990) to refer to the pacification of medieval society through the development of self-restraint, social regulation and increasing repugnance towards violence.

Cognition A somewhat inexact, indeterminate term that encompasses concepts such as memory, imagery, intelligence and reasoning. Often described as 'a synonym for thinking'.

Community notification Allowing communities to know when a sexual offender who may pose a risk has moved into their midst. Then policy is not pursued in the UK, but is in the USA where it is sometimes known as 'Megan's Law'. The policy is premised on the idea that information on the offender known to the professionals and practitioners working with the offender should not be held only by those professionals and practitioners and that with such 'notification' the community will be better able to protect itself.

Community penalties In its broadest sense, this term refers to any sentence that does not involve imprisonment and therefore includes cautions, discharges and fines as well as sentences involving supervision or monitoring. In its narrower sense, the term refers to Community Rehabilitation Orders (formerly probation orders), Community Punishment Orders (formerly community service orders), Community Punishment and Rehabilitation Orders (formerly combination orders), Drug Testing and Treatment Orders and Curfew Orders (with or without electronic monitoring).

Conscious mind Being aware (cognisant) of one's actions and emotions. Actions undertaken by the conscious mind are intentional.

Consumer expenditure (or in shorthand consumption): The money from income, savings, or from borrowing spent on the purchase of currently produced goods and services. Consumption tends to increase as income increases, but not by as much.

Corporate crime Illegal acts or omissions which are the result of deliberate decision-making or culpable negligence within a corporation.

Corporation Used here to denote all companies registered under the UK Companies Acts, from the smallest limited liability company to the largest multinational.

Corporatism A word used to describe an approach to youth justice based on centralization, government intervention and cooperation of agencies and professionals working towards common goals. Typically, it has also been associated with the use of targets, and prescribed ways of working.

Crime count The number of offences occurring within a given referent of time and space, for example, the number of burglary offences in England and Wales per year.

Crime frequency How the counts of criminal offences are distributed amongst a population, for example, how many people are victims, and how frequently are they victimized.

Crime markets A market that deals specifically with the acquisition, distribution and consumption of illegal goods and services.

Crime rate The measure that gives an index of crime occurring in a particular jurisdiction for a specific time period.

Crime statistics The accounts that the State compiles of the actions of its agencies concerning those acts which the law proscribes.

Crime victimization surveys Large-scale sample surveys of general populations whose purpose is to estimate, describe and explain the distribution of crime victimization and victims.

Crime flux A concept that defines the crime rate as a product of the prevalence of victims in the population, and the frequency with which they are victimized.

Criminal law This is the regulation of conduct by the creation of criminal offences—laws, made by Parliament, that forbid particular conduct and lay down punishments. Nowadays the courts no longer create new offences, although their decisions shape the boundaries of offences.

Criminological psychology A sub-discipline existing broadly at the interface between psychology and criminology that seeks to apply psychology to help explain criminal behaviour.

Criminological verstehen Sympathetic or affective understanding regarding the situated experiences and emotions of criminals, crime control agents and crime victims.

Cultural criminology A relatively new form of criminology that defines cultural dynamics as essential to the construction of crime and crime control, and so investigates the many intersections of crime and culture.

Culture The symbolic environment created by social groups; the meaningful way of life shared by group members.

Dangerousness An individual's actions or behaviour pattern considered dangerous to the safety of that individual or other people—a person may be so disposed by individual characteristics or by pre-disposing circumstances in their immediate environment—the behaviour is usually associated with elements of unpredictability.

Decarceration Refers to policies and practices that aim to reduce the numbers of offenders in prison by providing alternative measures for dealing with them in the community. Theoretically, the debate about decarceration was at its height in the 1960s and 1970s and included reduction in the use of other institutions, most notably psychiatric hospitals. With the dramatic increase in the prison population in the 1990s, the term and the debate has largely fallen into disuse.

Defence representation A key element of a fair trial is that of 'equality of arms'—that the prosecution and defence are allowed the same facilities to put their case. An individual defendant will never have the same resources as the State but the State must provide for adequate representation of offenders, whether in the police station or in court. The criminal justice system also provides for defendants to be assisted by lawyers, paid out of public funds.

Deterrence The idea that crime can be reduced if people fear the punishment they may receive if they offend.

Discipline A term used by Michel Foucault to describe a method by which some people can efficiently control others, and which he claims is at the heart of modern public institutions such as the prison, school and hospital. Discipline is the analysis and 'correction' of others' behaviour, especially in relation to time and space, and is a key part of his understanding of how surveillance operates and what it is trying to achieve.

Discrimination The unfavourable treatment based on a person's colour, age, sexuality, gender or ethnicity.

Diversion strategy Describes efforts to minimize young offenders' involvement with the formal youth justice system, steering them away from the more punitive sentences such as custody, and where possible keeping them out of the system entirely.

Edgework The momentary integration of subcultural practices with experiences of extreme risk and excitement.

Elder The blanket label of the 'elderly' can perpetuate a stereotype that the elderly population constitutes a homogeneous social group. The term elder will be used as a generic term to define those persons over the age of fifty in recognition of the positive aspects that older age can confer.

Empathy The ability to mentally identify with another person and thus understand how others feel.

Environmental criminology A form of criminology that focuses on the complex relationships that exist between crime, space and environment.

Ethnicity The problem that arises from using the biological concept of 'race' to describe social phenomena has led some theorists to reject the term 'race' in favour of 'ethnicity'. Like the terms 'race' and 'racism', 'ethnicity' has no universally agreed definition. The term ethnicity characterizes social groups based upon a shared identity rooted in geographical, cultural, historical factors and migratory patterns.

Ethnography A qualitative research methodology concerned with studying subjects within their own natural environment frequently involving detailed observation and in-depth interviews. Ethnographers seek to view the world through the eyes of their subjects.

'Fair trial' and criminal procedure Procedural laws govern the actions of law enforcement agencies. In the pre-trial process, such laws provide legal powers for the police enabling them to arrest and detain suspects. The rules also ensure that suspects are treated with due respect. Equally important are trial procedures—the idea of a 'fair trial' is enshrined in many human rights conventions and this idea governs such matters as the way in which defendants can defend themselves from accusations, the roles of the judge, as well as of the prosecuting or defending lawyers, the presentation of evidence, the questioning of witnesses and the taking of verdicts.

Fear of crime General term that suffers from lack of clarity in its definition. Generally taken to refer to concern, worry or anxiety about crime but there is research evidence that it may be a conduit for broader concerns about change and uncertainty. At the start of the twenty-first century the focus for the police has broadened to encompass a reassurance agenda as politicians struggle with falling recorded crime levels and rising levels of public anxiety.

Folk devil As constructed by the mass media and public officials, a public identity that comes to embody a larger sense of threat and social insecurity.

Functionalism A structuralist perspective, which argues that, although crime and deviance are problematic, they also serve a social function by contributing to the smooth running of the social system as a whole (see Chapter 4).

Gender A socially constructed phenomenon that refers to differences ascribed by society relating to expectations about appropriate social and cultural roles.

Gerontology Interest in the study of human ageing has grown steadily throughout the twenty-first century. Gerontology is a broad discipline, which encompasses psychological, biological and social analyses of ageing. It is also the study of social welfare and social policy focused on ageing. The various stands within gerontology seek to problematize the construction of ageing and to identify the conditions experienced by elders in society. Gerontology raises questions about the role of the State in management of old age to issues about the purpose of growing old within the context of a postmodern life-course.

Governance This is often used as a general term to denote governing strategies originating from inside and outside the State, though in this chapter is used more straightforwardly to refer to the constitutional and institutional arrangements for framing and monitoring the policies of the police.

Governmentality A term invented by Michel Foucault to describe certain specific techniques developed over the centuries by governments and the State, so as to exercise power over populations as a whole. It complements 'discipline', which refers to the operation of power at the level of public institutions.

Gross Domestic Product (GDP) The total value of all goods and services produced within a country during a specified period (most commonly per year).

Hegemonic masculinity The prevailing idealized cultural conception of dominant (hegemonic) masculinity involving the dominance of women, heterosexuality, the pursuit of sexual gratification and independence. This is a cultural resource enacted to maintain domination over 'subordinate masculinities' such as ethnic and sexual minorities.

Hegemony The dominance of one particular ideology, resulting in the empowerment of particular values, beliefs and practices over others and frequently resulting in the naturalization of those values, beliefs and practices throughout the social body.

History from below A form of historical narrative developed and popularized in the 1960s. This form of history focuses on the study and analysis of the lives of 'ordinary' individuals within society as well as individuals and regions that were not previously considered historically important. This has given rise to the important developments in such fields as women's history, black history, and gay and lesbian history.

Home Office Counting Rules Official instructions that set out how, and in what ways, incidents are to be recorded and counted as offences.

Ideal type An abstract model of a phenomenon which illustrates a generalization for descriptive purposes. For example, In the context of victimization, the 'ideal victim' is an innocent, elderly, vulnerable person. This does not imply that such people are typical of victims of crime—rather, it shows how many people think about victims and suggests a commonsense understanding which should be challenged and tested by research.

Incapacitation Punishment which calculates the risk of future crimes and uses a custodial setting to remove the offender from society to protect the public from further harm.

Institutionalized racism The term 'institutionalized racism' was first introduced in 1968 by Carmichael and Hamilton in their seminal text, *Black Power: The Politics of Liberation in America*. Common to most definitions of institutionalized racism is the collective failure of an organization to provide an appropriate service to people because of their colour, culture, or ethnic origin.

Intimate (domestic) violence Predominantly (but not exclusively) violence against women and children within the family, which can take many forms including physical assault, rape and sexual violence, psychological or emotional violence, torture, financial abuse including dowry-related violence, and control of movement and of social contacts.

Jurisprudence The science or philosophy of law.

Justice model One that places the offence at the centre, regarding it as an act of will. It is to be dealt with by punishment set to reflect the seriousness of the crime. The justice model also emphasizes the legal rights of young offenders, for example, to representation in court.

Labelling theory A criminological theory that locates the meaning of human activity not in the activity itself, but in others' reactions to it.

Late modernity A period in the historical development of capitalism characterized by individualization, globalization, personal insecurity, hyperconsumption and the decline of large-scale collective initiatives such as the welfare state.

Legal psychology A sub-discipline of psychology specifically concerned with the application of psychological knowledge and research to the process of law.

Liberal pluralist media theory A selection of approaches which view the media, more or less, as serving the interests of the majority by representing marginal views and holding the powerful to account, thus safeguarding the transparency and integrity of the democratic process.

Life-Course A term that has replaced the term life stages to reflect holistic understanding of the ageing process. The blurring of the life-course problematizes negative 'ageist' stereotypes and practices and in turn produces more accurate and positive images that imply that later life is a time for vitality, creativity, empowerment and resourcefulness—all attainable in old age.

Mafia A term often used to describe an organized crime group consisting of particular ethnic members, for example, Sicilian Mafia, Russian Mafia. It has also been used in reference to individuals and groups who deal specifically in illegal protection.

Managerialism The use of a more corporatist strategy to deal with crime. The 'managerial' approach aims not necessarily to deliver 'welfare' or 'justice', but to find the most efficient and effective way of managing a visible crime problem.

Media Any technological form of communication or expression designed to impart meaning (television, newspapers, Internet, radio, brochures, road signs, advertizing billboards).

Media loop A mediated representation that refers not to an external event, but to existing media representations; in this sense, an image of an image.

Meta-analyses When a number of studies on a particular research area are reviewed and assessed in a bid to find some overall conclusions.

Moral entrepreneur A powerful person or group seeking to impose a moral agenda by creating a new category of crime and crime control.

Moral panic As generated by the mass media and public authorities, the public's belief that a particular crime or criminal is symptomatic of larger moral failures and social harms.

National Crime Recording Standard A protocol to standardize crime recording practices amongst police forces, with effect from April 2002.

Neighbourhood Watch Voluntary organizations that are devoted to preventing crime and disorder in local neighbourhoods. Members are not expected to intervene in possible criminal incidents but to be the eyes and ears of the police by being alert to unusual activity. Grew rapidly in numbers during the 1980s as part of the Conservative government's emphasis on active citizenship.

Net-widening A term used to identify the counter-intuitive problem posed by the proliferation of 'alternatives' to prison. There is a risk that innovative non-custodial sentences might be used by sentencers for offenders who would previously have received *less* severe sentences rather than *more* severe sentences. If this happens, it means that *more*, rather than *fewer* offenders are likely to end up in prison. In this way, the *net* of criminal justice intervention is thrown *wider*.

Night-time economy Used to describe bars, pubs, nightclubs and fast-food outlets, often clustered in town and city centres.

Normalization thesis Associated with the work of Howard Parker and his colleagues who argue that drugs have become a central component of contemporary youth culture.

Nothing works The notion that became popular in the 1970s and 1980s that nothing could be done to reduce re-offending. It fitted well with the anti-welfare views of the time, and has now been replaced by the more nuanced view that some interventions work for some offenders in some situations.

Organizational culture Culture has been defined as 'the way we do things around here', and while organizations themselves tend to have their distinct cultures, these often take distinct forms within different parts of an organization.

Organizational structure Refers to the lines of authority, decision-making, accountability, management systems and the relationships between constituent parts of an organization.

Organized crime A generic description of any criminal activities carried out by a group of two or more people. Official usage of this term specifies that the groups engaged in these activities are motivated by profit, operate over a period of time and are willing to use violence as well as actively seeking to influence those across the legal divide such as the police, politicians, bankers and so on who can further their cause. Organized crime is not a legal term.

Patriarchy Refers to a system of social structure and practices in which men dominate.

Phenomenology A method of philosophical investigation that seeks to describe and understand experienced phenomena. Although phenomenological methodologies are deliberately complex and opaque, one could say that the 'goal' of phenomenology is to challenge and question the foundational knowledge claims.

Phrenology Phrenology is the study of the structure of the skull to determine a person's character and mental capacity. It is associated with the work of the Austrian physician Franz Joseph Gall (1758–1828). Gall was one of the first to consider the brain as the home of all mental activities.

Physiognomy Physiognomy is the interpretation of outward appearance, especially the features of the face, to discover a person's predominant temper and character.

Police The specialist state agency tasked with law enforcement and order maintenance.

Policing Organized and purposive forms of social control and regulation, involving surveillance and the threat of sanctions for discovered rule-breaking.

Positivism Positivism is a form of empiricism that was established by the sociologist Auguste Comte in the nineteenth century. Rejecting metaphysical or theological explanations, it attempted to emulate the methods of natural science. Thus only scientific or empirical investigation and observation will enable a true understanding of social structures and institutions.

Post-disciplinary Refers to theories of surveillance and/or punishment that derive from, and accept in part, Foucault's theory of technologies of power and of discipline, but which argue that the disciplinary historical phase is in the process of being superseded by a new technology of power.

Problem drug use Problem drug use involves dependency, regular excessive use or use which creates serious health risks (for example, injecting).

Proportionality A philosophical ideal stating that punishment should be proportionate to the criminal act.

Prosecution and trial In its technical sense, 'prosecution' means bringing an offender in front of a properly constituted tribunal (the magistrates' or Crown Court) in order to test the validity of a formal accusation made against the defendant. The obligation is on the State as prosecutor to satisfy the tribunal that the accusation is true beyond reasonable doubt. The preparation of a case for trial and the presentation of that case is predominantly undertaken by the Crown Prosecution Service, although other agencies such as Customs and Excise and Inland Revenue may take responsibility for mounting their own prosecutions.

Psychometrics The measurement (typically via questionnaires or inventories) of psychological characteristics such as intelligence, personality and creativity.

Punitive populism (or variants on it such as populist punitiveness, penal populism) The pursuit of a set of penal policies to win votes rather than to reduce crime rates or to promote justice. Central to this strategy is the support of imprisonment and, generally, the advocacy of tough measures to deal with offenders.

Qualitative analysis Research methodologies concerned with understanding and exploring conditions and phenomena which cannot be readily measured and reduced to statistical data—for example, emotions and subjective interpretations of meaning.

Quantitative analysis Research methodologies concerned with quantifying measurable aspects of social phenomena (crime, sentencing, victimization), typically through some form of counting and subsequent statistical manipulation.

Quantitative history Quantitative history involves the use of empirical, statistical historical data (such as census returns, crop yields, tax records) in the study of historical topics. It is often associated with the emergence of social history, which borrowed methodologies from the social sciences.

Race The terms race and ethnicity have been used interchangeably but are not synonymous. Current notions of race are centred exclusively on visible (usually skin colour) distinctions among populations, although its historical origins and usage were broader and included religious and linguistic groups (such as Jews or the Irish) who were considered to be 'races'.

Racism Many authors define racism as a 'doctrine, dogma, ideology, or set of beliefs'. All definitions of racism have a set of common themes—typically the belief that certain groups are innately, biologically, socially, morally superior to other groups, based upon an assumption held about them.

Racist violence Any incident, including threats, harassment, emotional and physical harm, which is perceived to be racist by the victim, or any other person.

Radical media theory A selection of approaches which view

the media, to varying degrees, as representing the interests of an elite minority to a subordinate majority, comprising a crucial part of the process through which elite ideological hegemony can be secured, maintained or, indeed, overthrown.

Rational choice theory of crime A classical model of human choice that assumes that offenders rationally calculate the costs and benefits of committing a crime. The rational choice theory is the leading perspective behind the majority of contemporary situational crime prevention initiatives.

Rational economic (wo)man An ideal type economists use to derive theories about human behaviour. The assumption is that, faced with choices and given their preferences, individuals will always act in such a way as to optimize their economic well-being. They weigh up the costs and benefits of different actions and choose the one that will leave them the best off.

Recession (economic recession) Defined formally by economists as occurring when the amount of goods and services produced by a country's economy falls in two successive quarters. A sustained recession, such as that in the 1930s, is often referred to as a depression. A recession will lead to fewer jobs and higher levels of unemployment.

Recreational drug use Characteristically centred on the use of cannabis and 'dance drugs' (for example, ecstasy), recreational drug use may be frequent but does not involve excessive use, dependency or serious risks to health.

Reflexive A heightened degree of self understanding and reflection about one's theorizing or particular standpoint/position; from the Latin term *Reflectere*, meaning 'to turn back on oneself'.

Regulation Within criminology, this term implies the control of business activity within the framework of a set of rules, by an agency or by dedicated personnel assigned to ensure compliance with those rules.

Rehabilitation The belief that it is possible to tackle the factors that cause offenders to commit crimes and so reduce or prevent re-offending. The focus is usually on individual factors such as employability, substance dependence and anger management.

Relativism The perspective that knowledge is relative and contingent rather than absolute and determined.

Resettlement Refers to a long tradition of work that is based on the effective reintegration of imprisoned offenders back into the community.

Restoration In the History of England the term 'Restoration' has a specific meaning in as much as it is used to describe the process whereby Charles II regained the English throne after the Parliamentarian rule in the wake of the English Civil War. More commonly, though, the Restoration period refers to the subsequent years of Charles II's reign (1660–85).

Restorative justice An approach to criminal justice which aims to restore victims, offenders and the wider community as far as possible to the position they were in before the offence was committed, by involving them in the decision-making process and attempting to reconcile their conflicts through informal (but structured) discussion. Mechanisms for implementing RJ include victim–offender mediation; direct or indirect reparation; family group conferences; changes to sentencing arrangements which involve wider community representation; and community involvement in supervising offenders using circles of support and accountability.

Retribution/Just desert Punishment that seeks to express social disapproval and concern but which is proportionate to the harm caused by the crime.

Revisionist history Historical revisionism is the re-examination and reviewing of the stories told as history with an eye to updating them with more recently discovered, more unbiased or more accurate information. Broadly, it is the approach that history as it has been traditionally told may not be entirely accurate and may be subject to review. Revisionist history challenges orthodox and traditional approaches to an historical problem. A revisionist history of crime offers new perspectives to the orthodox (often called *Whig*) version that many historians accept.

Risk assessment The activity of collating information on an individual, their immediate circumstances and social environment with a view to assessing the likelihood of particular behaviour patterns in the future. This may divide into clinical collection and assessment, and actuarial assessment; the latter implying a statistical analysis based on particular categories of people. In the case of sexual offenders this is an increasingly formalized and coordinated activity sometimes using risk assessment 'instruments'.

Risk factors Increasingly used to refer to individual or social factors which increase the probability of involvement in crime.

Risk management The activity of using a risk assessment to manage the future risk an individual may pose. In the case of sexual offending this is an increasingly formalized and coordinated activity involving various forms of containment and incapacitation to achieve public protection (for example, supervision, registration, routine surveillance, longer custodial or hospital detention).

'Rule of law' The idea of the 'rule of law' is that individuals and the State should regulate their conduct according to the law.

Laws must be created in a constitutionally proper fashion to be effective, normally through legislation passed by Parliament but such statutory offences can be contrasted with 'common law' offences which are based on the decisions of courts. Law enforcement agencies such as the police, the prosecution, the courts or prisons can only exercise their powers (such as those of investigation, trial or detention) where they have legal authority to do so.

Self-regulation Self-regulation refers to the expectation that most people are capable of complying with the law most of the time, not because of the fear of punishment, but because they have internalized the values and norms of society and consider that it is in their own interests, and the interests of those that matter to them, to comply. If they occasionally break the law, then it is assumed that this will produce a sufficient feeling of guilt and shame for them to *regulate* their behaviour without either restrictions or assistance from other people. The ultimate aim of criminal justice policy, therefore, is to produce *self-regulating* citizens who require minimal outside intervention to be law-abiding.

Sex Refers to biological criteria for classifying persons as male or female.

Sexism Refers to oppressive attitudes and behaviours directed towards either sex.

Sexual offending The commission of acts of a sexual nature against a person without that person's consent (for example, rape, indecent assault) or where that person lacks the capacity to consent (for example, because they are a child, have learning difficulties, or are otherwise incapacitated); these acts may be accompanied by violence or the threat of violence. The commission of acts of a sexual nature that are 'prohibited' by law (for example, between members of the same family, or abuse of a position of trust).

Situational crime prevention An approach to crime prevention involving the management, design or implementation of the immediate environment in which crimes occur in order to reduce opportunities for crime.

Social control A term used in various different ways in criminology. In the context of surveillance, its most frequent use is to claim (following Marxist theories of class conflict and domination) that the essential 'function' of surveillance is to help the State gather information on individuals or groups it perceives as representing a threat to its (class-based) interests, and/or to prevent such threats from arising in the first place.

Social exclusion A term used to describe people or areas suffering from a combination of problems such as unemployment, poor skills, low incomes, poor housing, high crime environments, bad health and family breakdown. It is distinguished from financial poverty and focused rather on constricted access to civil, political and social rights and opportunities.

Social interactionism A theoretical approach that stresses the interactions between individuals as 'symbolic and linguistic exchanges'. Within this rubric, crime is understood as a product of social interaction.

Style A symbolic medium for the display of collective identity and affiliation; style often serves also as the medium for others' attempts at surveillance and control.

Subculture The distinctive symbolic environment of a criminal group, often embodying language, rituals and symbols that, when considered in relation to the study of crime and deviance, run counter to the legal constraints and conventional understandings proffered by mainstream society.

Tautology/Tautological (In theoretical terms) something that relies upon circular reasoning.

Thatcherism A label given to a set of political value associated with Margaret Thatcher, the Conservative Prime Minister of the UK from 1979 until 1990. Economically committed to allowing markets to operate freely and opposed to supporting firms or industries that performed badly, its policies involved privatizing nationalized industries, reducing state expenditure particularly on welfare. Its advocates believed the Welfare State was to blame for the growth in a 'dependency culture' where people relied on State handouts rather than working and providing for themselves and their families.

Time series data Refers to data collected from a particular geographical unit—town, region or country—at fixed intervals—daily, weekly, monthly, quarterly, annually—for example, annual recorded crime in England for each year from 1950 to 2003. Time series analysis refers to statistical techniques that examine how the measurement varies over time. In contrast, cross-section data is collected for a particular time period across different geographic units, for example, recorded crime in each local authority in the UK in 2004.

Total institution An organization which controls all aspects of people's daily lives. Primarily associated with the work of sociologist Erving Goffman, who saw the total institution as a social microcosm which was controlled by an hegemony with clear hierarchies and sets of rules. Examples include prisons, schools, mental institutions and workhouses.

Traditional crime Those acts upon which criminal justice agencies—and criminologists—have typically focused their energies, such as interpersonal violence, theft, burglary, the use and distribution of illegal substances, public order offences, and so on; also frequently referred to as 'street' crime or 'conventional' crime.

Transnational organized crime A relatively recent term that is applied to activities carried out by crime groups across jurisdictions, either by the same group or in collaboration with others. It is intended to reflect the globalizing tendency of organized crime.

Unconscious mind The part of the mind that is inaccessible to the conscious mind but which still affects behaviour and emotions.

Unemployment The State of being available and able to work but unable to find a paid job. In practice, difficult to identify and measure. For example, government rules as to the meaning of 'available for work' or eligibility for benefit can change, altering the numbers counted as unemployed without the material position of any particular individual altering.

Verdicts and sentencing At the end of a trial, the magistrates (or the jury in a Crown Court) will bring in a verdict—this derives from the Latin for a 'true statement'. This verdict will be guilty or not guilty. After a verdict of guilty, the court will proceed to sentence. A sentence is a court order which specifies the penalty (from fines to community-based sanctions to imprisonment) to be imposed and which gives legal authority to agencies such as probation or the prison service to enforce that penalty.

Victim blaming Ways of thinking about the causes of criminal victimization which seek explanations from the individual victim's conduct and the victim's relationship with the offender, rather than looking for wider social factors which help to explain victimization. In the context of police investigations, victim blaming can take the form of disbelieving the victim's report of a crime being committed, or giving some types of incident lower priority on the grounds that the victim is less deserving than others.

Victim impact statements A mechanism for allowing victims of crime to give a written statement of the impact of the offence upon them, materially and emotionally, so that courts and other criminal justice agencies can take this information into account. An apparently straightforward and sensible innovation which has been controversial and largely ineffective in practice.

Victimology A sub-discipline of criminology. It is concerned with the study of victims of crime; the causes, nature and impact of victimization; and the dynamics of relationships between victims, offenders and the environments in which victimization occur.

Violence Behaviour that intentionally threatens or does physical harm, and involves the infliction of emotional, psychological, sexual, physical and material damage.

Welfare model One in which offending is taken to be a symptom of psychological or social deprivation. The response rests with providing expert-led treatment in order to meet the child's needs and so reduce offending.

Welfare State A State which takes the responsibility for providing basic services to its population. Through systems of social security it guarantees to meet people's basic needs for housing, health, education and income.

'What works' In its narrowest sense, 'What works' refers to a movement that emerged in the 1980s and 1990s in North America and spread worldwide. Its aim has been to revive interest in offender rehabilitation through the promotion of programmes for offenders, based on cognitive behavioural psychology and supported by scientific evidence of success in reducing rates of re-offending. The term is intended to counteract the claim that 'nothing works' in offender rehabilitation. In its broader sense, the term has come to refer to a very wide-ranging and controversial political and ideological agenda that emphasizes individual responsibility for offending and minimizes the role of social determinants.

Whig History A term used to describe the views of some eighteenth and nineteenth century British historians that British history was a march of progress whose inevitable outcome was the constitutional monarchy. It takes its name from the British Whigs, advocates of the power of Parliament, who opposed the Tories, supporters of the power of the King and the aristocracy. Whig history is criticized for its overemphasis of the roles played by key political figures and for downplaying the historical importance of the struggles between different classes and groups.

White-collar crime Offences committed by people of relatively high status or enjoying relatively high levels of trust, and made possible by their legitimate employment.

Rengert, G.F. 186
Ressler, R. 127
Rex, S. 541
Reynolds, E. 29
Richards, L. 213
Rider, A.O. 127
Rix, B. 189
Roberts, B. 162, 163, 172, 173, 376,
    388, 428
Roberts, C. 213
Roberts, P. 129
Robins, R.S. 315
Rock, P. 70, 159
Rogers, L. 502
Rogovin, C.H. 290
Rojek, C. 165
Ronfeldt, D. 313
Rose, N. 39, 477
Rosenfield, 414
Roshier, B. 64, 159
Ross, D. 168
Ross, S. 168
Rothman, D. 547
Rothman, M.B. 419
Rotter, J.B. 117
Rowe, M. 368
Rozenberg, J. 510
Ruberstein, D. 410
Ruggiero, V. 93, 268, 293, 301
Russell, N. 462
Rutter, M. 115
Ruxton, S. 389

S

Sabbagh, D. 333
Sacco, V.F. 414
Said, E. 93
Samenow, S.E. 120, 121
Sammons, A. 110, 112, 123, 130
Sampson, A. 204, 512
Sanber, A.A. 67
Sanchez-Meca, J. 125
Sanders, A. 495, 497, 502, 503, 514,
    521
Sanders, C.R. 85, 140, 154
Sapsford, R. 556
Sarat, A. 93
Sartre, J-P. 96
Sasson, T. 176
Saulsbury, W. 512
Saunders, R. 398
Savage, S. 520
Savolainen, J. 240
Schachtman, T. 127
Scheingold, S.A. 104

Schlesinger, P. 159, 172
Schmid, A. 309
Schneider, J. 189
Schrager, L.S. 268
Schwendiger, H. and J. 16
Schwitzgebel, R.K. 481
Scott-Fordham, A. 252
Scott, S. 397
Scull, M. 528
Seddon, T. 208, 209
Seidler, 355
Sellars, K. 6–7
Seymour, J. 54
Seymour, L. 214
Shakespeare, T. 494
Shapland, J. 354, 511
Sharpe, J.A. 22, 26, 29
Sharpe, K. 398
Shaw, C.R. 72, 328
Shaw, M. 437
Shearing, C. 509
Sheldon, W.H. 66, 111
Shepherd, E. 130
Sheptycki, J. 509, 514
Sherman, L.W. 73
Shine, J. 562
Shiner, M. 212–13, 214, 215
Shoemaker, R. 27, 29
Shore, H. 23, 24, 27
Short, E. 480
Short, J.F. 268, 272
Showalter, 352
Shute, J. 229
Sibbit, R. 238, 539–540
Signorielli, N. 171–2
Silverman, J. 173, 258, 259
Sim, J. 353, 409, 547
Simmel, 224
Simmons, J. 450
Simon, J. 253, 351, 476, 477
Simpson, S. 39
Skidmore, P. 161
Skinner, B.F. 116
Skiolnik, J. 514–5
Skogan, W.G. 49, 511
Slapper, G. 270, 271, 277, 280, 293
Sloan, J.J. 187
Smart, C. 77, 346, 351
Smith, C. 394
Smith, D. 226, 229, 234, 238, 239,
    291, 294, 297, 359, 360, 388,
    391, 393, 395, 512, 514, 517, 518,
    528
Smith, M. 192, 196
Smith, N. 206
Smith, S. 159

Smyth, J. 509
Snider, L. 267, 273, 277, 281
Socrates 3
Solomos, J. 369
Sommers, I. 353
Sondhi, A. 210
Sontag, S. 102
Soothill, K. 161
South, N. 186, 207
Spackman, P. 496
Spalek, B. 279
Sparks, R. 161, 176, 245, 405, 429
Sprinzak, E. 316, 317
St Augustine 13
Stack, S.A.
Stanko, E.O. 223, 230, 350, 353,
    356
Stanley, R.A. 126
Staub, H. 115
Stedman-Jones, G. 25
Steffan, E. 211
Steffensmeier, D.J. 334, 409
Steiner, G. 15
Stelfox, P. 296
Sterba, J.L. 310
Stevens, A. 211
Stevens, J.A. 127, 211
Stoltenberg, J. 354, 355, 356
Storch, R. 27, 30
Storr, A. 114
Strang, J. 210
Strentz, T. 127
Stretesky, P. 159
Stubbs, P. 512
Styles, J. 32
Sumner, C. 74, 475
Sumner, M. 215
Surrette, R. 354
Sutcliffe, F. 44
Sutherland, E. 72, 116, 267, 268,
    292, 298
Sutton, M. 189
Svedin, C.G. 248
Swanson, C.R. 127
Sykes, G.M. 74, 207
Symonds, P. 10
Szockyi, E. 276
Szwed, E. 388

T

Tapp, J.L. 129
Tappan, P. 7
Tarling, R. 44, 51, 359
Taylor, A. 206
Taylor, G. 44, 51